A Horse Around the House

❮❮❮

Round-hoofed, short-jointed, fetlocks shag and long
Broad breast, full eye, small head, and nostril wide,
High crest, short ears, straight legs, and passing strong,
Thin mane, thick tail, broad buttocks, tender hide.
Look, what a horse should have he did not lack
Save a proud rider on so proud a back.

Shakespeare
VENUS AND ADONIS (49, 50)

❮❮❮

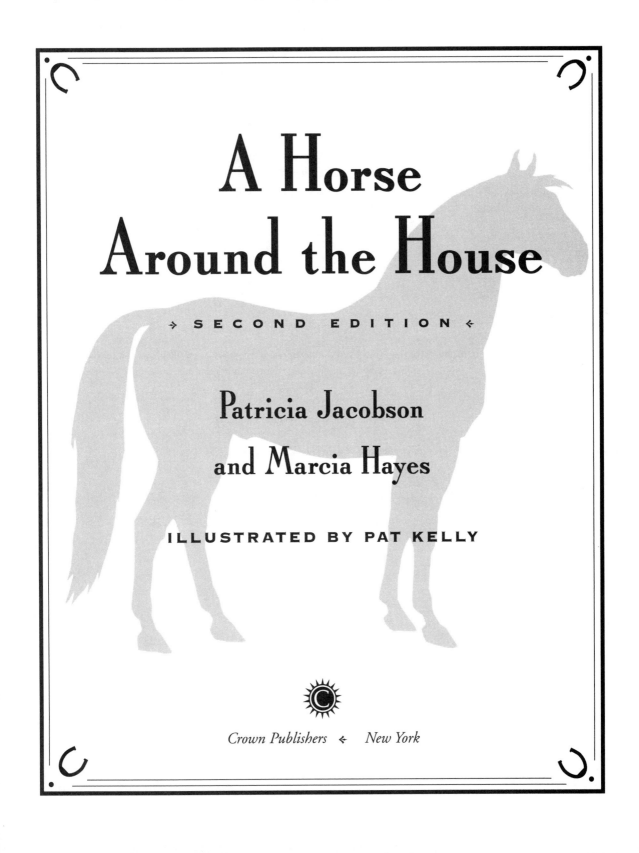

A Horse
Around the House

→ SECOND EDITION ←

Patricia Jacobson
and Marcia Hayes

ILLUSTRATED BY PAT KELLY

Crown Publishers → New York

Dedicated to my mother and father, whose love, humor, and
encouragement have enabled me to realize my potential.

P.K.J.

This book is not intended to replace the services of a veterinarian, nor is it meant to encourage diagnosis and treatment of illness, disease, or other medical problems. If you have any questions or concerns with any recommendation set forth in the following pages, you should consult your veterinarian.

Published by Crown Publishers, New York, New York. Member of Random House, Inc.

Random House, Inc. New York, Toronto, London, Sydney, Auckland
www.randomhouse.com

CROWN is a trademark and the Crown colophon is a registered trademark of Random House, Inc.

Originally published, in different form, in 1972 and 1978 by Crown Publishers.

Printed in the United States of America

Design by Cynthia Dunne

Library of Congress Cataloging-in-Publication Data
Jacobson, Patricia.
A horse around the house/by Patricia Jacobson and Marcia Hayes; illustrated by Pat Kelly.—2nd ed.
Includes bibliographical references and index.
1. Horses. I. Hayes, Marcia. II. Title.
SF285.3.J3   1999   636.1'08—dc21   98-28197

ISBN 0-517-70458-7

10 9 8 7 6 5 4 3 2

Acknowledgments

Patricia Jacobson

I owe lasting gratitude to a number of people for their abundant kindness and generosity in helping me compile the material for this second edition:

To Amy L. Grice, V.M.D., for her invaluable aid, contributions to and review of the health section, and suggestions on elder horse care. And to the always cheerful and ever-responsive staff at Rhinebeck Equine L.L.P. for their tireless help.

To Marsha Lancto, Sherri Lancto, and Gail Short for their extensive information and advice on tack and riding apparel. And to Jan Jacobson for sharing her expertise in saddle fitting. Also to Jennifer Van Deinse for her valuable review of the Miniature Horse material.

I particularly want to thank PJ Dempsey, the ultimate editor, to whom I am forever indebted for her creative suggestions, enthusiasm, and perseverance. Thanks is also due to Cindy Dunne, the designer of this edition, for giving *Horse Around the House* an entirely new look.

I also want to express my appreciation to my friends for their support and to all my teachers and students, past and present, from whom I've learned so much. I am deeply grateful to my loving friend and partner, Alan Cross, for his generous help, encouragement, and patience throughout the rewriting of this edition.

And above all, I wish to acknowledge all those wonderful horses that have contributed so much to the richness of my life and have provided the inspiration for this book.

Marcia Hayes

I would like to thank Michael Sheehan, Esq., who taught me basic DOS and about the ways of wayward computers, as well as Mike's assistant Terri Seca, who fielded frantic phone calls. Acknowledgments are also due to Barbara Scudder, chief Roxbury librarian, her assistant Doris Hewitt, and to the Roxbury Arts Group for emergency use of their computer. Thanks to Rick and Jennifer Maynard of the COET; kudos to Dr. John R. Fairbairn, D.V.M. (Cornell), who provided invaluable help; and thank you to those wonderful folks in the communications department of Cornell University.

A special thanks to Donald J. La Roca, assistant curator of arms and armors at the Metropolitan Museum of Art, for his help on the historical information in the tack section (and to Curator Emeritus Dr. Helmut Nichol for his help on the same in the previous editions).

Also thanks to Helen K. Gibble for her Trakehner information and to Dorothy Henshaw Patent and Wanda Litton for Miniature Horse input.

My personal thanks to my daughter, Pamela Hayes Baillie, a professional horse-woman and one of Pat's former students, for her suggestions. Finally, thanks to my husband, who put up with the chaos of a living-room office and provided emotional support and vitamins during the months I spent revising this volume.

Contents

Introduction

Quite a number of years have passed since the publication of the last revised edition of this book, during which time a great many discoveries and improvements have been made in the science of horse care, nutrition, and health, in new designs of equipment and riding attire, and in theories of training. Every month, it seems, one of the numerous horse magazines offers some new research on a health problem or eliminates an old axiom on horse care or feeding. These innovations affect the horse's welfare as well as the owner's pocketbook.

It is quite startling to realize that the United States has grown from a nation built on the horse's muscle and sweat to one that now has a multimillion-dollar pleasure horse industry. To take care of your own horse is really to get to know him. The hours we spend caring for and communicating with our equine friends are well worth the few hours we spend on their backs. There is nothing like the rapport that exists between you and your horse when he greets you at his stall door with a friendly nicker and a warm velvet muzzle, or when he comes flying up to the pasture gate sounding a welcome greeting.

My own romance with horses began when I was a young girl. Like many other horse-crazy kids, I was always thinking and reading about them. When not pretending to be one, I was sketching them (to the chagrin of many teachers) or dreaming about them. One of my favorite fantasies, when riding in a car, was to imagine myself on a horse, galloping along beside the car and jumping every obstacle along the path. I was definitely smitten!

Although I was fortunate enough to begin riding lessons in my preteens, they never quenched my desire to have a horse of my own. I couldn't wait until after school to rush to my girlfriend's barn to clean out her stalls and groom her horses. Living in a zoned suburban area made it impossible for me to keep one myself, and it wasn't until I was an adult and married that my dream of owning and caring for a horse became a reality. As my professional career accelerated, what began with one horse eventually grew into a full barn as I expanded into teaching, boarding, breeding, showing, and training my own and clients' horses. Many of my mistakes and on-the-job learning experiences and those of my students have contributed anecdotes to this book.

As more beginner and novice riders came for riding instruction, I found that for their safety as well as that of the horses, I had to teach a great deal of horse handling. A course on stable management (hands on, no riding) was the next logical step. At this point I'd put together a great deal of comprehensive material compiled from answers to questions and solutions to problems from new horse owners. Enter Marcia Hayes, the journalist. She was attending the stable management class as a neophyte horse owner while her son and daughter (the latter now a professional horsewoman herself) were taking riding lessons with me. Marcia said, "You really ought to put this into a book." And so began our collaboration, resulting in the first edition of *Horse Around the House* a year later.

After the book's publication my work expanded to include clinics, lectures, judging, managing, and consulting, all over the country. While I was judging in Arizona, a competitor came up to me at the end of the show, having recognized my name, and said that our book was her very first horse book and that she treasured it like a bible. When I was teaching a clinic in Colorado, a rider introduced himself and told me how helpful the book had been with his first horse. In Missouri a rider said she'd used it only that morning to braid her horse's mane. Over the years a number of college instructors have used it as a basic text for their stable management courses.

It is heartwarming and reassuring to know that *Horse Around the House* has fulfilled its intended goal and that my lifetime romance with the horse and my many years of experience as a professional horsewoman have positively influenced others. Now it only seems right to bring the book up to date for the sake of the wonderful animals that give so much of themselves for our pleasure and the enrichment of our lives.

Patricia Jacobson
KERHONKSON, NEW YORK

PART I

Hunting for a Horse

*When you are buying a Horse, take Care not to fall
in love with him, for when this passion hath once seized you,
you are no longer in a condition to judge his imperfections.*

Sieur de Sollesell (1617–1681)
THE COMPLEAT HORSEMAN OR PERFECT FARRIER
translated by Sir William Hope

✣ ✣ ✣

*Never believe a word any man says about a horse
he wishes to sell—not even a bishop.*

John Warde (1752–1838)

Horses Aren't House Pets

In order to thrive, horses need knowledgeable care and handling under conditions that simulate their natural state in the wild. Unlike dogs and cats, they never set foot in your house! The only exception might be the Miniature Horse, an appealing and relatively affordable pet. Standing two to three feet tall and weighing only 120 to 300 pounds, these diminutive creatures can be pastured three to an acre, need only good grass or hay, and can pull more than their own weight in harness.

By contrast, the average riding horse can weigh from 800 pounds to half a ton and stand from five to five and a half feet (or 14.2 to 16.2 hands) from ground to withers. He eats dozens of pounds of hay every day, along with several quarts of grain at each meal when working, and he's no house pet.

Even the smallest Shetland pony, docile looking and cute as he may be, can pull, pound for pound, as much weight as a 19-hand Clydesdale. That's horsepower. Just because you can look down on a horse doesn't mean you will be able to ride him or even lead him around easily.

In the euphoria of buying a first horse, these considerations are sometimes forgotten. A childhood diet of romantic stories and television westerns can leave the impression that horses are easy to ride and care for. Hollywood horses gallop non-stop for hours without being cooled down or watered; they respond to every spoken command, stop on a dime, and find their own way back to the barn.

Fictional expectations about equine behavior are dangerous and ultimately discouraging. The carefree cowboy riding into the Technicolor sunset belies the months spent schooling his horse and all the work that had to be done back at the ranch before he saddled up.

Although some horses are hardy enough to winter out on windy subzero pastures, they can also be delicate, complex, even eccentric creatures with very special needs. In their domestic state they depend entirely on their owners to meet these needs, all of which involves time and effort.

Hooves, probably the most vulnerable part of the horse, will need to be picked out every day and checked for signs of irregularity, particularly the hoof disease thrush. At least every six weeks, preferably once a month, the hooves should be trimmed by a good farrier.

A stabled horse will need daily grooming, not just for the sake of appearance but to ensure cleanliness and keep up circulation and muscle tone. You'll find your own muscle tone improving too, after the exertion of doing a good grooming job.

The most tedious task is cleaning, or mucking out, the stall. If the horse is inside only at night and turned out all day, you can get away with a daily cleaning. Stalls of continually stabled animals will need mucking out several times a day, each session taking about twenty minutes.

Riding equipment, or tack, needs regular cleaning, at least twice a week and preferably after each ride. Good tack is costly, and you protect your investment by keeping the leather supple and the metal parts gleaming.

After matters of routine maintenance, the next major consideration is money. Buying and keeping a horse is expensive, so before you take one home, it's wise to face some hard economic facts.

The initial purchase price of a horse can range from several thousand dollars to millions (although I assume you won't be buying a racehorse). After you get your new horse tucked away in the stable, you'll need to budget for a visit from the blacksmith, or farrier, every six weeks, with fees ranging from forty to a hundred dollars per house call, and for periodic vet's bills that will probably add up to more than two hundred dollars per year. Even a healthy horse needs annual shots and regular deworming in order to stay that way.

For the many hours and dollars spent, great rewards await the dedicated horse owner. No experience beats a trail ride on a crisp autumn day when your horse is in good condition and fine spirits, responding to every command. On a cold winter night it's enormously satisfying to bed your horse down on fresh straw and leave him happily munching a hot bran mash. Proper care and good training will foster a rapport worth far more than the effort it takes to achieve it.

But like anything worthwhile, this relationship won't come easily. Your horse needs regular care, day in and day out, twelve months a year. He can't be left in a kennel when you want to take a vacation, and a month in a boarding stable can cost as much as, or more than, the rent for a small apartment. Unless you have a pasture with a constant supply of fresh water, your horse can't be left alone for more than a day.

The responsible horse owner spends more time caring for his mount than riding him. If you live in a temperate climate with no access to an indoor ring, you will be working your horse regularly only six or seven months of the year. Even if you don't mind riding in the cold and snow, you will face days, sometimes weeks, when weather conditions won't permit it. This leaves a long, cold, dark period when your only reward will be a friendly whinny as you open the feed box with numbed hands.

Feeding a horse involves more than throwing a bale of hay into the stall twice a day. Hay has to be shaken out to rid it of dust and other particles that could be harmful if inhaled. Feed must be carefully measured, the amount determined by the horse's size and the work being done. To stay healthy and get full nutritive value from the feed, a horse should be dewormed every six weeks. His teeth must be checked periodically by a veterinarian and "floated," or filed, when necessary. All this takes time and knowledge.

Added to these expenses are the other basic costs of hay, grain, feed supplements, and bedding for the stall, along with tack, blankets, and medicines, and, if you don't already have facilities, materials for building and maintaining a stable, paddock, and pasture. While a stable can be as simple as an open shed, and a fence can be merely a single strand of electric wire, it still adds up. And up.

The price of hay, grain, and bedding will vary according to your location. In Connecticut a bag of feed might cost twice as much as in a grain-producing area of the Midwest, and a bale of hay that goes for a few dollars in the Northwest will cost more than thirty in Hawaii. Horse owners in rural areas will generally spend less if they can buy and store food supplies in bulk.

You must figure clothes, too, into your overall budget, bearing in mind that growing children will need riding outfits replaced each year. The type of riding you do will determine the appropriate attire. Even for casual English riding, you'll need breeches, jodhpurs or riding tights, boots, and gloves. Western pleasure gear is more simple, comprising a shirt, jeans, and boots, but in the show ring you'll need a dress shirt, hat, belt, and chaps. And the all-important safety helmet is a must for any type of riding.

All in all, the cost of keeping a horse at home, without skimping, will average about two hundred dollars a month in temperate rural areas. It will be considerably less in milder climates, and considerably more in the suburbs.

In addition to maintenance, the horse's conditioning has to be taken into account. Like people, horses need exercise to stay in shape. Regular exercise. This requires considerable discipline on your part. The horse should be exercised on a consistent basis—a requirement that deserves a lot of thought before you buy. Perhaps you won't be able to ride on Tuesdays, Thursdays, or any weekday. Maybe you'd prefer to go out for a long trail ride on Sunday afternoon and let your horse take it easy for the rest of the week. But a casual approach to riding is an invitation to disaster. For a horse out of condition, two hours on the trail or in the ring can result in strained muscles, saddle or girth sores, a pulled tendon, colic, or—in extreme cases—founder, a circulatory condition of the hoof that can cause permanent lameness.

I ask my students to imagine sitting around all week watching television until Sunday morning, then deciding to repent their slothful ways and going for a five-mile run. Unaccustomed to any activity, the sedentary muscular system will rebel against such vigorous exercise, becoming so strained and sore that the erstwhile couch potato won't be able to move again for another week. Think of horses as you would human athletes or dancers, whose bodies need to be gradually conditioned in order to strengthen and stretch tendons, ligaments, and muscles. After a week of lolling around the paddock, a horse asked to go on a Sunday afternoon trail ride will end up very sore and probably sick.

Riding isn't the only way to keep a horse fit—some large stables use the equine equivalent of a NordicTrack. But since all the alternatives involve a human presence, you might as well ride. It's more fun.

For safety's sake, the prospective horse owner needs to think about his or her riding skills, which should go beyond the ability to stay aboard a hack on a trail ride. Do you know how to cue a horse to trot/jog or canter/lope and maintain control at these gaits? If you don't know the basics, some formal riding instruction is mandatory. The more extensive your skills, the more pleasure you and your horse will derive from riding and the safer the experience will be.

Accomplished equestrians ride with seats balanced over the horse's center of gravity, independent of the hands and legs, so that signals given don't communicate conflicting messages. Only formal riding instruction can help achieve this. Knowing how to handle yourself and your horse in an assured and relaxed manner with regard to his and your safety takes training. Good instruction helps prevent dangerous situations from developing, assuring you of a longer and more fulfilling relationship with your new equine friend.

Unschooled riders have a fifty-fifty chance of purchasing a horse they can mount and control. Those who don't know how to saddle, bridle, or halter the animal, and who are ignorant of the correct riding signals, will see any previous training in the horse quickly nullified. As time goes by, you may spend more time on the ground than in the saddle—either unable to get on, unable to stay on, or too frustrated to keep trying. Most serious of all, you could get hurt.

If you buy a horse without knowing how to ride, groom, and feed it, you're beaten before you start. I know several people who bought horses cold, so to speak, always with distressing results. One beginning pupil came to my course on stable management to learn how to care for her first horse, a purebred Arabian stallion. Specifically, she wanted to know how to saddle and bridle him. But as the course wore on, it became apparent that the horse couldn't even be haltered and tied. Because stallions tend to be high spirited and unpredictable, the girl was afraid to get too close to him, and consequently she couldn't even groom him, let alone tack him up. Since she couldn't get a halter on, she wasn't able to lead him around. As a result the horse couldn't be taken outside and was becoming more and more unmanageable. Because their temperaments are generally unstable, stallions aren't recommended as mounts for novice riders. But this sort of dilemma is common to anyone whose knowledge of horses is based on romantic fiction instead of fact.

The girl was also reluctant to have the stallion gelded, arguing that it was unnatural. But faced with the prospect of a spirited horse becoming more and more unmanageable during a long, hard winter, she finally agreed to the operation. She has since taken riding lessons, her horse is being professionally trained, and she now enjoys him.

Putting an untrained rider on a green horse is almost equivalent to sending a novice skier down an advanced slope or throwing a nonswimmer into deep water. Actually, it's worse, because it involves a very strong animal with a mind of its own. Horses can sense when a person is afraid, putting the ignorant owner at risk for a lot of trouble. They're smart enough to take advantage of a situation that could endanger a neophyte rider.

For example, not knowing how to handle and care for a horse can be unhealthy and a liability to both horse and owner. Did you know that some horses are trained to tie with a halter, and others around the neck? If you try to neck-tie a horse that has been trained to a halter, he'll panic, pull back, and either rip the fence post out of the ground or choke himself. And unless you want a broken bridle, never tie a horse by the reins (even though you often see it done in the movies).

All horses are trained to be approached, mounted, and led from the near or left side—a custom derived from the military, when swords were carried on the left hip.

Should you approach or lead a trained horse from the off side, the animal could become confused and perhaps balk at being led.

When approaching a strange horse, be as wary as you would with a strange dog. Don't, for example, run up and pat him on the nose—many horses don't want to be touched there. If you want to show affection, speak softly and give him a gentle pat on the neck or shoulder of the near side, so he can see you, and always keep an eye on his ears, a barometer of mood.

I've often seen parents allow their children to pet a horse when his ears are laid flat back and his mouth is set in a menacing manner, apparently unaware that the animal's mood is anything but friendly. Experienced equestrians never take even the most docile horse for granted, and they learn to anticipate a horse's reactions and interpret his moods. If he's enjoying the attention, his ears will be upright or slightly forward.

Only spending time around horses with a good instructor will turn a novice into a relaxed and experienced horseperson. Riding lessons are costly, but your career as a horse owner cannot progress without them. Once you've found a good instructor, it's wise to take him or her along as a professional adviser when you go horse hunting. An instructor is likely to know the local dealers and will be able to judge your riding potential and help you pick the right horse. Not all teachers give instructions on horse care and stable management; if yours doesn't, there are alternatives. (See Chapter 28.)

Before you buy a horse, take into consideration all the perks and pitfalls of horse ownership. Ask yourself the following questions, and answer them honestly to make sure you can cope with these experiences:

• Would you be willing to get out of bed at two A.M. during a rainstorm to retrieve your horse from a neighbor's yard (usually a terrified, angry neighbor), then mend the fence through which he escaped?

• When it's twenty below zero and all the water pipes to your barn have frozen, would you be willing to cart two or three pails of water a day over the two hundred yards from your house to his stall?

• Would you have the stomach to hold your horse's tongue over on the side of his mouth (equine tongues are very large) while you pour a slug of whiskey down his throat to relieve colic (his kind of stomachache)? Then walk him around the paddock for an hour or more, no matter what the weather, even though all he wants to do is lie down?

• Could you help your horse get up from the stall when he's tried to roll and gotten himself pinned (cast) against the wall and is thrashing about in panic?

• Would you be willing to chip frozen manure from the stall floor and then dig a path through two feet of snow to the manure pile?

I could go on and on. But you get the idea. These situations aren't exaggerated—I've faced all of them and more during my years of horse ownership. If you're planning on getting more than one horse, you'll find that problems like these tend to multiply in proportion to the number of occupants in your stable.

If you're able to confront these frustrating prospects with equanimity, I'd say you have the stamina and dedication necessary for successful horse ownership. That being settled, we can get down to the business of choosing the right horse.

2

Where, What, and How Much?

Buying a horse is not something to be rushed into, by either personal whim or by pleading children. The first horse you see may capture your heart at three hundred yards, but don't reach for your checkbook until you've closely examined your prospective purchase for soundness, schooling, manners, temperament, conformation, and breeding. If you're not cautious, you're liable to end up getting stuck—like the person who bought the horse described in this advertisement:

> For Sale: Alert young trail horse for experienced rider. Gorgeous chestnut
> mare with white blaze. Goes English or Western. Sacrifice cheap.
> Will deliver.

Once you understand what to look for in a good horse, you'll never get excited by an ad like this again. Reading between the lines, you'll suspect that "alert" ("spirited" is more like it) is a euphemism for spooky or unmanageable. A horse that "goes English or Western" probably just goes, period; and an experienced rider is likely to be the only kind who could stay on for the trip. A low price tag ("Sacrifice cheap") often signals serious personality and/or behavior problems; and the offer of free delivery probably means she is probably next to impossible to load into a trailer.

Remember too that handsome is as handsome does. Good looks are significant only when accompanied by good training. A horse that is absolutely beautiful and absolutely unmanageable is absolutely worthless—except, perhaps, for breeding.

You can find a suitable horse through an ad, if you know how to read them, at a breeding farm, or through a dealer. Many owners and dealers now send videos to prospective buyers, an innovation that saves everyone concerned a lot of time. Inexperienced riders looking for a first horse should take a professional with them on their quest. But even with professional advice, auction sales are not a good bet for beginners. Bargains can be found at sales, of course. Some of the top horses in the country have been picked up at auctions for a song—but always by people who know what to look for.

Seattle Slew, the first undefeated horse to sweep the Triple Crown (in 1977), was purchased at public auction for $17,500 and was eventually syndicated as a breeding stallion for $12 million! Real Quiet, who was nosed out of a Triple Crown win in 1998, was bought as a yearling for $17,000.

Gordon Wright, a former coach of the U.S. Olympic Equestrian team, got his famous open jumper Sonny at a sheriff's auction for sixteen dollars. The horse had been found wandering along a back road in Westchester County, and no owner had come to claim him.

A horse named Sinjon, who was sold for $185 because of his reputation as a weaver, cribber, and general nuisance, went on to become the prizewinning mount of U.S. Olympic team members George Morris, Kathy Kusner, and Bill Steinkraus. Before his retirement Sinjon had helped Steinkraus win a fourth at the 1960 Rome Olympics, made seven trips to Europe, and was finally rewarded with the coveted King George V Cup, presented by Queen Elizabeth.

The Angel, a famous open jumper who won hundreds of ribbons at every top show in the country and holds the Haymond record for winning horse-of-the-year four times in a row, was discovered standing knee deep in manure in a milkman's broken-down barn. The Angel's stall was so dark that he was temporarily blinded, and he stumbled into the barn door when he was taken outside. Treatment by a veterinarian restored his vision, and he went on to become a champion.

Another famed open jumper, Snowman, began life as a plowhorse and was bought by Harry de Leyer just as he was being

loaded onto a truck bound for the dog-food factory. This eighty-dollar bargain was about to be sold for horsemeat because he kept jumping out of his pasture. He became the winner of the National Horse Show crown as well as the Professional Horsemen's Association champion. De Leyer later turned down an offer of fifty thousand for him.

These are wonderful stories, but they shouldn't get your hopes up. All these buyers were experienced horsepeople. The chances of you getting such a steal are very slim. Don't begin your search by looking for such a bargain, and be wary of any horse that is promoted as one.

Buying from a dealer can be tricky and isn't advised unless you have professional help. While most dealers are aboveboard and reliable, a few are definitely not. Only an experienced adviser will know the difference. An unscrupulous dealer, for example, might ride or lunge a high-spirited horse for several hours before your arrival, in order to pass him off to you as a quiet mount (when he's almost too exhausted to walk). Some have been known to drug sick horses with stimulants or antibiotics or to give tranquilizers to high-strung animals to make them appear normal. Others have given medications for various lamenesses that work a temporary cure. Butazolidin (Bute), a respectable medication when used properly, is sometimes used to obscure lameness.

If you suspect a horse is under the influence of a drug, ask your veterinarian to do a urine chemistry. Or take the horse home for a seventy-two-hour trial period, during which time most drugs will wear off. Beware of Bute under any circumstances where a dealer or stable owner stands to gain a great deal by peddling an unsound horse.

One girl I know bought a horse from the riding stable where she took lessons. Although she rode the horse several times a week, she never got a hint that he was unsound. When the stable was sold to another owner some months later, she was left with a $3,500 lame horse on her hands. The previous owner had dosed the horse's food with Bute every morning.

A reputable dealer, seeking future referrals from satisfied customers, will encourage a prospective buyer to vet a horse thoroughly to ensure that it is healthy and sound.

WHAT WILL YOU BE USING HIM FOR?

A lasting relationship with a horse depends on how well his conformation, training, and temperament meet the rider's needs. The time you spend anticipating these needs before making your choice is time well spent. Before shopping around, please give these questions some serious thought.

Will you be riding English or Western? Solely for pleasure or competing in a specialized discipline?

An English rider might decide to specialize in equitation, hunters, open jumping, combined training, or dressage. The Western rider might wish merely to pleasure-ride or to compete in reining, cutting, or barrel racing.

A horse's ability is determined by its conformation or physique, which in the case of purebreds has been developed over generations of selective breeding, producing equine types tailored to perform in specialized niches. Consequently, a horse that excels in dressage may be a dunce as a jumper, while a good cutting horse may not cut it on a hundred-mile endurance ride.

Once you've decided on a specialty, you can focus on finding a horse with abilities to match. This will narrow the field considerably. Reading between the lines of classified ads and asking the right questions will save hours, even weeks of random searching. When videos are available, you'll know how to evaluate them.

Some breeds, among them the European warmbloods favored in jumping, are all-around athletes—with price tags to match their exalted talents. Riders who decide to specialize usually want to show, and their choice of a horse will depend on the class of competition they enter. Equine breeding, conformation, and training make a significant difference at large, recognized shows.

Beginning riders, uncertain of how far they want to advance in their chosen specialty, should look for a mount that will help them perfect their skills. A purebred with impeccable credentials and perfect conformation is next to worthless as a first horse if its lack of training interferes with yours. It's better to gain experience before investing in a good-looking but hard-to-control mount. When that time comes, you may wish to resell your first horse to another eager novice.

Good equine manners, a quiet temperament, and suitability are all essential traits both inside and out of the ring. Show judges frown on skittish, ill-mannered horses and give points to those with conformations best suited to their competitive class. On the trail it's no pleasure to ride a spook who sees a ghost behind every bush or who lags behind because his build isn't up to the terrain.

Before you take out your checkbook, be sure to assess the personality, abilities, and soundness of a prospective purchase, both in the ring and on the trail, preferably in the company of a professional trained to spot potential problems.

When you're trying a horse out, don't forget about size. It sounds like an obvious thing to consider, but I've known people who bought horses without thinking about how they look astride them or considering whether they have the reach and strength to handle them on the ground.

HOW MUCH SHOULD YOU SPEND?

Owning a horse is a long-term commitment, so it makes sense to spend as much money on it as you can afford. A horse that satisfies your needs may range in price from a few thousand to several hundred thousand dollars. Half-breds and crossbreds are usually less expensive than purebreds. A horse that is mannerly and *well-trained* is a good choice for a beginner.

No matter what the purchase price, the cost of maintaining the horse will be the same. Half-bred horses and purebreds alike need the same food, shelter, and care. So if you can afford a more expensive mount, go for it.

Although the price of a horse depends primarily on breeding and/or conformation, it is also influenced by training, size, age, sex, and color. Since breeding affects conformation and is the most costly consideration, let's begin there.

WHAT BREED SHOULD YOU GET?

As I noted earlier, certain disciplines like jumping, dressage, and cutting require a certain type of conformation and disposition—ideal characteristics that have been integrated and honed by generations of selective breeding.

The Quarter Horse, for instance, has been selectively bred to achieve short bursts of speed over a quarter-mile, making him an excellent candidate for cutting and reining and the preferred mount in most serious Western competitions (although Arabians are favored in some areas).

For many years in this country Thoroughbreds dominated the hunter and jumper classes in the English show ring. They were the breed to ride if you wanted to catch a judge's eye. Nowadays, with the influx of European warmbloods, the picture is very different. The Thoroughbred is being outperformed by warmbloods like the Selle-Francais, Holsteiner, Hanoverian, and Dutch warmblood, all bred specifically for power over fences and elegant gaits, with the steady temperaments and stamina needed to undergo the hours of training that international competition demands. In jumping classes these European newcomers often outnumber Thoroughbreds, the latter being frequently crossed with warmbloods to produce superior hunter entries.

A rider who wants to compete in lower levels of dressage or combined training can choose just about any type of horse with suitable conformation and education. Those who aspire to international competition (and have bank accounts to match their ambition) should consider importing a horse from Europe. Because of a government-sponsored breeding program, Germans have dominated the international dressage ring for years, riding Hanoverians, Holsteiners, Westphalians, and

Trakehners. If you can afford to go shopping abroad, plan to spend at least $30,000 on an import.

A purebred with ideal conformation will usually cost more than a good-looking crossbred (a combination of two breeds like Connemara and Thoroughbred), a half-bred (one purebred parent), or a mixed breed (having three or more purebred ancestors). Grade horses have an uncertain and probably accidental ancestry, and—with the exception of mustangs—there aren't many around. Horse breeders can't afford to keep anything but purebred stallions, and the cost of breeding, raising, and training a horse is so high that it doesn't pay to raise a grade from infancy.

Because of a growing demand for horsemeat, more grades are found today on tables than in stables—a sad fate for these

THE WESTPHALIAN

dependable animals that were once the mainstay of the novice buyer market. The scarcity of grades has affected the economics of the equine industry, driving prices up as novices look elsewhere for a first mount. The best alternative is a half-bred; they are usually good looking, have a quieter disposition than a purebred, and are reasonably priced. (A half-bred hunter that looks like a Thoroughbred, however, will probably cost more.)

A first horse should be better educated than its rider. Good training, coupled with a quiet, trustworthy disposition, are the most important qualities a beginning rider should look for. A novice needs a mount that will build confidence and that is well trained to perform in the chosen specialty; the degree of training will depend on how far they want to advance. A green horse (a young horse or one of any age just starting its training) won't fit the beginner's bill (though an intermediate rider might decide that its potential talent justifies the extra time and/or money it will take to train it).

Schooled horses naturally cost more than green ones (a good deal more, in the case of purebreds), and the price will reflect the trainer's credentials. A horse schooled by an internationally known professional will have more star value than one trained by someone less well known, even if equally competent. Any horse with professional schooling is usually more valuable than one trained in the backyard by an amateur. Your professional adviser will be able to gauge the amount and quality of the schooling by putting the prospective purchase through its paces.

HOW MUCH TRAINING SHOULD HE HAVE?

HOW BIG?

The size of a horse is an aesthetic as well as a practical consideration. Not only will a petite woman of five feet or so look silly on a 16-hand hunter, she won't have the height to easily saddle, bridle, and groom it. Conversely, a six-foot-four man might look fine on a small horse with a barrel big enough to minimize the length of his legs, but he would cut an absurd figure in a hunter or dressage class astride anything under 16.2 hands. A Mutt and Jeff mismatch is sure to lose ribbons in the ring, if only because of the unsuitability of horse to rider.

Most horses entered in international competitions today measure more than 16 hands. But bigger isn't necessarily better, as Mickey Walsh proved in 1939, when he and his famous Connemara pony Little Squire won twenty-five blue ribbons and seven championships, including the National Open Jumping Championship at Madison Square Garden. In 1963 the 15-hand Connemara Dumdrum of Ireland was awarded England's prestigious King George V Cup for show jumping, and the 14.2-hand Thoroughbred-Connemara cross, Stroller, won a silver for the English show jumping team at the 1968 Olympics in Mexico.

HOW OLD?

While it isn't impossible to teach an old horse new tricks, it takes more time, energy, and patience than most riders care to expend. The muscular system of a mature horse is fully developed according to the way it has been used (or mis-used) during the preceding years. Although some breeds are fully mature at five years of age, many of the larger breeds don't reach maturity until seven. At this stage they should have finished their education and be ready for a full working schedule.

An ideal candidate for a first horse is a well-trained and sound aged veteran ten to fourteen years old. (*Aged,* in equine terminology, means any horse nine or older.) Aged horses are generally more reliable than young ones, and their years of experience will help young riders and novice adults gain the confidence they need to progress. For the novice-intermediate rider, a well-schooled horse seven to ten years old is a good choice. Properly cared for, these middle-aged horses will be ridable into their late teens and early twenties. Three horses in my barn, over twenty-one, are used regularly in the school, and I know of older ones that go on trail rides and win in competition.

I also strongly recommend sound, well-cared for seniors as safe, inexpensive mounts for novice adults who are primarily weekend riders. These old-timers are the closest thing to an insurance policy that a rider can get, and if properly cared for, they will provide three to eight years of pleasure while laying a foundation for the next level of horse.

Young horses between the age of three and five are generally less reliable because they have less training and are therefore less expensive than the usually more mentally and physically mature individual of six to nine years that has completed training and gained experience. An exception would be a green horse of unusual promise, in which case potential will determine price.

Registration, Brands, and Tattoos

When a horse is registered, its papers will list the year of foaling and the names of its sire and dam, as well as its sex, color, and markings. Purebreds of proven age and genealogy command the highest prices.

If you are considering purchasing a Thoroughbred without papers, check to see if it has a tattoo inside its upper lip. If so, the horse spent time on the track as a two- or three-year old (which doesn't always mean it has been actually raced). The tattooed letter in front of the numerals is a code for the year of foaling. A veterinarian or Thoroughbred trainer will be able to tell you the year. Standardbred stables also use tattoos.

Most registered Arabians are freeze-branded under the mane: An upright A denotes a purebred, and a horizontal or "lazy A," a half Arabian. The first two numbers after the letter are stacked, indicating the year of birth, followed by the registration number.

Freeze branding is also used on some Quarter Horses, Appaloosas, American Miniatures, American Performance Horses, Paints, Racking Horses, Standardbreds, Saddlebreds, Tennessee Walkers, North American Warmbloods, and Morgans. A state insignia precedes the horse's birth date and registration number, and the place of marking varies according to the state. Horses that are not breed-registered can be freeze-branded for identification purposes.

Teeth

The age of an unregistered horse is best determined by a close look at its teeth; hence the old adage "Never look a gift horse in the mouth." But dental examinations give only an approximate estimate of age, and the degree of accuracy decreases with advancing years and depends on the horse's diet and the care it has received. A wild horse that has foraged close to the ground in poor pasture will wear its teeth down faster than a racehorse that is fed alfalfa and has its teeth floated (filed) regularly. Despite these variables, dental condition is still the most commonly used indicator of age.

Horses' teeth have a limited period of growth, after which the crowns wear down with attrition and show markings characteristic of a certain age. Like people, horses lose their baby teeth (milk teeth) in

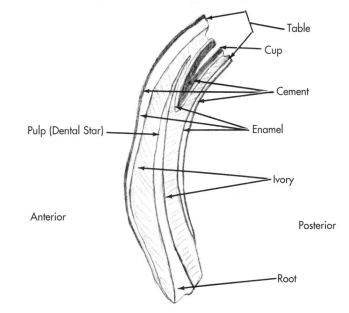

CROSS-SECTION SIDE VIEW OF PERMANENT FRONT TOOTH

Table
Cup
Cement
Pulp (Dental Star)
Enamel
Ivory
Anterior
Posterior
Root

Wearing surface of right front central tooth viewed from above is more horizontal in a younger horse, becoming triangular with age.

a specific order and grow permanent ones in the same sequence. Depending on the construction of the jaw, the mature teeth are then ground down in a fairly predictable way. The wearing surface, viewed from above when the jaw is open, is more or less horizontal in a young horse and becomes triangular with increasing age.

As a horse gets older, the tables of the lower incisors change from elliptical to round, to triangular, and finally to oval. At the age of seven, he begins to lose the "cups" on its central incisors, which wear down to rings of flat enamel. These rings erode further to expose the *dental star,* which becomes larger and more centrally located with advancing years. Over time the angle of the front teeth, which is close to a right angle in young horses, becomes increasingly acute.

At the age of ten, a dark line begins to form at the gum line on the outside of the horse's corner incisors. Named *Galvayne's groove,* after the Scottish veterinarian who used it to measure equine age at the turn of the century, this line gradually advances downward, extending to the middle of these teeth by age fifteen and reaching the bottom of the incisors five years later. By the twenty-fifth year, the upper half of Galvayne's groove has disappeared, and it is gone entirely by the age of thirty.

Galvayne claimed to be infallible in determining age by examining the wear on horses' teeth, but recent research at the University of Bristol disputes this boast. Scientists there question whether Galvayne ever used documented proof of the birth date of a horse to test his observations in a blind trial—the evidence indicates that he relied on hearsay instead. Still, researchers have concluded that dental examination remains the best practical technique for determining age, even though it is more of an "informed guess" than an accurate assessment.

SIDE VIEW—ANGLE OF INCIDENCE

| 3 years | 5 years | 9 years | 15 years |

Up to the age of seven, it's fairly easy to determine a horse's age, but it gets tricky after that. Unless you bring a professional along to "read" a prospect's teeth, you could find that your new eight-year-old is actually eighteen.

It's said that you can *tell* a gelding, *discuss* it with a stallion, but you *ask* a mare! As a rule, geldings are more tractable than mares or stallions, making them a better choice for a first horse. Some of my best school horses have been mares and they are preferred by many of my students, but they can be difficult, frequently having an attitude toward other horses, toward being curry-combed, or toward having their girths tightened. They may even resent the pressure of a rider's leg. This behavior isn't necessarily related to estrus. Some mares are just opinionated, but then, some riders enjoy the challenge.

Good breeding stock is expensive, so if you want a riding horse that will double as a broodmare, you should choose carefully, paying attention to pedigree.

A stallion is a poor choice for any but an experienced rider. He will probably require special handling, particularly around other horses; many stables refuse to board them. Unless a stallion's pedigree and performance record are impressive enough to rate keeping him for stud, he should be gelded. But when a stallion is kept as a stud, his price will probably be way beyond what the average buyer wants to spend. If your heart is set on owning a stallion, buy shares in a syndicate, and allow professionals to do the handling and showing. Meanwhile, keep looking for a gelding or a mare as a suitable riding horse.

Many riders, particularly beginners, won't need to worry about color. It doesn't make the slightest difference in a pleasure horse, unless the rider prefers a certain look; nor does it matter in those used for open jumping or combined training. In fact, I find that one of the pleasures of judging Horse Trials is the potpourri of colors, types, and breeds.

But riders who plan to show right away in hunter classes would be wise to choose a color traditional to the specialty: a basic bay, chestnut, brown, or gray. These colors shouldn't be embellished with too much "chrome" (slang for high white stockings and a wide, uneven blaze), which in excessive amounts will drive the price down. Some breeds go through trends and like a lot of white, but usually not over an eye or in stockings that extend over the knees.

Color gets costly when a breed is defined by it, including registered Albinos, Appaloosas, Buckskins, Palominos, Pintos, and Paints. In other breeds the cost of color is a matter of fashion.

Once you've carefully selected a list of candidates and made appointments to view them, you'll be eager to start making the rounds. Don't let enthusiasm blind you to first impressions. Before you enter a stable, look around to assess the condition of the grounds, buildings, and fencing—all indicate how the horse is being cared for. An unmowed lawn, sagging fencing, and buildings in need of paint don't bode well

WHAT GENDER?

WHAT COLOR?

HOW SHOULD YOU WINDOW-SHOP?

for the occupants of the barn. The stable itself should be clean and tidy, with stalls picked out and stablemates looking healthy and happy. Broken tack or filthy blankets are an indication that the horse's care is equally haphazard.

Giving a Horse the Once-Over

Before you ride a horse, you and your professional adviser will want to see him *in hand* (led out in either bridle or halter) and *set up* (standing on flat ground with weight distributed equally on all four feet).

While standing ten to fifteen feet away, give the horse a quick assessment, looking for overall balance and harmony in his parts as well as definition of his muscle and bone. Does the head look like it belongs to the body? Does the back of the body, from withers to loin, match the hindquarters? Or does the rear end seem to belong to a different horse? Each part of a horse should flow together harmoniously and smoothly.

The back should span approximately one-third of the horse's length. Very short backs tend to be tight and inflexible, while overly long ones are usually weak. A rear end lighter than the forehand will inhibit a horse's ability to come from behind and will cause his weight to fall forward.

Clearly defined, strong legs are a sign of good breeding, and like those of an athlete or dancer, they should be cleanly structured. As you view the horse close up and from a distance, muscle and bone should show well from all sides. Above all, the legs must be sturdy enough for the job the horse will perform.

Now that you've given him the once-over, we'll take a closer look at conformation.

Good breeding doesn't guarantee good conformation. Just as jug ears, narrow shoulders, or bow legs can run in some royal families, some purebreds will inherit the mule ears, U-necks, or pigeon toes of a poorly endowed forebear. Among humans, physical shortcomings don't affect social status, but they can affect a horse's soundness and its suitability to do the job.

Parts of His Body

HEAD. A large head usually suggests a lack of refinement somewhere in a horse's ancestry. Head shape varies from breed to breed; the dished profile of an Arab sharply contrasts with the Roman nose of some warmbloods. But the head should always set off and complement the body. A long, narrow head is usually attached to a body of similar proportions. A straight or slightly dished head is a nice complement to a small, square muzzle (of a size that would fit in a teacup, according to an old adage). A broad flat forehead and large eyes set well apart are desirable characteristics in most breeds. The eyes should be dark and clear, with no cloudiness. Small eyes or eyes with a lot of white around them usually indicate an unreliable temperament.

EARS. The ears ennoble a horse's expression and are excellent barometers of mood and degree of attention. They should sit well on the head at about a 45-degree angle and be in proportion to it. The expression in a horse's eyes, and the set of the animal's ears at rest and when you ride, will tell you a lot about his reliability and his ability to relax in the stable, ring, and field.

NECK. A horse uses his neck for balancing. A horse whose neck is too short or too thick will be laterally stiff, lack flexibility, and probably have a short, choppy stride. Thick-necked horses can be literally headstrong, constantly pulling on a rider's hands. They are difficult to control and consequently a nuisance to ride. Having too long a neck makes it difficult for a horse to balance and get his hindquarters under him, causing too much of his weight to be carried on the forehand.

All breeds should have some curve to the neck, although the muscle will be less clearly defined in horses that haven't been worked for a while. A neck that doesn't flow harmoniously into the withers,

like a U-neck, will interfere with movement and can cause breathing difficulties. The throatlatch should be trim and clean, allowing maximum flexibility at the poll.

Different riding disciplines require different head carriages. This is important to take into account because the way a horse naturally carries its neck can't be changed.

1. Ewe-neck, Roman nose, pig eye.

2. Short, thick neck, heavy through the throatlatch.

3. Well-crested neck with a good arch and a concave profile.

The neck of a dressage horse should be well up and arched; a hunter's, in contrast, should be almost level. Western pleasure horses carry their necks low and arched.

SHOULDERS. The ideal shoulder slopes from the withers to its midpoint at an angle of nearly 45 degrees, mirroring the pitch of the pastern.

This angle permits a long forward stride and allows a horse to easily raise its forelegs when jumping. A straight shoulder shortens the stride and inhibits freedom of movement, causing a choppy gait.

CHEST, RIBS, AND GIRTH. In human sprinters the size and strength of the upper body, rather than the length of the legs, determines speed over short distances. Likewise, horses that race short distances are distinguished by large, muscular chests. Quarter Horses, bred to race the quarter-mile, have relatively short, muscular legs beneath massive chests and barrels, with powerful hindquarters to match.

Look for a broad chest between forelegs spread well apart and a barrel ample enough at the girth to allow plenty of room for the heart and lungs. Some horses are too wide in front; while not a serious flaw, it looks awkward and can produce a lumbering canter and gallop.

Narrow-chested horses often have narrow ribs to match. This condition (called *slab-sided*) inhibits the oxygen intake and makes it difficult to keep a saddle in place, especially when the horse is jumping or going up and down hills. My daughter once borrowed a slab-sided horse for a trail ride and found that she had to dismount after every downhill trek to undo the girth and slide the saddle back into position. When the horse stopped to drink before crossing a stream, the saddle slipped forward, dumping her into the drink. A disproportionately shallow girth on a horse can also cause saddle sliding. An ample girth is a sign of quality, allowing plenty of room for heart and lungs—an obvious necessity for horses doing a lot of galloping or jumping.

WITHERS. The ridge between the shoulder blades marks the beginning of a horse's back and is its highest point of measurement as well. (Height is measured in hands from the bottom of the hoof to the top of the withers.) The withers should be clearly defined and pronounced enough to keep saddle and pad securely in place. Flat, fleshy withers allow the saddle to slide forward and interfere with shoulder movement, causing a horse to shorten its stride and can lead to lameness. Horses with the graceful, flowing stride characteristic of famous jumpers and flat racers almost always have well-developed withers.

BACK. The back of a horse must be well muscled and of a length that easily bears a rider's weight. Overly long backs strain easily, while horses with very short ones are less supple and tend to have choppier gaits. The back should be nearly level. *Roach* backs that curve up from the center tend to be rigid, causing jarring gaits. A back that is too hollow or *swaybacked,* a fault usually accompanied by an upright neck, will also be weak. A horse with any of these faults is difficult to collect and therefore unsuitable for anything but pleasure riding.

LEGS. Since every aspect of a horse's performance is affected by its legs, they rate an especially thorough examination. Viewing the horse from the front, drop an imaginary line down from the point of the shoulder to the ground. On a well-

FRONT VIEW CONFORMATION OF FORELEGS

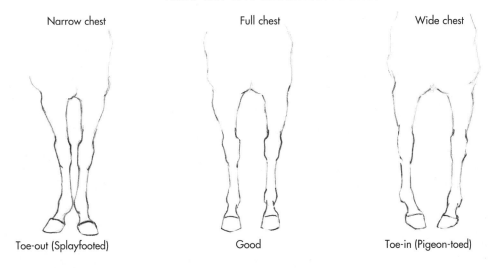

Narrow chest   Full chest   Wide chest

Toe-out (Splayfooted)   Good   Toe-in (Pigeon-toed)

balanced horse this line should bisect forearm, knee, and fetlock, ending at the center of the toe. Now move to the side, and draw another line from the center of the horse's shoulder down through the middle of the foreleg to the fetlock joint on the back of the heel. Do the same thing on the hind legs, dropping the line from the point of the buttock to the ground, running it against the back of or slightly behind the hock and cannon bone. Legs that pass this test are in good balance and are at less risk from stress injuries.

When knees fall behind the imaginary plumb line (a condition called *calf-kneed*), the body weight falls on the back of the joint, which is not built to absorb the greater shock of impact, straining muscle and cartilage. Less strain is put on knees that fall in front of the plumb line (*over-at-the-knee* or *buck-kneed*), so this defect is more acceptable if it isn't too extreme.

Knees should be well defined, clean, flat, and like all other joints, symmetrical and facing forward. Knee joints help to cushion the concussion of movement and should be structured to absorb shock equally.

The leg's primary shock absorber is the fetlock joint, which should be well defined—no wider than the leg above it—and should blend smoothly into the cannon bone with a gentle convex curve. Any old injuries in this area need to be carefully scrutinized by a veterinarian.

Proper functioning of the fetlock joint depends on whether the angle of the pastern below it is angled to absorb maximum shock. Pasterns should have a pitch of 45 to 50 degrees, allowing the ankle to flex downward as the horse's weight passes over its front end. An abnormally short pastern without enough slope can't do the job properly and, under continued stress, can cause arthritic conditions like ringbone.

Too long a pastern allows the ankle to drop too much, putting extra strain on

SIDE VIEW CONFORMATION OF FORELEGS

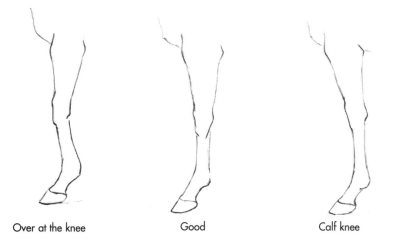

Over at the knee   Good   Calf knee

tendons and ligaments. The line of the pastern should be smooth and continuous. Any abrupt angle backward would put abnormal stress on the pastern bone and fetlock joint, leading to injury and unsoundness.

Horses that have been worked for a long time may develop wind puffs, small swellings above the ankle resulting from strain on the sheath encasing the flexor tendon. As long as the puffiness isn't hot or sore to the touch, this condition shouldn't cause trouble. But beware of lumps and bumps in the fetlock area—at the least this is an indication of severe wear and tear and, when located in the front, a sign of ringbone.

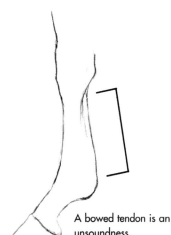

A bowed tendon is an unsoundness.

The knee is connected to the fetlock by the cannon bone. Running behind it like a cable is the flexor tendon. The line of the flexor should be neat and clean over its entire length, not slanting behind the horse's knee or bulging outward as it nears the fetlock joint. A slanted flexor tendon will be weak; one that is bulging or *bowed* indicates scar tissue beneath it left from a former injury. A bowed tendon is susceptible to reinjury, but if properly cared for, it can heal well, allowing the horse to return to competition and a full working schedule.

HOOVES. An old proverb cautions, "A horse is only as good as its worst foot." Ninety percent of all lameness occurs in the feet, the place where most irregularities are unacceptable. When you examine a horse, pay special attention to the conformation of the hooves, which carry all of the horse's weight and must be large enough to bear it. The front feet should be rounded, and the rear ones more oval. Each pair should match in size and conformation. Uneven angles or wear

 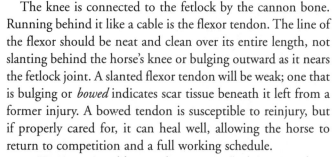

on a hoof are often just a sign of neglected feet, a bad blacksmith, or both. But a hoof that is noticeably smaller than its mate can affect the way a horse's weight is distributed, causing gaits to be uneven.

A foot that toes out places abnormal stress on the inside wall. One that toes in strains the outer wall. Both irregularities cause awkward movements: *winging* or *dishing* in horses that toe out, and *paddling* in those that toe in. A pigeon toe can be acceptable in a hunter or open jumper when it doesn't interfere with the way of going, but it would obviously not be desirable in any competition that gives points for conformation, and it could become a negative factor when gaits are affected.

The side of a hoof wall that is thickest and appears to flare out will bear the brunt of the landing foot. Ideally both sides of the hoof should have equal flare. A hoof wall that is too vertical will not support its full share of weight.

To equally distribute the shock of concussion through all four legs, the height of the heels must be the same. Heels that are too upright are usually too narrow as well and are prone to contracted heels or navicular problems.

Hooves should be free of vertical cracks extending into the coronary band or coming up from the bottom side of the toe. Deep cracks in these areas can lead to permanent lameness. Hoof walls that are dished or ridged are often an indication that the horse has "foundered" within the previous six months. (See the discussion of laminitis in Chapter 20.) In these cases an X-ray will be needed to check for possible interior damage. (Sometimes these abnormalities are merely an indication of a major change in diet or climate.)

The sole of the foot should be slightly cupped and the heel wide. A flat-footed horse with soles very close to the ground will be tender-footed and prone to stone bruises. A thin-soled horse will have similar problems. Either type would be a poor choice for the trail or as a field hunter or eventer. A dropped sole or a hoof separated from the wall is a sign of severe past foundering, and a horse with either condition should not even be considered.

The frog of the foot should be large, healthy looking, and pointed toward the toe to help the hoof absorb equal pressure on both sides. Watch out for mushy spots or drawn-up, atrophied areas. While you're examining the bottom of the foot, check to see if the shoes are evenly worn. Uneven wear can be a sign of soreness in the foot resulting in an uneven way of going.

VIEW FROM THE REAR

The power of a horse comes from the rear, his hindquarters driving the rest of the body forward like an engine. Hindquarters equally proportionate to the chest and midsection enhance the push and thrust a horse must have to excel in competition.

The shape of the rump varies from breed to breed. Round croups are favored in some, while the hindquarters of Arabians and some warmbloods are relatively flat. A too-steep croup that drops off sharply past the hindquarters is undesirable because it inhibits a horse's ability to push from behind.

While you are standing in back of the horse, once again imagine a line falling from the center of each hip (between the point of the hip and the tail on both sides)

REAR VIEW CONFORMATION OF HIND LEGS

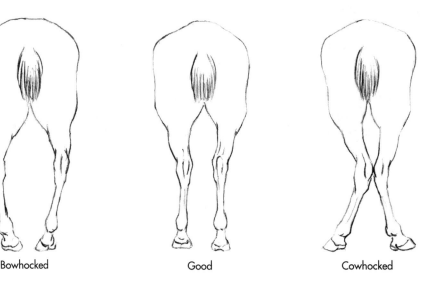

Bowhocked   Good   Cowhocked

HINDLEGS

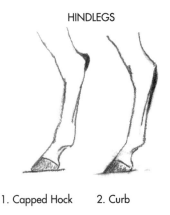

1. Capped Hock   2. Curb

Left Hind Leg
3. Bone Spavin   4. Bog Spavin

down the center of the hock and along the back of the cannon bone through the center of the fetlock, ending at the center of the heel. Hocks or cannons that slant outside the plumb line *(bowhocked)* or inside *(cowhocked)* put abnormal strain on the area. Severely cowhocked horses will eventually develop bog or bone spavins.

Viewed from the side, the hocks should look clean, with clearly defined bones, joints, and tendons. Viewed from the rear, the angle of the hock should be clear and should feel hard and smooth to the touch. A horse that has been competing for a while could show a little wear here, of the sort mentioned below.

Capped hocks, those enlarged at the point, are unsightly but won't affect soundness. Likewise, *curbed* hocks, enlarged plantar ligaments located a few inches below the point and caused by strain resulting from poor conformation, shouldn't cause a problem as long as they are cool and hard to the touch.

A *bog spavin* is a swelling slightly in front of and to the side of the hock and in an advanced state. It is a serious concern. *Bone spavins,* caused by extreme calcium buildup, are more difficult to spot. This irreversible condition, if suspected, calls for a flexion test and X-ray.

The hind legs, like the front, function as secondary shock absorbers, and their degree of angle is approximately the same. The pitch of stifle and hock also contributes to the power and efficiency of the hind end. When a horse is too straight behind, his back legs sit too far apart to absorb shock well. This flaw, called *post legged,* limits his ability to push his body forward and up—obviously an unacceptable defect in a jumper.

SIDE VIEW CONFORMATION OF HINDQUARTERS

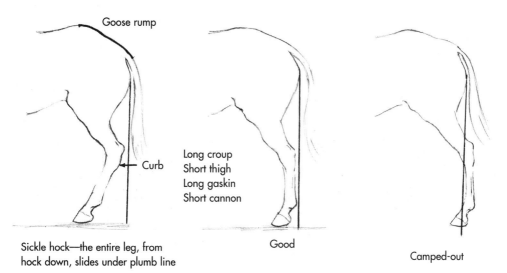

Goose rump

Curb

Long croup
Short thigh
Long gaskin
Short cannon

Sickle hock—the entire leg, from
hock down, slides under plumb line

Good

Camped-out

A horse with too much angle in his hind leg is called *sickle hocked*. In this condition the hock joint falls behind the imaginary line, and the cannon is pitched too far under the body, preventing the hindquarters from pushing off in a balanced, powerful manner. When a horse with this defect is asked to collect himself (carrying the hindquarters forward and under), the effort will irritate the joints between the small bones of the hock, causing their surfaces to roughen and calcium deposits to form. Eventually the joints will fuse into bone spavins.

Some deviations from the norm are more acceptable than others—another area where a professional can advise you. Any questions about back conformation should be brought to the vet's attention during the prepurchase exam.

Handsome Is as Handsome Does

After examining the prospect from all sides, have the horse walked or trotted out in hand onto flat, firm ground. Don't be shy about asking to see
him jogged out on a paved driveway. A reluctance to move out, or a show
of unevenness on a hard surface, is an indication of unsoundness.

When the horse trots out, watch him travel toward and away from you. Is his
movement straight? Does one leg move differently from its opposite? Does any leg
show unusual sideways movement? Are the front and hind legs too close together
or too far apart? And is there any interference, such as a hind hoof hitting or brushing a front leg? (Defects like this may show up as scuffed hair, thickened skin, even
scarring on the area being struck.)

WATCH THE HORSE PERFORM

If a prospective horse has met with your approval up to this point, it's time to see
him under saddle. Customarily the owner or handler will ride the horse first so you
can watch his performance.

A hunter prospect should be balanced at the canter, willing to take both leads,
and comfortable with flying changes. Hunters must be quiet and consistent over
fences and able to handle short or long combinations.

A dressage horse must have three pure, forward-moving gaits, be obedient to all
aids, and show above-average suppleness in turns and transitions. He should push
off from behind when lengthening his stride and come under from behind during
downward transitions. He must be further able to execute figures and movements
in keeping with his advertised level of training.

An event horse should be reasonably proficient at both dressage and jumping and, when facing obstacles in open country, must show boldness as well. Event fences are solid and of different heights, encountered on a variety of terrains along with other challenging problems. Although event courses vary in design and difficulty, geared to a horse's level of competition, a timid horse would be more likely to refuse jumps in the cross-country phase.

A pleasure horse should be obedient, mannerly, and comfortable to ride, as well as willing to stand or go wherever the rider directs him.

Before you put foot to stirrup, make sure you're not the one being taken. I hate to see a rider talked into buying a horse that they're afraid of and/or unable to ride.

TAKE HIM FOR A RIDE

Unfortunately, it happens all too often. Prospective buyers can become so entranced by good looks and impeccable pedigree that they forget to ask themselves the question that ought to precede any purchase: "Can I handle this horse, both on the ground and in the saddle?" Sadly, a few unscrupulous professionals, counting on a kickback from the sale, will encourage such matches, despite the buyer's misgivings.

Buying an unsuitable horse is a dead-end proposition: a drain on the buyer's confidence and pocketbook and a disservice to the animal. The fearful owner will gradually lose interest in the purchase, while the horse, not getting the attention and workouts he needs, will become increasingly neurotic. These sad situations usually end with the horse being given away or sold for far less than the purchase price. So after assessing the horse's abilities and temperament, take a close look at your own to make sure they're compatible.

Making a major purchase gives everyone a few jitters, but if they don't go away after ten minutes in the saddle, you should reconsider your choice. A horse that continues to make you nervous is unsuitable for you at this stage.

If this turns out to be the case, don't be embarrassed. Politely tell the owner of your decision, and move on to the next prospect. Look back on your negative decision as a positive experience. You've learned to evaluate conformation, performance, and suitability, reaching a mature decision based on this assessment. Future shopping trips should be a comparative piece of cake.

When you can't make up your mind about a horse, don't hesitate to take more time. Go back to the seller's farm for an unannounced visit and observe the horse in the pasture (a must for the one-horse owner). View the prospect in the stable, and watch him being led out of the stall, groomed and tacked up. Does he come shooting out of the stall like a cannonball? Does he cop an attitude when the cross-ties are clipped on and the currycomb approaches?

When riding the horse for a second time, do you find that he behaves differently, acting nervous and unsettled? If so, he was probably lunged or ridden for a while to calm him down before your last visit. Some horses do need to be lunged before they're ridden, but the owner should let you know this in advance. A buyer with limited time to ride may not want a horse that has to be worked every day or needs a half hour or more on the lunge to warm up.

VET HIM OUT

Once you've made your choice and agreed on price, a positive veterinarian check must be made before the sale is concluded. Try to be present for the checkup, both to ask questions about the results and to decide how far to pursue the examination, should something unusual turn up.

If any suspicious bumps are found on the hocks or pastern, or if the flexion tests suggest other difficulties, the veterinarian might suggest X-rays, which could cost more than a first-time buyer wants to spend.

Intermediate and advanced riders who are making a big investment in a horse that is to be used in major competitions will always want to have the feet and hocks X-rayed, if only as a future point of comparison.

Since no horse is perfect, the veterinarian can help you determine what irregularities you (and the horse) can live with. He or she will want to know what type of work the horse has been doing and what you will be doing with him, using the information as a checkpoint. The veterinarian will also call your attention to any unusual conformation defect that could affect the animal's health and soundness. Further examinations might be called for, depending on what is discovered during the first one and what you want to spend. Obviously a $50,000 horse will rate more extensive testing than one that costs $5,000.

TAKE HIM ON TRIAL

When it can be arranged, a trial period of one or two weeks, sometimes even longer, is the best possible way to check out an equine prospect. Unfortunately the advantages to the buyer are outweighed by the risk that the owner or dealer takes in loaning out an expensive animal. Many sellers refuse to send horses on trial. Others won't let a horse out of their sight without receiving notarized assurance that it will be boarded at a professionally run stable, along with a certified check for the full amount of the purchase price, to be forfeited should the horse meet with a fatal or crippling accident. It is also possible to take out an insurance policy for the purchase price to cover the horse during the trial period.

And accidents do happen. A friend, eager to make sure the horse she was selling was compatible with its prospective buyer, overlooked the young rider's inexperience and loaned her the animal without checking on how it would be cared for. Alas, the novice did the

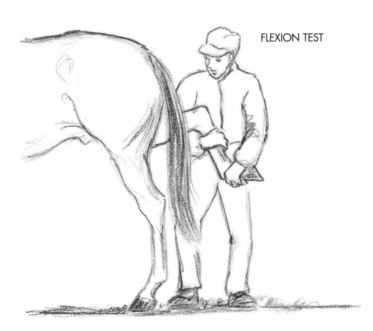

FLEXION TEST

unthinkable, turning the trial horse out to pasture with two others, who immediately took off after the stranger, chasing him into a corner. The panicked animal tried to jump the fence, failed to clear it, and ended up impaled on a post—with fatal results.

It's an awful story, but it explains why many sellers are reluctant to allow a trial period. (And it underscores one of the basic rules of horse ownership: Never put a new horse into a pasture with others.)

The Trial Period

If you can get a trial period, make the most of this opportunity to observe your prospect's behavior under every possible circumstance. Does the horse load well, travel well, and settle down quickly in new surroundings? Is he relaxed in the stall, during grooming, at feeding time, and when you turn him out? Does he conduct himself well around other horses in the ring and on the trail? Is his behavior consistent at different times of day? (To help in your evaluation, copy and enlarge the checklist at the end of this chapter and carry it with you, scoring behavior on a scale of 0 to 10.)

I usually like to give a horse a full day in a new barn before riding him, but if the trial period is for only a week, you won't want to waste any time. In that case, ride him for only a brief period on day one, increasing the duration of the workout as the week progresses.

An experienced horse can be expected to settle down quickly in new surroundings; a green horse might need more time. In the latter instance some unsettled behavior is acceptable—if it isn't too extreme and doesn't last too long.

When you first approach the horse in his new stall, does he come toward you with ears forward? Or does he swing his rump around and put his ears back? (A big zero on any scorecard.)

When you turn the prospect out to pasture, watch his behavior carefully. Does he jerk away from you at the gate? Does he settle down easily? A horse that tears around the pasture doing sliding stops and 160-degree turns is likely to injure or bruise himself. Bear in mind that some very valuable horses are rarely turned out and then only in the controlled environment of the arena, so be sure to ask about your prospect's recreational background.

Remember the tragic story about my friend's horse, and always turn a new horse out alone, preferably in a paddock or small area. The proximity of other horses, out of reach but close by, should help the newcomer relax.

When you turn a new horse out, keep the halter on in case catching him later becomes a problem. Hopefully it won't. Nothing is more annoying and time-consuming than stalking a reluctant horse. The equine game of evading capture is a difficult habit to change and rates a low two on my checklist. As you begin to check out the prospect's training, be sure to ride him alone and with other horses, before and after turnouts, and at different times of day. If trail rides will be part of his future, try him out on the most difficult of your preferred routes—down the road by the Joneses' woodpile (the one covered with a flapping tarp), past the Browns' free-ranging chickens (and the rooster who likes to perch on the rusty truck), and over the creaking wooden bridge. Take him through gates, over drainage ditches, and across streams. Watch his response to each visual challenge and physical obstacle.

Is he mannerly around the other horses, or do his ears flatten when another horse crowds him? Is he content to travel quietly behind the group, or does he continually jog and pull at the bit, calming down only when in the lead?

At the end of the trial period, evaluate your checklist. A score of five or better on each question is a passing grade. That and a subsequent bill of health from the veterinarian means that this is probably the horse for you.

If you need to compete with the horse before determining if he is what you are looking for, be sure to discuss this with the owner beforehand. The more a horse is moved around, the higher the risk.

PAPERS

When price is based on pedigree, be sure you have the papers in hand before the sale is concluded. (Papers are sometimes withheld for legal reasons, and you don't want to get mixed up in something like that.) In other cases you'll receive the papers after payment is made. Check to make sure the stated age of the horse is verified by the veterinarian. Then send a copy of the papers and other required information to the registry, assuring that your ownership is officially recorded.

INSURANCE

Most homeowners' policies cover personal liability for up to three horses, in case a visitor is injured by one of them on your property. The usual limit is $100,000, unless more coverage is requested.

If you have a very valuable horse, you might want to insure it with a company that specializes in livestock and/or equine insurance. The type and extent of coverage varies. Some firms, like the A-rated American Livestock Insurance Company, offer three separate policies: *full mortality,* which covers a horse's death from accident, sickness, or disease; *special accident,* when death is a result of any external or visible accident; and *specified peril* (limited risk), covering death resulting from fire, lightning, transit, and other perils you specify in the policy (such as drowning, shooting, or electrocution). Other agencies, like Dietrich and Company, offer a full mortality policy that covers special accidents and specified perils. This firm also has a two-hundred-dollar-deductible major medical program for horses that are valued at five thousand dollars or more, reimbursing owners for any reasonable, necessary, and customary veterinary charges, including surgery, that result from accident, injury, or illness. A comprehensive list of companies that insure horses appears in the directory of the American Horse Council. (See Appendix F.)

LEASING

At this stage of the game, you may decide that horse ownership is too big a commitment. You may be uncertain how well a horse will fit into your life structurally and financially. Perhaps you want to determine whether your child's interest in horses is a lasting enthusiasm. Or maybe an extensive search has revealed that the horse of your dreams is priced out of sight. In such cases, consider leasing a horse.

This is not an inexpensive alternative. The yearly cost of leasing is based on a percentage of the horse's value (often a third), and a leased horse costs as much to maintain as one you buy, needing the same examination and tryout beforehand, as well as a veterinarian check. In most cases the horse will be boarded out. Depending on where you live, such boarding can cost as much as or more than the rent on a small suburban apartment.

Some commercial stables lease horses for a year or a season. You can also make arrangements to lease with a private owner, who will likely want the horse boarded at a professionally run stable.

When you work out a mutually acceptable agreement, you might want to share the lease with another rider. I know of several co-lease arrangements that have worked out very well.

Unless you and the owner agree otherwise, the standard lease will hold you responsible for all aspects of the horse's care, including feeding, grooming, farrier costs, and veterinary care. Any special considerations, like the expensive food supplements or medication an older horse might need, must be thoroughly discussed with the owner, then spelled out in the lease. The document will be very thorough, itemizing the ways the horse will be used and specifying where responsibility lies in case of illness or injury. A notarized veterinary exam should accompany the lease.

The lease fee is usually paid in advance. Insurance is always advised for the period of the lease; in fact, most owners insist upon it. (See Chapter 22.)

EQUINE IDENTIFICATION

The horse thief, scourge of the Old West and archetypal villain of many a cowboy movie, is unfortunately still among us. Hundreds of cases of horse theft are reported nationwide each year. To address this historic Western problem, Arizona instituted a regional branding service even before it became a state.

In Iowa, which like many states east of the Rockies has no mandated system for checking and verifying ownership, a horse was stolen from a rodeo and discovered by his heartbroken owner seven years later at a rodeo in Colorado, having been sold numerous times in the interim. In this case the original owner was fortunately able to claim the horse legally because he had the original bill of sale, the health certificate, and the breed registration and had filed a police report at time of the theft. The horse was also branded.

Plain or chestnut horses with no white markings are prime targets for thieves and should have as much identification as possible. States like California, which at this writing has no brand inspection service that registers horses and verifies ownership at time of sale, are breeding grounds for thieves. Other Western states have varying systems of documentation that make ownership indisputable.

States without brand inspection laws claim they are impractical because stolen horses are usually moved out of state fast and cannot be tracked. Yet Colorado protects ownership within its borders by inspecting the brand of any horse hauled more than seventy-five miles from its home.

All states require a negative Coggins test, and most of them, a health certificate before a horse can be moved across state lines. Other paperwork is required in different parts of the country. So if you plan to travel out of your state, learn its requirements and those of any you may pass through.

The International Livestock Investigations Association in Denver (see Appendix F) has created a fax network for reporting livestock theft, giving quicker access to a horse's records and thereby speeding up the process of title search and recovery. Reports are circulated to law enforcement agencies in twenty-eight states, five Canadian provinces, and two states in northern Mexico.

Electronic microchip implantation is also being tried out as a unique and permanent identification marker. A tiny encoded capsule the size of a grain of rice can be implanted by injection into a horse's neck and read with a special handheld scanner. To date, the potential efficacy of these devices is undermined by the lack of uniform standards for both the scanners that activate the chips and the digits on the implants. And there are no laws requiring ownership verification of the person requesting the implant. Furthermore, although it takes only a second to inject the implant into the crest of the neck, it is subsequently hard to locate, and removal requires careful surgery.

On a more positive note, implants have been successful in curbing the spread of disease. When an outbreak of Equine Infectious Anemia (EIA) occurred in Louisiana in the late 1990s, owners of horses that were tested for it were encouraged by the Department of Agriculture to have a ten-dollar numbered microchip implanted, which recorded the brand or tattoo, Coggins test result, medical record, vital statistics, and ownership. EIA-positive horses were required by law to be euthanized, and the program markedly reduced the number of cases of the disease in the state.

Meanwhile, keeping updated records and marking animals with permanent identification like hot or freeze brands is the best way to protect and recover a lost or stolen horse. Photographs taken at several angles at different times of year can aid in identification and recovery. Documentation should include the breed registration, the bill of sale, health certificates, brand inspection papers, and veterinary records.

When you are staying overnight at a show ground, make sure the security is adequate, with a reliable night watchman who makes rounds. (Many owners or trainers with several horses have an attendant stay with them overnight.) Always leave your name and the phone number of where you're staying on the horse's stall door, in case of any problem or medical emergency.

SCORECARD OF BEHAVIOR ON TRIAL

(rated on scale of 0 to 10)

TRAILER

Wrapping legs before loading_____

Loading_____

Traveling_____

Unloading_____

After unloading_____

NEW SURROUNDINGS

Stable_____

Stall_____

Cross-ties_____

Grooming_____

Feeding_____

LEADING

To pasture_____

At gate_____

Releasing_____

Catching_____

IN PASTURE

Alone_____

With other horses_____

ON THE TRAIL

Mounting/dismounting_____

Alone_____

With other horses_____

Reaction to obstacles_____

Starting out_____

Returning_____

IN THE RING

Mounting/dismounting_____

Passing (in same direction and opposite)_____

In front_____

Behind_____

Alone_____

Over jumps_____

Around obstacles_____

PART II

Picking a Purebred

Pouter, tumbler, and fantail are from the same source;
The racer and hack may be traced to one horse;
So men were developed from monkeys, of course;
Which nobody can deny.

—Lord Charles Neaves, poetic comment on Darwin's
ORIGIN OF SPECIES

Survival of the Fittest

Some 53 million years and four geological epochs before man appeared on the earthly scene, the horse's evolution began. His most ancient fossilized forebear was the tiny *Hyracotherium,* formerly known as *Eohippus,* a creature eleven inches tall possessed of paws with four toes in front and three in back, an arrangement that gradually evolved into the hoof. About 20 million years ago, the earth's species began to diversify, producing successors with equally intriguing given names, like *Protohippus, Mesohippus,* and *Merychippus,* each

THE *EQUUS CABALLUS* VS. *HYRACOTHERIUM*

consolidating toes until the advent of the Pliocene and the emergence of the fully hooved *Equus caballus.*

For more than a hundred years, it was thought (and taught) that these pint-size equine ancestors grew progressively larger, succumbing in turn to extinction, until the emergence of *Equus,* whose greater size made him fittest to survive. But the "bigger the better" theory of evolution was recently challenged when a long-term study of fossil evidence made a compelling case for the coexistence of small, medium, and large equine lineages throughout most of horse history. It concluded that the survival of *Equus* was a matter not of superior size but of random circumstance. Supporting this theory are the cave paintings of Lascaux, France, made at the end of the last ice age in the late Pleistocene, which show both small and large horses.

Equus's forebears originated on the North and South American continents, migrating millions of years ago to Siberia across the land bridge that is now the Bering Strait. For reasons unknown those animals left behind became extinct, and the species continued its development in Asia, gradually spreading to the south and west. *Equus* didn't reappear in the Americas until the Spanish conquests of the sixteenth century.

Prehistoric man wasn't interested in horses, except as an occasional meal, so as *Homo sapiens* lumbered through the ages of stone and iron, *Equus* roamed untamed through different parts of the world, adapting to wide variations in environment. Horses were eventually domesticated in the copper age, more than six thousand years ago, predating the wheel as the first locomotive alternative to the human foot.

Variations within the species reflected adaptation to different climates, terrain, and available food supplies. The disproportionately large head of the Icelandic horse, for example, encases long nostrils (which evolved to disperse the chill air of its native Scandinavia) and a massive jaw (whose bigger teeth were needed to chew the tough grasses of his homeland and adopted country). Its short stocky body can survive on a minimum of food. Because of all the climbing the Icelandic does, it needs more weight in the forehand—the reason for the short, thick neck. Its heavy mane and forelock developed as protection against frigid winds; hard hooves were essential to negotiate rocky terrain; and hardiness, high intelligence, and keen eyesight were needed to cope with the harsh environment.

The Arabian developed in a very different world. Survival in a hot, arid climate, amid warring tribes, depended on swiftness and the ability to exist with a minimum of food and water. Since these horses often shared tents with their nomadic owners, geniality was at a premium, and Arabians today are noted for remarkably good dispositions.

Modern horse breeds are the result of a combination of social and natural selection. In ancient times horse breeders depended primarily on animals native to their vicinity, selectively bringing out the best of a breed's natural characteristics. Since most breeds were developed for a specific reason, some are more suitable than others for particular types of work. Many of the earliest domestic horses were used in war—from the steppes of Mongolia to the sands of Arabia. Speed and weight-carrying ability were vital, and horses were selectively bred for these traits and for

THE ICELANDIC HORSE

adaptability to their environment. Despite the Arab's relatively small size, his short back is adapted to carrying heavy loads. Some purebred Arabs even have one less vertebra than other breeds. During the Middle Ages, when knights fitted themselves and their horses out in hundreds of pounds of armor, they needed larger mounts to carry this immense weight while still moving with agility. The Shire was developed in England as a warhorse, after Henry VIII arbitrarily decreed that all horses under five feet (15 hands) had to be destroyed. Standing an average 18 hands high (six feet) and weighing as much as 2,200 pounds, Shires are still the largest draft horses in the world. The French developed the Percheron for the same bellicose purpose, while the Flemish horse became the Netherlands' answer to armor.

As agricultural methods became more advanced and gunpowder replaced lances, warhorses became lighter, and the remaining large horses were used to pull plows. Some large breeds, like the Belgian, were developed solely for farming. In the United States horses played an important historical role as a working animal. Some ponies toiled their entire lives in the coal mines, while huge teams did the work of bulldozers on the prairies, building beds for the first railroads. Workhorses pulled plows and threshers, and some walked in circles all day turning millstones.

The carriage horse, almost forgotten today, was the center of the horse market for centuries. Breeds like the Cleveland Bay (developed in Cleveland, England) and the Hackney were bred only for driving. The Cleveland Bay survived near extinction in the early twentieth century, and the high-stepping Hackney is now known primarily as a show animal. But the best blood of both horses has been passed on selectively to other breeds.

THE SHIRE

A breed is created when well-defined, genetically dominant (prepotent) characteristics distinguishing one animal from others of the same species are consistently transmitted to offspring over at least ten generations. In the past two centuries, many new breeds have been established. The term *purebred* should not be confused with the capital T of Thoroughbred, a specific breed developed in England for racing. A purebred is any horse of a distinct breed, from the Arabian to the Peruvian Paso, whose sires and dams are registered in the same studbook and has papers to prove it. The most popular purebreds have long and intricate genealogies.

The terms *hot blood, cold blood,* and *warmblood* denote the temperaments, metabolic rates, and conformation of different breeds. Hot- or full-blooded horses, like Arabians and Thoroughbreds, which have Oriental, Middle Eastern, or North African blood in their ancestry, tend to be high strung and refined. Cold-blooded horses are usually heavy-boned draft-type animals with relatively docile dispositions. Centuries ago European breeders began crossing cold bloods and hot bloods to produce horses of greater size and stamina and calmer temperaments, resulting in the warmblood breeds. As the need for them as farm and war animals diminished, their potential as superior international sport horses was developed. Warmbloods are now in demand all over the world for jumping, dressage, combined training, and driving competition.*

---

*Updated breed registries and associations lists may be obtained from the American Horse Council (see Appendix F) and from the *Encyclopedia of Associations,* available at your local library. Magazines and periodicals on specific breeds are listed in *Ulrich's International Periodicals Directory,* which is updated every year.

Andalusian or Lusitana

One of the oldest breeds in the world, the Andalusian is represented in early cave paintings. Some historians think these horses were ridden as early as 4000 B.C. When the Phoenicians arrived on the peninsula in 2000 B.C., the Iberian cavalry was already a formidable foe. Homer mentions Iberian horses in the *Iliad*, circa 1100 B.C. When the Moors invaded southern Iberia in the eighth century, they found their small Barbs no match for the nimble Spanish horses, and they crossed their desert breed with the lighter, more agile Iberian horses. By the time the Moors were driven from the region at the end of the fifteenth century, the Andalusian had been developed and perfected.

In Spain the breed is known as the Pura Raza Español or Pure Spanish Horse, in Portugal as the Pura Raca Lusitana or Lusitano. Its collective name, *Andalusian,* refers to the region in southern Spain where many of the best stud farms are located.

The breed first arrived in North America with Columbus. Prized for its beauty, docility, and obedience, the Andalusian has influenced light-horse breeds of every country. Studs were founded in Austria and Italy, leading to the creation of special breeds like the Lippizan, Neapolitan, and the Kladruper. In South America the Andalusian Horse Registry of the Americas maintains genealogies based on a complete set of registration books brought to the continent by the conquistadors. In the United States, Canada, and Mexico the only authentic registry is the American Andalusian Association, which also accepts horses with part Andalusian blood. Andalusians stand from 14.2 to 16 hands. White, gray, and bay are the most common colors for the breed, although some blacks and a few roans are registered. The head is fine with a slightly convex profile. Ears are short, neck well-arched, and withers clearly defined. The back is strong and sloped, the chest wide and well developed, and the quarters well rounded with a low-set tail. The legs are strong with broad joints.

Arabian

By retracing its history through drawings and paintings, historians have established that the Arabian is the oldest horse breed in the world with a definite name and registry. Its influence can be seen in almost every light-horse breed, all of which have been crossed with Arabians at one time or another to improve the strain. Thoroughbred, Standardbred, Hackney, and some Morgan lineages can be traced back to an Arab stud. Originating not on the Arabian peninsula but in Turkey, Syria, Iran, and Iraq, the Arab has been selectively bred over several thousand years to perpetuate its qualities of extreme endurance, sound wind, strong legs, speed, and ability to survive in the extreme heat and cold of the desert on a minimum of food. It is considered the first man-made breed, because of its total dependence on man for water and food in this harsh environment. The severe desert life with minimal care, combined with the hard work demanded of the war mares, produced a hardiness and constitution for which Arabians are renowned. This breed is famous for its convivial nature, developed over years of close association with man. Bedouins are said

THE ARABIAN

to have valued their horses more than their wives. The strict breeding standards that produced the modern Arabian were set by these nomads, who were fanatical guardians of the breed's purity. For centuries a mare and her future offspring were considered tainted if bred, even accidentally, to anything but a purebred Arabian stud. Because of this fatuous belief, many good horses were sold abroad for incredibly low prices.

The walk and gallop were the most useful gaits on desert terrain; the trot wasn't developed until later. In time the breed was exported to England, where it became the foundation of the racing Thoroughbred.

In the United States the Arabian excels in endurance and competitive trail rides. Its high intelligence is naturally suited to working cattle. The breed's even disposition and smooth gaits are also ideal for pleasure riding. A Thoroughbred crossed with an Anglo-Arab makes an excellent hunter or dressage horse. The Arabian-Morgan cross (Morab) is a popular all-around sport horse.

The ideal Arabian has a small head with a straight or preferably slightly concave (dished) profile, a small muzzle, large nostrils, and large round dark eyes with a short distance between the eye and the muzzle. The jowls are deep, and the ears small, thin, and well-shaped. The long, arched, smoothly muscled neck is set high on the withers. The back is short, and the croup level and ribs are well sprung, set off by clean legs with strong tendons. The tail is carried naturally high and "gaily"; the average height is 14.1 to 15.1 hands. The skin is dark and the coat fine. Arabians are found in all the solid colors. Black, rose-gray, and flaxen are less common colors peculiar to the breed.

Barb

The Barb, its desert neighbor the Arab, and the Andalusian are the world's oldest foundation breeds. All were strongly influenced by the Asian wild horse and/or the Tarpan before them. The breed is thought to have originated in Central Asia, brought into North Africa by traders and invaders, but it owes its name to the Berber tribesmen of Morocco, who rode these horses during the Muslim invasion of Spain in the eighth century. During that period the Barb was crossed with the Arab as well as the Andalusian, influencing the development of both breeds while retaining its own prepotent characteristics.

Barb or "Barbary" horses were imported to England in the late Middle Ages and became part of the foundation stock of the Thoroughbred. After later Muslim invasions of Europe, the breed was used to lighten the medieval French military charger, the Limousin, and by the sixteenth century it reached Ireland, where its influence can be seen in today's Connemara pony.

The Barb has a straight, sometimes convex profile, with an arched neck above prominent withers. Its powerful hindquarters slope from the croup to a low-set tail. The shoulders are long and muscular, and the chest is long and deep. The legs are slim and solid.

Thoroughbred

Developed in England in the early seventeenth century for racing, the Thoroughbred was founded on three imported Oriental sires: the Byerley Turk (1689), the Darley Arab (1706), and the Godolphin Barb (1724). These three studs are believed to have been bred to Oriental and English mares, producing offspring with superior speed and endurance. The most famous racehorses, like the legendary Eclipse, a descendant of the Darley Arab, can be traced directly to one of these founding sires.

Breeding is extremely important to Thoroughbred enthusiasts. They may or may not know how to ride, but they can quote pedigrees by the page and usually pick good bloodlines. A Thoroughbred with the right ancestry can command an incredible price at auction. In 1985 the yearling Seattle Dancer was sold for $13.1 million at the Keenland July yearling sale. Since stud fees can also be impressive, they are usually syndicated. A good stud normally breeds with forty mares a season. Fertility usually recedes as the stallion ages, but Man o' War stood through age twenty-five and Bull Lea was bred until he was nearly thirty.

Thoroughbreds were imported to the American colonies when mile racing began to rival the quarter-mile in popularity. The first noted stallion to come into the country was Diomed, sire of the first all-American Thoroughbred, Archie.

Archie and other descendants of these English imports became the foundation sires of several American breeds. Messenger fathered the Standardbred, Lexington the American Saddlebred, and Sir Archie and Janus founded the Quarter Horse.

Built for speed in racing on the flat, the long legs of the Thoroughbred are also suited to hunting and show jumping. But generations of inbreeding have made

THE THOROUGHBRED

them generally high strung, or hot. During the last quarter of the twentieth century, the breed has frequently been crossed with horses of steadier temperament, like the European warmbloods, to produce good hunters, dressage horses, show jumpers, and event horses. Thoroughbred–pony crosses produce elegant junior mounts.

Thoroughbreds range from 15 to 17 hands in height. The body is streamlined, with long, flat muscles. The head is wide between the ears, and the profile is either straight or dished, with nostrils capable of great expansion during exertion. Thoroughbreds have long, slender necks, and the withers are usually pronounced, with a good slope to the shoulder and considerable depth in the girth. The breed is quite long from hip to hock, with a generous gaskin. The legs are straight, with short, dense cannons, long forearms, and well-sloped long pasterns—all built for speed. Colors are usually solid, predominantly chestnuts, bays, blacks, browns, and occasionally grays.

POPULAR AMERICAN BREEDS

American Quarter Horse

Like the more recently developed Pony of the Americas and Morgans, the Quarter Horse, the most popular breed in the United States today, is all-American. Its origins can be traced to the Chickasaw Indian ponies of Carolina, Virginia, and Tennessee, all of which were noted for their speed and stamina. To improve these characteristics and develop a racing horse, the colonists crossed the ponies with English imports. By 1690 matched races for sizable purses were being held on the main streets of dozens of eastern communities, and special quarter-mile tracks were hacked out of the wilderness. Horses that excelled at this popular pastime were given the name, which, until the registry was established in Fort Worth in 1940, denoted type and racing skill rather than breed.

The Thoroughbred stallion Janus, foaled in 1750 and descended from an English import, was responsible for passing on many of the traits associated with the best Quarter Horses today. Because of his unusual conformation, Janus was considered something of a freak at the time, leading the Thoroughbred registry to formally disown him. Later on, as the breed gained in popularity, the registry relented to the point of taking credit for the Quarter Horse's development. Since then other Thoroughbred blood has been passed selectively into the breed to refine it. Quarter Horses gradually moved west with the population, working cattle during the day and racing at night. The best of them were usually put to stud to improve the breed's performance.

Among the outstanding Western sires were Copperbottom (1832), credited with passing along a keen cow sense to the breed, and Steel Dust (1849), whose speed was so legendary that for years Western Quarter Horses were called "steel dusters." Both horses are associated with Texas, where all of their get, or offspring, were foaled.

Truly an all-purpose breed, with the agility, speed, and intelligence needed for both Western sports and polo, the Quarter Horse has a calm disposition suited to pleasure riding and driving. As quarter-mile racing has come to equal flat racing in

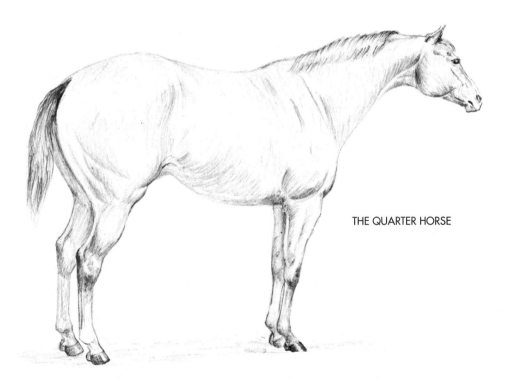

THE QUARTER HORSE

some parts of the country, in both popularity and size of purses paid, more Thoroughbred blood has been infused into the breed, changing the heavy, blocky conformation of the original type into a leggier, streamlined, taller animal. These horses are referred to as Appendix Quarter Horses. Along with their outstanding proficiency in cutting and reining, today's Quarter Horses are also winning ribbons in hunting, jumping, dressage, and junior equitation classes. They make excellent eventing mounts as well. Their even disposition makes them an ideal choice for a family pleasure horse.

The head of the Quarter Horse is short and wide and carried low, with small, alert ears and a short, square muzzle. Because Quarter Horses work with the head low, they have a distinct space between the large jawbone to allow for unrestricted breathing. The neck is of medium length, with a light arch, blending into deep-sloping shoulders. The chest is deep and broad, with large girth and wide-set forelegs. The breed's powerfully muscled forearms taper to the knee. The joints are smooth, the cannons short, and the pasterns of medium length. The feet are strong and round, with a well-opened heel. The back is short, close-coupled, and very full, with large muscles over the loins and well-sprung ribs.

Morgan

Everyone loves a mystery, and the ancestry of America's oldest breed continues to defy solution. Four plausible theories of the Morgan's origins have been advanced, but only the identity of the foundation sire is beyond dispute. He was a small, dark bay horse standing a scant 14 hands and weighing about a thousand pounds who was foaled in West Springfield, Massachusetts, in 1789 by a Vermont blacksmith, Justin Morgan, in repayment of a debt.

Morgan's horse quickly became legendary for his superior strength, intelligence, stamina, and speed at the trot. After working all week hauling logs, he showed no signs of fatigue, easily winning Saturday pulling contests and trotting races. As word of his exploits got around, the little stallion came into great demand at stud, standing under the name Figure for a mere two dollars. Not until his first owner's death did he assume the name Justin Morgan.

As Figure's get were seen to inherit his outstanding characteristics, particularly speed at the trot, the stallion became the talk of eastern horse circles. Registries for the fashionable Thoroughbred and Arabian began to take credit for the new breed's superior performance. More recently fans of the Quarter Horse have claimed Figure as one of their own. Equine historian Anthony Dent disagrees, advancing the opinion that the little stallion was descended from a Welsh cob, a distinct breed common in New England at the time. At this writing a full-page advertisement for the Morgan in *Equus* magazine refers to its Arabian and Barb ancestry.

The trouble with these claims and counterclaims is that Justin Morgan didn't look like a Thoroughbred, an Arab, or a Barb; nor did his immediate descendants. Rather, his prepotency suggested inbreeding and line breeding rather than a genetic mutant. According to author Bonnie Hendricks (see References) the Morgan in all probability descended from the then-popular Canadian Horse, a superb trotter and pacer imported by the thousands into the New England states during the colonial period. The Canadian's blocky build, crested neck, and powerful hindquarters are thought to derive from the Norfolk Trotter, Norwegian Fjord, and Friesian ancestors, the latter responsible for the breed's feathered legs and flowing mane and tail (and probably its nickname, the "Dutch Horse").

Throughout the last century it was the Morgan that pulled the buggy to church on Sunday after spending the week hauling logs, being ridden to town, and racing on Saturdays. The breed was greatly valued as a remount horse as well. The entire Vermont cavalry, some eleven hundred strong, was composed of Morgans.

The advent of the auto led to a rift among Morgan enthusiasts. A sizable group decided that the breed should be upgraded into a more serviceable saddle horse by cross-breeding with the American Saddlebred. Opponents worked to keep the line free of five-gaited blood and to improve rather than change the existing breed by introducing army remount stallions as sires, several of which carried Thoroughbred blood. The Archival Morgan Record was recently organized to preserve the original bloodlines of the Morgan breed. To certify a horse's bloodlines, its sire and dam must be DNA tested; or if they are dead, an affidavit by the owner is necessary.

The Morgan profile is straight, with wide-set eyes, powerful jaws ending in a

THE MORGAN

blunt muzzle, and short ears. The medium-size neck is heavily muscled and crested, with the head carried high. The back is fairly short and powerfully coupled at the hips. The croup slopes slightly, and the shoulders are built up into the withers. The barrel is well-rounded, set off by muscular thighs and gaskins, with a great deal of width in the chest. The legs have considerable length from elbow to knee and stifle to hock. Usually Morgans have a thick mane and tail, the latter set low but carried well. Their general appearance is powerful and stylish.

GAITED BREEDS

American Saddlebred

Originally called the Kentucky Saddlebred, the American Saddlebred was officially established and renamed in 1899, when seventeen foundation sires were selected from the best performers of the century. Then in 1908 all but the stallion Denmark (foaled in 1839) were eliminated from the registry, giving this horse credit for the entire breed. Fifty-five percent of the entries in the first volume of the Saddle Horse Registry can be traced directly back to him, and most of the best show horses today can be traced to either Denmark or another outstanding sire, Chief.

The Saddlebred evolved from a potpourri of breeds that included the Narragansett Pacer, the Canadian Horse, assorted Dutch horses, and the English Ambler—some no longer in existence. Morgan and Standardbred blood were later added to the blend. The ambling, lateral gait was cultivated at a time when people traveled great distances on horseback and comfort in the saddle was a major concern. Saddlebreds were also strong and hardy enough to be harnessed to a carriage or plow, but since the advent of the automobile and tractor, the breed has been primarily a show horse, shown at either three or five gaits under saddle and at a walk and trot in fine harness.

To accentuate their animated gaits, Saddlebreds' hooves are grown as long as eight inches for showing. The shoes often weigh twenty-five ounces each to encourage the high step and the long, reaching stride. To keep the tail high for shows, the depressor muscles at the base are cut, and a tail set used when the horse is idle. Switches or falls are sometimes added for extra fullness and/or length. Saddlebreds can be shown in three different ways. Three-gaited types wear a roached mane, with the top of the tail shaved clean before setting and the bottom pulled. Five-gaited types are shown with a full mane and tail, with a ribbon braided into both the forelock and the first section of the mane at the poll. Fine harness types that pull four-wheel carts also have full manes and tails.

A three-gaited saddle horse (often called a walk-trot horse) is shown at a walk, a trot, and a canter, all embellished with his high-stepping action. A five-gaited Saddlebred also has a slow gait, a comfortable stepping pace, and the rack or single-foot, a very fast four-beat gait.

The Saddlebred has a tapered head, with large, wide-set eyes, a fine muzzle, and small, slender ears. The long neck is well arched, and the throatlatch fine. The shoulders are well muscled and the chest wide, the back short and straight, and the barrel rounded, with a good, deep girth. The croup is set nearly horizontal, probably

THE AMERICAN SADDLEBRED

the straightest of any breed except the Arab. The tail is naturally high, and the legs are fine and shapely, with long, springy pasterns.

Peruvian Paso

Advertised as "the world's most comfortable horse," this elegant, high-stepping parade and pleasure horse has carried Peruvian plantation overseers on their daily rounds for more than four hundred years. Pasos were developed from Andalusians and Barbs imported to Peru in the early sixteenth century by Francisco Pizarro. They are distinguished by a smooth gait called the amble or *paso llano,* a four-beat running walk in which three feet are simultaneously off the ground; it can be maintained at a steady speed of eleven miles per hour over mountainous terrain and thirteen on the flat. The gait that sets them apart from their relative, the Paso Fino, is the *termino,* which complements their natural high-knee action, with front legs swinging high to the outside and reaching far forward, similar to the motion of a swimmer doing the crawl. The traditional riding attire is the poncho.

Pasos stand at between 14.1 and 15.1 hands and are found in all solid colors, from gray to roan. The head is small and narrow, and the profile straight or slightly convex. The eyes are rounded and set wide, and the nostrils are long and pro-

THE PERUVIAN PASO

nounced over the strong jaw. The neck is short, arched, and muscular, with a thick, flowing mane, and the chest is wide and well muscled. The withers are prominent and rounded, the back muscular and slightly concave, and the croup sloping and well muscled. The muscular legs have a short forearm, with long cannons in front and short ones in back, and sloped, flexible pasterns above small, strong hooves.

Paso Fino

A relative of the Peruvian paso, the Paso Fino originated in Puerto Rico. It has a four-beat gait that extends from the *paso fino* to the *paso corto* to the very fast *paso largo*. The Paso is younger than its Peruvian relative and may have derived in part from the Canadian Horse, which was exported in large numbers to the West Indies in the eighteenth and nineteenth centuries. Although the four-beat gait is inherited by all Pasos, no other breed is able to learn the "fine step" for which this breed is named.

Standardbred

The fastest breed at the trot and pace, used predominantly for high-stakes harness racing, it evolved in the nineteenth century, when horses were first required to meet a time standard to qualify. Pacers are slightly faster than trotters. In this gait the front and hind legs on the same side move forward together rather than diagonally, and horses wear special hobbles to encourage it. Trotters, once schooled in special weighted training shoes to encourage extension, have become so refined through breeding that these aids are usually no longer needed.

The best Standardbred trotters in the United States can all be traced to Messenger, a gray Thoroughbred stallion imported from England, where he had been known as a successful racehorse with an unusual ability to trot extremely fast. The name most commonly identified with the breed is Hambletonian, foaled in 1849; he sired more than forty horses that were able to trot or pace a mile in better than 2:30. Some 661 of his get have given record performances in their day, and one of the most famous races at the New Jersey Meadowlands (formerly in Goshen, New York) is called the Hambletonian.

The first horse to trot a mile in under three minutes was a gelding named Yankee, who set a record of 2:59 at the Harlem racetrack in 1806. But the greatest harness champion of all time was Dan Patch, who held the pacing record for thirty-three years (1905–1938), performing more miles under two minutes than any horse since.

Today's time standards differ according to the horse's age and the length and speed of the track. To qualify at the New Jersey Meadowlands, for instance, a pacer of four years or older must do a mile in 1:59. In 1996 four-year-old Jenna's Beach Boy beat the qualifying time by twelve seconds (1:47.3) to become the fastest pacer in the world.

Standardbred dispositions are generally steady and tractable, and they are often

THE STANDARDBRED

crossed with Thoroughbreds to produce good hunters. As the breed has become more refined, Standardbreds are increasingly being used as pleasure and show horses; they can be retrained for these purposes after a career on the track. Some have excelled in the show arena, most notably the famous Bionic Woman, ridden by Anne Kurinski of the United States Equestrian Team (USET). Those used as driving horses are trained to show a lot of knee action at the trot.

In the past many of these fine animals were shipped to the slaughterhouse when they became too old for the track, but now several agencies exist that will place them with responsible owners, to be retrained as show and pleasure horses. Several retirement homes cater only to over-the-hill trotters and pacers. (A list of these can be obtained from the American Horse Protection Association. See Appendix F.)

The Standardbred has a more angular, rugged build than the Thoroughbred and is closer to the ground. His long body and forearms are adapted to the long, flat stride needed for racing. The head is long and bony, often with a Roman nose.

Tennessee Walker

Like its Saddlebred ancestor, this breed was developed for utility, as a combination riding and light harness horse that could be used occasionally for farm work. Generations of selective breeding developed the three natural gaits for which the breed is known: the flat walk, the running walk, and the canter.

THE TENNESSEE WALKER

The flat walk is a smooth easy-to-sit four-beat gait accompanied with a rhythmic head nodding. The horse covers the ground at four to six miles per hour, with a large overstride (the hind foot overstepping the print of the front foot), which acts as a shock absorber to the seated rider.

The running walk is an accelerated gliding version of the flat walk at a speed of seven to ten miles per hour, with the overstride increasing from two to six feet beyond that of the flat walk stride. The canter, in keeping with the other gaits of the Tennessee Walker, is also extremely smooth. This slow, rhythmic, and rolling motion is frequently called a "rocking chair canter."

Tennessee Walkers were often referred to as Plantation Walkers because they could be ridden comfortably for hours between rows of crops by owners and overseers without tiring either horse or rider.

The Walker originated in the middle of his home state in the late nineteenth century, and its background derives from the Thoroughbred, Standardbred, Morgan, and a dash of Narragansett pacing blood. The first foundation sire was the black horse Arean, foaled in 1886. Tennessee Walkers make marvelous show horses, but primarily their biggest role today is as a pleasure horse. Their easy-to-sit gaits and docile temperament make them ideal trail horses. The saying goes, "Ride a Tennessee Walking Horse today; tomorrow you'll own one."

The Tennessee Walker is a slightly coarser, heavier horse than the American Saddlebred. Its conformation should be balanced with clean, hard legs; a short back; deep, full ribs; a well-proportioned chest with sloping, well-muscled shoulders; and a long, graceful neck setting off an intelligent head with well-shaped pointed ears and a large, expressive eye. Walkers come in a variety of colors, including palomino and a wide variety of roans. It's not uncommon to see white markings on their faces and legs. They average 15.2 hands and weigh up to twelve hundred pounds. Their manes and tails are always long and full. The tails are broken and set for show, but a great deal of effort is being made to discontinue this practice.

Albino

COLOR BREEDS

There is no recognized breed of pure Albino. All are pink-skinned, must have large blue or dark eyes (not pink), and can be registered under four different categories of hair color, ranging from pure white to cream. For this reason the breed is often referred to as the Dominant White Horse rather than the Albino.

The founding sire was Old King, foaled in 1906, but the registry was not established until 1937. A national recording club keeps records of any solid-color offspring of Albinos because they carry the gene and could produce a white foal.

Albinos are popular as parade and circus mounts, and there is no reason why they can't be used for English and Western pleasure or show riding.

Appaloosa

Ancient cave drawings found in France depict this uniquely spotted horse in existence as far back as forty thousand years ago. It also appears in Asian and Chinese art of a later period. Introduced to North America by the Spanish explorers, these colorful horses eventually spread to the Northwest. By about 1730 they had become the favored mounts of Native Americans.

Named by settlers, either after the Palouse region or the Palouse tribe, these horses were extremely popular among the Nez Percé and Palouse Indians of central Idaho, Oregon, and eastern Washington. The Nez Percé were the first to practice selective breeding, choosing spotted individuals that showed outstanding intelligence, speed, and endurance (and therefore ideal for hunting and racing). The Appaloosa's speed became legendary, enabling the Nez Percé to evade the U.S. Cavalry for a long time.

During the Indian wars the U.S. Cavalry chased the Nez Percé north toward the Canadian border, where the tribe, under the impression it had crossed over to sanctuary, actually set up camp a few miles south. The Nez Percé and most of their horses, comprising the entire original breed, were set upon by the cavalry and slaughtered. Those stallions spared by the army were gelded and given away to soldiers or settlers. Only a few horses escaped; these were crossed with draft animals to produce plow horses, causing the breed to degenerate. In 1938 the Appaloosa Horse Club was established, and Arab blood was introduced to upgrade it. Since then Appaloosas have been cross-bred with Quarter Horses for further refinement.

These unique horses are found in almost every discipline, including dressage, jumping, games, reining, roping, pleasure, and endurance riding and racing. Their quiet disposition also makes them gentle family horses.

Four types of marking are recognized, and registered Appaloosas may have any of the four or a mixture. A *blanket* is a white area on the rump, dotted with elon-

THE APPALOOSA

gated dark spots slightly larger than a fifty-cent piece. A *leopard* is all white with dark spots, and a type called the *snowflake* is dark with splashes of white. *Marbleized* can be dark with light spots or vice versa. Roans seem to predominate.

Three other characteristics help identify Appaloosas: mottled skin (usually around the muzzle and the genital area), white sclera (the area of the eye that circles the cornea), and striped hooves. In order to have a certified pedigree, a registered horse must have either a recognizable coat pattern or mottled skin and one more of the above characteristics.

Buckskin

Fabled for its resilience, this breed has been a favorite mount of generations of cowboys, and it is still in great demand in the West. Its colors, also seen in some Quarter Horses and mustangs that are descended from Spanish and colonial stock, range from light tan to dark bronze to lavender, slate, and mouse. The most common *dun* is peach gold, with a black mane and tail, zebra-like barring on the legs, and usually a dorsal stripe. *Red duns* are reddish brown, with a dark red mane, tail, and dorsal stripe. The relatively rare *grulla* (or *grullo,* as they are called by Quarter Horse owners) and *mouse dun* are slate or mouse colored, with black points and a dorsal stripe. The skin of all registered Buckskins is dark, with no white spots allowed on the coat.

The breed is descended from the Norwegian Fjord (Norwegian Dun), which was brought to America by European settlers. There it was cross-bred with mustang offspring of the ancient Spanish Sorraia breed, introduced by the conquistadors.

The American Buckskin Registry, founded in 1962, and the International Registry, established in 1971, accept all horses of good conformation that have no draft, pony, Pinto, Appaloosa, or Palomino ancestry. More than 90 percent of Buckskins are also registered with the American Quarter Horse Association. In 1997 there were eighteen thousand registered Buckskins in the United States and abroad.

Palomino

Registry requirements state that this breed, believed to be of largely Arabian ancestry, should be the color of a newly minted U.S. gold coin, or five shades lighter or darker. The mane and tail are white or silver, with no more than 15 percent dark hair allowed. No dark or light patches of hair should appear on the dorsal area, no zebra stripes, and no white markings should be anywhere except on face and legs. The eyes must be black, brown, or hazel. Most registered Palominos are Quarter Horses, with half-Arabs running second. The color is found in a few other breeds.

The Palomino Horse Breeders Association (PHBA) requires that horses in its registry must also be listed with another breed registry (like the Quarter Horse Association, the Jockey Club, or the Arab, American Saddlebred, Tennessee Walker, or Standardbred registry), or else have a sire or dam registered with the PHBA. Registered Palominos must be dark skinned. Mares and stallions, who might pass on the gene, cannot have Albino parents. (Geldings may, as long as they meet color and conformation standards.)

A Palomino bred with another Palomino is likely to produce offspring of the same color. A sorrel bred with a Palomino or an Albino bred with a chestnut has a fifty-fifty chance of getting the desired result.

Pinto and Paint

These legendary painted "ponies" of the West were prized by the Plains Indians, who often accented their brilliant colors with dye. Mutations in pigment that caused their odd coloration were recorded more than three thousand years ago in Egyptian, Persian, and Chinese art. During the invasions of the Roman Empire, circa A.D. 500, the Oriental ancestors of these breeds were brought to the Mediterranean, where they were crossed with Andalusians and other indigenous breeds and later brought to the Americas by early Spanish explorers.

The name *pinto* derives from the Spanish word *pintado,* or "painted," but the two should not be confused because not every pinto is a paint, although paints may also be registered as pintos. Pintos and Paints have their own separate registries, with their own requirements, distinctive body types, and specific color patterns. In researching this it is clear that you must contact either of the associations directly for detailed descriptions of each type (see Appendix F). The Pinto Horse Association (Pt HA) is a color registry in which horses can be of any breed except draft or Appaloosa if they meet the color pattern standards. The American Paint Horse Association (APHA) requires horses to be registered with either the American

THE OVERO AND THE TOBIANO

Quarter Horse Association, the Jockey Club, the APHA, or any combination of two of these and meet minimum color specifications.

Depending on the pattern of color, the two breeds are further classified as *Tobiano* (toe-bee-ah'-no) or *Overo* (oh-vair'-o). The Tobiano color pattern appears to be white with large spots of color that often overlap when there is a greater percentage of color than white. Spots of color usually originate from the head, chest, flank, and rump, often including the tail. The legs are generally white, giving the appearance of a white horse with large flowing spots. The Overo is a colored horse with white jagged spots that originate on the side or belly, spreading toward the neck, tail, legs, and back (almost never crossing the back). The color appears to frame the white spots. Often the tail, mane, and backline are dark, frequently with bald or white face and white legs.

The variety of sizes (which includes Miniature Horses) and conformation of Pintos and Paints means that there are types to suit everyone. They are excellent for pleasure riding, driving, racing, and endurance and suitable for all Western and English riding disciplines.

A relatively recent addition to these colorful horses is the *Pintabian* horse, or "Arabian with spots." The coloration must be that of a Tobiano. The breed was developed by continually crossing Tobianos back to purebred Arabians until the progeny were nearly 99 percent purebred Arabian. Their conformation should closely resemble that of the Arabian, including the distinctive dished face and large eye, arched neck, short back, level hip, and gaily carried tail. Pintabians' temperament, versatility, and intelligence make them ideally suited for family horses, pleasure riding, and competition.

THE MUSTANG

The distant ancestors of this feral breed were the Arabians, Barbs, and possibly Andalusians that Spanish invaders brought, first to Mexico (by Cortes) and later to the Southwest (by Coronado). By the end of the fifteenth century, wealthy Spaniards in the West owned many herds of horses. The Indians, realizing their potential, began to capture them and became accomplished horsemen in a remarkably short time. Riding without saddles or bridles, they grew adept at controlling their horses with seat and leg pressure alone, leaving their arms free for bows and arrows. Some of the horses managed to escape from both ranchers and Indians, becoming the ancestors of the wild mustang.

The Indians often selected horses as camouflage, picking colors that matched the season or terrain. They chose duns in the fall, white horses for the snow in winter, and blue roans for the sagegrass. They smeared pintos and grays with paint to blend with just about anything. White horses with roan freckles on the body and particularly over the ears and poll—a color pattern called *medicine hat*—were considered lucky and invulnerable in battle.

Still, the breed retained the appearance of its Spanish forebears until the nineteenth century, when mating with draft horses brought west by the pioneers caused its gradual degeneration. Then, too, with a few exceptions, Indian tribes were indif-

THE MUSTANG

ferent to the care and breeding of the horses, because so many were available. At the same time wranglers in search of mounts were cutting the best horses out of the wild herds, often killing the lead stallion to bring in the rest of the group, thus further weakening the breed.

At the turn of the twentieth century more than two million horses ran wild and unprotected. The migration of these expanding wild herds came into direct conflict with the business of raising beef cattle on the range and the development of land. The unprotected wild horses became fair game for anyone willing to round them up. Often with the most inhumane and crudest methods imaginable, entire herds were wiped out, reducing the population to a mere tens of thousands. In 1971, the Bureau of Land Management (BLM) stepped in with the Wild Horse and Burro Act to try to stabilize a deteriorating situation.

This BLM act still appears to be a work in progress, but many positive changes have occurred from its implementation, such as setting aside herd management areas, retaining an optimal herd size for each range, censuring the herd population with flyovers every one to three years, and establishing the Adopt-A-Horse program to reduce herd size. The latter program places young mustangs in pleasure horse situations and is now the only legal method of culling herds. If you are interested in the adoption program, contact BLM or Adopt-A-Horse (see Appendix F).

There are also many other civilian organizations concerned with the protection of these feral horses and burros, among them KBR (World of Wild Horses and Burros) and WHOA (Wild Horse Organized Assistance).

Although the older horses are more difficult to tame and train, mustangs do make good cow ponies and are outstanding as endurance horses. The breed has repeatedly won the famed Tevis Cup, the toughest endurance ride in the country, and has performed successfully in other disciplines.

Because for generations the best horses were destroyed or bred with other less hardy or cold-blooded breeds, mustangs are no longer as beautiful or rugged as they once were. Still, as with the Arab, only the hardiest have survived. The breed has remarkable endurance and an ability to live on what little land they have. Mustangs are small horses, generally not much above 14.2 hands, and they weigh seven to eight hundred pounds. The most common colors are dun, roan, and *grullo* (pronounced gru-yo). They are tough and wiry, with sinewy muscles and hard hooves, enabling them to be ridden unshod.

WARMBLOODS

After the need in Europe for heavy farm and military horses became almost obsolete, warmbloods were produced primarily as international sport horses, for show jumping, dressage, eventing, and driving. Warmbloods have from one-half to seven-eighths "hot blood." Unlike the Thoroughbred, Arab, or Morgan, the various warmblooded breeds do not have closed studbooks but continue to evolve with infusions of "outside" blood. Most warmblooded breeds have rigorous standards of testing and judging of conformation, performance, and breeding potential to select the best individuals for inclusion in their registries. These approved horses are then allowed to wear the specific brand of the breed.

Danish Warmblood

A relative newcomer to the international dressage and eventing arena, this breed is influenced by the Andalusian, which was crossed with German heavy horses in the fifteenth century to produce the Fredericksborg, its predecessor. The breed was more recently infused with Selle-Francais, Thoroughbred, and Trakehner blood. A stud was established in 1960.

Dutch Warmblood

This sport horse has achieved international competitive recognition in a relatively short time. It has been bred up from a farm and carriage horse to excel at dressage, jumping, eventing, and driving as well as ring and trail riding.

Dutch horses are bred in France, Germany, Sweden, Holland, and the United States; the combined European output of foals averages 90,000 annually. They are

THE DUTCH WARMBLOOD

exported to all parts of the world. Inspections are held throughout the Netherlands every year to evaluate and reward horses according to how well they fulfill the breeding goals of the oversight agencies. The test for breeding stallions is one of the most selective and rigorous in the world. Those of sufficient quality are inscribed in the studbook and usually branded. Outstanding stallions are predicated in the studbook with stars, while mares who excel at performance tests and have produced offspring superior in sport are graded either "preferent" or "prestatie."

Hanoverian

This breed bears the name of the German city where George II of England established the regional stud in 1735. It is still the world center for this tall, powerful breed that has achieved world-class fame for show jumping. The foundation sires were Holsteiner stallions. Norman, East Prussian, and Thoroughbred blood were subsequently mixed with the breed.

Originally bred as a farm horse and armored mount during the Middle Ages, the Hanoverian was modified to serve as an eighteenth-century cavalry mount and gained renown as an outstanding carriage horse. An infusion of refined Thoroughbred blood resulted in an even handsomer animal, with an energetic ground-covering trot and a smooth, rhythmic canter. Hanoverians are noted for their hardiness, which in combination with their heavier bone structure and conformation makes them ideal mounts for jumping, driving, and dressage. At the

THE HANOVERIAN

1976 Olympics the famous 17-hand Hanoverian Warwick Rex managed to negotiate an incredibly difficult course, winning the gold medal for jumping despite a viral infection that left him jaundiced and without his usual form.

The consistently outstanding performance of this breed is attributed to the particularly high standards of its testing program. The extensive efforts of the Hanoverian breeding program are also responsible for the distinctive conformation of these horses. This breed has been used to upgrade almost every other European warmblood breed.

From chest to croup the body resembles a rectangular outline (frame). The withers extend far back out of a sloping shoulder. The back is strong, with a broad, slightly rounded croup. The legs are strong and well-shaped, the hocks are clean and well-defined, and the hooves are clean and broad. The head is noble, with a large expressive eye depicting the calm sensible temperament. These horses are exceptionally strong and are endowed with large elastic movement.

The *Westphalian* is also rectangular in frame but is lighter in build and has a finer head than the Hanoverian. It ranks second to it in popularity and numbers within Germany. Westphalians range from 15.2 to 16.2 hands in height, excelling in dressage, show jumping, eventing, and driving. The famous Ahlerich, ridden by Reiner Klimke, was winner of the Olympic dressage gold metal for Germany in 1984.

Holstein or Holsteiner

Developed in the thirteenth century as a work and war horse, this breed pulled plows in peacetime and carried heavily armored feudal lords to battle. After the Reformation, when lighter horses were needed for cavalry, the breed was infused with Oriental, Spanish, and Neapolitan blood, and a stud was founded, resulting in the typical Holstein still seen today: a strong, large-framed horse with powerful gaits and a characteristic Roman nose.

By the sixteenth century Holsteins were in great demand throughout Europe as pleasure and cavalry mounts. The breed was severely decimated during the Napoleonic wars, then was rejuvenated with the infusion of English Thoroughbred blood. By the end of World War II, Holsteins were gaining a reputation as jumpers and show horses.

As more Thoroughbred blood has passed into the breed, it has become lighter, faster, and sportier looking. But Holsteins remain basically massive and muscular, with a deep chest, strong limbs, and excellent character and temperament. In spite of their size, they are extraordinarily graceful, excelling in dressage and show jumping.

Lippizan

Although these famous dressage horses are identified with the Spanish Riding School (the world's oldest equestrian academy), their origins are actually Austro-Hungarian.

The original stud was the royal and imperial court stud of Lippiza, established in 1580 and located in the mountainous Karst region, near what is now Trieste. When the Austro-Hungarian empire was divided, some Lippizans were brought to Austria, and others to Hungary, Yugoslavia, Czechoslovakia, and Romania. Today they are bred in many countries, but the worldwide population is not large, estimated at roughly three thousand.

The original breeding stock comprised nine Andalusian stallions and twenty-four Barb mares imported from Spain. Other breeds, predominantly Iberian and Arabian, were later infused to obtain today's Lippizan (which is classified as a heavy warmblood). The breed is divided into six main lines, named for their eighteenth- and nineteenth-century foundation sires: Conversano, Favory, Siglavy, Neapolitano, Pluto, and Maestro. Though born dark, most Lippizans gradually turn gray and then white between their fourth and seventh years. A few, particularly in the Neapolitano line, remain bay or black. Traditionally one black or bay horse is included in each performance of the Spanish Riding School.

During World War II Colonel Tempel Smith, serving under General George Patton, saved the Austrian Lippizans from conscription by the Russian military. The Spanish Riding School was put under the protection of the U.S. Army, and the stud, which had already been transferred to Czechoslovakia, was brought back to Austria under armed escort.

The neck of the Lippizan is set high and carried nobly, setting off a well-shaped head that often has a ramlike nose. The back is strong and muscular, ending in a

THE LIPPIZAN

powerful croup. The frame is rectangular, with a well-placed and silky tail. The limbs are compact and clearly defined, with clean haunches and well-formed hooves. The height is 15.1 to 16.2 hands.

Selle-Francais

Until 1958 all French riding horses except Arabians, Thoroughbreds, and Anglo-Arabs were called *demi sangs,* or "half breds." Since then competition horses have been known as French Saddlehorses, or *Chevaux de Selle-Francais.*

The line was founded in the early nineteenth century, when local mares in Normandy horse country were crossed with English Thoroughbreds, Norfolk Trotters, and English half-breds of predominantly Norfolk Roadster blood, to create two separate types: a racing trotter and a combination harness and riding horse. Both influenced the current breed, but after the Second World War more Thoroughbred blood was infused to increase speed, stamina, and jumping ability. Today most of these horses are used for show jumping, although a lighter type with more Thoroughbred blood is a popular competitor in cross-country racing.

Swedish Warmblood

Well known for over a century for its sensible attitude and powerful gaits, the Swedish warmblood is the product of a wide variety of imported horses, including the Andalusian and Friesian, that were crossed with native mares in the seventeenth century. The breed was later improved with Arabian, Hanoverian, Trakehner, and

Thoroughbred blood. Today it ranks with the top international competitors in all Olympic disciplines, winning medals in eventing and dressage. Studs at Stromsholm and Skane (the Royal Stud) demand performance tests and intensive examinations before horses are accepted for breeding.

Trakehner

Although this breed was known in the seventeenth century as mostly coach horses, official recognition wasn't received until 1732, when the Royal Stud was founded in Trakehnen (in what was then East Prussia) by King Friedrich Wilhelm I to breed remounts for his cavalry officers. Later in the century, hardier and faster horses were produced by adding Thoroughbred and Arab blood. When this role was no longer necessary, breeding goals were redirected toward dressage and show jumping.

Two world wars decimated the breed but ultimately improved its hardiness and endurance. The October 1944 evacuation of more than 26,000 horses (over 1,200 Trakehner geldings and broodmares, most in foal) from the East Prussian studs in three hours to avoid the advancing Russian troops began the exodus. The arduous two-and-one-half-month trek to reach the safety of Western Germany was over eight hundred miles long, through gunfire and bombing raids with a shortage of grain rations and no bulk feed, and is legendary in the history of the breed. Many foals died of starvation. Only seven hundred of the surviving broodmares were fit for breeding to the sixty Trakehner stallions that had been sent ahead. These hardy horses became the foundation stock of the breed in the West.

Like other warmbloods, this breed has also been enhanced and perpetuated by a strict testing and grading program. More than two hundred years of selective breeding and cross-breeding have helped to produce this all-around riding and driving

THE TRAKEHNER

horse. The breed is popular in many countries in the world and has the sixth-largest registry in the United States. These horses are solidly built, with a strong medium-length back, medium bone structure, and round, full ribs. The head is noble, with large eyes and a narrow muzzle set on a full crested neck and carried with style. The sloping shoulders, predominant withers, and correctly sloping pasterns make them elegant movers. Endowed with a floating trot, they are much sought after as three-day and dressage prospects.

The difference between a horse and a pony is sometimes blurred, and it can be confusing to the potential buyer. In England, where the Pony Club originated, all children's mounts are called ponies. In the United States and Canada, it is correct to call any equine under 14.2 hands a pony, but many registered breeds (like the Thoroughbred, Arabian, Quarter Horse, and Morgan) may measure less and still be called horses. The distinction is important to those who plan to show horses or ponies because rated horse shows have an age limit of eighteen years for riders in pony classes. A breed, like the Halflinger, recognized in Europe as horses, are relegated to pony status in the United States, unless officials at a given show rule differently.

As horses gained in popularity, the pony population zoomed. Imported ponies, including the Dartmoor breed, the Dales, the Fell, and the larger New Forest and English Hackney, come from all over the world. Everyone is familiar with the little Shetland from the Shetland Islands and the Welsh Mountain Pony from Wales; the Scottish Highland Pony is now almost as popular. Many of the larger ponies can be successfully crossed with Thoroughbreds or Arabians to produce a bigger and more refined show pony.

PONIES

Pony of the Americas

This first all-American pony breed was established in Mason City, Iowa, in 1954. The foundation sire, Black Hand, was a white Appaloosa with black egg-shaped markings on the loins, croup, and back; the dam was a Shetland. Ponies of the Americas have specific coloring that must meet the same requirements as the four Appaloosa types. Used for children who are too large to ride a small pony and not yet ready for a horse, the breed is also used for racing, pole bending, barrel racing, and all-around pleasure mounts. POAs are gaining in popularity in English show jumping and driving classes. The conformation varies, but the ideal is somewhere between an Arabian and a Quarter Horse.

Connemara

The Connemara pony is believed to be descended from Spanish horses rescued from ships wrecked off the rocky coast of Western Ireland in 1568. Bred in the county of Connaught, these horses were crossed with the native stock of Celtic ponies that date back to the fourth century B.C., when they were brought in by the Celts to pull war chariots and race. In the 1700s Thoroughbred and Arabian blood was introduced. By the early 1900s random breeding was diminishing the strong breed traits. A small group of quality ponies were selected and turned loose in the rough pastures and harsh weather to live and reproduce. The survivors preserved the prized Connemara characteristics: hardiness, stamina, agility, intelligence, and extraordinary jumping ability. The breed has been used to influence the renowned Irish hunter.

The Connemara is an outstanding jumper for his small size, between 12.2 and

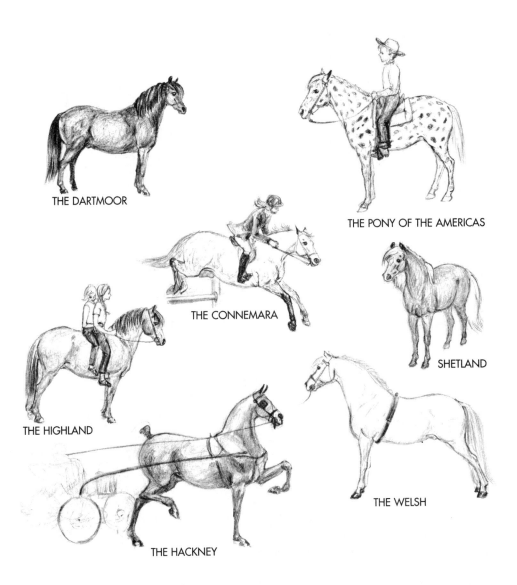

THE DARTMOOR

THE PONY OF THE AMERICAS

THE CONNEMARA

SHETLAND

THE HIGHLAND

THE WELSH

THE HACKNEY

14.2 hands. He is a compact pony with a deep chest and short, clean legs of ample bone. The head is handsome, of medium length, with a relatively lean neck and an abundant mane and tail. Now rare, the original coloring was dun. The most common color is gray, but black, bay, and brown are also seen.

Halflinger

Europe's answer to the Morgan, the Halflinger is prized for its versatility and docility, the latter developed over centuries of being housed in cramped barns and paddocked in enclosed front courtyards. Halflingers can be trained for dressage, driving, and hunting and as packhorses. They excel at endurance riding, showing only small increases in temperature and blood pressure.

Bred for centuries in Halfling, Austria, near the Italian border, this ancient breed originated in central Europe more than two thousand years ago. Roman invaders later cross-bred their Arabian stallions with the hardy Halfling mares, whose offspring they later used as cavalry mounts. The modern Halflinger dates back to 1870, when a local Halfling mare was bred to the Arabian stallion El Badavi. Purebreds of this new type must be traceable to El Badavi's get, the stallion Folie.

Halflingers are the most popular leisure-time horses in Europe, and they are becoming increasingly popular in the United States as well. They are famously long-lived, often continuing to work into their forties.

The breed is stocky and densely boned. Colors range from honey to dark brown. They have pure white manes and tails and a white stripe on the nose, ideally running its full length.

Norwegian Fjord

Looking much like the Asian wild horse, this dun-colored breed has had its mane roached, to resemble ancestors pictured on runestone carvings of the Vikings, who rode the ponies in battle.

Increasingly popular in Europe and the United States as a child's mount, the breed is used in driving competitions and endurance riding, doubling as a pack and plow pony. Even when worked hard, fjords need relatively little food to thrive.

THE MINIATURE HORSE

Once dismissed as passing curiosities, these little creatures, bred as pets and for show, are now a big business. Their registered numbers have grown from a few hundred to more than a hundred and fifty thousand in less than forty years. Smaller than traditional pony breeds (mature, they should not exceed 34 inches), they are always referred to as Miniature horses, never ponies. With nearly 400 years of selective breeding, they resemble scaled-down, well-proportioned versions of larger breeds.

There is some controversy about the exact lineage of Miniatures, but their descent from pit ponies imported from England and Western Europe (Holland, Belgium, and Germany) in the late nineteenth century is undisputed. Some breed enthusiasts believe that Miniatures trace back to the Renaissance, and even to ancient Egypt, although this cannot be documented in historical records.

In 1845 the Falabella family of Buenos Aires, Argentina, were first to selectively breed "mini horses" by crossing very small imported Shetland mares and native Criollas with an undersize Thoroughbred stallion. Falabellas are still the only distinct breed with pedigree records that go back 150 years.

Shortly after the First World War, Norman Fields of Bedford, Virginia, began importing ponies to work in the Appalachian mines. He started to breed for small size, producing an initial herd of fifty Miniatures. During the same period a West Virginia horse trader, Smith McCoy, discovered that the smallest ponies brought the best prices and began selling them to prospective breeders.

Although some Miniatures look like replicas of larger familiar breeds, their ancestry is always mixed. The American Miniature Horse Registry recognizes two types: the more refined Arabian or Thoroughbred type, and the stock type. The American Miniature Horse Association, founded in Texas in 1978, will accept only descendants of the sires and dams originally registered with them. Some horses are double registered.

Mature Miniatures that qualify for registration range from twenty-five to a maximum of thirty-four inches in height. They weigh between one and three hundred pounds. Their manes, tails, and hooves are thicker than those of larger equines. In harness most miniatures can easily pull the weight of an adult and are generally not ridden. They are noted for their gentle, playful temperament.

PART III

Eating Like a Horse

In Ireland, the general feed is raw potatoes. In Iceland, dried fish is employed as a provender; while during the needy period of the Crimean campaign, the English horses devoured the tails of their stable associates. . . . Why, therefore, are oats preferred as the fittest food for horses? Nature has sent food in abundance and variety. Is man justified when he first imprisons a life and then dooms it to subsist for the period of its being on a monotony of provender?

Dr. Edward Mayhew, Royal College of Veterinary Surgeons (nineteenth century)

Horses Are Grazing Animals

Real horses don't eat like proverbial horses. That is, they don't eat the way your uncle Harry eats when he wades into a fourth helping at Thanksgiving dinner and your aunt says, "Harry, you're eating like a horse." If a horse ate grain the way Harry eats candied yams, it would kill him. The equine stomach isn't big enough to handle large amounts of food at one feeding.

While horses do eat a lot, in their natural state they eat small amounts of food continually over extended periods of time. Put simply, horses are grazing animals.

Wild herds of horses once ranged over vast areas, eating a wide variety of vegetation during four distinct seasons of the year and drinking pure, mineral-rich water from natural sources. This indigenous diet has in modern times been severely restricted by domestication and confinement, limiting and often eliminating important vitamins and minerals. Modern industry and agriculture have had further adverse effects. Acid rain and fertilizers pollute hay, grain, and water. Nutrients are lost in the processing and storage of feeds, while the leaching of minerals from overworked soil depletes the quality of pasturage.

Wild and feral horses can choose from a diversified menu of plants and grasses— a high-fiber diet ideally suited to their digestive systems. Horses have small stomachs for their size, and their one-way digestive system works best when it is continually supplied with small amounts of food, as in grazing.

Everyone is aware that horses graze, but owners often fail to ponder its implications, mistakenly equating equine nutritional needs with their own. As a result, they overfeed their horses with too much protein and with rich, unnecessary supplements—an unnatural and potentially harmful diet.

Equine stomachs can't handle an overload; nor can they expel it by vomiting. The entrance to a horse's stomach is encircled by a strong muscle that admits food and fluids but prevents anything from going back out. Thus a horse can't even burp up excess stomach acid, let alone regurgitate disagreeable fodder.

So when a horse eats the wrong thing or even too much of the right things, the food is trapped in his stomach. It stacks up in soggy layers that his digestive system is unable to break down or expel, making him susceptible to several digestive problems. (Human stomachaches are minor maladies compared with the life-threatening equine disorder known as colic. See Chapter 19.) This vulnerability is heightened by any stressful situation, like a sudden change in the weather, not being properly cooled off after exercise, an aggressive horse in the pasture, or even a bumpy trip in a trailer.

Research has established that stressed-out horses become calmer on a low-protein, high-carbohydrate and -fiber diet. Too much protein will overload the kidneys as well as the stomach—an effect that will be unpleasantly noticeable when you shovel the very wet, acrid-smelling bedding into the wheelbarrow. (The price of feed rises along with its protein content—a big waste in both respects.)

Therefore, don't make the mistake of confusing equine dietary percentages with human ones. Carnivorous humans can tolerate a protein intake of 100 percent if they have to, but for herbivorous horses a mere 8 to 10 percent is the maximum. (A 2 to 4 percent exception can be made for some aged individuals. See Chapter 35.)

Forage is the foundation of a horse's diet, and nutritionists caution that protein-rich grain should be fed only when hay and pasture don't meet caloric requirements. Shortchanging fiber with too much grain and supplements will disrupt the ability of a horse's sensitive digestive system to absorb nutrients, leading to the problems mentioned before.

Once you understand how the equine digestive system functions, you'll be unlikely to confuse it with your own.

Teeth, of course, are the primary food processors, and digestive efficiency depends on their condition. Horses grasp food with the upper lip, aided by the tongue or front teeth, depending on the type of fodder. Before they chew hay or grain, they mix it with large quantities of saliva, which is secreted by three large salivary glands. These glands also produce a protein that helps break down starches. The salivary glands are usually stimulated by the water the horse drinks before eating.

The food then moves back in the mouth, where it is ground up, down, and finally sideways by the teeth. This lateral movement gradually wears down tooth enamel, creating sharp edges on the inside of the lower teeth and the outside of the uppers, often causing painful injuries to the tongue and cheeks unless filed regularly.

Horses eat slowly as a rule, in keeping with natural grazing habits suited to the configuration of their jaws. The upper mandible is larger than the lower, allowing them to chew on only one side at a time. Consuming a pound of hay can thus take from fifteen to twenty minutes (a pound of grain half that time). Some horses bolt their food, a habit that should and can be discouraged. (See page 106.)

Lubricated by all that saliva, the chewed food passes quickly through the pharynx. The automatic blocking action of the soft palate helps it along and prevents it from entering the windpipe and nasal passages or returning to the mouth. (This built-in safety valve also deters horses from breathing through the mouth.)

From the pharynx the food is propelled into the stomach by downward, wavelike contractions of the esophagus—the four-to-five-foot tube extending down the left

CHOWING DOWN

THE DIGESTIVE SYSTEM
1. Esophagus
2. Stomach
3. Small intestine
4. Cecum
5. Large intestine
6. Rectum

side of the neck. As mentioned earlier, the stomach is guarded by a powerful and involuntary ringlike muscle that marks the end of the one-way esophageal pathway and makes it impossible for a horse to vomit or belch. A relatively small equine stomach can handle only eight to seventeen quarts per feeding, depending on the size of the horse.

A horse's digestive system arranges food in layers: the most recently digested matter at the bottom, and the fully digested on top. The enzymes in the stomach wall mix with various gastric juices to break down proteins and fatty acids for later digestion, while its muscles contract and expand to expel excess or partially digested food. It takes twenty-four hours for all food to leave the stomach, making this stage of digestion a continuous process.

From the stomach the food passes into the small intestine—a misleading name for an organ seventy feet long and three to four inches wide, with a forty-eight-quart capacity. As the food navigates this tortuous route, enzymes are secreted to break it down further. Considering the length and narrowness of the organ, it isn't surprising that many digestive problems occur here, a twisted or telescoped intestine being among the most common.

Next stop on the alimentary canal is the four-compartment large intestine, site of the most important digestive activities. Here fatty acids are absorbed, amino acids and B vitamins are synthesized, and carbohydrates like starch and sugar are melded into energy-yielding fatty acids. Because of the enormous pressure that incoming food exerts on the small opening into the intestine's funnel-like compartments, the food can easily become impacted here.

Before it enters the rectum, all its fluid is reabsorbed into the waste of indigestible and/or undigested foods and cell residue cast off from intestinal walls. Healthy horses void anywhere from five to twelve pounds of manure daily, adding up to thirty-three to fifty pounds a week, depending on the animal's level of activity. This is something to consider if you're thinking of putting a stable in a residential area. That's a lot of fertilizer.

PORTION PLANNING

What and how much a horse should be fed is determined by his age, breed, and weight, as well as by the type and amount of work he is doing. Young horses have different dietary needs from older individuals and those in their prime.

Young horses, who reach half of their mature weight by the end of the first year and continue growing for another four to six years, have special dietary needs. Colts and fillies should be fed larger rations, with a higher percentage of protein during this period to promote proper bone formation—a process that isn't complete until the fifth or sixth year.

Aged horses also need special diets, depending on their condition. (Such diets will be discussed in Chapter 35.)

Large horses don't necessarily eat proportionately more than small ones. All pony breeds are notoriously "easy keepers," but so are all the big draft breeds. Thoroughbreds have the highest metabolic rate, burning nutrients the most quickly, while Standardbreds, Quarter Horses, Morgans, and other light breeds hold the middle ground. Arabians, like ponies, are easy keepers.

When figured into the cost of maintenance, dietary variations make a big difference. I once owned a Thoroughbred and a Quarter Horse of the same age, height, and weight, who did the same amount of work. The Thoroughbred needed twelve pounds of grain and twenty-five pounds of hay a day to maintain his weight, while the Quarter Horse thrived on only half that amount.

For reasons that the National Research Council has yet to pin down, metabolic rates can also vary widely among individuals of the same breed. So even if you feed your horse "by the book" for his age, weight, and breed, you might miss the mark. Only paying close attention to weight and condition will assure that he's getting a proper diet.

If you know what your horse ought to look like when he's in "good flesh," you'll probably have little difficulty telling if he's too fat or too thin just by taking a careful look at him. If his ribs are showing, he's too thin. If he has a noticeable belly, he's too fat. When in doubt, run your hand over his barrel. If you can feel (but not see) the ribs, his weight is normal. If you can't feel them, he's too fat.

Metabolic imbalance is a less visible problem. It might show up as an uncharacteristic lack of energy or a dull coat, but in most cases a horse that is energetic and appears well nourished is probably getting the right mix of vitamins and minerals.

On the other hand, a horse that looks too fat to you might be just right for his particular breed or build, while a thin horse might need medication, rather than food, to cure a low-grade infection that's sapping his strength. Never put your horse on a diet of any type before consulting the veterinarian.

If careful scrutiny detects any weight loss, take immediate steps to correct the situation before it gets out of hand. Horses can lose a hundred pounds before it becomes noticeable to the untrained eye, and by the time you can see a horse's ribs, he has lost so much weight that it could take more than six months to get him back in condition. In the case of older horses, who have less efficient digestive systems, it's extremely hard to put significant weight back on. The illustrations in these pages point out the trouble spots to watch for if you suspect your horse is losing weight.

Feeding a horse too much hay will give him the equivalent of a beer belly (in this case, a "hay belly"). Though hay bellies look superficially robust, they burn off in a hurry. It's possible to have all that weight down in the belly even while the ribs are showing above.

A hay belly shouldn't be confused with the full barrel of a mare in foal, which I mention here only because I've heard of a number of cases where knowledgeable people have confused these conditions. A few months after they put their horse on a diet, they walked into the stall one morning to hear the pitter-patter of little hooves.

For a horse in poor condition, adjust his diet accordingly. Gradually increase the

WEIGHING IN

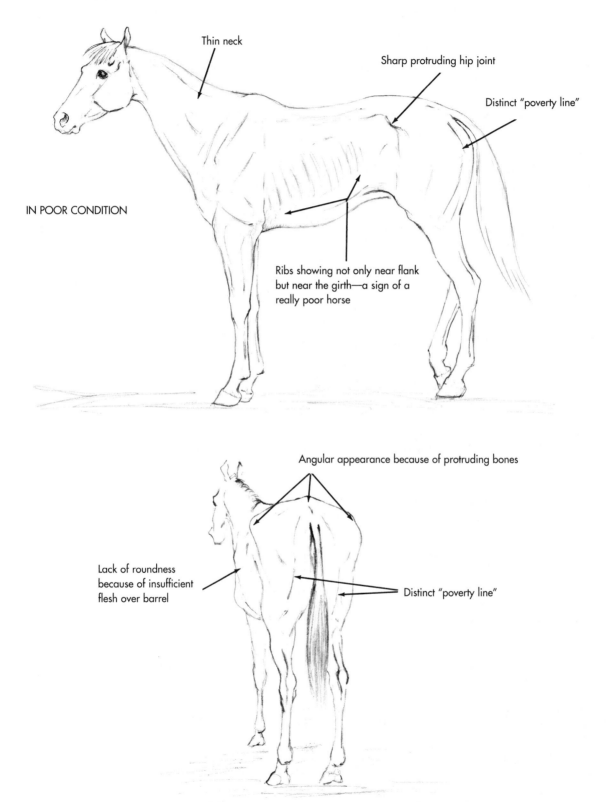

Thin neck

Sharp protruding hip joint

Distinct "poverty line"

IN POOR CONDITION

Ribs showing not only near flank
but near the girth—a sign of a
really poor horse

Angular appearance because of protruding bones

Lack of roundness
because of insufficient
flesh over barrel

Distinct "poverty line"

A HAY BELLY

feed, possibly add supplements, and extend the number of feedings each day to three or more. Conversely, for an overweight horse, decrease his food intake slowly, reducing his hay and grain rations by small amounts (about 10 percent of total volume each week) until he regains his figure. A horse should be lean and hard, rather than fat and soft. Overweight horses are far less agile than lean ones and are prone to founder and Monday morning sickness. (See Chapter 19.) Extra body weight puts a strain on the muscular and skeletal system and lowers fertility in broodmares and stallions.

A dieting horse can get very put out if he must watch his stablemates feast on regular meals. Keep weight watchers happy by adding low-calorie treats like chopped carrots and turnips to their grain.

You can gauge weight with a weight tape (purchased from a tack shop or neighborhood feed store), measuring in a circle around the girth, just behind the withers. Another option is to drive your empty trailer to the closest truck weighing station (your state police can direct you), record the weight, and then return with your horse aboard to weigh again.

The average light horse doing light work—like pleasure riding or low-level dressage—will need to eat from 1.5 to 2 percent of his body weight in feed daily: two-thirds of it in hay or equivalent fiber, and at least 8 percent in protein.

Equine intestines teem with diverse colonies of ravenous parasites waiting to cadge a meal. Botfly larvae and the eggs of large and small strongyles, roundworms, and tapeworms, to name just a few, will be first to feast on the nutrients of any fodder a horse eats, depriving the bloodstream of energy-producing elements that the horse needs for peak performance. These parasitic pests invade the mouth as eggs and larvae, swimming on a salivary sea into the hundred-foot alimentary canal, attaching themselves at various points along it, and burrowing in until they reach maturity

THE INSIDE STORY

NATIONAL RESEARCH COUNCIL

TABLE 5-4   EXPECTED FEED CONSUMPTION BY HORSES
(% body weight)[a]

	Forage	Concentrate	Total
Mature horses			
Maintenance	1.5–2.0	0–0.5	1.5–2.0
Mares, late gestation	1.0–1.5	0.5–1.0	1.5–2.0
Mares, early lactation	1.0–2.0	1.0–2.0	2.0–3.0
Mares, late lactation	1.0–2.0	0.5–1.5	2.0–2.5
Working horses			
Light work	1.0–2.0	0.5–1.0	1.5–2.5
Moderate work	1.0–2.0	0.75–1.5	1.75–2.5
Intense work	0.75–1.5	1.0–2.0	2.0–3.0
Young horses			
Nursing foal, 3 months	0	1.0–2.0	2.5–3.5
Weanling foal, 6 months	0.5–1.0	1.5–3.0	2.0–3.5
Yearling foal, 12 months	1.0–1.5	1.0–2.0	2.0–3.0
Long yearling, 18 months	1.0–1.5	1.0–1.5	2.0–2.5
Two-year-old (24 months)	1.0–1.5	1.0–1.5	1.75–2.5

[a]Air-dry feed (about 90% DM).

and are expelled in the feces. If left unchecked, these minuscule gourmands will permanently damage the horse's blood vessels and intestines, causing chronic digestive problems and general debilitation. Wormy horses have a lethargic attitude that translates into poor performance. Their coats are dull and resist shedding, potbellies swell under their visible ribs, and episodes of colic and diarrhea are frequent. To prevent these conditions, all horses must be regularly dewormed. (See Chapter 21.)

When food reaches the first stop on the alimentary canal, the billions of beneficial bacteria waiting in the highly acid stomach juices break it down, attacking in microorganic hordes of 200 million per gram. From the stomach foodstuffs travel to the small intestine, where liver secretions, pancreatic fluids, and enzymes join in the digestive fray, then on into the colon and cecum, where the action accelerates.

This "hind gut" is a giant fermentation tank. It holds up to thirty gallons of partially digested food, which it transforms into liquid nutrients that are then absorbed through the gut lining. For this job even larger forces are marshaled here: an army of 900 million microorganisms per gram. These legions of flora and fauna contain both beneficial and pathogenic bacteria, forty species of enzyme-secreting protozoa, and various mold-producing fungi, some familiar to all of us.

Among the yeasts produced are those used to culture yogurt, leaven bread, and ferment beer as well as penicillin. Some of the bacteria produce other natural antibiotics, along with B vitamins and acids that determine the gut's acid level (pH).

Digestive enzymes (all those names on food labels that end in *-ase*) are complex proteins that break down fiber and turn carbohydrates, crude proteins, and fats into easily absorbed simple sugars and amino and fatty acids.

To efficiently perform this final task of digestion, the fermenting microbial stew must maintain the pH (a mildly acidic 4 to 6 percent ratio in a healthy horse) with a delicate balance of benign and pathogenic ingredients. When this balance is upset, the animal won't get the nutrients it needs from food and may eat more in order to compensate, becoming a "hard keeper." Excess acid can also cause more serious symptoms of diarrhea, colic, and laminitis.

A number of factors can upset microbial balance, among them sudden changes in feed, a virus, a heavy load of parasites, deworming chemicals, and antibiotics, which kill beneficial bacteria along with their harmful targets. Unfortunately this balance is more quickly upset than restored. An abrupt change in feed, for instance, will cause changes in the hind gut and fecal output within three hours and major changes in the microorganic population within eight. But restoring the normal fermentation process takes several weeks, even with the special feed supplements now available to speed it along. These additives, which contain extra amounts of beneficial bacteria and yeasts, are called probiotics. Though they can curb colic and diarrhea within twenty-four hours, they require about three days to effect changes in the microbial balance and three weeks to reestablish gut fermentation.

Probiotics come as pastes, powders, or liquids and are added to some of the more expensive grain mixes and vitamin-mineral supplements. Most professional equestrians feel that, like other supplements, they should be used only on an as-needed basis. A horse in hard training, or one with a heavy competitive schedule that has him on the road eating different hay and water every weekend, would benefit from probiotics. The average pleasure horse or horse in light work probably doesn't need them.

BALANCING THE BACTERIA

Dietary Do's and Don'ts

To remain healthy, horses must be fed in accordance with their natural grazing habits, which means:

DO FEED LITTLE AND OFTEN. This feeding routine is an effort to imitate nature. At Saratoga and other racetracks, stable managers go all out to do so, feeding racing Thoroughbreds and Standardbreds six to eight times a day in small quantities. Frequent feedings enable a horse to get the most out of his food, which is particularly important for those who are high strung and have worked hard. Obviously the average horse owner would have difficulty keeping up with this kind of schedule and shouldn't try. Done correctly, feedings can be limited to two times a day. (The only time you might want to give your horse the racing Thoroughbred treatment is to fatten him up, as discussed in previous chapters.)

DO FEED PLENTY OF BULK FEED. A horse's digestive system won't function properly without bulk. Bulk feed is grass or hay. When grass isn't available, the horse should have access to hay at all times.

DO FEED ACCORDING TO WORK DONE. Decrease the grain rations and increase the bulk forage when the horse's work schedule is reduced. In hard winters when you won't be working your horse at all, he'll need little or no high-energy food. (See Chapter 33.)

DO WATER BEFORE FEEDING. Always do this to make sure food stays in your horse's stomach long enough for the nutrients to be fully absorbed. If you feed grain, hay, and then water afterward, the food will be washed through the system, and much of the vitamin and mineral content will be lost. A horse should be watered first, then given hay, followed by grain.

DO FEED ONLY CLEAN AND GOOD-QUALITY FOOD. Good-quality grain usually means good oats in the summer and a balanced blend of grains, corn, and meal in the winter. This will give the horse the right amount of protein, carbohydrates, fats, vitamins, and minerals to keep his condition up and his energy high. Food of good quality will be very palatable, with a high proportion of digestible nutrients. Your horse can get out of his feed only what's in it, so it's more economical in the long run to feed him clean, good food. Less will be wasted, and you won't run the chance of making him sick.

DO KEEP A REGULAR FEEDING SCHEDULE. This is very important if a horse is to keep his weight up and keep his *bloom* (having a glossy coat and healthy, vigorous appearance).

One pupil of mine used to feed her horse whenever she got around to it (sometimes at eight A.M., sometimes at noon), then complained constantly about how thin the mare was. Although I tactfully suggested the reason a number of times, the message didn't sink in until she went on summer vacation and sent her horse to a boarding stable for a month.

A good stable feeds in a businesslike way at precisely the same time every day. After only thirty days of regular feeding the mare returned home in full flesh and "blooming" with health. She hadn't been given any more grain or hay at the stable than she got at home, but she had been fed *on time*.

If a horse is accustomed to being fed at eight A.M. and six P.M. daily, his digestive juices will begin to flow at those hours, and he will be physically and psychologically prepared to utilize his food—relaxed and ready to eat. Some horses are so attuned to regular mealtimes that they will gallop the fence line furiously when the dinner hour is delayed.

So it's very important to avoid sudden changes in feeding times. Begin a routine and stick to it; do not vary it by more than fifteen minutes from day to day. This regularity is particularly important for underweight and nervous horses, who must be fed on time to stay in any kind of condition.

DON'TS

DON'T MAKE SUDDEN CHANGES IN THE TYPE OR AMOUNT OF FOOD. You can and should make seasonal adjustments gradually, extending them over a period of several weeks. But any sudden change, even a one-quart overnight increase in grain, could cause colic in a sensitive horse if there is no corresponding increase in work. Conversely, if a horse is standing idle for several days after very hard work, his grain must be reduced by 10 percent. In such an instance, don't be afraid to cut back suddenly on food to avoid azoturia or founder.

DON'T WORK A HORSE IMMEDIATELY AFTER A FULL MEAL. When a horse is idle, his blood supply is concentrated in the digestive system. During exercise it is converted to the lungs and muscles. Working a horse right after feeding could give him colic or founder.

DON'T FEED A HORSE IMMEDIATELY AFTER A WORKOUT. Wait at least an hour after he has been cooled out before feeding. A horse that isn't properly cooled down after a workout could develop colic or founder.

In order that your horse gets the most nourishment from his food, keeps his weight up, and stays in prime condition, he should be *dewormed* and have his *teeth checked regularly,* for reasons we have already discussed.

BALANCING THE EQUINE DIET

Protein

When an equine menu doesn't carry the right ratio of protein, carbohydrates, and fats, the horse's digestive system will go out of whack and his behavior may literally get out of hand. The playful expression "feeling his oats" takes on new and terrifying dimensions when an idle or lightly worked horse is fed a lot of high-protein feed. Protein converts to energy, a biochemical process that becomes spectacularly apparent if a horse eats too much of it. Lacking a constructive outlet for the surplus vitality, he will work it off by kicking, snorting, cribbing, weaving, and other obnoxious behavior. (See Chapter 36.) One mare I know just stands in her stall and bucks.

A few quarts of grain or pellet concentrates go a long way with some horses, particularly high-strung breeds like Thoroughbreds and Arabians. Thus fortified, they can make even the short trip from stable to pasture a hair-raising experience. If a horse can't gallop off or otherwise dissipate his excess energy, his digestive system will become overloaded, causing laminitis, colic, and other disorders. Studies at the University of Kentucky have demonstrated that horses on heavy protein diets, especially young ones, are much more susceptible to strangles, Potomac Horse Fever, epiphytis, and gastric ulcers.

IN GOOD CONDITION

All this should make it clear why it's important to feed a horse according to the work he has done and to accurately weigh grain and concentrates. A one-pound coffee can might do in a pinch, but a feed scoop with a built-in scale will give a precise measure.

Lush pasture and the hay harvested from it also contain protein, the amount depending on the types of grasses and legumes it contains. For some horses and all ponies and miniatures, such pasture and hay can be a complete alternative to grain. (Alfalfa hay, however, which has a very high protein content, is too hard on the kidneys of some older animals.)

The energy produced by protein fuels not only physical activity but breathing, digestion, and circulation. Energy is measured in units called *calories,* their value expressed in food that has been processed by the digestive system. Pasture and hay are relatively low in calories; grain and supplements are high. The amount of calories a horse burns will depend on his individual metabolic rate and the demands of the work he performs.

As we've seen, the equine digestive system isn't very efficient, and food needs a lot of processing before nutrients and caloric value can be utilized. Consequently horses need a much higher percentage of calories in proportion to their weight than humans do—an amount measured in *megacalories.*

Fats and Carbohydrates

Fats and carbohydrates are the other essential ingredients in the equine diet. Fat is more easily absorbed than protein and carbohydrates and therefore produces more energy per calorie, some of which is used to process the others. A horse's metabolic rate increases in order to digest these elements, producing heat, which is why corn is the recommended winter feed. It's higher in fat and lower in fiber than other grains, and it produces a lot of energy quickly, in smaller amounts, leaving more room in the stomach for heat-producing forage.

In temperate climates, where snowy winters prevent regular workouts, a horse's feed requirements may need further adjustment to provide him with enough energy. Sometimes a half-cup of safflower or peanut oil or other vegetable fat can be added to the rations to keep his weight up. Cornmeal and linseed meal will provide the same amount of fat (but shouldn't be fed in abundance to young horses because they affect the amino acid balance and block the absorption of fat-soluble A, D, and E vitamins, impairing bone growth). All the seed meals are wonderful restoratives for an equine coat. A few ounces of corn or soybean meal fed daily over a six-week period will bring out the shine.

Corn, wheat, rye, and barley also contain a high percentage of starch, the most common carbohydrate. Though all contain roughly the same amount of starch, they are very different in their appeal to individual appetites. Most horses like oats, wheat bran, and corn but will walk away from rye and barley. Keep in mind that almost all foods—grain or forage—contain nearly all the nutrients a horse needs in varying amounts.

When it's essential to bring a horse's weight up by increasing calories, do so gradually. Increase grain by half-pound increments over a three-to-seven-day period, depending on the horse. (Watch the consistency of the horse's manure to make sure you've got it right.) Do the same thing when switching from one type of hay to another—say, from timothy to alfalfa, or vice versa.

A lot of kindly old farmers would love a chance to unload last year's moldy hay on an unsuspecting neophyte. To avoid paying top dollar for an inferior product that could make your horse sick, it's important to learn how to tell good hay from bad. Ninety percent of equine food problems could be solved by feeding good-quality hay.

ALL ABOUT HAY

Hay is the primary source of roughage and bulk in the equine diet. Along with this essential fiber, it supplies calcium, phosphorus, several vitamins, and protein—the latter in amounts that depend on the type of hay and its maturity when cut.

In the northeastern United States the most common hay grasses are rye, timothy, bluegrass, bromegrass, orchard grass, and fescues. All of these are best when mixed with a legume—a leafy, succulent grass like alfalfa, trefoil, clover, or crown vetch. In the West lespedeza and some other vetches join the legume list. The best hay combination on the East Coast is a timothy-legume mix.

Apart from being a valuable addition to the pasture because they release nitrogen into the soil, legumes have a high protein, vitamin, and mineral content that balances the diet well by compensating for nutritional deficiencies in grain. This is particularly important for young horses and broodmares. Legumes are very rich in vitamin A (carotene) and those that have been field-cured have a high percentage of the sunshine vitamin, D. (Some dealers, however, cure their hay in the barn, which reduces the D content—a point worth checking out before buying.)

Alfalfa

Alfalfa is the most common legume hay. Its protein content is twice that of grass hay, which means it should make up only one-third to one-half of the daily ration. It is also twice as costly, putting it out of the range of some budgets, and has the laxative and urinary effect already mentioned. Because alfalfa weighs more than other grasses, it has less bulk, and restless horses fed on a large proportion of it are left chewing their fences.

Clover

Clover contains only two-thirds of the digestible protein of alfalfa, but it surpasses alfalfa in net energy value. Unfortunately, it isn't good for most horses, causing problems especially when it grows too high and comes into bloom. Some horses can't tolerate this legume at any stage of its growth and may become seriously ill, especially when the clover is wet. Alfalfa and clover contain more moisture than the other legumes, and unless they are cured until completely dry, they mold easily—which is the main thing to watch out for in this legume hay.

Trefoil

Trefoil prefers a different type of soil from alfalfa, which grows well in very damp, rich earth. Trefoil is hardier, doing well in dry, acid soil, and it doesn't need to be reseeded as often. A good growth of this legume, if fertilized, can last for twenty years without reseeding. Some farmers allow one cutting to go to seed in the field to promote thicker growth.

Because most of the essential nutrients in legumes and grasses are found in their leaves, the main characteristic to look for in all good hay is leafiness and greenness. It should still retain some color, be free of excess dust, and smell fragrant, with a sweet, fresh aroma. Brown or yellow hay with a dusty odor is either overmature or sun bleached—and therefore worthless.

TYPES OF LEGUME HAY

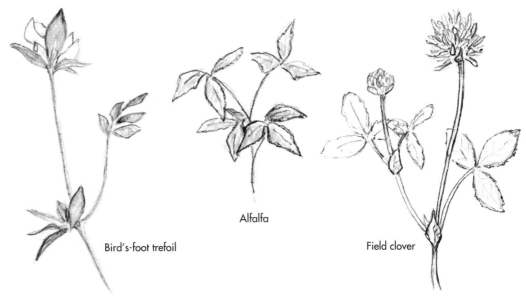

Bird's-foot trefoil

Alfalfa

Field clover

Timothy

Timothy is the standard grass hay used in the United States. It reaches its nutritional peak when the head is just beginning to merge through the blades. But harvesting at this early stage of growth produces less tonnage, so farmers often let the crop mature until its cash value increases by weight; meanwhile its nutritional value correspondingly decreases and often disappears entirely.

Selecting Hay

When selecting hay, open a bale. It should fall apart in sections (sometimes called flakes). Choose a section from the center of the bale, and shake it out to check for excess dust and to judge its leafiness and fragrance.

A heavy sweet or sour smell suggests that the hay was improperly dried, retaining too much moisture, and that it will become moldy. Hay that is already moldy will have white spots throughout. Both moldy and dusty hay can cause heaves or colic.

Hay should be free of foreign matter like weeds, stubble, and other refuse. On occasion I've opened up a bale to find old candy wrappers, crushed tin cans, and in one instance a dead mouse. These things can happen to otherwise good hay, but if you find such surprises in every bale, it's time to find another dealer.

Hay has little value as feed for horses unless it's cut at the proper stage of maturity, when it is highest in protein content, mineral-vitamin content, and digestibility. Harvested after its prime, it goes to seed. And after it lies in the field for more than a few days, exposed to sun, rain, or both, it quickly bleaches out and loses most if not all of its nutritive value. In wet weather a crop may sit in the fields getting drenched until it's worthless for anything but mulch. Sometimes even the most

TYPES OF GRASS HAY

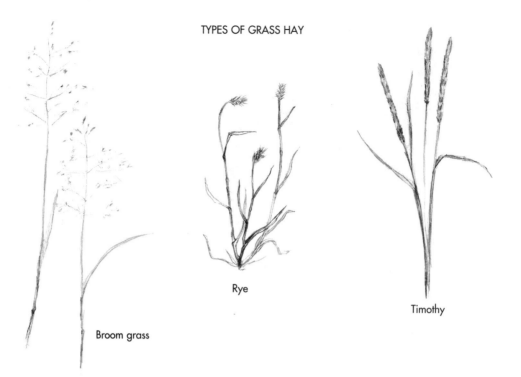

Rye

Timothy

Broom grass

experienced farmers can't bring in a good crop of hay if rain forces them to miss the weather window (a period of about a week) in which it should be cut and harvested.

After mowing, hay must be baled within three or four days during dry and prefer-ably breezy weather. With state-of the-art equipment some farmers can often get a field cut and baled in a day.

Periods of dry weather will stunt hay's growth. A poor harvest will drive up prices during the winter—unless the dealer is large enough to have hay dryers in his barn and special machines that crush the moisture out of stems.

Good hay is never cheap, even in the summer, and the best quality is always the most economical because there is almost no waste, and its high nutritive value will allow you to save on grain. The price is affected by three factors: the type of hay, when it was cut, and the time of year you are buying it. Summer prices are lower, so when you find a good source of hay, order in advance for the winter. In a good year a large farm may harvest as many as four hay crops, but in a bad year that yields only two good cuttings, midwinter prices will soar—that is, if you can find any hay to buy!

For those who live far from the hay dealer, shipping can get expensive. In such cases try to share a tractor truckload with a friend. Farmers in rural areas will often give a break on prices for customers who can bring their own truck into the fields at haying time and help load the bales. Finding and keeping a good source of hay is like discovering a hidden treasure—a secret you may be reluctant to share.

To assure that your carefully selected hay retains its quality, be sure to store it in a dry location. In a stable with no loft, stack the bales off the floor on wooden pallets to keep them from picking up moisture, which will spread to other bales, making all moldy.

In western cattle country and other areas where beef is raised, round hay bales of five to eight hundred pounds are available. They are rolled during dry weather (and stored under plastic tarps or in bale-sized drawstring bags) until they are needed, then are uncovered and left in the field for continuous feeding. But since they are intended for cattle, round bales are not as fastidiously dried as hay that is harvested for horses. And when stored under tarps in the open, they pick up moisture from the ground. You won't be able to examine the interior of these bales, so pay attention to how they roll off the truck when delivered. They should bounce as they hit the ground. Those that land with a thud are probably moldy.

Though round bales are cheaper per pound than square ones, they cost about the same in the long run because 20 to 30 percent will be lost through spoilage and scattering. (To minimize this loss, place round bales on the highest, driest spot in the pasture.) Because of their inferior quality, I really can't recommend round bales and would strongly advise against them for anyone with a high-performance horse.

COOL, CLEAR WATER

Fresh, clean water must be available to horses at all times in both stalls and turnout areas. A horse can drink from six to twenty gallons of water a day depending on the type of work he's doing, the weather, the amount of dry matter in his feed, and even his level of stress. The safest and most reliable way to keep the balance of fluids stable in your horse's body is to be aware of how much he drinks daily and to make sure he has enough water at all times. The best of all possible pastures will have a natural supply of water—a stream, a spring, a spring-fed pond, or a piped-in source. Some people like automatic systems because they keep water constantly accessible, but they have drawbacks too. (See Chapter 9.)

In the absence of an automatic watering system, fresh water must be supplied by hose to troughs, tubs, and buckets. These containers must be cleaned regularly to keep out dirt and bacteria. Drain and rinse containers outside before refilling them, and do likewise with buckets in the stall. Carelessness in this regard can be lethal. Several years ago at a large breeding farm where the horses drank continually from the same container, the water was allowed to become stagnant. One valuable animal was totally blinded, and several others had their eyesight seriously damaged by a virus that had invaded the putrid water.

Some horses like to dip hay into the water bucket before chewing it or to eat standing over it. You'll be amazed by the debris that accumulates at the bottom of the bucket after every meal.

Watering should be more frequent in the summer. We add a second bucket in each stall to make sure the horses have enough to drink. We do the same year round with horses that require more water. Of course the harder a horse is worked, the more water he'll need. And in very hot or humid weather, sufficient water intake becomes vitally important.

An automatic watering system is a substantial investment, so if you decide to buy one, make sure you get your money's worth. Choose the type that can be turned off manually. Should your horse become ill, you might need to monitor his water intake by using buckets. The automatic system should also have some kind of winter alarm device to let you know when the pipes are frozen.

Dehydration can cause serious problems in a horse. Without enough water his intestinal tract will perform sluggishly, and food cannot move through, causing constipation and impaction colic. As a dehydrated horse becomes increasingly uncomfortable, he will drink less and less water and eat more food, compounding and compacting the problem.

A good test for possible dehydration is to twist the skin on the middle of the horse's neck near the shoulder, then watch to see how quickly it subsides. If the skin stays pinched for more than two or three seconds, the horse is dehydrated.

Another way to detect dehydration is to check the horse's gums. To make this test more valid, be familiar with the normal color of the gums. Simply lift the upper lip—the gums should appear a consistent pale pink. Put your finger on the gum, and press firmly—the spot will turn pale. When you release it, the normal color should return within one or two seconds as the capillaries refill. If they do not, it may indicate dehydration or other circulatory problems.

A horse that is ridden hard, whether in a race, event, or endurance ride, should be monitored at intervals for dehydration. He loses fluid not only by sweating but also by expelling water vapors when exhaling. Even horses performing their regular work should be watched carefully in hot and humid weather. (See Chapter 30.)

Summer isn't the only season when dehydration can occur. During winter, ice must be chopped and removed from frozen buckets and tubs, or the horse will dehydrate fast. Streams and ponds must always be kept open in spots where horses can drink easily. In severe winter weather you might find it easier to place a small tub near the gate. To keep a container from freezing too rapidly, surround it with fresh manure (be sure to remove it in early spring, when parasites start to defrost), or use an insulated bucket with a floating cover.

Some discriminating horses refuse to drink ice cold water. This is a big nuisance. You can take off the chill with an electric heating device, similar to the one you use to heat coffee. (Make sure to remove it before the horse drinks!) An alternative is to change the water frequently as it gets icy. Don't make the mistake of offering the horse warm water. Tepid water freezes much more quickly (proving the principle of heat exchange), and the horse will come to prefer it—dooming you to a season of frigid forays between stable (or kitchen sink) and pasture.

Try tempting your finicky friend to drink icy water by adding a sweetener like dextrose powder or table sugar to it—about a cup per bucket. A quart of apple juice added to a bucket of water will usually entice a horse to drink up.

Heated watering systems for pastures are also available, but the price is out of reach for many horse owners, and it's often a major undertaking to get the proper wiring to the site.

Snow is not an acceptable substitute for water. Most horses will lick snow from time to time without doing themselves harm, but it lacks sufficient oxygen to quench thirst and may even increase it. Should the water supply freeze up, a horse may be tempted to gulp large quantities of snow—with disastrous consequences. When my stream froze over one frigid morning, one of our horses ate large amounts of snow and foundered with a temperature of 106 degrees.

SALT

Salt should also be available to your horse at all times, because it helps him retain water. More salt will be needed in the summer, when the horse is sweating.

This vital condiment is inexpensive and readily available in plain white bricks— or, if you prefer, in red, blue, and gold ones. The colored varieties contain different minerals and vitamins, all of them good supplements to the regular diet. Ask your veterinarian which one is best for your area.

In summer it's convenient to get large fifty-pound salt blocks, placing them in a sheltered spot to minimize erosion. Plastic holders can be purchased that will keep the blocks off the ground. Those with drainage holes are best, preventing water from accumulating at the bottom and dissolving the salt.

Feed stores and tack shops also stock four-pound salt bars, with holders that attach to the stall wall; some of them have separate sections on the side for mineral and vitamin powders.

FAST FODDER

Processing methods developed during the last quarter of the twentieth century have made it possible to provide horses with a square meal that doesn't include traditional forage. These streamlined alternatives to long-stem hay and legumes are cubes, pellets, extruded nuggets, and chopped or compressed hay. Many different brands are

out there to choose from, and new combinations appear on the market every year. Always remember that these feeds are only as good as the ingredients they contain.

Complete Feeds

For the most part, these concentrates combine forage and grain ingredients into a feed containing all the required nutrients, eliminating the need to feed the horse anything else. *Cubed complete feeds* resemble forage in texture and color, while the *pelleted* type looks more like grain. Forage pellets are sometimes combined with textured sweet feed or extruded nuggets of alfalfa or timothy. All this variety can get confusing, so be sure to read the labels carefully when you shop. Quality is imperative here. Each pellet or nugget can only be as nutritional as the quality of ingredients that went into it. A reputable supplier whose product is processed with quality control is essential to give your horse more bite for the buck.

Complete feeds are easier and cheaper to ship and store. They're also easier to chew, so less food is wasted. (Waste comprises 10 to 20 percent of total food intake, depending on the eating habits of the horse.) Both these factors will reduce feeding costs.

Finicky eaters will be tempted by the consistent levels of protein, fat, and fiber in these concentrates, as well as the taste and aroma of the molasses used to blend or bind them. They also won't be able to avoid feeds they don't like. Because complete feeds are lower in bulk, your horse will be trimmer, there will be less manure to muck out, and no dust and scattered stems to sweep up.

Compressed Hay Cubes

These cubes are usually straight alfalfa or a timothy-alfalfa mix, some with oat hay or whole corn plant added to them. Most cubes on the market are actually rectangles, about one and a half inches square and one to three inches long, and are sold in forty-to-fifty-pound bags (the size and weight depending on the manufacturer). Some companies offer different formulas for different ages and lifestyles. The manufacturing process is highly controlled, using only the best alfalfa and timothy, and the products are usually guaranteed to be dust and weed free.

These cubes are popular in the West and Southwest, where baled hay can get very expensive and difficult to find. One western company markets top alfalfa hay compressed into eighteen-inch cubes, banded together and sold in cardboard boxes with handholds. Compared with lugging around bales, lifting and loading these boxes is a luxury (and when you get home the back of the car doesn't look like it's been on a hayride). All in all, for the suburban horse owner who is showing and on the road a lot, compressed cubes are a welcome innovation. But because of this product's high concentration, it must be fed to the horse by weight instead of volume to avoid overfeeding and consequent digestive disorders.

When changing a horse's diet from hay to cubes, make sure the protein content of the compressed forage is equivalent to the long-stemmed hay you've been feeding. Then make the shift gradually, over a seven-to-ten-day period, substituting no more than two pounds of concentrated product each day. For several weeks after the switch, monitor your horse's weight carefully, watching for changes in the manure and in general health and behavior. If he gains weight, cut back accordingly on the weight of the processed feed, starting with 10 to 15 percent of what you were feeding per week.

Now comes the downside: The biggest drawback to using processed feeds is the price. All of them are very expensive, costing two or three times more than grain and baled hay. A secondary disadvantage is the shorter time it takes a horse to eat concentrated foods, increasing the chances that he will get bored and develop stable vices, such as weaving or chewing. As grazing animals, horses are happiest when they have something to munch on. When they are fed only concentrates, they may chew anything in sight—hay cribs, windowsills, trees, and fences. I know a few stables where complete feeds are used exclusively, and you can spot them just by walking in the door or looking at the trees and fences. Anticribbing sprays are available, but a horse deterred from that habit will probably find another objectionable way to pass the time. (See Chapter 36.)

Grains, Vitamins, and Supplements

GRAINS Unless you have a very small pony or a miniature who can get along on good hay alone, you'll also be making a substantial yearly investment in grain and/or mixed feeds.

Oats

Oats are the grain highest in protein and the lowest in heating carbohydrates. Also the oat hulls supply bulk that creates a loose mass in the digestive tract, whereas heavier foods like corn and barley tend to pack down. Oats are the best summer food for a horse (when you don't overdo it).

All oats should smell sweet and fresh and be plump in appearance, a mellow yellow in color, and free of excessive dust. Oats can be *cracked, crushed, flaked, crimped,* or *rolled* as well as *whole*—processes that improve digestibility by opening the hulls for easier chewing. The more involved the procedure, the more expensive it is, and all processed oats cost a lot more than whole oats. Some companies mix crimped oats with barley and molasses, a good food for fussy eaters. Triple-cleaned racehorse oats, more desirable because they're completely dust free, are the priciest of the lot.

Processed oats are of greatest benefit to horses that have dental problems or who gulp their food. More nutrients are extracted from crimped or rolled oats, which have been run through a machine to crush the hulls. Their high degree of digestibility makes these the preferred choice of many racehorse trainers.

If you live where winters are cold, switch your horse from oats to one of the mixed feeds mentioned earlier. These foods, available at all feed supply houses, are higher in the carbohydrates, fats, and oils that provide the energy needed and produce heat. Mixes are tailored to different age groups, and some are specifically prepared for broodmares. All contain dozens of different vitamins and minerals along with nourishing additives like hominy, soybeans, sesame oil, and wheat hulls.

A horse can get out of his food only what is in it. These values are expressed as total digestible nutrients (TDN). Because of its fat content, corn has the highest TDN of all feeds (80 percent), followed by oats (70 percent) and legume hay (52 percent). The chart on page 98 gives the TDN value of various feeds and will help you understand how an equine diet should be balanced.

Bran

Bran is the coarse outer coating of wheat. It must also be fed to a horse by weight. Served dry, straight from the bag, it is a bulky and palatable mild laxative. Fed hot and mixed with plenty of hot water and sweet feeds or a dash of molasses, it's a delicious treat for a cold winter night. (See page 106 for my favorite bran mash recipe.)

Barley

Barley has approximately the same TDN as oats. But fed alone, it tends to pack down too much in a horse's stomach, much as corn does, and could cause colic. Most horses don't like straight barley. It is usually present in more palatable mixed feeds and pellets.

Milo

Milo is a cereal grain, one of four varieties of sorghum common to the Southwest. It is highly drought resistant and can be grown on soil that is too thin for corn. Sweet sorghum, another variety, is ground to make molasses. Some 20 million acres of sorghums are grown in the United States. The grassy varieties are ground for silage (fermented fodder) or used for hay.

NATIONAL RESEARCH COUNCIL

DAILY NUTRIENT REQUIREMENTS OF HORSES (900-KG MATURE WEIGHT)

Animal	Weight (kg)	Daily Gain (kg)	DE (Mcal)	Crude Protein (g)	Lysine (g)	Calcium (g)	Phosphorus (g)	Magnesium (g)	Potassium (g)	Vitamin A (10³ IU)
Mature horses										
Maintenance	900		24.1	966	34	36	25	13.5	45.0	27
Stallions	900		30.2	1,207	42	37	26	13.9	45.9	40
(breeding season)										
Pregnant mares										
9 months	900		26.8	1.179	41	51	38	12.9	42.9	54
10 months			27.3	1,200	42	52	38	13.1	43.6	54
11 months			29.0	1,275	45	55	41	13.9	46.3	54
Lactating mares										
Foaling to 3 months	900		45.5	2,567	89	101	65	19.6	82.8	54
3 months to weaning	900		38.4	1,887	66	65	40	15.5	59.4	54
Working horses										
Light work[a]	900		30.2	1,207	42	37	26	13.9	45.9	40
Moderate work[b]	900		36.2	1,448	51	44	32	16.7	55.0	40
Intense work[c]	900		48.3	1,931	68	59	42	22.2	73.4	40
Growing horses										
Weanling, 4 months	275	1.30	23.1	1,154	48	53	29	5.8	17.7	12
Weanling, 6 months										
Moderate growth	335	0.95	23.4	1,171	49	44	24	6.2	19.6	15
Rapid growth	335	1.15	25.6	1,281	54	50	28	6.5	20.2	15
Yearling, 12 months										
Moderate growth	500	0.90	31.2	1,404	59	49	27	8.6	27.7	22
Rapid growth	500	1.05	33.5	1,509	64	54	30	8.8	28.2	22
Long yearling, 18 months										
Not in training	665	0.70	33.6	1,510	64	49	27	10.9	35.4	30
In training	665	0.70	43.9	1,975	83	64	35	14.2	46.2	30
Two-year-old, 24 months										
Not in training	760	0.45	31.1	1,322	53	45	25	12.0	39.4	34
In training	760	0.45	42.2	1,795	72	61	34	16.2	53.4	34

NOTE: Mares should gain weight during late gestation to compensate for tissue deposition. However, nutrient requirements are based on maintenance body weight.

[a]Examples are horses used in Western and English pleasure, bridle path hack, equitation, etc.

[b]Examples are horses used in ranch work, roping, cutting, barrel racing, jumping, etc.

[c]Examples are horses in race training, polo, etc.

Soybean Meal

It is high in TDN and has the highest digestible protein of all feeds. It can be successfully combined with bran as a mixed feed—the bran provides the bulk and soybean meal the nourishment.

Molasses

Molasses has 80 percent of the nutrient value of corn. Though it is most economical in the South, where the sweet sorghum is grown, it can be used anywhere to make grain more palatable, to stick pellets together, and to keep dust down. (Mineral oil and water can also be used for the latter purpose but isn't as nutritional.)

Whole Corn

Corn on the cob is not recommended except as an occasional before-dinner snack, cut into chewable chunks. The cob should be fed sparingly, like an apple. If your horse tends to gobble his food, never give him corn on the cob, and if he's prone to colic, don't feed him corn at all.

A friend of mine recently spent a dismal evening with the veterinarian trying to push a corncob down the throat of her miserable horse, who had swallowed it whole. A lot of people do feed their horses nothing but whole corn and get away with it, but it isn't worth the risk.

Some horse owners try to cut corners by feeding stale bread, corncobs mixed with beet pulp, and whole corn on the cob. The less said about bread the better. It just won't do.

Cracked or Rolled Corn

This corn can be added to mixed feed. Some horsepeople feel that shelled cracked corn isn't safe as an exclusive diet, claiming that it forms a doughy mass in a horse's stomach. Other equine nutritionists praise it as an excellent feed, even for racehorses.

Shelled Cracked Corn

This corn can be purchased for about half the price of oats, so you can save a quarter of the cost of grain by switching to it and halving the ration. Corn becomes heating only if the horse is eating more energy food than he needs, so take care to cut back on it in the summer, when he won't need as much heating food. If you plan to switch to corn, be sure to remember that feed is measured by weight, not by volume. Given the same ration (by volume) of corn as grain, a horse could founder. The coffee-can measure has been the undoing of many a horse, so weigh your horse's feed!

Almond Hulls

Yes, almond hulls. These are the fruit surrounding the nuts that are grown commercially in many areas of the world, including the American South and Southwest. Resembling a peach in taste and texture, the almond fruit is dried and processed into "hulls," which are then fed to cattle, goats, lambs, swine—and, since the mid-1990s, horses. Research at California State University at Fresno has established that the hulls of the high-quality nonpareil almond make a safe and palatable addition to alfalfa, when fed in a 45 percent ratio. Though their protein content is slightly under 10 percent, the horse will get a full complement of the nutrient when the hulls are mixed with that nourishing legume. In areas where almonds are grown, the hulls are an economical forage alternative. (Some 400,000 tons are produced annually in California.)

PROTEIN SUPPLEMENTS

Peanut oil, cottonseed, and linseed meals: Of the three, cottonseed is the closest to soybean meal in digestible protein. Both are valuable as feed additives for young horses, lactating mares, and mares in foal. All have high energy value. But never feed your horse too much of any of these supplements, which can cause digestive upsets if given in excess or too frequently.

FOOD AND VITAMIN SUPPLEMENTS

A horse that is getting a balanced diet probably won't need supplements. Food and vitamin supplements are designed for those obviously run-down, underweight, and undernourished animals who are unable to gain weight despite regular worming and adequate food. They are also indicated for young horses that need help in developing their full muscular and skeletal potential; for some older animals; and for those that have chemical imbalances that prevent the normal utilization of food.

Some supplements help a horse get the most out of the feed at hand. They come in syrups, liquids, powders, and pellets. Because they enable the horse to better utilize whatever he eats, you'll end up feeding him less over the long run. But supplements are expensive, and they're not magic potions, so don't expect overnight miracles after only a few feedings.

In addition to appetite-enhancing formulas, commercial supplements are available for a number of other purposes, among them to promote hoof growth, to grow a better coat, to enhance energy for better performance, to relieve stiffness in joints, to regulate hormones, and even to reduce aggression. But many of the available vitamin supplements are not necessary for the average horse. B_{12}, for instance, is used only for anemic horses and will not affect the blood count or increase the flow of oxygen to the veins of a normal animal, despite claims to the contrary. For run-down and anemic horses, brewer's yeast is the least expensive source of the B vitamins.

A horse that grazes on lush pasture gets all the A, D, and E vitamins he needs, and extras are completely unnecessary. The average horse needs 2,000 to 5,000 units of vitamin A daily, 200 to 500 units of vitamin D, and 20 to 50 units of vitamin E. When a horse is stabled, these vitamins can be added to his grain. But before rushing off to the nearest tack shop to buy them, check out feed stores, where the equivalent can usually be found for a quarter of the cost. Calf Manna, for example, gives the same nutritional boost to both colts and fillies.

Try not to give vitamins unnecessarily. I know of one overzealous woman who gave her new foal one of everything available in vitamins. The foal ended up with a

NATIONAL RESEARCH COUNCIL

OTHER MINERALS AND VITAMINS FOR HORSES AND PONIES (ON A DRY MATTER BASIS)

	Adequate Concentrations in Total Rations				Maximum Tolerance Levels
	Main-tenance	Pregnant and Lactating Mares	Growing Horses	Working Horses	
Minerals					
Sodium (%)	0.10	0.10	0.10	0.30	3[a]
Sulfur (%)	0.15	0.15	0.15	0.15	1.25
Iron (mg/kg)	40	50	50	40	1,000
Manganese (mg/kg)	40	40	40	40	1,000
Copper (mg/kg)	10	10	10	10	800
Zinc (mg/kg)	40	40	40	40	500
Selenium (mg/kg)	0.1	0.1	0.1	0.1	2.0
Iodine (mg/kg)	0.1–0.6	0.1–0.6	0.1–0.6	0.1–0.6	5.0
Cobalt (mg/kg)	0.1	0.1	0.1	0.1	10
Vitamins					
Vitamin A (IU/kg)	2,000	3,000	2,000	2,000	16,000
Vitamin D (IU/kg)[b]	300	600	800	300	2,200
Vitamin E (IU/kg)	50	80	80	80	1,000
Vitamin K (mg/kg)	[c]				
Thiamin (mg/kg)	3	3	3	5	3,000
Riboflavin (mg/kg)	2	2	2	2	
Niacin (mg/kg)					
Pantothenic acid (mg/kg)					
Pyridoxine (mg/kg)					
Biotin (mg/kg)					
Folacin (mg/kg)					
Vitamin B_{12} (μg/kg)					
Ascorbic acid (mg/kg)					
Choline (mg/kg)					

[a] As sodium chloride.

[b] Recommendations for horses not exposed to sunlight or to artificial light with an emission spectrum of 280–315 nm.

[c] Blank space indicates that data are insufficient to determine a requirement or maximum tolerable level.

skin condition, as a direct result of overdosing. Given in excess, vitamin D can be dangerous, causing calcification in the soft tissue.

Psyllium Husk Products

Given in periodic doses, these products can help prevent sand colic, a problem particularly familiar to horse owners in the Pacific coast, Florida, and the Southwest. But any horse that eats hay on the ground can also ingest a great deal of dirt, which can lead to an accumulation of sand and dirt in his intestine. On contact with fluid—in this case, the horse's saliva—psyllium swells and becomes a bulky, mucous mass and is able to capture and move sand or dirt through the horse's digestive tract. For this reason grain should never be wetted when psyllium products are added. The amount given per feeding depends on the product used.

Apple Cider Vinegar

Added to a horse's feed or water, this vinegar acts as a natural fly repellent, an old-timer's remedy that is quite effective. An eighth to a quarter cup per day in feed apparently changes the composition of the blood, causing the horse to smell differently to flies, which land but don't bite. Use only pure apple cider vinegar. The optimum amount is determined by what works for each individual.

To accustom a horse to the taste, add cider vinegar to his grain a few drops at a time, even disguised with a little molasses at first. Vinegar (cider or white) can also be added to his drinking water to disguise the taste and odor of water in a new environment. This approach is ideal for a fussy horse that won't drink "strange" water, risking dehydration and resulting constipation, which will interfere with his ability to perform. The amount of vinegar per bucket varies according to the horse's palate, but generally one or two tablespoons will neutralize the water sufficiently.

Don't be impressed by a long list of ingredients on a food supplement's package. Just because a product has thirty-five additives doesn't mean your horse needs them! Many supplements include a coat conditioner; others are conditioners only. If your horse's coat is scruffy and dull, corn oil is an inexpensive way to make it glossy, and it works just as well as a commercial coat conditioner, which costs more because the liquid is processed to powder form. On the track vegetable oil is commonly added to grain to make yearlings sleek before they're put up for auction. I recently used corn oil with great success on a middle-aged school horse named Moose, who became positively glamorous after his grain was enhanced with half a cup added twice daily to his feed for two weeks.

The list of supplements is endless and ever growing. Other benefits may include improved hoof growth, increased energy level, and reduced stiffness in joints. Discuss any supplement you plan to try with your veterinarian, who's familiar with both your horse and the ingredients in the various formulas.

Any horse with a respiratory or allergic problem needs a scientifically balanced diet to replace the hay or grain that his system can't tolerate.

Respond is one of several feeds you can buy for a wheezy or "heavey" horse, or for a horse recuperating from a respiratory illness with a temporary cough. It's expensive but well worth the cost if you can afford it.

If your budget won't stretch this far, consult your veterinarian. One of my students, a Cornell graduate, worked out an alternative to this expensive fare, consisting of three parts beet pulp, two parts sweet feed, one part alfalfa pellets, and eight ounces of Calf Manna twice daily.

Coughs and wheezes may also appear in dry weather, when the pasture has dried up and the hay in the barn has gathered dust. In cases of illness or dry weather, the horse should be treated as though he were heavey. If wetting down his feed does not suppress the problem, switch to an allergenic feed. If a respiratory condition is not treated aggressively, it may become permanent. Allergenic feeds usually clear up these temporary problems within a few weeks.

Aridity can also aggravate respiratory conditions, so be sure to wet down feeds during particularly dry spells. With one dust-sensitive horse, I've done this every summer and the regime has kept him cough-free. It's best to feed an allergic horse a commercial complete feed, because the ratio of vitamins and minerals is scientifically balanced.

Beet pulp, the leftover result of sugar-beet processing, has only an 8 percent protein content and is thus basically a fiber substitute, especially for horses that have allergic or respiratory problems and for old horses. It comes in two forms: loose, chopped, bagged dried bulk, and pellets. Both types must be mixed with water—an equal ratio of water for the loose type, and three parts water to one part of the pellet variety.

I've known horses whose chronic allergies to hay caused them to cough in short barks. The coughing stopped after they ate beet pulp. On a continual diet of beet pulp, wet feed, and supplements, they've done extremely well, staying in top condition for all types of strenuous competition. But the diet must be balanced with enough protein and vitamins to meet all the horse's nutritional needs.

Some people think beet pulp is an economical shortcut, and they use it as a substitute for grain during lean winter months. This is a mistake. A horse wintered on this type of feed program will lose a tremendous amount of weight and come into the spring looking wan and haggard, without the energy that grain or top-quality hay would have provided, and so run-down that he can't retain condition. I use beet pulp as a supplement under certain circumstances, as when hay is in short supply or of bad quality. Occasionally I've included it as part of the grain ration when a school horse gets a little too rambunctious in the winter. It's also ideal if a horse is recovering from an injury that doesn't allow him to be worked and his weight needs to be maintained without an increase in energy.

If your horse requires a diet of grain and pulp alone, be sure to increase the grain when he's working. For a large horse, a supplementary lunch is a must to compensate for the lack of hay in his diet. (It also keeps him from gnawing everything in sight.)

As the price of feed continues to climb, many horse owners are tempted to take money-saving shortcuts. After all, they reason, it's wasteful to throw away leftovers—so why not spread that slightly soiled hay or grain out for a horse to pick through? Don't do it! Never assume that a horse will pick out only the good food. Whether he is a naive young horse or a wise old glutton, he may gulp it all.

Always make sure that the food is clean and unspoiled and that the containers and dishes are scrubbed out regularly. Smell the feed before dishing it out. Bad feed has a sour smell and is guaranteed to make a horse sick. Handle the feed, and look at it. Don't use grain that's stuck together in a wad, feels wet, or has traces of mildew. Any feed that's below standard in any respect should be taken back to the store or thrown out—but never fed to your horse. The result could be fatal.

A few summers ago a large feed store down the road was selling off the last of its stock before reordering. I had the misfortune to buy some of this moldy grain, so I returned it and got it replaced. But another stable in the area was not as fussy in their feeding methods, and a young horse died.

Certain grains can be infected by parasites, rusts, and blights. If a dead animal lies undetected in hay or silage, botulism can develop from its spores—a toxin that doesn't affect taste or appearance and is usually odorless. So whenever animal remains are found in a bale of hay of a batch of grain, don't hesitate to throw the whole thing out.

Good food is cheap compared with the replacement costs of a horse and the guilt that comes with the realization that he's been killed by negligence.

When spring comes and the grass turns a luscious shade of green, it's tempting to throw open the barn doors and let your horse go out to graze until sundown. *Don't do it!* Remember the rule about not making sudden changes in feeding? Your horse has been on a hay and grain diet all winter, but the spring grass is far richer. It also has a much higher water content than dry hay. So for the first month of spring, introduce him to the pasture twenty minutes at a time, increasing the outing gradually by twenty minutes to a half hour each day for the first week. Watch his manure and his behavior to determine if the diet agrees with him. To reduce his appetite, fill him up with plenty of hay beforehand. Time spent in the pasture can be increased by a half hour to forty-five minutes in the second week and by the same amount in succeeding weeks. Spring grass is rich and lush, so it's better to be safe than sorry.

Even when a horse has been carefully reintroduced to the pasture, the high water content of the grass may have a laxative effect for a few days. If he seems all right otherwise, however, this is nothing to worry about.

By around the middle of August in the northern states, the pasture will be dried out and scuffed up, and your horse will need a hay supplement to get enough nourishment. If you have a small pasture, he may need it earlier. It's easy to tell whether pasture is sufficient just by looking at the grass. But as you survey it, remember that most horses refuse to eat where they urinate or defecate. What looks like lush grass to you may be off-limits to him. Mowing the pasture several times a summer will discourage undesirable weeds, and dragging it or picking it up on a regular basis helps to control parasites. Horses are apt to be less finicky when droppings are picked up. Between draggings, pick up the manure on a regular basis. (See Chapter 10.)

Those lucky enough to have the space can allot two separately fenced acres to each horse, rotating them every four weeks during the summer. While one pasture is in use, the other can be clipped, dragged, and allowed to regrow. A pleasure horse on good pasture often won't need grain, hay, or additives—only a free choice of mineral supplements in his salt block. But beware: Very few owners are blessed with pasture lush enough to sustain a horse throughout the summer. Don't make the mistake of thinking that a sweeping expanse of green alone will do the job. (See Appendix B.)

You'll be able to tell if pasture is adequate by your horse's condition. (See page 79.)

The best pasture is one that thrives in your area, depending on climate and soil. Bluegrass, for instance, is one of the prettiest of grasses, but in many areas it matures too quickly to sustain nutritive value. Your county extension service or soil and conservation service will give you free advice on what grasses to plant where.

Around mid-October in the North, and later if you live in milder climates, the grass will become so sparse that your horse will need a regular regime of grain and hay twice a day. By the end of the month, the menu should be gradually changed from the summer oat ration to the winter diet, a mixed, heating, or high-energy feed. The switch should be complete by mid-November. In the spring the procedure is reversed. If you're fortunate to live far enough south, no changes may be necessary.

HOT MEALS FOR HORSES

A hot meal a few times a month keeps a horse in top condition. Cooked grain is more easily digested than raw, and it's particularly good for old horses or those that have dental or digestive problems. But boiled feed has a relatively low energy value and shouldn't be fed to hardworking horses more than once a week.

Oats, whole or crimped, barley, linseed, and bran are all tasty choices, and each has a special nutritive effect. All boiled feeds, bran in particular, have helpful laxative properties, useful when a horse has been stabled for a long period. Cooking also swells feed and makes a meal go further. It helps finicky eaters regain their appetite and keeps body temperature up on cold days.

WHOLE OATS. These are the least expensive to buy but take the longest to cook—up to four hours of simmering before the husk cracks and exposes the grayish kernel. Costlier crimped oats take only about forty-five minutes to cook. Steamed oats don't stretch as far as boiled, but they have a great aroma and are an excellent feed for horses in training.

RAW LINSEED (FLAXSEED MEAL). This grain contains cyanide and must be thoroughly cooked to dispel the poison. (Linseed meal, oil, and cakes are already cooked.) When done, the husk cracks open, exposing a yellow kernel, and the liquid thickens into a gray, jellylike gruel. The grain expands to about two and a half times its normal volume. Linseed, as we have seen, is a supplement, not a whole food, and should be added to regular feed or mixed with dry bran.

BRAN MASH. This is a fine feed for a horse that's had a hard day hunting or showing. For a sick or tired horse, a hot bran mash is the equivalent of comforting milk toast. Try to serve it once a week in the fall and winter as a conditioner, laxative, and additional water source. Because of its laxative effect, your horse shouldn't be worked hard the day after his mash meal. Be absolutely sure that you *clean his feed dish thoroughly after he has eaten the mash.* Leftover residue from the bran itself or from additives, such as ingredients in some sweet feeds, can ferment when left in the dish and cause serious colic. It's not a good idea to add pellets, which will just dissolve into mush.

Basic bran mash recipe: Combine two parts hot water to one part bran, cover with a towel, and allow it to sit for forty-five minutes to an hour. By weight, the wet bran mash (with additives) should not exceed the weight of the horse's normal grain ration. To make it more palatable, you can add molasses, apples, oats, and sweet feed (not much). Other appetizing condiments such as Karo syrup and apple juice also work. When introducing mash for the first time, try mixing a small amount with a portion of the normal grain ration. Always be generous when adding water to dry bran, because when ingested too dry, bran can absorb moisture from the horse's digestive system—the reverse of your intention.

BARLEY. Cooked barley is an excellent way to put weight on a horse without heating him up. It's even good for show horses during the summer. But as a steady diet, it will make a fit horse fat and thick winded. It shouldn't be fed more than two or three times a week. Only whole barley should be used for cooking. The flakes turn into an unappetizing mush. Like oats, barley should be cooked until the husk cracks. It expands to about two and a half times its original volume.

STABLE MANNERS

Horses can be compared with humans in at least one respect: their eating habits. Some pick at their food, while others bolt it down. When food is gulped into the esophagus before it is sufficiently chewed, the digestive system can't do its work properly and nutrients are lost. Bolters tend to be undernourished and prone to colic.

Bolting

One sign that a horse is bolting is a substantial amount of whole grain and corn in his manure (which may also indicate dental problems). Once you are alerted, watch your horse as he feeds. If he seems to be consuming his food in record time, like an equine vacuum cleaner, slow him down. You can do it in any of several ways.

The old ploy of putting rocks in the feed bucket doesn't do the trick. Careful measurements made by Cornell University veterinarian Dr. Harold Hintz disproved the conventional wisdom, finding it has no effect on the rate of eating. But a veterinarian at the University of Tennessee found a method that does. Feeding small amounts of grain several times a day rather than in two large portions will raise a bolter's nutrition level, according to Dr. Frederick Harper. He cautions against using buckets for bolters. Instead, he says, feed should be spread thinly in a trough, so that the horse can get only a small amount with each bite. Feeding him hay before the grain rations will take the edge off his appetite.

Finicky Eaters

Finicky eaters sometimes play with their grain like a child toying with a bowl of spinach, often not finishing the entire ration at one feeding. Others may take a couple of hours to get the portion down, nibbling at it between sips of water and mouthfuls of hay. If you have several horses being fed in the pasture or an open shed, this habit can be infuriating. Unless you move the fussy eater at mealtime, he will just stand by watching his companions gobble the grain.

Horses with this habit usually can't afford to lose weight. Some may be high-strung, easily stressed animals. Others may be in poor health from a previously bad diet or lack of exercise. To whet a reluctant appetite, try a change of menu. Some foods are less palatable than others, and a picky eater may prefer sweet feed to pellets. Make feed more enticing by adding molasses, sugar, honey, or sliced-up carrots in amounts up to 5 percent of the total ration.

Sometimes a temporary stress or gastronomic trauma will turn a formerly finicky eater into a glutton. One Thoroughbred filly, who boarded at my stable for a while after a brief and stressful career on the racetrack, was a finicky eater. I tried all the gimmicks to get her to eat, even adding chopped-up carrots and turnips to the sweeteners as an extra enticement, but she still turned her nose up. A few weeks later, the same filly had to be confined to her stall for a few weeks to recuperate from an injury. Because she had to be kept as quiet as possible during her convalescence, I was forced to cut down on her grain. This bothered me because I'd worked so hard to build her weight up. But when she recovered and went back on full rations, this period of semistarvation paid off in an increased appetite verging on gluttony. Ever since then she's cleaned out her dish in record time.

Experts have endorsed fasting to achieve a good appetite, finding that horses who need to be fed a lot because of age, size, or work requirements have sharper appetites when put on a semifast once or twice a month. Many breeders and trainers do so to fend off the culinary blahs and keep the equine appetite keen.

SNACKS AND TREATS. These are an excellent way to lure a finicky eater to the feed dish, and they make nutritious appetizers for a normal eater as well as reward good behavior. An equine answer to the dog biscuit is marketed under a number of brand names, but all contain vitamins and minerals. They are available in apple, carrot, and sweet corn flavors, to be fed one or two at a time as an after-work treat.

Carrots are a particularly healthy snack. One pound contains 48 milligrams of carotene—enough to meet the daily requirements of a thousand-pound horse. (In contrast, a pound of field-grown timothy contains 2.1 milligrams.) Carrots are also high in calcium and phosphate. In the winter, when no green forage is available and horses are stabled a lot, one to two pounds of carrots daily will stimulate appetite, increase growth, add to bloom, and even increase fertility. When you feed them as part of the ration, slice them in small strips before mixing with the grain.

Other finely chopped root vegetables like turnips, parsnips, and sugar beets make palatable and nutritious additions to grain rations. Horses also like (and their stomachs can handle) apples, pears, peaches, and plums (with stones removed), and the meat of pumpkins, melons, and squash—all cut up into small portions. In Puerto Rico bananas are the favorite treat, and in Bermuda, fennel.

A track official who was entrusted with the care and feeding of some finicky horses slated to run in the Washington, D.C., International, says: "To satisfy the palates of our equine guests we've had to shop not only for carrots and apples but also lettuce, leeks, powdered milk, honey, eggs, and stout." The last item, as you may have guessed, was for an Irish horse.

PART IV

Housing Your Horse

*Now . . . Augeas's (stable) yard and
sheepfolds had not been cleared
away for many years, and though
its noisome stench did not affect
the beasts themselves, it spread
a pestilence across the whole
Peloponnese. Moreover the valley
pastures were so deep in dung
they could no longer be ploughed
for grain. Hercules hailed
Augeas from afar and undertook (him)
to cleanse the yard before
nightfall. . . . Augeas laughed incredulously.*

Robert Graves, GREEK MYTHS, vol. 2. In his fifth labor, Hercules had to divert two
rivers to clean King Augeas' incredibly dirty yards and stables—a chore he wouldn't
have faced if the king had practiced proper stable management.

Stable Stabling

Sooner or later, if your horse has any kind of imagination, you'll open up the stable one morning and find him waiting to greet you at the outside door. Twelve hours earlier he was neatly tucked away in his stall, with everything in apple-pie order. Now the stall door is hanging askew on one bent hinge. Your new saddle, stirrups amputated, is lying upside down in a pool of molasses. And everything else is smothered in a sea of hay. Ambling around happily in the midst of it all, molasses all over his muzzle and dripping from his mane, is your %*^%#@+#& horse!

Depending on how you keep your stable, these experiences will range from the merely hilarious (in retrospect) to the extremely dangerous. Unless your feed box or other storage area is horseproof, he has probably gorged himself on oats or something else and will need immediate treatment to prevent colic.

Stables, like ships, have a limited amount of space, and it must be utilized efficiently, with a place for everything and everything in its place—in a word, it must be kept shipshape. If tools haven't been put away properly, your horse may puncture his foot on a pitchfork or become tangled in some old strands of baling wire or string. The disaster potential is almost unlimited, as you'll learn the hard way if you fail to run a well-kept stable.

Tools should be hung on the wall in a convenient spot, removed from major traffic. Grooming tools should be in a grooming box, on a shelf, or in a tack trunk when not in use. Medicines should be kept in one spot, either in a cabinet or in a container on a convenience shelf. Supplements and messy additives like molasses should be kept in containers on a shelf or cupboard in the feed room or area.

Hay should be stored off the floor on wooden palettes in a separate building or another dry, well-ventilated area. Although it can be stored overhead in some barns, the dust and chaff will be detrimental to horses with respiratory problems.

If you are building a stable from scratch, you can provide for all these necessities. If you are converting an old building, you can improvise. A friend of mine went all out for her three horses, turning a lovely three-room guest cottage into a three-stall barn, complete with a view and indoor plumbing. (Overnight guests now have to put up with a sofa bed in the den.)

If you choose the third alternative—housing your horse in an open shed—you must make arrangements to store food, hay, and equipment in a separate building. Often part of a garage or another sound outbuilding can be set aside for this purpose.

FIELD KEEPING

Horses are by nature outdoor animals, and a lot of them prefer to remain outside most of the time. Most are hardy enough to need shelter only during severe weather—hailstorms, thundershowers, or winter winds—and in summer they need a place to escape heat and flies.

Sheds

On the theory that pasturing is better for equine health—aiding circulation, developing muscles, and strengthening legs and feet—more and more people, including most horse breeders, are using large open sheds to house horses individually and in groups. Sheds also keep building costs down, and less help is needed to maintain them. Using a run-in shed is the most economical way to house your horse, especially if you can build it yourself.

One of my horses would rather stay out in almost any weather (except freezing rain and extreme heat) than be stabled in a barn. I've seen him standing in howling blizzards, with a foot of snow piled on his back and icicles hanging from his nose. He's the healthiest horse I've ever owned and a very easy keeper.

"You never have unexpected vet's bills with field-kept horses," advises one breeder in my area, who uses large, sloping, three-sided sheds that open to the south. He advises building a shed at the highest point of the pasture, with a southern exposure to minimize wind and drifting snow, and allowing at least twelve by twelve feet of space for each horse. The ceiling should slope from at least twelve feet in front to nine or ten at the rear—high enough that the horse can't hit his head when he throws it back. He builds his own structures of one-by-sixteen green oak planks, the same size used on his fencing, and lines it with smooth plywood. The roofing is aluminum.

The sheds are built with a natural dirt floor, which must be thoroughly cleaned of manure once each season and disinfected (and mucked out regularly, of course). In the summer a sixteen-foot wooden overhang across the front entrance provides shade and keeps down flies.

The most durable, easily maintained, and expensive sheds are constructed of concrete blocks. Allow twelve by twelve feet of space per horse, with the roof sloping up from 10½ feet at the lower end to 12½ feet at the entrance. These vertical measurements, which also apply to wooden sheds, should allow for six to eight inches of bedding.

In the summer, unless each horse in your stable has at least two acres of good pasture, you will have to supplement the grass with hay. Five acres of grazing land per horse is ideal but is beyond the economic reach of most backyard horse owners. The larger the pasture, the more room available for rotation of grazing areas. Field-kept horses should have a shed in each area.

Should you decide to use a shed, your choice of bedding will likely depend on what's available. In Kentucky, for instance, some large horse farms use tobacco stems, which are very absorbent and heavy enough not to be blown around by the wind. In

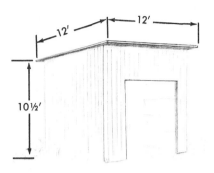

OPEN SHED

Hawaii and other sugar-producing areas, chopped sugarcane stalks are an absorbent choice. This type of bedding should be eight inches thick, and the top must be cleaned off and replaced at least every ten days. Because of their absorbency and easy handling, sawdust and wood shavings are also good choices if they are readily available. (See Chapter 10.)

Fat, aggressive horses should be kept in a separate shed area where they can be fed less, while skinny, timid horses will need a niche apart where they can eat more without constant harassment. Each group should have its own shed.

Hay cribs or nets should be kept inside, in a corner of the shed. A trough-shaped hay crib built in a field is not a good idea; nor is feeding hay on the ground, though it is often done. Horses tend to walk through the hay and soil it, wasting a great deal. Soiled hay in a small pasture is likely to be a repository for different stages of parasites.

When building an outside shed, make ample provision for hay storage in another building. Two tons of hay, for instance, take up approximately a thousand cubic feet. Before you buy a load and stick it away in an old chicken coop, make sure the floor of the storage area is dry and that the roof doesn't leak. You can also use one end of a garage or toolshed for keeping feed, storing it in plastic or galvanized pails with clamp-on lids that are rodent- and horseproof. Horses possess an uncanny ability to sense where feed is located, making it their first priority upon escape. Unopened feed bags are no insurance: Horses bite right through bags and drag them around.

Garage walls can also be used to hang grooming equipment and racks for bridles, halters, and saddles. To keep your shed in good order, you'll also need stable-cleaning supplies and equipment (discussed later in this chapter).

Construction Tips

As the cost of seasoned lumber continues to climb, you may want to buy green lumber and season it yourself. (You'll need two-by-fours and two-by-eights.) Seasoning takes at least six months but can save you approximately half the cost of finished wood. Rough hemlock lumber is less expensive than pine, and it seasons to a soft gray color. Just be sure, when you put it aside for seasoning, that it lies flat in a dry place to prevent warping or swelling.

Some people use unseasoned rough lumber for the outside of sheds, overlapping the boards with batten so the shrinking lumber won't leave gaps. But the protruding batten is a tempting target for horses that like to chew, and for that reason many breeders won't use it. Hemlock is supposed to be less appetizing than other woods, but I think it's better to use seasoned wood and not take a chance.

THE PERMANENT STABLE

Not all horses can put up with the outdoor life. Some are too highly bred and literally thin-skinned to tolerate prolonged exposure. They may not grow a sufficiently thick coat in the winter, or they may be especially sensitive to flies and need to be stabled during summer days. If you have doubts about your horse's ability to rough it, be sure to check with your veterinarian.

If you have the financial resources, you may want to build a permanent stable yourself. Figure out what features are essential at the start and what can be added later, planning accordingly. A number of firms sell prefabricated stables, for which a foundation must be built. You can get ideas from your friends' barns, and numerous reputable companies advertise building plans in leading horse publications. Before you start to build, be sure to check your local zoning ordinances. Make sure that horses and stables are permitted in your community (and if so, how many horses are allowed), and find out what distance the building must be from property lines.

A one-horse owner who is willing to go to the expense of building a stable may as well provide for the possibility of a second horse as well. You might decide to get a horse for your kids, breed a mare, or invite a boarder; and it's not too much more expensive. If you prefer not to do it now, build so you can add on later. Or build

RIDING HORSE BARN

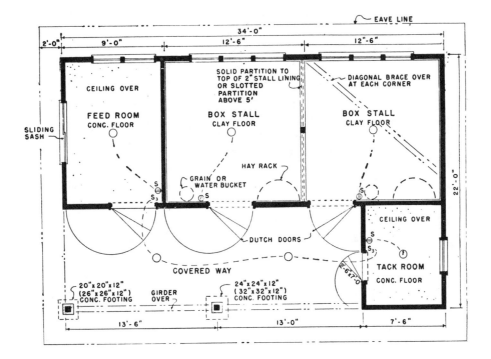

Courtesy U.S. Government Printing Office

the tack and feed areas to stall dimensions, for easy conversion. Here I'll assume that you're building a two- to four-horse stable.

Types of Barns

Your choice of construction methods and materials will be influenced by climate, cost, and appearance. Some popular choices:

POLE BARNS. These are among the most basic of horse barns. They are framed with pressure-treated wood or metal supports set into a concrete slab on the ground and roofed with trusses. They require no foundation, so they are relatively inexpensive. The price will depend on the cost of materials and labor in your area and on the complexity of your plan.

MODULAR BARNS. These barns are particularly popular in the Southwest and California. A framework of steel tubes and columns is bolted to concrete piers set in the ground. Prefabricated stalls, windows, and four-foot-wide roof and wall panels are bolted to the frame. The roof and wall panels are either steel or foam-filled sandwiches of steel and plywood. What modulars lack in looks, they make up for in flexibility. Sections can be added on easily, and stall walls and other components can be rearranged. Best of all, the whole thing can be unbolted and taken along if you move.

CONCRETE BLOCK BARNS. These are cooler in summer and therefore are popular in hot climates. They also have the advantage of being fire- and rotproof. Although they cost more in labor because a continuous foundation must be laid for the blocks, they are built to last. The blocks are filled with poured concrete to a height of five feet to make them shatterproof if a horse kicks out. Concrete is less desirable in cold climates, where moisture gets trapped and condenses in the walls.

Converting an Outbuilding

Many outbuildings can be converted to stables. Garages are the most commonly chosen for conversion, although I've seen a chicken coop and even the back of a large truck transformed for this purpose. Any structure will do if its dimensions are suitable, with doorways and ceilings high enough, the floor reinforceable, and the space large enough for a box stall (at least ten by ten to twelve by twelve feet). Never build a tie stall if you can possible find space for a box.

If the floor isn't sturdy enough to withstand 900 to 1,500 pounds, it has to be reinforced or rebuilt with sturdy wood framing and oak planks. If it's dirt, it should be dug up and underlaid with cinder or gravel for good drainage.

If you can arrange it, build a six-foot overhang on the outside to create a shady spot where the horse can be tied in the summertime.

STORAGE SPACE

Hay and Bedding

You should provide a separate area or an overhead storage space for hay and bedding. Figure on two tons of hay per horse per winter (from November to March in the Northeast) and a ton and a half of bedding, so you'll need at least 1,750 cubic feet of storage space for each animal. This will vary according to the size of the animal and the size of the stall to be bedded. If you plan to store hay in an extra stall in the barn, note that a twelve-by-twelve box, depending on its height, will hold about 180 bales.

Feed

If at all possible, keep feed sacks and/or containers inside a metal-lined feedbox, so they are off bounds for itinerant horses and rodents. When cold weather sets in, your stable will become a mecca for all kinds of creatures—mice, moles, voles, and worst of all, rats. Rodents can chew through feed sacks and plastic containers in no time, and other vermin can easily climb into uncovered feed cans and even bite your hand as you measure out grain.

Tack

Ideally, tack should be kept in a separate room, where it will stay clean, dry, and relatively warm. The temperature in the storage area shouldn't fall below 40 degrees, so you may have to take tack indoors during the winter months. If it is stored in the barn the rest of the year, make sure it is well out of nibbling distance. I once hung an expensive borrowed whip too close to a stall; by morning the bored occupant had reduced it to something resembling a piece of limp spaghetti.

For under five dollars, you can purchase metal bridle brackets. Hooks work fine for halters and lead ropes. For this purpose, we find that portable tack racks with four or five three-inch hooks, hung on each of our floor-to-ceiling stall doors, are extremely practical and also handy for hanging up fly masks and a small boot bucket. Some have hooks that fold flat when not in use.

A saddle should be kept on a saddle rack or holder. Most tack catalogs and shops carry inexpensive enamel-coated metal racks or plain wooden ones that fasten to the wall. A portable wooden saddle rack that folds flat when not in use and hooks to an upright position in a simple screw eye is easy and inexpensive to make. (See Appendix E.) We use sturdy enameled wall racks in the tack room and place portable wooden holders intermittently along the aisle for convenience.

Cleaning Supplies and Maintenance Tools

Every stable should have a special corner or wall where stable cleaning equipment and a toolbox is stored. It's essential to keep a few common tools on hand for the simple repairs that always come up around a stable or a pasture—a loose board, sagging fence, broken latch, or torn screen. You'll need:

- Large hammer
- Screwdriver
- Pair of pliers
- Pair of scissors (for string bales)
- Pair of wire cutters (for wire bales)
- Crowbar
- Box of assorted screws
- Box of assorted nails
- Roll of picture-hanging wire (for mending screens)
- Extra wire or tape for fence repairs
- Box of extra insulators for electric fence
- Posthole digger

When you're groping through a haystack, a pair of pliers can be as elusive as a needle, so try to get in the habit of returning everything to the toolbox after use. And I urge you to do your best to master the use of these tools. At least learn how to hold a hammer properly and drive a straight nail, in case a horse goes through a broken fence when a handyman isn't around.

Every stable should have an old feed sack hanging in a corner, or an extra garbage pail to hold old baling wire, string, and other refuse that could injure you or your horse if left on the floor.

Hoses

A hose is an essential piece of barn equipment. It is needed for keeping buckets filled year round, for washing horses, and for swabbing down stable floors in the summer. Provide a reel in a convenient place close to your water source so the hose can be coiled up out of the way when not in use. A flat hose that folds up is compact and easy to drain in winter. The twenty-five-foot type coils up into a small portable reel that's easy to bring indoors when not in use in the winter (to prevent freezing), and it's a must on the road.

Washing and Grooming

Try to provide a well-lit area for daily grooming, tacking up, shoeing, and veterinary visits. A wide aisle is adequate, but a large wash stall with a textured cement or asphalt floor and a drain is the best, enabling you to keep grooming tools and water in one place. A protected, out-of-the-way indoor area is especially important if you plan to have other boarders in your barn.

STABLE CONSTRUCTION

Location

In building a stable, location is the first consideration. To help you decide on a location, get tips on climate and prevailing winds from the local agricultural extension service in the United States or from a corresponding agency in other countries. The adjoining paddock area or stable yard should face south toward the sun and be sheltered from north winds. A well-planned air flow is necessary to a healthy environment; space doors and windows carefully and add cupolas or vents to take advantage of prevailing winds. Try to use natural lighting as much as possible, making the atmosphere cheerful for you and your horse. Horses don't like dark, closed places, which is why they're usually reluctant to enter trailers.

Ventilation

The movement of air through a barn regulates temperature and humidity. Try to have fresh air circulating through the stalls and aisles so that fumes from ammonia and manure don't hang in the atmosphere. Moving air also discourages condensation caused by differing inside and outside temperatures. The local extension service offers plans that solve these problems.

Ventilation can be provided by natural and/or mechanical means. Leaving windows, stable doors, and the tops of Dutch stall doors latched open is the simplest solution, as long as there isn't too much of a draft. To allow foul air to escape, place vents strategically or put louvered boards at the roof ridge or under the eaves. In a very hot climate, long, narrow, slotted vents placed about two feet above the stall floor will keep the stable well ventilated. Barns in the Southwest often have skylights that can be opened to help move the air. A number of my friends who have resurrected old stables in the Northeast have added a spinning cupola ventilator in the roof to push air through ridge vents. Fans and blowers can also be used to force air in and out of the barn. Air in stalls can be kept clean and moving by placing attic fans in the eaves above them.

Stalls

Box stalls should be as large as possible, allowing enough room for the horse to turn around in, relax, and be comfortable. Given a large enough space, some horses will defecate only in one small area, saving you mucking out time and bedding money. A ten-by-ten-foot stall is adequate, twelve is good, and twelve by fourteen or fourteen feet square even better. It will depend on the size of your horse. A small pony could get by in a nine-by-nine enclosure, but it's prudent to plan for the time when your child will outgrow him. Planning spaces in standard increments of four feet is most economical.

Straight stalls (five by eight feet) are not recommended. If you have one in an existing stable, use it to store hay and bedding or as a temporary quarters until you get a larger stall built. If your horse must be in a tie or straight stall temporarily, make sure that the tie ring and manger are at the proper height (three and a half feet from the floor). Your lead rope should be tied long enough to allow him to lie down, but not so long that his legs will get caught in it. When tying, use only a slipknot (see Appendix E) that can easily be released in an emergency (by you, not the horse). If your horse is a genius with knots as well as latches, he shouldn't be in a straight stall.

Aisles

The aisle should be wide enough for two horses to pass comfortably. The recommended width is twelve feet, which will allow a horse to be turned around and a tractor or manure spreader to be driven through.

Whether you have an aisle will depend on your location and the style and size of your barn. In the North it's handy to have sliding doors at each end of the barn to shut out winter winds. In hot climates like the South and Southwest, it's more desirable to have open sides or exterior side walls that stop short of the eaves and let air in at all times, with several feet of overhanging roof to keep the rain out. Southern stables have a high ceiling in lieu of a hayloft, some with a raised section in the center to let heat out and light in.

In colder climates a hayloft will insulate the area below. A ceiling loft should have a door or trapdoor conveniently located to dispense hay (which should be dropped during turnouts so the horse doesn't inhale the dust). To shed snow, a peaked roof is essential; be sure it's strong enough to handle the maximum snowfall recorded in your area. During a severe winter several years ago, blizzard after blizzard led to the downfall of roofs on two barns and three riding arenas within a twenty-five-mile radius of me. To forestall a cave-in, hire someone to shovel snow off the roof when it begins to pile up.

During rainstorms gutters are essential to keep water from pooling around the edges of the barn, where a horse can tramp through and make mudholes. They are especially important in the paddock areas adjoining the stalls.

Windows and Doors

Stall windows should be placed high on the wall, shielded inside with a grille (with maximum three-inch spacing) or a heavy screen. Windows that open outward and latch securely to the side of the building or sliding windows are safest. Fireproof metal frames are better than wood.

The door of a stall should be at least four and a half feet high, to prevent a horse of average size from putting his maximum weight against it or reaching out and pushing over the door to spar with passing stablemates. The hinges must be heavy and strong. The door should be at least four feet wide to allow the horse to pass through easily without scraping his hips. The height of the opening should be the same as the stable entrance, or a minimum of ten feet.

If you don't plan to build a stall door right away, you can get a heavy stall screen from a feed store or a livestock and tack catalog. They come in several different styles, one designed with a yoke for the horse's neck, and a variety of widths and lengths. These easy-to-handle, see-through steel screens also travel well and are simple to install on hanging brackets.

Doors can be purchased as complete units in standard four-foot widths in a variety of styles. Barn equipment companies advertise different types, including a whole install-it-yourself stall package. When ordering from a magazine advertisement, take into account the considerable cost of shipping; it might persuade you to build the door yourself.

It's convenient and pleasant for your horse to have a door that opens directly out to an individual paddock, allowing him to come and go at will. The paddock can be a relatively small area, as little as fifty feet square, either separate from or connected to the pasture by a gate—a place where your horse can be turned out on good days.

Portable metal fence panels are ideal for this purpose, making a pen of any size. They are a common means of fencing in the West and Southwest and are becoming more popular in the Northeast and other parts of the world as well.

Latches

For stable security, and to prevent the kind of fiasco described at the beginning of this chapter, latches are extremely important. Horseproof latches can be found at your local farm supply store or through tack catalogs, and saddlery supply houses sell special models. In some cases it's wise to put a latch on both the bottom and top of a Dutch stall door. Better yet, install a full-length sliding door with a secure latch. Make sure Dutch doors can be fastened back securely: Should a top door swing shut, it could tempt a horse to go under it and get into trouble.

There will always be some Houdinis of the horse world, with dexterous teeth and muzzles, who can undo even the most complex latches. I know because I own one. One of my horses has managed to figure out the combinations of the sturdiest devices on the market, even when a snap clip is added for extra protection. A neighbor has a horse equally adept—and he's generous as well: After making an escape, he lets all his stablemates out too.

About the only way to foil a horse like this is to put in a full-length door, or install another on top if it's not full length, so he can't get his head over the one at the bottom and fiddle with the latch.

Stall Guards

Stall guards are an excellent way to provide maximum ventilation in hot weather, either at home or during a show. They are safe, easy to install, and come in several styles: less expensive two-inch, three-tiered webbing strips; a four-tiered model that has canvas backing; and a heavier, more solid plastic type with cables molded inside. All attach to the stall door frame and can be adjusted from thirty-six- to forty-six-inch widths. Some are available in your stable colors, and some of the plastic styles can be custom monogrammed—a nice touch for showing.

For temperamental horses that value their privacy, stall guards can be used to close off the top of the door. One touchy mare with a foal, who objected to even a passing glance from her stablemates, was mollified by the addition of a stall guard at the top of her door. They are also useful if you have an open-top stall near your cross-ties with an inmate that likes to grab at the ties or nip at stablemates attached to them.

A few precautions: If you use a stall guard to close off the top of a door, be sure the bottom of the guard is flush with the door so your horse can't get his head caught between them. When used as a door substitute, make sure the guard is set high enough to prevent the horse from catching a pawing hoof in the canvas strips, but not so high that he will be tempted to follow the lead of one little Arab mare in our barn and duck under it.

Although I find stall guards invaluable in the summer, contributing to cooler stables and drier stalls, I don't leave horses alone behind them for long periods of time because of the possibility of injury. And I'm leery of using these devices at all with my more accident-prone horses, one of whom managed to get two front feet through a hay net hanging five feet off the ground from a tree. I shudder to think what he'd do with a stall guard. I also hesitate to use these devices with aggressive horses who are apt to lunge out at passersby, or with colts that might get tangled up in them out of curiosity.

Be sure to clip the stall guard back when you are leading the horse through the door, so there is no chance of him getting caught on it.

Screens made of lightweight steel are also nice for horses that like to see what's going on. There are many different styles, 36 by 52 inches, plain or with a yoke, and 45 by 52 inches, to name a few.

Lighting

For good visibility in the aisle, grooming area, and wash stall, try to incorporate a balance between natural and artificial light. A light in a fitted wire cage or recessed in the center of each stall ceiling works well.

When building a new barn or renovating an old one, give careful thought to the electrical system. Take into consideration the extra illumination and power you will need for winter water heaters and heat lamps (for a wash stall or foaling stall), along with outlets for clippers and vacuum. If you are planning to have a bathroom, tack room, or office, you will need additional lighting and heaters. And be sure to provide outlets for a hot water heater, washing machine, and dryer, which you may want to add in the future.

A very-well-lit area for grooming, veterinarian, and farrier work is a good idea, provided with both 110- and 220-volt outlets. Also consider outlets for a radio, flood lamps, hot plate, coffeepot, refrigerator, video camera, security system, and so forth. Plan for one or two floodlights above the outside doorways to illuminate those winter nights or days of competition, when you load your horse at dawn and unload after dark. Always plan for the future, allowing for ample expansion before the switch box is installed. In case of overload, the switch box should be separate from the house.

To eliminate the risk of fire, always have electrical wiring and outlets installed by a professional. Place all light fixtures as high as possible, either recessed or protected by grating or heavy screening. Make sure all inside and outside wires are enclosed in metal or hard-rubber conduits to protect them from sharp objects, including the teeth of mice and horses. Horses, especially young ones, are curious by nature. One bite into a hot wire could kill a horse and/or start a barn fire.

Any contact with an electrical appliance of 110 volts or more can kill a horse, so keep clippers, blowers, heating tape, tank heaters, and other electrical equipment in good working condition. Remember too that when a horse gets accidentally shocked and lives to recall it, he'll never go near that piece of equipment again. Equine memories are elephantine.

Skylights

A skylight can be made from the simplest corrugated fiberglass-reinforced plastic, a small dome, or a complex window package. All add a great amount of natural light. The types that open provide extra ventilation as well. Closed types can be covered with shades during the summer months to avoid the "greenhouse effect."

If you decide to install a skylight, have it done by a professional, with a guarantee that it won't leak. Unless it is expertly installed, with plenty of flashing and caulking set tightly around each nail and screw and along the edges, it will leak.

An alternative to using a skylight is to put a clear Plexiglas border on the top of the walls, just under the roof. Provided you don't have a long overhang, this border will let in plenty of light in the months when the sun is low, and it will be shady during the summer months, when the sun is high.

Partitions

Partitions or stall dividers can be built all the way to the ceiling, but I prefer to let light and air through by building them only four to six feet high. I top the wood partition with metal flashing to prevent chewing. You can also use heavy hardware cloth nailed down with brads to fill the space between stalls from the top of the partition to the ceiling. This will keep the horses from sparring between stalls. An alternative and more traditional partition topping is grillwork made of three-quarter-inch iron pipe; allow two inches of space between the pipe in stalls and three and a quarter inches on the aisles.

Flooring

Flooring can be constructed from different materials, depending on its location in the barn. It's possible to use concrete in the feed room, utility room, and wash stall; asphalt in the aisle ways; and clay in the stalls. On the whole, flooring should be easy to clean, withstand wear and tear, not retain odor or moisture, and offer drainage, traction, and some cushioning for equine feet and legs in the stall. These criteria are difficult to meet for those limited by budget or by materials available in their area.

No flooring will work without proper drainage, which you must take into account in the early stages of stable planning, when you are deciding on the location and design of the foundation. Ideally, a barn should be built on high, dry ground with a 2 to 6 percent slope away from the building in all directions for surface draining. The floor level should be eight to twelve inches above the outside ground level. But if a hillside or flat ground is your only option, then have some type of diversion drainage ditch dug around the back of the building.

Before putting in a stall floor, have the subsoil evaluated for its drainage capacity. For information on soil testing, once again, contact your local extension service or its equivalent. The agency will explain how to take a soil sample and will interpret the results. If you are fortunate enough to have well-drained soil, you can probably install flooring directly on top or over a thin layer of crushed rock, tamped flat. If the test indicates poor drainage, you will have to excavate from three to ten feet and put in layers of the better draining materials that are available in your area. Lay larger rocks at the bottom, then add crushed rock in decreasing sizes; allow one foot for the topsoil. It will settle better if you allow it to sit for several months before the floor is installed. For even better drainage, bury a network of interconnected Orangeburg or CVC perforated piping under the crushed stone, leading out from the stable.

To restore a floor in a building that is under renovation, it's usually easier to lay a mini–drainage field under each stall. This also works well when building an outdoor run-in shed. Simply dig a hole three and a half feet in diameter in the center of each stall area and fill it with gravel before you put down your flooring of choice. With other materials (wood, clay, asphalt, dirt, or synthetics like rubber mats), you need only six to twelve inches of different sizes of gravel in the center hole for adequate drainage.

ASPHALT. Asphalt is popular with many large stables as a flooring because of its strength and porosity, which allows drainage, and its texture, which offers some traction. It can also be comparatively easy to install, laying it over eighteen to twenty inches of gravel ("ones" and "twos," in gravel company jargon).

To maintain the porosity that makes it so desirable, asphalt requires regular, daily cleaning. After it is swept and cleaned, hose it down and spray it with disinfectant during mild weather. If manure piles up, the pores in the asphalt will clog, causing it to lose its resilience and drainage capacity. For this reason sawdust can't be used as a bedding over asphalt.

In heavily trafficked areas, asphalt compresses or corrodes. Some stables use solid rubber mats to prevent this. Asphalt is also hard to repair, tending to break in on the sides, and after two or three years the porous holes often seal up by themselves. Some professionals don't like it for this reason. Others object that the slight angle at which it's laid is bad for horses' feet and legs. Still others swear by it and wouldn't use anything else. Because of asphalt's rough, abrasive surface, the bedding must be at least eight to ten inches thick; straw is probably the best choice, though it is very expensive.

It's sometimes difficult to get hot asphalt delivered in the small quantities needed for a floor. A less expensive, do-it-yourself alternative is called cold patch—the stuff road crews use to make temporary repairs on macadam. Cold patch has the consistency of sandy cement. You can shovel it on top of the gravel, then roll it down with a large lawn roller and leave it to set for two or three days. Because this flooring is porous, urine seeps down into the gravel base and through the drains below, making it easy to hose down.

CARPETING. Believe it or not, many stables use indoor-outdoor carpeting laid down over well-drained concrete flooring. It was first used with great success on dairy farms; then a number of stables began using it with good results and the word spread. The carpet is soft under the hooves and can be hosed down without rotting.

CLAY. Clay is easy on the feet. It used to be the traditional flooring for horses, but it tends to get dug up, creating an uneven surface that forces a horse to assume awkward postures. To keep it level, new clay must be brought in every year to fill the holes, then leveled and tamped down—an expensive and time-consuming process. Clay must be underlain with good drainage.

CONCRETE. Concrete provides a permanent, low-maintenance floor. It should be installed on a slight slope with drains at the edges, and the surface should be scored for better traction. Concrete is a hard, cold, ungiving surface; you should use ten to twelve inches of bedding to assure the horse a comfortable surface. A stall that needs thorough disinfecting on a regular basis would be a good candidate for this material.

DIRT. Dirt floors are inefficient for the same reason as clay. People do use dirt because it is inexpensive and easily accessible. Dirt floors can be safe if heavily bedded down and well drained, with the generous subflooring described above. But the larvae of some parasites will burrow into dirt. To maintain hygiene, ten inches of the floor should be replaced every year—a real nuisance.

RUBBER MATS. Rubber mats are increasingly popular for stall floors. They are easy to install and clean, provide a resilient level surface, require less bedding, and are generally easier to maintain. When properly installed with good drainage underneath, they can cut bedding bills in half. When laid on top of clay, dirt, or stone dust, they help prevent uneven surface wear and provide a nice cushion for horses to stand on, thus protecting their joints and muscles. Mats are also excellent in wash stalls (with drains in the concrete underneath). Some barns use textured mats in aisleways.

Mats are installed in large sections; their size varies with manufacture. Usually one side is textured, and most horsemen, especially those with valuable horses or broodmares, want that side to face up. The smoother surface becomes slick when wet and is especially hazardous during foaling, when a mare or foal trying to rise can slip on the placental fluid.

Rubber mats come with smooth or interlocking edges. To prevent urine from getting underneath, either type should be installed very snugly against the wall and each other. Although the cost is high, the overall savings in bedding and everyday farm labor make mats a wise investment. They are available through farm supply houses and are advertised in most horse journals.

PLASTIC MATS. These are a recent favorite of some barns. Every section is composed of a raised grid with a drainage hole in the center of each square. When mats are laid down, the grids are filled with stone dust. These synthetic mats are suitable on top of clay, dirt, or stone dust stall floors.

STONE DUST. The fine screenings left over after rock crushing make a good flooring surface when underlain by coarser rock. Stone dust is very absorbent, but like clay, it is easily dug up.

WOOD. The only type of wood flooring sturdy enough to support a horse is two-by-four pressure-treated oak. To allow some moisture to drain through, you must drill holes in it and then maintain the holes with a dowel or screwdriver to prevent clogging. Wood's main disadvantage is that it rots after a few years and the boards have to be replaced. It's also slippery when wet, especially in combination with bedding like oat straw, and it's a hard surface for a horse to stand on for a long period.

Water Facilities

When planning a new stable, the source and accessibility of water is a primary consideration. Horses drink eight to twelve gallons of water a day and have to be washed periodically. If your utility room will include a washing machine, the well should produce enough gallons per minute to accommodate it.

Well water should be tested regularly for bacterial contamination and water quality. Even if your water is supplied by the community, it should be tested for purity. Springs and creeks should be checked for possible contamination, and ponds that serve as watering spots should be monitored in case they become stagnant. Your health department can help you with this.

In the stable providing water for your horse can be as simple as hanging a bucket on a ring with a snap. Make sure the bracket hangs low enough for easy drinking—at least three and a half feet from the floor. Putting buckets on the floor isn't a good idea because they fill with hay and bedding and are easily kicked over and stepped on in the night.

If you live south of the Mason-Dixon line and don't have to worry too much about freezing weather, you might want to invest in an automatic watering system for your barn. These are expensive but convenient. Many equestrians frown on them because one never knows how much a horse is drinking, and the amount is often an indicator of a pending health problem. Automatic waterers are usually gravity fed; they should be inspected daily and cleaned as regularly as water buckets.

Electrical water heaters are available for both indoor and outdoor watering. And if you're weary of breaking through ice on cold winter days, another alternative is a thermobucket, a plastic bucket inserted inside an insulated casing that can be mounted on the wall. To get a drink, the horse pushes against a disk floating on the surface. Thermobuckets can freeze in extremely cold weather, but it takes a long time, and they're easy to open up.

In colder climates running a pipe to the barn gets quite involved. To keep the pipe from freezing, it has to be sunk three feet below the frost line and either insulated or swathed with a heating cord (a large extension cord plugged into house current). But heating cords fail when the electricity does. And when the mercury is at ten below, it doesn't take long for a water pipe to freeze—and burst. After getting soaked a few times, you might find it easier to carry water from the house.

At my first barn, which housed eight horses, the electric heating cord to the barn failed during the course of an extraordinarily hectic midwinter week. My husband and I had to remove about twelve feet of cord and insulation and thaw out the frozen length of pipe with a small gas torch—a job that took more than three hours. Not until days later did we find the trouble spot, but in the meantime I had to cart sixteen pails of water a day two hundred yards from house to stable. To avoid a similar crisis, get a cord that has a thermostat, with a light that goes out when the cord isn't working—a very worthwhile investment.

The best solution for a year-round water supply is a hydrantlike, frost-free pump. These are housed below the frost line, drawing water up only when the spigot is turned; water drains out of the pipe after each use.

Feeders

Many types of grain and combination feed tubs are on the market. Some plastic types are designed to be attached to the corner of the stall; they have a feed ring that fits into the dish, slowing overly zealous eaters down and preventing feed from being pushed around and spilled on the floor. Extra large Duraflex tubs with rings are made to match water buckets and come in styles that fit in the corner or on the floor for ground feeding. You can purchase combination feeders that hold both grain and hay from most tack shops or farm supply stores, or through catalogs. These are designs that either fit the stall corner or are hung over a fence rail. Many professionals don't like these feeders because the hay compartment is too small for a full hay ration yet so deep that horses can't reach the bottom, wasting hay as a result. Types that fit in stall corners reach so high on the wall that putting hay in is awkward and messy, and some horses try to pull hay out of the top instead of the bottom, getting it all over themselves and the stall. Hay nets or racks are usually preferred.

Horsekeeping

You can keep stench and pestilence at bay with the right tools and a daily and weekly routine for keeping stables and pastures clean. Stalls and pasture pickups keep you fit while you keep an eye on stall and pasture maintenance. I often get my best thinking done while picking out stalls. And many of my best women friends would prefer cleaning the stable to cleaning the house.

MAINTENANCE ITEMS

Once your stable is built and occupied, you'll be faced with the daily chore of maintaining it, keeping the tack and feed rooms tidy, the stalls clean, and the bedding fresh. For cleaning, mucking out, and rebedding, these items make the job easier:

• Manure fork. The type varies according to the bedding you use. A ten-tined manure fork is good for straw and wood shavings. A fork with sixteen to twenty closely spaced tines is perfect for sawdust bedding.

• Thunderbolt Ultimate Sifter (optional). Shaped like a shovel but made of aluminum webbing, this tool holds manure while sawdust sifts through. It's handy for picking up manure in aisleways and pastures and for removing ice from water tanks in winter.

• Long-handled flat shovel

• Wheelbarrow. The size depends on the number of horses you have and what you can handle.

• Manure basket (skip and/or muck bucket). Though it is optional for a small stable, this basket can be a very handy piece of equipment anywhere. It's good for quick pickups at home or at shows.

• Broom

• PDZ or Stable Boy. Use this to dust on clean floors to absorb moisture and cut odor.

• Liquid disinfectant. This is for asphalt and cement floors and aisleways.

• Bedding.

Assuming that you're short of time, the fastest way to clean a stall is to work around a horse as he eats. Most horses will let you muck out anytime. You can take the skip bucket into the stall with you. Or place the wheelbarrow to block the stall door if necessary, or clip a simple stall guard to the rings on either side of the door. These plastic- or hose-covered chains with a clip on either end can be easily home made or purchased in a tack store or tack catalog.

CLEANING STALLS

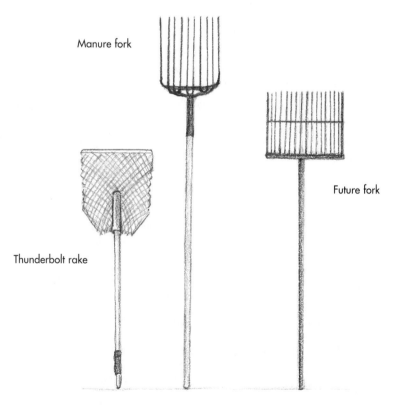

Manure fork

Future fork

Thunderbolt rake

As long as you handle the manure fork with care, any well-mannered horse will let you work close to him. Of course if he pins his ears back and it looks like you might be kicked or nipped, don't force the issue. Just feed your horse his grain in the stall, then put him outside with hay and water while you clean. But such a reaction means that your horse has a behavior problem that will have to be overcome in the interest of an enduring relationship.

The first step in cleaning a box stall is to pick up all the wet bedding and droppings with the manure fork and load them into the basket or wheelbarrow. When manure is frozen in winter, it's usually more convenient to shovel the droppings into the basket and carry them to the pile. Try to save as much bedding as possible, banking it up around the sides of the stall to dry while your horse is turned out for the day. Unless the weather is particularly cold or damp, it should be ready to reuse by nightfall. You'll see that some beddings dry more easily, making them more economical in the long run.

When you get to the bottom of the bedding, you may need a shovel to get the stall really clean. If moisture remains on the floor after the droppings are cleared away, sprinkle around some chaff from the hay or straw to absorb it, then shovel it up. As a finishing touch, you might want to sprinkle on either lime or a PDZ or Stable Boy sweetener to control odor and absorb any remaining moisture. Then let the surface dry out during the day. In the summer months it's a good idea to use a liquid disinfectant occasionally on asphalt, cement, or rubber mats and more frequently in aisles, but don't use it in the winter, when it might freeze.

Before letting your horse back in at night, push the banked-up bedding back into the center and add to it if necessary. Bedding should be from eight to ten inches thick on all flooring except rubber mats, where it can be a few inches less.

The stall should be cleaned every day, both to keep your horse cleaner and to dispel ammonia fumes, which can cause permanent respiratory damage. Urine-soaked manure will also erode a horse's hooves, causing thrush, which can destroy a horse's frog if not caught early. When a horse is stabled continuously, the stall should be picked out several times a day.

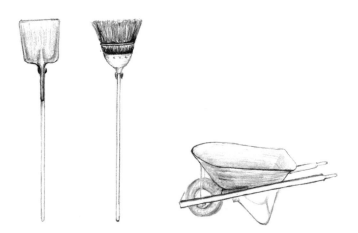

If your horse is in a tie stall (which I hope he isn't), there will be less bedding, making it simpler to clean. In the morning bank the damp bedding toward the front and against each side of the stall. At night make sure it's pushed far enough forward to give your horse a soft place to rest his knees when he lies down.

If you're around all day and want to do a super cleaning job, there are no limits to your fastidiousness. Like housekeepers, horsekeepers have their eccentricities, and some are almost compulsively neat. A really large stable hires help to do the major mucking out early in the morning and systematic picking up during the day, so a visitor seldom sees a soiled stall.

Every once in a while I run into someone who is sold on the theory that manure left in stalls during the winter will heat the stable as it rots. This is a dangerous old wives' tale. A horse left to stand in wet manure can develop thrush and a variety of unpleasant skin irritations. Manure is also infested with parasites in various stages, many of which survive over the winter. While leaving manure in the stall might seem like an easy way to get out of an unpleasant cold-weather job, not only does it put your horse's health at risk but you'll face a Herculean task of stable cleaning when spring rolls around. It's healthier, more economical, and in the long run easier to clean stalls daily.

Note: Never leave stable-cleaning tools in the stall with the horse, not even for a minute. It's an invitation to injury.

BEWARE OF BOOBY TRAPS

A veterinarian who has sewn up a lot of horses after accidents once told me that a lot of these mishaps could be avoided if owners would just put themselves in their horse's place. Stand in the middle of a stall, and consider your horse's natural habits. Think about the quick movements he makes, and look for things that could injure him—like a nail, a loose or projecting board, a poorly secured water pail, or an unprotected lightbulb.

Make sure that any stall or shed is flush with or sunk into the ground so the horse can't get his foot caught beneath it. A Dutch stall door should have a bottom latch for the same reason; otherwise a horse lying down could shove the door open at the bottom and get his foot trapped beneath it.

Make sure that Dutch doors fasten back securely. Should the top door swing shut, it could tempt the horse to go under it. When you use a stall guard, clip it to the side when you are leading the horse out. Likewise, clip the ropes at the back of a straight stall so the horse can't get tangled in passing.

Use rings with closed snaps to hold up buckets. Check your feed dishes to make sure a halter can't catch on any sharp edges of the hardware.

BEDDING DOWN

Bedding must be deep enough to allow a horse to lie down comfortably. Bedding of sawdust or wood shavings, for instance, should be four to six inches deep, and straw should be twice that. It's more economical to begin with too much than too little. A small amount of bedding will quickly get soiled and wet. Bedding should be banked during the day and the soiled portions shoveled up and discarded in the evening.

Common Bedding Materials

STRAW. When I am first bedding down a twelve-by-twelve stall in straw, I usually open up an entire sixty-pound bale. Depending on how neat your horse is (some will consistently leave their droppings in the same place), you will probably use three or four sixty-pound bales of straw per horse per week in a twelve-by-twelve stall, a major expense in some areas.

One disadvantage of straw is the difficulty of getting rid of it. It creates a much larger manure pile than other beddings, and because it's so bulky, many people don't like to use it on their gardens.

CHOPPED SUGARCANE. Available in sugar-growing areas like Hawaii and Florida, chopped sugarcane is highly absorbent but doesn't dry out as well as straw, and the wet bedding usually can't be reused unless you have a succession of warm, breezy days. Baled commercial brands of sugarcane are expensive if imported but economical when locally available.

WOOD SHAVINGS AND SAWDUST. Sometimes available from sawmills in lumbering areas, shavings and sawdust make more than adequate bedding if properly kiln dried. They are cheapest when purchased in quantity. In our area sawdust delivered by the truckload is the least expensive available bedding. If you have the storage space, sharing a tractor-trailer load of bagged wood shavings with friends can save money in the long run.

All these beddings tend to be dusty and aren't advised if your horse has allergic tendencies. Though shavings can be wetted down to eliminate dust, they aren't very absorbent and generally cannot be reused. They are also a storage problem. It takes a lot of shavings to make a soft bed, and they mat down quickly in the stall.

Other Beddings

PEANUT HULLS. Although they don't sound comfortable to lie on, peanut hulls are reasonably good for bedding. Like shavings, they are fairly inexpensive, particularly in areas where the nut is grown, but they are even less absorbent than shav-

ings and can never be reused. It takes a lot of peanut shells to bed a horse down comfortably, and picking them up is no fun—you need a shovel instead of a manure fork. Also some horses will eat peanut shells. (One of mine even likes peat moss.) So unless you live near a peanut farm, another type of bedding is probably preferable.

PEAT MOSS. The crème de la crème of beddings, peat moss was used in some of the most exclusive stables in the country but most is priced out of reach of any horse owner. (But even if money were no object, I'd still prefer straw.) It is the best bedding for allergic horses and is good for problem feet. Peat moss is also very easy to shovel up. But the dark color makes it difficult to distinguish it from manure when you're separating the bedding. And light-colored horses that lie down in peat moss will come up dusty.

The biggest thing going for peat moss is something that most people who can afford it don't care about: It makes your manure pile an asset rather than a liability, as we will see.

MANAGING MANURE

There is literally no getting around this subject, one of the biggest headaches of horse ownership, especially in suburban areas. Since the average horse produces about forty-five pounds of manure and urine a day, we are talking about more than eight tons of manure to dispose of a year. Aside from the fact that raw manure can leach nitrates into wells, water tables, and streams, you'll discover sooner rather than later that your neighbors are less than entranced with the sight and smell of that mushrooming pile steaming behind your stable.

Consequently you must consider the site of a manure pile carefully. The ideal solution is a covered pit, not a pile, built over concrete for easy removal and cleaning. But this arrangement is prohibitively costly for most horse owners, so let's consider the pile. It should be close enough to the barn to be easily reached by a wheelbarrow; accessible by truck; far enough from the stable and house to keep flies away; and located out of sight and downwind of neighbors. On properties of one or two acres, this is a difficult feat to perform.

One of the most efficient and inexpensive ways to eventually dispose of the sheer volume of manure is to compost. When done properly, with the right kind of bedding (which affects how quickly the mass will decompose), you can turn a massive pile of waste into an asset: smaller, lighter-weight, dark, loamy fertilizer that will have your neighbors pounding at your barn door.

Aerobic composting will raise the temperature enough to destroy some parasites, kill weed seeds, and eliminate some of the water weight. The amount of time it takes

depends on the ration of manure, bedding, moisture, oxygen, and microorganisms. The proportions of these and the temperature of the pile are critical to the amount of time it takes the pile to break down. The pile needs to maintain about 50 percent of its moisture and enough air that it doesn't get too hot too fast and destroy the microorganisms. It must have a specific ratio of nitrogen (found in manure) and carbon (found in bedding like straw and wood shavings and sawdust). Beddings that pack too tightly, like wood shavings and sawdust, do not allow air to circulate as well as straw does. The center of the pile heats the fastest and must be turned a number of times to have a good breakdown of ingredients. Breakdown can take as little as ninety days if properly constructed and maintained but averages 120 days; if left to fend for itself, the process can take as long as four years.

Advice, guidelines, publications, and even composting plans are available from your county agricultural extension service. Local libraries can suggest magazines on organic farming.

Come springtime, when the wind shifts, get on the phone and invite everyone within a quarter-mile radius to come over with a pickup truck. If you have seriously composted your manure, you may be able to sell it locally or have a landscaper arrange to take it away at no cost to you.

Sawdust, wood shavings, peanut hulls, and chopped sugarcane mixed with manure can also be used for mulch if they are not too hot (see above). Still, they're all a bit acid for this purpose. I've used well-rotted manure with either wood shavings or sawdust for years, testing to make sure the soil is balanced, with marvelous results.

Straw and cane manure make very bulky mulches, desirable only when soil needs lightening. Mushroom farms use them exclusively for this reason, and they might be an outlet for you, or a landscaper who wants to lighten up clay soil might be interested. If the pile is easily reached by truck, you probably won't have much of a problem.

If you're not composting, the manure pile should be cleaned up monthly, and more often in the warm months of the year, if possible. (Weekly cleanups are ideal but impossible for most people.) Having manure hauled away is usually expensive but may be your only alternative. Your cooperative extension agent can most likely help you find a local hauler.

FIREPROOFING

Millions of dollars and hundreds of valuable animals are lost every year in stable fires, 90 percent of them the result of human carelessness. Portable heaters are the leading cause, while cigarettes place second. (Don't even think of smoking anywhere near the barn, and take care not to overload fuse boxes with a lot of portable appliances.) Bad wiring, hot plates, and children playing with matches are the remaining leading causes of fire; the other 10 percent are the result of lightning, spontaneous combustion of hay, and arson.

Early detection is the key to preventing total loss, but make sure it never reaches that point by constructing and organizing your barn to prevent fire. Always have a plan of action ready should an accidental fire occur. Installing a telephone in your barn can save precious minutes. Post the number of the fire department above it, and make sure your name and box number can be seen clearly from both sides of your mailbox at night—especially important in a rural area.

Large stables can afford to install sprinkler systems. They are too pricey for the average backyard horse owner, but smoke detectors are inexpensive. They are battery operated, lasting about a year, and should be tested monthly to make sure they work. A detector can't put out a fire, but it will quickly alert you to one when you're in the vicinity of the barn.

More elaborate smoke/heat detectors can be set up to sound off in your house, and they are commercially monitored to alert the fire department. But they're so sensitive that other things will set them off unless the adjustment is just right. At a farm I used to manage, a newly installed system woke me up almost every night for two weeks, bringing the fire department out in full force on each occasion, until the alarm company finally worked the kinks out of the system.

Big stables that have suffered fire losses have some tips about fire prevention that can be incorporated into everyone's building plans. The insurance company that writes your policy will look at all the areas on this list closely, which will affect the rates. To qualify for insurance, then, you should follow these general rules:

• Try to build with concrete block exteriors.

• Treat stall partitions with noncombustible liquids (available through your local lumber supplier).

• Use fiberglass windows that won't explode under high heat, as glass does.

• Construct stables with fireguard, a specially treated, noncumbustible lumber, if you can afford it. The cost is high because it's treated under pressure.

• Thread wiring through metal conduit pipes, so that rodents and curious horses can't chew through it. This is a *must*.

• Have the wiring checked periodically by an electrician or other qualified professional who can spot any potential problems.

• Install a lightning rod on the stable roof. The most reliable kind should bear the label of Underwriters Lab, Inc., to ensure that it and the ground conductors have been made and installed to specifications.

• Be sure your stable roof is maintained in good condition and is able to hold up in high winds and under heavy snow (potentially lethal to horses below). A collapsed roof is an invitation to fire.

• Use fireproof asbestos shingles.

• Install all doors so they open quickly.

• Hang a halter and lead rope on each stall door for quick access.

• Move flammable debris like loose hay, scrap lumber, and oily rags away from the stable yard and barn perimeter.

• Store hay and bedding away from the stable area; keep only the minimum needed in the barn itself.

• Buy only well-cured hay, to prevent spontaneous ignition or combustion, which can happen in only a few hundred pounds of hay.

• Make sure a ten-pound fire extinguisher is hung at least every seventy-five feet. Water will work for wood, hay, and straw, but only the chemical extinguisher can contain gasoline and electrical fires.

• Check the extinguishers yourself every month to make sure the pressure gauge is in the green zone. They must be maintained professionally on an annual basis.

• Store a standard inch-and-a-half-diameter fire-fighting hose with a capacity of at least fifty feet on a mobile wheel.

• Post "no smoking" signs on every door and at other key points in the stable.

• Protect lightbulbs in stalls with heavy wire cages to keep them from breaking.

• House farm vehicles and any gas-powered equipment away from the barn. Gas, oil, and grease inevitably leak, creating a fire hazard.

• Pile manure well away from the barn, and remove it regularly. Manure piles can heat up, inviting spontaneous combustion.

• Mow grass closely around the barn, particularly in the dry season, to reduce the possibility of a spreading brush fire.

Fresh-cut hay should be cured on the field or in a haymow before baling. Watch all shipments of hay for six weeks after delivery for any signs of heating. Dampness on the surface and a fruity odor are the first signs of trouble. If you have any doubt about a load of hay, the National Fire Prevention Association suggests sticking a pipe several feet down into the bales and dropping in a thermometer tied to a string. If the temperature is 160 degrees Fahrenheit or more, you have cause for alarm and should phone the fire department immediately for advice.

Should the worst occur and fire breaks out in your stable, be ready for it. If you're in the house, call the fire department or dial the operator and ask her to report it. If you're in the stable, evacuate the horses before phoning. A horse in a burning stall must be out of there in less than thirty seconds.

Leading the Horse to Safety

This necessity raises the age-old problem of whether to halter a stabled horse. I prefer not to, and if you would rather not, or can't because of a skin irritation, have a halter or lead easily accessible on or beside the stall door. Practice putting the halter on in double time, getting a friend to time you with a stopwatch.

Because most horses panic when they see fire or smell smoke, keep a supply of towels or burlap bags ready for covering equine heads as they're led out. Keep the most high-strung horses near the door. (Some stables keep the most valuable horses there.) Any horse that puts up a fight about going out should be left until last. You don't want to waste precious minutes struggling with a temperamental horse when more docile ones can make a fast exit.

Always lead the horse away from the direction of the fire. Ideally, every stable should have two exit doors—a must if you're planning one from scratch. If fire seems to be spreading rapidly, don't worry about getting the horses to a fenced area. Just lead them to the door and let them loose.

Because even the most docile horses become nervous when they smell smoke, stable owners in western areas, where grass fires are common, evacuate their stock before the fire even comes close to the barn. If smoke from a nearby fire drifts your way, take the horses out to the paddock or pasture. It will be easier on their nerves and save wear and tear on the stable.

Fencing Around

When the weather gets warm enough for gardens to flourish, the irate phone calls start coming in from my neighbors. "Those damned horses of yours just trampled my tomatoes, and now they're in the marigolds" is a typical opener, followed by, "If you don't get them out of here right now, I'll shoot." From the descriptions given, it's impossible to tell whether the culprits belong to me, but I always run out to the pasture and count noses just in case they're mine—and occasionally they are.

Large, elegant stables and breeding farms never seem to have problems like this, probably because they have acres of rolling pastures and can afford the best kind of security available. They often have double fences between pastures—an expensive luxury for most one- or two-horse owners.

TYPES OF FENCING

Looks usually have little to do with the durability of a fence, which should meet the primary requirements of safety and strength.

MAN O' WAR FENCING. Named for the famous Derby winner and sire, this sturdy, handsome barrier has four horizontal boards supported by posts. It is sometimes electrified along the top for extra security. The fencing is sold in eight-foot sections. If you don't mind the expense, it's well worth the investment.

POSTS AND RAILS. This very popular type of fencing is very pretty but extremely expensive. A typical three-rail fence must be at least four feet high to hold a hunter. Despite their good looks, these fences have the disadvantage of splitting when a horse leans against them, and the rails can be worked loose from the posts, needing reinforcement with nails. Unless you have an exceptionally docile horse, a strand of electric wire should be run along the top of these fences to keep them intact.

ELECTRIC FENCING. Though not the prettiest, electric fencing is the cheapest, most reliable, and easiest type to install. Electric wire can be attached to pressurized wood posts sunk solidly in the ground or metal posts, which are easier to drive in. Wire-woven plastic tape, specially designed for this purpose, can be used as temporary fencing instead of wire.

FIBERGLASS RODS AND POSTS. This system can be used with wire-woven tape, but it isn't recommended for permanent fencing. A horse could easily become frightened and injure himself going through the lightweight barrier, dragging the tape and posts along. Fiberglass is better for dividing grazing areas within a solidly fenced pasture.

Unless you have a small pony, one strand of electric wire won't be enough. Two will be needed—the top strand about three and a half feet off the ground, and the other a foot under that. If you have a lot of land to fence, a special wire-tightening tool is useful.

Once the fence is up, it's important to remember that the wire or tape cannot touch any objects, including tall weeds, grass, nails, trees, or posts. If it touches anything except the insulator, the electricity will be grounded and lose its charge.

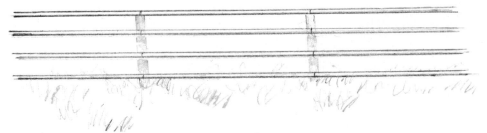

Man o' War fencing

All wire and tape should be very secure so that current doesn't "arc" or jump the faulty point, causing a short. This can also happen with rusty wire. Sanding them will make the connections clean.

These precautions are important for social as well as security reasons. Not only can shorts spark and cause a fire, but they create static in passing car radios and in house radios within a three-hundred-yard radius. I once returned from a vacation to hear that everyone in the immediate neighborhood had phoned the electric company to complain of faulty radio reception. For a while afterward I got phone calls whenever a favorite station buzzed out.

Try to avoid patching fences with small strands of wire. This dilutes the current and encourages the circuit to arc or short out. Try to use a single strand of wire for repairs, limiting patches to two or three per fence.

During the dry season a fire can be caused by a short or by dropping the electric wire on the ground when you open the gate. Even a little rust on the handle can cause a short that might ignite the dry grass.

If the fence shorts out, check the wires thoroughly, especially after a storm, to make sure no grass, sticks, or broken branches are touching them. Then take a close look at the transformer. I once did a careful two-hour examination of my fence after a storm but failed to find the short. When I took the transformer in for an appraisal, it turned out that a simple part needed replacement—a five-minute job.

Improper installation is the most common cause of fence failure. For a fence to work properly, it must have adequate grounding and a transformer large enough for the job. (One designed to charge fifteen miles of fence won't be able to handle twenty-five.) For best results, read your operation manual carefully.

An electric fence can be powered by outside battery transformers, solar packs with batteries that are recharged by sunlight (and can operate for three weeks in total darkness), or an electric transformer that plugs into your house or barn. Be sure to install a metal ground rod attached to the transformer, buried three or four feet deep in the ground.

When a battery-type transformer stops clicking, it's dead. This type should always be checked after a storm, when a short could drain the life out of the battery.

It sounds cruel, but when you first put a horse inside an electric fence, lead him

Split-rail fence with electric wire topping

up to it and let his nose touch the wire—to make sure he gets the idea. To avoid giving curious neighborhood children a jolt, buy a few warning signs at the feed store. (The voltage is 115.)

Above all, remember to check the fence regularly. A grounded or shorted electric fence is useless, a social nuisance, and as potentially dangerous as barbed wire. Some horses are extraordinarily intuitive about electric fences, ambling right through them as soon as the power goes off. And while equine escapes are often good for later laughs, I can't overstress how dangerous it is for horses to get loose on the road. In my area two horses were killed in one twenty-four-hour period after they got loose and ran onto the highway. Fencing should be thought of as a protective device that you, the owner, are responsible for keeping in good order.

All electric fence materials can be purchased at farm supply stores or through tack and farm supply catalogs.

BARBED WIRE. This is a horseman's nightmare! It's used almost exclusively in the West, being the only practical way to fence hundreds of acres, but many horses out there bear its scars. If you have a lot of acreage already fenced with barbed wire in good condition and want to risk using it, make sure the bottom strand is thirty inches from the ground so the horses can't snag a leg. (To get to the right height, you may want to clip off the bottom strand or remove it entirely.) But I hope it won't take a horse badly mangled by barbs to persuade you that barbed wire is a bad fencing choice. A horse that catches a leg in it and panics can literally tear himself apart.

BOARD FENCING. Reinforced with electric wiring, board fencing is a good-looking suburban compromise. If you want to cut a few corners, put up a three-board fence in the places where it shows, then run electric wiring around the other parts of the pasture hidden from view. The cost will depend on the thickness of the boards. Lumber is always expensive and costs a lot more when pressure treated.

Make sure that the ends of each board on the fence meet flush at the post on the outside. Overlapping boards on the inside leave protruding edges where a horse could snag himself.

Resist the temptation to skip the electric wire. Fences look prettier without it, but they will stay up much longer with it. Horses lean across unelectrified fences to graze, and if they see something particularly appetizing on the other side, they are capable of going right through it. A wooden arm with electric tape running on the inside, extending inward about a foot and a half, keeps horses off the fence and each other. It also prevents them from chewing or cribbing on the wooden fence when the pickings get slim.

If board fencing is painted or stained with whitewash, shingle stain, or other preservative, it will last longer. The ends of the posts can also be given a coat of wood preservative for longevity.

Use eight-foot posts, if possible, and sink them two to three feet into the ground for maximum strength. The boards come in twelve-foot sections, so it makes sense to set the posts six feet apart rather than cut off valuable wood. If you can find boards in fourteen-foot lengths, set your poles seven feet apart. Be sure to use thick wooden posts (four by four inches in circumference) for board fencing. Lighter posts, which can be used for electric fencing, will split when nailed.

A three-board fence, with the top board from four and a half to five feet off the ground, is the best choice. Boards should be three-quarters to one inch thick and six inches wide. Hemlock is good choice, being stronger and cheaper than pine. And for a long-lived fence, it's worth the time and mess to paint it all with wood preservative.

Unless you have a gas-driven posthole digger, digging is a tedious task. You might find that time saved by renting or hiring a gas-driven digger justifies the expense. Remember that postholes must be dug straight down. (Any angles will create problems when you put in the posts.) Rocks encountered en route are removed with a hand trowel or a crowbar, both essential to this venture. A long-handled trowel is also handy for removing loose dirt as you dig.

Before putting the pole in, place small stones mixed with dirt at the bottom to give the pole a firm foundation. As you refill the hole, pack the dirt and pebbles down with a trowel, using lemon-size stones to wedge the post in.

THE CENTAUR HTP. Each of these five-inch rails is made of three single-strand, 12.5-gauge galvanized steel wires encased in protective polymer. When a horse hits the fence, the rails flex and return to their original position, cushioning the impact. The manufacturers claim this fence will never rust, fade, crack, or peel, even in extreme temperatures, making it virtually maintenance free. They come in black or white and carry a twenty-year warranty.

SAFETY

Junk or farming equipment should not be kept where horses are stabled or pastured. I recently heard of a terrible accident where a horse caught his halter on a manure spreader that had been left in a pasture, ripping open the side of his face in struggling to get free. The smaller the area, the more care you should give to potential

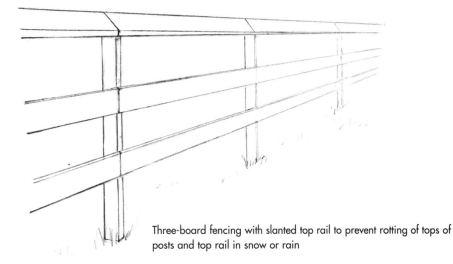

Three-board fencing with slanted top rail to prevent rotting of tops of posts and top rail in snow or rain

booby traps. Corrugated metal, for instance, often used for construction, should be checked for sharp edges or projections. If your pasture is within an arm's throw of a well-traveled road, check frequently for beer cans, bottles, and trash. Litterbugs seem to find pastures an inviting place to dump.

Make sure that guy wires from telephone poles and power lines don't protrude into the pasture. They're difficult for a running horse to see. Ideally, your fence should be built around them. If this isn't possible, tie strips of sheeting or colored plastic to the wires.

GATES

A gate can be as simple as two bars across an entrance of double posts with cross boards, but unless you have your horses on an honor system, I don't advise it. Bars are easily worked open by bored inmates. To make bars escape-proof, you must run *electric wire* across the bars and fasten it with a *rubber-handled hook* that can be opened and closed easily with one hand.

Wooden gates are fairly easy to construct. *Aluminum gates,* sold at most feed supply stores, are even better—lighter and easier to handle when you have a horse in tow, and they look nice. They should be hung with small horizontal slats at the bottom so the horse can't get his feet through. No bolts or sharp edges should protrude, and the opened gate should lie flush with the fence or building. Latches should be of the chain and snap types, which fall out of the way when the gate is open. When setting a gate, use carriage bolts with round heads.

The only way to find out whether a fence is adequate is to put your horse inside and see if he stays. If he's walking down the driveway a few hours later, you'll know you've failed. (Even if you don't see him make his exit, the neighbors will be sure to keep you informed of his progress.) Don't be discouraged. Check your fences to find where he got out and why; fix it, and try again.

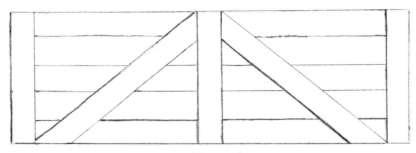

A type of homemade gate

**THUNDER-
STORMS**

Every year in the South and Southwest, particularly violent thunderstorms cause many livestock deaths. Horses instinctively gather in bunches for protection, and they are often drawn to a lone, tall tree for shelter. But these trees are often located near watering troughs or wire fences, which make superb lightning conductors, particularly in combination with wet ground and steel-shod hooves.

Electricity from lightning will follow metal fencing for a considerable distance, even traveling along power lines and down poles or brace wires. It can also strike tall trees and spread to the animals sheltered beneath them. A lightning bolt can bounce between animals, injuring or killing several in the group. You can avoid such a disaster by housing your horses in a safe, well-grounded building during electrical storms—preferably a wooden barn or else a well-grounded metal barn with lightning rods. Make sure the electrical conduits and water pipes are well grounded. It's worthwhile to have a qualified electrician make a safety inspection.

Try to install wood or vinyl fencing, and avoid having a single tree in the pasture where horses might congregate in a sudden storm. When forecasts call for stormy weather, keep horses out of any pasture near power lines.

**GREENER
PASTURES**

Overgrazing can turn a lush green pasture into bare, eroded acreage full of unpalatable and unnutritious weeds. Mowing won't restore the grass, but good agronomic management will preserve it.

Ways to Keep Grass Green

Ideally each horse should have a minimum of an acre and a half, preferably two, to graze on. This pasturage should be subdivided into smaller lots, so the horses can be rotated when one area is depleted. If you have more than one horse, these lots should be able to comfortably accommodate them, leaving room for a timid stablemate to elude a more aggressive one.

ROTATE PASTURE USE. Rotation can't keep parasites out of the pasture, but it can reduce their numbers. Given a choice, most horses won't eat where they defecate, doing so only when other grazing gets slim. Keeping the number of horses per acre to a minimum will make them less likely to graze on a contaminated area (with the exception of colts or fillies, who for some reason like eating manure).

USE TEMPORARY FENCING. Fiberglass posts with tape for an electric fence could be an option for dividing grazing lots. This fencing is gaining in popularity because it's easy to construct and move around. Many types of temporary fencing are listed in English and Western publications, made of a variety of materials and priced accordingly.

RESTRICT GRAZING TIME. If your total pasturage is limited, restrict grazing time so that a lot isn't depleted before the grass can grow back in the alternative area. New growth should reach at least four to six inches before it is grazed again. Pasture in which grazed areas of new forage are interspersed with tall, unappetizing weeds has been overgrazed. (Horses prefer to eat tender, immature forage.)

In early spring you don't want your horse to turn the pasture into a mudhole before the grass starts to grow. A paddock will provide turnout during these sloppy months. But because parasites thrive and reinfect small grassy areas, many experts advise putting cinders or fine gravel instead of grass in paddock areas.

A friend of mine in the suburbs with limited acreage keeps her pasture green by stabling her two horses in the wet spring and fall and at night, keeping the paddock and pasture picked up on a biweekly basis. So if you're willing to put in the effort, it's possible.

TEST THE SOIL YEARLY. If you have a large field, test the soil yearly to see if it is balanced enough to grow suitable pasture grasses.

LIMING. Liming should be done very early in the spring, even on top of the snow, which will carry it into the ground as it melts.

RESEEDING. Reseeding can also be done on the snow. But it will do no good unless your horse is kept off the new seedlings. A new pasture must be left ungrazed for a year to become firmly established.

PICK UP MANURE REGULARLY. Twice a week is recommended. This job is tedious but essential. Manure must be composted or disposed of properly; otherwise it kills grass and harbors parasites, which can reach the destructive phase sometime after the eggs are passed in the feces. If manure is hauled away before this phase is reached, they're harmless. Fresh manure should never be spread for fertilizer in a year when the pasture is being grazed. Although it is a great idea from a strictly pasture-management perspective—spreading organic matter, eliminating hot spots, and putting nutrients back into the soil—it still doesn't kill all the parasites. Only those exposed to sunlight and/or exceptionally dry conditions will perish. Eggs and larvae will remain encapsulated in manure balls, grass, and soil. (Your veterinarian should do a periodic fecal egg count to determine the extent of infestation.) To remove parasites, either mow the infested grass or plow it under and give the pasture a year's rest. Just dragging the field to scatter the manure so that grazing can continue will make it nearly impossible for the horses to avoid reinfecting themselves. Another way to break up the parasite life cycle is to rotate the pastures with other livestock, like sheep and cattle.

MAINTAIN A FRESH WATER SUPPLY. If you keep your horses close to the house, where you can see and enjoy them, it's usually practical to run a hose out to a large clean muck bucket (one used only for water) or a stock water tank (both available from farm suppliers or through tack catalogs). These watering troughs must be kept scrupulously clean. Algae and harmful bacteria accumulate rapidly in hot weather.

TEST PASTURE PONDS OR STREAMS FOR PURITY. Have this done by your local soil and conservation service agent. If a pond or stream is your only pasture water supply, be sure to recheck it often during the hot and dry months, in case it suddenly dries up or becomes stagnant. Horses drink more water in the summer because they perspire more. Fifty percent of a horse's weight is water, and leaving him without it for long periods causes serious dehydration.

Wetlands are another source of water, so take a second look at that perennial puddle in the middle of your pasture—it could prove an asset instead of a nuisance. It might look like an old swamp that needs filling in, but don't do it without checking with the soil and conservation service to avoid breaking a federal law. Any area wet enough to support vegetation is technically a wetland, protected by the government.

Horses have been happily grazing on wetlands since they first evolved, but state and local governments might place restrictions on this type of use. Check with your local conservation service or phone your regional U.S. Environmental Protection Agency office listed under U.S. offices in the telephone directory.

If you have an old pasture that needs a new lease on life or a new one that needs sowing, your county soil and conservation service can tell you what grasses grow best in your area. You should also have the soil tested by an agent to find out the appropriate level of fertilizer necessary to get the maximum growth out of your forage mixture. In the long run proper management techniques save money by increasing the nutritional value of pasture, saving on the cost of soil maintenance and improving property values.

PART V

The Well-Manicured Mount

Some glory in their birth, some in their skill,
Some in their wealth, some in their body's force;
Some in their garments, though new-fangled ill,
Some in their hawks and hounds, some in their horse . . .

Shakespeare, Sonnet 91

Guide to Grooming

In the era of the horse and buggy, grooming was something that grooms did, but today's average equestrians, beset by car and mortgage payments, can barely afford to keep a horse, let alone a groom, and must do most of the hard, dirty work themselves.

Appearance isn't the only reason to groom a horse. A daily once-over with currycomb and brush is essential to maintaining the animal's health during the riding season, keeping pores open, helping circulation, and maintaining muscle tone. It also assures cleanliness and affords you the opportunity to check your horse over for cuts, scratches, or other irritations. A thorough grooming obviously improves appearance, and a few extra things can also be done before a show, hunt, or other special occasion to make your mount look suitably glamorous.

In the animal world, grooming promotes friendliness as well as cleanliness, and so it is with you and your horse—an affectionate way to spend quality time and develop a trusting relationship.

Before you learn the basics of good grooming, you'll need to know how to lead, tie, and handle your horse so that he can be groomed properly. Every beginner I've taught has just assumed that all horses take naturally to being led and tied. They don't. Like everything else, it's a matter of training.

LEADING

Halters

A comfortable and well-fitted halter with a lead rope are basic necessities. Halters come in various materials, colors, and sizes that progress from pony, colt, and cob to standard and extra-large horse. (The cob is for horses with small heads, like

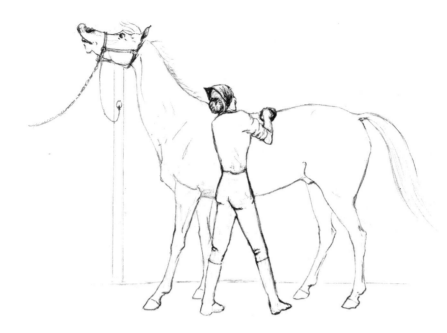

Arabians, or ponies with large ones.) Standard materials are leather, rope, nylon, and polyprohelene, which is softer than nylon. I personally prefer a halter that has buckles on the side and a clip under the chin for easy fastening. Nylon halters that open only on the top are awkward and time-consuming to fasten. Moreover they are dangerous, because they won't break in an emergency. I find it convenient to get a different-color halter and matching lead rope for each horse. Most horse owners will have a nylon halter for everyday use and a leather halter for show, the latter requiring the same care and maintenance as other tack. Also available are halters that resemble the cavesson of a bridle, designed especially for grooming; the lack of straps beneath the jowl makes it easier to clean the horse's head.

A good leather halter with brass fittings and a nameplate or the Western type with contrasting stitching and silver on the browband can cost as much as a bridle. Special halters used to show saddle horses in hand have patent leather designs on the browband and are equally expensive. Nylon halters are less costly and have various colors and patterns, from hearts and flowers to Indian motifs.

If a properly fitted halter still rubs and irritates a thin-skinned horse, Equi-Fleece tubing can be used to pad the cheekpieces, crown, and noseband. This material, which looks like sheepskin, is machine washable. Horses with very sensitive skin may need fleece on their bridles too (but not in the show ring).

Leads

The least expensive leads are made of rope, cotton, and nylon. Try to have several, and make sure that all have easy-to-snap clips. All leather leads cost more, and leather lead shanks (straps with chain) are far pricier still. I recommend lead shanks for small people, those with strong horses who try to lead them, and for young obstreperous animals. To assure firm and humane control of the horse, put the chain of the shank through the near side ring, and wrap it under the front of the noseband. Bring it through the opposite D-ring from inside to outside, then continue the shank up the side of the halter. Clip it to the outside of the ring just below the horse's ear. This applies pressure to the poll as well as to the nose.

Leather halter

Learning to Lead

To lead a horse properly, stand beside his shoulder on the near side, facing forward. Try not to turn and look at your horse as you walk, which might confuse him and cause him to stop. Stand far enough from his side that your lower arm is almost straight as you walk, allowing you both room to move ahead. Walking in front of a horse is a good way to get stepped on. Normally he'll do everything he can to avoid you, but he can't help it if you're directly in his path.

Remember to stay by his shoulder as you both walk forward. Walking ahead and pulling on the lead will cause him to draw back and refuse. If you do this often, your horse will become balky and impossible to lead. As you walk, hold the lead rope in your right hand about four to six inches beneath the snap; the remainder

Lead shank for control

The incorrect way to
lead a horse

should be gathered in your left hand so that neither of you will trip over it. Never wrap a lead around your hand.

In 4-H fitting and showmanship classes, entrants are judged by the way they lead their horses. When leading, your right leg should move forward simultaneously with the horse's near forefoot. If done the other way around, chances are good that his front foot will step on your toes. Never lead by the halter alone, which will tug on your horse's head and cause him to pull back, often with sufficient force to break your hold and get away. After doing this a few times, he'll realize that he has the muscular edge. A properly trained horse has been taught from early youth never to lean on a rope, and consequently he never gets to know his own strength. Horses that pull or drag you along get a failing grade in Leading 101 and will need a refresher course. The best spot for this is an enclosed area such as a paddock or riding ring. The horse should move when you move forward at his shoulder, stop when you do without having to be jerked or pulled, and stay in his own space, not barging into yours as you walk along.

If a horse has a problem going forward, a long whip like a dressage or driving whip can be used to move him along from behind. Hold the lead rope in the right hand and the slack in the left, along with the whip, which is pointed back toward the horse's hind legs. If the pace is a slow, normal walk, the command is a firm "walk." To get the pace to increase, say "walk on," and tap the horse gently on the hindquarters with the whip end, continuing to face forward as you do so.

If you will be doing some showing in hand, such as model or fitting and showmanship, you will need to add the trot to this training in exactly the same manner. Use the same procedure to teach the horse to trot in hand. While carrying the whip in your left hand for encouragement, begin by using the verbal command "trot."

Most horses that lunge will learn this quickly. If your horse still doesn't want to go forward, have another person walk a safe distance behind with the whip to give added incentive. When you want him to return to a walk, say "walk," drawing the word out, and give a little half-halt-like tug on the lead; at the same time bring the whip horizontally across his chest.

The ultimate goal is to keep the horse right by your shoulder the entire time, even during the transitions. Most horses will learn to do this easily. Besides being essential for model, breeding, and showmanship classes and for jogging out when they pin a hunter class, it's helpful to the veterinarian and farrier—a basic part of any horse's education.

To stop, say "whoa," and keep facing ahead. The goal is to have your horse keep pace with you as you move forward and to stop when you do without being hauled up short or dragging you. As he learns to do this, stop the voice commands and reward correct performance with praise, pats on the neck, and a treat if you're so inclined.

If stopping is a problem, or if the horse wants to lead *you* around, use a chain shank in company with a long whip. Carry the whip at your left side, holding it in the middle so you can bring it up and hold it horizontally across the horse's chest. Proceed until he pulls the lead taut, then stop and give a sharp "whoa" command, and at the same time give a sharp pull on the lead and place the whip horizontally across his chest. (The whip is not to strike him with but to block him.) Remember to stop him with a short jerk as soon as he begins to pull, then *immediately release the pressure.* Wait ten seconds or so, then resume walking (and gradually increase the standing time).

Because you'll spend more time leading than riding, undergoing this training is well worth the effort. Be sure to work with your horse on both sides. There are numerous situations in which leading from the off side is necessary—for instance, on the trail or loading onto a trailer. Set aside a special time for training on the lead, and be sure it takes place in an enclosed area where there are few distractions.

Excellent videos available by Linda Tellington Jones can be a big help. A special training technique she developed called TTEAM (yes, two T's) has received international recognition. You can purchase her books and videos at tack shops, through catalogs, and by direct mail. They deal with the handling of trained and problem horses on the ground, emphasizing a hands-on touch technique to relax the horse and gain his attention and trust.

Never pull against a horse; instead, behave like an immovable object, by not allowing him to move forward. Don't ever yank him around, or he'll respond the same way he does to heavy hands on his

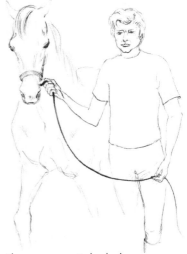

The proper way to lead a horse

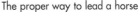

mouth—by ignoring or fighting you. Any amount of time spent correcting a lead-ing problem is time well spent and can save many hours of aggravation. To prevent bad habits from developing, stick with it.

I used to exercise a neurotic filly who had a number of phobias, among them a fear of being led. Taking her out of the barn was a hassle because the door was too narrow to accommodate both of us, so to avoid being crushed against the jamb, I had to walk in front. Whenever I made the move forward, she would freeze in her tracks, nearly pulling my arm out of the socket. This impasse was finally resolved by giving the lead rope plenty of slack—and it was helped along when a cooperative stablemate in a box stall by the door poked his head over the gate and bit her on the rump.

When you are leading your horse though a narrow opening, walk ahead, giving him a little slack rope, and keep the same pace. Don't pull the rope taut, or he'll stop and throw his head up. A lot of loading problems start when a rope is pulled too tight on the way into the trailer or van.

If your horse flunks this schooling lesson, life in the stable will be difficult, to say the least. One summer I boarded a mammoth 16-hand horse that weighed at least fifteen hundred pounds. In the working ring he appeared to be a real sweetheart, but I learned differently after his schooling session, when I led him into the stable. As we approached the stall door, I applied the customary restraint, but my boarder didn't get the message. He kept right on going, dragging me the entire length of the stable and stopping only when his nose touched the far wall. There we stood until I put the lead shank around his nose and got him in hand, and we began our first serious lesson in Leading 101. That's what can happen when a young horse discov-ers his strength and that he can lead a human around.

TYING

Just as you can't assume a horse knows how to be led, you can't assume he knows how to be tied. Never tie a horse by the bridle rein to a fence or hitching post—that's a sure way to break one or the other, probably both. So tied, a horse will panic and pull back until something gives, usually the reins. Western horses are usually taught to ground-tie.

If you're planning a trail ride or are in a riding situation where you will want to dismount and tie your horse, take along a lead rope and halter that can be slipped over the bridle.

Some English horses will tie only with a halter, while others won't tolerate any-thing but cross-ties. But no horse should ever be tied by the neck. Some Western horses neck-tie with a special knot called a bowline that won't slip no matter how hard he pulls, but an English horse tied this way would probably panic. A friend who rides Western once innocently neck-tied one of my horses. He pulled back hard enough to strangle himself, had we not cut the rope. (See Appendix E.)

When you are tying the end of the lead around a post or on a ring, be sure to make a slipknot, which can be easily pulled loose in an emergency. Leave about two feet of rope—enough for your horse to move his head but not enough to catch his legs. (See Appendix E.)

Even a horse that has been trained to tie can become a problem if you're sloppy about it. Rope that is too old or tied too loosely will encourage the horse to fool around and possibly break the lead. Once this happens a few times, he'll get the idea and become a chronic rope breaker.

Never tie a horse to a potentially movable object—like a wheelbarrow or mailbox—anything that can be pulled from its moorings. If the horse should start pulling, the bouncing object will frighten him into running in an effort to escape it. And the faster he goes, the more panicked he'll become.

Tie horses only to solid fence posts, never to boards or rails. And make sure the tie is of proper length, with a slip-knot for easy removal.

Never tie a horse with either a nylon or a leather lead, which can knot and not release. Use only a rope lead for tying.

Never tie a horse with a chain shank around his nose. It could cause him to pull back and injure the bridge of his nose. Use the shank for leading only, carrying a rope lead with you for tying.

For grooming, you'll need a convenient, light, roomy spot that offers easy access to your tools. The classic arrangement is to set up cross-ties in an aisle or a wash stall. Don't assume that every horse cross-ties—something that should be checked out before buying. If you're not sure how your horse will react to cross-ties, fasten the ends to the wall with baling twine that will break easily if he pulls; that way, if he does pull back, he won't hurt himself or you or break the halter or wall.

Often the only place to cross-tie is the stable aisle. Select a spot that isn't a major thoroughfare and that is free of hay bales, tack trunks, and cleaning equipment. Safety is the first order of business when you set up the ties. They must be higher than the horse's head, making it easy to unclip the snaps that attach to the muzzle rings on each side of the halter. The clips should be large and easy to release in a hurry without pinching your hand.

The ties can be heavy rope, nylon straps, or rubber. Some people prefer rubber ties, which give when a horse pulls back. These are sold in all tack shops as a pair, with proper safety snaps for wall and halter. Cross-ties should be attached to a ring tightly screwed into a wall stud. (Make sure you find the stud, or the horse could take a piece of the wall with him if he pulls back.) A heavy-duty safety clip should

CROSS-TIES

Cross-tied in an aisleway

be attached to the ring. In the case of a horse you can't trust with standard cross-ties, attach each one to the wall ring with a loop of baling twine. The twine will break quickly if the horse pulls back, saving the wall, cross-ties, halter, and even the horse from possible damage.

Some obstinate horses refuse to be cross-tied. One of them boards in my barn right now, a neurotic mare who was so traumatized by something in her past that she has to be held while being shod. She will stand only if a rope is loosely slid through one ring, but not secured. Another resident character is so high strung about cross-ties that he will sit back on his haunches suddenly if he is startled or upset. Out of cross-ties, he's no problem.

HANDLING YOUR HORSE

To groom a horse properly, you have to be able to work comfortably with him in close quarters. He should respond to your voice and be easy to halter, tie, and lead, moving over with a touch of the hand.

Whisper Sweet Nothings

Assuming that your new horse got good marks for grooming on the prepurchase checklist, he may still be a little nervous in new surroundings. When you enter his stall for the first time, keep your hands at your sides and speak in a reassuring, soothing voice. One young pupil of mine, not given to casual conversation, walked into his new horse's stall and announced: "How do you do. My name is Brian and my father owns a bakery. We live on Cherry Hill Drive." The horse turned toward him, ears forward, in a friendly manner. (Since the equine vocabulary is limited, it's not what you say but how you say it that counts.)

The tone of your voice and the way you move speak to equine confidence. A relaxed, self-assured horse will usually react, as Brian's did, by turning toward you with ears pricked forward. Others may walk right over when you approach the stall. When working around a horse, it's best to speak calmly and to always let the horse know where you are, talking and touching to keep him relaxed and attentive.

When you want your horse to move over in the stall or in cross-ties, put your hand against his shoulder or rump and firmly say "over." If you want him to back up, stand in front of him with one hand against his chest and the other on the bridge of his nose and say "back." When you walk behind him, keep your hand on his rump to let him know where you are, and pass close to him. That way he'll lack the leverage to hurt you if he gets startled and kicks out. If he does, the worst that can happen is a bump from a hock.

If your horse seems nervous as you work next to him, speak his name in a friendly voice and say "easy or "steady." Any well-mannered horse should respond to these simple word commands, and with patience and daily repetition, yours will too. Sometimes a little quiet music will do the trick.

As you approach a horse from the front, walk slowly and calmly. If you appear nervous, jumpy, or frightened, the mood will be conveyed to your horse, who may respond in kind. Always stay as calm as possible.

When walking up behind a horse in a straight stall, remember that his rear vision is limited. When he is facing straight ahead, he can't see all the way back. Although their rear vision is greater than ours, horses have a blind spot behind. So it's essential to speak as you come up from behind, to let him know you're there, then come up close and give a light pat on the rump.

A nine-year-old student of mine, who thought talking to a horse behind his back was silly, walked unannounced into the stall of the most docile, child-loving horse I own and got kicked in the stomach for her oversight. The mare was probably dozing at the time and became so startled that she acted reflexively, lashing out with a hind hoof in self-defense and knocking the girl to the floor. I don't know who was more shaken by the experience—the horse was as surprised as the student—but it was a dangerous way to learn a simple lesson.

I've stressed tying, leading, and general handling because of their basic importance, particularly for those who live in relatively isolated rural areas or have no help. It's no fun to spend half the day getting your horse into or out of his stable. Most horses are reasonable and enjoy human company, responding with obedience and affection when correctly handled.

A GROOMING GUIDE

Every horse should be thoroughly groomed before riding, and those on a regular work program should be groomed every day whether they are ridden or not. A horse is usually groomed thoroughly before working and then lightly groomed afterward, but some horse people do it the other way around, figuring that after work a horse's pores are fully open and his circulation has increased. Either way is okay as long as the horse is thoroughly clean before tacking up and his hooves are cleaned out before and after riding.

Grooming is a time-consuming job that requires energy from the arms and back. If you're not tired after grooming a horse, you probably haven't done a very good job. When I finish working on two or three horses, I usually don't feel very much like riding, but grooming is a chore that has to be done.

A word of caution: While your horse may express delight by arching his back as you curry him or by curling his lip into a classic horse laugh as you brush a favorite spot, always be wary of sensitive grooming areas. One Thoroughbred of mine was too thin-skinned to be curried at all. It was easy to tell how she felt about it by the set of her ears, which were pinned flat back on a tossing head, and her glare of displeasure when she spotted the currycomb. All thin-skinned horses should be groomed slowly and gently until you learn how sensitive they are. When the mud is two inches thick, it may be hard to restrain yourself, but your new horse will trust you more if you begin by handling him with care. A top-of-the-line shedding blade or currycomb, when wielded carefully, should do the job. The gentlest and least abrasive is a curry mitt, although it will take a little longer.

Basic Grooming

Stable aisles are lighter and roomier, but in a pinch you can groom your horse in the stall itself by tying him to a ring in his box or cross-tying him there. On nice warm days most horses can be tied to a secure post outside or, preferably, cross-tied in an outside wash area.

Grooming is a dirty job, so if you're wearing riding clothes, be sure to put on a grooming apron (an old smock or large sheet will do). Or you might prefer to put on old clothes and change afterward. A cap or scarf will help keep your hair clean.

Tools can be kept in a shoe bag or box, on a shelf, or on hooks close to the grooming area—someplace easy to get at when needed and where they are quickly replaced when the job is done. If you have no organized spot for your grooming tools, they will tend to get scattered about and eventually be buried under feed or mangled underfoot.

Portable grooming boxes are inexpensive and available at any tack shop or through riding catalogs. The most common resemble an open carpenter's toolbox. Others have hinged lids and come in many handy sizes and colors. Simpler alternatives like shoe bags are cheaper but lack portability and will need their pockets cleaned out regularly.

Necessary Items

- Hoofpick (the most efficient have a small, stiff brush attached)

- Rubber currycomb (or Grooma)

- Rubber curry mitt

- Stiff dandy brush (preferably wood-backed; quill or rice root bristles are best)

- Soft dandy brush

- Body brush

- Stable rubber (usually linen), or cloth toweling (old clean towels work fine)

- Water brush or bathing glove or currycomb with hose attachment

- Shedding blade

- Sweat scraper, or contoured sweat scraper

Optional Items
- Small electric clippers

- Heavy-duty body clippers

- Grooming vacuum cleaner (hand or floor model)

- Mane pulling knife

- Small wash bucket

- Sponges (several large and several small)

- Mane and tail comb, or small mane pulling comb.

- Hoof dressing (moisturizing or sealant, whichever is needed)

- Applicator brush, for hoof dressing

- Fly repellent with spray applicator and mitt or cloth

- Mane braiding kit

- Rubber braidbinders

- Vetrolin, or other body bracer

Vacuum Grooming

A grooming vacuum might seem like a luxury item, but to those who have them, they're indispensable. When bathing is out of season and your horse is shedding buckets of dirty or mud-caked hair, nothing takes the fluff and grime off a thick winter coat like a vacuum. The rubber currycomb and shedding blade attachments for these machines will do the job in half the time while minimizing airborne dust and debris, creating a cleaner environment for you and your horse. The more shedding hair you remove from your horse, the less will end up in your hair and on your clothes or on the saddle and blankets, making it easier on everyone concerned, including the washing machine. But when it comes to putting shine on a coat, nothing can compare to old-fashioned elbow grease, so to keep a coat at its glossiest, use the vacuum only every other day.

Select one that is recommended by owners and/or trainers, powerful enough to do the job, and easily maneuvered. The quieter the better. Some models are power efficient. Both handheld vacuums and floor models come with various grooming tools and weigh anywhere from twelve to eighty pounds. Most are covered by one-year warranties.

Not all horses will be vacuum friendly, so you may have to take some time to acquaint yours with the machine, in much the same way that you will accustom him to clippers. Allow the horse to look at the vacuum when it isn't running. Walk him past it, and let him stop and smell it, even touch it with his nose, before turning it

GROOMING TOOLS

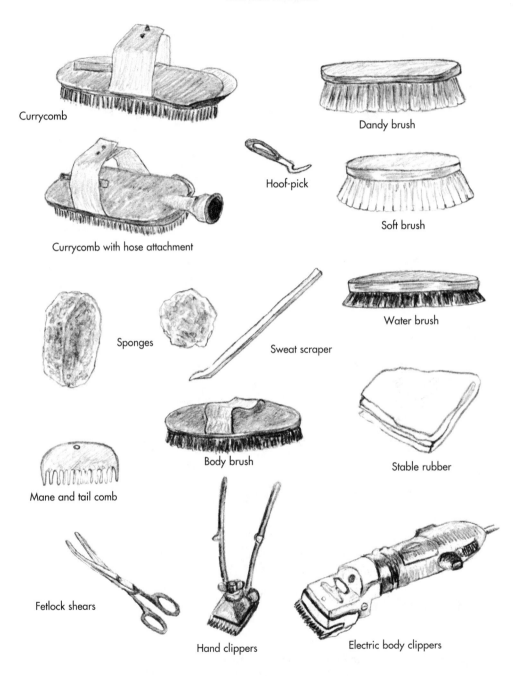

Currycomb

Dandy brush

Hoof-pick

Currycomb with hose attachment

Soft brush

Sponges

Sweat scraper

Water brush

Mane and tail comb

Body brush

Stable rubber

Fetlock shears

Hand clippers

Electric body clippers

on. Don't rush things. When he doesn't seem to mind the presence of the vacuum, groom him first with a familiar type of brush attachment with the motor turned off. When you move to the other side of the horse, roll the vacuum with you or slowly pass the hose over his back. This may take several days, but it's time well spent.

Next, let the horse hear the motor. Stand by his shoulder, holding the halter, when you turn it on. Let him listen for a few minutes, and move the vacuum around so he can get used to the sight and sound of it and the accompanying wires and hoses (that noisy monster with the big snake attached). Then begin grooming gradually, first laying the brush on the horse's shoulder. Don't try to do ribs, back, or head until you feel the horse is really comfortable with the machine. Many horses will adapt in a few sessions.

Be careful of the long cords and hose attached to portable vacuums, which can easily trip you up. Never use a vacuum on a wet horse or to suck water off the floor because of the danger of electric shock.

Take Your Pick

So you don't forget to do it afterward, begin each grooming session by picking out your horse's feet. This is really the most essential part of the process, because anything caught in the hoof will make a horse lame and unridable. I've found all sorts of strange things jammed into hooves—pieces of wire, old chunks of concrete, even a high heel from a woman's shoe. If a horse walked on any of them for any period of time, his foot would be bruised by the constant pressure, making him lame. Because of all the stuff that hooves can accumulate, it's a good policy to pick them out again after riding, especially when you've been on the trail.

To pick out, start with the near forefoot—the left front foot. Facing the back of your horse, lean your shoulder against his, pushing away from you. Then slide your hand down his leg and pick up the hoof. The force of your weight against his shoulder, not your hand, is what makes him raise his hoof.

CLEANING THE FEET

Picking out hoof

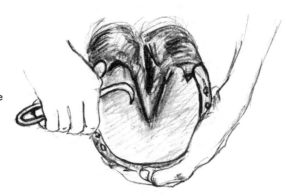

Use the pick going away from you along the side of the frog.

Lift the foot above the height of your knee and support it well with one hand as you pick out with the other. If you are holding the hoof too low, he will be tempted to put his foot down again. Once you have taught him to pick up his feet, you need only to slide a hand down his foot to make him lift it.

Use the pick going away from you along the side of the frog, digging out all manure and other foreign matter until the entire sole becomes visible. Also clean along the cleft of the frog. If the hoof smells bad and you see flaking on the sole, your horse probably has thrush and will need immediate treatment. (See Chapter 20.)

Still facing the rear, move down and do the near hind hoof, with your shoulder against your horse's rump. Leaning against him, run your hand down the leg and pick up the hoof. (You'll find the rear hooves harder work.) Pick the hoof up with your right hand, then reach over and grasp it underneath with your left, supporting it on the left knee as you work. (Be sure to have a comfortable position for yourself, to give the horse secure support as you clean. If he doesn't feel support, he'll try to put his foot down.) Repeat the entire procedure on the off side. Some hoof picks have a brush that allows you to brush out cleft and hoof; they are also handy for cleaning off dried mud before applying hoof dressing.

When grooming your horse for a show, finish the feet by taking a stiff scrub brush and washing the hooves thoroughly, leaving them to dry while you groom the rest of your horse. At the end brush on hoof dressing or black shoe polish if his hooves are dark. (See Chapter 17.)

When this routine is done on a daily basis, some horses become so accustomed to it that they automatically pick up their feet before you touch them.

Hoof Dressing

Hoof dressing can be used once or twice a week, both on the wall of the hoof and on the frog and sole. It not only improves appearance but keeps the hoof flexible, makes the frog more pliable, and keeps the heels from cracking. Before applying anything to the hoof, clean it with a brush and if necessary with water. Allow it to dry before you brush on dressing. Starting at the coronet band, work from top to bottom.

HOW TO PICK UP THE HIND LEG

Step 1

Step 2

Step 3

163

Some dressings can be sprayed on, while others are the consistency of ointment—they can be purchased in quart or gallon sizes. For horses with particularly dry feet, our farrier recommends a daily brushing of corn oil. It conditions the hooves just as well as commercial products. Some of the heavier hoof dressings have the opposite effect if they are used too often, sealing moisture out. (See page 222.) It is best to leave the application of hoof dressing until the end of the grooming process; that way the hooves have time to dry, and dirt and loose hair won't adhere to the dressing.

BODY CLEANING

Sponge Bath

If your horse has large manure or grass stains on his coat, start the grooming session by scrubbing down the area with a big body sponge or a section of a clean towel. Fill the washing pail with warm water. Rub the sponge or towel section with a mild soapy mix to pull the stain up, then apply a clean part of the towel to the spot. Do a little bit of your horse at a time. On light-colored horses it may help to sprinkle the stains with a little bran, which acts as a cleansing agent. Pale horses have a bothersome way of getting grass stains on their coats, which usually just have to be repeatedly worked over with mild soap until they disappear. After rinsing off the sponged areas, let the upper coat dry while you groom the rest. Dry shampoos on the market now are excellent for this purpose. (See page 175.)

Shedding Blade

Your horse will let you know when he starts to shed his winter coat by doing a lot of rolling around in the mud to quell the itching. This is the time to bring out

Applying the two-handled shedding blade

the shedding blade and currycomb, the only tools that can cope with that mud-caked hair.

Shedding blades come in one- and two-handled models. Another type has two handles that convert to one by tucking the other under a strap. Go very easy with this tool on the sensitive underbelly and on the flank, and don't use it on the face or below the knees and hocks. Some horses dislike the shedding blade so much that you may be forced to do the job with only a stiff brush, rubber curry, and a lot of elbow grease.

Currycomb and Mitt

The most efficient and professional way to work with the curry is to hold it in your right hand, with a dandy brush in your left, cleaning it against the brush as you work. Begin at the top of the neck (poll) on the near side and work toward the back, currying in a circular, counterclockwise motion against the hair—literally rubbing it the wrong way. This works dirt to the surface and stimulates circulation.

Work over the muscular parts of the body vigorously, but go lightly over the sensitive places like the flank and belly. A rubber currycomb is more pliable and less likely to irritate than a plastic one. Never use a metal currycomb except as a tool for cleaning the curry or stiff brush during grooming or for shedding out a horse. They are much too harsh for even a thick-skinned horse, and if there are scabs or scars under the coat, the metal teeth could open them up and cause infection. As the curry gets dirty, which will happen dozens of times in the course of a grooming, rub it against the dandy brush, cleaning both at the same time. Do not use the curry on the face (unless you're using a mitt, and then go very gently), the legs below the knee, or the rear belly. Be sure, however, to curry between the front legs and carefully under the girth and along the flanks.

Some horses are ticklish. You'll soon learn if yours is one of them if she squeals, pins back her ears, tosses her head, bares her teeth, or tries to cowkick you. So pay attention! Should the horse try to bite or kick, always punish her quickly with a sharp "no!" Sometimes a hard slap on the rump, neck, or shoulder, depending on where you're standing, will show her that this behavior is not acceptable. Then proceed again in a slower, gentler manner. It depends on the horse. But in the future, respect her wishes (and protect yourself) by being aware of the speed and pressure you are applying. With mares especially (you'll notice I used that gender), act as if you have all day, even if you don't, and remember to converse with her as you groom. It's not what you say but the tone you use.

As you've probably realized by now, or will when spring brings shedding coats and mud, a good currying job takes a lot of time and muscle.

Stiff Dandy Brush

This brush is used to brush mud and dirt from the places you can't curry: hocks, fetlocks, pasterns, and hind legs. It is also for drawing out dirt raised to the body surface by the curry. After brushing dirt and mud from the uncurried areas, begin again at the near poll, and brush with short, snapping strokes, this time going with the hair to get to the skin between hairs and sweep out the dirt. The stiff dandy is also used to brush the roots of mane and tail and to help train the mane over to the off side, but do not use it on the face. As you brush, hold the currycomb in your left hand and clean the dandy against it.

Soft Dandy Brush

This is the next tool to use. I prefer to use two of them, one in each hand, cleaning them against each other as I work. Start out by gently brushing your horse's face and around his ears. Then smooth down the mane and the tail. Starting at the near poll again, do the body with alternate, swift downward strokes to pull out any remaining dust and dirt and really put a gleam on the coat. Use less vigor around the flanks and belly area.

Body Brush

These are sometimes used in lieu of the soft dandies. Some grooms feel that the shorter hairs of the body brush penetrate more easily to remove scurf and bring oil to the surface. It's really a matter of personal choice. I prefer the soft dandies.

Stable Rubber

This is the English term for the linen towels that are used to bring out a high gloss on the coat—the final grooming touch. Follow the brushing with a thorough, energetic wipe with a clean towel or stable rubber, which squeezes the oil out of the glands of the skin, making the coat shine.

Cactus Cloth

If you have one, use a cactus cloth next. Its ancestor is the English *wisp*, a handmade straw grooming tool used as a massage to harden muscles, stimulate skin, put extra polish on a horse's coat, and condition muscles at the same time. It's also helpful for rubbing a horse down after using the sweat scraper. Some equestrians still fashion homemade wisps from straw, but cactus cloths are just as good.

The cactus cloth should be dampened and applied with a lot of pressure, followed by a long, sweeping motion—a procedure called *banging* or *strapping*. Like its cousin the wisp, it is applied in a rhythmic manner that causes the horse to contract and relax his muscles in sync with the pressure and sweep. It should be applied gently at first, using only a dozen strokes; then gradually increase the downward pressure and number of strokes.

Not all horses are candidates for the cactus cloth, but for those who enjoy it, you can build the strokes up to thirty per grooming, putting your entire body weight into the banging. This will actually build muscle on a horse that is flabby—and will develop yours too.

Small Sponges

Some people prefer to use these first in a grooming. I think it's better to use them last to pick up any dust that may have settled on the soft parts of your horse. Use one sponge to gently wipe debris away from his eyes and nostrils. (You can also use a damp, clean towel or disposable cotton balls here.) This area is especially important to keep clean in the summer, when the secretions around equine eyes and noses attract flies. Not only are flies annoying to the horse, they are a source of parasitic infection.

With the other sponge, clean the dock area beneath the tail. When cleaning a gelding, be sure to periodically wash the sheath and penis. If not done regularly, urine and scale will accumulate, causing swelling and soreness, in extreme cases blocking the urinary tract. When the genital area is cleansed carefully with warm water and mild or antibacterial soap, most horses won't object. (If you're not comfortable about doing this, ask your veterinarian or another knowledgeable horse person to show you.) Some special products have been designed to clean this area.

REPELLENTS

Tracking Ticks

Ticks, particularly the deer ticks that carry Lyme disease, are a serious problem in many areas. If you live in one of them, watching out for these parasites will become part of your regular grooming routine, and your grooming kit should include a small jar or can of alcohol, cotton swabs, tweezers, and some rubber gloves. Be diligent in your search. Along with Lyme disease, ticks can carry other diseases that are infectious to humans as well as horses—which is why it's important to wear gloves and disinfect the area where the tick was attached. Wash your hands thoroughly afterward.

Ticks can be found almost anywhere on the body, including the legs, belly, chest, dock, or crest of the mane. When you find one, put on the gloves, pick off the entire tick with tweezers, put it in the jar of alcohol, dab the bitten area with alcohol, and search for more. If the head breaks off, you will have to dig for the rest of the tick. To prevent infection, make sure you get it all.

If your horse is frequently infested with ticks, be sure to have him tested for Lyme disease once a year. You can put a repellent spray on your horse before going out on the trail.

Foiling Flies

During the fly season, finish up the grooming by wiping or spraying on (if your horse will tolerate sprays) a fly repellent, being careful never to spray around the face. I like to keep sprays handy in different places like the grooming area, the pasture gate, and the riding ring, ready for a quick once-over. A lot of repellent can get wasted when using sprays. Children often get carried away and end up spraying everything but the horse. Sprays are convenient and efficient when used correctly (and the bottles can be rinsed out and saved for reuse with diluted concentrates.) A repellent-soaked rag kept in a plastic bag or covered coffee can in the tack room is handy for head areas. Just make sure, when you use a rag or mitt, not to get any of the chemical in the horse's eyes. Special fly-stick applicators can be used on face areas.

Some repellents are diluted with water, and you can prepare them in various strengths to suit the sensitivity of your horse's skin; others, which are oil-based, can be applied directly from the can. An application of undiluted concentrate could cause serious skin problems, so make sure you know what kind you have, and read the directions carefully. Repellents can often be found on sale during the off-season. By all means buy the largest size—it's more economical in the long run.

If your horse is particularly sensitive to flies, tossing his head and generally unable to pay attention to the work at hand, a *fly bonnet* for his ears may be just the thing, especially the type with strings that hang down; they act as an additional forelock and reinforce the natural protection it offers to eyes and ears. A variety of fly masks and bonnets designed for turnout are sold at tack shops—welcome innovations to improve the summer comfort level. (See page 433 for more about fly control wear.)

Flies seem to become immune to some sprays after a few months, so it's a good idea to switch brands midway through the summer. Always try a new type out on a small area of the horse's body first to make sure he isn't allergic to it. If he is, it would cause him to break out in hives.

Many of my clients have had luck mixing their own fly sprays, using natural products like vinegar, which is believed to change the composition of a horse's sweat. While these environmentally correct potions seem to work pretty well, the horses sprayed with them smell to me like salads! Then of course there is the old-time remedy of feeding the horse a vinegar solution (one part vinegar to two parts water), to make his body unappetizing to flies.

Shaving Off Botfly Eggs

In the summer this is an absolutely essential part of every grooming job. Bots are a seasonal plague that can seriously debilitate a horse. They lay one egg on each hair; an accumulation of them looks rather like pollen. The best method of control is a good worming program. (See Chapter 21.) But you can make a considerable dent in the bot population during your regular grooming session. Using a botfly knife or razor (a single- or double-edged holder with blade) dipped in kerosene (to kill eggs), shave off the areas where the new eggs are deposited every day. It's very important to keep up with this. Left to their own devices, bots can be lethal.

c h a p t e r

13

Bathing, Sponging, and Dry Shampoos

**SPONGING
DOWN**

The method and degree of sponging will vary with the temperature. On a mild fall or spring day when you come in from a ride, just sponge off the areas that are sweaty or wet—under the saddle and girth, between the front and back legs, and possibly on the chest and areas of the neck. The water should be clean and lukewarm. Scrape off excess water with the sweat scraper, and rub dry with a towel. If the coat is still damp, throw on an *antisweat sheet,* to be worn in the stall until the coat dries. A lightweight *stable sheet* with clumps of hay or straw underneath to allow air to circulate is just as effective.

Cool Weather

When the weather is cool, place a *wool cooler* over your horse to prevent a rapid loss of body heat. Most of my clients like to take this opportunity to spend quality time with their horses, hand grazing them as they dry. Once dry, the coat should be brushed out so it fluffs up to keep him warm.

Warm Weather

When the weather is warm, bring the water up to body temperature, and sponge it on lavishly. The hotter and more humid it gets, the cooler the water. Many horses enjoy being hosed down, which is really helpful in extreme heat. Heatstroke is a danger when temperatures soar into the nineties, with humidity to match. Running a cold hose behind a horse's elbow, behind the ear, and on the chest helps, but the best way to bring body temperature down is to hose the large muscle masses, doing one side at a time, and scrape off immediately so the water doesn't reheat from the horse's body temperature.

After sloshing water all over his body (making sure to include the belly between the front and hind legs and the dock), use a smaller, dampened sponge to do the head. Be particularly careful not to get any water in the eyes and ears, to which many horses object. Wipe the nostrils, around the mouth, under the jaw, and any place where the tack came in contact. If the horse takes exception even to the small sponge, gently use a damp towel. Now remove all the excess water from the body, using the sweat scraper on all the large, muscular contours. (I prefer the squeegee type.) Finish off by drying the head with a clean towel.

When a horse is overheated and blowing from extremely hard or fast work, his breath and body temperature should return to nearly normal before you sponge him. Loosen the girth first, and keep the horse moving to avoid tying up or founder. On cool or windy days, throw a sheet or cooler over him and allow the horse to cool down slowly at a walk, but not to stand. Only when he has his breath back and body temperature feels normal should you untack and begin to sponge.

When you're sponging in normal summer weather and don't have access to warm water, put a few buckets of clean water in a sunny spot early in the morning. (This is also a good trick to remember at a show or other type of competition.) Before sponging, add a capful of a body brace like Vetrolin, which cools and soothes tired, sore muscles and smells great besides, to each bucket of water.

Endurance riders have found that putting a little salt in the horse's sponging water toughens sensitive areas of his skin. Numerous body braces and washes will cool, invigorate, stimulate, or soothe stiff, sore muscles when you add a small amount to the sponge water after a workout.

Unlike shampooing, sponging down with clean water after exercise won't dull the coat. It will keep the skin clean and in good condition, promote circulation under the saddle area, and keep the coat shiny by removing the salt. Dried sweat and salt left in the coat attracts flies and will make a horse want to rub and scratch himself. When exposed to strong sunlight, sweat-stained areas will become sun-bleached. So it really pays to do a thorough job of sponging.

Many horses don't care for dripping water around their ears and eyes, in which case you can substitute a wet towel for a sponge. In summertime some horses will not only tolerate but enjoy being hosed down, a particular treat in very hot, humid weather—and fun for you too. Some will even drink from the running hose.

After the sponge bath lead your horse around awhile to graze until he dries out completely. If you let him out to pasture immediately, the first thing he'll do is roll, leaving you with a double grooming job the next day.

In early spring and late fall, your horse will catch cold if bathed this way. To prevent a chill, rub him down with straw or clean towels and walk him around as he dries, then groom him lightly. When it's cold and your horse is still slightly damp, blanket him and push wads of straw up underneath it to cover his back. Air can then circulate under the damp blanket, creating a thermal layer that will keep him warm.

The other alternative is to use an antisweat sheet that allows air to get under and dry him off. When it is very cold, place a wool cooler over the sheet to keep the horse from drying too quickly. You can also put this antisweat sheet under a regular blanket until the horse is completely dry.

BATHING THE HORSE

Late spring, once the weather warms up enough, is a good time to give your horse a bath to clean away accumulated dirt and scurf. Keep in mind that bathing dulls the coat, temporarily removing the oil, and it can also dry the skin. Glands beneath the skin produce an oily, water-repellent lubricant called *sebum* that brings a shine to the coat as well as inhibiting fungal and bacterial growth. If too much accumulates, the coat will get sticky and attract dirt. If you're planning to show and your horse's color requires a serious bath, bathe him two or three days beforehand, to allow his coat to regain its sheen.

If your horse's skin appears scaly or flaky, a medicated shampoo might be in order. If the condition of the skin is particularly dry or the coat isn't in top condition, supplements or nutritional boosts may be needed. (See Chapter 8.) This should also be discussed with your veterinarian.

The best bathing facility is a well-drained indoor *wash stall* with a textured concrete floor or rubber mats to prevent slipping and, ideally, with shelves where every-thing is at arm's length. Otherwise you can set up an outside wash area with a tex-tured macadam or even crushed-stone floor that will drain and allow your horse to stand on a flat surface. (Of course, you will sometimes be restricted by the weather conditions.) There should be shelter on one or two sides and some way to safely cross-tie the horse and obtain easy access to a hose and warm water. Cold water does not dissolve oil and dirt. If hot tap water isn't available, a few hours beforehand, fill three or four buckets with water and place them in a sunny spot to warm them up. If the sun isn't warm enough outside to do this, it is not warm enough for a bath outdoors.

Have the following items assembled and handy: Your favorite *sweat scraper* (mine looks like a squeegee and has rubber on one end that slides easily over the contours of the horse's body), your *shampoo* of choice, a *rubber curry mitt or currycomb, large, medium,* and *small sponges, towels,* and a *water brush. Three to five buckets of warm water* should stand ready to use. (Rinsing uses lots.) Oh, and be sure to dress for the occasion—your horse will not be the only one getting wet! Old clothes and Wellingtons are a good choice.

In order for the shampoo to reach the skin and do a proper job, thoroughly *groom the horse before bathing him.* Remove as much body hair as you can with the rubber currycomb, and use the mitt for the face, flank, and legs. (Most horses enjoy this.) Do any clipping from fetlocks, throat, under the jaw, and bridle path beforehand. Choose either a mild nondetergent or, if needed, a medicated shampoo from the many that are available at tack shops. Spring is an ideal time to use a medicated shampoo; those that contain iodine will help clear up itchy fungal and bacterial skin conditions that make a horse rub.

Some equine shampoos and conditioners contain proteins, oils, and other sub-stances—like collagen, coconut oil or lanolin, and aloe vera—to condition the rough surfaces of every hair shaft on the coat so that it lies smoothly against the next. Some shampoos are formulated for light or gray horses, containing a bluing agent that dissolves yellow urine and leather stains and brings the coat back a shade closer to white. Recycled spray bottles are good containers for diluted shampoo, allowing you to direct it exactly where you want it. Or you can make a bucket of soapy water and begin.

Some people begin by getting the legs wet first. I usually start with the mane and tail, so the horse won't be chilled by the end of the bath. Make sure to get into the roots of the mane and tail, to get to the source of the dirt. You may need the brush here, but use it carefully so you don't pull out hair. If your horse is light colored and his tail is discolored from manure stains, start there and allow the soap to stay on the tail for five or ten minutes while you work on the rest of the horse. You can dunk the body of the tail into a bucket and rub shampoo in by hand. For really dark grass stains, rub in old-fashioned brown soap, and allow it to stay on for fifteen minutes or so before rinsing.

Using the large sponge, start near the top of the horse's neck on the near side just as you would for grooming. Sponge on the soapy water, and curry it into a lather as you go. It's a good idea to mentally divide the horse into sections, soaping and rinsing one at a time. Otherwise the soaped area will start to dry while you're working on the offside. If you are using the spray bottle technique instead of a pail of soapy water, wet the areas of the body first with the large sponge, apply shampoo, and scrub until the coat is thoroughly saturated. Then scrub and scrub some more. (By now your horse should be really enjoying this.) Rinse over and over until the water is completely clear. For bathing the body, you may find it helpful to use a currycomb with a water attachment. If your horse seems shy about it, use it around him for a few days before the big bath until he becomes accustomed to it. This attachment will save a lot of rinsing time.

Use a smaller sponge for the head, being very careful not to get soap in the horse's eyes, ears, and nostrils. If the small sponge makes your horse nervous around the eyes, ears, and nose, use a damp towel. You can use earplugs if he is especially sensitive to dripping water around the ears. (Earplugs are also useful to screen out the noise of clipping.) Make sure to clean behind the ears—the repository for all that mud he's been rolling in. Go slowly on the head, and again, be sure to rinse thoroughly. Finish up by scrubbing and rinsing the legs and hooves. When you're through, the coat should be squeaky clean. When both the weather and the water are warm enough, it's easiest to rinse with a hose. When the entire bath is finished, rinse him down all over again, then scrape off the excess water with a sweat scraper.

If you choose, now is the time to use a *rinse solution* over the entire body (but not the head). I use liniment and Calgon (the water softener, not to be confused with calgonite), which is also handy for sponging away bridle or saddle marks after work and for quick rinses of the mane and tail. One teaspoon per gallon is adequate unless the water is very hard, when you'll need two. A capful of liniment per gallon helps blood circulation under the skin surface, acting like a skin brace. Don't use a conditioner or creme rinses on the mane or tail if you are planning to braid.

Rinse again until the water is clear, then take off the excess water with a sweat scraper and apply a *conditioning rinse* the same way. Again make sure to remove all conditioned rinse water with the scraper. Some conditioners will help prevent a long mane from getting tangled. If the mane and tail need a little moisturizing, a light coat of baby oil will do the job. Dry the legs and hooves thoroughly with towels to discourage scratches, chapped heels, and hoof deterioration. Apply hoof dressing or sealant, whichever is needed. (See Chapter 17.)

For a dazzling coat, you can now apply a *finisher*. Most finishers contain silicone and give hair a sparkling shine that lasts up to a week and repels stains and moisture. But silicone creates a slippery surface, so stay clear of the saddle area. Some finishers contain sunscreen to keep coats from bleaching out.

Silicone coat sprays will help return that shine to the coat and mane and tail, but they also make a coat and mane and tail slick, so beware! A talented young pupil of mine got completely carried away with one of these products before showing her pony in a halter class. She won that class, but in the bareback competition, where she'd previously been undefeated, she slipped and slid all over the pony's back, breaking her winning streak.

How often should you wash your horse? It really depends on his color and how clean he keeps himself. Some horses are naturally sloppy and seem always to have grass and manure stains on their coats. Spot baths can take care of this. For the average riding horse, two or three full baths a year are usually plenty.

A bath will take a few hours. Be sure that you give your grooming tools a good scrubbing too. You wouldn't want to groom a clean horse with a dirty curry any more than you would use a soiled brush on your own freshly washed hair. Be sure your horse is thoroughly dry before turning him out, otherwise I can almost guarantee that he'll find the muddiest or dirtiest spot to roll in.

By *hot toweling* with a terry-cloth hand towel, a bucket of too-hot-to-touch water, and rubber gloves, you can get him clean in cold weather. First thoroughly curry your horse's entire body with a rubber curry or vacuum to bring all the dirt to the surface. On the mane and tail, use an old hairbrush to get to the deep-down dirt. Then put a little Vetrolin in your hot water, don your rubber gloves, and dunk the towel, wringing it out well so that it's hot but not wet. Working quickly so that the water doesn't cool, spread the towel on the area you're cleaning first, and allow it to steam for about five seconds until the hair stands on end. Then rub vigorously against the hair for ten to fifteen seconds. Moisten the towel again and move to another spot. It will take seven or eight applications to cover the entire body.

The face and forelock can be done in one application. (Most horses enjoy the facial.) The mane and tail should be done a section at a time. If your towels were hot enough, the coat should be dry by the time you've finished with the tail. Finish by brushing the hair smooth with a soft, clean brush.

Dry shampoos can be used in cold weather or at times when water isn't handy and sweat or manure stains need to be removed—before entering the show ring or on occasions when the horse can't get wet. A number of good products efficiently remove dust, scurf, dry sweat marks, or those difficult green stains. They're particularly good on long, thick winter coats that are in dire need of a cleaning.

Try to avoid dry shampoos with too much oil, which attracts dirt after you clean, or too much soap, which leaves an itchy residue. A few leave the coat slippery, making it difficult to keep a saddle in place. Though nominally dry, most of these products are wet. One exception, called Radiance, is sprinkled on, rubbed in with fingers or rubber curry, then brushed out of the coat with a clean, stiff body brush.

Another type that appeals to me because of its all-natural ingredients and rosewater smell is Cowboy Magic Green Spot Remover, which leaves the coat soft, shiny, and resistant to dirt buildup, seeming to last for days. It's easy to apply by spraying it on a cloth or directly onto the horse, and a little bit goes a long way. It also gets your hands clean after a vigorous grooming or tack cleaning session.

TOO COLD FOR A BATH?

**CATCHING
THE JUDGE'S
EYE**

Years of showing have taught me many lessons about getting ready for the big event and the measures that can be taken to make sure a horse will enter the ring looking glamorous, and to make the owner feel secure in the knowledge that the horse looks his best.

You can bathe a dark horse several days before the show and blanket him at night with a very lightweight cotton sheet to protect him from dirt in the interim. But a light-colored horse is almost impossible to keep clean for more than a day. To show off his beauty at its palest and most pristine, use the finishers (except under the saddle area and mane and tail if braiding). This will simplify spot bathing the morning or afternoon before you take your horse into the ring. To recapture the coat's natural sheen, spray or rub on more silicone coat conditioner while the coat is drying. Along with making the coat shiny and soft, these sprays will repel dirt and make it easier to wipe off stains and grime.

As the former owner of a light Palomino, I assure you that these pale horses can and will get messed up in any number of ways during a night, or even during a few minutes in a stall. But there are a few precautions you can take. After he's had his bath and has been sprayed with a silicone product to simplify spot removal, while his mane is still wet, you can braid him. Or leave it until the day of the show, covering him with a hood for the night to keep the mane clean and laid over. Don't leave him alone for a minute until he's been covered with a light cotton sheet and a hood and had his tail wrapped and turned up like a mud knot, with a cotton sock over that and *another* bandage on top for sure protection.

If a single hair is left exposed, you're sure to find it stained with manure when you arrive, dressed to the nines, ready to lead him out of the stall. I once put my horse back in the stall in the morning after his final grooming while I made a quick phone call. Five minutes later I returned to find him lying down, his cotton sheet scrunched up beneath him, with manure stains all over his rump—another good reason to keep stalls picked up at all times.

Even when you take all these precautions, schedule a half hour before loading your horse to do patch cleaning jobs. In really desperate cases, when you're on a tight schedule and have to braid that white mane the night before, you can put a lightweight hood over his entire head. Then pick out the stall carefully before going to bed. And pray.

A sheet, a tail bag, and a face hood are the next best thing to putting him in a plastic bag. I usually left my horse's tail in the bag until we reached the show grounds. And I had my helper (anyone with a light-colored horse needs one) carry along a towel for emergency use. After seeing him shrouded in his green hood and blanket, my children dubbed him the Green Hornet.

A horse of any color should have his hooves scrubbed and washed off the night before. In the morning brush or wipe them off again, and pick them out. When the hooves are completely dry, brush on a liquid hoof dressing. They come in black, brown, and clear and are guaranteed to make the dullest hoof shine.

Apply the dressing evenly and carefully to the entire hoof, including the heels.

Make sure all the hooves are dry before you return the horse to his stall, lead him to the yard, or apply leg wraps for traveling. A wet hoof dressing will pick up dust and dirt and stick to bandages, but it's worth the extra trouble because it definitely makes a horse look spiffier.

The night before the show is the time to organize and set out your show grooming kit, along with clean tack, riding clothes, two buckets (one for drinking, one for washing), and a hay net.

If the budget allows, and you do enough showing, it's convenient to keep this separate set of grooming items in a special box:

- Hoof pick

- Currycomb

- Dandy brush

- Two soft brushes or a soft body brush

- Mane and tail comb

- Two sponges (one for body, one for face)

- Three or four all-purpose towels (good for everything from rubbing a horse down to wiping boots and tack)

- Fly repellent and applicator (during fly season)

- Sweat scraper

- Small plastic bottle of shampoo (a must for pale horses)

- Saddle soap and sponge (for quick tack jobs)

- Modified first-aid kit (containing wound dressing and bandages)

- Extra braiding materials (such as elastics, thread, needles, and yarn for last-minute mane and tail repairs)

In the cavalry an inspecting officer would run his white-gloved hand over a horse's coat. In grooming classes at horse shows, the judges do the same but with bare hands. Both gloves and hands better remain clean!

When you think you're through grooming, be sure to check between the horse's front legs, inside the hind, and under the girth area to make sure you've done a thorough job. There's a lot to a horse, and it's easy to overlook some of it.

Because she couldn't see that high, one little girl in my stable management class consistently forgot to groom her pony behind his ears. 4-H and Pony Club fitting and showmanship classes are very thorough about these forgotten areas, always checking behind ears and under the dock and belly. These areas are important because a horse can get bridle sores from a buildup of mud behind the ears and saddle sores from accumulated mud in the girth area.

PASSING MUSTER

Mane and Tail

When a horse is shown, the mane and tail must be coiffed in the style preferred for that particular breed and/or class. Many breeds, among them the Arabian, Morgan, Palomino, Paso Fino, and Peruvian Paso, are shown with a naturally full mane and tail. Most Western horses and those used for hunting, jumping, eventing, and dressage should have a short, neatly pulled mane. A roached mane is preferred on ranch and rodeo horses, polo ponies, and three-gaited American Saddlebreds. All working Western breeds have the mane clipped at the withers and along the bridle path to prevent ropes from getting tangled. In English competition the mane is pulled and braided or worn loose. Whatever the style of mane and tail, all require regular care and periodic pulling, trimming, and brushing to maintain their special look.

CARE OF THE MANE AND TAIL

The mane and tail should be groomed just before you near the end of the grooming procedure; which brush you use will depend on how dirty the mane and tail are. If the mane is covered with mud, it can be brushed out gently with a body brush or a soft hairbrush. When brushing it, make sure to get down to the roots and work methodically down the neck. This may involve flipping the mane over to the wrong side and really getting underneath it, then brushing it back over in layers.

Trying to comb or brush out knots has messed up many a mane. The teeth of a comb or the abrasive bristles of a stiff brush will pull out hair. Instead, *separate the hairs with your fingers,* untangling a few at a time. When you remove all the knots, gently brush the mane with a soft brush. Afterward apply water or hairdresser's gel to make it lie flat.

For most English disciplines the horse's mane is worn on the right side. Western horses' manes are generally worn on the left. So it's wise in your daily grooming

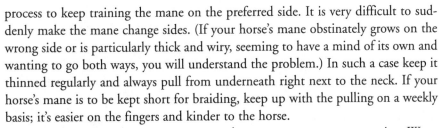

1. Natural full mane and forelock (as seen on an Arab type).

2. Roached mane (worn by three-gaited American Saddlebred).

3. Pulled mane (as seen on hunter type and some Quarter Horses).

process to keep training the mane on the preferred side. It is very difficult to suddenly make the mane change sides. (If your horse's mane obstinately grows on the wrong side or is particularly thick and wiry, seeming to have a mind of its own and wanting to go both ways, you will understand the problem.) In such a case keep it thinned regularly and always pull from underneath right next to the neck. If your horse's mane is to be kept short for braiding, keep up with the pulling on a weekly basis; it's easier on the fingers and kinder to the horse.

To help train a stubborn mane, you may have to resort to some aggression. Water won't do the trick. Part it in even one-to-two-inch segments, and wet the mane. Braid it over to the side on which you want it to stay, and put an elastic at the end, like a pigtail. Leaving these in for a few days usually gets results. (Don't leave them in too long, or your horse will roll and/or rub, and the mane will end up in worse shape than before.) If pigtails don't seem to do the trick the first time, take them out and redo them every few days. Should the mane still refuse to submit, get some *hairdresser's gel* and a *mane tamer* (a kind of equine hairnet, sometimes called a *sleezy*).

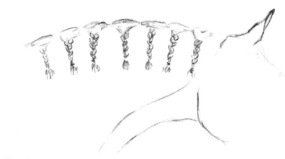

WET AND BRAIDED MANE

"MANE TAMER" OR "SLEEZY"

After finishing the braids described above, cover them with setting gel and put the mane tamer over all. But don't leave the tamer on for long, lest it rub the mane out in spots. It's best used for short periods—for instance, during one or two classes before yours at a show. Setting gel is also good for a long mane, keeping it neat and lying correctly.

Pulling the Mane

Horses never get their manes *cut;* rather, they are *pulled* out by the roots to create a more natural look. This process is used to create the short manes worn by hunters, dressage, event, and most Western mounts. Some horses have thick, bristly manes, while others are thin and stringy. Keeping a mane short and neat requires as much time and attention as maintaining the natural look.

Pulling is done by hand, with the aid of a small metal *pulling comb* or *pulling knife.* The number 10 blade from a body clipper also makes an excellent pulling tool. For a particularly long mane, start with a pair of *thinning shears.* Try to keep up with mane maintenance when you do your daily grooming. Unless the bridle path is clipped regularly, your horse will end up with a mohawk.

When pulling a mane, begin with the longest part, and try to get it all even. You can measure it with a tape. The desired length is four to six inches, depending on the size of the horse. Always work from underneath, so the top hair will fall over and lie flat.

Take a small section of hair, and tease it with your comb (combing backward until it frizzes). Continue until you're down to three or four hairs. Wrap these around your fingers or a little comb, and pull straight up. You're both shortening and thinning at the same time—a tedious process when the mane has been growing all winter. It's also hard on the hands; thin gloves are recommended.

After you have thinned the mane, use the number 10 clipper blade for shortening. Hold the blade with teeth angled slightly downward, and feather it up and down so that the hair is severed at slightly different lengths. You can also use thinning shears for this purpose, particularly when the mane is very long. First run them along about an inch lower than you want the finished mane to end. Then pull the mane by hand to create a natural look on the ends.

Yes!

No!

Most horses are fairly good about having their manes pulled—if you don't overdo it. Taking on a greatly overgrown mane in one session is a sure way to make your horse learn to hate it. Even though a horse has fewer nerve endings at the end of his hair roots than we do, some will toss their heads or pin their ears back as you pull. Using hot towels to soften the mane along the roots seems to help, and at least one authority thinks liniment is the best answer. A minority of very sensitive horses will have to be tranquilized. I find that with these sensitive horses doing a little at a time, rather than waiting until the mane is too far gone, is the best policy.

Though manes are usually kept at a three-and-a-half-to-six-inch length, there is no hard-and-fast rule. A longer mane might look better on a huge warmblood, while a shorter one would be more flattering to a small, dainty pony. When you're doing a lot of showing and the mane needs constant braiding, it's better to be on the short side.

A *roached* mane is easy to clip, but returning one to its former shining glory is the toughest task an equine hairstylist can undertake. As the tightly trimmed hairs begin to grow upward, your horse will sport a "punk" look for quite a few weeks, followed by a long period when the mane sticks up like an upside-down broom. It will take six months to a year before the hairs start to tilt right or left— or both!

Depending on which way you want the mane to go, coax it by starting to pull the underside hairs to the left or right as soon as there is enough mane to make small braids. Then wet the hair, apply setting gel, braid tightly, and secure the braids with elastic bands. Let them dangle until you undo them and repeat the process a few days later. Give the same treatment to a short mane that is undecided about which direction to take.

The *forelock,* a natural shield for eyes and ears, should be left pretty much as it is. One that is too full may need a little gentle pulling, and a very wide one can be clipped very carefully on either side. A forelock is easily shaped, but it's also one of a horse's most charming features—so don't get carried away.

Grooming the Tail

The tail should be untangled only by hand in order to keep the hair intact. (A *silicone spray* will help to separate the hairs.) Hold the body of the tail in one hand, and separate it into small sections with your fingers, untangling a few strands at a time. When the body or skirt of the tail is untangled, groom it down to the roots with a hairbrush or body brush, starting at the top and working down. This area must be dirt free if the tail is to stay clean.

BRAIDING

For showing English, hunting, or other special occasions when you want to put that added touch to your turnout, braiding is the answer. In many disciplines it is customary to braid both the mane and the tail; in others the tail is merely pulled and shaped at the top. It is traditional to not braid the tail in dressage, for instance, because braiding causes the horse to tighten his tail, preventing it from swinging freely from its base to emphasize its supple back. It is important to *be familiar with the current approved turnout for your discipline.*

Braiding the Mane

The number of braids in the mane will depend on the length and width of your horse's neck and the thickness of the mane itself. In the English tradition, from whence braiding came, seven to eleven braids were customary, with stallions and geldings having an odd number and mares an even number. In the United States twenty-five to thirty braids is the average number, and nobody really counts.

An elegant neck with an attractive head is set off by a good braiding job. A large number of narrow braids can extend the line of a short horse's neck, while a larger neck will be set off by fewer, slightly thicker braids.

Before beginning the mane, make sure it is clean right down to the roots, pulled to three and a half to four inches in length, and even in length and thickness all the way down the neck. (See page 180.) A thin mane is better short; otherwise, the braids will look skinny. Conversely, a thick mane will look better if it is a little longer.

Do not combine braiding with pulling. A horse that dislikes having his mane pulled will confuse the two and end up not standing for braiding—a real nuisance! Put the horse in a quiet, well-lit place. Have braiding tools at hand. Ideal for this is a carpenter's apron or something similar, so that everything is in easy reach and won't get knocked over. You can buy a mane-braiding kit or make do easily with household items.

Braiding Items

1. A mane and tail comb, and a human hairbrush (with bristles).
2. A *pull-through:* that is, a large blunt needle, like a crochet needle, a rug hook, or a ready-made one (available in tack shops). You can make one yourself from bailing wire or a hanger. Shape it into a large needle with the wire end down; cover the sharp ends with vinyl tape. Thread the eye with yarn.
3. A long hair clip or two (for holding back the next piece of mane).
4. Blunt-end scissors (if you're using yarn or finishing with tape).
5. Yarn, elastics, and/or adhesive tape, depending on what you decide to use. The color should be as close to your horse's mane color as possible The tape is usually white except for special situations (see continental braid, page 187).
6. Something solid and flat to stand on.
7. Water in a small bucket, and a small sponge.

Braiding (manes) is often made easier by using the little bandettes that tack stores carry in a variety of horse colors.

How to Braid

BEFORE BRAIDING. If you're using yarn, cut it into two-to-two-and-a-half-foot lengths, depending on the texture of your horse's mane. A thick wiry mane holds better if the yarn is added in close to the beginning of the braid; thus you will need a longer piece.

Saturate the mane with water before you begin. (By no means use a silicone spray; it will be too slippery.) Have water and a small sponge handy to keep dampening the mane as you go; it will help keeps things tight.

BRAIDING MANE

Step 1

Step 2

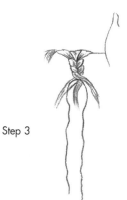

Step 3

Step 7

STEP 1. Measure off a one- or two-inch section of mane, clipping the end of the rest out of your way with the long hair clip.

STEP 2. Divide this section into three equal parts with the comb or your fingers. Begin braiding, being aware of starting each braid with the same piece (usually the right, then left, and so on), so each braid is uniform. Braid as tightly as you can, pulling downward to keep the braid tight, straight, and flat.

STEP 3. About halfway down, or closer to the top if the mane is thick and wiry, add yarn folded in half with the fold against the piece to be crossed over next in the braid.

STEP 4. Split the yarn between two sections to help to keep the braid more secure. Braid all the way down until you run out of mane.

STEP 5. Loop the remaining yarn around the braid end, and pull it tight to tie the braid off. If you are using elastics instead of yarn, just *eliminate* adding yarn in step 3 and finish by folding the tiny end over toward you and wrapping it firmly with an elastic.

STEP 6. Leaving the braid in this stage, undo the hair clip from the neighboring mane, and move on to that section, continuing as before, making sure to measure the section so it is the same size as the last and securing off the next piece. When the entire mane is done to step 5, take the pull-through and insert it through the top of the center of the first braid at the crest, loop first. Insert the yarn through the loop of the pull-through in the back of the braid.

STEP 7. Bring it back through, bringing yarn with it. Seat the end of the braid firmly against the back of the braid. If you are using elastics, just fold the braid in half, keeping the narrower end in back, and secure it in place firmly with another elastic, as close to the neck as possible, and include the hidden end. Make sure at this point to press the braid into position so it lies flat on the side of the horse's neck.

STEP 8. If you're using yarn, remove the pull-through and divide the two pieces of the yarn ends. Cross them over in back of the braid, and tie them with a single knot, to keep everything in place. Then bring the two pieces forward, cross them over each other, and tie them again in back. This should be about a half to three-quarters of an inch down the braid.

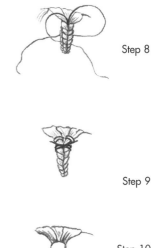

Step 8

STEP 9. Finish with a square knot in front over other yarn, and cut the ends to no less than a quarter of an inch so they don't come loose.

Step 9

STEP 10. For dressage braids, all these steps are the same, with this additional step: Cut a long piece of white tape and wrap it at least one and a half times around the braid, covering the yarn or elastics.

Step 10

You can braid the forelock in the same manner, or use a raised French braid similar to the one on the tail. I prefer the latter, and I like to see the forelock braided when the mane is, but in some disciplines it is not necessary. Braiding (manes) is made easier by using little bandettes that tack stores carry in a variety of horse colors.

Banded Western Mane

Banded Western manes are relatively short and simple. The mane should be thinned and pulled until it is even in thickness and length. Then wet it down and separate it into half-inch segments. Determine the number of banded sections in the mane by the length of the horse's neck and the thickness of the mane. A plastic four-inch-long comb called a *braid aid* is the perfect tool for this job. They come in different widths depending on the size locks you wish. Usually the mane is banded into forty to fifty sections with the two inches of mane at the withers left unbanded. Keeping the mane flat on the neck, dampen it with water or mane spray. Band each section with a small elastic braid binder in a color matching the mane, as close to the root as possible so that the mane lies flat. These can be left in for showing or removed just before the class. Again, be sure to know the correct turnout for the classes you enter.

Andalusian or Viennese Braid (French Braid)

These braids are seen in many old paintings and are thought to have originated with the Lippizans of the Spanish Riding School. Ancient origins and elegant appearance aside, their primary purpose is practical. In this age, when horses are valued as much for their versatility as for breeding, the Andalusian braid pulls the long, flowing manes of Arabians, Morgans, and Andalusians decoratively out of the way

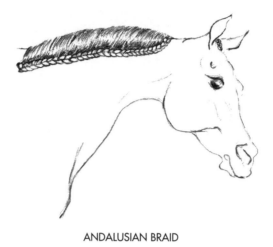

ANDALUSIAN BRAID

for stadium jumping and hunt seat equitation classes. Long tresses are an obvious hazard when hunting or competing in a cross-country event, and they don't have the workmanlike appearance required in hunter equitation classes. In dressage, where grooming is next to godliness, this braid helps long locks look tidy and allow the judge to see the horse's neck.

It is not an easy braid to master. My first attempt fell out in the middle of a dressage class before a particularly distinguished judge. Since then I've learned some tricks the hard way, but because of that experience I recommend you do several practice sessions at home before taking this braid into the ring. Its elegant look makes it definitely worth doing.

Before starting the Andalusian braid, check the mane to make sure it is of an even thickness. A mane that is too thick will be unwieldy, and one of uneven thickness will make the finished braid lumpy.

Begin by brushing the mane out thoroughly, removing all tangles. Then wet the mane down. Don't use Show Sheen or another conditioner on the mane when braiding—it will make the hair too slippery and hard to handle. Once the braid is finished, spray on a conditioner.

Starting at the top, pick up a section of mane an inch wide or a little larger, depending on its thickness. Divide this section into three pieces, then cross the right strand over the middle, followed by the left. Pick up another piece, and add it to the middle strand. Then cross the right section, followed by the left, over the middle again, picking up another piece to add to the center. Continue down the mane in this fashion, always keeping three strands in your hand and pulling them tight as you go along.

Be sure not to get ahead of the piece of hair being braided, or you'll end up with a sag. The finished braid can slant down gradually, starting about an inch from the crest of the neck to five inches near the withers; or in the more current fashion, stay very close (about two inches) to the neck, and keep it even. You can finish off the end with a rubber band or by sewing it up, selecting a color that matches the mane. Using a piece of matching yarn to weave into the braid will give you a tighter braid. The French braid is similar, but it is as short and close to the mane as possible and even all the way along.

Continental Braid

During my Arabian horse period, I became adept at making this type of braid, which resembles a weaving more than a braid. It is particularly attractive on horses with traditionally long manes in a contrasting color to the neck. It's quite simple, requiring only a small mane and tail comb, a lot of elastic braiding bands (preferably matching the color of the mane), and a roll of either matching or contrasting, black or white plastic mending tape a half- to a quarter-inch thick. (Please, no color for dressage classes!)

Part and divide the mane into equal one-inch sections with the small comb. Secure each section with an elastic about an inch below the crest of the neck, and wrap it neatly with the tape. Divide each section in half, banding it to the next until the braid matches the length of the one above it. Again secure each one with elastic and cover with a piece of tape. Now you'll begin to see the pattern. One more split is made and secured as above. The final segment is left hanging but is also wrapped with elastic and tape. The finished work of art is very attractive and enhances the picture of a nice top line in a dressage test.

Braiding the Tail

The tail is braided in the reverse direction of the pigtails people wear. The strands go under

CONTINENTAL BRAID

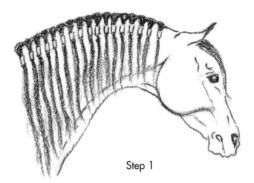

Step 1

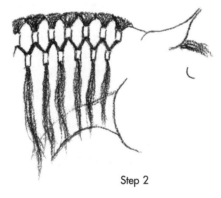

Step 2

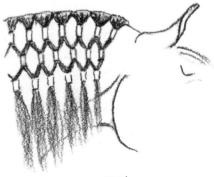

Finish

Starting a braid   Completing a braid

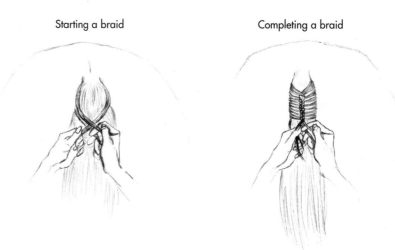

instead of over. Comb three thin strands of hair from the outside of the tail root. Starting at the top, begin your braid. Keep the strands parallel to the ground, and continue down the tail, adding equal-size hair sections as you proceed. Be sure to keep the braid in the center and tight so it won't be crooked or sag. Finish just before the end of the bone (depending on the thickness and the length of the remaining body of tail). When finished, the raised braid is on top of the tail. You'll have a long braid left that can be either tucked under and sewn, or rolled. Sewing looks neater, and when you do it this way, you can put a slipknot at the end so the braid can be easily undone without cutting the tail hairs.

Horses ample in the aft look more refined with longer, smaller tail braids, while small rumps are enhanced by larger, shorter braids.

All mane and tail braids should be as tight as possible. If they are at all loose, they won't hold. After you finish the tail, wet and wrap it with a tail bandage until you get to the show. Always bring mane and tail repair equipment with you.

FULL MANES AND TAILS

The Natural Look

"Natural look" is a misnomer, because nothing is natural about the perfect full manes and flowing tails so admired in show rings. Tails take several years to grow out, and they can be destroyed in only a few hours by burdock, bushes, and rough fencing in the pasture. A tail that is allowed to grow full must be clean, conditioned, wrapped, and maintained regularly. Otherwise you'll find your horse rubbing it against fence posts or trees (which could also be a sign of worms; see Chapter 21) until the ends break off and it sticks out awkwardly on top. When this happens, it's a long wait before the new hair grows out.

Most pleasure horses wear a "natural" mane that belies the back-to-nature look of an animal that has been rolling in the mud or playing "chewy" with a buddy in the pasture. The mane must be kept unsnarled and clean; it must be of fairly equal

Tucked under

Rolled

Short braid for a light horse

Longer braid for a heavy horse

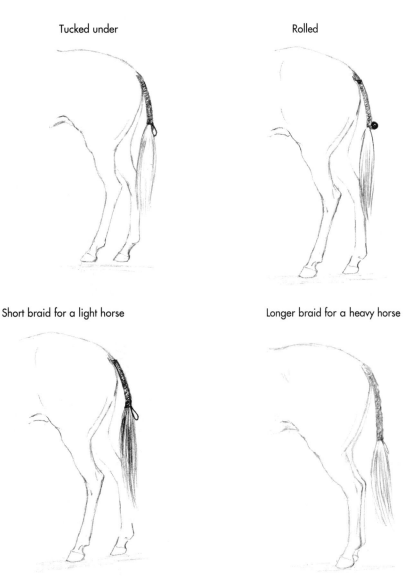

thickness and shaped to follow the curve of the neck from poll to withers, with the longest hairs at the point of the shoulder.

A full mane and a touch-the-ground tail require a great deal of time and effort to maintain. Achieving this elegant look requires systematic shampooing, conditioning, untangling, braiding, and wrapping. The skin on the neck and dock must be kept clean and conditioned, both to maintain the length and texture of the mane and tail and to make sure it's not dry and scaly, tempting the horse to rub them.

Always use a soft brush, and then only at the roots. Combs break hairs and so are never used if you want the mane or tail to stay long. Any *tangles must be undone*

NATURAL VS. NATURAL

with your fingers in small sections of three or four hairs at a time. Depending on the number of snarls, this can take hours if you haven't kept up with it. The job is finally done when dry hairs hang long and free from the neck and tail. (A hair dryer is a big help here if your horse will stand still for it.)

When the weather is too cold for shampooing, take a soft brush, along with a towel or sponge, and work your way along the roots until all the skin is clean—brushing only the skin, not the precious hairs.

A long mane can now be loosely braided to keep it orderly. Work in strips of the same cotton sheeting you'll use to wrap the tail (see below). If the mane tangles easily, divide it into four-inch sections before braiding for easier handling. These mane braids should be left long, not folded under.

Tail Wraps

Once the tail is clean and tangle-free, protect the fruit of your labors with a tail wrap. Rip or cut a piece of flannel or cotton sheeting into strips about two to three inches wide and four feet long. Beginning at the dock, divide the body of the tail into equal sections, and loosely braid them until you get about a fifth of the way down. At that point start to work in the flannel sheeting, beginning in the middle. Bring it around from the back on either side to become part of the braid, covering the hair as you get toward the end.

When you finish braiding, two ends of sheeting will be left dangling. You can end the procedure here by making a slipknot around the bottom of the braid with one

PROTECTIVE TAIL WRAP FOR THE NATURAL LOOK

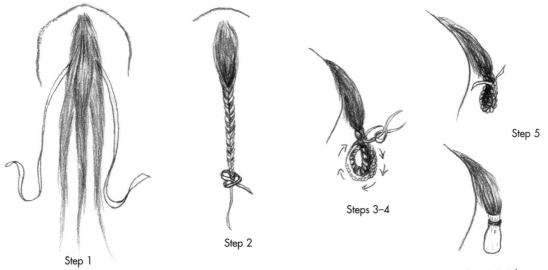

Step 5

Steps 3–4

Step 2

Step 1

Step 6 Finish

end of the sheet and tying the other to it. Fold the tail under by passing the bottom of the braid up and through the looser plait at the top, bringing the two ends of the sheeting around and tying. To make sure the folded tail stays clean, cover it with a cotton sock, secured with Vetwrap and/or self-adhesive tape below the dock.

A wrapped tail can be left up for regular riding and let down at show time. But don't leave it this way for more than ten days, or the hair will start to get brittle and fall out in hunks instead of strands. In a week to ten days the whole tail will need to be unplaited and redone; this time add a little conditioner if the hairs are very dry.

While wrapping protects the tail, it leaves a horse unprotected during fly season. You may want to consider if it's wise to turn out a tail-wrapped horse at all. Certainly don't turn him out if the flies are really heavy; he can be hurt and irritated by the weight of his own bagged tails as he swings it to ward off flies. Some owners get around this problem by dressing the horse in a fly sheet and adding insect strips or extra repellent-soaked cotton strips to the tail bandage.

Tail Bandages

Tail bandages are used when you are shipping a horse, when you want to keep a braided tail neat and tidy before a show, or when you want the top hair to lie flat as you shape the tail. For shipping, an inexpensive Neoprene tail wrap with a Velcro fastener is easy to get on and off. An old-fashioned tail bandage used for the other purposes is made of plain cotton knit. Wrap it around the tail, starting a little above the bottom, and overlap as you move upward. Midway up the tail, take a two-inch piece of hair, and leave it out. Continue wrapping up, taking pieces of hair to the right or left of the first one, until you reach the top of the tail. Then start back down again, folding the hair back and under as you wrap down. When you run out of bandage—usually at about the middle of the tail—secure it with string or Velcro.

Braided tails are wrapped a little differently. Proceed the same way as with the full tail, but do not work in any hair until you reach the top. Then wrap it downward just a few inches, securing it at the end. An Ace bandage can be used as long as it is never pulled tight; it should be unwound, not pulled off.

Tail wraps are also useful when a mare is being bred or prepared for foaling.

Mud Knots

To keep your horse's tail up and out of the way when you're clipping or he's out in muddy weather, braid it into a mud knot. After you brush out the tail, begin at the base of the bone, and braid it as a woman would her hair. Eight inches from the bottom, stop and divide the remaining hair into two sections, or "strings." Then fold the braid in half, below the bone.

TAIL WRAPS

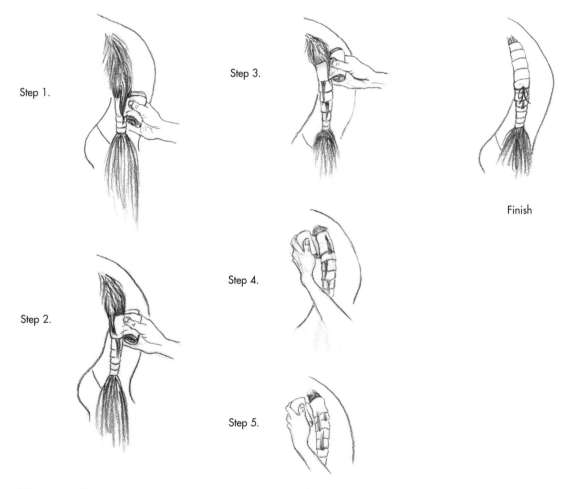

Step 1.

Step 2.

Step 3.

Step 4.

Step 5.

Finish

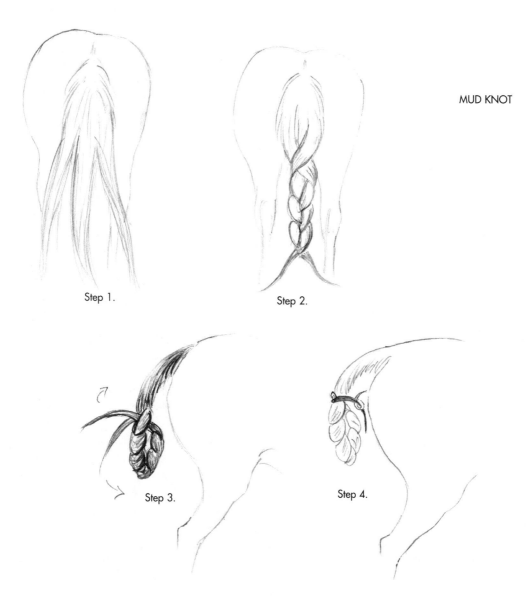

MUD KNOT

Step 1.

Step 2.

Step 3.

Step 4.

Take the two strings behind the tail bone, and push them through the unbraided hair around the bone. Cross over and go back through again to the back, and tie in a single running knot. Then put on an elastic band, tucking the remaining ends anywhere in back where they can be conveniently hidden. In sloppy weather at a hunt or show, this is a good way to save yourself work. It doesn't look as good as a braided tail, but like the trace clip, it's functional.

TYPES OF TAILS

Tapered

Dressage

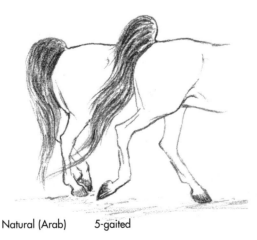

Natural (Arab)   5-gaited

Tapered and Banged Tails

For many classes, including hunters, dressage, and Western sports, the tail style is smooth and slim at the top and tapered or banged (straight) at the bottom. Tapered looks best on a horse with a thin tail, while banged is more becoming for horses with fuller tails and powerful hindquarters. In this country banged tails are cut to the bottom of the fetlock joint, but the English prefer them at hock level.

To make a cut that will stay even when the horse is in motion, the bottom of the tail must be angled. This is easier said than done. You will need a helper to hold the tail up, as a moving horse would carry it.

I recently witnessed the sorry aftermath of a solo effort to bang a tail. The owner put it over her shoulder and cut away—and away—to try and get it "even." Finally it looked like a bottle brush that ended five inches above the hocks. It will take several years of growing to make that tail look respectable again.

Dressage Tails

The tails of dressage horses are customarily pulled at the top to look slimmer and are tapered with the curve and carriage of the tail—a natural, graceful look. These tails are pulled short along the sides (about four and a half to six inches, depending on the animal's size and carriage), beginning at the top and ending at the point where the tail curves over. The bottom of the tail is banged or tapered, depending on its thickness. Thin tails look better tapered.

The shaping of the top of a dressage horse's full tail can add to the grace and beauty of his movement and accent his suppleness. Traditionally the sides of the dock are plucked by hand, often using pliers to grasp the shorter hairs—a tedious job that should be spread out over a two- or three-week period. Some horses won't tolerate it. Clippers are faster and more comfortable for the horse.

Whatever method you use, you must prepare the tail first. After shampooing it thoroughly, use a silicone spray to ease the separating of hairs (as discussed earlier), but not if you are going to pluck or pull by hand. Don't begin untangling until it's completely dry. Once the hairs are separated and hanging straight, run the mane and tail comb through to make sure the entire tail is tangle free.

Before shaving, get the top of the tail to lie flat so you can see what you are doing when you start to clip or pluck. Covering the tail with a damp tail bandage an hour or so before you start helps a great deal; of course, take it off when you're ready to start.

TRIM AND SHAVE FOR DOCK OF DRESSAGE HORSE

STEP 1. The area to be plucked or clipped is triangular in shape. Plan to clip the tail a week to ten days before competition so the new hair has a chance to grow in and lie flat, looking natural rather than bristly.

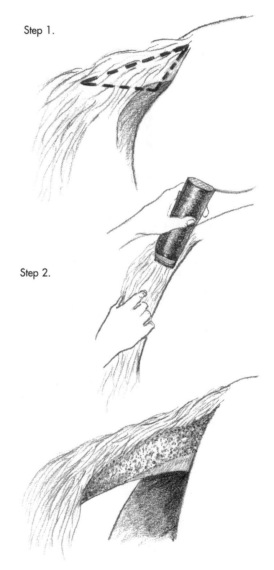

Step 1.

STEP 2. Hold your trimming clippers close to the rump and low on the tail root. Slowly shave in the direction the hair grows along the imaginary triangle; allow some hair at the top of the root of the tail, so it will look more natural when you train it with a tail bandage to cover the shaved section. You may need to pluck some of those untrainable hairs if they don't cooperate.

Step 2.

STEP 3. After brushing away excess hair, apply a mixture of one part baby oil to three parts water to the newly shaved area for a few days. This will discourage tail rubbing as new itchy hair grows in, and it will help hair to stay down. It's also a good time to bang the tail anew or to redo it.

Step 3.

Trimming and Body Clipping

TRIMMING

Most of us take special pride in the appearance of our horses, and trimming is one way to keep them neat and tidy. During the winter a horse needs a heavy coat as protection against mud and snow, while the shaggy "feathers" on the lower leg deflect water from the fetlock. Hairs on the muzzle and the insides of ears and nostrils, which protect against gnats and flies in summer, do double duty in keeping out winter cold and wind. Horses that aren't worked in winter need trimming only on the bridle path, an inch or two behind the poll, for easier haltering.

When showing breeds like the Arabian, Palomino, and Morgan, you can cut back the bridle path as much as seven or eight inches, to show off the head and neck. All horses will need their feathers and whiskers trimmed and the mane cut back two or three inches on the withers. The degree of trimming will depend on where you'll be showing.

In 4-H shows a close ear trim is optional, but I wouldn't opt for it because sensitive equine ears really suffer from flies. For this reason, the Pony Club will mark it against you if you shave the insides of ears. The only place ear shaving is mandatory is in a model class, where you'll be marked down for not doing it, and then you leave a triangle of hair to accent the tip of each ear.

The Pony Club will also give bad marks for clipped feelers and muzzle whiskers on the same grounds: that they serve a natural function. But 4-H will count it against you if you don't trim them.

BODY CLIPPING

For those of us who compete, hunt, or use indoor rings during the winter, all that extra hair is a nuisance to both horse and rider. Not only is it difficult to groom, it is detrimental to the animal when he works up a sweat. Long coats stay damp and clammy, taking a long time to dry out, absorbing heat from the body in cold air and causing a chill or worse.

In winter a full or partial body clip is given, depending on the circumstances. A shorter coat dries quickly, looks better, and is more easily groomed. The drawback for horses getting a hunter or other full body clip is that they must be blanketed when they're not working.

Body clips are not recommended in the spring because clipping off the tips of the ingrowing summer coat makes it look dull.

Trace Clipping

The term trace clipping derives from the days when draft horses were clipped to the level of the traces. This clip takes various forms today in different parts of this country and the world at large. The main objective is to clip the areas of the horse that should dry most quickly, leaving as much protection as possible on rump, back, and loins for slow work. Even a modest trace clip shaves under the neck, chest, part of the belly, and behind the elbow. In all these clips the hair on the legs is left long as protection against brush and mud.

Clippers

A number of different types of clipper are available to make the job of trimming or body clipping a relatively simple chore.

Trace Clip

Slip Clip   Blanket Clip

A *small, very quiet electric clipper* can be used for trimming just the muzzle, ears, bridle path, and legs. They come with an assortment of blades for each purpose. A wireless, battery-operated clipper sold in most tack shops gives you the option of clipping anytime, anywhere. A superdeluxe model can even be mounted on the wall.

You will need a *large, heavy-duty clipper* for body clipping, roaching manes, and on particularly furry legs. This is more expensive and generally noisier than the trimming type. It's best to purchase one with variable speeds that get quieter as they go slower—an important consideration when working on a young or green horse experiencing them for the first time.

Most large clippers are also air-cooled to prevent overheating. This feature should be maintained by keeping the air screen free of horse hair; clean it with an old toothbrush as you work. Whatever type of clipper you buy, be sure to read the maintenance instructions carefully to protect this substantial investment.

A good clipper has a selection of blades in different sizes, each specifically tailored for coarse, medium, fine, or extrafine work. I find it convenient to keep two sets of blades, since they get dull after several body clips and need to be sent away for sharpening. The instructions for some brands of clipper warn customers to send the blades only to an authorized dealer for proper sharpening, but friends who have gone this route tell me it takes several weeks to get them back from the dealer and costs more than having them sharpened locally.

Dull or dirty blades leave tracks, don't cut cleanly, and make clippers heat up. You can dispel dirt easily by dipping the blades in kerosene or commercial blade wash and keeping them well oiled at their lubrication point. Cleaning and lubricating are necessary before, during, and after use.

A valuable clipper accessory to help in winter clipping is a *snap-on comb* that attaches to the bottom blade and allows you to regulate the length of hair as you cut. Instead of a trace clip, the comb allows you the option of shortening the hair from one inch to one-sixteenth and gives a neater trim while still maintaining protective hair.

Preparation

For the clipper to do an efficient job, your horse must be really clean. Mud, dried sweat, scurf, and the like will clog the teeth and dull the blades, causing the instrument to seize up and leave unsightly tracks.

Select a flat, light area near an electrical outlet to do your clipping. It's not always advisable to tie or cross-tie a horse unless you're certain he'll behave well. If you need assistance, have an experienced person available to help, particularly when you are giving a horse his first clip and when you're tackling the loose-skin areas under the neck and chest and behind the elbow. You will need a helper to stretch some of these areas to accommodate the clipper.

Keep handy your dandy brush, several towels, lubrication oil, an old toothbrush, and a blade wash (or a shallow can with kerosene in it) for blade cleaning. (And double-check your blades to make sure they're sharp before you begin!) When doing a trace clip of any kind, you'll need either chalk, masking tape, or a water-soluble Magic Marker that shows up against the horse's coat. I prefer chalk.

Never try to rush the job. Even for an old hand, a body clip can take three or four hours, and you may not be able to finish in one day. Every twenty to thirty minutes you'll need to stop and allow the clippers to cool, giving both of you a break. When trimming a horse, particularly a shy one, it's best not to put him in cross-ties but have someone hold him instead.

Before you clip a horse for the first time, you have to make sure he will allow you to touch all the areas to be clipped. Take time beforehand to get him accustomed to the look and smell of the clippers while they're turned off, and touch his body with them. Turn the sound on well away from his body at first, running the clippers at the quietest slow speed.

Next let him feel the vibration. Hold the clippers on low, and run the back of your hand slowly over his shoulder so he can feel the vibration. When you start to clip, select a neutral place like the shoulder or lower neck until he gets used to it.

Before beginning a hunter clip or one of the trace clips, draw a line with the chalk or marker along the edge of the area you won't be clipping. Make sure to look at the lines from front and back to keep things symmetrical. Then tie the tail in a mud knot or wrap to keep it out of the way while you're clipping.

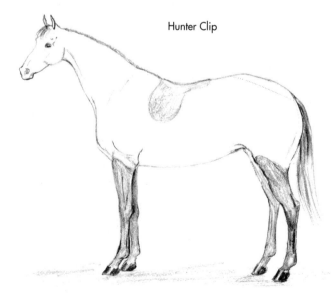

Hunter Clip

Techniques

For a full body clip and a partial and/or trace clip, the clipper follows the direction

Stretching neck area

of the hair as you cut, including the swirls at the flanks. Try to keep steady pressure on the clipper as you work, overlapping each previous row as you proceed to avoid tracks.

When marking the top of stocking lines in front or breeches in back for the clipper to follow, it works best to cut the line with one smooth sweep. Again, make sure the marks are even when you view them from the front and the back.

In areas of loose skin, pull it taut with your free hand, or have an assistant help you. It's difficult to do the girth area under the elbow alone. A helper can extend the foreleg out and up, pulling the skin taut in the area as you clip. When clipping next to the mane, make sure you don't accidentally clip the mane itself and create a bristly fringe that won't lie flat in the future.

If you're marking for a saddle patch on a body clip, use the pattern of a small saddle pad, cut slightly smaller so that it won't show under the real pad. You should also mark the upside-down V at the top of the tail before you clip. For body and hunter clips, do the entire head using the smaller, quieter clipper, with fine or very fine blades. Encouraging your horse to keep his head low will make this part of the job a lot easier. If he won't cooperate, some restraint, like a twitch, may be necessary.

Most clippers will get hot after a long period of use. Turning them off allows you and your horse to take a break while you clean the blades, brush the air screens to let them cool, and brush off horse sections you've already clipped to get rid of excess hair.

BLANKETING

The degree of clip determines whether a horse should wear a winter blanket all the time or just at night when not working. A full body clip requires constant blanketing with a change of blankets for indoors and outdoors. The most modified trace clip probably won't need a blanket at all, or not in the daytime. The horse should always be thoroughly dry before blanketing. While he cools down after work, an antisweat sheet can be used with a wool cooler over it in winter. (See Chapter 25.)

In the spring, to force a coat to shed early, you can start blanketing in early March (in the North) if you haven't been already. Be careful, though, that the horse does not get overheated underneath and end up standing in a wet blanket. By the end of March, the blanketed horse's coat will be way ahead in the shedding process. Clipping, as I mentioned earlier, isn't recommended at this point.

Palominos and chestnuts can become sun-bleached in the pasture; a light cotton blanket will help them keep their color. It will also keep a light horse clean before a show.

When you don't want to clip a winter coat, you can prevent it from growing to angora length with sheets and blankets. As soon as the nights start to get cool, the horse's hypothalamus gland will kick in, triggering hair growth. When the temperature drops below 60 degrees, begin covering him with a light stable sheet. As the weather gets progressively cooler, increase the blanket weight gradually, putting on heavier ones until you end up with two heavy blankets, a liner, and even a hood to guarantee that the neck and head hair length will match the coat.

Horses with naturally short winter coats need to be treated like clipped ones and shouldn't stand without being covered. In general, blanketing requires attention, care, and knowledge. The blankets must be kept clean, fit properly, and be removed during warm spells or augmented in a sudden cold snap.

Some show barns and breeding farms simulate changes in climate to stimulate the hypothalamus. By keeping the lights on from six A.M. to nine P.M. and keeping the stable temperature about 45 degrees, the horse's system is fooled into thinking summer's coming. This artificial stimulus coaxes a show horse to shed his winter coats in January. In breeding stables, where early foaling is desirable, a mare's seasonal cycle is altered by this method, allowing her to be bred earlier.

PART VI

It's All Riding on the Hoof

Now I submit that the first thing a man who owns a horse should obtain is knowledge of the foot and the best method of protecting it; because it is the foot and the condition of it on which depends the value of the animal, whether he be kept for pleasure or profit. . . . A horse without sound feet is no horse at all.

—W. H. Murray
THE PERFECT HORSE, 1873

Why, When, and How to Shoe

Back in the days when broncos had hooves instead of engines, village smithies stood under spreading chestnut trees forging, among other things, horseshoes. Though telephone directory listings for Smith attest to a past ubiquity, the craftsmen themselves are as rare today as American chestnuts. And reliable farriers—the proper name for today's horse-shoeing specialists—are as overbooked as good carpenters, plumbers, hairdressers, and anyone else with skills essential to modern living.

How do you tell a good farrier from a poor one? The farrier's experience or lack of it is the basic yardstick of performance. Be skeptical of recent graduates from farrier school who boast of their prowess at corrective shoeing. Blacksmiths are not magicians. A good one can only compensate for conformation faults, not permanently correct them.

Ask for recommendations from friends, your veterinarian, and large stables in your area. When you do manage to find a good smith, go out of your way to ensure continued services. Be considerate of your farrier and treat him or her like the professionals they are, and they will arrive promptly when scheduled and more likely be available for emergencies. Here are some tips: Have your horse in his stall, ready for his appointment. If he's difficult to handle during shoeing, make arrangements to have someone competent there to hold him, if you can't. If he threw a shoe, leave it in a conspicuous place for your farrier. Most important of all, have a well-lit, flat, confined area, preferably with cross-ties, where your horse will stand quietly and your farrier can comfortably work.

WHY SHOE? In their original state horses roamed over soft, clean ground and grazed on nutrient-rich grass that grew good horn. Hooves were worn down gradually and evenly, maintaining balance, and natural growth processes allowed the areas receiving the greatest stress and wear to grow back the fastest. But these horses moved at a slower pace and didn't carry hundreds of pounds on their backs every day. Not long after equine domestication began, humans realized the need to protect the feet of riding and pack animals. Six thousand years ago Asian horses wore protective booties made of hide or woven from plants.

Horseshoes were first introduced on Roman roadways, around the second century. They were covered with "hippo sandals" similar to those of their riders, fastened with leather straps. Later on farmers in northern Europe found that the horses they used for agriculture and transport had trouble getting a toehold on road surfaces and often became lame and unsound when their porous hooves were softened by long days of pulling plows through damp earth. By the sixth century horseshoes were being nailed onto equine feet, becoming a common practice by the eleventh.

The first horseshoes were comparatively lightweight and were made of bronze, with a scalloped rim and six nail holes. They were succeeded by heavier, round-edged, eight-hole types. By the twelfth century the English were using iron to cast both coins and horseshoes (and even accepted the latter as currency for the payment of taxes). A century later blacksmiths were producing ready-made shoes in different sizes, called by the kegs in which they were transported. Hot-shoeing didn't become widespread until the sixteenth century in France and Great Britain, when the word *farrier* (and the French verb *ferrer*) were first coined from the Latin *ferrum* ("iron") to describe the specialized craft. A machine that forged horseshoes was invented in the mid–nineteenth century and was used by Union forces during the American Civil War, giving them a major advantage over the Confederacy.

Shoeing is an essential but unnatural procedure. The nails damage and add to the vulnerability of horn already weakened by a heavy artificial diet and the enforced idleness of the stall. But these detrimental effects are outweighed by shoeing's advantages. Shoes can be used to rehabilitate the hoof or help conformation defects. They can relieve the pain of deep cracks, corns, bruised soles, or pulled tendons; and they can help change a gait or action and compensate for faults. Shoes can also affect the length of the stride by maintaining, shortening, or extending it. The long, low, reaching stride of the Standardbred is augmented by putting more weight on the toe of the shoe, while Western horses that do little trotting have hooves trimmed close all around and light shoes to produce a short stride, close to the ground, suitable for the jog and lope. Light shoes improve the performance of racehorses, and adding weights behind the heel makes the hoof "fold" or curl under, accentuating the naturally flashy action of park-type saddle horses. Compared with the sixteen-ounce weight of an average shoe, Saddlebred shoes weigh twenty-two ounces or more, and those worn by Tennessee Walkers about thirty.

Some horses and ponies don't need to be shod. Most pony breeds evolved in rocky terrain, and their feet are extremely hard, as are those of mustangs. As long as their feet are trimmed properly, these animals can be ridden barefoot all the time.

Short toe—as on a Quarter Horse

Long toe—as on a three- or five-gaited American Saddlebred

Uneven hooves cause awkward action, straining tendons and leading to unsoundness. Trimming allows a horse to stand square and upright. Horn grows as much as half an inch a month and must be trimmed regularly to keep the wall from breaking off, chipping, or wearing irregularly. If a heel or toe is allowed to wear away, the angle of the foot changes, putting an unnatural stress on the legs.

YOUR FARRIER AND YOU

Professionals like to work with professionals, so you'll be much more likely to engage a competent farrier if you understand what his job is about and call him on a regular basis. An owner who calls up once or twice a year, usually a few days before a show or hunt, is a blacksmith's bane. It has nothing to do with money—good farriers always have more work than they can handle. Rather, a regular shoeing schedule ensures a farrier a sound hoof on which to best display his craft. When a horse is shod only a few times a year, a lot of hoof has to be trimmed at once, which changes the way a horse moves and can cause lameness. The farrier doesn't want to be blamed for your carelessness.

Farriers also know that infrequently shod horses often present behavior problems. If your horse gives the farrier a hard time, you can expect that appropriate disciplinary methods will be used to make him stand and hold his feet up properly. With a real problem horse, a twitch may have to be employed, a device that puts pressure on a horse's lip—cruel but effective. Remember that the physical safety of the farrier is more important than your horse's feelings. Mine told me about one night-

Hopefully not like this

mare of a horse who would submit to shoeing only when tied and thrown on his side, with the owner sitting on his head to keep him down. I've known others that were the most lovable animals in the world around anyone but a blacksmith.

Problems like these can be prevented if the horse's feet are handled daily and properly cared for from early infancy. A young foal should have his feet handled almost from the day of birth to educate him to stand for the blacksmith. His feet should be trimmed regularly until he is weaned and thereafter at regular intervals through maturity to assure proper wear and correct balance. And they should be picked out daily.

Whenever I judge fitting and showmanship classes at 4-H shows, I always ask the child to pick up the horse's feet—to see if they're clean, of course, but also to find out whether he or she does the job properly and if the horse's reaction indicates that he's used to having it done regularly. If your horse gives you or the farrier a hard time, you should begin this essential training all over again. Work on it every day, at first giving a carrot or some other treat only for every foot picked up *without* a hassle.

Depending on individual problems and how much your horse is used, four to six weeks is the maximum time to allow between shoeings. Unshod hooves should be trimmed equally often, and young horses under the age of five often need more frequent attention.

Some horses have exceptionally thin hoof walls, making it difficult to keep shoes on. Often these horses will lose a shoe before the farrier is due and go lame immediately thereafter. In such cases frequent shoeing—as often as every three weeks—is advisable. If you let more time go by before reshoeing, the nails will pinch the wall against the sensitive laminae, causing a short stride or general tenderness and lameness (like someone wearing a tight shoe).

If this sounds like your horse, it might be a good idea to keep an equine spare tire on hand, called an Easy Boot, to protect the hoof when a shoe is lost. (See Chapter 20.) If you don't have one, confine your horse to a stall or soft-surfaced paddock or pen until the shoe can be replaced.

Hooves should be cleaned daily and kept from drying out. "A horse is only as good as his worst foot" goes the old adage, and none will be very good without regular care.

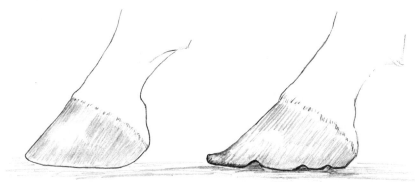

Trimmed Foot—Standing Square   Untrimmed Foot Showing Irregular Wear

KNOWING WHEN TO SHOE

How do you know when new shoes are needed? If you're unsure, there are several things to look and listen for:

ANGLE OF THE HOOF. An untrimmed hoof will distort the angle, which should be the same as the pastern, around 45 degrees. An uneven wearing-away of the heel or toe will put a strain on a horse's tendons and joints, showing up in an awkward stance.

CLINKING SHOES. I hope this extreme hasn't been reached, because it means your horse is long overdue for shoeing. A shoe that is as loose as this can shift on the foot, causing bruised soles or corns. Even worse, he could step on it with the other foot and tear it off, ripping the wall in the process—a farrier's nightmare.

MISSING SHOE. When a horse has lost a shoe, it's best not to ride him at all, especially if it is a front shoe that has been thrown. An unshod hoof will wear down and chip, and the sole can become bruised and tender. If you let it go too long, the farrier may have a problem getting a new shoe on. Above all, never jump a horse that is missing a front shoe. The difference in weight and height between the two feet will throw his balance way off and affect the way his legs absorb concussion. If you must ride, use an Easy Boot to protect the foot, or make your own with a piece of toweling, duct-taping it to the bottom of the foot. (But don't ride with the home-made type.)

RISEN CLINCHES. The clinch is the turned-over end of the nail used in shoeing. If it sticks up a quarter of an inch above the hoof, it's definitely time to reshoe.

STUMBLING. I've had several horses who would remind me when they needed to be shod by their gait. If your normally surefooted horse starts to stumble, check the calendar; his toes may be overgrown.

THIN SPOT ON SHOE. Worn-down spots on the toes or quarters or heels of a shoe indicate the need for reshoeing. Worn shoes can't be reused.

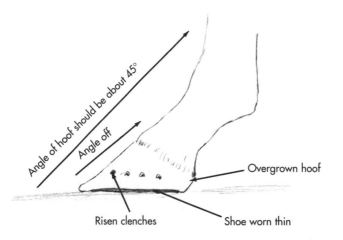

Angle of hoof should be about 45°

Angle off

Overgrown hoof

Risen clenches

Shoe worn thin

By the time the blacksmith arrives, you should have cross-tied or tied your horse in a well-lit, roomy area on a flat, dry surface where work can be done efficiently. The farrier begins by removing the shoes. He cuts the clenches so they won't damage the hoof wall when the nails are taken out. Using pincers, he then pries out the nails and pulls the shoes. If they haven't been badly worn, the shoes can usually be reused.

To prepare a hoof for shoeing, he clips back the excess wall to its correct length. Then he cuts away the old sole and frog with a drawing knife and uses a rasp to flatten the bearing surface of the wall—the part that rests on the ground.

If a piece of the wall has been torn out and not enough surface is left to properly seat the shoe, the farrier can build up the hoof with plastic and acrylic fill. He molds one of these materials to the hoof and covers it with duct tape until it dries. After about fifteen minutes the tape is removed, and the artificial section is rasped to conform with the rest of the hoof.

When a horse is just getting a trim, the farrier finishes the job off at this point by rounding off the rim of the wall. If he is making the hoof ready for the shoe, he flattens it. Then he measures the hoof and selects the largest shoe closest to it in size. If the heels are too narrow or too wide, he shapes them to the right dimension with an anvil and hammer. Shoes should always be made to fit the hoof—the hoof should not be rasped away to fit a shoe.

The farrier drives the nails in lightly at first until he finds the right spot; then he hammers them all the way in, making sure the angle is right so the nail doesn't come out too near the edge or too high up. Mechanically speaking, the shoe is kept on by friction between it and the hoof wall. Thus the more contact between the two, the better the friction.

If nails are too close to the edge, a shoe can be easily pulled off, splitting the hoof. If they are too high, they can pinch and put pressure on the laminae, causing lameness. Rather than risk this problem, an inexperienced farrier often places the nails too low. (A recent study found that clinches as long as the width of the nail can withstand 920 pounds of pressure on the shoe, while smaller or shorter

PREPARATION FOR SHOEING

1. Trimming away old sole with drawing knife

2. Cutting away excess hoof with hoof cutters

3. Rasping heel of hoof

4. Trying on shoes to find the largest

5. Nailing shoe

6. Cutting nail ends with claw hammer

ones can take only 370 pounds of pressure before the shoe comes off.) There is no magic potion for keeping shoes on. Climate, nutrition, condition of the hoof, and how it was shod can all contribute to a horse throwing a shoe. A healthy hoof, maintained with regular trims and resets by a good farrier, has the best chance of holding a shoe.

The farrier's final job is to cut off the protruding nail point with a claw hammer. He uses the clinching bar to bend the end down into a clinch that secures the nail and keeps it from slipping back through. Before he bends it, he rasps a small area below the nail so the clench will lie smooth. As a finishing touch, he rasps off the clinches and files the edge of the hoof flush with the shoe to keep it from splitting off.

If you have a regular blacksmith and are on a regular shoeing schedule, he can usually be counted on to show up at the agreed-upon date and hour. But not all farriers are equally efficient, and it's a good idea to phone and confirm his ETA beforehand.

7. Filing nail groove

8. Seating nail head in nail groove

9. Clenching nail with hammer

Your farrier sometimes takes a vacation too, and during this time your horse could pull a shoe. Or perhaps you notice that one is clanking, loose, or bent enough to be easily torn off, potentially damaging a hoof wall or leg. In these cases, you'll just have to fill in for the farrier and take the shoe off yourself. Don't panic. You can do it easily if you have a standard eight-inch file, a small pry bar (Wunderbar), and a claw hammer in your toolbox (or two claw hammers if you don't have a pry bar).

Stand in a comfortable position, and support the problem foot on your knee or set it on a large block of wood. With the file remove the bent-over part of each nail (clinch) with a back-and-forth motion parallel to the ground. Continue all the way around the hoof, taking care not to gouge it, until the clinches are gone.

Now insert the edge of the pry bar (or second claw hammer) between the shoe and the hoof, right behind the last nail on the outside. Don't put pressure on the sole; just tap the bar gently enough to work the shoe away from the wall, then lift it enough to loosen the nail. With the hammer tap the shoe between the nails until it lies flat against the hoof wall and the nails protrude enough to be hooked at the head with the claw hammer and pulled out. The shoe will then come off easily without damaging the hoof. Save the shoe. Even if it's twisted, the farrier can reshape it on his anvil.

Some owners like to give their horse's feet a rest during the slack season by leaving the feet unshod but *trimmed*. The time and duration of this pedal vacation depend on climate. In temperate regions, winter is a convenient time for those who don't plan to ride frequently. An occasional barefoot ride in the snow won't damage hooves.

A rest period allows hooves to expand and the frog and foot to return to their natural, healthy stage, but regular trimming is still essential. Working cowhands generally don't shoe their horses unless they will be doing a lot of riding on the road or other hard surfaces.

Because of the long toes that certain park horses must grow for show, it's impossible to give their feet a rest. It takes months for these toes to grow to the desired length of six to eight inches, and without shoes the end of the hoof would quickly chip off.

How much does shoeing cost? Readers advise me that it varies greatly according to area of the country, the type of shoes the horse requires for his work, and/or climate.

REMOVING A SHOE YOURSELF

GIVING FEET A REST

Evaluating the Hoof

A healthy hoof should be full, round, open at the heel, and proportionate to the horse's size. Very large feet are usually a sign of poor breeding. They look ungainly and result in a clumsy stride. Small feet, though they look cute and delicate, are also inefficient and portend unsoundness. A large horse with tiny feet will have an oversize share of foot problems. The shape of the hoof, too, affects both its ability to absorb shock and the horse's stride; its configuration determines the point at which the leg breaks over. If the inner or outer quarter is higher, which happens when a horse toes in or out, the stride will not come straight through in front, instead swing out or in.

A horse should stand evenly on all four feet, with the front hooves squarely on the ground. Although they often shift their back legs, healthy horses never lift the front feet in like manner. The equine center of gravity is located just behind the withers. Consequently a horse takes about 20 percent more of his weight on the round front hooves. The more oval hind hooves initiate the thrust necessary for forward movement.

A normal, properly maintained hoof should be centered under the leg so that when viewed from the front, a straight line could be drawn down from the middle of the knee, bisecting it. Seen from the side, the hoof position should match the natural angle of the pastern and cannon, the foot centered under the leg.

Assuming that your horse has no conformation faults in his limbs, balancing the feet is a simple matter of trimming to maintain the normal angle of the pastern bones and create a continuous line from ankle to toe. (See Chapter 16.) A horse with too much heel will have a pastern that buckles forward, putting a strain on tendons and ligaments. On a horse with too little heel or too much toe, the bones of the foot will buckle backward, causing strained flexor tendons—the large, important tendons in the horse's legs—and making the animal forge. Either of these problems will cause a horse to stumble and put excessive strain on the wrong parts of the leg.

Step back and look at your horse from the front. If the inside of the wall of his hoof is too high, the ankle will buckle outward. Too much foot on the outside will make the ankle buckle in. If either condition is neglected, a horse could end up with strained tendons and ligaments, contracted heels, and faulty gaits like paddling or interfering.

Forging—Hind Toe Striking Front Toe

Once a hoof is out of line, the imbalance reinforces itself with every step taken. The horse's weight has been redistributed and will rapidly wear away that area of the hoof carrying the burden, taking a toll on the entire leg (much as a run-down heel on a human shoe distorts and strains the spine).

Conformation defects in ankles, knees, hocks, or stifles can put abnormal strain on different areas of the hoof, wearing them away—in this case, the symptom rather than the cause—but the result is the same: uneven distribution of weight. The important difference is that a normal hoof can be corrected with trimming, while one worn from a conformation fault can be trimmed only to look presentable, not to correct the fault. Most so-called "corrective shoeing" to restore natural balance and angle is done in the trimming, not the shoeing. Changes must be made gradually during successive visits by the farrier to avoid causing soreness or lameness.

FAULTS OF GAIT AND CONFORMATION

Brushing is often a fault of splayfooted horses, who are likely to brush the inside of either the front or back fetlock when the hind legs reach through. They will need boots for protection. Younger or green horses that aren't fully muscled or well balanced may brush the front or hind legs against each other.

Overreaching or *forging* is just that—an overreaching stride that causes the toe of the hind foot to reach out and hit the back of the foot in front and (occasionally) its opposite. Young horses sometimes have such a stride because they are unbalanced. Often training will help the problem. Shoeing also helps, and in some situations quarter boots are the answer. (See Chapter 25.)

Pigeon toes and *splayfeet* are usually conformation faults of the front feet that strain tendons, joints, and ligaments in the forehand. Often, however, a slight tendency to toe in or out is aggravated by improper and/or infrequent trimming of a young horse's feet. These faults can't be corrected in older horses, but they can be improved by trimming the hooves to distribute the weight equally on the front feet. In some cases special corrective shoes are helpful, but usually shoes of this sort only add more lateral motion like winging or paddling.

Rope walking or *plaiting* horses place one foot in front of the other, causing stum-

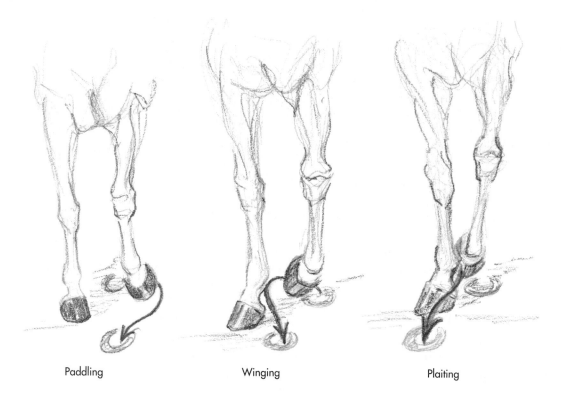

Paddling   Winging   Plaiting

bling and interference. This problem is seen in both base-narrow and wide-chested horses who toe out or toe in.

Speedy cutting, a fault most common in Standardbred trotters, occurs when the front feet clip the inside of the back ankles or just below them.

Crossfiring is a fault in some pacers, whose back feet clip the inside of the front feet.

Winging feet swing inward in flight, landing outside their normal track and often interfering. This is usually a fault of horses that toe out or have narrow chests.

Paddling feet swing outward and land inside the normal track—a fault found in horses that are wide in front or toe in.

PARTS OF THE HOOF AND HOW THEY WORK

The *wall,* or horny outer shell of the hoof, protects the sensitive inner tissue and gives under the full impact of a horse's weight. Its quality determines the strength of the hoof. For expansion and flexibility to be sustained, the hoof cannot be allowed to dry out.

The *paripole* is a glossy, natural, waterproof varnish on the outside of the entire hoof wall. It retains moisture and keeps the foot pliable. When it is damaged by standing in the toxins that accumulate in urine and manure, the hoof looses its elasticity and will dry and crack. Standing for long periods of time on sandy or dusty soil or dry bedding like wood shavings will also draw moisture through the coronary band, as will inflammation caused by work on hard roads or constant stamping at flies on dry ground. This protective coating can also be abraded by sand, stones, dry grass—or worse, sandpapering the hoof, which is sometimes done in a misguided attempt to produce a smooth, show-ring appearance. Farriers are (or should be) careful not to rasp away large portions of the paripole when shoeing. Moisture is naturally balanced in the hoof by correct diet and circulation, stimulated by exercise to help blood travel through the foot, feeding and moisturizing it from within, and by external sources like dew, stream water, or mud. Hooves that are too dry and hard can become bruised inside and cracked outside, causing some of the problems discussed in Chapter 20, and those that are too moist and soft will break up under the slightest impact. To help maintain the natural moisture balance, hoof dressings, packs, and polishes can be applied. (See page 222.)

The *coronary band* is the area where the top of the hoof meets the hair. Any injury here is considered serious because it will interfere with the horn-secreting tissues, affecting the normal development of the hoof wall as it grows down. Moisturizers should be concentrated at the coronary band to be effective.

The *white line* is the thin boundary line between the wall and the sole—actually a continuation of the laminae on the inside of the hoof. Bars give added strength to the outer wall and protect the heels from extreme wear.

The *frog* acts as an elastic cushion that absorbs concussion when a hoof strikes the ground, protecting the leg from the full shock of impact. The frog should always be in contact with the ground when a horse is standing. If it is allowed to dry out, it will shrink and lose contact, causing contracted heels. If it is too wet, which happens when a horse stands on muddy ground or in manure for long periods, the frog will rot and develop thrush, a condition described in Chapter 20. Some idle horses

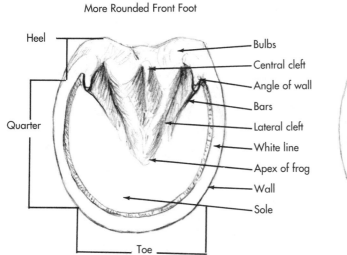

More Rounded Front Foot

Heel

Quarter

Toe

Bulbs

Central cleft

Angle of wall

Bars

Lateral cleft

White line

Apex of frog

Wall

Sole

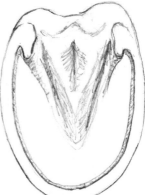

More Oval Hind Foot

shed their frogs several times a year, but this process is usually gradual and barely noticeable in those getting the right amount of exercise.

The *sole* is a horny, slightly concave structure that protects the inner tissues of the foot, helping to support the hoof. It is soft enough to maintain a flexible wall that will give when the horse puts his foot down.

The *plantar cushion,* which can't be seen, is a fibrous, fatty mass, located inside the hoof above the frog. It is the real inner cushion of the foot that the frog acts against. It pushes outward when pressure is greatest and contains glands that keep the frog supplied with moisture, assuring its elasticity.

The *coffin bone* forms the internal bony foundation of the hoof. When a horse founders, this bone tips down, causing the sole to drop and separate from the wall— a condition called *seedy toe.*

The *lateral cartilage,* attached to the upper rear edge of the coffin bone above the coronet, is an important aid to the expansion and flexion of the hoof on impact.

TYPES OF SHOES, PADS, AND OTHER ACCESSORIES

In the old days horses were taken to a smith's shop, where shoes were forged and put on the hoof still sizzling. Many farriers and horsemen believe that shoes adhere better with this method. Nail holes are made while the shoe is still hot, just after measuring the foot. Although some farriers still do *hot shoeing,* most will bring a variety of shoes to your stable and shape them with hammer and anvil—known conversely as *cold shoeing.*

The weight of the average-size *keg,* or ready-made steel shoe, is about sixteen ounces. (They now come in twenty-five- and fifty-pound boxes instead of kegs.) Those who can afford it use lighter handmade shoes, which give a better fit and are particularly good for young horses because they interfere less with their natural stride.

Today's horseshoes are available in many styles, including wide-webbed *racing plates, wedged heels,* and *egg-bar shoes* (the latter resembling round doughnuts, used for orthopedic conditions like navicular disease and laminitis), all made of aluminum. Extremely lightweight aircraft-quality aluminum alloys that resist wear and last up to eight weeks under normal riding conditions are popular with performance-oriented horse owners. *Titanium shoes,* highly resistant to abrasion and available in traditional and egg-bar style, are equally popular, particularly for eventing.

Just about every shape and style imaginable is available. There are shoes with clips for horses who have difficulty keeping shoes on, and some have creased grooves extending down both branches of the shoe so the farrier can countersink nails for better traction. Other traction devices are *heel calks* that act like cleats on a soccer shoe, and *rim shoes* with a deep groove all around. Western horses that make a lot of long, sliding stops can be outfitted with wide, *flat sliding plates.*

Composite horseshoes, usually made from a combination of aluminum, steel, and rubber or plastic compounds like urethane, can be nailed or glued on and are in demand for jumping, endurance riding, and racing because of their excellent traction. *Glue-on shoes* were developed to help get horses with hoof problems back to work, giving the farrier another option when nails are out of the question.

Special, very expensive, *two-part shoes* have a shapable steel base, nailed to the hoof and covered by a plastic shoe that the owner can replace or change at any time.

The farrier's trade has a few useful shoe accessories you should know about:

Borium

Borium is the name given to small knobs of metal, made of hard bits of carbide set in steel, that give an excellent bite on ice and don't wear as fast as steel calks. When borium is used on the heel and toe, combined with a convex bubble pad, it makes an excellent winter shoe that prevents slipping and keeps snow from balling up in the foot. The only thing against it is that the knobs raise the hoof off the ground, lessening pressure on the frog and reducing heel expansion, but under certain conditions they're indispensable.

Calks

Calks are cleats at the heel and toe that give a better grip on the ground or ice. They also provide traction when a horse is jumping, hunting, barrel racing, pole bending, or carrying weighted shoes. They can be turned over from the steel of the shoe itself or screwed or welded on. Some of these have a larger metal center that doesn't wear away as fast as the rest of the shoe. In the old days farmers used to have the calk points on the shoes of draft horses sharpened in the winter to prevent slipping.

Clips

Clips are low, broad triangular pieces of metal that the farrier draws from the shoe. They lie flat against the hoof wall and prevent the shoe from slipping. Front shoes usually have a single toe clip; hind shoes have two quarter clips. They are used on horses who gallop over rough ground, and up- and downhill. They help keep shoes on. Horses with poor feet, thin, shelly, crumbly, or cracked walls will routinely need clips to keep shoes secure. This may also be necessary for horses that live in extremely humid climates or where the ground is soggy.

Studs

When a horse is required to do figures on hard ground or to jump off a tight, fast turn, studs are excellent for that extra traction. That is why they are popular in combined training, endurance riding, and dressage.

The rider can attach them to any kind of shoe after stud holes have been drilled by the farrier, who may suggest adding clips to help hold the toe against the added stopping force of the studs. Studs come in many sizes, but the holes and threads are all the same. When they are taken off, the holes are plugged with rubber or cotton treated with WD-40 oil to keep them from filling with dirt or pebbles.

Before inserting the studs of choice, remove the plugs with a large horseshoe nail or a very small screwdriver. Then use the screw tap to clean the threads of any dirt that may have worked its way around the plug. When the hole is clean, screw the stud in by hand as far as you can. Do the final tightening with a vise grip, or adjustable wrench, until there is no space between the bottom of the stud head and the shoe. It takes about twenty minutes to a half hour to clean treads and insert studs. Reverse the sequence when you take them off after the competition.

Using a larger stud than needed can hinder a horse's normal stride and put him at risk of tearing off a shoe or pulling a tendon. Wearing them too long can make his feet sore, just as a woman accustomed to sneakers will get sore feet after a day in high heels. Studs are usually inserted just before a class or event begins.

Swedge Shoes

These shoes have a small crevice running around the middle to give it more bite. They are relatively light and are frequently used on Standardbred trotters and pacers, often on hunters, reining horses, and barrel racers. Sometimes calks are added.

Tungsten Carbide

Tungsten carbide is preferred by some as an alternative to borium. Members of the mounted police patrol in Wichita, Kansas, found that this element, melted onto horseshoes in four spots, gives exceptional traction on concrete, asphalt, brick, and icy city streets in winter. They claim that the cleatlike traction of shoes treated with tungsten carbide gives greater safety and wears longer than borium.

Pads

To pad or not to pad really depends on many factors, not least the genetic makeup of your horse's foot, the condition of the hoof itself, and the type of surfaces you'll be riding him on. The most common reasons for putting an extra layer

Keg Shoe

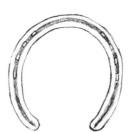

Swedge Shoe

Shoe with Borium

Toe Clip

Quarter Clip

Borium

between your horse's hoof and the ground are *shock absorption, protecting the sole,* and *therapeutic purposes.*

When a horse is being worked for long periods of time on hard, rocky, or gravelly terrain, pads are a welcome addition to healthy feet. Flat and harness racers sting their unprotected soles on track surfaces; field hunters never know what type of footing they will encounter during a day's hunt; and trail and endurance horses risk stone bruises as they traverse rough and rocky trails. They all can be protected by these shock-absorbing hoof pads. Pads can also help prevent arthritis, navicular disease, road founder, and other problems associated with excessive concussion. They can protect the feet of a horse recovering from injury as well.

The downside is that pads can put horseshoe nails under stress, pushing them up and down as the pad compresses, expands, and wobbles back and forth, enlarging holes and loosening clinches until the nail may actually snap from metal fatigue. Also a pair of pads can add an extra twenty to thirty dollars more to your shoeing bill, depending on the material and style.

And pads do interfere with the natural expanding and compressing action of the hoof, which stimulates the flow of blood to the leg. So you should give careful thought to their use. Your farrier and your veterinarian can advise you. Because the design and the material of pads vary according to function, professional advice is recommended, so that the right pad is chosen for the particular problem.

Some of the types of pads available are listed below. Usually full pads are applied with some kind of packing material to *keep feet clean, control bacteria,* and *cushion* them.

Bubble pads have a convex bubble that protrudes in the center of the pad, which is great for keeping snow from packing up inside and turning the pad into an ice ball. They give the horse traction and prevent him from slipping and sliding—a terrifying experience on or off his back. If you're a serious cold weather rider, it's worth paying the extra dollars more for the snow-resistant pads.

Flat pads consist of an even thickness of material. They are used to relieve concussion and protect the sole from bruising on a thin-soled horse or for cushioning on unusually hard or rocky terrain.

Leather pads are often used on Hackneys, Saddlebreds, and other park-type horses with long toes to build up the hoof, when added weight is needed to alter their way of going. Pads cover the entire sole, and pieces of it can be used over the larger covering to build up the heel.

There are two drawbacks to these pads; their smoothness replaces the traction of the cupped-and-treaded hoof bottom, and they are relatively heavy.

Plastic pads, which serve the same purpose as leather ones, are available in a number of new types that are highly durable and are superior as shock absorbers. Made of polyurethane and packed with silicone gel, many endurance and trail riders prefer them for their ability to withstand the rigors of rocky going. They tend to be lighter in weight, and some have a texture to aid traction.

Rim pads fit under the edge of the shoe, leaving the frog exposed, which allows better traction and also serves as a shock absorber. Racehorse trainers, unwilling to add a lot of extra weight or give up traction, usually prefer these pads.

Rubber pads are used primarily for horses ridden on the road, notably driving horses. They keep the hoof from slipping, absorb some of the impact of the foot on the hard surface, and keep the heel from getting sore. For frequent use on a hard road, a tip shoe, worn just on the toe, will allow the back of the pad to connect with the road, providing give and traction.

Tube pads, or hoof grips, are antisnowball pads that prevent a buildup of snow in the bottom of horse's foot—the plague of ardent winter riders. These pads have a thin flat rim that slips under the shoe and is riveted into place at the back of the shoe. The tube portion fits against the edge of the shoe and is flexible with each step the horse takes, pushing out the snow. They are particularly useful in hard-packed snow. The bottom of the pad is open, unlike the bubble pad. Thus it is accessible for easy cleaning and allows air circulation when thrush is a problem.

Wedge pads provide varying degrees of elevation. One end of the pad is thicker than the other. They are frequently used when the horse's heel or toe needs to be raised for therapeutic purposes. They can also help raise one side of the heel when needed.

HOOF DRESSINGS, PACKS, AND POLISHES

These products and potions all have the same purpose: to maintain moisture balance in the hooves so they remain pliable without becoming too dry or too soft. Dry hooves, as mentioned earlier, transfer concussion to the interior of the foot, causing bruising inside and cracking outside. Hooves that are too soft will break up under the slightest impact. Both the wall and the sole, the hoof's tough, insensitive outer structures, should be pliable enough to give a little each time the foot strikes the ground, absorbing shock and protecting sensitive inner tissue from trauma. Under ideal conditions, the hoof maintains its own perfect balance, but this is seldom the case in the real world, where dressings, packs, and moisturizers are needed to restore the wall and sole and keep them lubricated.

Hoof Dressings

These are either *sealants* or *moisturizers*. Feet that are too moist will need a sealant. Overly moist hooves have walls that give under your thumb when you press down and flaky horn around nail holes that won't hold a shoe properly. The frog is mushy and the outer layer of the sole scrapes off easily with the hoof pick. Fine cracks in the hoof wall frequently accompany this condition. For this type of problem, a petroleum-, mineral oil–, or beeswax-based sealant is used. The base of these dressings is what keeps moisture out or in. Since all ingredients aren't listed on the labels, you should know what they look and smell like.

Sealants tend to be dark in color, and those that have petroleum bases have a distinctly sharp odor like creosote or auto lubricants. (But don't try to economize with motor oil, which has harmful chemical additives.)

Dry feet don't necessarily show severe cracks, but the frog will become almost as inflexible as the wall of the hoof, and when you tap the sole with your hoof pick, it will echo. This condition will need a dressing to provide moisture and a sealant to hold it in. Lanolin-based products and those with mink oil, fish oil, wheat germ oil, or aloe fall into this category. They will smell milder and have a creamy appearance reminiscent of lard or fat. (In fact, lanolin is the fatty substance found in sheep wool.)

A *moisturizer* should be applied evenly (but not excessively) to the areas where moisture enters the hoof: the coronary band and across the heel and sole. Then use a sealant on the hoof wall to keep the dressing in. A sealant should also be applied after a horse with dry hooves has had a bath or has come in from a wet pasture. Conversely, a horse with soft feet should have a sealant put on before bathing or going out on wet grass.

The moisture balance of normal hooves will also change under certain conditions. Keep this point in mind when you come in from a long ride on a sandy trail or a paved road, when a moisturizer will be in order. But in wet weather, when fields are sloppy for days on end, use a sealant before you turn your horse out.

Before applying a dressing, make sure the hoof is clean, by brushing or washing off any mud or manure. Cross-tie your horse on a clean flat surface, preferably the aisle of the barn, with a piece of brown paper bag or a feed sack underfoot to keep a darker dressing from staining the floor. Before riding or turning him out, allow the dressing to dry or soak in, depending on the type; otherwise everything from horse hair to hay will stick to them.

Hoof Packings

Packings of commercial clay products or pine tar are used to moisten soles. Both types are packed into the hoof. A piece of cardboard or brown paper cut to size is taped to the bottom of the hoof to trap moisture in during the twenty-four hours the packing stays in. No packings should be used excessively, and they shouldn't be used at all on horses prone to thrush.

Venice turpentine in its pure state is used to toughen tender soles. It has a dehydrating effect and shouldn't be used on a daily basis.

Hoof Polishes

Polishes are usually acetone-based and are applied strictly for cosmetic reasons, to make feet shine. Some people use liquid shoe polish. Although a lot of people do it, particularly before a halter class, never use sandpaper or a wire brush before polishing—it's a sure way to dry out a hoof. A nail brush or toothbrush will do just as good a job.

PART VII

Healthy as a Horse

*He will rarely consult his own interest who,
not having had the advantage of a veterinarian
education, undertakes the treatment of any of
the serious diseases of the horse.*

THE HORSE, published under the superintendent of the Society
for the Diffusion of Useful Knowledge, London, 1831

Symptoms and Injuries

Uncharacteristic behavior is usually the first sign of equine illness or lameness and will be obvious to conscientious owners who know their horses well and can distinguish between the abnormal and the merely odd.

Many horses have unusual habits or personality traits that might be mistaken for maladies by those unfamiliar with their normal behavior, but by adhering to a strict schedule of stable management and observing your horse thoughtfully on a daily basis, you will be able to tell the difference. Some horses, for instance, like to take a morning nap in the stall right after breakfast. Others snore raucously as they sleep. One Palomino I know takes sunbaths in the pasture at high noon, looking to all appearances stone dead.

When behavior such as this happens all the time, it's normal. But if your horse lies down at an unexpected time or place and seems very restless, it may be a sign of illness. Likewise, finicky eaters are normally picky at mealtime, but when a horse who usually eats voraciously suddenly loses interest in his food, he should be watched carefully. Or if your horse customarily greets you at the stall door with a bright eye and friendly nicker, you have reason to suspect something wrong on a morning when he fails to appear. If he stands with ears at half-mast looking miserable, something is definitely awry.

In most cases it's a good idea to take your horse's temperature and/or pulse before phoning the veterinarian. Some symptoms will call for your attention and further observation. Any two together will require an immediate call to the veterinarian, as will any obvious injuries. Never try taking matters into your own hands.

**COMMON
SYMPTOMS
AND INJURIES**

Interpreting the signs of illness and determining the extent of an injury requires a tremendous amount of experience, for example:

- Deep cuts or punctures, excessive bleeding

- Lameness, odd stance, or reluctance to move

- Signs of distress, anxiety, or discomfort

- Discoloring of normally pink tissue of gums, nostril, and inner eye

- Abnormal color, consistency, and/or volume of feces and urine

- Listlessness or lack of interest in food

- Unusual sweating

- Temperature over 102.5 degrees

- Increased pulse rate

- Discharge from nose or eyes

- Persistent coughing

- Swellings or bruises

- Heat in feet or legs

- Bare or scabby spots on skin

TAKING READINGS

Know What's Normal

Be familiar with your horse's physiological signs. Know his normal pulse rate, temperature, and respiration rate (the latter being twelve to fourteen breaths a minute for a normal horse). Also take note of the normal color of the mucous membranes around the eyes, nose, and mouth, which reveal the amount of oxygen in the blood and the rate of blood flow. The gums should be pinkish with a slight yellow tinge. Check your horse's gums periodically when he's healthy, so you are aware of their normal color. If you press the gum with your finger, it should turn white or light in color, returning to normal within one and a half seconds. Gums that are very pale, dark red, or bluish are abnormal, as are those that take more than three seconds to recolor.

Temperature

A normal temperature for a horse is 99.5–100.5 degrees and may reach 101 in the afternoon. In extremely hot or humid weather or after a very hard workout (racing, cross-country phase of combined training, or an endurance race), the temperature could reach 102 or 102.5. Any reading above that will need the veterinarian's attention. A temperatures over 106.0 is cause for serious concern and from 110 to 112 degrees will cause brain damage and death. Veterinarians know several ways to bring a high temperature down quickly, so the sooner the feverish horse is treated, the better.

Special large-animal thermometers are available with a hole in one end to tie a string to, which can then be clipped to the tail. (It should be a must in your first-aid kit.) Make sure your horse is securely held, tied, or cross-tied. After shaking down the thermometer, rub Vaseline on the nub end and insert it gently into the

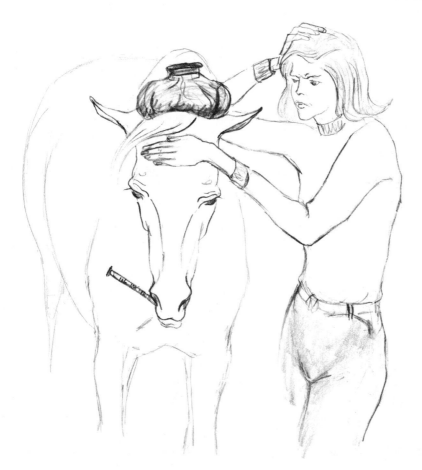

anus. Stand close to and slightly to the side of the horse's rump in case he kicks out. Leave the thermometer in for two or three minutes.

Pulse

The pulse is taken on the artery under and inside the jawbone. The normal pulse for a horse is 44 beats—give or take a few—per minute; but if he's excited or afraid, or has a fever, stomach disturbance, or infection, it can range anywhere from 23 to 70 beats per minute. With serious colic the heart rate can be 80 to 120. A strong, pounding pulse in the foot may indicate that the horse has an inflammation. It can be felt on the sides of the pastern both medially and laterally.

Pulses are often taken during endurance rides and combined events. The recovery rate of the pulse indicates a horse's general condition, as it does in humans.

To get a normal pulse rate, pick a time when your horse is relaxed, then take the pulse several times a day over a two- or three-day period, when he's at his leisure. That will give you a normal average to compare against the abnormal.

**YOUR FIRST-
AID KIT**

You will be able to treat some ailments under the vet's instruction. For simple first-aid treatment, the following items should be included in your stable medicine chest:

- Cotton roll

- Vetrap

- Elasticon

- Gauze pads (variety of sizes)

- Gauze wrap

- Adhesive wrap and adhesive tape

- Leg wraps

- Sharp scissors

- Thermometer (rectal type, with string attached)

- Surgical scrub and antiseptic solution

- Latex gloves

- Flashlight and spare batteries

- Marker pen (permanent ink type)

- Hemostats (clamps used to hold skin together)

**MINOR
AILMENTS**

It's important for you to know the most common horse ailments so you can take the proper precautions. By no means should you become your own diagnostician.

Colds

Horses get them too. They are caused by respiratory viruses and can progress to secondary bacterial infections. The symptoms are similar to the human varieties. A cold can begin with a nasal discharge, a persistent cough, a temperature, general listlessness, and lack of interest in food. Your veterinarian can prescribe appropriate treatment.

To prevent colds, don't allow your horse to be put away hot after work; always cool him out thoroughly. Don't let him stand in drafts, and keep his resistance up by proper feeding. If he gets overtired or chilled, perhaps from standing around in a wet or damp blanket, you're inviting a cold. Make sure the drinking water is germ free by keeping buckets and troughs clean.

Cuts

No matter how hard we try to create a safe environment, horses will find ways to cut themselves. A wound can range from a clean slice, a triangular flap, or an abrasion to a torn eyelid or nostril, even a two-inch nail protruding from the bottom of the hoof. Try to assess the extent of the injury before phoning the veterinarian, so that when you do call, you can describe the location and size of the injury, the amount of bleeding, the degree of lameness and/or swelling, and any exposure of bones, tendons, or muscles.

With a clean cut or a tear, the immediate danger is excessive bleeding. If the blood is bright red and spurting out, an artery has been severed, and the flow must be immediately stopped with pressure applied manually or with a bandage. If bleeding continues, add a folded towel on top. Do not apply a tourniquet, as it impedes blood flow to the entire limb. A loss of blood flow for fifteen minutes will cause the tissues in the hoof to die, which in turn could cause a loss of the hoof within five or ten days.

Less serious wounds need to be cleaned out immediately to reduce the chance of infection. Wait for the veterinarian before clipping around the wound. Meanwhile, cold-hose with clean running water for fifteen or twenty minutes. Never rub, or you may push the dirt in. In this kind of emergency, a syringe of water is helpful for flushing out the wound. After cleaning, spray or dab on a disinfectant solution or antiseptic powder (available from the veterinarian). If your horse is afraid of being sprayed, put the disinfectant on a cloth and dab it on. After cleaning, cover a wound on a lower leg with a bandage so it stays clean until your veterinarian arrives.

Puncture Wounds

Noticing the location of a puncture wound is critical because a wound over a joint or tendon sheath can be life-threatening or, at the very least, might cause permanent lameness if infection occurs. These wounds nearly always produce swelling and soreness, though sometimes the puncture itself is invisible. If a wound is very swollen and/or oozing pus, it is likely to have occurred more than twelve hours before and is almost certainly infected. Puncture wounds are never sutured.

Swelling should be soaked in Epsom salts or packed with ice, depending on the type of injury. Sometimes running a cold hose on the swelling, applying an ice pack, or, when the injury is low, standing a horse in a running stream is effective until the veterinarian comes. If you have any doubt about whether a horse has had an annual tetanus shot, have the veterinarian give another one. Tetanus bacteria thrive in the anaerobic environment of a puncture wound, which closes over quickly at the top.

Eye Problems

Eyes should *never* be treated without your veterinarian's guidance. Should you find one or both eyes red, swollen, tearing excessively, or with a blue opaque haze, call your veterinarian. In a single eye any of these symptoms often indicate a corneal abrasion or ulceration from contact with a foreign object. Never apply a treatment that would be used for human eyes, because equine eyes are not the same, and you could inadvertently cause permanent damage.

During the fly season, when horses swing their heads around swiftly to remove flies, corneal abrasions are common from abrupt contact with ordinary grasses and hay. The veterinarian should determine the extent of the problem before medication is applied. Steroids are used only in special situations, and never if the cornea is not intact. The cornea can degenerate rapidly. Corneal ulcerations are treated with antibiotics and anti-inflammatories, as is conjunctivitis. Should a foreign body become embedded in the cornea, it must be removed by the veterinarian with a sharp dissection or flushing.

Redness of the whites of the eyes and excessive discharge in both eyes, particularly during fly season, may indicate conjunctivitis. If one or both eyes are swollen, weeping, painful, and/or have a blue haze, it may be *uveitis,* known as "moon blindness," a serious condition that can lead to blindness if not treated immediately and properly. A wide variety of medications are used depending on the severity and chonicity of the disease.

Lyme Disease

A bacterium carried by deer ticks is the cause of Lyme disease. In areas where the disease is endemic, up to 60 percent of the deer tick population may be carriers. First recognized in humans living in Lyme, Connecticut, in 1973, the disease has since been reported in forty-nine states and is one of the most commonly reported tick-borne diseases to affect pets and livestock as well as humans. The tiny parasites measure only one-eighth inch in length and can appear anywhere on a horse, but they are most often found under the lower jaw, the underside of the chest and abdomen, the legs, and in the mane and tail.

It is important to find and remove deer ticks within the first twenty-four hours after they have attached themselves. When a tick is removed, it should be preserved in alcohol and dated, and the area where it was picked up should be recorded. Even if your horse exhibits symptoms a week or more later, report it to your veterinarian, and have the preserved tick positively identified.

Some fly sprays will repel and kill deer ticks, but too much of it too often can be toxic, so be sure to follow the manufacturer's directions. Spray before riding out in an endemic area, and stay out of tall grass.

If the test is positive, the horse is treated with antibiotics, and if his condition improves after treatment, he is assumed to have the disease. Another antibody test is needed a few months later to check on the efficacy of the treatment. It may take a few months to a year before the antibody level returns to normal.

Lyme disease is difficult to diagnose in horses (and humans) because it frequently mimics other problems like lameness, laminitis, swollen joints, low-grade fever, eye problems, muscle soreness, depression, a reluctance to work—even encephalitis. To test for this elusive disease, a blood sample and sometimes a joint tap is taken.

Dental Problems

Teeth, when neglected, can be the primary cause of nutritional deficiencies and digestive disorders. As mentioned earlier, food is chewed by the back teeth, which grind it up, down, and finally sideways before it is swallowed. This lateral movement creates sharp edges on the inside of lower and the outside of upper teeth, which can cause painful injuries to tongue and cheeks unless teeth are regularly filed (called floating).

Pointed teeth are obviously inefficient, as well as painful, grinding instruments. Horses so afflicted will chew food too slowly and waste a lot of it in the process, "quidding" or dribbling feed or half-chewed hay from the mouth. Fodder that isn't

Floating Teeth

ground up enough to break the surfaces of food particles can't be efficiently broken down by digestive juices when it reaches the stomach and loses nutritive value.

A horse with bad teeth won't gain weight no matter how much you feed him, and depending on the extent of dental impairment, he may have great trouble eating or possibly not want to eat at all. If your horse salivates a lot, drops large portions of grain as he chews, or twists his neck and head while eating, chances are he needs his teeth *floated* (filed with an instrument called a float). Unless he is obviously in pain and/or has great difficulty chewing, however, a special visit from the veterinarian won't be necessary. Teeth can be examined and treated during scheduled immunizations. Elderly horses have special dental problems that are discussed in Chapter 35.

Common Ailments

I gnorance of the equine digestive process and/or carelessness in measuring forage and grain can cause a number of potentially lethal ailments. As we've already seen in Chapters 6 and 7, the diet of the domestic horse must be in keeping with his natural habit of eating little and often, and the amount of feed should be determined by the amount of work done.

DIGESTIVE DISORDERS

Azoturia

This was once called "Monday morning sickness," a common disorder among farm horses that were worked very hard during the week, then stabled over the weekend but fed the same working food ration. On Monday morning, soon after starting work, the horse would break out in a cold sweat and his back legs would stiffen. Known as "tying up," it is more common now when horses are worked hard in deep sand or snow. But it can also occur if a horse is worked too hard after being stabled (and/or overfed) for an extended period. Azoturia affects the muscles, particularly those of the loins and quarters.

To alleviate the symptoms, stop working your horse immediately and keep him warm and quiet. To prevent the disease, be sure your horse gets regular exercise and is being fed according to the work done. And when starting work after a period of idleness, always warm him up slowly.

Colic

A horse's peculiar one-way digestive system makes him particularly prone to digestive disorders. One of the most common such disorders, and therefore the most important to learn to recognize, is colic.

Colic is a clinical sign of pain caused when the abdominal wall stretches, putting pressure on its sensitive nerve endings. (A lot of other ailments are also accompanied by this affliction.) The symptoms are restlessness, biting or kicking at the flank, turning the head toward the abdomen, tossing the head, and a recurring desire to lie down and roll. When a horse is off his feed, listless, and has a high pulse rate, suspect colic. The temperature and respiration rate may increase, the stomach may distend, and the mucous membranes may turn very pale. Failure to defecate within a twenty-four-hour period implies a blockage. Colic kills more mature horses than any other ailment.

Colic can be caused by any number of things, from poor feeding practices to a sudden change in the weather. It can be quite mild, like a stomachache, or extremely serious and even lethal.

A horse with a simple flatulent colic will usually respond to a mild analgesic and light walking. You'll notice his discomfort by his compulsion to lie down and by his subsequent extreme restlessness. Veterinarian monitoring is also needed to determine if the horse needs to be sent out for surgery. Waiting too long could make it too late. If you suspect colic, call your veterinarian immediately. In the meantime, keep your horse moving and prevent him from lying down and rolling, which could complicate the problem by adding a twisted gut.

In any case of colic, the veterinarian will tell you to walk your horse, and perhaps prescribe a dose of milk of magnesia or another colic medicine—even whiskey— before he gets there.

Some horses are more susceptible to colic than others. It cannot always easily be avoided. Even some of the best-managed farms in the country experience a case every year or so. And a deathly colic can occur even when everything is done correctly.

On one of my first mornings on the job managing a large Arabian farm, I found a prize mare down with colic. I couldn't locate anything in the medicine chest to give her some immediate relief before the veterinarian arrived. Being a nondrinker, I had no liquor on hand, so while my son walked the mare, I trekked around the new neighborhood, door to door, asking if anyone could spare a bottle of whiskey. I got some very odd glances before an understanding horse-owning neighbor finally provided a bottle.

IF YOU SUSPECT COLIC. The best treatment for colic is early detection and care. When you describe your horse's symptoms to the veterinarian, be sure to:

• Say how long the horse has appeared ill, and the signs.

• Describe any changes in his disposition.

• Mention any noticeable change in pulse, respiration, or temperature.

• Discuss any variations in feeding or turnout routines.

• Describe any medication you are currently giving the horse.

COLIC SURGERY. Unfortunately those serious colics that may need surgery start out the same way as the mild types, not showing their severity for hours. Once these signs do occur, the only solution is immediate surgery. Waste no time getting your horse to the nearest clinic that can handle this kind of emergency (and learn its location the day you bring your new horse home).

Surgery costs anywhere from $3,500 to $6,500, and postsurgery complications can sometimes add on thousands more. It is wise to think this issue through before colic hits, when you're coolheaded, practical minded, and emotion free. Keep in mind that some colic surgery is not successful, leaving the bereaved owner a huge bill and a dead horse. Referral clinics are usually hours away, so early veterinarian assessment is important in making a timely decision.

It's important to tell the veterinarian if you can't afford surgery, because a lot more painkillers can be administered without fear of covering up a surgical lesion. If surgery is imminent, fewer drugs will be administered, and frequent rectal exams will be given to assure prompt referral.

The best solution to colic is prevention. Pay careful attention to your feeding program, and make sure the horse is dewormed regularly. (See Chapter 21.) Keep plenty of fresh water available, and always cool him out properly.

Types of Colic

GASTRIC. With gastric colic an overloading of the stomach with fine, indigestible material creates sudden and intense pain.

SPASMODIC. This type is characterized by loud bubbling, popping, gurgling noises in the stomach. It is most frequently caused by a sudden change in food, a long cold drink of water, or the fatigue of being overworked after a period of idleness.

IMPACTION. This colic is an acute obstruction (either partial or complete) of

Colic Pain

the intestines. The pain is mild and persistent, and a horse so afflicted will act in a dull and depressed manner.

THROMBOEMBOLIC. In the severest form of colic a blood clot obstructs arterial flow to the bowel. Sometimes it is caused by strongyle worms. (See Chapter 21.) The blood supply to the stomach comes from only one artery, and when parasites damage its walls, the blood flow is cut off, causing permanent damage that eventually leads to gangrene and death.

TORSION. The design of the gastrointestinal system allows gas to lift sections of the bowel into abnormal positions, called *displacement.* The displaced bowel can then spin around on the axis of its blood supply, a condition called torsion. Without surgery, torsion colic is fatal within two or three hours of the event. Because of the few attachments of gastrointestinal components to other organs, the bowels can slosh around into very abnormal positions.

RECURRENT. This type of colic can result from a parasite infection, an impaction, and irregular feeding or overfeeding.

SAND. This impaction is caused by grazing on pastures with sandy soil. It is particularly common in parts of Florida, the Pacific coast, and the Southwest. Fecal testing for parasites will detect sand. To see if your horse is a sand consumer, collect a fecal pile that hasn't contacted the soil (say, when your horse is in cross-ties or on a rubber mat). Place the feces in a five-gallon pail and fill it with water. Then stir with a sweat scraper, breaking the manure apart and distributing it uniformly through the water. Tip the bucket, letting the runny waste go down the drain and leaving the solid material at the bottom. Repeat the process of washing and dumping until only sand is left at the bottom of the pail. If you come up with more than one-eighth of a cup, there is probably some in the intestine too, and your veterinarian should be advised. To help prevent sand colic, don't feed your horse in a sandy area. Instead, make an area under the feeder out of concrete, planks, or rubber mats. Feed him only clean hay, and have plenty of clean, fresh water available, along with a salt and mineral block. And of course adhere to a regular deworming program. Fecal testing for parasites will also detect sand. Periodic doses of supplements containing psyllium husk are used as a preventive measure.

IMMUNIZA-TIONS

Vaccinations are a vital part of good horse management, an integral part of a program that includes regular deworming, an ample supply of clean water, good nutrition, and a safe environment to ensure that you and your horse will spend many happy, productive years together. Nothing will prevent some destructive diseases as easily and effectively as regular immunizations, which provide a protective barrier against tetanus, encephalomyelitis, influenza, rhinopneumonitis, rabies, strangles, and Potomac Horse Fever, to name the most common bacterial and viral afflictions.

Vaccines contain specific bacteria or viruses that have been inactivated or modified so they won't cause actual disease. They are injected into the muscle so they absorb slowly; and they create antibodies to combat themselves. Usually two doses administered at three- or four-week intervals are needed to provoke an adequate immune response. These antibodies decline over time, needing booster shots at regular intervals to reinforce immunity—once a year in the case of tetanus and rabies, and more frequently for other diseases.

Vaccinations don't provide 100 percent protection. Depending on the severity of the disease, they may only decrease its virulence, not prevent it completely. The type of vaccination program to follow will depend on environment, age, use, exposure risk, geographic location, and the value of the animal. Consult your local equine veterinarian to determine what best suits your horse's individual needs. Keep in mind that some horses get reactions to shots and that different batches of vaccine may affect one differently from another. Always keep a close eye on your horse for a few days after any immunization.

At the Arabian farm where I worked, all the horses were vaccinated for "rhino." The next day one of the stable girls came running up to me in hysterics, exclaiming that a valuable yearling colt named Whizz Kid was having a fit in his paddock. I tore over there and confirmed that his behavior was indeed bizarre. The colt came toward me, his head tilted to the left, took three short steps, and then turned a complete circle, continuing in a leftward spiral until he reached the fence. An examination showed that the left side of his neck was a flat, swollen mass around the site of the injection. It prevented him from stretching his neck on the left, causing it to tilt, and it impaired the left shoulder movement, impelling him to circle in that direction. Our veterinarian subsequently informed me that other horses had reacted to this particular batch of vaccine, though in a less spectacular fashion. A few days after getting topical treatments on his neck, Whizz Kid was flying around the paddock with his usual exuberance.

INFECTIOUS DISEASES

Encephalomyelitis

Commonly known as sleeping sickness, encephalomyelitis is actually a group of viruses that attack the brain. The two most common types are Western Equine Encephalomyelitis (WEE) and EEE, the eastern variety. WEE has been diagnosed throughout North America, while EEE appears only in the East and Southeast. A recent outbreak of VEE, the Venezuelan version, was reported in Mexico but hasn't been seen in the United States for many years. The virus is usually transmitted by mosquitoes, which acquire it from birds and rodents. Humans are also susceptible.

The initial symptoms, all resulting from the degeneration of the brain, include fever, depression, and loss of appetite. In later stages a horse might develop a staggering walk and will eventually become paralyzed. The mortality rate from WEE is about 50 percent and 70 to 90 percent with EEE or VEE.

Vaccinate your horse annually against these viruses, preferably in the spring, before the mosquitoes become active. In some areas of the South and West, your veterinarian may recommend a booster in the fall for extra protection. In our northeastern corridor a three-in-one combination is given, covering EEE, WEE, and tetanus.

Equine Infectious Anemia

An average of two thousand cases of this incurable viral disease are identified yearly in the United States alone, making it a major threat to the worldwide horse population. Although most infected horses show no symptoms, they remain carriers for life, endangering others in close proximity. In consequence, the U.S. Department of Agriculture and state animal health regulatory agencies require either euthanasia or strict lifelong quarantine for horses that test positive for EIA.

Sometimes called *swamp fever,* this disease weakens the equine immune system, leaving it vulnerable to secondary infections like bronchopneumonia, which can also be fatal. EIA has three forms: *acute,* in which the virus multiplies and harms the immune system and others; *chronic,* which vacillates between remission and the acute disease; and *inapparent,* in which a horse is a carrier with no apparent symptoms.

It is legally mandatory to report any case of the disease both to state veterinarians and to the federal Animal and Plant Health Inspection Service office. Horses testing positive are required to be permanently identified by branding, tattooing, or in some cases electric implants and then permanently quarantined.

The virus is transmitted by horseflies, deerflies, mosquitoes, and other blood-sucking insects who carry it in the residual blood on their mouth parts. (People can also spread it by using a single needle on a number of horses.)

The only accurate way to determine whether a horse is infected with the EIA virus is a Coggins test, in which blood samples are examined for the presence of antibodies specific to the disease. A negative reading is a clean bill of health. These tests, developed by Dr. Leroy Coggins, are made annually and are required of all horses imported or transported to another state. Each state has its own specific requirements regarding shipping horses interstate, intrastate, and in change of ownership. You should become familiar with your state's requirements and any that you plan to visit. Most equine competitions require a negative Coggins certificate to enter. Since the 1970s, when one million carriers were detected by this method, rigorous owner cooperation to limit the disease with Coggins testing has reduced that number by 99 percent.

Equine Protozoal Myeloencephalitis

This parasitic disease affects the neurological system of a horse, causing either permanent disability or death. EPM is endemic in all areas of the United States that have opossums. This carrier passes the egglike oocytes in its feces, which a horse might then ingest when grazing or eating contaminated feed. Birds are secondary carriers, spreading the disease by picking up the oocytes in feed or water. When the birds die, the lethal protozoa lie dormant in the skeletal muscle tissue in the form of sarcocysts until a possum eats the carrion, continuing the cycle.

The horse is a dead-end host. The quantity of the protozoa ingested will determine the severity of the disease. About 40 percent of horses seem to have an effective immune response to the parasite, but for reasons that are unclear, it can also be present in an equine system for some time before the disease develops. EPM can develop swiftly or slowly, and stress is believed to contribute to susceptibility. The protozoa migrate to the central nervous system, causing swelling, hemorrhaging, and degeneration of the affected nerves and spinal cord. The horse may appear slightly lame or out of balance or sometimes unable to stand at all. Other symptoms are a rapid onset of blindness and difficulty swallowing. Because of the variety of places to which the protozoa can migrate, the effects on the nervous system vary, making diagnosis difficult and easily mistaken for other conditions. The earlier the disease is detected, the easier it is to treat.

When EPM is suspected, the horse is given a blood test called a *Western blot*, which detects antibodies to *Sarcocystis neurona*. Usually a negative result means EPM is not present. The test is useful only if the horse is negative, because 40 percent of positive horses may not be sick. A more definitive diagnosis can be made by giving a standing sedated horse a spinal tap from the lumbosacral area and analyzing the fluid. Or an atlanto-occipital tap can be done when the horse is anesthetized.

The current treatment, which costs from $200 to $350 a month, is oral doses of pyrimethamine and sulfadiazine. Owners are usually advised to supplement the diet with folic acid, to avoid anemia, and with vitamin E to counter inflammation of the nervous system. Horses with severe cases are also given intravenous DMSO for several days and Bute or Banamine. Only 10 to 20 percent of horses treated for EPM will return to former use. Others may have to retrain new nerve cells to take on the jobs of the cells that were destroyed. The process of recovery, much like that of a stroke victim, is slow, and some horses never completely regain their former function. One out of five never recovers and has to be put down.

As of this writing, no vaccine against EPM is available. The most effective prevention is control of the opossum population. Opossums are nocturnal and often difficult to detect. Keep feed covered, and check for fecal contaminants. Heat-processed feed is excellent because any sporocysts that might have been present have been destroyed by the high temperatures. Accessible garbage, or cat or dog food left outside, will tempt this undesirable marsupial. Many authorities recommend using humane traps, turning the opossums loose a few miles from equine habitats. (Since the animals stay within a 150-acre range for their entire life, there is no guarantee against their return.)

The best prevention is to keep a close and vigilant eye on your horse's behavior and physical condition. New drugs are being tested to combat this disease, but none have yet reached the market.

Influenza

Influenza is one of the most common and highly contagious equine respiratory diseases. The airborne virus can be transmitted by coughing or snorting over a distance as great as thirty yards. Horses under a lot of stress from traveling, competition, and exposure to a changing population of horses are most likely to contract it.

Symptoms are similar to those of a human cold: dry cough, nasal discharge, fever, depression, and loss of appetite. With rest and proper care the horse should recover in about ten days. When this period of convalescence is allowed, the disease is usually not life threatening. But if ignored, influenza can linger on for weeks or even months, developing into chronic allergic lung disease. (See page 242.) Horses in the stressful situations mentioned above should be revaccinated every two to four months. Equine flu viruses change constantly, as they do in human populations, and the vaccines to combat them are not long-lasting. Horses that travel a lot should be periodically immunized against the type or types of virus currently prevalent, and your veterinarian can advise you how often this should be. In our area, influenza/rhinopneumonitis are given in one shot.

Potomac Horse Fever

This noncontagious disease causes depression, fever, and anorexia, followed by diarrhea and then by laminitis, particularly if its first subtle stages are ignored. Treatment for PHF is usually successful if it is begun early in the course of the disease, but it's expensive, requiring intravenous antibiotics and fluids for three to seven days. Vaccination for PHF in the spring is most effective in preventing and/or dramatically reducing its severity.

Rabies

This frightening disease is more common in some areas than others, but all pet animals and livestock should be immunized against it. Horses, cattle, sheep, and goats must receive annual vaccinations. Though horses are seldom infected, the disease is always fatal, so don't take any chances. Even a vaccinated animal must receive a booster rabies shot within five days if it is bitten or comes in contact with a rabid animal. An unvaccinated animal in the same circumstances would be either euthanized or quarantined for six months. (State laws differ on this.) Rabies can be transmitted from horses to humans.

Rhinopneumonitis

Rhino invades the respiratory tract in two distinct types, number 1 and number 4, which cause two different diseases. Although both cause respiratory problems, number 1 rhino may also cause abortion, foal death, and paralysis. All mares in foal must be immunized against it, as should foals, weanlings, yearlings, and other young horses. Pregnant mares should be vaccinated at least in the fifth, seventh, and ninth months of gestation; youngsters will need booster shots every two or three months, depending on their circumstances. Rhino is spread by air and direct contact with secretions, utensils, or drinking water. The more benign type, number 4, can also cause lingering respiratory problems. It may not be apparent in carrier animals.

Strangles (Distemper, Shipping Fever)

The symptoms of strangles may vary, but this upper respiratory infection is caused by a single bacterium: *Streptococcus equi*. The first symptoms are high temperature, fast breathing, and general listlessness, usually followed by a nasal discharge and swelling of the lymph nodes under the jaw, which frequently abscess. This disease is highly contagious and dangerous, so if any of these symptoms appear, you should immediately call in the veterinarian to administer antibiotics and show you how to treat any abscesses. A horse recuperating from strangles should have complete rest and fresh drinking water at all times. He should be given light feed, like a bran mash, and be kept warm and away from drafts. Strangles came to be known as shipping fever because of its prevalence among horses transported long distances, when resistance is lowered by nervousness and fatigue. If you buy a horse from a large stable or a dealer, he may bring along a new strain of respiratory virus. If you have other horses, keep new arrivals separate in a different building and pasture for a minimum of two weeks until the danger period is past. There is a vaccination for strangles, but it may cause some side effects, so discuss the risks versus benefits with your veterinarian.

Tetanus (Lockjaw)

Tetanus is caused by toxin-producing bacteria present in the intestinal tract of many animals. It is found in abundance where horses live. Its anaerobic spores can exist for years under the soil or in other airless environments, entering the body through a wound, laceration, or the umbilicus of a newborn foal.

Symptoms include muscle stiffness and rigidity, flared nostrils, hypersensitivity, and legs stiffly held in a sawhorse stance. The muscles in the jaw and face stiffen to a point where the horse can't eat or drink.

Though not contagious, the disease poses a constant threat to horses as well as humans, most of whom will die if infected. To prevent tenanus, your horse should be immunized annually.

RESPIRATORY AILMENTS

Allergic Lung Disease/Chronic Obstructive Pulmonary Disease

These new tongue-twisting names refer to a condition once known as *heaves*. It is now called simply COPD. The ailment develops when a susceptible individual is exposed to allergens such as dust, molds, or other air pollutants, causing an inflammatory reaction in the lungs. If not controlled, this inflammation will scar and stiffen once-elastic lung tissue, making breathing difficult. As the asthmatic condition causes air cells in the lungs to become overinflamed, the horse must take in extra air and then use his stomach muscles to force it out. Eventually respiration will become so impaired that the horse will have difficulty eating without distress. A bad bronchitis might also develop into chronic heaves.

Like a human with emphysema, a horse with heaves destroys air sacs every time he coughs. The lungs lose their normal elasticity, and the affected animal breathes in and out with two distinct movements. This strain on the lungs causes a barrel chest, and the forced pushing-out of air causes an enlargement of the stomach muscles called a *heave line*. Heavey horses may tire easily and will have a deep, barking, persistent cough. They have difficulty breathing during even moderate exercise. (Breathing will be hurried, with nostrils dilated.) In severe cases the nostrils become extremely distended, even when the horse is idle. Some separate ailments, like sinusitis, pneumonia, and anemia, are secondary results of a respiratory system weakened by heaves.

Careful treatment when this disease develops can prevent its progression and allow the horse to live a full life span. If not too advanced, it can be arrested with proper attention. The veterinarian may tell you to eliminate hay temporarily (possibly permanently) and substitute a special feed, like pellet concentrates. Even a slight cough should be checked out by the veterinarian and treated.

Roaring and Whistling

These are two different stages of a single disorder, resulting from a paralysis of the nerves that power the vocal cord muscles. In mild cases the affected horse makes a whistling sound when he inhales; in severe cases he emits a loud wheeze, known as roaring. Don't confuse this condition with the normal snorting sound made by an excited horse. Roaring occurs only during inhalation. Sometimes the disorder will follow a case of strangles. The condition is often found in Thoroughbreds and very large horses. Ponies rarely suffer from roaring or whistling—why, no one knows.

Bed Itch

Bed itch, a form of dermatitis, produces crusty, sore spots on parts of the skin that have come in contact with soiled bedding, typically thighs and elbows. Keep the stall clean and contact your veterinarian for medication.

Chain-curb Gall

This condition can be caused by a twisted curb chain or a strap that is too tight. The resulting inflammation is similar to a saddle sore. The best medicine for saddle sores and galls is to prevent them by systematically conditioning and grooming your horse and making sure that all tack is carefully fitted and adjusted.

Mud Fever or Rain Rot

Rain rot is a crusted, painful infectious skin inflammation caused by a microorganism called *Dermatophilus* that thrives on damp coats. When it drizzles but doesn't rain hard enough to thoroughly cleanse a coat or when snow melt dampens it, this organism starts to reproduce, causing scabbing and hair loss, usually in the areas of water runoff. The condition is most common in winter or early spring when horses with time off do a lot of standing around outdoors.

Mud fever can be prevented by keeping equine legs as clean and dry as possible. In wet weather, hose off accumulated mud, and hand-dry the legs with a towel or a hair dryer. Then keep the horse inside for a while. Never let a horse stand for days in wet mud.

SKIN PROBLEMS

The infection is best combated with an iodine-based shampoo, after discussing the frequency of treatment with your veterinarian. Rain rot can be transmitted, so be careful not to use the same grooming tools or equipment on other horses. As the infected horse heals, disinfect the grooming tools with a mixture of three parts water to one part bleach.

Ringworm

This fungus shows up like raised circles on bare skin, developing into lesions covered with a grayish crust when a horse rubs or scratches them. The crust can then spread to other areas the horse touches. This condition is highly contagious (especially on grooming tools and tack) to people as well as other horses, and it should be treated immediately by your veterinarian. Fortunately it is not very common and is mostly limited to young horses, generally clearing up in two to three weeks.

Saddle Sores and Galls

Saddle sores are usually caused by ill-fitting equipment, but they can also appear on an out-of-condition horse that has been ridden hard or on one that has not been thoroughly or carefully groomed. The girth of the saddle may pinch or rub the skin, making a raw spot. A saddle that doesn't fit properly or has pads that are too small or improperly placed may cause soreness or bruising. Most saddle sores occur in the small area where the tree has pressed down on the withers or back, leaving a welt that gradually reduces in size and eventually becomes concave as pressure is removed. The hair around this type of sore will turn white.

Another easily irritated area is beneath the cantle, where sores can be caused when a rider sits too far back and doesn't balance correctly, bouncing around rather than redistributing weight in the center of the saddle. Equine backs take a beating from poor horsemanship. Many years ago the U.S. Army designed the uncomfortable McClellan saddle specifically to protect the backs of cavalry horses from green troops by distributing the weight evenly, thereby absorbing the concussion of bouncing derrieres.

If they go unattended, saddle sores can become very nasty and difficult to heal. The usual and most important treatment, which you can do yourself, is to give the area a rest and apply a drying medication. When a sore is swollen but not open, soak the area or apply an ice pack. Sometimes a warm water and salt bath is effective. Your veterinarian can suggest the best treatment.

If you absolutely have to use a horse before a saddle sore has completely healed, cut a hole in a thick saddle pad to relieve the pressure. But it is far better to let the horse rest until the sore is fully healed, because the saddle pad can slip and make the sore worse.

Scratches

This scabby and/or oozing skin inflammation, which appears on the back of the pastern above the heels, is sometimes called *greasy heel.* The condition is painful and can cause lameness when scabs form and crack or become infected and bleeding and oozing. It is thought to be caused by loss of protective skin oil when a horse is over-exposed to moisture such as a muddy pasture or windy winter weather. In my experience horses with white skin are more susceptible, but those of any color can become victims if the conditions are right.

Try to treat scratches before it really takes hold, and keep a vigilant watch on the legs of horses that are especially prone to getting it. Keep the pastern clean and dry, but not so excessively dry that it removes the natural oils from the horse's skin. A mild form of scratches can be compared to chapped hands that people get in winter. In some cases it may be helpful to protect the affected area with a coating of Vaseline or Desitin, checking it at least once a day and wiping accumulated dirt off and applying fresh ointment. If cracked skin appears, trim away excess hair carefully with scissors. Wash the area gently with a mild soap or Betadine scrub, removing only scabs that will come off easily. Use clean towels or a hair dryer to *dry off* the area thoroughly (wetness is what probably started it in the first place) before applying the antibacterial ointment recommended by your veterinarian. This procedure will also help to prevent further spreading.

When a thick scab has formed, the horse can be very sore. Apply ichthammol ointment after cleaning and drying the area. Cover with a plastic wrap, then wrap a cotton quilt bandage over it and secure the area with a standing leg bandage. (See Chapter 20.)

Moistening or antibiotic creams may clear up scratches in some cases, but quite a number of horses who contract it continue to have chronic or acute problems. Be sure to confer with your veterinarian if this is the case.

Sunburn

Sunburn is indicated by red, swollen skin and is caused either by direct sun or an allergic reaction to light, triggered by certain foods like buckwheat and St. John's wort. (See Appendix B.) Several other grasses, as well as some weeds, will irritate the skin when wet. Because any number of things could cause sunburnlike irritation, any red or swollen area should be seen by the veterinarian.

Lips, nose, eyelids, parts of the ear, and other areas where the hair is thin can also burn if they are pink or lacking in pigment. Even the underparts of the horse—udder, sheath, and beneath the tail—can burn in winter from sun reflecting off the snow. This is unusual, but it can happen when a horse is taken from a shady area and exposed to intense sunlight for a long time.

Pale horses like Albinos, Palominos, cremes, and Tobiano Pintos and Paints are the most likely to get their skin burned and coats faded by the sun. Take care to work them only in the morning or late afternoon when the sun's rays are weakest. When not being worked, these horses should be blanketed with a light cotton sheet. A white face should be protected with sunblock, which is included in some fly repellent ointments.

In severe cases of sunburn, a veterinarian may use corticosteroids. In less serious cases the horse is kept in a dark stall and turned out only in the evening until he's completely healed. Human cooling ointments or sprays can be applied to affected areas. Preventive human ointments can also be used.

GENETIC DISORDERS

Purebreds have been carefully selected to pass on their best characteristics to the next generation. But this can backfire and perpetuate genetic disorders. If you are planning to purchase an Arabian or a Quarter Horse for breeding purposes, be aware of two genetic disorders: combined immunodeficiency (CID) in Arabians, and hyperkalemic periodic paralysis (HYPP) in Quarter Horses.

Only 3 percent of Arabians carry CID, which affects the immune system, causing the death of foals by inhibiting their ability to produce a specific type of white blood cell. Removal of this disease defense makes the foal vulnerable to infection from organisms encountered every day in soil, water, and air. There is no treatment for this condition.

CID is caused by an inherited recessive gene carried in both the mare and stallion. A horse with the CID defect has a 50 percent chance of passing it on. When bred to another carrier, the chances of producing a CID foal are one in four. After more than twenty years of research, an expensive DNA test to check breeding stock has been developed. If breeders are conscientious and CID carriers are not bred, this disorder can be eliminated.

HYPP began with a gene mutation in the Quarter Horse stallion Impressive. It is estimated that due to the popularity of Impressive and his offspring, about 100,000 Quarter Horses carry the gene. At least one parent of an affected animal must carry the abnormal gene and be affected to pass it on.

The symptoms of this disorder are intermittent attacks of muscle tremors, localized shaking, trembling, weakness, disorientation, or convulsions. In severe cases an unpredictable attack of paralysis can lead to collapse and sudden death, usually from cardiac arrest and/or respiratory failure. The horse is affected for life, with symptoms that sometimes decrease with age. It also appears that the disease can be associated with stress, intensive training, dietary changes, illness, or disease.

To control this inherited malady, a horse to be used for breeding should be tested. Beginning in 1999, the American Quarter Horse Association will require all foals to be tested prior to registration, in hopes of eliminating this disorder.

Leg and Foot Problems

Lameness

Lameness is defined as an alteration in gait. It can be caused by pain in other parts of the body (neck, withers, shoulders, back, loin, or hips), as well as in the foot or leg. Identifying the source is essential to proper treatment. Lameness can be deceptive; it appears only when a horse is under saddle and then is evident only by a barely detectable shortening of the stride. Or it may be obvious to a rider only when trotting or when he circles in one direction, going downhill or working on a hard surface. Owners and trainers familiar with a horse's normal way of going can usually pick up on any irregularity.

The trot is usually the best gait for evaluating lameness because of its two-beat character and stride pattern. The irregularity will show up in an abnormal distribution of weight between the diagonally opposite legs. Your veterinarian may want to see the horse move on both a hard and a soft surface to evaluate the extent of injury. He or she will observe the horse at the walk and trot, from the front, back, and both sides. A shortening of stride, irregular foot placement, head bobbing, stiffness, and weight shifting are signs that aid in the diagnosis.

When a horse is being ridden, lameness can usually be detected by an uneven stride or an unnatural bobbing of the head. Dismount immediately, and check to see if a stone has lodged in your horse's shoe. On hunts and trail rides, remember to carry a hoof pick with you for this purpose.

Lameness is sometimes barely detectable, but in other cases it is so severe that the horse is unable to put any weight on the affected limb. Based on the initial exam, your veterinarian may recommend further tests like a radiograph, nerve or joint

PARTS OF SKELETON AND INTERIOR OF HOOF

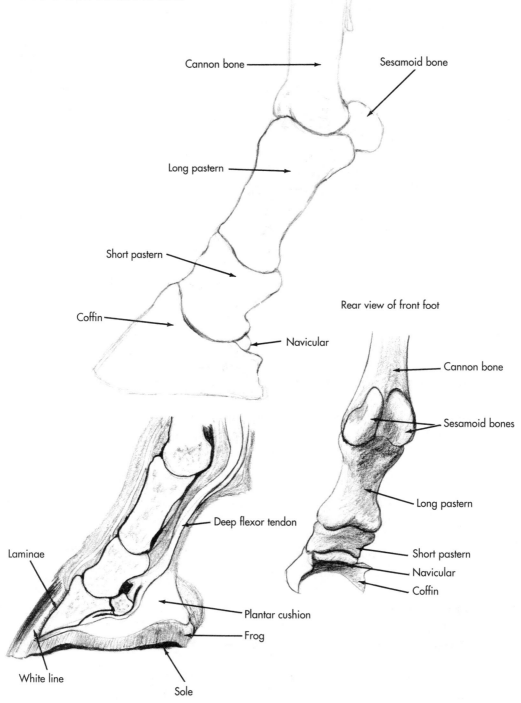

Cannon bone

Sesamoid bone

Long pastern

Short pastern

Coffin

Navicular

Rear view of front foot

Cannon bone

Sesamoid bones

Long pastern

Short pastern

Navicular

Coffin

Deep flexor tendon

Laminae

Plantar cushion

Frog

White line

Sole

block, arthroscopy, ultrasound, or blood, synovial (joint fluid), and tissue samples. Before resorting to any tests, he or she will do a thorough hands-on exam, palpating muscles, joints, bones, and tendons in the suspect area for evidence of pain, heat, swelling, or other abnormalities. Hoof testers are often used to apply pressure to the soles of the feet in order to detect undue sensitivity or pain. Or the veterinarian may hold the horse's leg in a flexed position for about ninety seconds, then release it and immediately trot him away. If this is the affected area, signs of pain are usually very apparent in weight shifting or irregular movement.

If you can find no obvious reason for a horse's lameness, jog him out on a level or uphill stretch. Each time the sound front leg hits the ground, his head will nod. If the lameness is behind, he will put most of his weight on the sound leg. To find the right spot, run your hands simultaneously down both front or back legs, and try to notice differences. Compare them for heat bumps, swellings, or obvious signs of sensitivity. Sometimes several of these symptoms will be present; in rare cases, none. In any case call your veterinarian, and follow his or her directions closely. Try not to rush the horse back to work. Along with correct diagnosis and proper treatment, rest and time are the best cure.

Cocked Ankles

Cocked ankles are a common condition among young horses that haven't had enough exercise and/or a proper diet and regular trimming. The condition distorts the horse's way of standing.

Ringbone

This arthritic condition occurs on the bottom or top of the pastern joint. It is caused in some cases by a conformation fault (like toeing in), but usually it is a result of hard work or old age. It shows as stiffness in the joint and can be confirmed with X-rays. Medication can be used to mask the symptoms, but for buying and selling purposes, ringbone is considered an unsoundness.

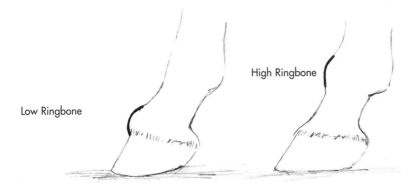

Low Ringbone

High Ringbone

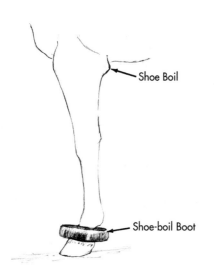

Shoe Boil

Shoe-boil Boot

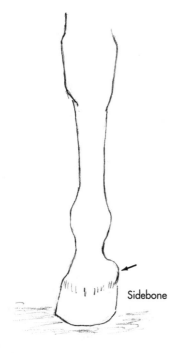

Sidebone

Shoe Boils

These fluid-filled areas or lumps on the elbow of the front legs will develop when a horse that is lying down repeatedly bangs the elbow with his front hoof. This can be prevented by using a shoe-boil boot: a round of canvas roll that fits over the lower pastern, keeping the hoof from the elbow. Shoe boils can be drained and injected with steroids, but the boot needs to be used to avoid recurrence. Although these boils don't cause lameness, they are very unsightly.

Sidebones

Also considered an unsoundness, sidebones are a hardening of the lateral cartilage inside the coffin bone. They can be caused by serious conformation defects and also may occur in racehorses that have been worked too early and others whose feet interfere (hit themselves) at fast gaits. In a few instances, this condition, like ringbone, can be inherited. A horse thus affected tends to walk on his toes or shuffle.

Sprains

A sprain will usually cause a horse to become quite lame. It may look very serious: within a few hours the affected area will begin to heat and swell up. A sprain can result from a sudden movement, a fall, or a quick turn on muddy ground. Overgrown toes can also put more stress on tendons and ligaments, causing a sprain. Jog your horse out to find out which limb is affected, and call the veterinarian, who may recommend an overnight poultice or a hosing down.

Splints

Splints are inflammations of the ligament that hold the splint bone to the cannon bone. A fairly common condition, it can be caused by a simple accident, like bumping a rail when jumping, or doing too much work over hard ground. After the initial period of swelling, calcification usually occurs. Once the heat is down, splints won't interfere with a horse's way of going—as long as they are not involved with or close to a joint or tendon.

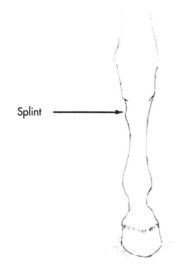

Splint

Stocking Up

Many horses that are left standing idle for long periods after hard work will get edema in the legs. They are generally not lame. The usual cause of the problem is poor circulation sometimes resulting from conformation faults. To keep the legs from filling up with fluid, be sure to walk your horse out well after working. Usually after ten or fifteen minutes of warm-up work, a stocked-up horse will come down to normal. A support bandage, the equine equivalent of Supp-Hose, called Equihose, will help this condition. So will a stable bandage (described later in this chapter).

HOCK PROBLEMS

Several of these conditions are similar to bursitis and arthritis in humans. Some are considered a serious unsoundness, while others are blemishes that don't interfere with a horse's way of going.

Bog Spavin

This is caused by a buildup of excessive fluid in the joint capsule at the front end and sides of the hock. Again, it is usually the result of a conformation fault like a straight hock. This condition usually doesn't make a horse lame. (See Chapter 3.)

Bone Spavin (Jack Spavin)

This problem is more serious and is usually considered an unsoundness. It is arthritis of the hock, and it often occurs when a horse is subjected to too much heavy strain—for instance, working a long time in very heavy, deep footing. (See page 28.)

Because these faults put abnormal stress on the hock, sickle-hocked or cow-hocked horses are more susceptible to this disorder. To detect jack spavin, hold your horse's hind leg and fold it under for a few minutes, then trot him out. Any stiffness will be immediately apparent in his gait.

Capped Hock

This swelling is caused by an injured bursa (one of the fluid sacs that surround various joints, tendons, and ligaments) at the point of the hock, causing it to secrete an abnormal amount of fluid. It's like the human condition "water on the knee" (in this case, water on the hock!). (See Chapter 3.)

Curbs

Curbs are inflammations of the plantar ligament behind the hock. They are seen mostly in Standardbreds, sometimes in Thoroughbreds, and are usually due to poor conformation (like sickle hocks or cow hocks). (See page 28.)

Progressive Arthritic Hock Changes

These changes frequently occur as horses age. The cartilage pads and synovial membranes that cushion and lubricate the joint don't regenerate as quickly. Sometimes this condition is the result of wear and tear from the stress of hard work or competition, or the changes may occur because of conformation faults that reduce a joint's effectiveness. When a horse is under stress from hard work, inflamed joints and tissues release destructive enzymes, causing more rapid degeneration.

A horse may react to this painful condition by being unable to track up anymore, refusing to move out, or in the case of a hunter or jumper, switching leads before taking a fence to lessen the strain on his sore back legs.

To rule out other problems before making a diagnosis, your veterinarian will do flexion tests and analyze the horse on the lunge or under saddle to locate the site of the pain, perhaps taking an X-ray of the hock to make sure that that's where the trouble lies.

Once he confirms the diagnosis, your veterinarian has a number of different treatment options, depending on the severity of the condition. They could include poulticing with DMSO (available through your veterinarian) or medicating temporarily with phenylbutazone (Butazolidin, or Bute) or another painkiller. In more severe cases, injections into the joint itself may be suggested and/or food supplements prescribed. Intravenous hylaronic acid, known as Legend, has been a wonderful solution for a number of my clients' horses.

The most effective supplements have an active component of complex sugar molecules called glycosaminoglycans, or (mercifully) GAGs for short. They are produced by cells in the cartilage of all mammals to promote its growth. Under normal conditions the cells manufacture enough of these molecules to keep up with ordinary wear and tear, but when cartilage starts to degenerate from inflammation and/or arthritis, GAG production lags behind. Oral supplements bond chemically with destructive enzymes and incapacitate them, giving the body a chance to catch up and repair damaged tissues.

When one of these supplements is mixed with a horse's grain, the benefits will begin to show within four to six weeks. During this period the horse is usually dropped back to lighter work. His back and hip muscles can be affected by hock soreness. Acupuncture and/or massage by a licensed practitioner can speed up the healing process.

Several horses in my barn have used GAG products with great success. Some seem to work better than others for certain individuals; a product that is healing for one horse may not have the same result with another. If your horse has not improved by six weeks on supplements, the joint should be reevaluated by the veterinarian.

Thoroughpin

This is a swelling in the lubricating sheath that surrounds the tendons on the sides and back of the hock. Usually caused by overexertion, the swelling is soft and spongy to the touch. Contact your veterinarian for the proper treatment.

There are numerous hoof problems and diseases to watch out for, and most will require the attention of a veterinarian.

HOOF TROUBLES

Abscesses

One of the common causes of lameness, an abscess can be caused by just about any injury to the foot—a nail prick during shoeing, tearing off a shoe accidentally, a piece of sand or gravel in a cracked hoof wall, or severe bruising of the sole. A puncture can close up quickly, trapping bacteria in the sole and often going unnoticed until a week or two has passed and the horse suddenly comes up very lame. A severe bruise produces blood in the interior of the hoof that puts pressure on the surrounding tissue, causing microcracks through which bacteria gain access.

Abscesses usually cause heat in the foot and a pulse above the heel. When the veterinarian or farrier pares away the sole to the afflicted spot, releasing all the pus from it, relief comes quickly. But without proper drainage the abscess will follow the path of least resistance and break out at the coronary band, usually at the heel. To draw out the infection, the foot must be soaked in hot water and Epsom salts for about

Soaking foot = abscess

Easy boot

twenty minutes several times a day. Then apply a poultice like ichthammol over the wound area, covering it with several gauze pads, and wrap the whole hoof, including the entire sole area, with a wide, self-sticking tape like Vetwrap. You can put an Easy Boot over the bandage to keep the area completely protected while the poultice does its job, allowing the horse to be turned out during the healing process. In these cases make sure your horse's tetanus shot is current.

Bruised Soles

A bruised sole can be caused by a sharp object, like a stone lodged in the crevice of the frog, or by an ill-fitting shoe. Rocky or frozen ground can be enough to bruise a thin sole. A horse with this injury may be lame, and the foot will be tender to the touch, sometimes with a reddish mark. The bruising occurs in the deep, sensitive tissue covering the coffin bone, known as the *sensitive sole*. Horses with flat feet are prone to stone bruises and should be protected with leather or plastic pads.

Contracted Heels

This problem results when the frog loses contact with the ground, leaving the outer wall to bear the brunt of impact. This puts severe strain on the leg and can lead to chronic lameness and navicular disease. The most common cause of contracted heels is an overly long toe that unbalances the hoof, which then loses its ability to expand under the horse's weight. Very hard or dry hooves transfer the concussion of movement inside the foot, causing interior bruising, outside cracking, and eventually lameness, unless corrected by proper trimming and shoeing. Make sure the shoe is large enough for the foot and not too narrow in the heel.

Corns

A corn is the outer manifestation of a bruise, a discolored area of the sole, usually between the bar and the wall. Because of its location, it does not heal as easily as those bruises of the sensitive sole within. A *dry corn* is a bruised area in the sensitive tissue. It shows up as red staining, coming from dried blood inside the sole. A *moist corn* is more serious, the result of fluid seeping beneath the sole. If it is allowed to become infected and abscessed, this condition can be very dangerous, causing permanent damage to inner tissues.

Laminitis or Founder

Pushing an unfit horse at a fast pace for long periods until he dropped or foundered, which happened often during turn-of-the-century military operations, probably gave rise to the name of this hoof disease. It can also be a result of feeding a horse beyond his daily maintenance requirements, stabling him without proper exercise, or giving him too much rich green grass in the spring. (Fat ponies are particularly liable to *grass founder*.) Acute cases of founder are usually caused by excessive feeding, fast work on a hard surface, or drinking large quantities of cold water after working hard. Sometimes it develops as a complication following another disease. Founder causes an inflammation of the sensitive laminae on one or more feet, usually the front. The horse will be very lame and in pain, and his feet will be not only hot but sensitive to the touch as the expanding laminae press against the wall and sole, causing extreme discomfort. Secretariat was a victim of this dreadful disease.

Founder

The temperature of a foundering horse may go as high as 106 degrees, and he will sweat profusely. In chronic cases the hooves can become so distorted that the sole separates entirely from the wall, the hoof dishes inward, the toe curls up, and the sole drops down—a condition called *seedy toe*. A horse that has foundered badly will have very clearly defined markings on his hooves. Normally any rings there will parallel the coronet, but founder rings tend to cluster up around it and drop down toward the heel in back. Fever and changes in nutrition will also create rings, but this type parallels the coronet farther down. For an acute case of founder, apply wet, cold packs to the feet, or stand your horse in wet clay or a cold stream until the veterinarian arrives. For a chronic case, special trimming and shoes will be required after the temperature has been stabilized and the horse is on the mend. A horse that founders badly will probably never be completely sound again.

Laminitis is considered chronic when the coffin bone rotates, a situation that occurs when the tissues or laminae connecting the coffin bone to the hoof wall weaken and actually break down. This breakdown is caused by toxins, especially histamine, which change the permeability of the blood vessels in the tissue. It could happen from three days to a few weeks after the onset of the disease. The catalyst is probably too much grain, lush pasture, or other trauma to the sensitive laminae. Veterinarians consider laminitis an elusive, little-understood disease, and many questions about it remain to be answered. Early detection is the key to preventing serious damage, so if you even suspect founder, consider it an emergency, and don't hesitate to call the veterinarian. It could make the difference between a healthy horse and one that is permanently unsound.

When laminitis is suspected, some vets will recommend soaking the hoof in Epsom salts to help remove those inflaming toxins. Others might tell you to walk your horse out twice a day to restore circulation. Whatever the advice, follow it to the letter.

Navicular Disease

The degeneration of the navicular bone is usually the result of a direct or indirect trauma to interior or exterior tissues, caused by a conformation fault that puts severe stress on the bone, shoeing that leaves a heel too high, a long period of fast work on a hard surface, or intense work after days of rest. Sometimes it is a secondary result of contracted heels. One symptom of an affected front foot is *pointing,* when a horse shifts his weight back to relieve the pain in the front feet.

Normally this very small bone inside the hoof acts as a pulley to change the direction of the tendons on the back of the leg, but a direct or indirect injury to the deep flexor tendon, the irregular development of the bone, an inhibited vascular supply, or the aftermath of a previous infectious disease like strangles can interfere with this function. Some horses are not permanently disabled by the disease and can resume activity with the aid of a good veterinarian or a farrier. The angle of the foot can be raised and degree pads added to relieve pressure and encourage circulation to the navicular area. Many vets recommend the daily use of isoxsuprine hydrochloride with a tablet of Bute the day before and after strenuous activity. But the pain of severe degeneration can be relieved only by cutting the nerve to the heel so the horse doesn't feel it *(nerving)*.

Quarter Cracks (Sand Cracks)

These vertical cracks on either side of the hoof or toes (toe cracks) are caused by drying out. When a crack extends to the hairline, dirt and sand may work their way up into the coronet, where they fester and lead to lameness. Some horses, perhaps because of a deficiency of the paripole, are more prone to cracked hooves than others. As weight bears down on a hoof, a sand crack will open and close, exposing sensitive underlying tissues to infection if deep enough. The hoof will eventually grow new horn to repair the damage, but the process takes eight months to a year depending on diet and environment. The most serious cracks are those extending from the coronary band to the area where new hoof is made, crippling the ability to produce horn and resulting in a permanent fissure on the wall.

Cracked hooves are treated like dry ones. In addition, some blacksmiths advise shoeing to keep the crack from widening, and plastic is sometimes used to fill very

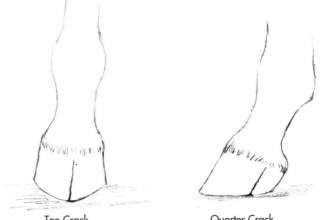

Toe Crack   Quarter Crack

wide cracks. Standardbred and Thoroughbred farriers do this with fiberglass patching material (called quarter-crack patches). Special trimming to take stress off the area is usually effective. The problem may not be as serious as it looks. A lot of horses continue to function well even with severely cracked hooves.

Quittor

Quittor is a fistula sore on the coronet. It can be caused by a blow from a horse's own foot or from pus working up from another hoof injury, like a corn, a nail puncture, or a piece of sand in a crack that becomes embedded in the hairline and festers. This ailment is painful and usually causes lameness. A veterinarian's attention will be needed, and a poultice will probably be recommended.

A Quittor

Rings and Ridges

Rings and ridges on the hooves give a visual, chronological history of your horse's medical problems. As it grows, the hoof records each injury and illness, as well as the nutritional status of itself and the entire horse. Inflammation is the chief cause of most hoof irregularities, and when the coronary band is affected, it produces thicker (but not healthier) horn with rings, ridges, or bumps. If the band is not receiving proper nutrition, it produces thinner horn, which appears as a groove. Repeated, evenly spaced rings and ridges record a repeated cycle of inflammation and recovery that weakens hooves and makes them brittle. Rings that are numerous and farther apart at the heel than the toe are a sign of chronic laminitis. Loss of circulation in the toe area may also cause it to dish in. Long after a horse has recovered from a serious illness, like a respiratory infection, a single distinct ring around each of the four hooves will be visible as its calling card. A trauma caused by abscess or injury to the coronary band could show up as a bump of a single bulge that descends as the hoof grows, weakening the wall and eventually cracking. Once any inflammation has receded, the hoof growth returns to normal. Any defects will migrate down the hoof, where they will be worn down or trimmed away, but the process takes nearly a year.

Thrush

Thrush is a rotting of the tissue around the frog, causing it to darken and soften. Sometimes a thick black discharge is present. It usually begins in the cleft of the frog and extends into the bars and sole. Severe cases are caused by damp, dirty conditions in a stall or paddock, but mild ones are common in the spring and other extended periods of wet weather. Some horses are prone to thrush even when kept in the best of environments. Thrush is easily detected by the foul smell it gives to the hoof. Mild cases can be successfully treated with a daily sprinkling of Kopertex or other commercial remedies available through your veterinarian or local tack shop. If unchecked, the disease can involve the frog and the horse will go lame. Keeping your horse's stall and turnout area as clean and dry as possible and cleaning the feet daily are the best preventives.

White Line Disease

This bacterial-fungal invasion of the white portion of the hoof horn was described by the Scottish veterinarian who first identified it as *horn-digesting bacteria*. Other researchers have isolated various fungal agents, but it is still not known whether they are part of the cause or an effect; nor is it known how the disease spreads. But the result is certain: devastating destruction of the hoof wall. This disease is most prevalent in hot, humid areas of the United States, but it has also appeared on the New England coast and in Texas, Arizona, and California. Early symptoms resemble the effects of poor nutrition or excessive selenium in the diet and can be easily misinterpreted. Hoof walls show uneven growth rings and may look flaky and crumble easily, especially around nail holes. As the condition progresses, it destroys the hoof wall in a triangular pattern, with the apex near the coronary band. Affected horses are sometimes misdiagnosed as foundered because they go lame and experience some type of extreme rotation, and because the hoof feels warm to the touch over the apex of the frog—all symptoms of laminitis.

The telltale difference between this disease and laminitis is the character of the gas pocket caused by the bacteria and fungi. It creates a bulge extending down one side of the hoof wall (the result of unattached horn continuing to grow), while the opposite side looks dished. Because the white zone has been destroyed, the outer horn has no support when it grows out. The dish forms when the bone drops away from the involved side, causing the opposite hoof wall to cave in. Although the bulge and other characteristics of the disease can be spotted early, only your veterinarian or farrier will be able to give an accurate diagnosis. The affected wall will have to be cut away with a tool called a Dremel and the area treated. Unless the condition is caught in its first stages, a horse must be sidelined for several months while the hoof heals.

BANDAGING

Special leg bandages are made for horses, with ties or Velcro to hold them firmly in place. They are used over cotton batting or cotton wrap and give real protection to the leg.

Before starting to bandage, put your horse in cross-ties. Don't park yourself on the floor where he might kick you if irritated; instead, crouch down so you can easily get out of the way. Begin by putting the cotton batting over the cannon bone. Have your bandage rolled and ready to go, with the Velcro or ties on the inside of the roll. Start in the middle of the leg, and wrap down to the top of the fetlock and then back up again. The bandage should be firm but not tight.

Cold Water Bandages

These are used to cool hot or strained muscles and reduce swelling. They are wraps with convenient pockets for ice or compresses, designed for humans, that stay cold for twenty minutes after application. When a compress warms up, it can be returned to the freezer to chill out again. Poultices that substitute for ice are also used to cool and tighten muscles. The pain of strained or swollen legs can be relieved until the veterinarian arrives by hosing them down.

If none of these medicinal wraps are available, there are some homemade alternatives. You can cut up quilted padding from an old mattress cover or other source and use it as a wrap, applying it underneath a regular stable bandage. (Don't use cotton, which dissolves quickly.) Wrap the leg as you would for an exercise bandage, but make it a little looser and include the ankle. (You want to be able to pour in crushed ice or hose water down into the bandage; hence the looseness.) You can also use a cotton pad soaked in ice water before wrapping.

Another alternative, as good as cold water hosing, is an ice-filled rubber wrap. I've made these by cutting off about three feet of tire tubing and slipping it around the horse's leg, securing it with a cotton leg bandage at the bottom and top and filling it with cracked ice all around. Or if the strain is lower down, you can tie it at the bottom under the hooves with bailing twine so your horse can stand in it. A commercial five-pound bag of ice will last in the tubing for several hours.

This bandage works wonders, quickly reducing swelling and getting rid of inflammation and heat. I've found it most effective on horses that have just pulled a tendon. When treated promptly with ice or cold water, they usually recover in three to five days. Of course any of these treatments should be approved by your veterinarian.

Hot Water Bandages

Except for their temperature, these are identical to cold water bandages. The wrap is soaked first in hot water, then applied; a dry outer bandage is placed over it and a poultice like ichthammol is used to draw out any abscess or infection. Instead of resoaking the same pad and applying it again, hot water wraps are changed frequently to keep maximum heat on the affected area.

Exercise Bandages

These are used occasionally when riding to give support and reinforce weak tendons, as decoration for a parade, or to protect legs from brambles or thorns. Only the area from below the knee to the top of the fetlock is covered with bandage (polo wrap), as with a stable bandage. The bandage should be applied quite firmly, taking care not to restrict the joint, finishing in the center of the cannon bone. (See Chapter 25 for an illustration and directions.)

Poultices

A poultice is a treatment for a punctured or abscessed foot. After the veterinarian has diagnosed the condition and thoroughly cleaned out the affected foot, soak the foot in warm water and Epsom salts for at least twenty minutes to draw out the infection. Then apply a poultice paste. I use smelly old ichthammol, slathering it over the area, then covering it with several large gauze pads. I top it all off with Vetwrap, which should completely cover the sole of the foot and be secured by wrapping the entire hoof.

The safest and best cover for this dressing is a heavy rubber Easy Boot. It is kept firmly in place by a spring clip and is available in different sizes, a handy item to have around any barn. You can turn a horse out in a boot without worrying about whether it will come off. It is easily slipped on in an emergency, should a horse with tender soles lose a shoe. Sometimes a shoe is accidentally torn off, leaving the hoof wall vulnerable to chipping or breaking down.

Murphy's law seems to take over in crises like this, which have a way of occurring a few days before a competition when all the farriers are "out in the field." Provided a horse isn't lame, he can be exercised in the boot and your training program won't be interrupted.

If you haven't gotten around to buying these boots, a temporary solution in an emergency is a piece of heavy cloth cut to fit the sole of the foot over the paste and fastened in place with good old duct tape.

Spider Bandages

A spider bandage is excellent for a wound at the joint. It is cut from a burlap bag, and sections of the material are then loop-tied down the leg to hold the underlying batting firmly in place. Ready-made joint wraps are also available at tack shops and through mail-order catalogs.

Support Bandages (Standing Wraps)

These bandages are used to prevent edema (stocking up) from building up in a horse's legs after he has been standing in the barn overnight after a workout. They are also frequently used when a horse receives a leg injury and the veterinarian does not want the swelling to extend to the lower leg. A large cotton wrap can be purchased at your tack supplier. These are about 16 by 30 inches or larger, are quilted and/or filled with fiber fills of poly and nylon, and are wrapped next to the leg to form the under layer. A leg wrap (a polo wrap or one that is even wider but *not elastic*) is wrapped over it to keep it in place. All of these wraps are washable. Nonsterile, bleached cotton can be purchased in a roll that is not washable, but it is not as practical or economical in the long run.

Trucking and Stable Bandages

Use these for protection in trucking or vanning a horse or to keep him from stocking up during a prolonged period in the stall. Wrap the cotton from a point below the knee right down to the coronet, making sure it covers the horse's heels to protect them from injury in shipping. Beginning at the middle of the cannon, work down to the coronet and then back up. You may have to use two bandages to cover the entire lower leg, but don't wrap it too tightly or the bandage will leave a mark on the leg or cause the leg to fill up when the bandage is removed. A bandage should

SPIDER BANDAGE

1. Feed bag

2. Cut strips on sides about 1 inch wide

3. Wrap cotton or gauze around leg

4. Fold ties over one another . . .

5. . . . covering ends as you descend

6. Tie in bow at end, cutting off all remaining ends

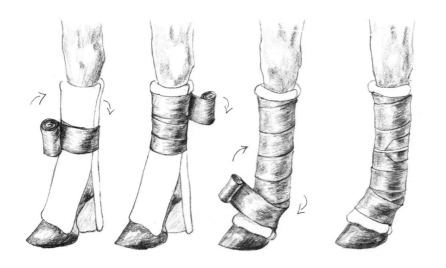

Stable and Transportation Bandage

tie or fasten on the inside or outside of the leg, never on the front or back. To further protect the coronary area, use a quarter boot with a trucking wrap. Ready-made shipping wraps are available at tack shops and through tack catalogs. They protect hocks and hooves as well as legs with easy-to-attach Velcro. These wraps are generously padded on the inside and easy to wipe clean on the outside; they come in a variety of styles, sizes, and colors.

WATER THERAPY

Pool Therapy

You can lead a horse to water, but can you make him swim in it? Nine out of ten horses don't need much persuading, enjoying this new conditioning method from the start. Originally used by racehorse trainers to keep horses fit while they recovered from foot or leg injuries, its beneficial effects on the cardiovascular and respiratory systems have made it more widely popular, particularly for horses prone to joint stress or bowed tendons or those recovering from knee chips or joint surgery. Many trainers have horses do laps in a pool three or four times a week to prepare them for competitive driving, combined training, and other rigorous disciplines. On one famous Arabian horse farm I visited in the Southwest, champion show stock were accompanied to a circular pool twice a week by handlers, who stood on a circular platform in the middle and used a long pole to guide them in the water.

One Olympic three-day event rider has a lake in her backyard that she uses to supplement trot and galloping work in the summer. She continues the program at an indoor equine pool in a neighboring town in the winter.

Swimming is particularly beneficial for older horses. It reduces their riding time by 30 percent while still maintaining fitness. Ten minutes of swimming equals four miles of track work. Ten minutes is the maximum time a horse can do this kind of exercise without overexerting the cardiovascular system, according to Tufts University Equine Sports Medicine director Dr. Howard Seeherman.

Like any other kind of exercise, pool therapy should be introduced in small doses of no more than two minutes, gradually working up to ten. If you would like to augment your regular training with an aquatic program, consult your veterinarian and other area trainers to get a picture of the risks and benefits of this type of work.

Whirlpools

Circulating water in which the horse stands is another therapy, used particularly for tendon and ligament injuries. Whirlpool boots, available at tack shops or through catalogs, are an inexpensive alternative.

Parasites

More than 150 types of internal parasites and numerous external parasites exist. So the odds are good that your horse will be exposed to at least one of them. Each parasite species, whether fly, lice, tick, stomach worm, botfly, or bloodworm, has a subspecies, making the whole subject quite complex. Bloodworms, for instance, come in forty different varieties. The important thing to remember is that all are harmful at particular stages of their development cycle, and that your horse must be kept as free of them as possible, with regular dewormings and good barn and pasture hygiene. Horses that aren't dewormed regularly, with attention to the various larvae stages, can be permanently damaged by internal parasites. Prevention should be a paramount concern of every horse owner. By the time the need for treatment becomes obvious, most of the damage has already been done.

It's hard to believe that these tiny organisms can cause the death of a fifteen-hundred-pound horse, but they are one of the primary cause of disabling or fatal illness. To reduce the number and variety of parasites around your stable, you can take some of the following precautions:

• Store grain in covered containers, so that flies, birds, and rodents—all carriers—can't reach them.

• Clean stalls and change bedding often, to reduce chances of fecal contamination.

• In each dirt floor stall replace ten inches of surface soil with fresh clean soil each year to get rid of the larvae that burrow into it.

• Remove manure from small pastures and corrals twice a week and either spread it on a field not in use or put it on the manure pile.

• Mow or harrow pastures regularly to break up manure piles and expose parasite eggs and larvae to the elements.

• Don't allow the horse to drink from accumulated puddles in the barnyard, since they are contaminated by manure drainage. (They won't be tempted to if fresh water is always available.)

• Spread gravel or fine shale on corrals and paddocks to prevent the horse from eating infested grass.

• Keep the stable and surrounding areas free of manure, soiled bedding, and wasted food, to prevent flies from breeding.

• To break the life cycle of parasites, rotate pastures as often as possible. Allow livestock such as sheep or cattle to graze them, which interrupts the life cycle of equine parasites.

• Prevent overgrazing by keeping to a minimum the number of horses on acreage. This will also reduce fecal contamination.

• Remove botfly eggs regularly from the horse's coat to prevent ingestion.

• Rotate dewormer chemicals, not just brand names, to prevent chemical resistance from developing.

• Consult your veterinarian to set up an effective deworming schedule for the horse.

INTERNAL PARASITES

All horses have them. They enter a horse through the mouth in a number of devious, invisible ways—as eggs, larvae, or adults, carried on the heads of face flies, on blades of grass, or on birds and rodents. Many of these parasitic pests may be present in the horse at any one time and in different stages. Some species can lay more than 200,000 eggs a day, escalating their danger quickly. Different parasites damage the horse's blood vessels, lungs, liver, stomach, and intestines. Many species swim on salivary seas into the hundred-foot alimentary canal, burrowing into walls or tissues along the way until they reach maturity and are expelled through the manure. The most damage is caused in the larval stage of their reproductive cycle, when they penetrate host tissue and organs, leaving scars in their wake.

In sufficient quantities internal parasites cause severe physical strain, undermining performance, preventing proper utilization of food, and often causing permanent damage such as obstructions and ulcerations within the digestive tract or to blood vessels in the intestines, resulting in colic, periodic lameness, a chronic cough, or bronchitis. Eventually they can kill a horse if they are uncontrolled. Bloodworms, which can affect circulation, in extreme cases can cause death from blood clots. Internal parasites are especially lethal in young horses. They penetrate the liver and the lungs. From the age of one month until a year, foals should be dewormed every thirty days to ensure good health.

Other worms produce toxins that destroy red blood cells, leading to anemia. Immature worms migrating through body tissues also open the way for bacteria and fungi to enter the system and cause other diseases.

Telltale Signs That a Horse Is Wormy

- Dull, rough coat
- Frequent tail rubbing
- Lethargic attitude and performance notably off
- Decreased appetite
- Weight loss with no change in diet
- Potbelly
- Frequent colic or diarrhea
- Coughing and/or nasal discharge
- Sores on the skin

Strongyles

LARGE STRONGYLES. These include a variety of species; the most common is the bloodworm. It can cause blood clots in the arteries from scar tissue left behind after larval migration. Any severe loss of blood supply to any portion of the gut causes death to the intestine, resulting in colic, shock, and death of the horse from the overwhelming toxicity.

The larvae are picked up in spring from the pasture, migrate through the gut wall, develop for months in the arteries, then migrate to the intestines where they produce eggs. (The female can lay up to five thousand per day.) The eggs are deposited into the pasture, where they hatch in early spring to resume the cycle again.

SMALL STRONGYLES. These larvae are also ingested orally. They bury themselves in cysts in the walls of the large colon, where they can even evade dewormers. When they burst to release the larvae for their next stage of development, they can also cause extensive edema and hemorrhage. This causes severe inflammation and damage to the absorptive surface of the intestine. Some of the larvae may remain in hibernation in cysts for extended periods. In early spring a massive release of larvae can cause acute diarrhea. Small strongyle larvae also cause weight loss and chronic colic.

Ascarids

The eggshell that protects ascarid larvae enables them to survive in the horse's environment for years. A mature female ascarid can lay millions of eggs in a lifetime and over a period of time may contaminate a large part of the horse's environment. The sticky coating of the egg enables it to adhere to any surface, including the horse himself, or on the teat of a nursing mare. When the egg is ingested, a larva emerges and penetrates the small intestinal wall, then migrates to the horse's liver, through the circulatory system, and to the lungs. There the larva is coughed up and swallowed into

THE MOST COMMON AND TROUBLESOME WORMS

the intestines, where it matures. Ascarids are primarily a danger to foals, who eventually become immune to them as they mature. The larvae's lung migration can cause a nasal discharge with respiratory complications. As they move through the liver and the lung, tissue damage occurs, lung damage predisposing foal to pneumonia. In the digestive tract they may cause diarrhea or constipation with colic. A heavy infestation of ascarid adults can result in a complete blockage or rupture of the intestine.

Pinworms

These worms are about two or three inches long and are one of the few parasites that can be easily spotted in manure by the naked eye. When the egg is ingested, the larvae are released into the small intestine, where they migrate to the cecum and large intestine. There they mature and pass out through the rectum. The female cements her eggs to the anus area, which irritates and causes the horse to rub its tail. As the eggs dry, they detach by the thousands, falling to the ground or being expelled in manure to begin the cycle again.

Botflies

The adult botfly looks like a honeybee as it darts and hovers around a horse's legs, usually in mid- or late summer. It lays its tiny yellow eggs on the hair of the forelegs, belly, flanks, mane, and occasionally shoulder.

When a horse's saliva touches the area where the eggs have been deposited, it warms them and stimulates hatching. The larvae then start their migration in the mouth, burrowing into either the tongue or gum and then working their way down into the stomach. They attach themselves to the stomach or gastric walls and migrate through surrounding tissues. There they remain for nine to eleven months inside the host horse until they reach maturity and pass out through the manure. After one to two months the adult flies emerge to begin the next generation.

Tapeworms

A forage mite ingests tapeworm eggs, which develop into cysticercoids over two to four months. A horse ingests the mite. After one or two months, the adult tapeworm matures in the horse's intestine. These tapeworms are most destructive at the junction of the small intestine and cecum, where they can cause ulceration, inflammation, and a serious condition where the bowel telescopes in on itself. Mature segments are passed in the feces, releasing the eggs, continuing the cycle. The worms seem to appear less in the spring but increase as the season progresses. For this reason treatment is best attempted in the fall.

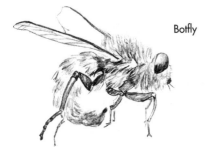

Botfly

Stomach Worms

The worm larvae ingested by the horse migrate to the stomach, where they live (hence their name), develop into adults, reproduce, and then pass out in the feces. These worm larvae are in turn ingested by the larvae of the house or stable fly when they feed on the feces. When these larvae mature, they migrate to the fly's labium, ready for deposit when the fly lights near the horse's mouth, resuming the cycle.

Sometimes the flies deposit stomach worm larvae around an eye or in open wounds. The latter will penetrate damaged skin, feeding there and enlarging the area, resulting in *summer sores*. Although this prevents the cycle from continuing, the resulting sores can become seriously infected if unattended and the skin can become ulcerated and/or granulated.

DEWORMING

The destructive reproductive cycles of parasites can be interrupted only by deworming the horse at least every eight weeks with different chemicals, rotating the type used in order to target specific parasites at the right time. Foals are very susceptible to parasite infestation and will need deworming every month until they are weaned and every six weeks thereafter during the first year. Older horses become more prone to parasites in their late teens and will likewise benefit from a six-week deworming program, as will those suffering from digestive tract problems. Fecal analysis should be done periodically by your veterinarian to help you regulate this.

A six-week schedule is also advised in a crowded turnout area and/or situations with a continuing change of population. Conversely, less frequent dewormings of six times a year would be appropriate in a large pasture area with a consistent population of the same horses. A quarterly program can even be sufficient when several years of fecal exams have shown egg counts to be low.

In a barn full of horses, all should be dewormed at the same time, to prevent any surviving parasites from migrating to an untreated host and then reinfecting other stablemates. And if any neighboring stables are less than conscientious about deworming, you may have to step up your botfly control program from two to four times a year.

Different dewormers are designed for different parasites, and some are safer and more palatable than others. Read labels, and be aware of which chemicals eliminate which parasites at what stage. Depending on their strength, these drugs should be rotated as often as each deworming or as seldom as once a year. The most formidable parasitic villains are strongyles, roundworms, and pinworms, which must be treated at each regular deworming session. Generally bots need be targeted only in spring and fall and tapeworms in the late fall.

Ivermectin and *Strongid* are the dewormers most often used. Ivermectin is not effective against tapeworms, which are more prevalent in wetter southern areas. The procedure with Strongid is to double-dose either orally or by stomach tube (in which case, because of the large volume, your veterinarian will do the procedure), in either late fall or winter if a fecal exam reveals that your horse has been exposed to worm-carrying mites during the summer.

Unfortunately some parasites can develop strains resistant to dewormers, in which case a stronger and/or different chemical must be used. Small strongyles can become resistant to benzimidazoles. Ivermectin appears to be the only chemical

Tube Worming

proven not to have resistance problems, and although it is expensive, it would be the most appropriate to use in a nonrotation program.

Most dewormers come as pastes or pellets. The easiest to use is paste in a syringe-type tube. When a large volume is administered to an uncooperative horse or to one who has food in his mouth, it can get messy. In this case, to avoid getting paste all over yourself, rinse out the horse's mouth with several syringes of water and wait until it drips out. Then squirt in the dewormer. Pellets are designed to be fed mixed in the grain, but some finicky horses may take exception to the added medicine and refuse to eat.

The amount of dewormer given is determined by weight—another good reason to have a weight tape around. Syringes that are used to administer chemical paste have a weight table on the tube.

Before using a syringe, spend some time with your horse. Handle his muzzle, and slowly rub his nose and lips with the empty tube to get him used to it. That way you won't have a fight on your hands every two months.

Many professionals support the use of the daily dewormers Strongid C and Strongid C2X, which have been recently introduced. They are growing in popularity because they also appear to reduce the incidence of colic. Both are administered as feed additives mixed in the horse's grain. Although expensive, they are particularly effective in situations where overcrowding is unavoidable and contamination inevitable. But they do not kill botflies, which must still be targeted in spring and fall with Ivermectin. For the adult horse, daily doses of Strongid C should be supplemented in the spring and fall with Ivermectin paste to control botflies. But if you're giving a double-dose paste for tapeworms, the daily Strongid wormer should be stopped for five days before and after.

The best testimonial to the use of these daily dewormers is a study done by Dr. Mat Reeves at the Michigan State University College of Veterinary Medicine. He found that horses on Strongid C were nine times less likely to develop colic than horses receiving other dewormers.

A daily dewormer fed to a young horse will ensure optimum growth; manufacturers claim that feed bills will be lower, energy levels higher, and weight will increase in horses of all ages. In spite of the extra expense, which is about fifty cents per horse per day, the large farms that use the Strongids swear by them.

The only concern about daily dewormers to date is the possibility that resistance will develop against them. So far no such instance has been documented. There is, however, proof that horses on Strongid C have a better food utilization ratio, and many owners and trainers using the product report other benefits, such as improved coat condition and better general fitness.

As in any maintenance program, your veterinarian should be consulted before you embark on a deworming program. He or she will advise you about the medicines most appropriate for your area and your horse and how often to use them.

Flies

Flies have developed in numerous shapes and sizes, all of them a constant irritation and some of them potentially dangerous. Whether horn flies, house flies, blowflies, deerflies, horseflies, face flies, or stable flies, they all either bite or suck blood. The biting varieties carry diseases like sleeping sickness. Blowflies, common to some areas of the country, lay eggs in wounds. The screwworm feeds on live tissues and can be fatal. House, stable, and horn flies usually lay eggs on any moist material available—rotting vegetation, manure, or spilled grain. Face flies are the ones that lay eggs on fresh manure and carry the worms on their heads. Deer- and horseflies leave their eggs near water, either in swamps, high grass, or salt marshes, which is why they always seem to be around when you go swimming.

To control flies, keep manure and other likely breeding materials away from the stable. Keep stalls clean, along with feed dishes and buckets. In the northeastern United States horseflies grow as large as three inches in length. They dive-bomb their targets, and four or five of them can literally drive a horse up—and over—a wall. (Once these flies land, they're easy to kill.) On a hot day a horse that is turned

EXTERNAL PARASITES

out and bothered by flies can lose a lot of weight as he races around and works himself into a lather trying to avoid them, risking injury as he flees. I've seen horses throw themselves into thick bramble bushes just to scrape flies off. The conscientious owner will put a horse out at night and bring him in during the day. Fly bonnets, fly sheets especially for turnout, and even fly leg wraps are available to relieve horses of this problem.

Flies are one of the biggest nuisances in any stable. Keeping them off your horse and under control requires time, ingenuity, and the right fly spray. It's exasperating to spray a horse and then watch the flies start to land again before you even put the cap back on the bottle. Every serious horseman I know pays careful attention to getting the right kind of spray, one that will last and be tolerated by equine skin. Flies seem to build up an immunity to sprays as they do to certain kinds of dewormers. A spray that works wonders in June may not be effective by August.

Automatic fly spray misters are fairly common in our northeastern area of the country. A pipe is installed along the barn ceiling above the stalls and is set to release a fine mist of nontoxic repellent at timed intervals. Very efficient *fly traps* are also available.

Some Fly-Prevention Hints

• Clean and groom your horse before every workout and wash him afterward, paying particular attention to removing dried sweat.

• Keep the stable clean, cool, and dark during the hot months.

• Keep the manure pile as far from the barn as possible.

• Keep pastures dragged and paddocks picked up, so they don't become a breeding ground for flies or attract other insects.

• In the summer, stable the horse in the morning and turn him out in the late afternoon. This will keep him relatively relaxed and fly-free.

• Apply fly spray to a horse before turning him out.

• Use fly bonnets or sheets if they help.

Some horses have extremely sensitive skin and will become allergic to sprays as well as to flies. A sign of allergy is large hivelike welts where a spray has been applied. Always test a new spray on a small area of the skin before covering the whole body.

Some horses are afraid of being sprayed. If you can't train him to get used to it, you must wipe on the solution with a rag. To accustom a jittery horse to spraying, hold him on a lead (never in cross-ties). Stand away from the horse, and spray into the air to accustom him to the sound. Start with the shoulder, and slowly work your way over the body. On the head use a mild solution, and gently wipe it on, or use a deodorant stick–type repellent, wiping it around the face area and under the jaw. Pay special attention to the underside of the stomach and to the sheath of a gelding and the teats of a mare, both of which must be kept clean.

For those who like to experiment, I've heard of one Thoroughbred breeder who uses a sheep-dip bath in lieu of fly spray, claiming that it keeps horses fly-free for three or four days without any allergic reactions. But this bath could be too strong for your horse, so be careful to test the solution first on a small section of skin.

An alternative is to add cider vinegar to the feed and water, which changes the composition of the blood and deters flies, who land but don't bite. (See Chapter 8.)

Some fly sprays are oil based and last longer than the water-soluble variety, but they also attract dirt. You can place flytraps in your barn, and a portable or electric fogging machine. You can also spray the interior manually with a solution like Baytex or Cygon. Take care to thoroughly spray the ceiling, walls, and around the doors and

FLY BONNETS FOR RIDING

windows. One gallon of the solution covers five hundred square feet of surface. In a four- to six-horse barn, you may wish to install ceiling pipes that are designed to release nontoxic fly spray at periodic intervals.

For a horse that is field-kept all the time, leave his mane and tail long during the summer months for fly protection. It helps to turn a horse out with a friend, so they can protect one another with their switching tails. Some vets suggest keeping whiskers long to protect against face flies. A shed is recommended for summer as well as winter, to give the horse a shady, relatively fly-free haven.

When riding your horse in fly weather, try to pick a good time of day—early in the morning or late afternoon—in a pleasant spot, preferably on high, shady ground, away from swamp or marshy areas. You can get a net bonnet to fit over the horse's ears to give him fly protection. It's helpful to carry a fly switch (or pick a leafy branch) especially to ward off deerflies, the nasty little brown ones.

Some horses become neurotic about flies, tossing their heads even when there isn't a fly in sight. This habit usually disappears with the passing of the fly season. Several friends own horses that have a seasonal fly neurosis, and they have learned to live with it. One such horse was so disturbed by flies that he had to be sent to Cornell for treatment.

Horse Lice

Horse lice live on the hair of a horse, biting, sucking his blood, causing bare spots, and making him itch, rub, and bite the affected area. This parasite is usually spread by direct contact with an infested animal or by dirty tack and grooming tools.

Shampoos have been developed to kill lice, but be sure to have your veterinarian check a suspected case first.

Mites

These bloodsuckers are not always visible to the naked eye. They lay eggs in furrows of the skin, causing irritation and inflammation and making a horse itch. Call the veterinarian for a mite check if scaly-looking skin develops and your horse is scratching the area with his teeth or rubbing it against a post or wall.

Ticks

As we've seen, ticks can be a real problem in some parts of the country. Deer ticks should be removed with tweezers; then apply Ichthammol to the area. Preserve the ticks in alcohol and report to health authorities. (See Chapter 18, under "Lyme Disease.")

Keeping the Veterinarian Happy

When the veterinarian has to be called, give the symptoms as calmly and objectively as you can over the phone. Make sure you do business with one regular veterinarian. (Don't frantically call all the numbers in the yellow pages and see who gets there first.) When he or she arrives, unless there is something you can do to help, stay out of the way until the examination is completed. The veterinarian can't listen to you and your horse's stomach and respiration at the same time. When the exam is finished, you'll have all the answers to the questions you wanted to ask.

If you are asked to hold your horse, try to keep him as quiet as possible. Some horses are terrified of veterinarians. If yours is one of them, warn the doctor and then be as reassuring but as firm with your horse as you can. Speak to him in soothing tones, or scratch him on his favorite spot to calm him down.

A horse with a severe veterinarian complex may need a more aggressive restraint, like a twitch, to make him stand for examination and treatment. While it may seem cruel, remember that your horse's health, possibly his life, is at stake. The more thorough the examination, the more accurate the diagnosis. Keep in mind that the doctor's physical safety, like the blacksmith's, may depend on your learning how to hold a twitch properly. The veterinarian is there to do a job. If you haven't done yours, which is to manage and train your horse properly, you will have to suffer the consequences.

My veterinarian once apologized for being rough with our brutish 17-hand colt. (Three of us were holding him at the time.) Actually I was delighted with his handling because one of his problems had been that no one had been strong enough to force him to behave.

THE TWITCH

PUTTING ON A TWITCH

When applying a twitch, be sure to approach your horse calmly. Gently pat his nose, then grasp a large portion of his muzzle (the top lip, between the nostrils) firmly in your hand. Avoid grasping the nostrils themselves, which will interfere with his breathing and cause him to panic. With your other hand, slide the chain over the muzzle and secure it by twisting the chain on the end of the long handle. This should be enough to keep any horse quiet for twenty minutes to a half hour. Be careful—some horses strike out at the person holding the twitch.

PREVENTION IS THE BEST CURE

Preventing disease is obviously preferable to waiting until a horse gets sick. Apart from its economic benefits, effective prevention means that you don't lose time nursing and taking care of a sick horse—and losing the use of him during his convalescence.

The best prevention is to feed your horse properly—meaning a balanced diet—to provide clean and sanitary facilities, to control parasites, and to keep him outdoors as much as possible with room to exercise. He should also be groomed regularly and worked enough to keep physically fit.

Remember that you alone are responsible for your horse's well-being, so try to anticipate possible difficulties before they occur. Seventy-five percent of all calls to veterinarians, my own included, are the result of some carelessness on the part of the owner. With more foresight, they could have been avoided.

The cost of a horse call will vary, depending on how far away from the veterinarian you live and what part of the country you live in. The basic price won't include shots or other medications he prescribes, which also vary widely. To keep expenses down, consider enrolling in a managed care plan. Consult your veterinarian to see if one is available.

Equine health management organizations (HMOs) are individually structured programs of preventive medicine with fixed yearly fees. They are catching on fast throughout the United States, and the biggest complaint seems to be that there aren't enough of them.

Designed like HMOs for people, these convenient plans save time and money while reassuring subscribers that equine health needs are in the hands of professionals. Although they don't offer the financial protection of medical insurance, they offer routine preventive services at less cost than those provided by an individual veterinarian.

Advance payments are rewarded with discounts. Some plans also offer discounts for farm calls and veterinary services not included in the program.

Programs vary in price and services offered. An average plan might include:

• Spring and fall vaccinations

• Semiannual physical and dental checkups and dewormings

• Two paste dewormers for you to administer between veterinary visits

• Free farm calls

• Free advice on minor health problems

A cheaper alternative would include two exams and the semiannual dewormings but a less comprehensive package of immunization and only a 50 percent discount for farm calls. Normally each additional horse is covered at a lower rate.

Pricier plans include floating teeth, with sedation provided if needed, sheath cleaning for male horses, and four fecal tests for parasite eggs and sand. Some programs offer 10 percent discounts for services they don't cover, sales on health care products (buy three, get one free), and in some cases below-catalog prices on medicine and equipment if cash payments are made on the spot.

Veterinarians are happy with HMOs because bills are paid up front, relieving them of collection chores. Moreover, they are able to access their patients at regular intervals, which gives them a chance to observe and treat potential problems before they escalate. These plans claim that the emphasis on prevention results in less need for diagnosis and treatment of medical emergencies; colic cases are far less frequent and when they do occur are less severe. Equine HMOs are available through some insurance companies.

Alternative practitioners believe their therapies can get to the root of a problem without medications, which they believe merely mask symptoms and cause damaging side effects. Many of my clients, especially those competing in dressage, have used massage, chiropractic, and acupuncture to relieve specific problems. I have also used energy work and magnetic therapy, getting positive results in almost every case. Frequently the best results are achieved with a combination of traditional and alternative methods.

Once considered too far out to be taken seriously, alternative equine therapies are now accepted and recommended by many veterinarians, and some procedures are taught in leading agricultural colleges. In 1997 the American Veterinary Medical Association (AVMA) issued guidelines for these therapies, available only to veterinarians. (See Appendix F for the addresses of the AVMA and other alternative therapy associations.)

Certified practitioners of the various alternative therapies are listed in the directories of their associations and societies that represent them.

If you are considering using alternative therapy for the first time, it's best to get a conventional medical diagnosis first. Ask your veterinarian to recommend a qualified practitioner who can work with him or her to coordinate an effective therapy program. (Some veterinarians are negative about alternative therapy, in which case you can refer to one of the organizations listed in Appendix F.)

Acupuncture

Legend has it that horses were the first beneficiaries of acupuncture, when Mongolian warriors observed that lame horses ridden into battle became sound after being struck by arrows in certain parts of the body. It is established that acupuncture was practiced in China during the Tang and Chou dynasties two to three thousand years ago, and some scholars believe its origins date back even earlier to Tibet and northern India.

The modern name for this treatment derives from the Latin words *acus* ("needle") and *pungare* ("to pierce"). Acupuncturists insert solid metal needles at specific locations on the body to diagnose, prevent, and treat disease.

Acupuncture is now a generally accepted medical practice in the Western world. Practitioners have augmented its effectiveness by applying light electrical currents to needles, injecting vitamin B_{12} at the puncture points to prolong the restorative effects, and using laser beams as an added stimulus.

Traditional Chinese medicine teaches that disease is a result of an imbalance of an electrical life force, or *chi*, which is transmitted through twelve major channels called meridians and two others that carry positive and negative charges (yin and yang). The acupoints are distributed along these channels to boost and regulate energy flow. Any disruption of the normal flow will short-circuit the electrical system and cause malfunction, much as a highway accident interrupts the normal flow of traffic.

In horses, as in humans, disruption of energy flow can be caused by chemical imbalance, viral or bacterial infection, malnutrition, or environmental or psychological stress. The acupuncturist locates problem areas, then inserts and twirls the needles to block pain signals from body to brain and stimulate natural pain-relieving chemicals (endorphins), starting a chain reaction that begins the healing process.

There are no absolutes in acupuncture. Each practitioner develops individual diagnostic and therapeutic techniques. Usually two or four weekly or monthly treatments will show results. Sometimes the practitioner will show you how to press specific acupoints for temporary follow-up relief. Very active horses may need maintenance treatment every two to four months to remain pain free.

Practitioners are certified by the International Veterinary Acupuncture Society, which maintains a directory. (See Appendix F.)

Chiropractic

Chiropractic can help a horse with chronic back or neck soreness, unevenness in any gait, shortness of stride, and even resistance to bending and collection, when these disorders don't respond to conventional treatment or massage. And as part of a regular maintenance program, it can prevent small problems from getting bigger.

Misalignment of the spinal vertebrae affects nerves within the spinal column and those that branch from it, restricting normal motion because of pain and tension in the back and legs.

A trained equine chiropractor observes your horse standing and moving, then palpates the spinal column to detect any misalignments or abnormalities. Manual pressure is applied to restore vertebral alignment but should not include violent joint "manipulations," which could cause permanent injury. After three or four treatment sessions, you should see improvement.

Frequently acupuncture is used first and then chiropractic work is done, enabling the horse's body to be more susceptible to the realignments. I have seen wonderful results with both the combination and the individual methods.

Energy Balancing

Energy balancing is a hands-on therapy done by a trained practitioner who reestablishes the energy flow between and within muscles throughout the horse's entire body. The practitioner relieves pain by removing muscle spasms, blocks, and tension that interfere with the horse's movement and/or comfort and in turn his attitude. Horses are usually very responsive to the treatment. I have seen very positive results on a number of clients' horses and our school horses. Some of my friends have studied it and use the method on their own horses with great success. One of the most noticeable differences, after a treatment, is that the horse moves more freely. Several books are available on the subject.

Herbology

Herbs are the basis of a number of modern drugs, and they have been used for thousands of years in their natural state to treat a variety of ailments. Valerian, passionflower, and hops have a soothing, anti-inflammatory effect on many horses and are a gentler alternative to Bute, which can damage an equine stomach if used extensively. Other herbs can enhance the ability of the digestive system to utilize nutrients, boost the immune system, and help to eliminate toxins from the body.

Plant substances are given internally and externally, fresh or dried, as extracts, oils, teas, or infusions and creams, starting with a low dosage and gradually building it up. Herbs act more slowly than synthetic drugs and affect each horse differently. Because of these diverse reactions, no herb treatment should be attempted without a veterinarian's okay. He or she should be familiar with herbal and homeopathic remedies.

Veterinary herbologists aren't certified, but some holistic practitioners use herbs. Ask your veterinarian how to contact the American Holistic Veterinary Medical Association.

Homeopathy

This medical theory is based on the same premises that led to the development of vaccines—that the same substances causing various diseases will, in diluted form, stimulate the immune system to fight off illness. However, homeopathy also includes quick and effective first-aid treatment for scrapes, bruises, and stings. Chronic ailments may take six months to a year to resolve. Certified practitioners are registered with the Academy of Veterinary Homeopathy. (See Appendix F.)

Massage

Massage is used to manually compress and release muscles and thereby stimulate blood circulation, flush out toxins, speed healing, and relieve pain and stiffness. It can also ease spasms and cramps, restoring elasticity to overworked or stressed muscles and relaxing a horse, which helps to prevent injury and improve performance. A qualified masseuse feels a horse's muscles for tightness (trigger points), then massages the location with knuckles, elbows, or hands. Marked improvement can be seen after three or four sessions and can be maintained with less frequent follow-ups. There are many good massage therapists that do equines, canines, and humans in most areas of the United States. Speak with professionals in your area to find out whom they recommend for your horse.

Making Waves

The different energy wavelengths of ultrasound, electromagnetism, and laser and light-emitting diodes (LED) are used to promote faster recovery from illness and injury. Some expensive high-tech therapeutic gadgets have been developed by owners and trainers and are available for sale, rental, or lease to qualified professionals.

ULTRASOUND. Inaudible sound waves penetrate deep into tissues to create a warming effect that relieves muscle soreness and improves circulation around injured ligaments and tendons, preventing edema. Because it generates its own heat in the tissues, ultrasound requires caution, particularly around contained sacs of fluid like hematomas. The area to be treated should be clipped and a lubricating gel applied to the skin to assure good contact with the instrument.

LASER AND LIGHT-EMITTING DIODES (LED). Although the light-wave energy of a therapeutic laser penetrates only an eighth of an inch into a horse's skin, it creates a ripple effect that goes much deeper to speed healing, discourage the formation of proud flesh, and flush out edema (fluid swelling) by increasing blood supply to the area. LED uses the same wavelengths, but the beam is less focused, needing longer exposure.

Magnetic Therapy

This gentle, painless procedure works on soft tissue, ligament, and bone damage, soothing aching joints and muscles, increasing circulation, and reducing swelling. It is a well-known therapy worldwide and was only recently introduced here. Blood is chock-full of electrically charged particles that react to the magnet, which widens blood vessels and allows more blood into the area, stimulating the healing process. Magnetic boots and wraps should be used as directed and under veterinarian supervision. Magnetic blankets have insertion pockets for coils or magnets to treat withers, stifles, shoulders, and back; they come with separate specially shaped wraps for knees, hocks, and tendons. To effectively penetrate tissues in target areas, the devices must be worn for several hours. When using magnets, leave them on for short periods of time at first, and gradually increase to the maximum time prescribed by your veterinarian or the manufacturer. Boots, wraps, and blankets are available in tack shops or directly from manufacturers, advertised in many horse publications. They are also recommend by many well-known professionals.

PART VIII

Talking Tack

The gemmy bridle glittered free
Like to some branch or stars we see
Hung in the golden galaxy
The bridle bells rang merrily
As he rode down to Camelot
And from his blazon'd baldric slung
A mighty silver bugle hung,
And as he rode, his armour rung,
Beside remote Shalott

—Alfred Lord Tennyson
THE LADY OF SHALOTT

Saddling Up

Medieval war saddlery, the direct ancestor of modern Western tack, was the most elegant and impressive in the history of horsemanship and, despite all its bulk and glitter, was highly functional. Heavily armored knights needed the deep seat, curved pommel, and high cantle to support their weight and keep them from being unseated by a blow from an opponent's lance. Better balance was achieved during a charge with long stirrups. The force of the ponderous battle horse, combined with several hundred pounds of heavy armor, all focused on the point of a lance, making a secure seat of the utmost importance. The impact was roughly equivalent to two speeding cars crashing head-on. Medieval warriors used a curb bridle to control their spirited stallions. (Geldings were sometimes used but were less prestigious mounts.) The horse responded to an ancient version of the neck rein, the reins being held in one hand, leaving the other free for the sword or lance.

The noseband, used today to help keep a horse's mouth closed over the bit, may have had its origin in the muzzle worn by such a warhorse to keep him from biting when he was off the battlefield. The horses, trained to fight along with the knights, were taught to bite and strike at opponents with their front legs. In fact, many of the elaborate exercises, or airs above the ground (performed today by the Austrian Lippizans at the famous Spanish Riding School in Vienna), originated in battle, where they were developed to terrify foot soldiers. Controlling these spirited animals with a single hand while weighted down by armor and with a heavy lance tucked under one arm required a high degree of horsemanship. Knights have been unfairly depicted in much popular fiction as deadweights in the saddle, moving like robots. In fact, considering their handicaps, they were surprisingly dexterous.

When the Moors invaded Spain in the eighth century, their small, fast horses, light saddles, and more agile style of riding gave them a tactical advantage over the Spanish knights. The invaders rode with short stirrups (consisting in those days of leather straps, or surcingles, that held the point of the rider's toes) and perched lightly on their saddles. They often dropped the reins over the necks of their mounts as they used their bows and arrows. Metal stirrups were introduced in the last half of the eleventh century, providing more support for the armored riders, who could now wield longer, heavier lances, carrying them low rather than above the shoulder.

During seven centuries of occupation, the Spanish crossed their heavier horses with the lighter desert breeds and adopted much of Moorish culture, including its finely carved leather work, which was widely used on saddles and bridles. When the Spanish invaded the Americas in the fifteenth century, they rode in on these elaborately carved war saddles, with long stirrups, using the traditional neck rein.

The war saddle that gave security to the knights has, in modern form, done the same thing for the cowboy. Wranglers need a deep seat and long stirrups to brace themselves against the weight of a dropped steer. Equally important, the seat and wide swells are comfortable, allowing the saddle to serve as a rider's chair for days at a stretch.

The rest of the modern Western saddle is equally functional. The *horn,* with the opening at the fork, is designed to hold the lariat. After a steer has been downed, the cowboy wraps the rope around the *pommel* to create tension, against which a horse is trained to pull—playing the steer almost like a fish. The *flank girth* prevents the saddle from flipping up in back with the impact of the dropped animal.

Wooden stirrups, originally carved out of light wood, were traditionally accompanied in the Old West by *tapaderos* or hoods, which protected feet from brush and thorns and kept them warm and dry. The *fenders* protected a rider's legs from the substantial amount of sweat a horse built up during a day of working cattle.

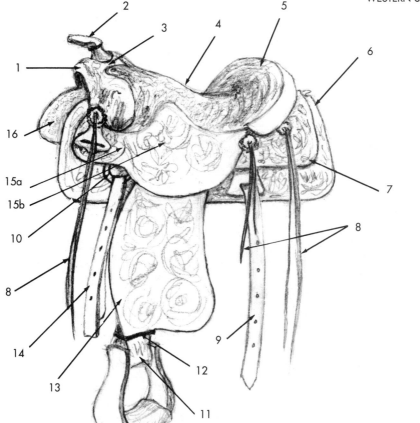

WESTERN SADDLE

1. Pommel
2. Horn
3. Fork
4. Seat
5. Cantle
6. Skirt
7. Back housing (or back jockey)
8. Lace strings
9. Leather flank girth billet
10. Dee ring
11. Stirrup leather
12. Stirrup leather keeper
13. Fender or Sudadero stirrup
14. Front tie strap or cinch strap
15a. Front jockey
15b. Seat jockey
16. Wool lining

Rawhide strings fastened to the saddle could hold all the gear a cowboy might need on a long drive—slicker, bedroll, saddlebags, food, utensils, and rifle scabbard.

Because the condition of a horse's back was vital on a long ride, a cowboy was careful to protect it. In addition to the lining of the saddle, a thick *Navajo blanket* was customarily used as a saddle pad—an article of trade common in the Old West and still made for this purpose today on reservations.

In parts of the West and Midwest where cattle are still worked from horseback, the cowboy's tack is as functional as ever. Although to eastern eyes wranglers appear to be more lackadaisical about some aspects of horse care, cowboys are very concerned about how their saddles are made and how they fit the horse—often having them custom made.

The Tree

A saddle is only as good as its understructure. Because many different types of Western saddles are available to fit a variety of sizes of equine and human builds, attention needs to be paid to the foundation of the saddle—the tree. Originally saddle trees were made of wood wrapped in rawhide. To lighten and strengthen the trees, Western saddle makers now frequently reinforce them with molded plastic, or wood with fiberglass, at critical stress points.

The most important feature of stability in this saddle's understructure is the positioning of the cinch rings. In the past they were usually located in the middle of the saddle, where they could cause it to tip forward, throwing the rider and horse off balance. The placement of the two rings or a single ring determines the stability of the saddle on the horse's back and the amount of freedom it allows the rider's leg. Moving a single cinch ring closer to the front of the saddle, just below and a little behind the fork, adds stability. With double rings the front ring can be placed the same way, and the second ring just below the cantle, either parallel with the front ring or higher. Each affects the way a saddle rides during work. (See 294, "Fitting the Saddle.")

Types of Western Saddles

Rodeo riders prefer a more decorative saddle, while roping contestants might prefer a close variation on the traditional *stock saddle,* with a longer, thicker horn, narrow pommel, and more sloping swells. A *barrel racing saddle* is lighter overall with a higher cantle and a more vertical fork to help the rider, usually female, in tight turns. The thinner, smaller horn provides a good place to grip, and thinner stirrups are lighter. (One cinch ring is most appropriate here.) The opposite extreme is the old-type bronco-riding saddle, with swells eight inches high and twenty-four inches wide.

The *utility stock saddle,* as the name implies, is a no-nonsense sturdy saddle crafted of good leather that's comfortable for both the horse and rider. It is unencumbered by excessive ornamentation and limited to just essential trappings. In other words, it's designed to withstand days of working in the saddle in all kinds of conditions. This saddle shouldn't be confused with the ornate saddles worn in

parades, covered with silver, that rival medieval battle garb in weight. A *show saddle* often features elaborate leather tooling with silver or other bright metal embellishing the swells, horn, cantle, and skirts. Some have suede seats and cutout skirts, giving the rider closer leg contact with the horse.

For *cutting* and *reining,* the saddles are designed with a flat low seat to keep the rider close to the horse. For cutting, the pommel is smaller and the horn is narrow and vertical for gripping. Reining saddles' horns are generally small and low to keep the reining hand mobile. The cutting saddle tends to be heavier, with fenders that move freely over a cutout skirt.

A *roping saddle* requires double cinch rings for stability when the calf hits the end of the rope. A heavier, stronger saddle, its flatter seat with lower forks makes quick dismounting easier. The fenders are extra wide. The horn is very strong and thick, usually wrapped with rubber or leather to withstand the abrasive rope.

Reflecting the trend toward pleasure riding instead of work on horseback, another type of saddle has been created with a flat seat much like that of an English saddle. Called a *balanced ride* or *horsemanship saddle,* it puts the rider in the center of the horse rather than back closer to the cantle, as with the traditional stock saddle. This saddle is popular with Western riders in the East and is spreading across the country.

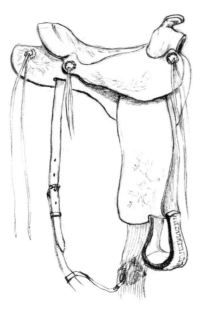

Balanced Ride Saddle

For pleasure riding and trail riding, a Western saddle should fit the horse and rider well. (See page 294, "Fitting the Saddle," and page 298, "Fitting the Saddle to the Rider.") Any combination of these styles can be chosen. Comfort is the chief concern. A lightweight saddle is easier on both horse and rider. Many feature well-padded seats and a horn of medium height that is easy to hold.

The cost of an average Western saddle used for pleasure riding can range from less than five hundred dollars in the West to three times that in the East. The price depends on the basic design and intricacy of the workmanship and the amount of silver on a show saddle. The average size for an adult rider is fifteen inches, measured back to front from the center of the cantle to the center of the pommel. A saddle for a large adult would measure an inch more, a youth saddle an inch less.

Western saddles come complete with all fittings except cinches. These are available in a variety of materials and styles. (See "Girths: Western," page 303.)

Western Saddle Blankets and Rugs

The most widely used Western blanket is the wool *Navajo rug*. While the single type is less expensive, double wool is a better buy because it absorbs 80 percent of its own weight in moisture (a horse's back gets moist, not wet), and its porosity allows air to circulate. The tiny barbs of the wool fiber actually grip the hair on an equine back, preventing slippage. Wool's resiliency makes it last longer, and it gets softer as it wears. These ideal blankets also resist dirt penetration and don't soil quickly; cleaning them is a simple matter of hosing them down and hanging them out to dry.

Another top-of-the-line Western blanket is fleece- or wool-lined with a felt filler and leather patches over the girth area. These are kept clean by hosing and brushing. The orthopedic pad of pile fabric, sometimes referred to as a *cool back,* is washing machine and dryer safe. For showing, blankets can be ordered in your favorite colors or those of your stable. Styles of saddles and colors of saddles and blankets change with fashion, just as in other disciplines. If you're planning to show, observe the classes you intend to enter, and if you don't have access to a professional trainer, read the rulebook before going out and purchasing equipment. Knowledgeable personnel at a good tack shop can also be extremely helpful.

The English and northern European saddle had several prototypes. During the Middle Ages light saddles with low cantles and narrow-to-nonexistent pommels were widely used for sport and pleasure riding. Wealthy knights owned three horses and three saddles: one for battle, one for sport, and one for everyday use. Even the knight who could afford only a single horse owned a change of tack.

In the jousting arena knights would choose their saddles along with their weapons. Unlike cantles of war saddles, cantles in sporting events were always low, the object being to unseat rather than kill. A well-placed thrust from a lance would send an opponent sailing over his horse's croup. The height of the pommel depended on the weapons used and the nerve of the knight. Saddles with low pommels were less secure and therefore more sporting. They also provided more room for maneuvering a sword or lance.

In the fifteenth century the Hungarian cavalry, which was unarmored and used bows and arrows, rode with a light, elegantly crafted saddle that had a pommel but no cantle. The saddle was flat, with only a slight depression for the rider's seat. During the same period saddles with lower pommels and cantles were used for hunting throughout Europe and the British Isles.

The modern English and European saddles with low pommels were developed in the eighteenth century to put maximum demands on the skills of the rider. Today a wide variety of English saddles are manufactured in many different countries to meet the requirements of the various riding disciplines. Their prices range from three hundred to more than three thousand dollars depending on the style, materials, and saddle maker. They include saddles for jumping, cross-country, and endurance riding, along with special types for horses with animated gaits, and others designed to fit closely to a horse's back, allowing complete freedom of movement for dressage.

Once you select the right type of saddle for your discipline, you must make sure that it fits both you and your horse well. A bad fit will affect your riding and his way of going—even causing lameness. Despite the fact that saddles come in different seat sizes to accommodate the rider and at least three tree widths for equine backs, different makes will fit different breeds better than others. It's wise to seek professional advice before making this substantial investment.

Types of English Saddles

PARK SADDLE. This ordinary English saddle, minus knee rolls, is customary for saddle-seat riders. It is cut straight from the pommel down, with very long, wide flaps. It has either a very low pommel or is cut back in front to allow for the high neck carriage and big shoulder movement of park horses. The center of the seat is closer to the cantle so that the rider interferes as little as possible with the action of his horse. When a rider posts in a park saddle, he stays behind the motion of the horse. These saddles are made of very thin leather, bringing the rider's legs as close as possible to the horse. Although great for the show ring, they give a rider very little support on the trail.

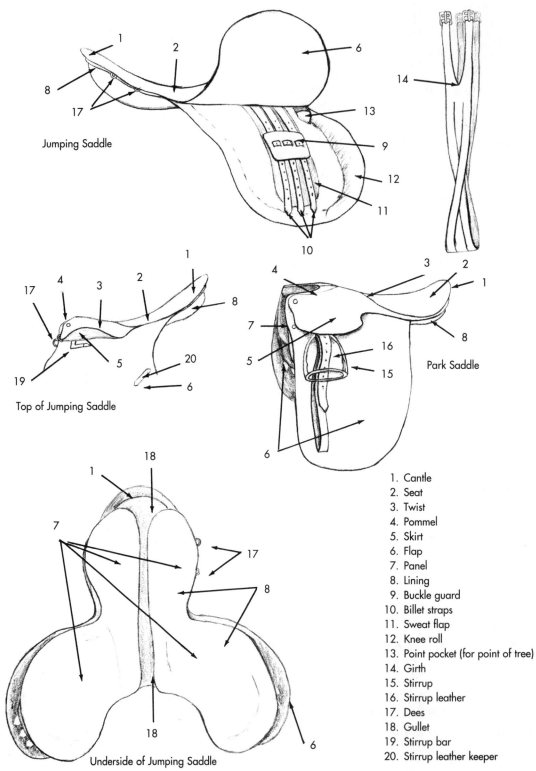

ENGLISH SADDLE

Chafless Girth Contour

Jumping Saddle

Top of Jumping Saddle

Park Saddle

Underside of Jumping Saddle

1. Cantle
2. Seat
3. Twist
4. Pommel
5. Skirt
6. Flap
7. Panel
8. Lining
9. Buckle guard
10. Billet straps
11. Sweat flap
12. Knee roll
13. Point pocket (for point of tree)
14. Girth
15. Stirrup
16. Stirrup leather
17. Dees
18. Gullet
19. Stirrup bar
20. Stirrup leather keeper

DRESSAGE SADDLE. This saddle is designed to give the rider a deep, soft seat correctly balanced for comfort and closeness. Long, soft flaps with long billets are usually preferred because they allow closer contact of the rider's leg. Some have a billet both under the pommel and toward the rear, helping to stabilize and distribute the rider's weight more evenly and promoting close contact.

Special attention is given to the flocking in the panels, which should mold to the horse's back, helping to distribute weight evenly and avoiding any pressure points that would impair movement. Wool is the best filling, molding to the horse's back with wear.

JUMPING SADDLE. This saddle has the deepest part in the center, with a low pommel and a narrow twist (the area between the pommel and the seat). The seat is wide and soft, shallower than either the all-purpose or the dressage saddle. The flaps are cut forward to better accommodate the rider's forward leg position. It comes with or without padding at the knee.

The ideal jumping saddle gives the rider balance when sitting down and support when jumping. The panels should be padded well and broad enough to allow the horse to move naturally, without putting stress on pressure points that might interfere with his performance. The channel or gullet should be high enough not to touch the horse's back during jumping. Generally a lightweight saddle with minimum leather between you and your horse is most desirable.

ALL-PURPOSE SADDLE. This saddle has flaps long enough for dressage, a seat deep enough for cross-country riding, and flaps forward enough for jumping. Knee flaps are often molded to conform to the shape of the rider's leg, helping them to stay in place. The panel and gullet meet the same requirements as the jumping saddle, and both are available with suede knee rolls, which theoretically lock with the suede of the rider's breeches.

AUSTRALIAN STOCK SADDLE OR AUSSIE SADDLE. This saddle fits closer than a Western saddle and is more secure than an English saddle. Available in both Western stock and English styles and designed with deep, padded seats for those who log many hours on horseback, it has become an outstanding favorite with trail and endurance riders and mounted patrols. It covers the maximum of the horse's back to reduce pressure and has numerous D-rings for attaching provisions needed for a long day's ride.

ENDURANCE AND TRAIL SADDLES. These are made for those who ride for many hours at a stretch and require the ultimate in a comfortable seat and a good distribution of weight on the horse's back. Many styles have an extension below the cantle, with extra D-rings for carrying needed items.

If you are buying your first saddle and don't plan to start off right away in big competition, a secondhand saddle of good make will be a better choice than a new one of inferior quality. Fine secondhand German, British, and French saddles are often advertised in saddle shops and circulars, and it's possible to pick up a quality model for half its original price. Often the seller is letting the saddle go because he or she

CHOOSING THE RIGHT SADDLE

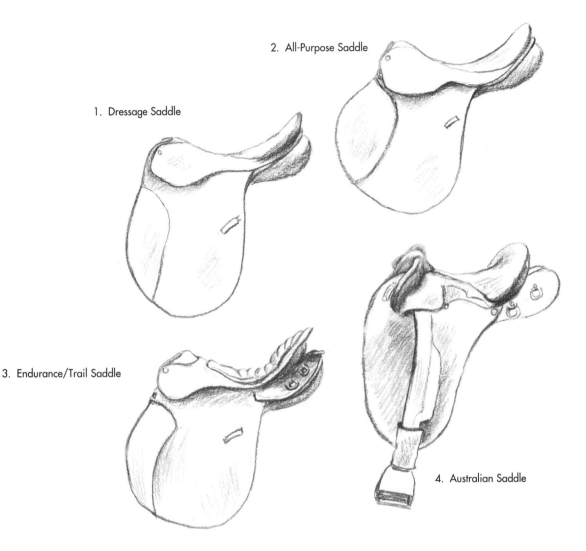

2. All-Purpose Saddle

1. Dressage Saddle

3. Endurance/Trail Saddle

4. Australian Saddle

needs a different type; consequently the tack will have been well cared for. Always make sure that the *stitching* is sound and the tree isn't broken. On a new saddle, the stitching should be even and firm. The *dyeing* of the leather should be even and of better color with increasing price.

Make sure that the saddle fits both you and your horse. An ill-fitting saddle that is too large or too small for you will keep you fighting to hold your balance. (See page 298, "Fitting the Saddle to the Rider.") And if it doesn't fit your horse correctly, it can interfere with his movement and give him a sore back. (See page 296, "Measuring for the Saddle.") If you're new to riding, get a professional trainer, an experienced saddle fitter from a tack shop, or a saddle specialist to help you. A saddle that doesn't fit is worthless.

What Makes a Quality Saddle

Saddle prices vary according to the overall design, the quality and type of leather used, the length and intricacy of the tanning process, the shape and material of the tree, the type of flocking used, the workmanship, and the reputation of the company that makes them. Nowadays saddle making is so sophisticated that many new saddles don't even have to be "broken in." The manufacturer may even request that you don't oil a new saddle because the elaborate tanning process renders it ready to ride as is.

Since custom-made imported saddles can cost as much as four thousand dollars, it behooves a buyer to pay close attention to selection, fitting, and care. Prices have risen so much in the past three decades that I've been offered double the price paid for a Passier purchased used in the mid-1970s.

Leather is tanned through two different processes, each of which gives it a particular color. *Bark curing* (or tanning), which leaves leather with a brownish color, takes cleaning and oiling well and absorbs oil better than the *chrome* method of curing, which is characterized by a greenish color. Different parts of a hide are used for saddles; the most preferred is taken from the hindquarter, which has little stretch and is most durable.

Saddle makers grade leather according to the country it comes from and the curing methods employed there. Of the five grades, the poorest quality is Indian leather, which is tanned in clay vats, comes out very dry, and is unable to absorb oil, making it prone to cracking and further drying. Fourth-grade Japanese leather has poor strength; the fibers separate, tear, and stretch easily. Southern European leather is considered third grade because it is hard, often has grub holes in it, and needs a lot of work to make it pliable. Some South American leather is top quality, some is third grade. The best quality, both first and second grade, comes from England, Germany, and the United States, where tanning processes create an unblemished, soft, and pliable product. Unfortunately no government-regulated grading program exists, and the consumer has no way of determining leather quality.

Some leather that starts out feeling hard will eventually soften to a glovelike pliability without too much breaking in. Another type may feel great at first but become flabby and thin with wear. Usually a knowledgeable person at your tack shop can tell you which will wear the best.

When buying a new saddle, observe the consistency and texture of the leather. Quality leather is treated with mutton lard to keep it from drying out or cracking, helping to preserve the leather and making it more malleable. This *tallow* is the whitish substance often seen on new saddles. It's an essential part of the leather-treating process that literally feeds the leather, and some of the excess tallow forms a coating on the surface. It should be rubbed in with your bare hands on both sides of the saddle. The warmth of your hand will help to soften the accumulated waxy substance, helping it to blend in.

Some saddles are constructed from as many as five types of skins from three different animals. One manufacturer uses well-stretched pigskin in the seat and thick cowhide for the skirts, with a pliable horsehide panel on the underside. (Horsehide is used because it wears longer and doesn't crack from the horse's sweat.)

Types of Trees (English Saddles)

The *frame* or the *tree* of the saddle, along with the quality of the leather, is of primary importance and has a lot to do with the price you pay. The cheapest frame is *laminated plywood* without any steel reinforcement, the type used on many Argentine saddles and the reason they open up with wear (a condition called *treespread*). Some Argentine saddle trees are reinforced with fragile barrel-hoop wire.

One of the best types of wooden tree is made of *hickory and birch* and reinforced with flexible *spring steel*. A leather tree is a comfortable alternative but expensive. *Fiberglass* trees get high marks for durability, but I find them very hard on the seat, and the screws become loose as the threads wear out. A broken fiberglass tree is virtually irreparable, and if the stirrup bars need to be reattached, it will have to be sent back to the factory because of special tools required.

Stuffing the Panels

One of the most important parts of the saddle is where it makes contact with the horse's back. The *panels* on the underside of a well-made saddle should be firm but soft, evenly distributing weight over the back so that one spot doesn't receive more pressure than another, causing soreness in the back or shoulder and/or eventual lameness. The construction of these panels affects both a horse's gaits and his desire to move forward willingly.

Poorly made saddle panels can be stuffed with anything that happens to be on hand. Less expensive makes are stuffed with *foam,* a *foam/felt combination,* or other *synthetic material.* More expensive saddles are stuffed with *wool flocking,* an organic material that molds to the shape of a horse's back after several rides. After a few years or more, depending on the amount of hours you put in riding, your saddle panels may get lumpy or develop thin spots. They will then need restuffing. (Any good saddle repair agent can do this.)

Foam stuffing is an advantage when you're riding more than one horse and don't want the individual fit that wool offers. Foam/felt panels are not supposed to compress. But when they do need replacement, the process is more expensive than reflocking.

Some good saddles have Irish *linen webbing* with several layers of *canvas.* Others have a *foam-rubber* pad under the seat to spare the rider from the hard frame of the saddle.

FITTING THE SADDLE

People have been riding for thousands of years without understanding the physical effects of the saddle on a horse—an often inhumane oversight that has undermined many an athletic performance. Over the past century riders buying mass-produced saddles have rarely paid attention to properly fitting them because physical damage from bad tailoring takes a while to show up. When a problem became apparent, the equestrian would buy another saddle and then another until he or she had a collection of them—an expensive learning experience.

Before the twentieth century, horses were the principal mode of transportation and were ridden for many hours a day. Riders bought saddles from the local saddler, not a tack shop, taking their horse along so the craftsman could fit the tree and then build around it, padding the panels to conform to the individual equine back. In those days horses tended to be regionally grouped by type and build, reflecting the demands and interests of the area in which they were selectively bred. The backs of these breeds were consequently similar in shape, and saddlers accustomed to working with familiar dorsal conformations designed their saddles accordingly, making individual adjustments to a basic pattern. If a saddle didn't fit properly because of an error in construction or a change in equine conformation, the rider returned to have it readjusted. But the same saddle always remained with the same horse.

Eventually saddle design evolved into three basic patterns: English, Western, and Australian. Some saddle trees are rigid, some are flexible, and others have rigid trees with flexible panels. Flocking, or stuffing, is thicker in some saddles and can be adjusted in some of them but not others. Despite the variations, no one saddle design has proved superior over time.

Today, when breeds are not specific to one area and there are cross-breds, one size does not fit all. A saddle manufactured in England might be purchased in Montana for a Quarter Horse or Arabian or in Canada for a Thoroughbred or Shire cross. To make sure an "off-the-rack" saddle will fit, you must try it out on a horse before purchasing it and have it readjusted, if necessary, by a saddle-fitting specialist. At a recent saddle-fitting seminar, where participants were asked to bring their saddles in, it was amazing to see how many didn't fit either the horse, the rider, or both. One poor fellow arrived with a very expensive, spanking-new hand-tooled-leather-and-silver-decorated Western saddle that turned out to be the wrong size for his horse.

The Science of Saddlery

The important and complex subject of saddle fitting was neglected for years, during which time we were all taught to position the pommel of a saddle as close as possible to the horse's withers so that the girth would fall a few fingers' width away from the elbow. Unfortunately we weren't told about measuring the width and curve of the horse's back, the correct height of the pommel, or the balance and stability of the saddle when in place—omissions that have caused decades of discomfort to horses and riders. Nowadays, with the high cost of a saddle, fitting is finally getting long-deserved attention.

A poorly fitted saddle can cause deep muscle damage, a sore back, lameness, uneven gaits—and a horse with an attitude. Pressure in the wrong places will also decrease circulation and imperceptibly damage hair follicles to a point where the pigmentation process is altered and hairs grow in white. To avoid these problems, a saddle must be sized to the horse's individual conformation, with weight distributed evenly over the bearing surfaces at no more than one and a half pounds per square inch.

Skin and muscle tissue need a constant, intermittent flow of blood to remain healthy and maintain metabolism, a need that increases during strenuous exercise.

If saddle pressure exceeds the blood pressure and the structural strength of the capillaries beneath it, the vessels collapse, depriving the blood of oxygen, nutrients, and the ability to expel waste products. Saddle fitting is the management of this pressure on the horse's back.

Clinical studies have established that surface pressure on equine spinal vertebrae increases three to five times internally, putting enormous strain on the latissimus dorsi muscle that lies adjacent to the spinal column. The weight, seat, and ability of the rider has a significant influence on the amount of pressure the saddle exerts on equine tissue and the degree to which it affects spinal curvature. A saddle that fits perfectly with a light rider in the seat may cause damaging pressure on the back when a heavier rider is aboard.

The effect of a rider's weight is compounded by his level of competence and seat in the saddle. In contrast to the deep seat of Western and dressage riders, English riders in jumping, hunting, and eventing tend to ride more forward in the saddle. An unbalanced novice rider may lean too far to the back or slightly to one side. The better the rider, the better they handle their weight on a moving horse. A well-trained heavyweight rider will be easier on a horse's back than a less competent lightweight.

Measuring for the Saddle

English saddles have always come in narrow, medium, and wide tree sizes to accommodate different widths of withers. But today's designers of both English and Western saddles give equal consideration to the width and curve of the horse's back. Leading saddle makers ask customers to take these measurements with a flexible drawing tool called a French curve and transfer them to cardboard before sending in the order.

When measuring for a saddle of any type, *stand your horse squarely on flat ground* and place the saddle on his back *with tree resting behind the shoulder blade.* (If you are in doubt where this is, run your fingers down the shoulder from the withers until you feel a large bone curving toward the back.) Knee flaps can cover the shoulder *as long as they don't inhibit the full four-inch range of movement.*

The *tree size and the shape of the metal dead plate* inside the front of the saddle *must conform to the shape of your horse's withers,* allowing *three to three and a half finger widths* to be slipped between them and the underside of the pommel. If four or more fingers can fit there, the tree is too narrow and will sit too high. If two fingers or less fit in the opening, the tree is too wide. Remember that the added weight of the rider will press the tree closer, and that a new saddle will gradually settle a half inch or more when broken in.

Now take a look at the *balance* of the saddle from the side. The lowest point should be at the center, with pommel and cantle in most cases at the same level. (The cantle may be higher on some horses, depending on conformation and saddle style.) If the lowest point of the saddle is too far back, the rider's weight will be correspondingly off center, sending legs forward and making her struggle to stay in bal-

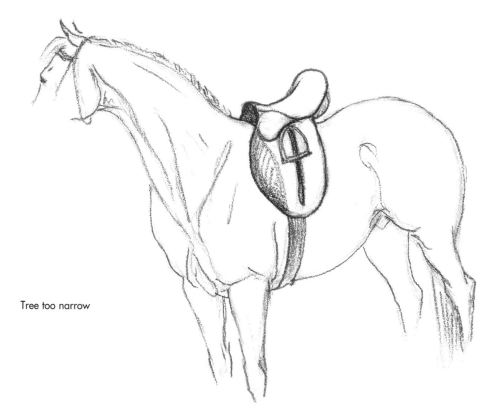

Tree too narrow

ance, bumping around on the horse's back, affecting the rhythm and regularity of his gaits, and making him uncomfortable. If the saddle is too far forward, the reverse will happen, with the rider fighting to keep her legs under and down and at risk of catapulting over the horse's neck in a jumping situation. Some custom saddles can be readjusted to their center by adding or taking out the wool flocking.

The next consideration is the *stability* of the saddle on the back. When you put your hands under it, the panels must rest evenly, with the same pressure at all points. When you press down on the pommel, the cantle shouldn't rock up (or vice versa); nor should the saddle rock when pressed diagonally. Saddles and equine backs aren't always symmetrical. These discrepancies can usually be corrected.

The extent to which a horse flexes his back affects the fit of a saddle, so it must be tested in motion. A dressage horse, for instance, really rounds up the back during exercises; space allowed under the side panels when he's standing will fill up nicely when he's working.

In determining whether a saddle fits, first assess how your horse feels about it. Run your fingers down either side of the spine, pressing near the withers, in the center, and where the cantle would rest. If your horse hollows his back, flattens his ears, kicks out, or otherwise says "ouch," the saddle you've been using has been hurting

Tree too wide

him. If your saddle is an old one, make sure the tree isn't cracked or broken, and run your hands along the paneling to see if it's too hard or, worse, uneven in spots. If these aren't the problem, and the fault lies in uneven weight distribution, you'll need a new saddle.

A poorly fitted saddle can't be fixed with saddle pads, which weren't even used until the beginning of the twentieth century. Until then, sweat from a horse's back helped contour the saddle. Even today riding without a saddle pad for a time is sometimes advised to break in new wool-flocked saddles (of course wiping them off after use).

Equine anatomy changes with maturity and with work. This is particularly true of horses being schooled in dressage, where bodies change after a year or two of the demanding work, needing new or reflocked saddles. If your horse is under five years of age, it would be wise to buy a good used saddle and wait until his body matures before making that big investment.

FITTING THE SADDLE TO THE RIDER

A saddle should allow the rider to *sit naturally* in the deepest point of the seat, at the center, with a *hand width between the back of the seat and the cantle.* Some makes and styles of saddle will fit differently. A seventeen-inch jumping saddle that fits perfectly may be a full or half size too small in a dressage type, where the smaller seat would force you to sit at the slope of the cantle, pushing you painfully into the pommel at a sitting trot or canter. Measure a saddle with a tape from the button, or saddle nail, on either side of the pommel to the center of the cantle. Some Western saddles may sit you closer to the cantle rather than in the center.

The *width of the seat* is as important as the length. If too wide, the outside edges will rub the buttocks; if too narrow, legs won't grip effectively and the buttocks will overlap unattractively. Women should make sure that the seams of the saddle don't overlap with the underpants line, which can cause chafing and extreme discomfort.

The *depth of the seat* varies with different disciplines. A shallow, flatter seat is best for jumping, allowing a rider to comfortably hold a two- or three-point position. A deeper seat is used for dressage, where the rider must be balanced, with back straight, in the ideal center.

Always take a new saddle for a test ride. You shouldn't make such a costly decision on the basis of a stationary ride on a tack shop "horse." Most good shops will let you try out a saddle, taking a cash deposit or charging your credit card during the tryout. (If yours doesn't allow this, go elsewhere.) To avoid leaving marks on the saddle, put a hole in the bottom of some old (clean) socks, and slip them over the stirrup leathers.

The *twist* of the saddle, directly behind the pommel, will be very uncomfortable if it is too high. Riders who jump will want a flatter twist to get easily into jumping position. Too wide a twist will strain groin muscles in the effort to encircle it. Too narrow a twist will be just as uncomfortable and feel extremely insecure.

The placement and thickness of *knee rolls* under the saddle skirt is a matter of personal choice. Saddle makers offer a number of configurations that you can try out, and they're easy to customize. Riders with heavier thighs will be more comfortable with smaller knee rolls; long-legged riders like them placed fairly high.

Stirrup bars can be recessed so the buckles don't rub the inner thigh. On dressage saddles they are placed farther back so a rider can maintain the classic hip-over-heel alignment. *Billets* on dressage saddles are unusually long, giving closer contact with the horse. Although they can't be adjusted from the saddle, this inconvenience is offset by the lack of lumpiness under the leg. Long billets require a girth twenty inches shorter than the regular hunter type, and some saddles with universal billets are suited to both girths. On some saddles the front billet runs at an angle to the back of the flap to keep the saddle from rocking or creeping forward. Others have flap straps that fasten over the girth to keep the saddle skirts down.

Saddle too small for rider

FITTINGS | New English saddles are usually sold without fittings, meaning without stirrups, stirrup pads, and girths.

Stirrups

Falling off a horse is one of the accepted risks of riding, but having a foot caught in a stirrup and being dragged by your horse is unacceptable. It is easily avoided if you take the precautions of making sure your stirrups fit properly and always riding with the stirrup bar open.

With your riding boots on, take the measurement for your stirrups across the widest part of your foot. Add one inch beyond that, and you have your stirrup size, which will correspond to its interior measurement. When in doubt, go toward large. But be careful in measuring children's sizes because a small foot can slide through an oversize iron. (There are special smaller stirrups for children.)

STIRRUPS—FIT AND TYPES

Stirrup fits correctly, allowing enough space on side of foot

Stirrup is too large

Stirrup is too small

Safety stirrup

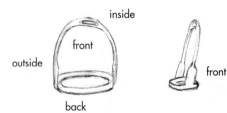

inside

outside   front

back

Offset Stirrup—Two Views

front

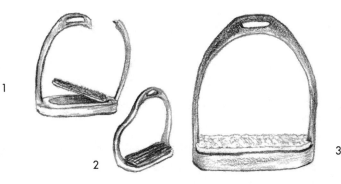

1. Jointed Stirrup
2. "S" Stirrup
3. Fillis Stirrup

ENGLISH. Most stirrups come in stainless steel or a rustproof nickel plate, while the heavier ones are the most comfortable. The most popular traditional stirrups are the *Fillis* style, which have a slim appearance, are weighted at the bottom, and usually have white rubber pads. Another type are *offset* stirrups, which help a rider keep heels down and the lower leg on the horse.

Safety stirrups, open on one side, have a keeper at the bottom that houses a *large rubber band seated in a notch* at the top. Although not guaranteed by independent testing, these stirrups do decrease the chance of injury and are a very good idea for children. The rubber bands and tabs that hold them are all replaceable and inexpensive.

For adults who wish for a safer stirrup, an iron with a sculptured *S-curve* on the outside allows ample room for the front part of the foot to slide out in an emergency. These are popular in Europe and with fox hunters. They are not advised for children because their tiny feet could slip through.

On other brands of quick-release stirrups, the outside of the metal pops out, but these pose a risk if a horse should run loose and they're banging at his sides. The crème de la crème of all safety designs is the *Herm Sprenger* jointed stirrup, shaped to help the rider keep heels down and relieve calf pressure, while preventing feet from being hung up in a fall. These are favored by leading European eventers and open jumpers and can cost more than two hundred dollars. Less expensive brands of jointed stirrups are available that aid the rider in keeping heels down. Some riders claim that they relieve pressure not only on the back but on knees and ankles as well. Although not all brands can be classified as safety stirrups, these *flexible* stirrups have a joint that allows them to rotate down, enabling the rider to keep a deeper heel and a steadier, more classical leg position over fences. As a riding instructor, I must add that these stirrups are more appropriate for the rider who has already mastered the fundamentals of balance and keeping the heels down.

WESTERN. Traditionally made of wood, Western stirrups are now also made of nylon and Ralide (synthetic materials) and are wrapped in leather or rawhide. Hard wood stirrups are either plain or wrapped in leather or rawhide. Another type is made of metal and laced with leather.

The Western type closest to English safety stirrups is *covered* or *hooded*. Usually seen on children's saddles, they derive from the *tapaderos* on Spanish saddles, the forefather of today's Western saddles. They protected the rider's feet as he worked cattle through brush and cactus. As a safety feature, Western stirrups can prevent the rider's foot from slipping through the stirrup and getting caught. The heel of the Western boot helps too.

Stirrup Pads

Pads made of white or black rubber help keep the English rider's foot in place in stirrups. Some have an abrasive nonslip surface for a better grip. *D'angles pads* are designed with a ribbed and angled surface. They help the rider maintain a more stable, balanced leg by keeping the foot inclined at the proper angle.

For both English and Western stirrups, an appropriately styled *fleece-lined foot warmer* will fit over the stirrup to keep the foot warm in winter.

Stirrup leathers for the English saddle can be purchased in short lengths and narrow widths of less than an inch for a child. Average leathers are one inch wide by 54 inches long but are available in narrower widths of three-quarters and seven-eighths and lengths of 60, 64, and 68 inches for the tall dressage rider. For showing in your own saddle, it's a good idea to neatly cut off the ends of the leathers so the excess doesn't flap out of the keeper.

For closer and more comfortable leg contact with your horse, without interference from the stirrup buckle, use the type of stirrup that adjusts at the bottom of the leather near the top of the stirrup with a loop that slips over the stirrup bar. Most leathers come in different shades of brown, from very light to very dark, and in black, so be careful to choose one that matches your saddle. Extension leathers, which can be taken up once you're in the saddle, are good for mounting those extra-tall horses.

Girths

ENGLISH. The girth, which keeps the saddle secure, must be comfortable and fit the horse properly. It should also be durable and smooth, not bulky, and easy to keep clean. It should be cleaned after each ride, just as the horse's girth area should be kept clean and free of dirt and dried sweat. I always check the girth area with my bare hand before securing the girth to make sure it is really clean and smooth. Dirt particles left on the hair here can be rubbed into the skin, causing a girth sore, fungus, or other skin problem that could put your horse out of commission for weeks while it heals.

Girths are available in many styles and materials, but for safety and fit I prefer a leather contour with one end that has two elastic straps—making it more durable and therefore desirable. Buckles that are rounded at the tops don't cut into billets, and tongs are easier to secure if they're seated in the leather rather than sliding around. (You will need this feature when you tighten the girth from the saddle.) Select a girth large enough so that the buckles can be secured in the middle of the billets, not at the very top or the very bottom. When tightening the girth up from the saddle, nothing is more irritating than finding that the last hole is already taken. Girths also affect whether a saddle sits in the center of the horse's back or tilts to one side. To assure the right balance, do it up to approximately the same holes on each side.

Straight girths tend to interfere with the horse's elbow, although these days most of the leather ones are cut a little narrower or are contoured. Many girths are now made of synthetic materials such as neoprene, which a lot of riders prefer, claiming that they're chafeless and very easy to keep clean. Washable white string and mohair girths are chosen for their comfort. They provide even pressure. All others come in black and shades of brown to match the saddle.

With the growing interest in dressage, short girths have become popular, and the extra-long billets allow maximum contact for the rider's leg. Shorter girths are available with and without elastic, in an assortment of sizes and in brown or black to match your saddle. Some girths have a loop for an overgirth—of special interest to eventers and competitive trail riders. They match the saddle or come in colors for variety. Some dressage saddles have an extra-long strap attached to the bottom of the long flaps, which act as an overgirth.

To prevent chafing and girth sores, many English riders use slip-on girth covers or guards—a real asset for thin-skinned horses. They are made from a variety of materials, most of them washable, and they come in different sizes to fit both traditional and small dressage girths. Some are made of Equigel; another type, from Germany, is made of a synthetic material that offers ventilation and has an antibacterial, slip-resistant surface.

WESTERN. As many different materials are used for Western girths as for English ones, including leather, mohair, cotton, cord, neoprene, and other synthetic materials that are easy to clean and maintain. Neoprene and the synthetics need only brushing off and a little soap and water. Other girths are made of combination materials, such as washable fleece on one side and an easy-to-clean synthetic material on the reverse. Western girths come in all sizes too, just like their English counterparts. The price varies according to the material and whether they have buckles.

Certain styles are designed for specific disciplines. A girth for roping horses is almost double in width at its center, with rings front and back. The breastplate attaches to the ring in the front; the back girth to the one in back. When the steer hits the end of the rope, all these features, including the double-center width, come into play to keep the saddle in place.

Saddle Pads

No matter what type of saddle you use, a pad is essential to protect it and the horse's back. A variety

MOHAIR CINCHES

With Buckle

Without Buckle

of therapeutic pads, like the *gel pad,* are designed specifically for horses with back problems. (They should be considered only a temporary solution.) Saddle pads of many materials are made for both English and Western saddles. Square and contour pads are used for daily riding. Supplemental pads of closed-cell foam, vinyl, gel, and other materials go over the conventional pads to adjust a saddle that doesn't fit correctly or to protect a sensitive back. Always keep in mind, though, that all the padding in the world is not going to improve a saddle that doesn't fit properly in the first place.

In selecting a pad for everyday riding, the main considerations are fit, durability, and weight. A pad that is too thick will distance you from the feel of your horse. Softer, plusher types are assumed to be better, but the buyer overlooks what happens to them after mounting and considerable use. Any material will be compressed and made denser by the weight of the saddle. Even gel pads get forced away from a saddle's high spots, usually bottoming out with time. High spots on felt, foam, and sheepskin pads get pressed down more than low ones, making them harder and denser in the area where softness is needed. If the saddle fits properly, your best bets are a *cotton fleece* pad for jumping, a *cotton or cotton combination* pad for dressage, and a *wool or wool combination* for Western riding.

For jumping, a form-fitting pad is more functional and more attractive. They fit the shape of the saddle, with just a few inches peeking around the edges. Washable Air-flo pads made of equi-fleece are designed for minimum slippage and maximum breathability.

Pads with wool on the bottom and fleece on top are ideal in terms of absorption and ventilation, but to prevent both from slipping, leading riders recommend that you place a moistened chamois (or synthetic) on the horse's back under a well-fitted saddle pad and saddle.

Dressage riders can choose from a variety of square pads and contour pads, shaped to fit the withers. Cotton is the best material, being the most breathable, durable, and comfortable. It has the added advantage of being easily washable. The usual colors are black or white, but pads can be purchased in a number of conservative colors with or without contrasting piping and even in plaids.

The pad should be long enough to prevent the saddle flaps from touching your horse's sides or other parts of the saddle from contacting his back, but it should not be so long that it hangs too far down below the flaps; two inches is fine. Most pads have either girth, billet loops, or both to help keep the pad in place. Special pads for endurance and trail riding are thicker and softer, designed to keep the equine back cool and the weight evenly dispersed, with pockets in back for carrying supplies.

SEAT SAVERS. Made of sheepskin or fleece, for both English and Western saddles, these pads are soft under the seat and warm for winter riding. They also prevent slipping. They come in black, white, or brown and are easily secured over the saddle seat.

SIT TIGHT. Don't laugh. Top dressage, jumper, and event riders who are willing to spend extra money for those full-seat breeches will also want the best and most consistent contact possible with the saddle, and that means a saddle grip product. Resembling a wax, it can be carried in the pocket and rubbed into the saddle just before you compete. It helps the jumper-rider to maintain a two-point position over a massive oxer or drop fence and is a real asset to the event rider splashing through water obstacles or any rider competing out in the rain. It is also used by dressage riders who want to feel glued to the saddle. Some use a saddle grip to improve the contact of leather gloves on leather reins.

Every type of English and Western saddle, bridle, halter, girth, breastplate, martingale, and even hackamore is now available in a synthetic material, often in a wide range of colors. All are extremely long-lasting and lightweight, requiring little maintenance. Best of all, they're inexpensive—an ideal choice for the novice or for the rider who wants to branch out into a new discipline but doesn't have the budget for two sets of leather tack.

Though not as popular in the show ring, endurance, trail, and event riders find synthetics ideal for their sports. They are about two-thirds lighter than leather and require just a scrub with soapy water to make them look like new—a real time saver. Many have wool-stuffed panels that are designed to conform to the horse's back. The softer-than-leather gel seats are a real asset for equestrians who spend long hours in the saddle.

Among the synthetic materials used for saddles, bridles, and fittings are Wintec; Biothane, a polyurethane-coated strapping that doesn't tear, fray, or soak up moisture; and weather- and mildew-resistant nylon, which is supple and resists breakage. A particularly popular item for endurance, eventing, and trail riders is a bridle of synthetic material that converts to a secure halter, with a detachable bit and convertible head stall. Synthetic saddles don't have the resale value of traditional leather ones, but they will last just as long if properly cared for. For a few hundred dollars more, you can buy a middle-grade leather saddle that can be sold later when you move up to a better one.

What to Look For

1. Overall appearance. It's impossible to return the tallow to dried-out tack. The drying-out process begins with cracking, so you can check for cracks by bending back the saddle's skirts, billets, and stirrup straps. Cracked billets can't be restored to usable condition, and they are expensive to replace. So don't even consider buying a used saddle that is dried out and cracked.
2. Leather thickness. The thickness of the leather is no indication of its quality. Thin leather is frequently superior. The part of the animal from which the piece is cut and the tallow are the most important factors.
3. Stitches. Good saddles should have a variety of stitching lengths. Areas that take strain are usually sewn with a long stitch that takes fewer holes, while spots that bear less strain have more stitches. Any ornamentation should also be closely stitched.
4. Quality of tree. Be sure to check the tree to make sure it is sound. If it is broken, the saddle is worthless. It should also be symmetrical.

5. Condition of panels. See if the panels are too hard or lumpy in some places and lacking stuffing in others. If the saddle is uneven on either side, that should also be considered. All these factors are fixable if the saddle has been flocked with wool, but it definitely should be considered in the price. Reflocking can cost well over a hundred dollars.

6. Protruding nails. Make sure there are no protruding nails underneath the gullet area of the saddle that could come in contact and injure your horse's back.

Once again, if you're new to riding, it would be wise to have your instructor look the used saddle over first. Even a good used saddle can be expensive.

TACKING UP

It's somehow comforting to know that a few pounds of leather and steel link modern equestrians and those of the Greek cavalry. In Xenophon's time (circa 400 B.C.), bridles were put on exactly as they are today. In the third century B.C., equine equipment was almost as light as it is now, consisting of a leather saddle with a wooden tree and rudimentary stirrups.

But by the middle of the fourteenth century, horses were as heavily armored as the knights astride them, and tacking up had become a major production. Wealthier knights had three grooms for the task, one to hold the horse while his fellows put on the steel plate poitrel, the horse's breastplate; the crupper, which covered the entire hindquarters; the saddle, with a pommel and cantle of steel; the crinet, which protected the horse's neck; the chamfron, to mask its head and protect its ears; and an escutcheon, showing the knight's coat of arms as a browpiece. By the time the armored rider and horse were ready to ride out, their tack weighed in the neighborhood of an additional four hundred pounds. Fortunately over the centuries most tack has been streamlined for the various disciplines, and except for elaborate saddles, adorned with silver worn by parade horses, you do not require a weight lifter or a crane to saddle up your horse.

Preparation for Saddling

Both English and Western saddles are put on over the saddle pad. Before you saddle up, make sure your horse is secured by a lead rope or in cross-ties. Then slide the saddle pad into place, beginning in front of the withers and moving it back toward the rump until it's in the right position. Make sure that it lies smooth and straight on both sides. Some English saddle pads have loops at the girth and/or tabs that fit over the billets to keep them in place.

If your saddle has been put away properly, the girth will be folded up over the seat or hung up separately (and stirrups on English saddles run up). On an English saddle the stirrups on both sides will remain run up until you're ready to mount. The off stirrup on a Western saddle can be hooked over the horn when you are putting the saddle on to keep it out of the way and prevent it from hitting the horse as you swing the saddle over his back.

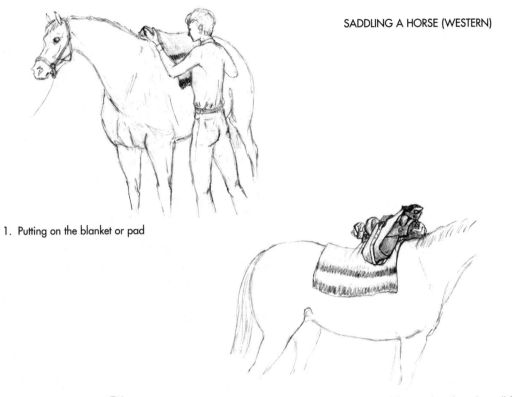

SADDLING A HORSE (WESTERN)

1. Putting on the blanket or pad

2. Saddle on, placed gently, well forward of its final position (slide into place), stirrup resting on horn, girth over the saddle to avoid hitting horse

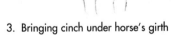

3. Bringing cinch under horse's girth

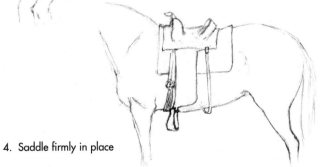

4. Saddle firmly in place

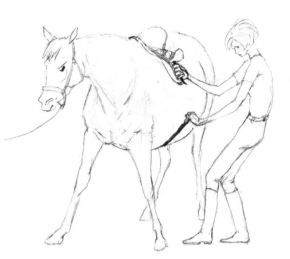

Blowing Out

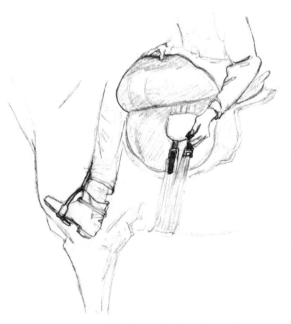

Correct Way to Adjust the Girth When Mounted

Saddling Up

After you have positioned the saddle pad in the center of the horse's back, gently put on the saddle, working it from front to back. (The girth should be separate or lying across the seat of the saddle.) If you see that the saddle is too far back, lift it and reposition it. Never slide it forward—that will push the horse's hair in the wrong direction and cause saddle sores.

Moving to the off side, drop the girth or cinch down (and on a Western saddle, the stirrup also), or attach the girth to the off side. Be sure to leave it long enough to reach the billets on the opposite side. (If the girth has elastic on one end, the elastic attaches on the near side.) Return to the near shoulder, and bring the girth under. Secure it enough to keep the saddle in place for the time being. Now, circling around the front, go to the off side again to make sure the saddle pad and the girth are lying flat and sitting straight.

Wait until the bridle is on before you tighten the girth another notch or two. Do not secure it to the right notch for riding until just before you are ready to mount. Never attempt to get the girth as high as it will go on the first try. Some horses have extremely sensitive backs, and this is no way to find out if yours is one of them. A horse may object to an abruptly tightened girth by cow-kicking, biting, or in extreme cases developing a *cold back*—humping his back and jumping straight-legged into the air like a bucking bronco when the saddle goes on or, worse yet, when you mount. A young horse who has a saddle suddenly slapped on his back and a girth pulled up tight is likely to react this way. But in most situations your horse will probably forewarn you of his displeasure by pinning back his ears and becoming restless. While it's obviously unsafe to mount or ride with a loose girth, think of your horse's comfort, and take it up in stages. It helps to walk a sensitive horse around in hand and slowly take up the girth or cinch before mounting.

The same treatment works if your horse is one of those that blows out (fills up with air like a balloon) when the girth is first buckled and then gradually returns to his normal size. Taking your time tightening the girth will give him the chance to relax and "depuff." If you use a martingale or tie-down, put it on before you attach the girth or cinch on both sides. (When you remove tack, the procedure is reversed and these come off first.)

Try to have the girth attached equally on both sides so you don't end up in the last hole on the near side and find that it needs to be tightened another notch after you've mounted. (This is nearly impossible to do on the nonelastic girths, and you will probably have to dismount and readjust it from the ground.) If your horse has put on a few inches around the middle over the winter, you can purchase a girth extender.

Putting on the Bridle

After you unsnap the lead rope or cross-ties, put the reins of the bridle over the horse's head, before you remove the halter (so you have something to hold him with if he decides to walk away). Face forward, with your right shoulder by the near side of his head, with the crownpiece of the bridle held in your right hand. Slip your

Correct Way to Put on a Bridle

The Interdental Space
and Bar of the Jaw

right arm under the throatlatch so your horse's head is looking over your right shoulder and the bridle is under his nose. Now take the bit across your left palm, with thumb and index finger supporting it at each end. As you bring it up toward the horse's mouth, balance the bit on your palm and stick your thumb in the near side of his mouth on the bottom bar of the jaw in the interdental space between the molars and incisors. As soon as he opens his mouth, gently slip the bit in. (Jamming it against the teeth is a sure way to make him resist the bit.) By feel, slide the crownpiece just as gently over his ears, one at a time, beginning with the right one.

A Pelham, Kimberwick, or curb bit should have its curb chain (or strap on a Western bridle) fastened next. Before you hook or buckle it, make sure the strap or chain is lying flat and is adjusted so that it is not too tight, to allow the bit to operate correctly. Adjust the cavesson or noseband the same way, remembering to put the straps on the inside of the cheekpieces, allowing space for two fingers between it and the horse's jaw (if it is a flash or drop noseband, allow space for one finger; crank nosebands should be snug). Attach a standing martingale or tie-down to the cavesson or noseband at this point.

Next, hook up the throatlatch, taking care that the leather is flat, with no twists, and loose enough to allow a hand to slide palm-down between it and the horse's throat; otherwise it could interfere with his breathing. Going around to the front of the horse, smooth out the forelock and make sure everything is sitting straight, and that the browband isn't drooping over one eye.

Horses are well disposed to bridling; some even lower their heads and open their mouths for the bit. A few will throw their heads back to avoid it, probably because of a bad experience. If your horse is balky about bridling, it's worth spending a few weeks and using some patience (and offering bribes of carrots, grain, or molasses with the bit) to change his attitude.

After tacking up, you may want to leave your horse in his stall for a few minutes before riding. If so, put a halter over the bridle to keep the ends of the reins from catching on anything in the stall. Then run up the stirrups or twist reins under his neck, and secure one loop in the throatlatch. (See page 384.) (If they dropped down on his neck, he could step on them.) English riders should always keep the stirrups run up until they are ready to mount to prevent them from swinging and catching on objects when a horse is being led or tied.

Sliding the Crownpiece over the Right Ear by Feel

UNTACKING

After you have dismounted from a ride, loosen the girth a few notches before you walk your horse out so that circulation can return to his back. Some endurance riders feel so strongly about the bad effects of removing a saddle too quickly that they will leave it on for an hour or more after working a horse, loosening the girth then lifting it up off the back after dismounting to allow circulation to be restored. In the Vermont hundred-mile ride, a few conscientious souls leave saddles on for several hours, loosening the girth one hole at a time.

After you dismount from an English saddle, before you move your horse even a step, immediately run up the stirrups. (Dangling stirrups can catch on the oddest things; I've seen one horse bang his nose on one while trying to bite a fly.) Before you run them up on the off side, bring the reins over the horse's head and hold them. Then return to the near side, loosen the girth, and hand-walk him until he's cool before untacking. If the weather is cool, throw a cooler over him to prevent a loss of body heat as he cools down. When he's thoroughly cool, remove the bridle first, slip on the halter, and cross-tie him; then remove the saddle, placing it on a collapsible saddle rack. (See Appendix E for an easy-to-make variety.) While he's tied, give him a rubdown or sponge bath, depending on the weather, then untie and hand-walk him until he's dry before returning him to the stall.

After you take care of your horse, take care of your tack. Good tack is expensive and can last for years if it is well cared for. Racks and/or holders, available at any tack outlet, are easy for a handyperson to make. The best kind is open at the bottom, allowing air in to dry the underside and lining. Cover the saddle with a commercial cover or clean towel. (For instructions on how to make your own saddle cover, see Appendix D.)

24

Bridles, Bits, Breastplates, Martingales, and Whips

In the Middle Ages, when blacksmiths were concerned more with appearances than with humaneness, horses were fitted out with a variety of decorative but torturous mouthpieces. Forged out of gold and ingeniously carved in the shape of monsters, dragons, and flowers, the beauty of the bits masked the terrible toll they took on a horse's mouth. The characteristics of these harsh bits can still be seen in some contemporary Western bits.

BRIDLES

A basic bridle is made up of a bit, reins, and a headstall. The latter comprises two *cheekpieces;* a *crownpiece* (sometimes called a headpiece); a *throatlatch,* which keeps the bridle from being pulled off the horse's head; and a headband or *browband,* which prevents the bridle from slipping too far back off the poll. The English *cavesson* or Western *noseband* keep the mouth closed and are also where the standing *martingale* (or tie-down) attaches. On an English bridle the crownpiece and throatlatch are generally in one piece, fastening to the cheekpieces, which are attached to the bit. It fits over the horse's head behind his ears and is held in place by the headband in front and the throatlatch, which fastens loosely under the horse's throat.

The cavesson is of one piece, with a strap going up over the horse's head and another that fits around the nose. It slips through the insides of the crownpiece and is worn under the cheekpieces. The *reins* attach to the bit, giving the rider direct communication with the horse's mouth.

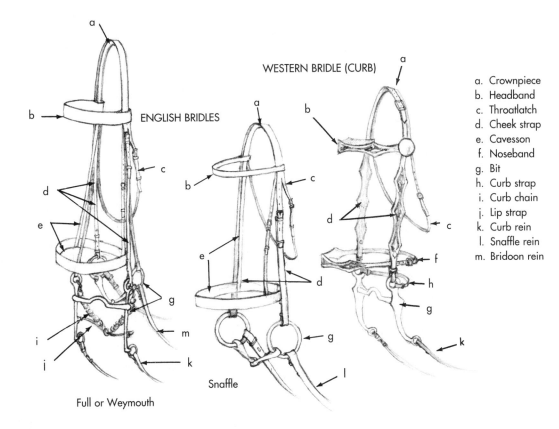

WESTERN BRIDLE (CURB)

ENGLISH BRIDLES

a. Crownpiece
b. Headband
c. Throatlatch
d. Cheek strap
e. Cavesson
f. Noseband
g. Bit
h. Curb strap
i. Curb chain
j. Lip strap
k. Curb rein
l. Snaffle rein
m. Bridoon rein

Full or Weymouth

Snaffle

Tips for Fitting a Bridle

As with saddles, the quality of the leather determines the softness and comfort of a bridle. A poorly fitted bridle can rub and irritate the horse, causing him to resent bridling and toss his head when working under saddle. An ill-fitting bridle doesn't add a thing to the head of any horse and can actually detract from an attractive one. Conversely, a well-made, properly fitted bridle can enhance a head and lend elegance to the overall picture.

Good-quality leather on a bridle should appear smooth throughout. The stitching should be consistent and run parallel to the straps. Skimpy stitches weaken a bridle. Leather should be tapered and thinned at junctures, not bulky.

When putting on a bridle, fasten the buckles at the level of the horse's eye, but never in the last hole (if you need to, go to the next-size bridle). The throatlatch should be attached at that same alignment with the eye, without a lot of excess leather hanging down. When a bridle is on, all the loose ends should be put home in their respective keepers, so they're not dangling loose. (Many cheap bridles make the keepers so tight, the leather ends don't fit.) The attached throatlatch should allow enough room for the width of your hand or four fingers to fit between the leather and midway down the horse's jaw. You don't want it so tight that it interferes with your horse's breathing or neck flexion. A finger should fit under the browband; if it is too tight, it will pinch or rub; if too loose, it will sag.

When fitting a double bridle, the additional cheekpiece should be behind and in back of the cheekpiece for the curb. (See page 317, "Fitting a Bit.")

The top of the cavesson should lie just a finger's width below the cheekbone. (Frequently these are set too low.) It should fit snugly, two fingers' width, attaching under the jaw at the center. The wider and softer the cavesson is, the more comfortable it is for the horse. The back of the cavesson is where the standing martingale is attached, if you're using one.

Instead of a cavesson sometimes a *dropped noseband* is used to keep the horse's mouth closed, allowing the bit to function more efficiently. They often tend to be too big across the nose, with straps that drop too acutely, interfering with the action of the bit. Now they have mostly been replaced with the *flash noseband,* which fits and adjusts better. This ordinary-looking noseband has a loop sewn into the bottom of the center front, allowing a smaller strap, or flash, to slip through, converting it into a dropped noseband. The flash is fastened firmly on the near side below the bit, with only a finger's width between it and the nose. It should be snug but should not pull the cavesson out of place. Remember that one of the main functions of the flash is to keep the mouth closed, not interfere with breathing.

An alternative is a *converter,* a small sliding strap that buckles on the center of the noseband and turns any regular cavesson into a flash. It can be purchased at any tack shop.

Flash Noseband

CRANK NOSEBAND. This expensive device looks like a plain noseband but offers combined leverage to keep the horse's mouth closed. Some have extra padding at the rear for a more comfortable fit. More severe types are studded or chain-lined. Like the flash, these fasten firmly, with a finger's width between it and the back of the horse's nose.

FIGURE-EIGHT NOSEBAND. These come in two types. One has a sliding crown that can be adjusted to fit different horses; on the other, the crown is attached to rings. These are used on event horses and racehorses to keep the mouth closed without obstructing breathing. If you are showing, find out what type of noseband is allowed in your discipline. Dropped nosebands are not permitted in hunter classes and are frowned on in the field, but crank nosebands are allowed. Jumpers are allowed any type; the flash cavesson is preferred because a standing martingale can be attached to a noseband. When governed by American Horse Show Association rules, dressage horses can use any type of dropped noseband, but at Fédération Équestre Internationale (FEI) upper levels, where double bridles are used, only cavessons are allowed. Event horses must follow dressage rules for that phase of the competition, but they can use any type of dropped noseband for the jumping sections.

The reins should be long enough to allow your horse to stretch his head down at a free walk, but not so long that they become tangled in your knee or stirrup. Pay attention to this especially with children and ponies. Keep your extra rein on the opposite side of your crop to prevent them from becoming tangled. In the ring the crop is usually carried on the inside of the circle, while extra rein is on the outside.

A snaffle bit calls for a single rein, buckled rather than sewn at the center. This allows each

Figure Eight Noseband

side to be slipped through the rings of a running martingale if necessary. Many people prefer to buy plaited or braided reins for a better grip. A narrow three-quarter-inch rein is a good size for a woman's hand; children, who have trouble holding thick reins, will need them thinner. Riders who have difficulty keeping their reins even or at the correct length can select a type with corresponding notches of leather or nylon at even intervals near the end closest to the buckle.

Two reins are used on a full bridle and a Pelham: a snaffle or bradoon and a curb. A narrow rein, sewn at the center, is buckled to the curb. This rein is usually an eighth of an inch thinner than the snaffle or bridoon rein, which attaches to the snaffle or bradoon bit and buckles in the center. Its width varies, depending on the rider and the situation. Braided or laced reins are often employed on the snaffle bit for easier handling when hunting or jumping.

While most cheekpieces and reins buckle, they can also be sewn onto the bridle and together, a requirement for certain show classes (like Corinthian hunter). Reins made of cotton webbing or with rubber handgrips give a better grip for jumping and are preferred for endurance riding, the cross-country phase of eventing, and open jumping, but they are not permitted in hunter classes. Be sure to wear gloves with these reins, otherwise they will burn your hands.

BITS

Bits vary as much as bridles, the type depending on how the horse is being used and the degree of training of both the horse and the rider. But all are variations on just two styles: the *snaffle* and the *curb*.

A number of factors need to be considered when you are selecting a bit. First be aware of the areas of your horse's mouth that will be affected by it: the *interdental space,* which is the large toothless gap between his front teeth (incisors) and his back

English bridles with bits (all Pelhams and curb bits are
used with curb chains and lip straps, and Kimberwicks
are used with curb chains alone)

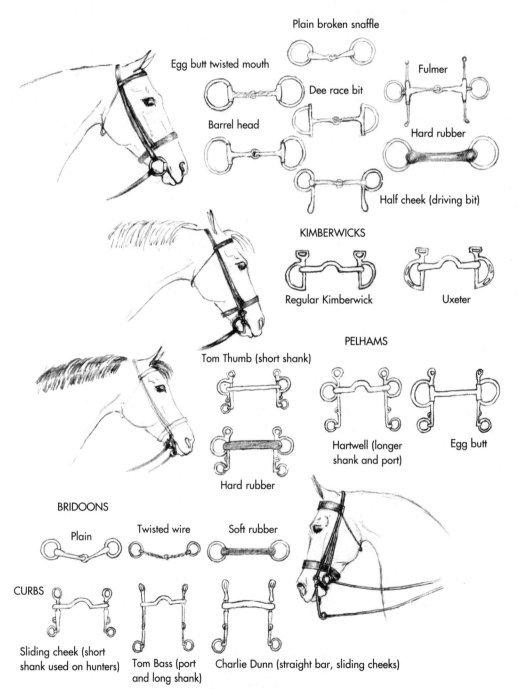

SNAFFLES

Plain broken snaffle

Egg butt twisted mouth

Dee race bit

Fulmer

Barrel head

Hard rubber

Half cheek (driving bit)

KIMBERWICKS

Regular Kimberwick

Uxeter

PELHAMS

Tom Thumb (short shank)

Hartwell (longer
shank and port)

Egg butt

Hard rubber

BRIDOONS

Plain

Twisted wire

Soft rubber

CURBS

Sliding cheek (short
shank used on hunters)

Tom Bass (port
and long shank)

Charlie Dunn (straight bar, sliding cheeks)

teeth (molars); the *bars* of the mouth (jawbones); the *palate* (roof of the mouth); and the tongue. Also affected are the lips, cheeks, and *poll*. A bit that doesn't fit properly or is poorly designed or inappropriate for your horse can cause behavior problems and injure his mouth.

Selecting a Bit

When buying your first English or Western bit, ask your riding instructor to help you in the selection. Because a horse's mouth can be ruined by a mouthpiece that is too harsh or ill fitting, he should be ridden in the lightest bit he can be controlled in. If you are showing, be familiar not only with the rules but with the acceptable bits in your discipline. Also, keep up to date—they do change.

Fitting a Bit

To fit a bit, first stimulate one with a piece of baling twine about a foot and a half long; knot it about six inches from the end, and slide it through the mouth at the bars like a bit. When the knot is flush with the lips on one corner, tie another knot at the same point on the opposite side. Remove the twine, measure between the two knots, add a half inch, and you have your horse's bit size.

When a snaffle bit is in place, it should cause a single wrinkle at the corners of the mouth. (Pelhams, curbs, and Kimberwicks shouldn't wrinkle the corners.) If it is too narrow, its rings will pinch the corners and cause sores; if it is too wide, the joint will hit the roof of the mouth, allowing too much play sideways. If it hangs too low, the ineffective bit will hang loosely in the horse's mouth, hitting his incisors and encouraging him to fiddle with it. Sometimes he will shake it between his teeth to hear the noise.

A horse dissatisfied with the bit might throw his head, pull against the reins, open and close his mouth excessively, and generally act uncomfortable. If it's too sharp, he may tuck his nose behind the vertical. He may salivate excessively, tossing his head and pulling at the bit as though trying to get more rein. Factors other than the bit could be involved—teeth problems, a green mouth, or an inexperienced rider using too long or short a rein. The bit may be aggravating an old mouth injury or irritating a wolf tooth. Your horse is telling you something in the only way he knows how, so pay attention. Whatever the source of the problem, consult with a professional before experimenting with different types of bits.

In a double bridle the two bits should be wide enough that the lips of the horse are not being pinched. Because the bits work together, take care not to get the snaffle too high; keep it at the same height it would be in a regular snaffle bridle. The smaller rings of the bradoon prevent it from interfering with the curb.

Before you make a permanent switch to a new type of bit, see if you can borrow one like it to try out. Again, seek professional advice to be sure it's the horse's problem and not yours. Be sure the mouthpieces, particularly on a jointed snaffle, are symmetrical and smooth.

English Bridles

A complete English bridle without a bit will vary in price according to the workmanship and quality of the leather, which can be raised, "fancy raised," or black leather, with white trim for the dressage horse. If you plan to do a lot of showing, it's a good idea to have two bridles, one for everyday schooling and a better one for show. When selecting a show bridle, choose one that sets off your horse's head. A large head would look better in wider leather, while a thinner, finer, raised-leather bridle is more becoming to a small head. Good-quality leather is softer and more comfortable for your horse.

English Bits

SNAFFLE. The snaffle is a nonleverage bit that works by direct pressure from a single rein attached to each side. Although other types of bits have come and gone over the centuries, the snaffle has stood its ground. Similar designs have been with us for many thousands of years, and they were so widely used in so many early cultures that it's impossible to pinpoint one place of origin.

The snaffle is a mainstay in racing, eventing, jumping, and dressage. It is usually used as a first bit and training tool in all disciplines, both English and Western. Although considered the mildest form of bit, different snaffle designs can have a varied effect on horses' mouths. They were basically designed to work on the corners of the mouth, not the bars. Snaffles today come in all shapes and sizes; some apply more emphasis on the lips, others on the bars and tongue. Variations of design affect the function of the bit. Smooth and unjoined mouthpieces are milder than twisted ones. A straight or slightly curved bar *(mullen-mouth)* is milder because the horse can use his tongue and push against the bit, evading some of the action. Fixed rings, as opposed to loose rings, influence the way the horse will take hold of the bit and move at the poll.

The mildest type of bit is a *jointed* (or broken) *snaffle* with loose rings. It acts on the tongue, the corners of the mouth, or the lips. This is the best choice for a young horse with a sensitive mouth or an inexperienced rider who has yet to develop a light touch with his hands. Combined with a dropped noseband (to keep the horse's mouth closed), a snaffle can control almost any horse. In addition, it allows the rider to maintain a steady light contact with the horse's mouth. It also has a lifting action on the head, especially when combined with a curb bit in a full bridle.

For ages it was an accepted fact that a thick mouthpiece was milder because it spread the pressure on the corners of the mouth while a narrower one was sharper. Recent research has shown that a wide mouthpiece can be too large for some of the lighter breeds, like Arabians and Saddlebreds, who have a small or narrow mouth and a shallow palate. These mouths are more comfortable with slimmer bits that allow sufficient room for the tongue. Too thick a bit can actually prevent a horse from closing its mouth, drying it out—particularly in arid climates—and causing bruising of the bars.

Some very mild snaffles have a *straight bar* of soft rubber, hard rubber, plastic, or metal. The rubber and plastic types are used primarily on horses with very sensitive mouths or on those recovering from a mouth injury whom you would like to have accept and trust the bit. I've had horses that chewed right through a plastic or soft rubber bit. In those instances I moved on to a mild, hollow-mouthed snaffle.

Copper bits are used because their taste encourages the horse to chew the bit, causing him to salivate and maintain a soft mouth. The saliva acts as a lubricant, cushioning the movement of the bit in his mouth. The most severe snaffle is a *twisted wire* mouthpiece. This type of bit should be used only by experienced riders, as it can ruin a mouth.

A *full cheek* or *half cheek* can point up or down or both ways and prevent the rings of the bit from sliding through the horse's mouth. By applying pressure to the cheeks, it encourages the horse to bend laterally. A keeper added to the cheekpiece on each side of the bridle will keep the top vertical piece of the full cheek bit in place. Egg butts and D's, names describing the shape of the rings, are fixed, encouraging the horse to take hold of the bit—often desirable in a racing. The egg butt snaffle rings should be molded smoothly into the mouthpiece, not pinching the corners of the horse's lips—one of the problems with some ill-fitting but popular loose ring snaffles. Many trainers like to use lightweight hollow mouth bits on young or green horses; they look exactly like the solid ones.

Double-jointed snaffles like the Dr. Bristol, French, and KK are quite popular with dressage riders and are spreading over into other disciplines. The shape of the additional center joint affects the way it acts in the mouth, and some horses seem to like it because it allows more room for the tongue. The Dr. Bristol has a long flat center piece, more severe than the smaller, smoother, rounded one on the French snaffle. The KK bit is good for very young or sensitive mouths because the center piece is small and lies flat on the tongue. As with all other bits, the rider's expertise will affect the severity of the double-jointed snaffle. A beginner who uses the reins as a means of balance can turn the mildest bit into a weapon.

We now come to the *bridoon,* which is usually a narrow snaffle used in combination with a curb bit, part of the full bridle (double bridle or Weymouth). This bit can be handled either separately or simultaneously. The *full bridle* is considered the most complex and yet most flexible of all the English bridles.

CURB. The curb can be the most severe of bits if improperly used. In experi-

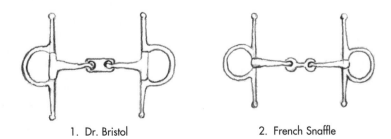

1. Dr. Bristol   2. French Snaffle

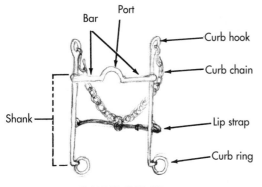

Port

Bar

Curb hook

Curb chain

Shank

Lip strap

Curb ring

ENGLISH CURB BIT

enced hands, however, and in combination with a bridoon, it will enable the rider to get the most advanced kind of performance from a horse. Originally used for hunting, these bridles are now favored in upper-level dressage and most saddle horse and park horse classes. It is used by itself in Western riding but not in English riding.

The mouthpiece of the bar (and port, if there is one) of the curb acts on the anatomical bars and the tongue. As with the snaffle, the degree of severity depends on the curb's shape. The wider and shallower the mouthpiece, the milder it will be. The narrower and steeper the port, the harsher it will be.

The curb bit draws in the chin of the horse and makes it flex at the poll. The shank, in conjunction with the curb chain, acts like a fulcrum, putting pressure on the bars and tongue. The longer the shank, the tighter the curb chain will get and the more severe the pressure—with no extra effort on the rider's part.

The curb chain, used with curb, Pelham, and Kimberwick bits, should not cut into a horse's chin. It should fit comfortably in the curb groove, located under the chin. When too taut, the chain can cause curb galls. A horse with sensitive skin will need a curb-chain guard made of leather or rubber.

In a full bridle, the bridoon goes on top and the curb on the bottom. Each bit has its own crownpiece; the one attached to the curb has the throatlatch and the browband. A lip strap is usually added to keep the curb chain and bit in place.

The *Pelham,* a kind of cross between snaffle and curb, acts a little like both and ends up being less effective than either. Yet some horses will go better in a Pelham than in a snaffle, so this type of bit has become a necessary evil. Pelhams come with short or long shanks and have mouthpieces of varying thickness. They are straight, broken, or have a port.

Some horses that do well in the schooling ring on just a snaffle with a dropped noseband are hunted, jumped, and ridden on the trail with a Pelham because the bit gives the rider greater control. However, the double reins used on a Pelham are difficult for many children to handle. For this reason, a child or an inexperienced rider may find it easier to use a *converter*—a leather loop between the snaffle and the curb rings, to which a single rein attaches. Although it does simplify control, this device robs the bit of its versatility.

Kimberwicks are one-rein bits that combine the properties of the snaffle and curb, providing more control than the ordinary snaffle. But in inexperienced hands the exaggerated port on the mouthpiece (varying in severity), combined with the curb chain, tends to make a horse overflex or pull, drawing his chin in too far.

Unfortunately this type of bit is being used more and more frequently by novice riders. While some horses do well in this bit, usually they will do just as well in a snaffle after a little work. But like the Pelham, the Kimberwick does give greater control, especially for riding in the open.

Western Bridles

BOSAL. The bosal (pronounced *boh-zahl*), used as a training device on most Western horses, is a braided rawhide band that attaches to a headstall and goes around the nose. The reins are tied to the bosal with a special knot called a *fiador*, which determines the amount of pressure a horse receives on the rear of the jaw and behind the poll. A lot of people prefer the bosal to a hackamore because it doesn't squeeze the nose. A horse can be trained to neck-rein nicely with a bosal. When a young horse is being taught to stop with this device, the rider doesn't pull but uses an alternating action with each rein. Pulling on the nose will have the same deterrent effect as pulling on the mouth.

HACKAMORE. The hackamore puts a squeezing action on the nose. It has a piece that goes across the nose, along with a curb strap and shanks. Some cutting horses get so involved in their work that they get angry at errant cattle and give them a nip—behavior that counts against them in competition. These horses have to be schooled in tight hackamores to train them not to bite.

SPLIT-EARED. The simplest kind of Western bridle is the split-eared type—a simple headstall with no throatlatch. Most Western horses are shown or worked in the split-eared bridle because it is more workmanlike and neater in appearance. It is easy to put on and slips off easily instead of breaking in an emergency—if, for instance, a ground-tied horse becomes frightened and steps on the reins.

Some riders use a bridle that includes a noseband and a throatlatch, similar to the English style. These bridles are often elaborate, with tooling and studs decorating the wide leather pieces.

Western Bits

GRAZING BIT. The innovative grazing bit has a broken mouthpiece and shanks that bend back when the horse puts his head down to graze. I don't like them because they encourage a bad habit.

ROPING BIT. Roping bits have two shanks that curve down and meet together with a ring below the chin. This keeps the rope from getting caught in the shanks when working cattle. Most cowboys today use steel bits with a medium port and a medium-long shank.

SPADE BIT. The spade bit is a severe device that looks as harsh as it must feel in a horse's mouth when an inexperienced rider has the reins. If used properly, a horse can be trained not to fight it, but in the hands of a novice it can be a disaster.

HACKAMORE BIT. The hackamore bit is sometimes used on working cow horses and often on roping horses in competition to keep the mouth from

WESTERN BRIDLES, BITS, AND REINS

WESTERN BRIDLES AND BITS

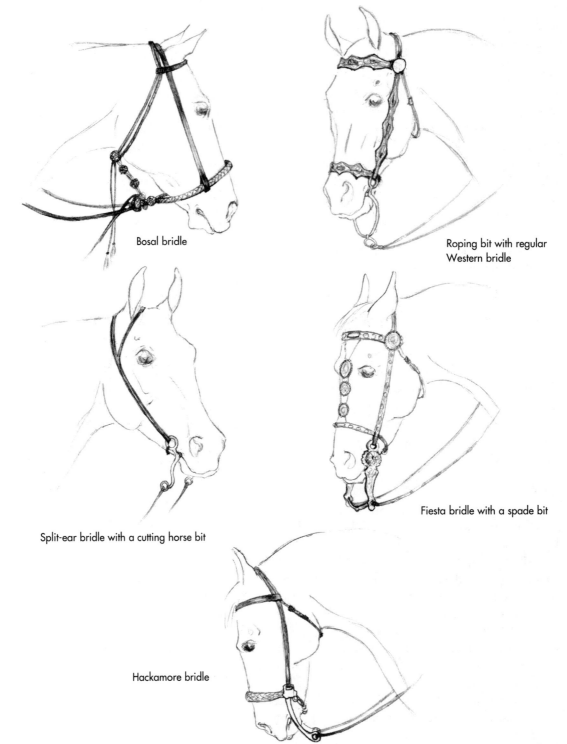

Bosal bridle

Roping bit with regular
Western bridle

Split-ear bridle with a cutting horse bit

Fiesta bridle with a spade bit

Hackamore bridle

receiving the full brunt of the rider's pressure on the reins during sudden stops. Like English bits, the longer and straighter the shank in combination with the curb chain, the more severe the bit; and the narrower and steeper the port, the harsher it is.

Western Reins

The Western rider has both narrow and wide reins to choose from, the selection depending on how the reins feel in his hand. They are made of leather, rope (like the bosal), and horsehair, for decorative purposes. Except for those on a roping bridle, Western reins are usually long and split in the middle. Roping reins are short, in a continuous loop so they can be dropped during roping and recovered quickly, accommodating the rider, who leans forward over his horse's neck. *Romel* reins, seen in the show ring, particularly in Arabian and Morgan classes, are also a continuous loop, but they have a tail in the middle with a popper on the end. The rider carries the rein in one hand and the tail in the other. These reins are usually very decorative, of braided rope or nylon, sometimes with silver ferrules, and they often have a matching browband. They snap on or attach to the bit with hobble straps.

BREAST-PLATES

Breastplates, hooked to D's on the front of the saddle, are used on horses with very heavy or undefined withers to keep the saddle from sliding back. Traditionally used for hunting, to keep the saddle from slipping when galloping up- and downhill, they are equally useful in strenuous cross-country riding. This equipment is visually pleasing in the show ring, helping the neck to appear shorter and adding to a workmanlike turnout.

Western horses with heavy or undefined withers also use a breastplate for keeping the saddle in place when doing quick turns or maneuvers, as is required in roping, barrel racing, or cutting cattle.

Breast Collars and Breast Girths

These are used in conjunction with breastplates to keep the saddle forward on horses that have high withers or are lightly built behind the saddle. A breast collar attaches to saddle D-rings like a breastplate, but it doesn't attach to the girth. The breast girth, considered a safer piece of equipment, attaches to the stirrup bars (which won't pull out), still allowing the horse freedom of shoulder movement. They are often made of elastic and widely used for endurance, racing, show jumping, and eventing.

MARTINGALES AND TIE-DOWNS

Any horse that has a headsetting problem and attempts to escape mouth pressure by raising his head too high is a candidate for a martingale, which helps to keep the head down. I prefer to use a standing martingale, which influences the head directly without interfering with the mouth.

In hunter classes over fences, a standing martingale is often used to give a horse a more traditional appearance. Make sure it fits properly and has a stopper (the lit-

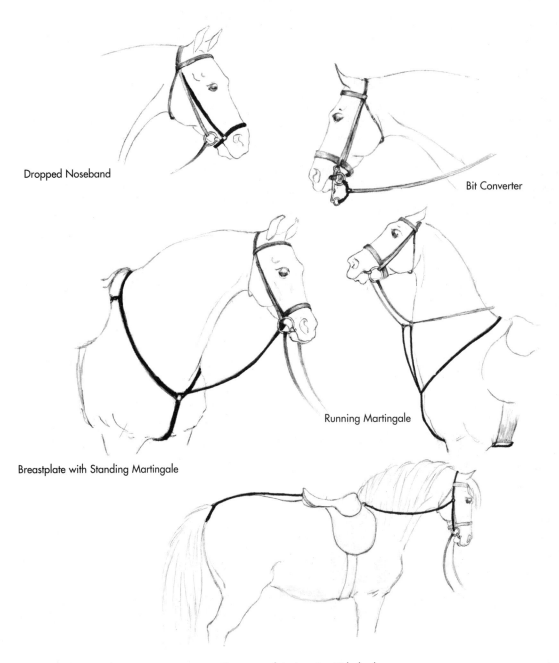

Dropped Noseband

Bit Converter

Breastplate with Standing Martingale

Running Martingale

Crupper and Antigrazing Sidecheck

tle rubber doughnut) at the junction of the two chest straps. When attaching the martingale to the girth and cavesson, have your horse stand with his head in a natural position, and push up the strap between the chest and cavesson until it just touches the throatlatch. The stopper keeps the strap from sliding. The standing martingale loop is slipped onto the back of the cavesson and puts pressure on the nose rather than the mouth to keep the head down. Any horse with a ewe-neck will probably need one, but they are not permitted in certain show classes.

The Western equivalent of this device is the tie-down, which also attaches to the noseband. It is particularly effective in keeping the nose down during quick stops and rollbacks.

The running martingale is used in situations where the horse needs freedom of head and neck and only occasional restriction. Instead of the single piece of leather used in the standing martingale, it has two straps, each with a ring. The snaffle reins are unbuckled, slipped through the rings, and buckled again. Because it puts direct pressure on the bars of the mouth, this type of martingale should be used only by experienced riders with educated hands. It's best to get expert advice before using one.

Running martingales are frequently used as an early training device for show horses like Arabs, Morgans, and Saddlebreds to teach them how to set their heads for pleasure or park horse classes. They are also employed in open jumping and the jumping phases of eventing, where any interference with head and neck movement is undesirable. A martingale or tie-down can be used with a breastplate and can be purchased as an attachment.

If you're showing, be aware that martingales of any type are prohibited in horsemanship on the flat, pleasure classes like road hack and bridlepath hack. They are not permitted in dressage. In hunter classes over fences, only standing martingales are allowed. Jumping classes that follow FEI rules and the jumping phases of three-day events permit only running martingales.

Cruppers

Cruppers hook to a D on the cantle of the saddle and loop under the tail to keep the saddle from sliding forward. They are normally used to compensate for lack of form in the shoulder, withers, or barrel of a horse or pony, keeping a saddle from sliding forward on long downhill treks or trail rides in steep mountain country.

Take time to accustom your horse or pony to the crupper before heading for the hills, or the ride may get more exciting than expected. Put the tail over the crupper first, and apply a little pressure before attaching it and riding off. Better yet, lunge the horse with the crupper and saddle on to make sure he accepts the strap under his tail.

Antigrazing Sidechecks

These are usually used on hungry ponies that take advantage of their young riders by stopping unexpectedly to graze. The sidecheck attaches to the bit, preventing the head from being lowered suddenly. In lieu of buying one, I've had success using

CRUPPERS AND ANTI-GRAZING SIDECHECKS

a checkrein from an old driving harness, attached to a regular bit and set loosely. Sidechecks come halfway up the cheeks and are hooked to the D's on the saddle, allowing normal head carriage but keeping the pony's head from dropping below the chest.

WHIPS

Types of Whips and Their Uses

Among English riders, a whip is also referred to as a *crop, stick,* or *bat.* Western equivalents are the *quirt* (a piece of braided leather with more flexibility than an English crop, which is carried on the saddle when not in use) and the *romal,* a special type of quirt that attaches to roping reins and is required in some Western classes.

Different types of English crops accompany different riding styles. (Saddle seat riders carry a long whip.) Schooling a young or green horse without a crop is very difficult, and most English trainers carry one. However, they do make some horses extremely tense and nervous and must be used with discretion in these cases. Some horses won't tolerate them at all. But even the most hot-blooded mount will have lazy moments, and when a horse is not immediately responsive to normal aids, he must be punished with a firm smack behind the saddle. (Never use a crop on the neck or around the head.) The short, light, twelve-inch-long bat is used to give a quick, noisy slap when needed by hunt seat riders. A heavier, longer (about thirty inches) racing bat is often used by event or jumper riders. The more generic lightweight crop, most frequently used, is about twenty inches long.

Although the crop is an invaluable part of any rider's equipment, it must never be used as a substitute for correct seat and leg aids. Nor should it be expected to make up for inadequate training. Remember to always use this aid with discretion. If your horse is frightened of an obstacle, for instance, give him time to look it over before employing the crop.

Everyday English riding crops should be easy to carry and feel comfortable in your hand. Though it takes practice, an experienced rider should be able to carry and use a crop in either hand to discipline the horse on either side.

DRESSAGE WHIPS. The length of these whips varies from 36 inches to 60 inches, allowing a rider to influence his mount's hindquarters without removing his hands from the reins. A whip under 48 inches should work just fine for the average dressage rider. Longer types over 54 inches are usually used for ground work. (The trainer stands on the ground and taps the horse on the hocks, cannon, or croup for more engagement, especially when teaching the piaffe.) Long whips tend to be more flexible and fit around the horse; the shorter ones are stiffer. In competitions where whips are permitted, a length of 48 inches, including the lash, is the limit.

Weight and balance are the primary considerations in the selection of a dressage whip, which is held where the handle meets the shaft. If it is too heavy or improperly balanced, the whip will feel awkward and you are likely to drop it. The length and stiffness will vary according to the sensitivity of the horse. A poky warmblood may respond better to a stiffer whip, while a more sensitive Thoroughbred could become very testy and respond more positively to one that is lighter and more flexible. Above all, the whip must be comfortable for you and your horse.

DRIVING WHIPS. Driving whips are about five and a half feet long with a lash four to eight inches or longer. The whip is held toward the top of the stock, near the ferrule, and is not used on the horse's back or hindquarters but behind the backpad and on the sides, approximately where the rider's leg would fall. Driving whips are safety devices, not offensive weapons, and should be carried and used accordingly.

A trained driver will use the whip to give signals. Slapping the horse with the reins and yelling "yah" is acceptable only in Hollywood westerns. Off the set it's a good way to get a kick in the buckboard.

LUNGE WHIPS. Staffs and lashes of lunge whips come in different lengths. Some come apart to fit into your tack trunk for traveling. The weight of the lunge whip in your hand is extremely important when you choose one. If it's too heavy or not well balanced, your wrist will ache at the end of a lunging session. Pick up the whip, and flick it to see how it feels. With practice, the popper at the end will pop with the snap of your wrist. (First practice on your own without the horse.) Keep in mind that the length of the staff and the lash will depend on the size of the horse you'll be lunging. A pony, for instance, would not need the extra length of lash or staff that a large warmblood would require. Whips come in nylon and other synthetics, with colors ranging from black to a complete rainbow assortment.

POPPERS. Lunge, dressage, and driving whips all have poppers on the end, most of which can be replaced. The replacements are very easy to slip onto the end of a compatible whip. Poppers come in different lengths, so choose carefully. A short one is best for a dressage whip, and longer ones for the driving and lunging whips.

Care of Whips

All whips should be stored on a rack, not left leaning against a wall or lying on the floor. Because they are so long, some extra care should be taken with dressage, driving, and lunge whips when not in use. Most have fiberglass centers and are easily broken if stepped on or caught in a door. And they will bend out of shape if stood up in a corner. Beware of barn cats, which have an affinity for the long lashes, easily destroying and reducing them into frayed tassels. (I have a particularly playful cat who likes to run after the end of the whip when I'm in the midst of lunging!)

Whips with short lashes can be hung on broom-type wall brackets, handle up and lash down. Long-lashed whips are best stored flat or in a whip bracket with a spool for the lash. (It's possible to use a tuna or cat food can as a spool, letting the extra lash hang down around the perimeter.)

SPURS

Spurs are an advanced piece of equipment, comparable to a full bridle. They don't belong on the feet of a beginning or novice rider. They should be worn only by an equestrian balanced enough to keep legs quiet and in proper position (especially not toeing out, which would keep poking the spurs into the horse's sides). Used improperly, spurs can become a destructive substitute for the training of horse and rider, and they will numb a mount to correct leg aids. Used with care, however, spurs are helpful for keeping a horse up on the bit and, with some, are essential for jumping.

Spur on Right Foot

Most English spurs have blunt ends, and some have very tiny rowels. The most sensible are dressage and offside schooling spurs whose projections are slightly to the inside of the rider's heel rather than at the center. Western spurs have larger rowels than the English type and are usually made of aluminum.

When putting spurs on, the buckles should be on the outside of the boot, with both strap and spur pointing down. If the strap is too long, trim it so that no more than an inch is visible past the last keeper.

Boots, Wraps, and Blankets

Equine legs and feet take the most pounding when a horse performs at speed, making fast turns and quick stops. When jumping fences, the impact of a rail can sting a hoof or a leg. Young and green horses in training frequently overreach (forge) as they learn to balance. Boots are designed to protect extremities during strenuous work and competition. Some people use them on young, rambunctious, or extremely valuable horses when they turn them out in the pasture, to prevent injuries.

Fitting Boots

To get the right fit, first measure the length of the horse's cannon, then the circumference of the cannon bone, midway between the knee and the fetlock. These boots should fit snugly, exerting even pressure all around. If they are too loose, they will wrinkle, buckle, and shift around or down the horse's leg, causing abrasion. (Should sand work its way under a loose boot, it could cause a gall.) Check the boots both during warm-up and after the horse has been worked to make sure they are still firmly in place. Remove them immediately after a workout.

Before putting on any boot, make sure both it and your horse's legs are clean and dry. The latter is easier to accomplish when hair is kept at a medium length. If it is allowed to grow too long, hair is difficult to keep clean; if too short, it can rub. When Velcro becomes filled with debris, you can scrub it clean with a toothbrush to restore its grip.

When boots made of any synthetic material get covered with mud, hose or wash them off immediately. If warm soapy water is available, scrub them with a stiff brush kept just for that purpose, then rinse them thoroughly. Hang them somewhere

BOOTS

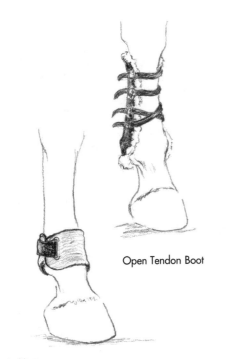

Open Tendon Boot

Ankle Boot

where they can dry completely before your next ride. Wet boots can rub skin raw. Leather- and/or fleece-lined boots must dry completely before you brush them off with a stiff brush. The leather portions are treated like any other piece of leather tack and not allowed to become dried and cracked. (See Chapter 27.) Given good care, leather boots should last for years; only the elastic, Velcro, straps, and buckles should need occasional replacement.

Types of Boots

ANKLE BOOTS OR CUFFS. These boots are used primarily on the hind legs of jumpers to prevent interference. They are available in an inexpensive feltlike material (used mainly in the ring), thick neoprene with leather at the ankle and a Velcro closure, and a top-quality leather type with lamb's wool lining.

BELL BOOTS OR QUARTER BOOTS. These boots protect the pastern and bulb of the heel from overreaching or other irregularities caused by faulty gaits or conformation defects. Done consistently, such interference can create a raw, sore spot that puts the horse out of commission until it heals. Many owners and trainers also use these boots to protect the feet during shipping. To determine whether your horse needs them for riding, observe his movements on a lunge line and consult with your trainer and/or veterinarian.

Bell boots are available in small, medium, and large sizes and have numerous designs, with a variety of fasteners. They fit around the lower pastern, just above the coronary band, and should be of a size large enough to allow a finger to slip under the top of the boot. *Rubber* bell boots slip over the feet. These can be something of a nuisance to put on, but soaking them in hot water before tacking up softens them, making the job easier.

Split boots of *leather and synthetic* materials come with many different types of fastenings, including leather hooks, leather buckles, and Velcro. The best are those with the double, under-and-over Velcro tabs. Those with single Velcro tabs don't hold up too well after an accumulation of water and mud penetrates the fastenings. (At the end of one day of fence judging at a cross-country event, I found half a dozen assorted bells dispersed around the exit path of a water jump—all with Velcro closures.) One precaution: Be aware, when riding for a long period of time in very muddy or wet going, that the friction on rubber bell boots can chafe and rub the pastern raw, causing more problems than they prevent.

BRUSHING BOOTS. Made of leather or neoprene, these boots are designed to keep the inside of the front fetlocks from hitting or brushing by the diagonal or opposite rear hoof or shoe. This problem commonly causes injury in horses engaged

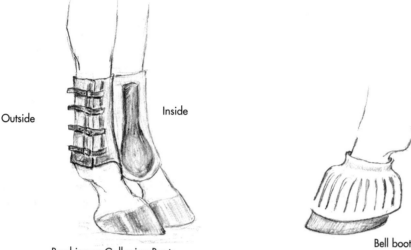

Outside

Inside

Brushing or Galloping Boots

Bell boot

in hunting, eventing, or doing other vigorous work. One type used in stadium jumping is open at the front to discourage the horse from hitting the rails (it stings if he does), while at the same time protecting those precious foreleg tendons.

FETLOCK RING. Sometimes called a donut, a fetlock ring is a rubber ring worn around the pastern when the horse is not being ridden, to prevent interference.

GALLOPING BOOTS. These boots, which wrap completely around the leg to protect the tendon, ankle, and lower part of the leg, should be fitted to the leg's contour toward the back, snug but not so tight that they rub or chafe the skin. They come with a variety of fasteners, and some are machine washable. The expensive leather type requires more care, and those with fleece lining don't do well in water and mud, requiring a lot of maintenance. Most of these boots come in three sizes. Some horses may need different sizes in front and back.

When a horse needs extra protection for field, trail, or cross-country work, or even for everyday training and exercise, galloping boots are excellent. Their ounces of protection are worth a pound of cure. For horses who travel close in front or behind, they're a must. When schooling a horse over jumps, it's foolish not to protect both his front and back legs with boots. Underweight or out-of-condition horses sometimes have a tendency to brush their heels or ankles together behind. Galloping boots should be used in these cases, at least until the horse gets into better shape. Once he becomes balanced through training and weight increases, the problem may or may not improve. As a general rule I use them on all horses when schooling on the flat or jumping and in jumping competition when rules permit. Many different kinds and sizes of brushing or galloping boots are available, made of leather, felt, or synthetic materials with different means of attachment. They may buckle or attach on the side with straps on the outside of the leg, or toward the rear or in front, depending on the function of the boot. I don't advise the felt kind, which

Support Boot

stretch when wet, keep coming unfastened, and don't last long. Leather boots are expensive, and the price increases with their length.

OVERREACH OR PETAL BELL BOOTS. These boots cover the sensitive areas of the heel and coronet and are popular for showing and schooling. They're quickly taken on and off; the petals slide easily on and off the strap to make them smaller or larger so that one size fits. You can also create your own color combinations from a wide selection of hues.

PROTECTIVE OR SPORT BOOTS. These boots extend down over the fetlock joint to support and protect the tendons and ligaments of the lower limb during strenuous activity. They are usually made of a stretchy, durable, nonporous product like neoprene, which won't absorb moisture or harbor bacteria. Lightweight sport boots are more flexible and fit snugly. The heavyweight boots have two layers of lining and provide added thickness to protect tendons and ligaments.

SHIPPING BOOTS. These boots are an expensive but necessary investment for those who will be doing a lot of trailering. Protecting your horse's most vulnerable attribute, his legs, is easy with strong, well-made, correctly sized shipping boots that cover the hocks, knees, cannon bones, tendons, heels, and coronary bands when properly fitted. Make sure the bottoms are tough and resistant to urine and manure. The boots should be interfaced with a fill and soft lining and fit well, so they won't rub or shift. Be aware that some boots are stiffer than others, which may affect your horse's desire to go forward (as in loading). If these boots make your horse's legs sweat, wrap them underneath in cotton. Before his maiden voyage, accustom him to shipping boots for a few weeks in his stall so he won't be kicking or stomping in the trailer and injuring himself because of the unfamiliar boots.

WRAPS

Exercise bandages or polo wraps serve the same purpose as galloping boots, but they don't offer as much protection for jumping and cross-country riding. Often used by dressage riders to protect the legs of horses in training and available in a variety of colors, they are made of a soft, fluffy, brushed-polyester knit and are usually about five inches wide and nine feet long.

Sometimes referred to as galloping bandages, polo wraps for exercise are not used with quilts; nor should they be confused with therapeutic bandages, which give support. These wraps protect your horse's lower leg, between knee and pastern, from hits on fence rails when jumping, and also from hitting himself when lunging and doing flatwork. Velcro closures sometimes come undone when they lose their stick. Putting a strip of masking tape around the whole leg and over the Velcro can help keep them from coming unwrapped. Because they can slip down when wet, causing a horse to trip, they shouldn't be used during turnout.

Wrapping Wraps

One method of wrapping is from front to back. Wind up to about an inch under the knee, then wind down to the fetlock joint, then back up to midcannon where you started, fastening with Velcro either inside or outside. When tightening a wrap, always pull against the front of the leg (cannon bone), never against the tendon, and make it firm but not too tight. When you take it off, roll the wrap up so that the next time you put it on, the Velcro will be at the end of the bandage.

This exercise wrap will also help protect the tendon:

1. Holding the rolled wrap in your right hand, pull about six inches extra (a flap) around the right front leg to behind the knee. (You will use this later.)
2. Keep this flap out of the way as you begin wrapping the bandage down in a spiral motion, overlapping by about an inch. Hold the wrap straight up and down as you roll, and pull it snug against the cannon, not the tendon. At the ankle, take one turn.
3. Let the six-inch flap down now to cover the tendon, creating an extra layer there. Continue wrapping up the leg, keeping everything smooth as you wind.
4. Wrap the polo back up the leg in the same manner, covering the flap until you finish just below the knee. Secure with the Velcro closure.

Traditional exercise wraps are started in the middle of the leg on the inside, wrapped downward, overlapping in the manner described above, and figure-eighting the fetlock joint so movement isn't impaired. Then reverse, continuing back up the leg to just below the knee, again reversing and wrapping downward to the area where you began. Secure the wrap with its *clean* Velcro tab, which can be reinforced with masking tape for extra security.

Exercise Wrap That Helps Protect the Tendon

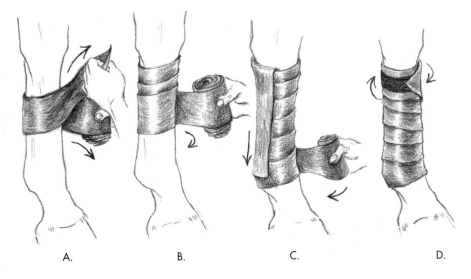

A.   B.   C.   D.

BLANKETS

Does your horse need a blanket? If he has a thick, woolly coat and you ride only sporadically during the winter, probably not. Whether you clip your horse, the type of clip you give him, and how regularly you ride will determine whether he needs blanketing indoors and/or outdoors. Regular grooming takes away the dirt and oil that contribute to his natural insulation. Putting a blanket on a horse squashes the insulating layer of warm air trapped between his coat and skin, taking away this natural protection but not fully replacing it. Once blanketing has begun, a horse will become accustomed to the artificial warmth, and it must be continued.

Selecting the Right Blanket

With dozens of types and designs to choose from, shopping for the right blankets can be a confusing task. Lightweight varieties, which include fly sheets and scrims, are called stable sheets. Heavier types are referred to as *turnout rugs* or simply blankets. One of the elegant *coolers* available is the Irish linen *antisweat sheet*; and a recent addition to the wardrobe of a well-dressed horse is *liners*—the equine equivalent of underwear.

Buying the best-quality blankets you can afford will save money in the long run because they fit better, last longer, and are easier to care for. It's not necessary to replace them every year with the newest fashion fad. A few well-made blankets will do the job nicely and economically for quite a few years—unless you happen to have one of those horses that are particularly hard on blankets.

When selecting a blanket, pay attention to its construction. Feel the material to make sure it's durable, heavy, and of good quality, with tight, regular stitching. The number and placement of surcingles depends on the style of the blanket; some are better suited than others to different conformations. Many owners and trainers prefer a style that is cut back or scooped across the withers; others swear by the straight style with a contour peak. It's essential to have a good fit at the shoulders and chest for your horse's comfort. A gusset at the shoulders, a smooth lining, and extra padding at the withers will help to avoid rubbing marks. You may have to try several out before deciding which is more suitable for your horse. An ill-fitting blanket or incorrectly fastened one can cause irritation to the horse if it rubs, slides around, or is too tight. Your horse can become entangled in surcingles and in leg straps if a blanket is too loose. Fastening it too tightly at the chest or at the surcingles will create too much stress and will be likely to break at the first good roll.

Whether a horse is inside or outdoors, his clothing can be customized to suit the temperature by layering. In very cold weather a liner and lighter blankets can be put on under a turnout rug. On milder days the rug alone will do.

Types of Blankets

STABLE SHEETS. These lightweight coverings will protect a horse from flies, dust, and drafts during warm weather and double as a liner under a heavy winter blanket, keeping both coat and blankets clean. Every equine wardrobe should include one. Sheets, a lot easier to wash than blankets, must be kept scrupulously

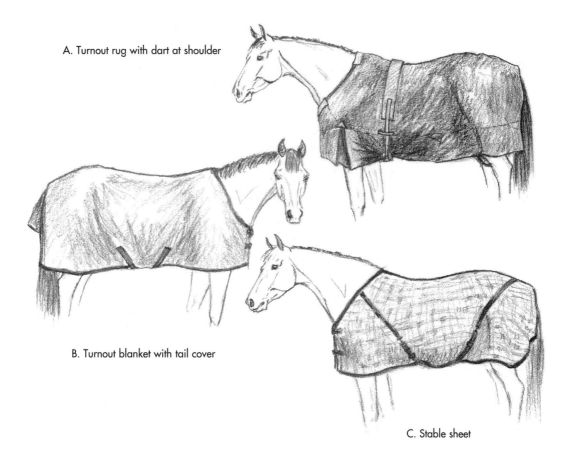

A. Turnout rug with dart at shoulder

B. Turnout blanket with tail cover

C. Stable sheet

clean to avoid skin problems. Stable sheets are often used under blankets after exercise to absorb or "wick up" moisture from the horse's back, insulating warm muscles from the moist blanket, thereby preventing dampness and chilling. They serve the same purpose as "thatching" after a hunt, when layers of straw are put on the horse's back and covered by a burlap rug, felt side out.

FLY SHEETS. Fly sheets are perforated with tiny holes that admit air—but not flies—to the horse's back. They are lightweight and cool, made of a "breathable" fabric like cotton or polyester or a mix of the two. They must be tough enough to withstand the occasional reflexive bite at a fly. Some fly sheets, designed solely for stabled horses, are quite flimsy. Those used during turnout must have leg straps strong enough to withstand stomping and rolling.

Numerous types of fly sheet are available for thin-skinned horses. They are usually made of some type of mesh and have adjustable leg straps to secure them during turnout. A special lightweight-mesh *leg wrap* will keep a horse from stomping at flies. It can be augmented with a *fly mask* that covers only eyes and ears or with a *hood* that attaches to the shoulder and withers and also covers the neck.

For riding, ear guards and/or nets or bonnets that don't cover the eyes are available. They tie under the neck and are extremely effective on horses doing outside work during the height of the fly season. Though not appropriate in the show ring, they are acceptable in most jumper classes.

STABLE BLANKETS. Stable blankets are made of a durable material like nylon, acrylic, or canvas and are lined with cotton, flannel, Thinsulate, fleece, wool, or a synthetic. Some are filled with Poly-Fil or fiberfill.

DRESS BLANKETS. These are fancier and are made of 100 percent wool. They are the preferred second layer in England and Ireland, used over a stable blanket, when the weather is cold.

TURNOUT RUGS. These rugs keep a horse warm, dry, and comfortable if he spends most of the day outside. It must be of rugged construction, weatherproof (which doesn't mean completely waterproof), and large enough to accommodate one or two stable blankets underneath. Be sure to choose a type with sturdy leg straps to prevent slipping and twisting.

Rugs come in weights appropriate to different weather. The heavier waterproof rugs, while warmer, don't breathe as well as nonwaterproof types. Waterproof blankets cannot be dry-cleaned, only brushed off until thoroughly cleaned or rewaterproofed with a special sealant. The other, lighter types are machine washable, though not as warm.

When shopping for a turnout rug, choose a design suited to your horse's contours. (Some rugs fit certain builds better than others.) Select one that buckles easily in front, with front panels that overlap to keep the chest covered and sides long enough to protect the horse's belly. Nylon lining at the shoulder and withers will minimize hair loss when the horse moves. If you buy a waterproof rug with a tail flap, be sure to adjust it so the horse can lift his tail to defecate.

SHOULDER GUARDS. Available in different sizes at most tack stores or through catalogs, shoulder guards are made of a soft, stretchy fabric that fits the contour of a horse's shoulder and allows complete freedom of movement. Designed to protect the shoulders from chafing, they are worn under a blanket. They come in a variety of conservative colors as well as some pretty wild patterns.

COOLERS AND ANTISWEAT SHEETS. These sheets, made of a natural material like wool or cotton, are most efficient at wicking away moisture. Used after exercise, they prevent a chill by keeping the coat from getting clammy. Antisweat sheets of cotton, polyester, or a combination thereof have holes, while coolers are a solid piece of cloth, usually wool, a wool blend, or a synthetic with wicking ability. Make sure that you get one large enough and long enough to really do its job. Some of the bargain-basement varieties skimp on fabric. On the other hand, if you have a horse of one of the smaller breeds, you don't want him tripping on the hem. For the closest size, carefully follow the manufacturer's directions.

RAIN SHEETS. Lightweight and water repellent, these sheets are great when

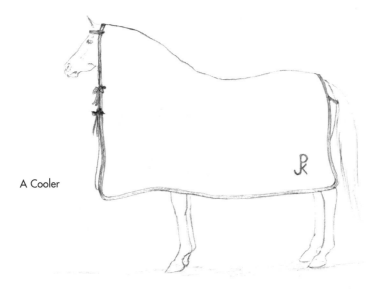

A Cooler

you're trying to keep a horse covered from poll to tail and keep tack dry before or after competition. Many styles are designed for turnout, and a few are even designed for riding. It is important that they be breathable, quiet when the horse moves, and fit well. For turnout, some are reinforced at the withers with fleece to prevent rubbing and have an elastic inset at the chest and on the surcingles, allowing for more unhindered movement. Pay attention to a sheet's water-repellent capabilities; if it has seams, see that they are sealed or taped to be assured that rain won't seep in. Low surcingles and leg straps keep a blanket secure. In cool climates a sheet with a liner is a good investment. For easy maintenance, lean toward a sheet that tolerates a warm water wash. Horses have an affinity for rolling in mud, so frequent launderings will be needed.

QUARTER SHEETS. Also called *half sheets* and *exercise rugs, quarter sheets* keep your equine's back and loins warm during exercise in cold and/or damp weather and help him to cool down gradually after a hard workout. They come in several different styles: one attaches at the girth with a loop, another has a slit for the girth to slide through, and yet another, European style is cut away behind the girth, giving the rider closer leg contact. Some are shaped nicely to the horse's back and tend not to bunch up under the girth. Quarter sheets that reach past the dock usually have a tail cord to keep them in place. Several types have strings for tying so you can roll the sheet up against the cantle when you don't need it and roll it down when you do.

These sheets are made of fabrics like wool, Polarfleece, or Coretex that have enough substance to retain heat while also allowing sweat to wick away from the skin during strenuous exercise, thereby preventing chills and tightening of muscles from too quick a cool-down—a real asset when riding outdoors on a cold, windy day. Some styles fit certain conformations better than others. A quarter sheet should

Quarter Sheet

fold up easily when the horse gets warm. We use them a great deal in winter, riding indoors and out, when temperatures go below freezing.

Fitting the Blanket

If a blanket is to fit your horse properly, he must be measured for it beforehand. Some manufacturers give instructions on how to measure for their particular blanket. Follow them! Even though the instructions all start at the same place, they differ on where to end the measurement. So if you're already set on a specific label, be sure to follow its directions for measuring. If it provides none, the procedure is simple: Take a flat, sixty-inch tape measure and begin at the center of the horse's chest, level with the point of the shoulder. Keeping the tape flat and parallel to the ground, continue to the flank, following the contour of the barrel, until you run out of tape. Mark the spot with your finger and start again, continuing the tape around the hip area to the center of the tail. Add this second measurement to the tape's sixty inches to get the blanket size. If you arrive at an uneven number, round it out to the next even one. (For instance, a seventy-six-inch measurement would be a size eighty blanket.) The average mature horse is between size seventy and eighty.

Before you try a new blanket on your horse, make sure to put a cooler or light sheet between your horse and the merchandise, so it can be returned if it doesn't fit.

If you have a new or young horse who isn't used to a turnout sheet or rug (with those scary dangling leg straps), take time to accustom him to the unfamiliar clothing. Have a helper hold him in his stall while you touch him with the blanket and let him smell it. Fold the blanket in half, put it gently across his back, and have the helper move him forward a few steps to get him used to the feeling. Then quietly unfold it, hooking the chest straps and surcingles before walking him forward again.

If your horse is an old hand at blanketing, the fitting process won't take long. Once the blanket is on, secure the front buckles, followed by the surcingle. Then unclip one snap from each leg strap and pass the straps around each hind leg, either fastening each to its own side, looping one through its mate on the opposite leg, or crisscrossing them so they attach to the ring on the opposite leg. Either alternative prevents the straps from rubbing the legs and keeps the horse from getting caught in one if he lies down or rolls.

Leg straps need to be loose enough to allow comfortable movement, but they should not hang down near the hocks, where a foot could get caught. If a strap is too tight, it will pull the blanket backward as a horse moves, putting pressure on the shoulder. It's a good idea to put a horse on a lunge when you try out a new blanket to see how it fits him in motion.

Even when the size is right, a blanket may not fit properly. The same size eighty that looks like a second skin on a Thoroughbred may not work on a Quarter Horse of the same measurement. Problems usually occur at the neck opening, which should lie three to five inches in front of the withers, depending on the horse's natural head carriage. This will allow the blanket to move forward and give the neck and shoulders enough room when he lies down. If the blanket is too open above and/or around the neck, it will slip back and rub off hair as it tightens at the shoulders. If it hangs more than one or two inches below the neck in front, it can pull against the points of the shoulder, restricting chest muscles as the horse moves. Be sure that the chest buckles close the front of the blanket, so the chest is always covered.

If the fit is okay except at the shoulder, a dressmaker or blanket repair service can take a dart about halfway up each shoulder to adjust the neck opening. You can try this out by pinning the darts with diaper pins (making sure it isn't too tight at the chest) and working him again on the lunge to test the fit. This is time well spent. Nothing is more frustrating then realizing, in the middle of a long cold winter, that your horse's blanket doesn't fit.

Removing the Blanket

When removing the blanket, reverse the procedure for putting it on. Begin by unsnapping the leg straps and clipping them to their rings so they don't hang loose. Then undo the surcingle and the front clips. If it's pliable enough, fold the back of the blanket a third of the way to the front, fold the front third back, and gently lift it off his back. (All the while, give lots of praise and reassurance to a young or green horse.)

Blanket Care

After you take the blanket off, hang it up to air—in the sun, when possible. Then fold it over a blanket bar or rack. Make sure all blankets are scrupulously clean before you store them in a plastic bag or trunk at the end of the season. If you aren't going to clean it yourself, there are services that professionally clean horse blankets. But don't send them a blanket that shouldn't be dry-cleaned!

A decent blanket is costly, but properly cleaned and maintained, it will last many seasons. Keep an eye on its condition, especially on all fastenings and hardware and all attachment areas, which take the most stress. Make any necessary repairs immediately. During the season keep an extra blanket on hand for an emergency, such as sending one out for repair. Keep a spare *elastic surcingle* and *elastic leg straps* (with a clip on each end) on hand in case of breakage, which I can almost guarantee will occur during the worst cold snap or snowstorm.

For quick emergency repair for a small or large tear, nothing beats duct tape. I have temporarily repaired tears up to three feet long by cross-hatching the tape vertically and horizontally, so the tape is sticking to itself. (That's what makes it hold.) First brush the absolutely dry blanket as clean as possible. This unattractive but workable remedy can hold a blanket for several days (depending on the size of the tear), until you get another one and repair the torn one.

Read the manufacturer's cleaning instructions at purchase time (and make sure they fit your lifestyle). Then reread them when the blanket needs to be cleaned. Not all blankets can be machine-washed; detergents can remove the waterproofing. Some cannot be dry-cleaned for the same reason. You can purchase waterproofing products from your tack shop, but make sure to find one compatible with your particular blanket.

Usually stable sheets, antisweat sheets, and rain sheets are machine washable. Cover the surcingles with socks to save the interior of your machine. For sheets with particularly stubborn stains, apply a mild soap to the spots, then allow them to soak in cold water for twenty minutes or so. That usually dissolves them. A wool blanket needs to be dry-cleaned or washed in cold water once a year.

To help a blanket stay cleaner longer when it can't be washed, I brush it briskly while it is still on the horse, then remove it and lay it on the floor, repeating the process with a stiff brush or broom, attempting to remove every particle of dirt and/or manure. When a blanket is beyond this point, covered with wet mud, I remove it from the horse and hang somewhere to thoroughly dry, inside and out.

Pay attention to the inside of a heavy turnout rug, which can take more than twenty-four hours to dry. (Remember that extra blanket I mentioned earlier? This is when it comes in handy.) Once the blanket is completely dry, brush it off with a stiff brush. A heavy blanket that can tolerate washing can also be washed by hand with a mild soap and brush and laid out on the floor, as described above.

Harnesses and Carts

As the dual pleasures of riding and driving gain in popularity, harness makers are enjoying a renaissance. Harnesses can be purchased from any of the leading tack distributors, but for a less expensive source try tack shops located in the Amish areas of Pennsylvania, Ohio, and Illinois. Since the Amish travel only by horse-drawn vehicles, their harnesses are sure to be safe and utilitarian. Several friends have bought very good harnesses at auctions, sometimes selecting them for the rare hardware alone, then having the harness rebuilt by a craftsman expert enough to copy the style. An elaborate custom-made harness can cost several thousand dollars.

A secondhand harness should be checked out as thoroughly as a used saddle. Make sure the leather isn't dry or cracked, that the stitching is secure, and that all the hardware is there. The leather should be pliable, and the fittings and hardware in top condition. Every piece of this elaborate equipment has a purpose, which won't be fulfilled unless all are in good shape.

Harnesses come in a variety of styles and strengths. The different thicknesses and widths of the pieces are suited to different types and weights of carriage. A two-wheeled wire jogging or pleasure cart used close to the ground in a show ring needs only a thin, one-inch breast-collar harness, while a four-wheel one- to two-seat buckboard or Stanhope gig would take a breast-collar harness of heavier, thicker dimensions. Most pleasure harnesses are intended for use on light- to midweight wooden-wheeled jog or road carts. Before you buy, be sure to check how much weight a harness is designed to pull. Whether new or secondhand, a harness has to

HARNESSES

be fitted correctly. An ill-fitting harness can cause sores, discomfort, and pain, any of which could sour a horse.

Fitting the Harness

Depending on the type of harness you select, the *collar* or *breast collar*—overlaid by the *hames,* a brass fitting that encircles the collar, to which the traces are attached—is put on first. Initially the collar is placed over the horse's head upside down, with the traces still attached but crossed over the neck so they won't get stepped on. Then it's turned over at the top part of the neck and slid down into position. Breast collars are recommended for novice drivers, who often start with secondhand harnesses.

The importance of fitting a collar properly cannot be overstated. It should lie flat and comfortably on your horse's shoulders and be roomy enough at the bottom that it doesn't press on the windpipe or pinch the skin. (You should be able to slip a hand between the collar and the neck.) You may find that a collar that fits your horse early in the season, when he's not in peak condition, will be too tight in July when his muscles have developed and filled out.

The breast collar is placed over the head and fitted so it lies above the point of the shoulder. If too low, the collar will rub; if too high, it will interfere with breathing. Both breast and neck collars must be kept immaculately clean. A dirty collar will cause sores.

After fitting the collar, place the saddle pad on your horse's back, leaving it unfastened until the tail is placed through the crupper. (If your horse is new to driving, take care to place the crupper on lightly, and have someone standing near his head in case he acts up.) Unlike a riding saddle pad, the harness pad should be placed a good four to five inches on the back behind the elbow. The girth is then tightened.

The strap between the saddle and the crupper must not be too tight, or it will put stress on the dock of the horse's tail, chafing it and possibly causing him to kick. The crupper should be kept clean and pliable to prevent irritation.

Breeching is used to hold back a heavier carriage traveling over hilly terrain, but it isn't necessary on a light cart or a show buggy rolling on flat ground. After placing it around the horse's rump and running the breeching strap through the backstrap, put on the bridle in the usual manner.

The type of bit you use will depend on your horse's mouth and the type of driving you plan to do. The bits most commonly used are half-cheek, straight bar, snaffle, Liverpool, or Buxton. The latter two are most popular because they can be adjusted at several points, allowing the driver maximum control.

Blinkers are necessary to keep a horse from being distracted by passing events, to keep him from seeing the moving wheels (which create the illusion of overtaking him when in motion), and to keep his mind on the driver—especially on a busy road. They should be centered, facing ahead, so the horse can't see above, below, or around them, and they should neither flap nor be so tight that they press on the eyes or eyelashes. An improper adjustment can be disastrous. The most experienced

PARTS OF A HARNESS

1. Blinker
2. Blinker stay
3. Rosette
4. Terret ring
5. Rein
6. Liverpool bit
7. Backpad
8. Back strap
9. Crupper
10. Loin strap
11. Breeching
12. Breeching strap
13. Trace

14. Belly band
15. Girth
16. Shaft loop
17. False martingale
18. Hames
19. Bottom hame strap or chain
20. Wrap strap
21. Shaft
22. Collar
23. Bearing rein or checkrein
24. Bearing rein drop
25. Bearing rein hook

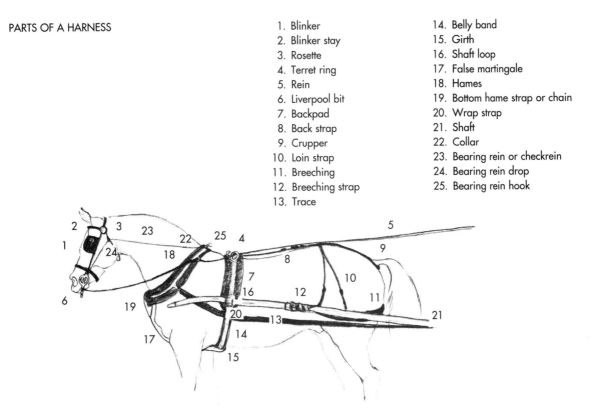

driving horse can become terrified if a flapping blinker allows him to see the cart.

The *checkrein* is an optional piece of equipment, but it is required in some competitions. Many driving advocates believe that a properly trained driving horse should be balanced well enough to carry himself without the aid of a checkrein.

Once the bridle is on, thread the reins through the terrets and attach them to the bit and bridle in that order. (This procedure is reversed when you unhook the harness.)

Now attach the cart to the harness. It's easier and safer to have two people do this (especially if the horse and/or driver is inexperienced), with a third person standing at the horse's head to hold him. Pull the cart slowly up behind the horse. Raise shafts in position to run through the loops or *tugs* (on the saddle pad) on both sides of the horse. Always attach both shafts at once, to avoid complications should your horse become restless and move forward.

Hook up each set of straps (traces, breeching, or tug wraps—whatever your harness has) before starting on the next. Uncross the traces and run them through the loops on the shafts, if there are any, then hook the traces to the trees in back so they are nearly taut when the shaft tip is at the point of the shoulder. After both traces are attached, secure the breeching by slipping it through a metal eye or leather loop, then wrapping it around the shaft, encircling the traces three times and buckling it to itself. To adjust this properly, push the cart forward about four inches until the breeching presses against the horse's hindquarters.

Your driving safety will depend on properly attaching and adjusting the harness. Driving equipment is reinforced in those places that receive the most stress, but if it is hooked up incorrectly, the stress will be shifted to the wrong spots, and not even the most expensive harness will hold up under the strain. Nor will leather or hardware be able to withstand the pull of a cart that is too heavy for the harness.

One word of caution: If your horse is new, and you've been told he drives, and you are inexperienced, *do not* attempt to hitch him up, let alone drive him. That is an accident waiting to happen! Get a professional who drives or another experienced person to "road test" your horse for you. They can do some preliminary exercises with the animal to see if driving really is part of his repertoire. (See Chapter 30.) I have witnessed and heard about too many hair-raising driving accidents with trained horses and ponies not to take this aspect very seriously. Now, as driving has become more popular, there are numerous opportunities to learn the art of driving from a professional at a driving clinic.

Care of the Harness

In past centuries, when carriages were the main form of transport, elegant stables stored harnesses in glass cases to protect them. It isn't necessary to go to this extreme, but keeping the harness clean and dry is essential. For cleaning, follow the same procedures as you would for the rest of your tack. (See Chapter 27.) Special harness hooks can be purchased at a tack shop or they can be homemade by copying a form in wood from a catalog. The backpad, collar, and attachments should be hung up carefully so they don't pull out of shape.

SELECTING A CART

Compared with the elegant victorias, landaus, and phaetons that used to travel American highways, the spartan show buggies seen in fine harness classes today are mere skeletons. Before the internal combustion engine made them obsolete, hundreds of types of buggies, carts, and sleighs were manufactured by different carriage makers. Many were nearly identical in construction and purpose but were given different names by their builders (some of which, like *station wagon* and *coupe,* were later adopted by car manufacturers).

Pleasure drivers can choose nearly any type of vehicle they fancy, but if you intend to show, you should read the rule books carefully before selecting a cart or buggy. Each breed has different regulations, requiring different harnesses and vehicles.

The most rugged, durable, and inexpensive cart for pleasure driving is the high wooden-wheeled type with hard rubber tires, variously known as a *jogging cart, road cart, breaking cart,* or *cross-country cart.* Another type often used by beginners on flat ground only is a one-seated, light jogging cart with bicyclelike wheels, available at most established tack shops. For beginning horses, two-wheeled carts are considered safer than four-wheeled buggies; they're also more maneuverable.

Any cart should be well sprung, to be comfortable for passengers and evenly balanced for the horse. It should fit your horse in size so that the shafts are level and correctly balanced when the horse is hitched. If the wheels have no rubber, you will probably want to have it fitted to them. (Iron wheels are all right for driving on grass, but rubber is a must on roads; it is not only quieter but more shock absorbent.) Because of the growing interest in driving, wheel making is reviving as a business, particularly in New England. Wheel makers can also be found in Amish country.

You can pick up an antique cart at an auction (or sometimes in the back of a friend's barn). Driving publications and newsletters advertise used carts in their classified sections. If you do locate a gem of an old cart at auction, make sure to check it out carefully before you make a bid. Here are some key points to consider:

• Does it fit your horse?

• Are the shafts level at the point of the shoulder where the horse is hitched?

• Can the shafts be altered in height, length, and width to suit different horses?

• Are the wheels evenly balanced when the cart is viewed from behind?

• Is there any looseness in the spokes or dry rot? (Rotten wood can be replaced, and loose-spoked wheels can be soaked in water to swell and tighten the wood.)

• Is the cart sound?

• How much restoration does the vehicle need—just refinishing or major reconstruction?

There are a number of publications to help the do-it-yourselfer restore old carts and buggies.

Tack Shouldn't Be Tacky

Equestrians may differ on the details of caring for tack, but all agree that the life of the rider and the comfort of the horse depend on its upkeep. Usually the second-largest expense for the horse owner, tack, when properly cared for, can last for decades. After investing several hundred dollars in a bridle or several thousand in a saddle, you'll want to preserve them with the right leather care products.

To understand why tack needs regular care and feeding, reflect on the fact that the hides that were used to make your saddle and bridle once housed a living animal, whose blood vessels, sweat glands, and subcutaneous fat kept the skin moisturized. After skinning, the hide was scraped, stretched, dried, and tanned with acidic organic extracts like oak bark to produce a supple but firm light-colored leather. Deprived of a natural supply of nutrients to keep it healthy, leather will, without assistance, eventually become dry and brittle in an arid climate or mildewed and rotten in a damp one.

In damp parts of the world like the Pacific Northwest and Hawaii, saddle oils contain fungicides to prevent mildew. (If mildew does show up on a moist, well-oiled saddle, it's easy to wipe off.) In arid areas leather needs to be kept clean and lightly oiled. Alkaline dust dries out leather quickly and should be wiped off after each ride. Tack should never be stored in a hot car trunk or attic, where leather fibers would become dry and shrink, causing protein bonds to break and permanently damaging the leather's internal structure and strength.

**CARING FOR
YOUR TACK**

Regular cleaning and periodic conditioning are necessary to keep leather in good condition. Wipe off tack after every use to remove dirt and sweat on which bacteria grow, harming leather and stitching. To prevent leather fibers from drying out and separating, condition the leather several times a year to replace lost moisture and oils.

Cleaners

Dirt, grime, and salts can impregnate leather and cut through the fibers like microscopic knives, tearing and weakening it and drawing the oils out. Cleaners remove these destructive agents. When choosing a cleaner, read the label to find the type with a neutral pH (7 to 9) that minimizes breakage of leather fibers. Many soaps have a high alkalinity, which can weaken the protein bonds in acidic leather. Castile soap, originally made with olive oil but now comprising other vegetable oils, is a traditional leather cleaner with a neutral pH.

In the final stage of the leather-making process, the stiff hides are removed from the tanning solution and tumbled in a water-and-fat emulsion to lubricate fibers and make the final product pliable. These oils oxidize over time and must be replenished if leather is to stay supple. The amount of oil to apply will depend on the condition of the leather. In general, leather absorbs what it needs, and any residue can be wiped off the next day with a damp sponge. But be careful not to use too much. If excessively lubricated, the fibers can stretch and separate, becoming weak and mushy. And too much paste conditioner becomes very sticky, building up in stitching lines and crevices.

Conditioners

Conditioners are available as oils, nonoily liquids, and pastes. The most common is neat's-foot oil, *neat* being the old English word for "oxen." This product was originally made by boiling cattle hooves and rendering the oil. Nowadays it is made from liquefied lard or pig fat. A more expensive type is 100 percent pure fat, yet another mixes animal fat with petroleum-based mineral oils. Animal fat and mineral oils behave differently on leather, the former dispersing to a certain point and going no further, the latter spreading through the fibers indefinitely and tending to darken the leather. To apply a neat's-foot oil product most efficiently, pour some into a small container and paint it on your tack with a small brush. Apply paste products with the fingers (body warmth helps to melt the substance into the leather) and in thin coats; old-timers recommend doing this outside in the heat of the sun, to help drive the lubricants into leather. When applying any conditioner, make certain to reach every surface. Wipe off the excess, especially along stitching lines, where an accumulation could hold dirt and bacteria, deteriorating the stitching. An old toothbrush can help in this endeavor.

SUEDE. Never use a cleaner or conditioner on suede. Instead, rub talcum onto suede areas and brush it off.

SADDLE SOAP. Traditionally a one-step product, saddle soap combines cleaning and conditioning ingredients: mild glycerin soap mixed with oils, fats, and waxes. In most instances, a little saddle soap and a lot of rubbing will produce fairly clean leather, made supple by the added fats and oils. Work saddle soap into a lather, then rub some into the leather, working it around to lift the dirt. Be sure to wring out the sponge or rag often, to keep excess water from carrying the alkaline soap deeply into the fibers and flushing out the tannic acid (which will make the water look brown). Rinse the sponge frequently in clear water, and squeeze it out to wipe away excess soap lather.

MINK OIL. Chemically similar to neat's-foot oil, mink oil is a good conditioner for saddles that will be stored for the winter. Varying from a light, thin oil to a thick, greaselike cream, it is an excellent waterproofing agent and will not clog leather's pores.

ATOM WAX. This product is recommended for Western show saddles, where a high shine is desired. Although highly waterproof, it seals leather pores, trapping perspiration and leading to odor and mildew problems. It can also be very slippery, so some people use *beeswax,* which is also waterproof but doesn't hold a shine as well.

CLEANING YOUR TACK

Equipment

A special stand called a *saddle horse* is designed to rest a saddle on while cleaning. Some saddle horses are made of wood; others, constructed of galvanized tubular steel, even come with folding wheels, making them easy to store and handy for traveling. As a homemade alternative, place two tall chairs back to back, and fold a towel or sheet over the tops to make a padding thick enough to protect the saddle gullet. You can use inexpensive tack hooks to hold the bridle high enough to keep the reins off the ground and facilitate the cleaning of all bridle parts, stirrup leathers, and leather girths.

Set aside an area in the stable or house where you can work easily. If you are in the house, spread out newspapers on the floor where you'll be working.

You'll need the following equipment for cleaning your tack:

• Saddle soap, in a tin or as glycerin (or a spray bottle of liquid saddle soap)

• Small sponge (to apply the soap)

• Rough towel (for wiping away dirt)

• Chamois cloth (used damp, for drying leather)

• Metal polish (for stirrups, bits, and metal surfaces)

• Neat's-foot oil or Lexol (for dry leather)

• Wooden matches (to clean soap and dirt from holes of stirrup leathers, metal D's, and chains)

• Flannel rags (for shining metal)

• Towel scraps (for applying oil)

• Old toothbrush or nail brush (to scrub metal, remove excess paste from stitching, or remove dirt from tooling in Western saddle)

• Pail of clean lukewarm water (changed frequently)

• Optional equipment: Saddle-cleaning stand; tack cleaning hook

Cleaning the Saddle

English and Western saddles have different parts, but the cleaning procedure is basically the same. Put the saddle on the "horse" (cleaning stand). Remove all the leather fittings from an English saddle, hanging them by their buckles on the tack hook, which should be hung high enough that the fittings hook at shoulder level and don't drag on the floor. Put the stirrups aside with the metal parts of the bridle (bit and curb chain, if you have one), to be cleaned later. A leather girth should be treated like the rest of the saddle. It's a good time to clean any other leather tack as well.

If the girth is made of cloth or other washable material, brush it off, making sure to get off any dried mud. Then soak it in cool water and mild soap for a few hours. If it is badly soiled, work soap into the soiled areas by hand, then soak it overnight.

Washable saddle pads can be handled the same way. After soaking, machine-wash the girth and saddle pad in cool water with mild soap or cold-water detergent. (A harsh detergent might irritate your horse's skin.) Remember, by the way, that each horse should have his own saddle pad to prevent the spread of any skin conditions.

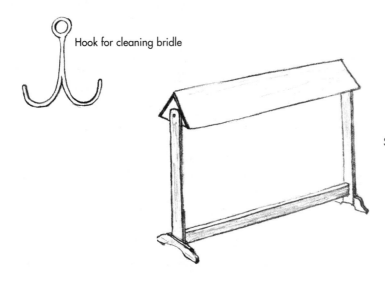

Hook for cleaning bridle

Saddle horse for cleaning saddle

Turn the saddle over on its tree (commercial stands conveniently reverse to a trough for this purpose), and wipe the entire panel with lukewarm water on a clean, rough towel or sponge. After scrubbing really hard to get all the dirt out, immediately wipe it dry with a chamois. Then turn your saddle over and repeat the process on the top, under the skirt, the flaps, billet straps, and buckle guard. At this point any leather area that seems particularly dry should get an application of neat's-foot oil, Lexol, or other conditioner. But put very little, if any, on the seat itself or the outside flaps, where it will soil your clothing.

Saddle-soaping is the next step. Before applying the soap, the saddle should be completely free of dust and dirt, or it will rub them in further. Wet the soap, thus keeping the sponge barely damp during the application. Don't strive to work up a lather. If you do, it's a sign that the sponge is too wet. Use a towel to squeeze excess water out.

After soaping, your saddle should glow and smell clean. Leave it on the stand until you're through with the fittings, which can be done separately or with the bridle pieces. The martingale or tie-down should also be soaped and dried carefully.

A Western saddle is cleaned in a manner similar to an English, unless you don't wish to darken it. In that case use the special waxes that help to keep leather looking new—a current trend. A Western saddle does not need to be taken apart for cleaning like an English saddle.

Cleaning Tooling and Silver

Use the same technique for cleaning tooling as you would for cleaning saddle or bridle leather, only use a clean toothbrush or nail brush for working into crevices. Work around silver carefully when cleaning leather. Use silver polish for the silver, being careful not to get any on the leather. When possible, use a clean cloth (even thin plastic wrap) to isolate silver from leather. Do this job slowly and carefully. A good saddle cover with a soft interior will help to protect silver from tarnishing when the saddle isn't in use.

Cleaning the Bridle

The easiest way to clean a dirty bridle is to take it apart completely. Before doing so, a novice horse owner should pay careful attention to the way it fits together and note the holes into which the crownpiece buckles. Also note the direction of the bit and how the reins are hooked to it. I see many interesting variations after well-meaning students clean a bridle.

Hang the bridle pieces and fittings from the tack hook, and wash them off one at a time with a damp sponge, drying them immediately with a chamois cloth. Use wooden matches to remove dirt from the holes of stirrup leathers and bridle pieces, then apply saddle soap, working it in well. Afterward use matchsticks to remove any excess soap.

All metal parts, including the bit, stirrups, and curb chain, can now be washed and scrubbed with a brush (a toothbrush is also good for this), removing the dirt from the recesses. If the stirrups have rubber treads, wash them with a brush and laundry soap, and set them aside to dry while you apply the metal polish.

Swab metal polish generously on each piece, and shine it vigorously with a clean flannel cloth. When the metal is gleaming, replace the stirrups on the leathers and reinsert the rubber treads. Put the stirrups and leathers back on the saddle, switching sides to equalize any stretching of the leathers caused by mounting.

Tack must be cleaned regularly to keep it soft and pliable. If neglected, it will dry out, rot, and break. Before riding, reins and billet straps should always be checked for worn stitching. Should any be found, repair immediately to avoid an accident.

A *saddle cover,* available in many styles and a range of colors and color combinations, will keep your saddle clean and dust free when not in use. Some Western saddle covers completely cover the saddle, stirrups and all, while other types do not. Saddle covers can even be monogrammed. Some zip-on styles have handles for easy transport.

Waterproof covers for English saddles have openings for stirrup leathers, allowing you to ride in the rain and protect your saddle at the same time. Rain is very hard on tack, severely drying it out.

Lay the clean girth over the top of the saddle, with each end running through the stirrups. Put it up with the clean saddle pad on top and a saddle cover over all. Or hang it up on the hook under your bridle. When the bridle is correctly put back together, adjust the crownpiece in the same holes. Then put your bridle up as you would after a ride.

A bridle should be hung up neatly when not in use, an attractive workmanlike way to keep the tack room looking tidy. Traditionally an English bridle is put up by wrapping the throatlatch around it in a figure eight, looping the reins through and putting the cavesson around everything. This arrangement is ideal when you're

PUTTING UP TACK

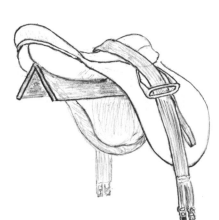

Saddle and bridle put up correctly

Bridle Bracket

traveling to a show and have numerous bridles to carry; it prevents them from tangling up. (Nowadays bridle bags serve the same purpose for both English and Western bridles.)

In tack rooms with lots of space, bridles are hung sufficiently high to allow the reins to hang straight down without touching the floor. Attractive steel bridle brackets can be purchased for under five dollars, although numerous, fancier styles are also available.

Other equipment can be hung neatly on hooks. Most metal bridle brackets have an additional hook that is perfect for hanging up a martingale, breastplate, girth, or what have you.

TACK IDENTIFICATION AND INSURANCE

Always store tack in a closed room with a good lock. Tack is expensive and a desirable target for thieves. It's possible to insure tack under your homeowners' policy even when it isn't stored at your place of residence. Just make sure your boarding barn is within the mileage range specified by the insurance coverage and that any horse shows you plan to attend are also within the limits. To insure tack, simply declare it with your insurance agent.

Commercial stables sometimes offer tack lockers on which you can install your own lock. And some tack shops offer a holder with a bracket that comes down over the saddle, locking it in place. One sad owner who lost a valuable silver-trimmed Western saddle and bridle to thieves who broke into a locked tack room, told me that she now marks every piece of equipment, right down to the last thirty-nine-cent hoof pick. She marks her saddle on the stirrup bar with an engraving tool and has a shoemaker stamp her initials underneath all leather pieces of her tack.

In some areas it's possible to have a microchip inserted into the tree in the cantle of your saddle for permanent identification. Saddlers and microchip companies that do this advertise in horse publications and charge a minimal amount for insertion.

PART IX

Education and Exercise for You and Your Horse

It is here gentlemen that practice, example and experience are worth more than words. . . . I am warning you that the horse will use any trick he can, like tossing his read, resisting the aids, or champing the bit. When he resorts to this, however, or to any such maneuver, you must reprimand him in a stern and angry tone of voice, shouting roughly and menacingly, using whatever words come to mind—like "come on, get on, get going you traitor, rebel! About face, turn, stop, turn this way, turn that." . . . ! and more of the same, so that your shouts are tremendously intimidating. Keep on with this until he gets it right.

Federico Grisone
RULES FOR RIDING, 1561

✢✢✢

The seat on a horse makes gentlemen of some and grooms of others.

Cervantes
DON QUIXOTE

Instruction: Who and Where

In countless romantic novels and films, an aggressive, untrained equestrian wannabe leaps onto an unbroken horse—usually a stallion—and subdues him after a brief, hair-raising battle of wills. Such dramatizations have convinced a lot of inexperienced riders that bravery and power are a winning combination in any saddle. In real life they're not.

Brute strength and courage have little to do with good horsemanship. Some of the greatest riders in the world are relative lightweights, like petite Kathy Kusner, who rode burly 17-hand mounts to one Olympic victory after another. Steeplechase riders, who take high-strung racehorses over the most treacherous jumps in the world, have a weight limit of 126 pounds. All competitors do have an oversize share of nerve, but the basic component is talent and acquired skill.

Films and books aren't entirely responsible for all the misconceptions about horsemanship. The art of riding is often confused with an activity that passes for it on public hacking trails. The novice who rents a horse at a public stable often returns from the outing convinced that riding involves little more than an ability to hang on while the horse follows his friends down the trail. These Sunday riders may feel in control, but if all the other horses in the party decided to return to the barn, the riders would quickly discover how illusory this feeling is. Horses at most public stables, who have been ridden by hundreds of bad riders, are numb to the aids and signals to which a well-trained horse responds. The mouths of these unfortunate animals have been pulled and their sides kicked so often that all their senses are deadened. A few years at a hacking stable will drain all the spirit out of most horses or, in the case of high-strung animals, make them hopelessly neurotic.

A good riding horse is the product of intensive training, tuned and polished like

a fine violin. In comparison, a hacking stable horse is an out-of-tune player piano, programmed to repeat the same tinny tune over and over. A pleasant riding horse moves forward willingly, responding to the rider's weight and a light touch of the leg and rein. Gaits should be smooth and elastic; this sometimes comes naturally but sometimes has to be taught. To school a horse properly, the rider himself must be well trained. If not, any training the horse has had will disappear quickly and be replaced by bad habits. I constantly remind my students that each time a horse is ridden, he is being trained—or untrained.

Great riders don't master their horses, they play them—much as musicians play their instruments. The finer the rider, the better the melody, and the better the instrument, the finer the harmony. Both horse and rider must be in tune. And like other artists, good equestrians are always striving to improve their mastery of the art. Some riders, like some musicians, are more talented than others. All have their limitations. It helps to know, by working with an instructor, what your limitations are. Spending tens of thousands on the equine equivalent of a Stradivarius is pointless if you can't play it to maximum effect. Plenty of good horses are out there, with capabilities suited to every riding level.

BASIC TRAINING

Riding aids are a nonverbal language that you must understand in order to communicate with your horse. To school a horse correctly, you need to know some of the basic physical "vocabulary" of this language. Five natural aids are at your disposal: your voice, hands, legs, seat, and weight. You need to sit comfortably and correctly at all gaits using these aids. And whether you ride English or Western, you should know something about the way a horse moves, with his center of balance slightly behind the withers. A horse propels himself from behind, collecting himself at different gaits by bringing his hindquarters well under him. A good rider knows how to encourage this natural motion to achieve balance, lightness, and a rhythmic gait.

This training can't be accomplished alone. Although books and videotapes can be helpful teaching supplements, neither can substitute for good instruction. Where do you find it? There is no shortage of riding instructors, some excellent, some dreadful. They can be found in private stables, exclusive clubs, riding centers, summer camps, and 4-H or Pony Clubs. Let's explore a few of these options and discuss how the novice can differentiate between good and bad.

Children's Instruction

SUMMER CAMPS. Many summer camps specialize in riding. Some, with long-standing reputations for excellence, offer training over a period of two weeks to two months. On a local level riding schools often run summer day camps, sometimes providing one week of intensive training that includes one or two riding lessons a day in combination with supervised, hands-on training in horse care. Sending a child to a good riding camp is one way to find out if he or she is really serious about taking care of a horse or pony.

Saddle Seat

Make sure beforehand that the excellent rider or professional advertised in the camp brochure will actually be teaching your child. Two friends who sent their daughters to an expensive riding camp in upstate New York found, when they visited, that the professional praised so highly in the promotional literature was teaching only eight of the 175 campers. The balance were being "taught" by far less qualified counselors who knew little more than their thirteen-year-old students. Apart from the expense, an experience like this could be a big setback for a child who is a serious rider. As my friends said later: "We could have spent the same amount of money for three or four private lessons a week."

Be wary of camps that offer riding along with thirty other activities. Such places often have a few undistinguished horses tacked up half-English and half-Western and an instructor who may have taken a few riding lessons in the course of his career as a tennis player.

Stock Seat

4-H CLUBS. A less expensive alternative for children under eighteen is a 4-H club. 4-H is free and encourages both English and Western riding as well as driving. Some very active 4-H clubs have regular clinics in which members learn riding theory, stable management, and horse care. Often local veterinarians are called in to lecture, and relevant films or videos are shown.

Sponsored by the U.S. Department of Agriculture and administered locally on a county level, these clubs have a lot of good things going for them. Members are required, for instance, to keep a practical yearly record of the cost of maintaining their mounts, listing the price and contents of feed, bedding, shoeing, pasturing, and equipment. Children must also record the cost and frequency of visits from the veterinarian, the number of horse shows, clinics, and trail rides they've attended, and other significant experiences with their mounts during the year. This record must be submitted before prize money is awarded at county 4-H shows.

At the beginning of every 4-H show, members are encouraged to enter fitting and showmanship classes, where they are judged on grooming, the horse's condition, cleanliness of equipment, and personal neatness. This is a wonderful way to encourage good stable management and good grooming. All junior shows should require it as a prerequisite to competition.

4-H also has a top-notch horse science program, and a variety of valuable literature about horse care is available free through the clubs or your county agricultural department.

My only reservation about 4-H—which I hesitate to mention because the organization is otherwise marvelous—is that it tends to be inconsistent about basic standards of horsemanship and horse care. 4-H stipulates no standard way of bridling and saddling a horse, and no standard riding techniques or rules for proper horse care. It all depends on the personal preference of the volunteer instructors available in any given area.

PONY CLUBS. Pony Clubs, which teach only English riding, require a nominal fee for registration, half of which goes to the national club. *Pony,* by the way, is used here in the English sense, meaning a child's mount of any size. The clubs were started in England and are now popular in many countries.

Pony Club instructors are also volunteers, but they are trained in the club methods. They work from specific standards set by the national Pony Club, which is based on British Horse Society standards. Children are rated at different levels in riding ability and are given written tests of skill at practical tasks like grooming, stable management, cleaning tack, and health and care of horses (shoeing, feeding, and bandaging). A child who is better at horse management than riding will have this talent recognized.

The clubs emphasize team rather than individual performance. At rallies, members compete in teams, which are judged on care of stalls, tack, horse, and grooming tools and equipment. They then compete in a three-phase riding event, similar to combined training, geared to their own level of riding ability. Club members also attend lectures and seminars by veterinarians and farriers.

Adult Instruction

4-H and Pony Clubs accept only youngsters, so where do you go if you're married, middle-aged, and want to begin or renew your acquaintance with riding and horse care?

RIDING OR EQUESTRIAN CENTERS. These are a good but expensive choice for beginning riders of all ages. They are usually centrally located and advertise in most weekly and monthly horse journals. An adult riding program is a good way for the older novice to learn what equine ownership will entail. Some stables offer intensive three-day weekend programs for adults.

Any competent teacher will be glad to accept an older pupil, and there's no age limit for beginners. Some of my novice pupils have been in their late sixties. Riding clubs, centers, academies, and stables are within easy traveling distance in most parts of the country, and some offer beginning through advanced instruction.

Courses in stable management are fewer and farther between. Some colleges, particularly at the community level, offer adult education courses on the subject. I've been surprised at the large turnout at an evening course I teach—an indication of the need for this type of instruction. If the colleges in your area can't help, try calling a nearby riding academy or Pony Club to see if you can observe some of their stable management courses. Or phone individual instructors and explain your plight. Most will be very helpful.

EDUCATIONAL VIDEOTAPES. These are not a substitute for instruction. Excellent videos are available to aid you in further understanding of specific riding disciplines. They can be purchased through horse publications, tack catalogs, and tack shops. Two shops in the Northeast rent and sell videos. One dressage and combined training association, to which I belong, rents videos to its members from their extensive, constantly expanding library. During long winter months my students and I view select videos at potluck get-togethers.

CLINICS. A clinic is somewhat like a master class. A well-known visiting professional comes in for a day or more and teaches his or her discipline. The organizer arranges the schedule, collects the fees, and pays the instructor. In some more isolated areas of the country, it is their only opportunity to be exposed to quality instruction. Even though switching from one instructor to another can be confusing, clinics are of unquestionable value. But be selective when choosing one. Some tips to help you evaluate a clinic:

• Who or what reliable organization is sponsoring the instructor?

• Does the instructor have a background familiar to you? Where and with whom has he or she studied, and are they able to ride the discipline they teach?

• What is the exact purpose of the clinic? What is the level of riders accepted for it, and how many students return?

• Will there be teaching on several levels, and what is the cost?

• Has the instructor had group teaching experience? Many teachers are great in a one-on-one situation but can't relate their ideas to a group.

If you have doubts about riding in a clinic, audit it from the sidelines. A receptive student can learn a lot just by watching. Take notes, particularly if the instructor is dealing with a horse or rider with problems similar to your own, and ask questions afterward. And when you *are* riding in a clinic, it's helpful to make notes on everything immediately afterward so you can refer to them when you get home. Often so much information is given that it tends to be forgotten if you don't write it down.

I had the frustrating experience of participating in a clinic conducted by an internationally famous and beautiful rider who couldn't communicate his knowledge, so he left me feeling disappointed. Conversely, I've been delighted, when just auditing a clinic, to be able to absorb vast amounts of material because of the instructor's skill at articulating it.

Choosing the Right Instructor for You

Look around for a while before you sign up with an instructor. Visit riding schools and observe their classes (phoning in advance, of course). Make sure the teacher specializes in the English or Western discipline you want to learn. Explain your goals to the instructor, who needs to know whether you'll be riding for fun or show. And don't be afraid to ask about his or her professional background. Riding instruction is a business, and you won't offend anyone by asking for credentials—unless there aren't any, in which case you can expect a defensive or evasive reaction.

By observing some lessons and/or training sessions, the level of competence exhibited by students will give you an idea of the teacher's qualifications. Afterward you might want to chat with one or two of them to see how confident they feel about the instruction, how long they've been studying, and how they feel about their progress.

Instructors must be able to ride competently in the disciplines they teach. Unfortunately this isn't always the case. Several certification programs have been developed in the United States to establish standards of instruction, all modeled after those of the British Horse Society. (One of these, sponsored by the United States Dressage Federation, was set up by leading American dressage riders and instructors. This organization also offers adult summer camp programs in different parts of the country. See Appendix F.)

In another certification program, by the American Riding Instructors Association (ARIA), instructors are rated by nationally known professionals for proficiency in the discipline they will teach. ARIA covers just about every specialty: hunt seat, endurance riding, combined training, dressage, driving, mounted patrol, open jumpers, recreational riding, saddle seat, stock seat, sidesaddle, and vaulting.

If an instructor is uncertified, it doesn't mean he or she is unqualified or incompetent. Many leading instructors in the United States are not certified; but by the same token, not everyone advertised as an instructor is qualified to teach.

If you think an instructor may be right for you, watch him or her teach several classes at different levels, not just beginners, to give you an idea of their eye, their knowledge, and how well they communicate. (A superb rider without communication skills is useless as a teacher.)

Good instructors must be able to teach as well as they ride, and their attitude should be positive and constructive. Like math or music, riding is based on theory, and a teacher should give full explanations to any questions asked. Evasions or comments like "It's that way because I say so" are good reasons to be skeptical about an instructor's qualifications. It's also possible that a personality clash will interfere with your learning process. You'll want a teacher who will encourage, inspire, and stretch your abilities to their maximum.

A teacher should demand respect but not be authoritarian to the point of intimidation. Some instructors seem to take a student's errors as a personal affront. Beginning riders are sufficiently unsure of themselves without having to contend with a temperamental teacher—particularly at today's rates. A teacher who makes you tense by constantly yelling or making sarcastic remarks takes the fun out of riding.

Any good riding instructor will be teaching a cross section of pupils of varying ability. If class after class contains only beginners, it could be a sign that the instructor isn't up to more advanced students. A mixture of adults and children at different levels is a good sign.

When you visit an instructor's stable for the first time, look closely at the condition of the horses, stalls, tack, and riding facilities. The surroundings need not be elegant, but the horses and equipment will be in good condition if the teacher is good at his or her job. If the stalls are knee-deep in manure, their occupants dull-coated and underweight, and the tack dried out and held together with pins, take yourself elsewhere.

After you select a stable and sign up for classes, you may be asked to take an evaluation lesson—a good idea if you'll be riding in a group. The instructor will be able to focus on you alone, assessing your skills and weaknesses in order to place you with riders of equal ability. In turn, you will get a chance to give the teacher a tryout. Do you like the teaching technique? Do you understand the instructions? If not, this solo lesson is an opportunity to have unfamiliar terms explained and instructions clarified. See if the instructor can do this for you.

A complete beginner should be assigned a quiet mount, and instruction should be begun on a lunge line. Some stables have specialists who teach only beginning riding. Beginners should make a commitment of one or two lessons a week for a year or more if their goal is to ride competently. Those with previous training should plan on taking a lesson once or twice weekly for at least three or four months. By repeating the basics often, you'll gain confidence and show substantial progress in a relatively short time.

RIDER FITNESS

To stay fit, an equestrian has to do more than ride. Nearly all Olympic contenders do some form of aerobic exercise or work out in other ways, realizing that a fit, athletic appearance enhances the whole competitive picture. Nothing looks worse than an overweight, out-of-condition rider puffing, perspiring, and trying to push an unbalanced horse through a dressage test. It's not a pretty scene; nor is it fair to the horse or the sport.

From a horse's point of view, it's much easier to obey clearly expressed aids from a balanced, coordinated rider than to try to follow garbled messages transmitted by someone sliding around in the saddle. Neither humans nor horses are naturally straight and symmetrical; both have to work to maintain the right balance. If rider and horse are both weak on the left, for instance, strength on that side will have to be increased through exercise. An unfit rider won't have the flexibility or muscle to keep himself or his horse in balance.

It's terribly frustrating for a student who has finally managed to get balanced and coordinated at a sitting trot to collapse like a flat tire because his weak muscles are unable to sustain the position (thereby losing the feel and continuity it has taken so long to attain). Lessons are a waste of time if a rider's body isn't fit enough to carry out the instructions. Riding involves a lot more than just sitting in the saddle. Students of dressage know that a one-hour workout is as hard on them as it is on their horse. The less fit the rider, the more difficult it will be to sustain a relaxed,

supple position and give distinct aids that your horse can recognize. Even a light-weight rider can control a massive warmblood if her body is centered over strong stomach muscles that support her back, seat, thighs, and lower legs.

Eventing is even more rigorous. It's said that to compete effectively with one horse in a three-day event, you should condition two horses and jog in your spare time. In the last half-mile of the cross-country phase, a rider must still have enough energy to stay in a balanced position, taking the load off the back of his tired horse. At this stage of the competition, an overtired rider on an equally tired horse can be an encumbrance instead of an asset.

Endurance riders must cover a hundred miles a day in some competitions, dismounting frequently to lead their horses downhill after grueling climbs through mountainous terrain. They also need to be in tiptop shape and pursue other forms of exercise to attain it.

The goal of any supplemental exercise program is to make soft, flabby muscles supple and strong. A lack of elasticity and strength in major muscles will prevent the rider from following and feeling the horse's motion. Beginning riders, who tend to brace and grip to secure their position in the saddle, will find that a rigid posture has the opposite effect. Novices are more likely to get thrown when a horse suddenly bolts, or "spooks," at the sight of an unfamiliar object because their stiff muscles aren't able to react quickly enough to the horse's movement. Even experienced riders lack suppleness when they fail to keep up with other forms of exercise. Granted that your body does get some exercise in the daily routine of grooming, tacking, working out, cooling down, and cleaning up, these chores don't improve your upper body strength, your endurance, or your cardiovascular system. Many exercise options abound, among them gyms with personal trainers, jogging, or serious power walking with barbells, lifting them as you step along. I prefer a combination of swimming, t'ai chi, and yoga. Exercise machines work if you stick with a regular workout schedule.

After watching my dressage instructor doing familiar ballet leg stretches on a fence rail before mounting up, I realized the importance of a warm-up and designed exercises for my students to perform on the horse at the beginning of each lesson. These suppling exercises help loosen muscles up and are a particularly effective way to get novices to relax, take their minds off their jobs or other commitments, and focus on riding. Sometimes it's even necessary to remind students to breathe normally. (Some hold their breath as they try to maintain the right position.)

Outside the ring, take ten to twenty minutes a day to do some active, passive, and contraction/relaxation stretching exercises to work all the major muscles that you use in riding. Active stretching, like leg raises, is done against gravity. Passive stretching, like toe touches, goes with gravity and tightens muscles. Allow the weight of your body to help you reach and breathe, hanging down as far as you can for about five seconds without bouncing. Contract/relax stretching works against another force—an object or person. Begin by doing a few of each stretch exercise every day, gradually increasing the number. Any of these programs will lead to a healthier you, a happier horse, and a safer ride.

Schooling Your Horse:

The Essentials

No matter what work you do with your horse, he'll do it better if you ride and school him consistently. That's assuming that he went through basic training before you bought him. If not, you could be in for a lot of headaches. Every riding horse should know some universal equine ABCs. The days of taking a seven-year-old horse off the range, slapping a saddle on his back, and bucking around a corral until he's broken are long past. These days Western horses are trained when they're young, then turned out to pasture again until mature and strong enough for a full day's work.

**WHAT IS AN
EDUCATED
HORSE?**

Any well-educated horse has been voice-trained from birth and handled and haltered since he was a few days old. How do you know if your horse has gotten an elementary education? Here are a few telling tests, put in boldface type to emphasize the correct way a horse should respond in each situation. If he doesn't, the problems should be corrected, probably with help of a professional, in the interest of a pleasant riding experience. This usually means ring work under supervision, but you may want to send your horse away to be trained. In other instances, riders of intermediate skill can retrain a horse and correct some of these faults, if they have the knowledge, the patience, and the time—as well as a professional available to advise and/or supervise.

1. Does he **lead forward willingly,** stopping when you stop or when you say "whoa"?
2. Does he **stand for mounting** or gallop off as soon as you get your toe in the stirrup?
3. Will he **move forward with only a slight pressure from your inner calf,** or does it take a major effort to get him to budge?
4. Does he **walk or trot briskly forward, maintaining a consistent balance and rhythmic tempo in response to light leg and following seat?** Or do you feel you have to pump him with your seat, bang him with your legs, or flail him with a crop?
5. Does he **halt readily when your hands and body stop following the motion** of his head and neck and when contact between your hand and the bit is lightly connected? Or do you feel like your arms are being pulled out of their sockets with pounds of weight pulling on the reins?
6. Does he **bend into every turn, with his nose, neck, and spine following in an even curve,** and with his hind feet following in the line with his front feet? Or is he counterbent, with his head, neck, and shoulder going in the opposite direction of the turn?
7. Does your horse **move in the direction indicated, when you turn your upper body and apply leg and rein pressure for the turn?** or does he lean against your leg, or fail to respond at all?
8. Does he **depart promptly on cue on the correct lead into a steady, balanced canter?** Or does he run into canter through the trot for twenty or thirty yards?
9. Once **cantering, is he light and balanced,** underneath you as well as in your hands, with his **hindquarters well under him,** maintaining a **balanced, rhythmic three-beat gait?** Or does he give you four or five different speeds, causing you to use your hands for balance and making it very difficult to sit securely?

Before you correct your horse's faults or continue his schooling, you should know about his elementary education. By understanding how a horse has been trained, you'll see what grades he may have failed along the way. Training is a step-by-step process. If you skip steps one and two, five and six won't take.

THE ABC'S OF TRAINING

Leading

The first lesson for the foal is learning to lead. (How well this is done can affect many other areas of training later on). It is taught by looping a rope (a clothesline will do) around the rump, bringing the end up, and slipping it through the halter ring, a device called a *come along*. The trainer, standing beside the foal's shoulder facing forward, says "walk." If he then resists or starts to move backward, the trainer pulls forward on the rope, bringing pressure to bear on the rump, thereby moving him from behind. (Often the mare is led in front of the young foal at first as an added inducement.)

Learning to lead with a come along

If done properly, the foal never has a chance to learn that he can pull back. From the start, he's impelled forward by pressure from the rear, *never by pulling on his head.* In this initial stage of training, he's also learning the first two voice commands: "walk" and "whoa."

This kindergarten lesson is also a young horse's first confrontation with punishment and reward. In training a horse, punishment doesn't mean beating. It consists of applying pressure to various points on his body; the reward is the release of this pressure. In the lesson just illustrated, the punishment would be the tightened rope around the foal's rump. The reward is twofold: the release of pressure, and a pat on the neck or a word of encouragement. The reward system is vital to later personality development, particularly with a high-strung horse. A heavy-handed, impatient trainer can create all kinds of complexes in an impressionable animal.

Early in his training, a foal is introduced to the whip (referred to in some training programs as a *wand* or a *flag*). This is often done in halter training, when the rope is removed from his rump and is replaced with a lead snapped on the halter. The trainer uses the whip as an artificial extension of his arm. As he leads the foal with his right hand, he carries the whip in his left. Should the young horse not move forward briskly enough, the trainer will, without looking back, move his whip hand behind him and touch the horse lightly on his hindquarters. Proper use of the whip is crucial to the animal's developing personality. If used correctly, there is no reason for a young horse to be frightened of a whip.

In his first year, as he is handled daily in grooming, a yearling will also be taught the commands "stand," "back," and "over." He will be introduced to the saddle or surcingle and a comfortable, simplified bridle with a mouthing bit with keys (little metal bars that hang from the center of the bit, encouraging the horse to chew on the mouthpiece) or other mild rubber snaffle. Western horses are usually introduced to the bosal first and may not have a bit in their mouths for several years, at which time it is often a simple snaffle.

Lunging

During the next stage of training, usually at the end of his first year, the young horse is taught to lunge. The trainer's aim here is quite different from lunging as a means of light exercise or to further school a horse (discussed later in this chapter). Obedience, balance, and tempo of gaits are the trainer's main concerns.

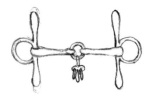

Mouthing Bit and Keys

Once he's been lunged, the young horse learns that he is expected to move in a circle in both directions around his trainer. At that point he is acquainted with more new voice commands—"walk on," "reverse," "trot," and much later, "canter." The trainer becomes familiar with the young horse's temperament and natural way of moving, concentrating on helping him establish rhythm and balance at the various gaits.

The equipment for lunging is a bridle or lunge cavesson, side reins, and a surcingle (or training roller). Elastic side reins or those with a rubber donut are connected from the surcingle to the bit. They are quite loose at first and are shortened gradually, notch by notch, during the weeks of training, so that the horse gets used to the feeling of a little pressure on the bit. The elastic reins give with the movement of the head and neck, and he learns to flex or give with the bit. (See "Lunging as Light Exercise" in Chapter 30.)

Schooling schedules at this age should be simple, short, clear and should be consistent in duration and frequency. This is essential if a colt or filly is to leave each lesson refreshed, encouraged, and eager to return to please his trainer rather than ending up exhausted, confused, bored, or balky.

Side Reins and Training Surcingle

Long Reining

The next step in a young horse's education is to learn to steer. Some trainers do this from the ground, running long reins through the run-up stirrups on the saddle. The trainer handles the reins walking four or five feet behind the horse. This can be continued right into driving training, eventually hitching the horse to a light cart. (See "Driving" in Chapter 30.)

Directed from behind by voice commands, the horse learns to walk forward and turn right and left by pressure on each rein and/or release of the opposite rein. The normal reaction is to move in the direction the head is turned. The youngster is taught to move forward into a walk or trot with light contact on the reins and rein pressure that he can associate with the already familiar voice commands "walk," "whoa," and "back."

Though long reining from the ground is a classical teaching method, some trainers frown on it, claiming it puts too uneven a contact on the horse's mouth. These people teach steering directly from the horse's back, with the use of either a leading rein or an opening rein, taking the left rein out to the left for a left turn and vice versa, softening contact on the right rein to allow the horse to turn its head to the left.

Long Reining

Adding Weight

Sometime between the second and third year, the horse is introduced to the weight of a rider on his back. This process isn't usually accompanied by the bucks and snorts one might expect from seeing wild horses broken in TV westerns. For months the young horse has become familiar with saddle and bridle while lunging and, just as important, has experienced the gradual tightening of the girth.

It's essential that the latter process be performed correctly. Buckling a girth to its tightest fit when the saddle is first put on is the worst mistake a trainer can make. The horse will remember the discomfort the next time he's saddled and will tense up, shake his head, pin back his ears, and sometimes cow-kick—becoming what is known as a *girthy* horse. In the extreme, he could develop a resistance to being mounted or, worse yet, start bucking as soon as a rider sets a foot in the stirrup or swings into the saddle—called a *cold back*. Once a horse succeeds in dislodging a rider, this behavior is difficult to change.

To avoid this potential problem, I make a point of adjusting the girth on young or very sensitive horses several times when they're in cross-ties and three or four times while I'm lunging them.

Preparatory to mounting a young horse for the first time, the rider has gradually leaned more and more weight on the horse's back. Once in the saddle, the rider takes up the reins and is walked around on a lead or lunged by an assistant. At this final stage of elementary training, the voice commands that the horse has learned are synchronized with legs, weight, rein, and seat aids. For instance, when the rider says "walk," he applies calf and seat pressure and softens rein contact. When he says "whoa," he stops the movements of his hands, braces back, and stops, following with his seat simultaneously. The young horse now associates the physical aids with the familiar oral ones.

In the next several weeks, the horse is taught to trot and eventually to canter; the rider's body reinforces the familiar voice aids. Voice commands are gradually eliminated as the horse responds and understands the rider's aids. It takes a while for the young horse to become accustomed to balancing the rider's weight on his back at all three gaits.

Canter work is not usually begun until the horse is able to execute simple figures in the ring at a balanced trot. When he can maintain tempo and stay balanced while trotting in circles, and half circles, making diagonal changes of direction and performing simple transitions, he is ready. He should bend around the rider's inside leg on a circle, so that the entire spine, from the base of the tail to the poll, is curved in the direction of the turn and each hind leg is following the corresponding foreleg on the circle. All this strengthens and helps him balance better, preparing him for the more difficult three-beat canter.

This has been a highly simplified explanation of how a colt or filly is first trained—a task that should be undertaken only by an experienced rider. But it will give you an idea of what your horse should have learned and what gaps in his education may need to be filled in before he goes on to advanced and more specialized training in disciplines suited to his breeding and temperament.

Designing the Workplace

To keep your horse in condition and responsive to your commands, he should be worked or schooled at least four times a week within some type of enclosure, so his attention is focused on you rather than on the inviting pasture next door. A flat, smooth rectangular area, preferably enclosed, with good footing can make an enormous difference in the quality of training and subsequent performance in competition.

The Riding Ring

The riding ring should be level across the working area, with a slight pitch of about a foot (per 100 feet) toward one corner. Or it can have a crest in the middle and drop a foot to the outside perimeters to allow for drainage. After the area is graded and all loose stones picked up, a three-inch layer of stone dust is spread on and packed down with a steamroller. This makes a sturdy, long-lasting base—the key to a good riding ring—over which the footing of your choice can be laid down. Dressage riders, who need a light, springy, dust-free footing, usually opt for a two-to-three-inch layer of sand. Those who are jumping prefer a footing that gives without being too soft, doesn't compact, and has good traction—either shavings, shredded bark, or rubber. (Some are made of recycled tire treads or sneakers to a depth of three to five inches.) For driving, a heavy, firm mixture of dirt and shavings about two or three inches deep is ideal. Each type of footing has its drawbacks, not the least of which is cost. Investigate other arenas in your area, and find out what other riders in your specialty favor before making a choice.

I've found that washed sand is best for my teaching and training. Like all footings, it needs to be dragged regularly to maintain quality; the frequency of this procedure will depend on use. To make spreading and leveling easier, the initial footing should be put down after the posts are sunk and before the side boards are in place. This investment in footing may seem high, but for long-term training it's a good one, often allowing those without access to an indoor ring to exercise and train soon after a heavy rain or snowfall.

The Fence

If an arena is to be really serviceable, it needs a fence supported by eight-foot posts, spaced eight feet apart, and sunk at least three feet in the ground, with boards on the inside to create a flat interior enclosure. The top rail is five feet high with a foot and a half between it and the one below. It's a good idea to place a bottom board flush with the ground to prevent sand or other footing from washing away. This is an ideal, long-lasting work area, but if posts and rails aren't in your budget, the outer perimeter can be "fenced" with cinder blocks stood on end at intervals of a length that can accommodate "posts" of PVC pipe suspended between them, making a good all-purpose schooling area that can be replaced, when budget permits, with posts and rails.

Before you can do any kind of work on your horse, he *must* be taught to stand for mounting and dismounting. This is not only a functional necessity and a sign of good manners but a must in any type of pleasure riding, showing, or hunting—in short, for every situation. Nothing is more annoying than a horse that backs away as you try to mount. If your horse hasn't already learned this elementary lesson, it's worth all of your time to teach it.

To keep mounting a pleasant and comfortable experience, use a mounting block, which is easier for you and better for the horse's back. They're available in most tack stores and catalogs (or you can make one).

Hold the reins in your left hand, at the length you will be using for riding, so your horse won't be tempted to move forward. (Try not to mount a horse with reins too long or with one rein longer than the other.) If you're carrying a whip, it goes in your left hand, fingers around the handle (not through the loop if there is one), with whip end hanging down. Both stirrups should be down and in your correct riding length before mounting. On an English saddle, you do this by extending your arm until the fingertips are on the safety bar of the saddle. Pull the leather taut until the bottom of the stirrup is under your armpit. This will be approximately the right length. For normal English riding, the bottom of the stirrup should touch the bottom of your ankle bone when you're mounted. Dressage riders will want them a hole or two longer, depending on their level of training, and jumping riders a hole shorter.

If you prefer to adjust the stirrups from the saddle, keep your foot in the stirrup, but lighten the weight, move your thigh back so you can reach the stirrup leather buckle, pull it down a little below the bar, unbuckle the leather, adjust it to the right length, and return it to its original position.

**MOUNTING
AND
DISMOUNTING**

Measuring Stirrup Before Mounting

Adjusting Stirrup While Mounted

When you mount, never allow your horse to drop his head to graze. Aside from getting the bit dirty, this is bad manners and potentially a dangerous habit, especially in a child's mount. Although some Western bits are especially designed for grazing, with movable shanks that bend back, encouraging this habit only invites the danger of the horse stepping on the reins and breaking them and/or becoming frightened and bolting.

After you've mounted, your horse should remain standing until you give him a specific signal to move forward.

THE GAITS

Up until now I've spoken in general of the three basic gaits that can be improved to some extent with good training. (Some horses are naturally better balanced, more athletic, or simply better movers than others because of their breeding and conformation.) As mentioned in Chapter 2, specific disciplines prefer a different quality of movement.

Walk

The walk is probably one of the most abused of all gaits. Unless they are aware of its importance, most riders use it as a transition to rest when going from one gait to another, or to cool the horse out in the ring, or on the way home on the trail. The *free walk* is close to the one that we all use when we allow a horse to relax and stretch out with his head lowered on a loose rein. A good free walk needs to have the horse stepping deeply under his body, producing a good overtrack from the reach of the hind leg and the stretching of the back.

The walk should cover the ground in a forward, clear four-beat rhythm with the quality of a march. A foreleg and hind leg on the same side should not land simultaneously. This lateral movement is a serious fault in horses that are not gaited.

Apart from the free walk, there are three walks developed in dressage: *medium, collected,* and *extended.* The medium walk is the one most horses assume naturally when asked to walk under saddle; the rider keeps light contact with the horse's mouth. The walk should be even, relaxed, and rhythmic and have energy in each step; the hind foot should touch the ground in front of the footprints of the forefeet (called *overtracking*).

The collected and extended walks require a horse to be advanced enough in training to accept sufficient contact on the bit and to be strong enough in hip, stifle, and hocks to engage his hindquarters. In the collected walk the energy and power of the engagement produce

The Walk

more bending in the joints, but because of the shorter steps, the horse carries himself more upright. In an extended walk the power is used to carry the horse forward to cover as much ground as possible, with each stride overtracking sometimes by more than a foot; the horse also stretches its head and neck and remains on contact.

Trot

The trot is probably the most important of the three gaits, and because it is the one in which the horse has the best balance, it is best for training in almost all phases of riding. It is a two-beat diagonal gait in which the horse alternates from one diagonal pair of legs to the other. Rhythm and elasticity should be its chief characteristics, but speed and animation can vary a great deal between individual horses and breeds. There are basically four trots: *working, collected, extended,* and *racing.*

The working trot is what most horses naturally perform. The speed is about eight miles per hour with a stride nine to ten feet long. The hind feet can overstep the front feet by a few inches or as much as a foot. It is a balanced and energetic gait that a fit horse can keep up for many miles. The U.S. Cavalry used it for almost all traveling, rarely galloping.

The collected trot seen in dressage has the same power as the extended trot, but here the hocks, stifle, and hip are bending and carrying more of the horse's weight, making him lighter and higher in front rather than carrying him farther forward. The hind leg lands behind the footprint of the front foot. Although the forward movement is less, the power (or impulsion) is being applied for a greater lift.

A Good Working Trot

Another trot, the *medium trot*, is seen in dressage and falls between a working and extended trot. The horse tends to be rounder (not as long as in the extended trot) and should push off from his hindquarters.

Unlike the collected trot of dressage horses, the jog, a very slow, short trot used by Western horses, should have little animation. The jog should be close to the ground with little knee or hock action with the horse taking short, smooth steps forward.

Nor is the extended trot something every horse does. It can take extensive training, muscle development, and conditioning. During the extended trot there is a moment of suspension when all four feet are off the ground—not usually the case in the working or collected trot. When a horse extends the trot, he can lengthen his stride to a point where he oversteps by as much as several feet (the distance the body travels while the trot is in its suspended phase). The horse may travel from twelve to twenty miles per hour as he lengthens his body and lowers his hindquarters.

The racing trot, a specialty of the Standardbred and rarely performed by most horses, has a speed of up to thirty miles per hour, a stride of fifteen to twenty feet, and an overstep of as much as six feet. The horse covers ground faster, not by speeding up leg movements but by lengthening his stride, increasing his thrust off the hind legs and adding a longer period of suspension.

Canter

The canter (or lope), a slow, collected gallop, is a three-beat gait that should be forward, rhythmic, and light. Footfalls for the *right lead* are: strike off with the left hind, then the diagonal left pair, consisting of left fore and right hind, then the right fore, followed by a period of suspension when all four feet are off the ground. A horse should be on the right lead when traveling clockwise and vice versa.

The canter should have an even rhythm and be balanced in both directions. The horse should be comfortable on both leads and willing to work them on command. Frequently a horse is better balanced on one side. By using suppling exercises of circles, figures, and changes of tempo to shorten and lengthen the stride, the canter can be improved. A weak side can be strengthened by making sure the horse is straight, with hind legs traveling in the same track as the front. Work over the cavalletti at the trot can also help build up the horse behind, enabling him to carry himself better at a canter.

Like the walk and the trot, the canter also has four variations: *medium, extended, collected,* and the *gallop,* with other variations in between. Any good hunter or jumper should be able to lengthen or shorten his stride on command to adjust to distances between fences quickly, just as a good cutting horse adjusts instinctively to the movements and speed of the cow.

In the medium canter (between the extended canter and the regular or working canter), the thrust coming from the hindquarters extends and lifts the frame of the horse. In the extended canter the horse covers as much ground as possible. This is similar to the hand gallop in hunter classes, but here the horse is on the forehand, unlike dressage horses who must be light on the forehand, maintaining rhythm and balance while pushing from the hindquarters.

Right Lead Canter

The collected canter has some of the characteristics of the collected walk and trot. The stride is short but the gait is light, and the horse is very active in the hindquarters and very free at the shoulder. In this gait, the impulsion lifts the horse, rather than carrying him so far forward.

The countercanter, when the horse canters on the left lead while traveling clockwise and vice versa, is used as a training exercise to develop and improve balance and collection. It should not be confused with cross-cantering, in which a horse mistakenly mixes its leads, cantering on one in the front and another in the back, producing a ragged, unbalanced gait that is severely penalized in all disciplines.

Flying Changes

Flying changes are changes of lead in midair while cantering, usually when the horse is changing from one bend to the other or one circle to another. This is a more advanced form of training and should not be taught until the horse is balanced, relaxed, and steady on both leads. It is essential for all hunters, jumpers, and Western horses. In the higher levels of dressage, flying changes are developed further into a series of every fourth, third, and second stride. The training reaches its epitome when a Grand Prix competitor performs fifteen single lead changes on a straight line.

Full Gallop

At very high speeds the gallop becomes a four-beat instead of a three-beat gait, again followed by a moment of suspension. Secretariat, who still holds the one-and-a-half-mile record at the gallop, covered the distance at the 1973 Belmont Stakes in two minutes, twenty-four seconds, winning the Triple Crown by thirty lengths. He was traveling at 37.5 miles per hour!

•chapter•

30

Conditioning, Exercise, and Gymnastics

Your horse's health, happiness, and habits depend on regular exercise. While the casual workouts he gets from strolling around a pasture strengthens his legs, bones, lungs, and muscles, it can never replace the rigor of a regular workout in the ring or on the trail, which account for the long, hard, rippling muscles of a healthy horse, building wind while improving manners and discipline.

In its simplest form equine exercise is the natural act of walking and grazing. Unless your horse is particularly delicate, he will stay much healthier by spending most of his time outdoors. Left standing in the stall without regular exercise, he will become irritable and soft, and his legs may even stock up from poor circulation brought on by forced idleness.

In temperate climates with harsh winters, horses often have to be stabled for extended periods, and when they are turned out, deep snow can inhibit exercise. By the time spring finally rolls around, a winter-weary horse will be full of energy, but not fit enough to resume an intensive exercise program until he is gradually conditioned for it.

THE GOAL OF CONDITIONING

The goal of conditioning is to gradually increase the stress on a horse's muscular system until he adapts to an exercise. If a workout isn't strenuous enough, no conditioning will occur. If you overdo it and exert a horse beyond his current capacity, he may break down physically and/or metabolically. Consequently you should evaluate your horse carefully before beginning a conditioning program, paying close attention to his overall appearance and muscle tone.

This is a good time to learn his resting body temperature, pulse rate, and respiration per minute for future reference. Circulation should also be evaluated by firmly pressing your thumb to your horse's gum. When you remove it, the white spot should return to its original color in two to three seconds. Also pay attention to whether the joints are filling and heating up. Compare the horse's normal amount of fluid retention and heat before and several hours after work.

As a horse becomes more fit, the consistency of his sweat will change from sticky, smelly paste to a thin, watery, odorless liquid, the sign of the way a good conditioning program affects the whole horse. But each equine system is different, and parts of it respond more slowly than others to exercise. An effective program must keep his weakest link in mind.

It takes about six weeks to two months to get a mature horse relatively fit on a planned conditioning program, keeping in mind that diet and daily grooming also play an important role. For adequate conditioning, workouts should be scheduled at least three days a week, preferably six, with a free day or light exercise on the others. Light exercise is a short, relaxed trail ride, an easy hack in the ring, or in a pinch a half hour to forty-five minutes on the lunge.

Three different types of work should be done in a conditioning program. *Slow work* over a long distance provides steady aerobic exercise. Long periods of *walking* build muscle and are very calming for a young or green animal. (Some show and racing stables feel so strongly about its beneficial effects that they invest thousands of dollars in walking machines that lead a horse around and around before and after a workout.) *Strenuous work,* which includes interval training and repetition, puts higher demands on the system, and *maximal work,* designed to develop speed and agility, pushes a horse to the highest level of exertion.

THE EQUINE EXERCISE PROGRAM

After a vigorous grooming to stimulate circulation, begin each exercise session with a conscientious warm-up. The best way to prevent injury and illness, a warm-up will dissipate fluids that have built up in legs and lungs during inactivity, open capillaries, lubricate joints, and sharpen neuromuscular reflexes. You can prepare the horse for the work ahead by stretching his legs or doing what I refer to as "carrot stretches" with my students. You can also massage his back and neck and do tummy lifts (curling fingers under the ridge of the stomach and pressing up). Or you can hand walk, lunge, or ride to warm him up.

If you have a nearby trail, a short ride before going into the ring is a good introduction to work, relaxing you and your horse physically and mentally. Always begin at a slow walk, building up to a faster one. This will loosen his muscles progressively and gradually raise his heartbeat, respiration, and body temperature. Create warm-ups to suit your horse's temperament and build, following them with a carefully thought-out exercise session.

While conditioning your horse, make his exercise interesting by alternating ring

Carrot Stretch A

work with hacking on the trail. When work is dull, horses get bored and often display their displeasure by shying or resisting aids. In the ring use a variety of transitions from one gait to another, figures, changes of direction, and transitions within gaits (to working to lengthened trot, with a transition to walk or halt). Vary sitting to the trot and posting (when the horse isn't young or green) at the ordinary trot, as well as lengthening it to see if he accepts this and maintains the same tempo and balance. The same thing can be done at the canter. The only limits to the routine are your imagination and the horse's ability.

Once he has been trained, a horse being shown on weekends in hunter or jumper classes doesn't have to be worked over fences the week before. Some hacking, in combination with well-designed ring work, will keep the competitor supple and fresh. The same goes for dressage competition. The horse doesn't need to practice the tests over and over again until he anticipates movements and figures. Instead, practice suppling exercises and parts of the test that are giving you trouble at different areas of the ring and at different letters. This helps to keep your horse listening to you rather than one step ahead, anticipating and tensing up for that exciting canter depart at C.

Before you begin a riding session, have a definite plan of work in mind. Choose one exercise, like bending, and work on it in all gaits in both directions for an entire

Carrot Stretch B

session. Know your horse's physical and mental limitations, and never drill and drill. If your horse does something particularly well, reward him with pats and praise. Even if you cut the workout a little short, end it on a good note as positive reinforcement for a job well done.

When introducing a new movement, do it clearly and gradually rather than insisting on perfection the first time. Help the horse to understand what you're asking of him, and if he performs the first step well, let him know. Improvement comes in small increments—one of the biggest lessons I've learned from years of dressage training. When a horse is physically and mentally relaxed and tuned in to your aids, an initial improvement of 1 to 3 percent each week will leap to 15 or 25 percent when the performance plateau is reached—the time when a horse's body is strong enough to perform the movement with ease and he understands it completely.

The Cavalletti

Unsurpassed as a schooling device, the cavalletti can help train a horse to balance himself at the trot by encouraging him to round his back, use his hocks, and stretch his head and neck. They are also a basic tool for teaching a horse (and rider) to jump.

Cavallettis can be simple and inexpensive, constructed of six-to-eight-foot rails of equal diameter (they can be as thick as a fence post, but the diameter must be consistent), spaced at an equal distance. They can be flat on the ground or suspended

Going over Cavallettis in a Good Rhythmic Trot

about six inches above it on wood or plastic supports laid on level ground, secured so they won't move—which is especially important if you're schooling from the saddle. If they are raised, the rails should be parallel to the ground. Ideally, either type should be positioned in the center of the ring to allow a horse to turn in alternate directions after traversing them. When this isn't possible, the rails should be worked in both directions.

When taking your horse over a cavalletti for the first time, lay a single rail on the ground and let him get used to walking over it first. Then add another rail approximately four feet away. Although this is the trot distance, it accustoms him to the process.

Once your horse is able to walk over two rails straight, trot them. When he can do this quietly and at the same speed, add a third and fourth at the same distance. If he overreaches, extend the second rail a bit farther. Horses' strides vary, but when rails are properly adjusted, they should be able to trot between them without hitting them.

Four rails usually precede a training crossbar jump. More than four cavalletti rails are used in flat work when trying to improve a horse's rhythm and balance at a trot. Keep in mind that raised rails are much more strenuous for a horse, and don't overdo the exercise. Trot over it just a few times at first, gradually building up to a maximum of a dozen passes. The cavalletti can also help lengthen and shorten his strides.

Once you've received basic instruction in jumping, a combination of fences spaced at specific distances (called a jumping gymnastic), based on the cavalletti, is used to train your horse to quickly adjust to different intervals between fences. A basic setup would be to lay six rails at equal four-foot intervals on the ground, putting a set of jump standards or plastic jump blocks (advertised in catalogs and many horse publications) at either side of rail six. Then pick up rails five and six and cross them between the blocks, beginning the crossbar at six inches and working up from there. The low point of the cross invites the horse to stay centered when he's jumping, and an extra ground rail placed nine feet from the landing side will help him to remain balanced after taking the fence. An eight-foot space between the fourth rail and the crossbar jump will give him room to take off. If your horse is new to jumping, place an extra ground rail about six inches in front of the cross rails to give him a ground line for takeoff, in which case you will need to readjust the preceding ground rails so the distance is correct.

Beyond the first one, you can set up as many as jumps as you have room for and can afford. By adding another crossbar jump nine feet from the landing ground rail on the first one, you are beginning to build a schooling combination. You can expand it to higher, wider jumps. But distances between fences are critical, and I advise you to get professional instruction when you're setting them up. Otherwise your horse might get frightened of jumping. These exercises should really be done under professional supervision.

Practice jumps can vary between two and a half and three and a half feet high and simulate type of jumps you may face in the ring or hunt field. Try to have a variety of jumps so your horse will gain confidence and won't hesitate to jump obstacles he'll encounter at shows and hunts.

Be sure to take temperature into consideration when you plan any exercise program. In very hot summer climates like the South and Southwest, trainers get up at four in the morning to work horses and are finished by nine. Here in the Northeast we ride early in the morning or, during heat waves, in the late afternoon. Although a certain amount of work in moderate heat and humidity can help a horse develop tolerance to it, over a certain point it prevents the equine cooling system from operating effectively. A combined temperature and humidity value over 140 degrees causes a lot of sweating but inhibits self-cooling in any horse, no matter how fit. Past this point, sweating won't cool a horse at all, and ice water must be sponged on large muscle groups as well as poll and chest, applying it continuously and immediately scraping off after each sponging so the water doesn't heat up again.

Whatever the outside temperature, a horse must be walked after exercise to bring his body temperature down, normalize his respiration and pulse, relax his muscles, and minimize toxic metabolic by-products like lactic acid. This is accomplished by gradually slowing blood circulation to normal. Too abrupt a change in circulation, which occurs if a horse is stabled right after a hard workout, will at the very least cause sore and stiff muscles and at worst founder and/or colic.

Begin the cooling-down process while you are still mounted. Walk your horse on a level area, allowing him to relax on a long rein, stretch his head and neck, and walk long and low. If the weather is cold, place a folded cooler across his croup, sitting on it to keep it in place. After walking him for ten minutes or so, dismount, loosen the girth, lift the saddle off his back, and then replace it. This will relieve pressure on his back muscles while keeping them warm, allowing circulation to return slowly.

Depending on the weather or season, put a cooler of appropriate weight over the saddle and horse to cool the body down gradually. After walking the horse awhile, put a hand on his chest. If it's still hot, keep walking him. When his temperature is normal, walk him some more until he's completely cool before allowing him to stand for sponging or rubbing down, checking him as you do this to make sure he doesn't reheat. (If he does, immediately go back to walking.)

When the horse is completely cool, remove the saddle and rub or brush it and the girth area vigorously. Or if temperature allows, give your horse a warm-water sponge bath, removing all tack marks so that nothing is left to dry and cake on the skin. His legs should then be towel-dried to restore circulation and prevent filling or chilling. Afterward, depending on the weather, put the cooler or sheet back on, and walk the horse until he's dry. Offer sips of water while you walk him out until his pulse and respiration return to normal (pulse 30 to 48 beats per minute, respiration 8 to 16 breaths per minute).

DRIVING
YOUR HORSE

Driving is a great way to get acquainted with a young horse and build a sound base for later training under saddle. Depending on his build, you can start a two-year-old horse in driving a year or even two before he can be ridden. When taught correctly, driving instills obedience and balance, builds muscles, and develops the mouth of the horse.

Once you're sure that a young or mature horse is familiar with all the steps of training on the lunge line, responds to all verbal commands (particularly "whoa" and "stand"), and is performing all steps of long reining, including circles and turns, he's ready for harness. This is done gradually, introducing no more than one or two pieces of the harness at each schooling session. (See Chapter 26.) Some individual parts may take longer than a single session. Give special attention to the crupper—hold the tail carefully when you put it on. When in place, it shouldn't pinch, pull, or rub if your horse is to accept it in a relaxed manner. It's a good idea to lunge him with this on, to accustom him to the feel of it when he's in motion.

Always take your time when introducing a horse to harness. Many amateurs have excellent driving horses because they've spent time on each training step to give the animals a solid foundation.

To familiarize a horse with the action of the shafts, short poles that run the length of the horse's body are attached to the harness, slipping them through the tugs and tying them to the breeching with baling twine. After that, the horse is ground driven to accustom him to the poles flopping and slapping at his sides.

At this point you can also simulate the noise the cart will make out on the highway later on. A friend of mine ties cans full of rocks to her belt, which rattle ominously as she steers her horse on the long reins. This lesson is essential to accustom a driving horse to the sound of the rumbling cart behind him, which blinkers prevent him from seeing.

Before they actually hitch the horse to the cart (described in Chapter 26), many people use a *travois,* an easily constructed, stretcherlike device. Green wood is recommended for the frame so that the poles will have some resilience and won't break. A travois makes a noise similar to a cart and slides sideways when the horse turns, but it won't turn over and won't go in reverse, should he try to back up.

Before you hitch up the travois for the first time, let your horse look it over closely. Then, as you lower the poles into the tugs, have a helper stand at his head.

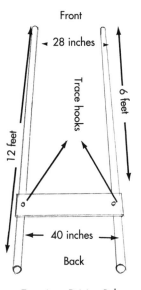

Front

← 28 inches →

6 feet

Trace hooks

12 feet

← 40 inches →

Back

Travois or Driving Poles

Never back a horse into the poles; rather, bring them up high, then lower them into position and slip them through the harness tugs. (Use the same procedure when hitching a horse to the cart.) The travois is used until the horse is completely relaxed with it and able to do the simple exercises he performed on the long reins.

Patience and thorough attention to detail produce a calm driving horse. It's not worth it to rush training. I've been told by driving enthusiasts that once a horse runs away, he is no longer safe to drive. A runaway in harness is more dangerous than one under saddle. So if you don't have the time to teach your horse carefully, be sure to find a qualified person who will.

If your horse is a young or green animal, he may dash into the ring for the morning workout full of more energy than you care to manage from his back. Nippy weather will have the same effect on horses of any age. When you don't have time to turn a horse out for a few hours to work off the excess steam, lunging is a good way to take the edge off and calm him down.

This routine warm-up procedure can also be used as a light workout on days when there isn't enough time to ride, or when he's recuperating from certain types of sickness or injury. It's an excellent way to reinforce training, establishing obedience as well as tempo, rhythm, and bending.

Twenty minutes a day is sufficient for a light workout, extending it to forty-five minutes on days you won't be riding. But limit the first few learning sessions to ten or fifteen minutes, as you would teaching any other exercise.

Apart from your halter, bridle, and saddle, lunging can be taught with a minimum of equipment. You'll need to purchase a *lunge whip,* a lightweight cotton web *lunge line* with a snap, and for English riding horses, a set of *side reins.* Some of the latter have elastic ends that attach to the bit and are made of leather or nylon. Others have a rubber doughnut in the center of the leather rein. When attached to the bit and saddle, the give-and-take simulates the light contact of the rider's hands on the reins to which a well-trained English horse responds. Used properly, they can also teach a horse to stretch his neck and use his back.

Optional equipment, to take the place of a bridle, is a *lunge cavesson,* which has a solid noseband with three rings. By attaching the lunge line to the middle ring, you can reverse your horse on the circle without leaving your place at the center. However desirable, this piece of equipment is not essential.

LUNGING AS LIGHT EXERCISE

Lunging cavesson with lunge line

Before you start to lunge a horse for the first time, get him acquainted with the whip. Let him look at it close up, smell it, and get accustomed to its light touch on different parts of his body. Don't rush things. With an extremely tense or timid horse, the process could take up to a week.

The first step in a lunging session is to bridle and saddle your horse and wrap his legs with exercise bandages or boots for protection. Secure the stirrups on a Western saddle with a thong under the belly that attaches to the bottom of each stirrup. For an English saddle, you can purchase an elastic strap with a snap on each end that stretches over it and attaches to the top of the run-up stirrups on each side. Or you can run stirrups up as illustrated, to prevent them from sliding down during lunging.

The bridle reins should be placed over the horse's head and twisted under his neck to take up the slack, catching one of the loops through the throatlatch of the bridle. Attach the lunge line by running it through the snaffle ring on the near side, over the top of the poll, and down, securing it to the top of the snaffle ring on the off side. Each time you reverse, you must undo and reverse the lunge line.

If possible, choose an enclosed area and work a fifteen-to-twenty-meter circle. If your horse is new to this, it is a must that area be enclosed; and keeping the circle on the small side gives you better control. Make all the verbal commands loud, clear,

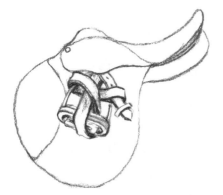

Stirrups Secured for Lunging

Bridle Reins Secured for Lunging

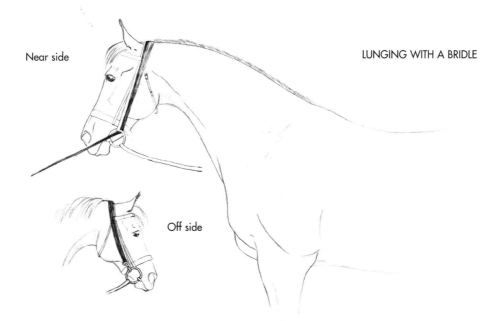

Near side

LUNGING WITH A BRIDLE

Off side

and crisp. When you want the horse to slow down, let your voice drop at the end of the command "slow," drawing the word out to communicate its meaning. Upward transitions—"walk," "trot," and eventually "canter"—should be loud and sharp. The tone of your voice is an effective tool. Clucking can be used (sparingly) to encourage him to move out.

To get more forward impulsion, you can use "walk on" and "trot on" in conjunction with the whip. In theory the whip keeps the horse out on the circle, replacing the rider's leg as an aid to move him forward. Pointing the whip at the front of his nose will slow or stop him. I also use the position of the whip to indicate the gait I want (discussed below).

Begin by lunging your horse to the left, with the line in your left hand and whip in the right. Never, under any circumstances, coil the remaining lunge line around your hand, wrist, or body. I've heard too many horror stories about people (who should have known better) being dragged on the lunge line by a frightened horse.

The lunge line is like a rein. You need to keep steady contact with the horse's mouth as he's circumventing you—not so tight that he pulls you off your feet, but not so loose that it sags on the ground. Extra line can be folded in a ribbonlike manner in either hand. Some experts specify the whip hand, but I find this extremely awkward. The extra line should be held so it can feed out of your hand in equal sections and not get caught underfoot.

The hardest thing to remember when you're just learning to lunge is to stay in the center of the circle and pivot. Let the horse move around you, rather than moving in and out, as you increase and decrease pressure on the line (which only encourages the horse to do it more). When standing in the center of your circle, stay in

line with the center of the saddle, with your whip pointing at his hip, forming a triangle with the lunge line attached to his head. If the horse starts to move in, point the whip at the shoulder. (If necessary, actually touch him there to encourage him to stay out.)

A horse that pulls out on the perimeter or speeds up can be given the equivalent of a half-halt rein signal (in this case, a quick tug with a release), along with an appropriate verbal command if he's too fast.

By using clear commands and body language with your horse, he will gradually begin to understand. If he's too slow, flick the whip at him or even touch him lightly on the rump, but try to avoid cracking it continually. All horses that I've trained to the lunge learn that the whip pointed at the hip means *trot;* at the hind fetlock, *walk.* A vertical whip means *canter,* and a whip pointed at the nose means *slow down* and accompanies all downward transitions, including *halt* or *whoa.*

Horses familiar with side reins should be warmed up for about five minutes before you attach them. Never lead a horse with side reins or attach them in the barn. Attach them to the girth first and clip them to the saddle D-rings until you are ready to use them. (If the side reins in their last hole are still too short, attachments especially for this purpose can be purchased.) When the procedure is new to your horse, wait and attach them at the end of the lunging session.

To begin your horse on side reins, try one at a time, beginning with the outside one first. Attach one end to the girth or ring on surcingle, allowing enough rein to enable the horse to turn his head slightly in the opposite direction and not feel too restricted; then attach the elastic end to the bit. Lunge him at the walk and trot for a few minutes until he accepts this arrangement. If he does, then attach the other side rein at the same length.

Over a period of time, you will gradually work the horse up to a point where the side reins create a straight line from bit to girth, similar to the pressure a horse feels on the bit when you're riding, and he continues to willingly move forward. If they are too tight, the horse will show his irritation in a number of ways—refusing to move forward, dropping his nose behind the vertical (overflexing), or at the worst extreme, rearing or running backward and pulling you with him (in which case you should follow, not pull back). Try to avoid the latter by taking plenty of time to introduce the side reins; do not set them too short, and be sensitive to your horse's attitude toward them.

Other lunging tips: Encourage your horse to maintain a steady tempo at all paces. Make sure he's pushing from behind and tracking up at the trot (hind foot stepping into the track of the front). Try to work him several times in both directions, especially on his stiffer side. If he's extremely stiff on one side, you can let out the opposite side rein and shorten the one on the inside. But do this with extreme care later in the lunging session and only when he's comfortable with the entire procedure.

When your horse is lunging well on both sides at both the walk and the trot, you can add the canter. Usually I increase the size of the circle to give the horse more room. Other excellent training exercises on the lunge are transitions within the trot, shortening and lengthening the gaits as you contract or expand the circle.

Even on a pleasure outing, when you're not actively working your horse, he shouldn't be allowed to stumble along at a lazy walk or to set his own pace at a poky trot. Bad habits start this way. Remember that you're reinforcing good or bad training every time you ride.

Trail riding can be a relaxed hack, a warm-up or cooling-off period, or a way to challenge your horse by riding over uneven terrain—a more stimulating environment than the ring. It helps to keep him fresh while improving balance, fitness, and athletic ability. The varied footing of hilly terrain and open fields develops forwardness, boldness, and mutual trust. The sudden appearance of a running deer, the flurry of a surprised grouse, even a tree or a small stream across the trail teaches your horse to listen and be obedient, strengthening the bond between you.

A lot can be accomplished on a trail ride. Keeping the same speed while going up and down hills is difficult. Turns and diagonal lines on a hillside are even harder. Check out the area first for chuckholes and other dangers, and make sure your horse is fit enough for the ride you plan. Don't do this type of exercise with a very green horse.

Uneven terrain will help the horse develop balance and agility. A few good climbs up a steep slope are excellent for his hindquarters and back and shoulders—good training for a jumper, eventer, dressage, or cutting horse and a pleasant variation from his regular routine as well.

When riding uphill, help your horse. Rise up out of your saddle, and get seat and weight up off your horse's back without hanging over his neck. If you're riding English, assume a jumping position; the horse needs his hindquarters free in order to push himself up.

TRAIL RIDING AS EXERCISE

Correct riding position downhill—rider's body
perpendicular to horse

Correct riding position uphill—rider's weight off seat
In both instances the horse is free to use his
hindquarters to help himself

Going downhill, keep your weight centered and your legs well under you. Your seat should be perpendicular to the horse, over his center of gravity, in your normal riding position, with your lower leg at the girth. This will leave his hindquarters free to maneuver. Allow him some freedom in the head and neck (his balancing mechanism), keeping only enough light contact with the mouth to hold him together.

Trot him on the trail at a brisk eight miles an hour. He'll try to slow down when he's tired, but this is just the time to push him out a little and really make him work. That way he learns to keep a steady pace. If you ride English, be sure to alternate the diagonals you post on to keep the horse from becoming one-sided.

When your horse is up to it, a long canter will do wonders for his wind. Remember to canter on both leads, and don't overdo it. You can tell by his breathing when he's had enough.

An English or Western horse should know what to do when confronted with an obstacle on a trail: walk or trot over it quietly. A horse that is trained to jump will not jump an obstacle unless it is big enough to merit the endeavor. A well-trained hunter is recognized by his ability to clear jumps with a minimum of effort and no more than a safe margin between him and the obstacle. Green horses tend to pop over fallen logs like rabbits.

One Western rider I know takes her horse out on ten- and twenty-mile rides the day before a show to relax him. Of course, her horse is in excellent condition and has been carefully built up to this type of work, and her specialty is endurance riding.

RIDING IN COMPANY

If your horse is going to be used around other horses—at horse shows, hunts, or trail rides—part of his schooling needs to be done in company. Nothing is more annoying to fellow riders than a horse who keeps overtaking and bumping those in

front of him, who gets spooked by everything, or who is so neurotic about being left behind that he jogs all the time or kicks out at horses behind him.

A good trail horse should be able to follow as well as lead. He should take the commonplace in stride, not shying at signs, mailboxes, garbage cans, bridges, trucks, or cars. But even the most sedate horse can be startled by a sudden run-in with an unknown or unexpected object. My quiet, well-mannered horse once froze at the

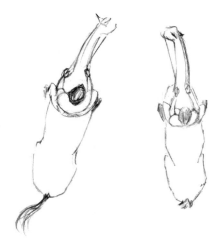

Passing on a trail, rider at left turns his horse's
head toward and rump away from other horse.

sight of a woman pushing an elegant black baby carriage down a country road. He
began trembling, blowing out of his nose and rolling his eyes at this strange, hooded
apparition. Once you know what your horse has experienced before, you can anticipate his fright at the sight of something new.

When riding down the road in a group, go single file, leaving a one-horse distance between each of you. Be sure to observe state laws regarding traffic. And if you
must go on a heavily trafficked road, walk. Trotting or cantering is dangerous near
traffic, and paved surface is hard on a horse's feet and legs. If your horse shied or
slipped on macadam or concrete, it could be disastrous for you both; and the fall of
horse and/or rider on a busy road could be fatal.

Take nothing for granted on the road. Lots of riders assume that cars will slow
down for them. They don't. Some motorists seem to get a kick out of stepping on
the gas as they approach a horse and rider—or blowing the horn. Try to select roads
with a decent shoulder, giving you an avenue of escape should one of these callous
drivers tear by.

Have it understood among your group that the lead rider will notify everyone,
by voice or hand signal, when they are to change gaits. If riders at the front suddenly break into a canter, those at the rear may not be ready and could get hurt.

Should someone fall off on a trail ride, the rest of the group should stop immediately to investigate and give aid. This will also encourage the riderless horse to
rejoin the group, or stop and graze instead of bolting.

If at some point you decide to ride two abreast on the trail (not on the road),
keep about three feet between you so your stirrups won't hook and your horses can't
bite. Be aware of your horse's mood. Remember that flattened ears and bared teeth
are not a friendly demeanor. Should your horse take offense at being passed, stop
and use leg pressure to turn him so his head faces the other horse and his hindquar-

Pulley Rein—Setting Left Hand on Horse's Withers and Pulling Up on Right Rein

ters are turned away. When passing an unfamiliar horse, be sure to leave more than kicking distance between you. And if you have a horse that kicks in these situations, place a red ribbon on his tail—the traditional warning to others—and stay at the end of the line. By observing these and other simple courtesies on the trail, you can make a ride pleasant for all concerned.

Don't ever race on the trail. Your horse should become accustomed to holding steady gaits in company, and the lead horse should set the pace with gaits that aren't too slow or too fast. Should your horse ever decide to take off at a gallop, you can stop him by applying a pulley rein, setting one rein short and pulling up with the other. This throws the horse off balance and will usually stop him. An effective alternative is to turn him in smaller and smaller circles until he has to stop. Always punish this kind of behavior when you do eventually stop: Make him stand and then back him up. (It may be time to go back to the ring for a little homework.)

If you plan to ride on a private road or trail, always ask permission. Treat the land with respect, avoiding lawns, gardens, and field crops. The surest way to lose riding privileges is to ride across a beautiful lawn or newly planted field. Always close gates behind you, and be courteous if you encounter the owner. When I use a private trail during the season, I always send a Christmas card with a sincere thank-you.

PART X

Attire, Competition, and Events

. . . On Saturdays, most everyone is well turned out; proper clothing is worn, horses are braided, tack is clean. During the week, however, only a few make an effort to be presentable. . . . Ninety percent of the members feel that they must be someone with their bizarre equine wardrobes. Only the Master and a handful of the Field observe the dress code. The Master is always correct, her horses impeccably clean, their manes and tails meticulously braided, her person neat and attractive. . . . I appreciate her conscientiousness. . . . As for the individuals in the field, shape up or ship out!

Letter from a "traditionalist" to *The Chronicle of the Horse*

Clothes for Riding

The timeless elegance of equestrian sports is reflected in the traditional dress of each discipline. The clothing is so comfortable and flattering to male and female figures alike that the fashion industry has coopted it. Couturiers like Ralph Lauren and Hermès have taken frocked coats and high-backed breeches from show ring to runway, and recently JCPenney introduced an off-the-rack Hunt Club label.

While it's nice to know that one could go to tea at the Pierre in a hacking jacket, jodhpurs, and high boots, it's more satisfying to use riding dress for riding and to understand the purpose it serves. Adhering to the concept that form follows function, riding attire is designed primarily to be practical. Just as certain bits go with certain bridles and specific trims are typical of specific breeds, particular clothes are more appropriate to one riding situation than another—for practical as well as traditional reasons. Comfort and utility should be the criteria by which riding clothes are chosen.

Most regulation attire, however elegant and expensive, was originally designed with function in mind. The scarlet coats worn by members of a foxhunt, for example, were intended to distinguish them from harriers (rabbit hunters) and stag hunters. Many centuries earlier, when saddles and stirrups were introduced in Asia, tribesmen there were the first to wear boots and trousers to keep their legs and seats from chafing against the leather.

Most qualified instructors insist that students attend a lesson in safe, comfortable riding attire. Even for the first few lessons, when a student is deciding whether or not to continue, safety helmet, suitable footwear, and comfortable long pants are a must. I've cautioned many students who insisted on riding in jeans not specifically

designed for riding—only to complain later of sores on the inside of their legs—that riding clothes are designed for riding, so why not use them?

These days, with such an inexpensive assortment of comfortable riding outfits to choose from, even riding sneakers, there's no excuse for incorrect attire. Modern equestrian clothing not only costs less now but is extremely comfortable. Modeled after biking, hiking, and skiing apparel, it's made in easy styles and lightweight fabrics designed to both absorb moisture and retain warmth.

From the first beginner lesson on, I insist that all students wear hard shoes or boots and a helmet with harness. After the initial trial period, I recommend riding tights or breeches and riding sneakers or paddock boots (if high boots are beyond a student's budget). So far no one has complained, and all have mentioned how comfortable the clothes are.

Unfortunately the rural dress code still prevails in some areas. In the summer barefoot or sandaled riders clad in bathing suits or shorts can often be seen galloping down country roads, hair streaming in the wind. What might look like a lot of fun to a passing motorist will be anything but when these riders wake up the next day to find their knees and thighs rubbed raw. Bare feet, sandals, and regular sneakers have no place around a thousand-pound horse wearing metal shoes. And they offer no security in the stirrups, tending to slide right through them. Only high boots give the best protection to toes and feet, and they are more inclined to stay put in the stirrups.

Novice horse owners often forget about attire when they are figuring the cost of

their new sport. The most expensive, long-term investment of any beginner's riding kit will be a helmet and boots. Appropriate pants, shirt, and probably gloves are the only other apparel you'll need to start off with, and these come in a variety of styles and price ranges.

Since the 1980s, when a growing number of riding fatalities prompted a series of studies on the subject, hat and helmet design has undergone enormous change, and the riding public now accepts protective headgear as an essential part of the equestrian wardrobe. More than 60 percent of horse-related deaths result from head injuries, and they have caused long-term or permanent brain damage in countless other careless riders—a grim reminder to never ride without a helmet or hard hat. No matter how mild-mannered a horse may be, accidents can happen at the most unexpected times.

It's vital to remember that you can fall off a horse even at a walk. After years of

**HARD HATS
AND
HELMETS**

breaking and training horses, showing, hunting, and cross-country riding and eventing, the most serious riding accident of my career occurred when I was walking a horse back to the stable one cold, gray December morning. We were only two hundred yards from home, walking on the narrow shoulder of the road, when a pickup truck came flying up behind us, and the young mare became frightened and bolted. With a fence on one side and the macadam road on the other, there was no room to maneuver. So I had nanoseconds to decide whether to hop off and try to hold her and risk the chance that she would bolt in front of the truck, or stay on and try to control her from the saddle. I chose the latter option but didn't stay on long. She bolted sideways and I slid off, holding on to the reins to keep her from running out on the road—and dislocating a shoulder in the process. My head hit hard, but the helmet I always wear protected it, and I was fortunately able to lead the mare home. The driver never stopped. Accidents like this are impossible to anticipate. You can fall off a horse anytime, anywhere, and odds are good that you'll land on your head. A helmet can be a life-saver.

Though used only for jumping in the past, helmets are worn today for endurance riding, in saddle seat and Western classes—even in combined carriage driving. Two styles of helmet are designed for Western pleasure riding, and protective headgear is permitted in all American Horse Shows Association (AHSA) Western shows. In any AHSA-sponsored show, junior riders may not compete unless they are wearing an approved helmet. But tradition is difficult to change, and some judges oriented more to fashion than to safety still frown on hunt seat riders wearing approved helmets with harness because they're larger and less handsome than the old-fashioned velvet caps. The American Society for Testing and Materials (ASTM) began setting standards for certifying helmets in the 1980s. The Safety Equipment Institute now does the testing, inspecting both the manufacturing plants and the product. Whatever helmet or hat you choose, make sure it is ASTM-SEI approved. Others may be less expensive and look prettier but are worthless if they don't do the job. Just reflect on the price of a head injury.

Some approved schooling helmets are vented and lightweight. Others look like jockey or motorcycle helmets. If the shiny synthetic black and white materials don't appeal to you, colored hats for schooling and cloth covers are available in different colors and color combinations. Polarfleece helmet covers designed for winter riding will let your riding helmet double as a winter hat. All of these items are washable, and many are designed for ventilated helmets. More expensive velvet-covered helmets are for showing. When putting on a helmet, make sure the harness is correctly and firmly fastened. A chin cup is safer than a strap.

Approved Helmet and Protective Vest

Riding Pants

Riding pants were traditionally divided into only two categories: breeches and jodhpurs, both conservatively tailored and colored black, white, or beige. But new styles and fabrics borrowed from other sports, along with the influence of German-style breeches, have revolutionized the market. For schooling there are a variety of close-fitting, lightweight, and comfortable stretch pants to choose from, available in a kaleidoscope of colors and designs. One popular type of pant with shoulder straps (or suspenders) was derived from tights worn by jazz dancers.

BREECHES. Breeches used to mean pants that were worn only with high boots and flared at the hip, ending at the top of the ankle and secured from the midcalf down with buttons, laces, or zippers. But the breeches and riding tights used for schooling are made of the new four-way stretch fabrics and often don't need closures on the legs. These often come with stirrups or have fastenings made of Velcro. Breeches and tights can be worn with either high boots or paddock boots. Those showing in hunt classes wear breeches in the usual assortment of conservative colors. White and off-white are the biggest favorites, as they are for dressage riders. Kentucky-style jodhpurs are worn for show by saddle-seat riders. They have a fitted hip and leg and flare at the ankle to accommodate jodhpur boots.

Lightweight *insulated pants* with leg zippers, designed to be worn alone or over others for winter riding, are also called breeches. Incredibly warm Polartec four-way stretch breeches and another style lined with this insulating fabric are designed for cold-weather riding.

FULL- OR HALF-SEAT LEATHER BREECHES. This innovation was introduced by German dressage designers. The more expensive full-seat type helps the rider stay close to the saddle. A less pricey variation, perfect for schooling, is made of a synthetic look-alike fabric in a range of colors. Stretch riding tights designed for summer use often have synthetic full seats in complementary colors perforated for ventilation. These have matching tank or halter tops for more comfortable schooling in the hot months.

Concern for riding comfort has encouraged more utilitarian designs and fabrics, and today's riding pants suit every size and preference. Many different types of waist closures, some elastic, are designed for women; a style with pleats in front fits full feminine figures.

Boots

JODHPUR BOOTS. These boots are the correct footwear for saddle-seat classes and are often worn by children in hunter classes, who wear jodhpurs with a garter strap under the knee to keep the pants in place. The boots are made in patent leather for showing in saddle-seat classes and regular black or brown leather with elastic or zippers at the ankle for show, schooling, and pleasure riding.

FULL-LENGTH BOOTS. These boots were originally developed to protect the rider's leg and serve as a riding aid. A well-fitted boot that is secure on the foot helps the leg to remain in its most effective position. Unlike the human leg muscle, the boot's long, stiff surface lends a uniform driving power to the muscles and nerve endings in your horse's sides, affecting his forward movement.

Boots that are too pliable and/or don't fit properly can make your position less stable, interfering with leg aids. Unsupported ankles will cause legs to move around, making the rider grip to stay secure—interpreted by the horse as a "go forward" signal.

When boots are too tight they restrict movement, causing numbness in the foot, ankle, or leg, followed by blisters on toes, ankles, or heels. Those too narrow in the toe can cause bunions, hammertoes, or severe ingrown toenails. If, after trying them on, you find that you have hard-to-fit feet or calves, you'll need custom- or semi-custom-made boots. Although more expensive than the presized, off-the-shelf brands, you'll save money and avoid discomfort in the long run.

SEMICUSTOM BOOTS. These boots are a compromise, offering standard foot sizes to match custom calf measurements or vice versa. Custom boots, frequently called made-to-measure, are constructed to fit individual feet and legs. (Be sure to follow the manufacturer's directions to the letter when measuring yourself for custom boots.)

Try on boots at the end of the day when your feet are largest, using baby powder or silicone spray or thin plastic produce bags to help slip them on and off. Wear riding socks and breeches, of course, and be sure to walk in the boots and ride in them. Boots that fit well should be snug across the instep and wide enough in front to

High Boot

Newmarket Boot

Field Boot

Jodhpur Boot with Elastic Ankle

Laced Riding Boot

allow you to fan your toes out. In the saddle, your heel should stay down in the bottom of the boot, not slide up. The tall part of the boot, or the shaft, should be snug at the calf and not slip down. Although they do slip down a little when broken in (usually an inch or an inch and a half), the shaft should be as tall as possible, coming to the bottom of the kneecap in front and to the point where it bends in back, without restricting knee movement.

FIELD BOOTS. These boots come in both black and brown. The former are worn in hunter classes, the latter in informal shows or for casual wear.

PADDOCK BOOTS. Heeled and usually made of leather, these boots are worn with jodhpurs, riding tights, or chaps for schooling. They lace higher above the ankle to give more support than jodhpur boots and are usually made of heavier leather that offers more foot protection. (Tall paddock boots are in fashion, so be sure to get the kind designed for riding.) Waterproof, insulated paddock boots made of leather or synthetic materials are worn in the winter with chaps or insulated pants.

RIDING SNEAKERS. These are too soft to offer the same protection as tall leather boots or paddock boots, but many riders now wear them for everyday riding. They do give ankle support and are cooler in hot weather. But they lack the leg contact, toe protection, and stirrup safety of boots. Endurance and trail riders use them a lot, finding them perfect for their purposes. Because they're lightweight and comfortable, I find riding sneakers comfortable for teaching in mild weather. They come in a variety of colors to match today's riding clothes and are about the same price as regular high-quality sneakers. Some are designed to go with half-chaps.

RUBBERS. Rubbers come in all sizes to fit over boots, protecting them from manure, water, and mud when you're not riding. But left on for extended periods, they will damage leather and stitching and leave marks.

TALL BLACK BOOTS. These boots, without laces, are traditional for dressage, and the favored style has a "Spanish cut," curving up on the outside of the top of the calf to give an elegant look to the leg. Many are designed with a stirrup rest on the back of the heel. Those who plan to show should invest in a pair of well-fitted, tall leather boots, which really add to the turnout, or overall appearance, of horse and rider. But footwear, however elegant, can't replace riding lessons. As one judge put it: "Your boots shouldn't look more beautiful than your riding."

WINTER BOOTS. Winter boots are designed to keep your feet warm in subzero temperatures. Nonleather, waterproof, and insulated, they are inexpensive and come in tall or paddock styles. When the temperatures start sliding, I wouldn't dream of going out without them. For those preferring a more elegant look, insulated black or brown leather paddock boots with or without matching half-chaps are available as well.

WELLINGTONS. These traditional English rubber boots have a heavy tread designed for wearing around the barn, particularly when mucking out stalls, and for walking to and from the pasture in muddy weather. They are heavy, not as tall or well fitted at the top as high boots, and they are not meant to be ridden in. A pair of these over heavy socks will keep feet dry and warm, saving wear and tear on regular riding boots.

WET WEATHER BOOTS. These boots are made of rubber or vinyl with reinforced toes. They tend to be short in the shaft and often fit loosely around the calf, which is unflattering to the rider's leg. They also lack the support of the stiffer leather boot and tend to be hot in warm weather, causing feet to sweat, and cold in low temperatures. Many riders choose them as an inexpensive answer to a high boot but they rarely fit as well as leather ones do, and some judges frown on them.

Boot Care

Manufacturers claim that with proper care, the life span of custom or semicustom boots is five to ten years, and two to three years for the ready-to-wear type. Boots for riding should not be worn when cleaning stalls; urine and manure will damage the leather. When walking in them, take care not to shuffle, which wears down heels and toes unevenly.

In wet, muddy, and cold weather, wear rubbers to protect the boots and keep your feet warm. Never put boots away wet, and always use boot trees, which keep the ankles from breaking down and wrinkling as the boots dry and makes them easier to clean. Use leather-cleaning products recommended by the boot manufacturer, and be meticulous when cleaning the inner calf and ankle, where sweat accumulates.

Boots should be stored shaft down on special boot brackets designed to promote air circulation, available through tack shops and catalogs. Compared with the purchase price, the cost of taking proper care of boots is a small one.

BOOT TREES, JACKS, AND PULLS. *Boot trees* of wood, metal, or plastic should always be put in boots after they are taken off. They facilitate cleaning, prevent boots from breaking down and wrinkling at the ankle, and keep the shaft straight.

Boot pulls are traditional English hooks with handles that slip into the loops on either side of the boot to help you slide it on. These are invaluable, and my advice is "Never leave home without them." I keep an extra set in the car.

A *boot jack* is just as essential for getting boots off. Boots that fit well have one drawback: they can't be removed easily without a jack. I suggest getting two, in wood or plastic, one for home and another for the car.

Chaps

ENGLISH CHAPS. English chaps are ideal for winter or cool-weather riding. They are adapted from the Western style and unfringed, with a more conservative cut and more subdued color selection. The suede adheres to leather- or suede-seated saddles, helping the rider to sit closer to the saddle. The chaps are warm, comfortable, and easy to put on, and they can be worn over fitted jeans, riding pants, or riding tights. A word of caution: If you're in the habit of using them for schooling and plan to be in a show, stop wearing them for several days before the competition. You'll need to get reaccustomed to the looser feel of breeches in the saddle.

Exercise Chaps Used by English Riders

HALF CHAPS. Covering the lower leg from knee to ankle, half chaps probably evolved from leggings. Today they are worn over riding pants, with sneakers, jodhpurs, or paddock boots, to give a smoother leg surface against the horse (though not as consistent as the uniformity of a tall riding boot). The more expensive leather half chaps are stiffer and give the appearance of a tall fitted boot. These are usually available in black or brown, come in different lengths, and have a stirrup that slips over the boot. They zip up the outside and are most often secured with Velcro straps. Those of better quality are reinforced on the inside leg.

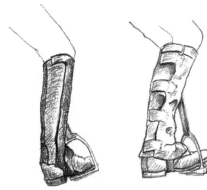

A. Leather Half Chaps   B. Suede Half Chaps

Body Protector Vests

The greatest number of nonfatal riding injuries affect the upper body, trunk, and torso. Since 1996 the American Horse Shows Association has required all riders competing in the cross-country phase of combined training to wear a protective body vest. (See illustration page 398.) Although they don't offer the same degree of protection that helmets give to the head, they do soften the blow of falling and reduce the severity of broken bones and bruising. (But they can't protect internal organs or prevent rotation and flexion of spine injury.)

British Equestrian Trade Association (BETA) standards require a vest to cover the torso, to the bottom of the rib cage in front and over the kidneys in back. Some of the materials used are the same found in bulletproof vests and in those worn by rodeo riders to protect themselves from the bull's horns. Their density makes these vests terribly hot, and some riders put them in ice chests before donning them for competition (a practice that isn't encouraged because of the possibly harmful affect of moisture on the composition of the material).

Despite complaints that vests should be more protective of the lower rib cage, abdomen, and pelvis, a vest is a worthwhile investment for a rider who does a lot of jumping or cross-country competing. They range in price from two to three hundred dollars.

Gloves

Gloves are essential for riding and driving. Apart from keeping the hands relatively clean, they give a firmer hold of the reins, protect hands from blisters, keep them warm so they can function when it's cold, and prevent slipping when it's hot. In pleasure or show ring driving, they also give a finished, smart look to your attire. Although required in only a few areas of showing—among them saddle-seat classes and all FEI dressage classes—most riders wear them whether they are showing or not. Once accustomed to gloves, one feels undressed without them. They should always be worn when lunging or long-reining a horse.

Gloves come in all weights and sizes and a variety of colors in the synthetic materials. Cotton string gloves, with leather on palms and between the fingers, are ideal for warm weather. For winter wear warm, soft synthetic gloves reinforced with leather, or riding mittens with the pinkie separated and the grip reinforced. Leather gloves, always good for fall and spring riding, are more expensive but give a nice feel of the reins. If showing, you will want to have one or two pairs of gloves just for that purpose. (I go through at least two a season.) White, which looks well with white breeches, is traditional for dressage riders, but it calls attention to the hands. Unless their hands are really excellent and quiet, lower-level riders are better off with a well-fitted pair of black gloves.

Undergarments

Undergarments that rub or bind cause blisters and sores and make riding a nightmare. Equestrian clothing manufacturers have developed a variety of highly comfortable undergarments, including panties for women with extra padding and above-the-knee pant liners in lightweight stretch fabrics that eliminate panty lines. Special sports bras give extra support.

Silk or silklike underwear, socks, and glove liners are designed for winter riding, and socks that pull moisture from the skin are comfortable in the summer. (Some have black shafts that blend in with the top of your boots.)

BACK SUPPORTS. These are available in styles that can be worn under or over your clothes. They are excellent for weak or sore lower backs, as knee supports are for problem knees.

Shirts and Jackets

These should be well-fitted and comfortable, allowing you to move your shoulders and arms easily without feeling restricted. When jumping and reaching forward in a crest release, the sleeves should still keep the wrists covered, and the jacket shouldn't climb up the waist. The length of the jacket should be appropriate for your height and fitted at the waist to allow ample breathing room. To keep a jacket clean at a show, put it on just before entering the ring and remove it as soon as the class is over.

Most of us compete in hot weather, when cotton is the best choice for a shirt and jacket. Sleeves can be long or short but must not be absent. (When a show committee announces that riders can go jacketless, it doesn't mean sleeveless.)

Hunter riders can choose from a variety of jacket styles and colors, dark green and blue being most popular. Dressage riders are limited to black and dark blue. Anyone planning to compete should read the rule book section on attire before shopping. Even within specific disciplines, certain classes may require a slightly different form of dress. Many casual riding jackets available from tack shops and through catalogs can also be worn as regular sport jackets.

POLARTEC. These shirts, jackets, and vests work well for winter riding, either individually or in layers. A down vest is always a good selection for a layered winter wardrobe. When working indoors in the winter, I wear a silk or cotton turtleneck over a sleeveless thermal underwear top and a long Polartec shirt or wool sweater over that, topped by a down vest and heavy jacket. By the middle of the workout, I'm down to the shirt or sweater. While cooling the horse down, I put the vest back on (usually throwing a folded cooler across my horse's hindquarters at the same time), then wear my jacket over my shoulders as I walk him out.

Driving Attire

This can be any comfortable, practical, attractive clothing. In shows, the type of horse you drive and the class will determine the formality of your dress. Driving colors are traditionally conservative and the clothes are tailored. Derbies are traditional headgear for men, and floppy-brimmed hats for women. A sport jacket or suit is acceptable in all but the most formal classes.

A lap robe, knee rug, or apron is usually required in competition to protect the driver's clothes from road dust, keep off the chill, and prevent clothes from being stained with harness-dressing oil. Coverings should be dark and blend with the upholstery. In short, "ladies" and "gentlemen" are expected to live up to that description when they drive.

WESTERN RIDING CLOTHES

The highly decorative, spangled, sequined outfits traditionally worn by women in barrel-racing contests were designed in the past to add a little sparkle to Western rodeos, which began as a dusty, colorless, predominantly male sport. For many years this kind of dress carried over to other riders in the show ring, where many contestants showed up in floppy earrings, balloon sleeves, sequined vests, and other flashy adornments. Later on, Western show dress went through a conservative period, in which riders favored tailored suits and color-coordinated hats and shirts similar to everyday dress. Today's show ring outfits are brighter and more colorful again; the blouses, shirts, and vests are designed to catch the judge's eye in equitation classes, bearing little resemblance to outfits worn on the range.

The working Western rider maintains just about the same wardrobe favored in years past—jeans, chaps, denim shirt, neckerchief, hat, and comfortable boots—just as practical now as they were then. Like his equipment, a cowboy's clothes are all highly functional.

Chaps

Originally intended to protect legs from prickly thorns and brush while insulating them from wind, rain, and cold, chaps were formerly made of wool for maximum protection. Nowadays they are usually made of suede and can be quite elaborate. Chaps are well tailored and should end below the heel when the rider is mounted, adding a long, elegant look to the leg.

Western Chaps

Fitted Western Frontier–Style Jeans or Pants

For showing, these pants are worn under chaps, which are mandatory in all classes except equitation. In some shows women wear dress pants with a dress blouse. A decorative or plain suede vest is often worn over a dress shirt, with or without other accessories like scarf, choker, rosette, or silver pin at the collar.

Western show riders sometimes wear the dressier Western *frontier suit* for halter classes, a tailored jacket with matching, straight frontier pants or frontier pants with a vest and neck accessory. In other classes, particularly Quarter Horse equitation, women don a sparkling bright-colored dress blouse or shirt, often set off by a contrasting vest. All Western riders complete their costume with a wide belt and large buckle, usually made of silver.

Men's Frontier Pants

Boots

Boots used to be shorter in the old days, largely because they were easier to put on. The heel was also higher, to keep the foot from being pulled through the stirrup when roping. High heels also dug more effectively into the ground when a wrangler was "running down the rope" on a steer. Modern Western boots have a variety of heel sizes and come in different heights, colors, and styles, many elaborately tooled. A good pair can cost hundreds of dollars; the price depends on the hand carving and the skins used.

Rubbers for protection against mud and rain are especially contoured for a pointed toe and are sold in Western tack and apparel shops.

Neckerchiefs

Bandits weren't the only ones to pull a neckerchief over their nose. All working cowboys did and still do in hot, dusty weather or windstorms, especially when riding behind a herd of cattle to keep the dust and dirt out of their mouths and noses.

Fancy Western Boots

Hats

Hats were designed with a wide brim to act as a sunshade during long summer days on the trail. The high crown allows air to circulate underneath and keep the head cool. "Ten-gallon hats" were so called because they were often used to drink from—by both cowboys and horses. A hat and chaps are usually worn when working cattle and in shows or at rodeos. In hot climates a hat is a welcome partner.

Gloves

Leather gloves are less popular today than synthetics, which breathe better, absorb moisture in hot weather, come lined for winter riding, and are washable. Most Western gloves are handmade, so check the stitching carefully.

In roping classes gloves protect against burns, and some are designed especially for this purpose, with palms of leather or synthetic leather to give extra strength and protection while allowing a good feel of the rope. Other working and roping gloves are made from goatskin or kangaroo hide, soft leather that molds to a rider's hand; a particularly popular type is made of aquasuede, with a pad on the inside of each palm. For summer there are cotton string and stronger poly-cotton gloves. All-weather gloves, which are supple, wash easily, and wear like iron, were recently developed for jockeys who wanted a warm glove that gave them the same feel of the reins as the summerweight. Most Western-wear stores carry a few of these styles, and a tack shop can order others for you.

HAIRSTYLES

Whether the riding style is English or Western, women's hair should be tied back in a braid or bun, or worn in a hairnet. Flowing locks may be fashionable at times among both sexes, but they are not very practical in the saddle, tending to fall in a rider's eyes or mouth when he or she is jumping or trying to circumvent a barrel in record time. Also, long hair looks terrible straggling out from under a hat. Most show classes call for a neat, workmanlike appearance, and that includes hair.

Many attractive hair nets have been designed for English and Western women riders. Resembling a snood, they come complete with a tailored bow to contain long hair and are available in tack shops or through catalogs. Both English and Western lady riders wear snoods with modest ornamentation. Women with especially long hair who usually wear it in a long braid down the back may need a hat a size larger for showing, doubling the braid back and under to keep it tidy.

JEWELRY

The English rider wears a pin on a stock or choker. Originally the stock was an emergency leg wrap worn with a large safety pin to secure it, and one sign of an educated rider was whether he or she could tie a stock from scratch. These days stocks can be put on in one pretied piece that's secured behind the neck, and plain safety pins have been replaced with more decorative ones.

Women with pierced ears frequently wear earrings when showing in many of the English classes, but they are always conservative and never of the dangling variety.

Women in Western pleasure and equitation classes wear jewelry as an integral part of their attire. Earrings, often large but not dangling, are required. These are usually made of silver or semiprecious stones like turquoise, the color coordinated with the rider's outfit. Frequently a matching neck ornament is worn. Both men and women wear a decorative belt buckle, usually of silver, to set off the whole outfit.

·chapter·

32

Events and Competitions

FOX-HUNTING

Tallyho

In past centuries, when foxhunting was the prerogative of the landed gentry, it was fashionable in London and Dublin salons to make snide remarks about the sport. Oscar Wilde delighted society by referring to foxhunters as the "unspeakable in pursuit of the inedible," and the sport has been maligned by some circles ever since—usually by people who know nothing about it.

Some hunting enthusiasts feel that the hunt field is the best possible training ground for junior riders. Hunting demands a high degree of equestrian skill, as much as or more than riding on the flat or jumping in a show ring. Hunters are all-around equestrians who know the importance of keeping their mounts and equipment in top condition. And riding cross-country demands quick thinking and concentration to cope with a variety of changing situations.

Although some conservationists and animal rights groups deplore foxhunting as a cruel and exclusive sport, many hunts today are *drag hunts,* in which a burlap bag partly soaked in fox urine is dragged over the field for the hounds to follow. When a live animal is used, he eludes the hounds and "goes to ground" 99 percent of the time.

Where foxes are hunted, they are nurtured by huntsmen, who put food out for them during lean winters and keep an eye on their condition. Those that give the best "run" have often been around for years, learning to be "wily as a fox."

Hunting is exclusive in the sense that it takes money to pursue it, but it is no more expensive than sailing, skiing, golfing, or sports car racing. It also keeps lands open, natural, and maintained.

Membership fees are about equal to those of any other club, and all hunts welcome visitors during the year. Some sponsor junior hunts for young riders and special hunts for adult novices. Those who don't want to hunt actively can follow by car or can "hilltop" on horseback, led by a hunt member on a parallel route, from which they can watch the action and jump a few low fences if desired.

Hunts depend on the goodwill and support of their communities to exist, and usually half their budgets are raised through public events like rummage sales, hunter trials, and auctions. Members go to great effort to keep the fields up and the fences mended.

Joining a Hunt

If you'd like to participate in a local hunt, begin by calling the hunt secretary. Ask if you may hunt on the next visitors' day and what the cap fee is. You'll probably be sent a fixture card, stating the time and place of the meet.

On the day of the hunt, arrive a half hour early, neatly and properly turned out. Mount up before the meet begins. Introduce yourself to the master (who may be a woman). Pay the capping fee (which was originally collected in the huntsman's cap) to one of the staff soon after their arrival. Check with the secretary to be sure.

Visitors stay to the rear of the field during a hunt, and juniors ride at the very end. Leave at least one horse length between riders when hacking. Never talk during a check (an interruption of the chase), when the huntsman has to listen carefully to the hounds.

Hunting Attire

At a formal hunt and on opening day of the season, horses are braided up and members and guests wear regulation dress. (Guests wear a black melton jacket, fawn or canary breeches, canary vest, riding shirt with stock and black boots, and a derby.) Less formal clothes are worn in midweek. During the cubing season in late summer, when the young hounds are being trained, a "ratcatcher outfit" is worn—usually a tweed jacket, brown boots, an ordinary hard hunt cap, and a casual (ratcatcher) shirt.

Velvet hunt caps or hard hats are worn only by members of the staff and children during a hunt. Though derbies are traditional for others in the field, most informed riders wear regulation headgear these days.

Before scarlet became traditional for experienced members of a hunt, the colors of the master's livery were worn. This tradition is still followed in parts of England, where yellow, blue, and several other colors are used. Scarlet coats are often called "Pink" coats, the name of a fashionable nineteenth-century English tailor, not a color. Much of the clothing and equipment originally worn was very functional. The stock was a long, white linen bandage worn around a rider's neck in case he or his horse was injured. It fastens with a plain gold bandage pin, worn horizontally. Leather sandwich cases and brandy flasks are carried on the saddle so that members can have a drink or a snack during long hours in the field.

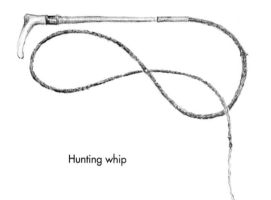

Hunting whip

In A shows (see page 412), special classes restricted to hunt members are judged on the appointments of riders, who are required to wear formal attire suited to their position in the hunt. Bridles must be sewn, an extra pair of gloves tucked away under the girth, and the sandwich case and flask filled with traditional contents—ham or cheese, and brandy. All this is carefully checked out by the judge.

Hunt Staff

Members of the hunt staff include the *huntsman,* who carries wire cutters and a pocketknife; and the *master,* who carries the horn if he is hunting the hounds. If a professional huntsman is employed, he will carry the horn, and the *whippers-in* will carry a set of couples (a brace used to keep two hounds together) and spare stirrup leathers draped over the right shoulder and buckled under the left arm. All staff members carry hunting whips with long thongs, used to control the hounds; these have a horned handle that's also handy for opening gates.

SHOWING OFF

A horse show is a good place to measure your progress as a rider and to compare your horse and his skills with others. Above all, it is a challenge. Even when a class is based on the performance of your horse, it is your riding ability that will bring out his best. Of course, winning a ribbon is also great for the ego, and depending on the rating of the show, getting pinned can increase the value of your horse. At its best, showing is great fun. At worst, it's a neurotic pastime where winning becomes the only thing that counts and sportsmanship is forgotten.

Many national organizations—among them the American Horse Shows Association, the American Quarter Horse Association, and the United States Dressage Federation—sponsor horse shows all over the country. Riders and horses can accumulate points in specific divisions that make them eligible to compete for that year's national championship awards at a specified location in the country. Some shows are referred to as "recognized." These are given under the auspices of the AHSA, which keeps a record of the proceedings; members can accumulate points, qualifying them for championship classes in the larger shows around the country.

In many areas where horses are abundant, other organizations sponsor horse shows on a local level, offering an opportunity for the less experienced rider or green horse to compete. Pony Clubs, 4-H clubs, charities, and riding clubs and associations, as well as schools and fraternal organizations, all underwrite the cost of unrecognized schooling shows. Entry fees at smaller shows are usually less than those at larger, recognized ones. Your local tack shop is a good place to get a listing of local shows. Many areas have regional horse organizations that sponsor shows, clinics, and other educational events. By becoming a member of the American Horse Shows Association (see Appendix F), you will receive a rule book that covers all the disciplines and a monthly publication giving show listings.

Entering a Show

Before you enter your first few shows, go over the prize list with your instructor/ trainer to pick classes suited to both you and your horse. For a competition where the entries must be mailed in by a closing date, particularly a dressage or combined training competition, try to get your entry in ahead of that date. Because of the time requirements, this type of competition can handle only a certain number of entries, and even small shows are often filled before the deadline (in which case you'll have to go on a waiting list). Popular recognized events and dressage shows can be counted on to fill up before the closing date.

If you or your horse are unable to attend for reasons of ill health, be sure to phone the secretary to "scratch" (withdraw) your entry so someone on the waiting list can take your place. If your horse is ill or injured, *getting a vet's certificate to the show committee within a specified time* will usually entitle you to a partial refund.

If you are new to showing, select classes in which you feel confident. Because of the additional pressure on both rider and horse in a show setting, enter classes in which you'll use familiar, comfortable skills. If your horse is accustomed to jumping two feet six inches at home, for instance, don't start him at three feet in the show. And if you're working first level dressage at home, enter training level classes to give you and your horse a chance.

Preparing for a Show

Three to four days before leaving for a show, bathe and trim your horse. The day before, lay out all freshly cleaned tack and clothing. Load the trailer with tack and equipment, have the truck gassed up, and check the tires and oil. Braiding can be done the night before a show, but bring along extra elastics, yarn, or tape for patching up. If you are stabling overnight at the show grounds, make sure to bring hay, grain, and stall-cleaning tools, a muck bucket, water and wash buckets, and extra bedding. (Or phone in advance to reserve extra bedding.) No matter what the weatherman says, always toss in rain gear. To complete your preparations, pack folding chairs and a cooler for drinks and food. Try to persuade a friend to come with you to act as groom. Many of my students share this task with each other, alternately showing and grooming. It takes a lot of pressure off.

For all combined events and dressage shows, you will either be sent your riding times or told when to call to get them. Plan your arrival accordingly. When practical, come in the night or afternoon before a competition. It's a good way to accustom your horse to new surroundings and gives eventing riders a chance to walk the cross-country course a few extra times. If the show is nearby, arrive several hours before your first class, allowing plenty of time to pick up the show packet (which includes your number, class times, ring numbers, a show schedule,

and other necessary materials). At a regular show allow ample time to make your entries and get your numbers.

After cleaning up your horse and laying out jacket and number, warm him up. Lunge him, if this is part of the usual warm-up routine—if you want to perform at your best, this isn't a time to cut corners. Then take him to the warm-up area so he becomes acclimated to it. Make sure to wear your helmet, and have your friend bring a clean jacket, the number, a rag to wipe off boots at the last minute, and a brush and towel for a final polish for your horse. When it's that kind of day, don't forget fly spray.

When warming up for a jumping class, make sure to use the practice fences set up in the schooling arena, keeping a careful eye out for other riders. Combined training riders must remember to jump only those practice fences with red on the right. (A mistake here will get you disqualified.) Be ready at the in gate a few minutes before you are due. Before you enter the ring, take a few quiet minutes alone with your horse to focus on what you're about to do, review your course or your test in your mind, and tune in to your horse. Be sure your number is on and secure and the correct one for the class. Have your assistant give you and your horse a last-minute once-over to be sure everything is clean and tidy. When you do enter the ring, smile, do your best, and enjoy your ride. Good luck!

RECOGNIZED SHOWS

Recognized shows are sponsored by the American Horse Shows Association and are governed by its rules, with regulations for all breed categories and all English and Western classes. Each discipline is divided into divisions to cover the full spectrum of skill levels for ponies, horses, and riders. Shows are rated *A, B,* or *C,* relative to the number of classes in each division and the amount of prize money to be awarded. Often the *A* shows will last three days to a week. Sometimes recognized shows have a combination of *A, B,* and *C* divisions.

A division is a group of classes designated for a specific breed, type of horse, or type of riding. Each competes for its own champion and reserve champion. There are divisions for Arabians and half-Arabs, for Quarter Horses and hunters, for saddle-seat, pleasure riding, and Western stock. Some *A* shows break these divisions down still further, perhaps offering classes for Arabian mares or green conformation hunters. Often there are age and experience limitations for both horses and riders. For example, there are classes for twelve years and under and for novice or maiden equestrians (a designation that refers to the number of blue ribbons a rider has won in that class).

Because the best riders in the country appear at AHSA shows, competition is stiff and the horses entered are usually expensive and well bred. By winning divisions and specific classes in various regions of the country and accumulating enough points, you and your horse can become eligible for national championship competitions. A rider new to showing might find it less intimidating to begin at a local schooling show, where you will be governed by the same rules but will compete against riders and/or horses of similar experience.

The AHSA charges a nominal fee for membership and admits juniors (anyone under eighteen as of January 1 of any given year) at half price. Members are entitled to the monthly magazine *Horse Show,* which lists results from all recognized shows, and a yearly rule book with a calendar of all shows, their location, and the names, addresses, and ratings of the licensed judges and ring stewards.

Entry fees for individual classes in AHSA shows are more expensive than in schooling shows because of the number of licensed officials required, the high cost of running a show, and the elevated status of the classes. (Championship and stake classes, which offer cash prizes and more classes, cost more.) Higher rates prevail at A shows, where cash prizes are largest and the rating the highest. In all recognized competitions, entry fees must be mailed in in advance by a certain deadline. Even schooling dressage shows and events require early entries to facilitate time scheduling. Where post entries are allowed, you are charged extra at the secretary's stand.

Dressage

Dressage is a classical form of equestrian competition that goes as far back as written history. Though it has yet to attain the following in the United States that it has in Europe, the discipline is becoming increasingly popular with American riders. Many all-breed shows, particularly those for the Morgan and Arabian, include dressage in their programs, and there are even Western classes in the discipline.

Dressage seeks to develop a harmony between a horse's physique and his ability. Its goal is to make him calm, loose, and flexible, appearing to act of his own accord by submitting confidently, attentively, and generously to the imperceptible control of the rider. Horse and rider are tested at many levels. Training level from first

TYPES OF COMPETITION

A. Hunt Seat Rider

B. Dressage Rider

to fourth is governed by AHSA rules, while the Prix St. Georges through Grand Prix levels are governed by Fédération Equestrie International (FEI) rules. At each level except the third, there are four AHSA tests, which progress with the development of the horse's gaits and his ability to move forward straight and to bend in accordance with curved lines. As a horse progresses, he becomes stronger, carrying more of his weight on the hindquarters as well as maintaining an increasingly soft contact with the bit.

Another competition is the *Kur,* or freestyle, which is usually performed at the first level and up (the upper level being the most exciting). It is choreographed by the rider to incorporate required movements at each specific level and set to music of his or her choice. In a dressage test, rider and horse are judged individually on each movement, based on a score of zero to ten, with five a passing grade. Some of the more important movements are multiplied by two. These always include the last category of the tests, called *collective marks,* when the judge scores the quality of the horse's gaits, submissiveness, and impulsion and the rider's position and use of aids. The final score is then converted to a percentage. This is an encouraging form of competition in which riders essentially compete with themselves and get a sense of achievement as the percentages mount from show to show.

Combined Training

Combined training originated in the cavalry, where horses were expected to prove obedient and disciplined in dressage and close-order drill on the parade ground, while showing the boldness, endurance, and speed necessary to carry dispatches long distances over rough ground in the shortest period of time. Stadium jumping became a way to entertain troops at Sunday shows, while demonstrating that a horse still had the fitness and stamina to finish the demanding course after the punishing fifteen-to-twenty-mile ride of the previous day. Since the U.S. equestrian team won the world championship for eventing in 1975 and the Olympic gold medal in 1976, more and more amateur riders have taken up this exciting sport, which has three types: horse trials, two-day events, and three-day events. Each includes distinct tests in three phases: dressage, cross-country, and show jumping. (The dressage test is always first, but the latter two can be run in either order.) Many one-day events are locally sponsored. Of the three, the cross-country phase has the most influence on the score, with the dressage test second in importance and show jumping last. In cold climates winter events are limited to two phases: dressage and show jumping. Sometimes for schooling purposes just the cross-country phase will be run midseason.

Combined training is governed by the U.S. Combined Training Association (USCTA) rule book. Advanced, intermediate, preliminary, training, and novice levels are offered. To encourage amateurs to participate, organizers frequently offer divisions specifically for novice or beginning novice horses and riders. In the *dressage* test, the complexity of exercises and gaits performed are determined by the competition level and judged in the same way as the tests described earlier. A good dressage test is an excellent start on the road to a blue ribbon.

The *cross-country* test is designed to prove the speed, endurance, and jumping ability of a well-trained and conditioned horse. It also demonstrates the rider's riding skill and ability to pace the horse. As the divisions progress from novice to advanced, the type, number, width, and height of the obstacles increase, along with the required speed. The optimum time is based on the distance of the course and the speed a horse should average at a specific level.

International and some national competitions divide the endurance test into four timed phases: roads and tracks, which is done at a trot or slow canter; the steeplechase course, ridden at a gallop; and another roads and tracks, immediately afterward. The last and most demanding phase is performed at a gallop over a cross-country course that has as many as thirty-five jumps. It is preceded by a required ten-minute rest stop, during which each horse is given a complete veterinary check and is washed and scraped down; his shoes are studded and legs greased to allow him to slide over any jump he takes a bit too low.

Unlike collapsible show jumps, eventing obstacles are bone-cracking solid. Natural terrain and modified natural jumps, like ditches, banks, and water, are all integrated according to the level of difficulty. Penalties are given for any refusal or fall at a fence and for crossing the finish line a quarter second or more over the optimal time. At the highest levels of combined training, riders are also penalized for finishing the cross-country phase under the optimal time. All in all, it is the most exciting yet most demanding phase of the competition.

Show jumping or *stadium jumping* is a test to prove the suppleness, obedience, and jumping ability of a horse over a course of a variety of obstacles. It also demonstrates the rider's knowledge of pace and skill of handling the horse in a jumping arena. The length of the course, the type and number of obstacles, and the speed required are determined by the level

Cross-Country Phase in Combined Training

of competition. All phases of combined training are scored by penalty points, not positive ones. Thus the horse and rider with the fewest penalties will win.

Although it requires considerable time to condition yourself and your horse, combined training is a lot of fun. And because it involves all aspects of training and management, it's a great learning experience and confidence builder. Even if eliminated from an event, you can come home feeling that you've learned a lot about yourself and your horse. Just the process of teaching him to jump over a ditch or into water is a big training step forward.

4-H Competitions

4-H Clubs, financed by the U.S. Department of Agriculture, run shows all over the country, ranging from small local competitions to county and state fairs. At times these are run according to the 4-H's own rules. The prize list will note if a show follows AHSA or American Quarter Horse Association rules.

Many 4-H shows use the democratic Danish system of judging, which in effect enables a child to compete against himself—easy on a young ego. In any given class, for example, there might be five or six blue-ribbon winners, rated first blue, second blue, and so on, with a cash prize for each at county and state fairs. Or the judge might decide that none of the riders deserved a blue, that all were riding on a red level instead. This method of judging increases the chances that a child riding a swaybacked, Roman-nosed horse will win a ribbon. Cash prizes give children an opportunity to earn money for clothes and riding equipment and/or to cover show expenses.

4-H class divisions are often different from regular horse shows. Some classes are open to all children under eighteen, and a child of ten could find himself competing with a teenager. Equitation classes are sometimes split into pony and horse divisions, even though they are judged only on the rider. In general these shows are well run and fun to go to. Points accumulated at local 4-H competitions will determine whether a child is eligible for the state fair championship. You can get in touch with the 4-H clubs in your area by phoning the local county cooperative extension service.

Pony Club

Pony Clubs do sponsor horse shows, but they focus more on team competitions and games. At rallies the members compete in teams. Sportsmanship, animal care, and riding skills, rather than winning, are emphasized. Experienced members and volunteer adults help teach newcomers.

Despite the relative competence and expense of their mounts, children can compete equally against each other in Pony Clubs because of the strong emphasis on stable management. In addition to a written test, club rallies are judged on dressage, cross-country, and stable management. After several years in this group, a child can become a competent all-around equestrian.

Pony Club is a volunteer organization to which parents and interested adults contribute their time. In the past many professionals donated time, but the current economic climate has changed, and consequently riding instruction is inconsistent in some areas of the country.

For a list of Pony Clubs, write to the United States Pony Club. (See Appendix F.)

Not to be confused with the National Cutting Horse Association, which sponsors cutting events open to all breeds, the AQHA sponsors a variety of shows and contests open only to Quarter Horses. It awards points for ability and conformation, in order to maintain and promote the breed's high quality.

To receive a championship award or register of merit listing, a horse must win a required number of points at halter and performance. The number of points awarded is determined by the number of entries in a class. The approved performance events are cutting, reining, roping, working cow horse, barrel racing, English pleasure, Western pleasure, Western riding, and pleasure driving.

While the AQHA has its own rule book, some of its shows are given under AHSA auspices, in which points can be accumulated toward AHSA Association shows. Free rule books are given to paid-up members.

Other Breed Programs

Many other breeds have similar programs to honor and encourage outstanding individuals in the breed. I chose the Quarter Horse as an example because it is the most popular pleasure horse breed in the United States. If these programs interest you, check with your horse's registry office to see what awards are available.

Whether or not a show is recognized, its judge will be selected from a roster put together by the American Horse Shows Association or another accredited national equestrian organization. Judges are trained and tested by the ASHA, then rated with a small *r* (recorded) and a large *R* (registered) next to the classes listed in their specialty. Dressage judges also have an *S* (senior) rating.

A good judge is quick and decisive. Those who work a class for an excessively long time are generally less competent. After showing for a while, you'll get to know the various judges and learn their likes and dislikes. Judges do have their prejudices, and if you don't agree with the choices of a particular judge, simply avoid those shows. If you decide to go anyway and aren't pinned, demonstrate good sportsmanship. A surprising number of people—often adults whose children are riding— will upbraid a judge for failing to place them or their children. Granted, some judges are better than others and subjective factors do enter in. But most of them are highly qualified equestrians with a great deal of knowledge and experience. Try not to take it as a personal affront when the day isn't filled with ribbons.

Parents who take it hard when their child doesn't win are breeding bad sportsmanship by emphasizing competition and victory instead of the fun and challenge of showing. Sour grapes behavior usually stems from a lack of knowledge and an inability to see a child objectively. Sometimes overly enthusiastic parents (and, I'm sad to say, trainers, too) put their children in classes or shows way beyond the capability of

THE AMERICAN QUARTER HORSE ASSOCIATION

TAKING A LOOK AT THE JUDGE

the horse or rider. Observing at a number of horse shows and learning how and what a class is judged on will help you develop a more educated eye.

If you're really puzzled by the way a judge has placed a class, or if you would like constructive criticism of your performance, there is no harm in speaking to him or her at a convenient moment (at the end of the day when a show is over) and in a reasonable manner. I encourage pupils to speak to the judge at the end of the show if they don't understand the way a class was placed. A lot can be gained by finding out where you or your horse went wrong, and a good judge will usually keep notes on their cards rating performance in each class. Advice from a parent or instructor that a child has not absorbed will often sink in when phrased differently by a judge. Remember, too, that there is a certain element of luck at a show. In some classes a judge can't see everything that's going on in the ring at a given time. Although you may have seen the winning horse cantering on the wrong lead, its rider managed to correct the fault before the judge spotted it. A smartly turned-out rider, mounted on a well-bred, nicely coordinated animal, is going to make a better overall picture than a rider of the same ability riding a homely, backyard horse.

If showing doesn't appeal to you, you can compete or participate in many other challenging events that demonstrate the capabilities of you and your horse.

OTHER TYPES OF COMPETITION

Gymkhanas

Gymkhanas are like field days—a group of informal games, with classes like barrel racing or pole bending for Western riders and English egg and spoon races and musical chairs (using feed bags in lieu of chairs). In saddling and bridling classes, riders are sometimes asked to ride to one end of the ring bareback, using halter and lead shank, to saddle and bridle their horse, and then to race back. The number of classes is limited only by the imagination of the sponsors. In one California show competitors rode bareback tandem, back to back, and were judged on their seats at the walk, trot, and canter. Gymkhanas are particularly good for children and adults with limited riding experience. They always have lots of strictly fun classes that give everyone an equal opportunity to place.

Endurance and Competitive Trail Rides

These rides probably originated in Middle Europe around the turn of the century, when members of the Prussian cavalry rode from Vienna to Berlin within a set period; the winner was the officer who came closest to the prescribed time. The U.S. Cavalry adopted the sport in the 1920s, sponsoring five-day, three-hundred-mile endurance rides, during which a horse was expected to average sixty miles a day.

The Green Mountain Horse Association took over the sport in 1936, becoming the first civilian organization to sponsor a competitive trail ride. One of the most famous in the country is the Vermont One-Hundred-Mile Ride, on which competitors cover forty miles on the first two days and twenty on the third. The first forty miles must be covered in not less than six and a half hours and not more than seven. The twenty-mile stretch, usually the most grueling part of the test, is to be completed in not less than two and a half hours and in no more than three.

One of the toughest of the dozens of national endurance rides staged every year is the California Tevis Cup. Competitors must ride one hundred miles from Lake Tahoe, California, to Auburn, California, in twenty-four hours or less. The trail follows an old 1849 miners' road, climbing to 9,500 feet at one point and descending 12,250 feet at another. The strain taxes the limits of any horse's capabilities.

Competitors in any of these rides must be all-around equestrians who know how to put a horse in top condition before the event and how to pace and care for him during the ride. The winning horse in any endurance ride has traveled the course in the fastest time and arrived in the best condition.

Competitive trail rides require entrants to arrive at the finish line within a set time, not the fastest. They also judge the condition of the horse. In both endurance and competitive rides, each horse is thoroughly examined by a veterinarian before starting out and again at various points along the route and at the finish. Both types of competition are open to English and Western riders. Awards are sometimes given to breeds that place highest in any given race (like Arabs, Morgans, Thoroughbreds, and Quarter Horses).

In addition to soundness, appropriate conformation, and willingness to move forward, an endurance horse must have the desire to eat and drink even when exhausted—a trait that prevents dehydration and helps the animal to recuperate faster. In some parts of the country, there are shorter endurance and competitive rides of twenty-five to fifty miles that a rider can cut his teeth on. Some enthusiasts use these rides to condition their horses for the longer rides.

Hunter Pace and Hunter Trials

Usually sponsored by active hunts to raise money, these events are open in most cases to seasoned horses that have hunted regularly in the field. A Hunter Trial is held over typical hunting country: a course of uneven terrain with natural obstacles, generally one or two miles long. Trials are great fun for competitors and spectators alike. It's a delight to see eager riders and keen horses working over natural country.

Trials have a variety of classes for junior hunters as well as for the field, staff members, and tandem teams of three hunters. Entrants are judged on the horse's manners, way of going, and suitability as a hunter.

In a *Hunter Pace* riders on fit hunters go out in tandem pairs across a marked course of typical hunting country, usually five to seven miles long. (Sometimes there are modified courses for horses that have not hunted regularly.) This event requires that a rider be skillful in pacing his horse. The top teams must navigate the course in an ideal time, which is usually determined by a team of riders who rode the course earlier in the day and sealed their time in an envelope. Sometimes the course is ridden in advance by a member of the hosting team, whose time is revealed after all the teams have finished. Occasionally the winners are selected by taking the average time of all the teams after they have completed the course. The winner is the team that has come closest to the average time. Hunter paces also have a "race for the mask" (meaning the face of the fox), in which the object is to travel the course as quickly as possible. This pace derives from the importance of staff members staying up with the hounds during a hunt.

The type of field hunter that excels in these competitions is rarely the same as those seen in the ribbons in hunter classes at A shows. Field hunters are more rugged and usually less high-strung then their more aristocratic namesakes that grace the show ring.

You need to determine which type of competition suits you, your horse, and your pocketbook. Not only is competition an excellent way to improve your skills, but it puts you in situations with a lot of like-minded people. Recognized shows offer a lot of top competition, so to do well you must have excellent instruction, lots of experience, and a suitable horse. Showing on a regular circuit is expensive; the costs of entries, stabling, and vanning require you to plan a budget and adhere to it, as well as your training program. A few talented youngsters have made it on a shoestring by working part time or becoming working students and picking up horses to ride along the way, but they are rare exceptions.

If competition is not for you, don't feel bad. You can enjoy many rewarding years of riding and caring for your horse without having to ever set foot in the show ring.

PART XI

Horse for All Seasons

"I don't think a man like me ought to marry. 'osses require a man's undivided attention, morning noon and night. Now, of course, a man is bound to pay his wife some little attention, as the saying is, and what he gives to his wife he must take away from his 'osses."

F.M. Lutyens
MR. SPINKS AND HIS HOUNDS

✦✦✦

Quake in the present winter's state, and wish that warmer days would come.

Shakespeare
CYMBELINE

Winter, Spring, Summer, Fall

On days when icicles sprout from equine nostrils and you have to skate to the pasture with an ax to liberate water from a frozen pond or stream, even the most dedicated equestrian may slide to a stop and wonder if it's all worthwhile. Winter can get to the best of us, but by preparing for the worst, we can survive it with equanimity, if not a smile. And we who must suffer through sleet, blizzards, Arctic clippers, and other hibernal caprices should be aware that our horses don't like it much either and can get just as sick from seasonal diseases as we do.

While humans enjoy the comforts of heated homes, thermal underwear, lotions, and flu shots to ward off cold-weather maladies, horses are commonly thought to be better at eluding illness because they grow their own winter coat. Although they are unquestionably hardier than humans under harsh conditions, even horses that live in areas where temperatures seldom drop below freezing can come down with equine versions of our seasonal plagues: colds, flu, and chapped skin, along with other conditions like rain rot and scratches. And at the end of a long, hard winter, they can show all the symptoms of cabin fever.

Owners ignorant of the problems that cold weather can bring may inadvertently provoke them with good but misguided intentions, covering a favorite mount's natural insulation with thick blankets, sealing him in an airtight barn, and feeding him too many scoops of grain. This effort to keep a horse warm, dry, and fat will instead make him very uncomfortable and probably sick.

The equine circulatory system adapts quickly to seasonal change. A regulator in the brain called the hypothalamus keeps body temperature within a few degrees of the normal 99 by monitoring the temperature of the blood pumped through it. If blood returning from the extremities is too hot or too cold, the hypothalamus prompts compensatory behavioral or biological changes, shutting down when the temperature returns to normal.

In autumn this internal thermometer triggers the hormones that cause the coat to grow heavy and coarse, and it slows metabolism to create a greater capacity for the storage of insulating fat. Other reactivated hormones encourage retention of water and nutrients. Finally, the blood vessels near the skin actually retreat from the surface to the warmer ambience below.

Hibernal Health

A heavy winter coat, waterlogged with snowmelt and left to steam-dry slowly in a humid barn, joins with the warm, damp, skin below to create the perfect anaerobic incubators in which mud fever, rain rot, and bed itch can develop. The noxious result is collectively known as skin crud.

Long hair on the fetlocks normally deflects water from that area, but thin-skinned horses with shorter hair are vulnerable in winter to *scratches*—scabby pustules that form around the pastern from too much moisture (water or mud). (See Chapter 19.) As a preventive, horses that are normally turned out all the time need to be brought in at some point during the day, their legs hand-dried, and antifungal or antibacterial powder or ointment applied.

Preventing skin problems in winter is largely a matter of cleanliness and diligence. The majority can be prevented by keeping everything with which a horse comes into contact clean and dry. Blankets, tack, grooming equipment, and living quarters can be breeding grounds for bacteria, viruses, and fungi that will reinfect horses unless they are eliminated by disinfecting or other strategies. If any horse in your barn contracts a skin disease, consult your veterinarian about the most effective treatment to undertake. If the conditions is contagious, keep all his grooming tools, blankets, and other equipment away from other horses.

The most common contagious diseases, like influenza and rhino, seldom strike an isolated home stable but pose a real threat when a horse goes on the road. Vaccination at appropriate intervals is the best protection for any horse who will be traveling in the winter. (See Chapter 19.) Always isolate any new horse entering your barn.

Hibernizing Your Horse's Habitat

Begin winter preparations early with a survey of the water supply. Horses drink less in cold weather because they sweat less, but they must have water available at all times to provide them with the moisture they need for normal digestion and elimination.

If faucets and pumps are to withstand subzero temperatures, they should be sunk below the frost line and located near an outlet with a ground-fault interrupter (GFI) circuit, available at hardware stores. This system permits de-icers, heat tape, and bucket warmers to be plugged in while preventing electrocution if a horse should bite the wire. (See Chapter 11.)

Next, make sure your electrical system has enough amps to supply the power needed for these devices, as well as lights and clippers. While days are still long, repair the fixtures and replace the lightbulbs, so you won't have to fumble around in the dark later on.

Clean turnout sheds, and check to make sure there are no broken boards, protruding nails, or other potential hazards. Likewise for stalls and fences. Your horse will be spending a lot of winter time in the stall, and uneven flooring puts exceptional stress on legs, so make sure it's level. Even rubber mats may need shoring up.

In late fall it's a good idea to have your manure pile removed so you won't have to force the wheelbarrow up frozen, snowcapped banks. Keep the paths to it, to the paddock, and to the pasture open with sand or rock salt stored in a convenient place outside the barn exit, and have shovels standing ready by the inside door. Because rock salt kills grass, I prefer to use sand, covering the pile with a tarp to keep it dry.

In areas where drainage is a problem, deepen ditches or install French drains or culvert pipes before the ground freezes. Boggy turf harbors bacteria, pulls shoes, and strains tendons.

If you don't have a loft or separate area for the storage of hay and bedding, keep bales off the ground with wooden pallets, available free from nurseries and hardware stores. Cover the bales with a plastic tarp, and anchor it with large stones or staked ropes. Always order sufficient hay well in advance so you don't run out in February and have to buy overpriced midwinter dregs.

Be sure to contract a plowing service before they all get overbooked. In areas of heavy snowfall, you may find it more economical to plow yourself. In either case be careful to protect curbs and gardens with tall driveway markers.

Keeping Your Horse Fit

Exercise is the best preventive medicine. To remain acclimated to cold weather, keep his digestive juices flowing, and stay generally fit, a horse should be turned out regularly and worked when possible. If you have no access to an indoor arena, the winter workouts you give your horse will require courage and ingenuity, but the extra effort will pay off in toned equine muscles that are better able to withstand stress and fatigue—and a happier, healthier horse when spring finally arrives.

A large pasture doesn't guarantee that the horse will use the space to work out by himself. With no grass to entice him forward, a mature horse may well spend winter days just standing around. A horse should never be left standing in a field without a wind break, lest he get chilled and catch cold.

To encourage mobility when the snow gets really deep, plow some areas of the pasture and paddock. When successive snowstorms outpace your plowing capacity, lead your horse back and forth on a cleared driveway for half an hour or more each day.

If you cannot ride indoors, it could be not days but weeks before you can squeeze in a ride between snowstorms. The horse will be full of energy, yet not fit enough to do much hard work. When the weather finally gives you a break, don't expect to hop on your horse for a pleasant outing. He'll be rarin' to go—and might decide

not to take you along for the ride. If you do manage to hang on, the riding experience will be far from pleasant. With this in mind, try to keep an area cleared where he can be lunged regularly for exercise and reminded that he's a riding horse.

Create a workout area with hoof tracks by making successive circles in the snow until the ring packs down. In the past doing this has permitted me to ride on a regular basis in the heavy winter months. When an area became too rutted, I moved on to another part of the field and repeated the process. If you have a plow, make a wide ring and keep it ridable with applications of manure and some wood shavings or chips. Neither alternative is perfect, and really harsh weather sometimes makes any riding impossible, but every little bit of exercise helps. I think of this as maintenance riding, not serious training.

Extreme cold is stressful for a horse, and stiff muscles are easily damaged. Don't ride hard in weather below twenty degrees, and tailor workouts to dropping temperatures: the lower they get, the less work he should do. Ride with a quarter sheet (see Chapter 25), or warm up and cool down with a folded cooler over his loin and rump.

When you do ride, lunge your horse first to settle him down. Warm-up time should be double that needed in mild weather and twice as slow, so muscles can stretch gradually. Making large circles at a slow or moderate gait is easier on his body and probably his mind as well. Make quick transitions before starting to work on speed, collection, and jumping. With most horses it's best to keep the routine predictable, repeating exercises he's used to. Hot or quick horses generally pay better attention when their routines are more varied.

In winter horses are more susceptible to "early tying up" or azoturia. (See Chapter 19.) Symptoms are violent muscle cramping, usually in the hindquarters, which will show up early during the workout in short, stiff strides or complete immobility,

Warming Up or
Cooling Down in
Winter with Cooler
Folded Across Rump

accompanied by labored breathing and excessive sweating. The precise cause of this condition hasn't been determined, but most afflicted horses have been fed too much carbohydrate for their level of activity.

This brings us once more to the rule of *feeding according to work done.* When winter riding schedules are unavoidably erratic, it's best to reduce or entirely eliminate grain rations on days when a horse is idle. A "hard keeper" should have his hay rations increased and a half cup of corn added to a small serving of grain twice a day. This will reduce the risk of colic and quell the equine urge to burn off extra energy by galloping full tilt across slippery or pockmarked pastures. An exuberant, out-of-shape horse taking an exhilarating romp in deep snow can also tie up, strain a ligament, or pull a tendon.

Low-Temperature Diets

Colic is the most common cold-weather ailment. In winter months the number of cases of impaction colic reported to health authorities increases sharply. (Sand colic is more prevalent in Florida and the Southwest in this season.) Because horses drink less during the winter, their food is drier and moves sluggishly through the intestines, where it's liable to impact at some point along the way. (See Chapter 19.)

To prevent colic, it's crucial to encourage your horse to drink water, even if you have to chop through ice two or three times a day to keep the natural sources open. Keep the water in troughs or buckets above 40 degrees if possible. An investment in heaters costs less than the emotional price you will pay when a horse with impaction colic has to be nursed for days (and is possibly lost).

When temperatures start to drop, reach for hay, not grain. The act of eating roughage creates warmth, which increases as the forage ferments in the stomach. If the digestive system needs a boost, probiotic supplements will encourage the growth of microorganisms that break down food, and a hot bran mash once a week will help to keep the digestive processes moving. (See Chapter 8.)

A properly blanketed horse with a normal winter coat and access to a windbreak can withstand temperatures as low as 40 degrees below zero. Except in periods of heavy, cold rain, stinging sleet, or high windchill, most horses fare better outside than in.

Watch out for weight loss, which can be concealed under that heavy winter coat. As you run your hand from the point of the shoulder to the point of the hip, the ribs closest to the elbow should be covered with insulating fat, and only the last three or four should be palpable to the touch. An underweight horse will lose more heat and expend more calories just to keep warm. His weight can be built up, even in frigid weather, with sufficient feed, deworming, and dental care, allowing him to retain the fat he needs to fuel him through a tough winter.

Windchill has to be factored into temperature readings, adjusting bulk rations upward with increasing cold. To figure out how much additional hay is needed, subtract the wind velocity from the air temperature, increasing hay rations one percent for each degree below freezing. For instance, if it is 40 degrees outside with the wind blowing at a brisk twenty miles per hour, the temperature will really feel like twenty degrees. A horse normally fed thirty pounds of hay a day will need three and a half pounds more to keep pace with his body's additional heating demands.

Breathing Easy

Horses are supersensitive to airborne irritants like dust, ammonia, and mold, which can irritate respiratory membranes and leave them open to bronchitis and other infections. When you can smell ammonia in bedding, the level is probably sufficient to damage equine lungs.

Good ventilation is essential. It's always better to add a blanket and open a window than to close a horse in an airtight barn. A large equine body beneath a relatively small surface area generates a lot of heat and loses it slowly.

Daily cleaning and airing is a must in winter stable management. If your barn lacks enough doors and windows to allow air to circulate, you may have to install a fan or build vents under roof peaks to keep it moving. Take care that it doesn't cause a draft where your horse is standing.

Chilling Out

Cooling a horse down properly after winter exercise is vital. Mechanisms that disperse heat from an active body don't naturally reverse themselves fast enough to the heat-conserving mode, and below-normal temperatures will weaken the immune system.

Like the winter warm-up, the winter cool-down should take twice as long as in good weather. If a horse's skin is cold to the touch, walk him out in a cooler, tied or clipped close at the chest. These large, usually wool blankets are designed to hold in body heat, allowing the horse to readjust slowly and avoid chill. An Irish linen sheet underneath, or some bunches of loose straw or hay between a wet coat and cooler, will promote circulation and allow the hair to dry and fluff out. (See Chapter 25.)

Covering All the Angles

A horse not doing regular work is best left in his natural unclipped state. Blankets won't be necessary because the heavy winter coat will give him adequate protection against the elements, with dust, scurf, and skin oil providing an extra shield. Groom your horse once a day, if possible, to check on his general health and maintain the social bond.

To keep a horse that is normally blanketed from getting chilled during before-and-after-work wintertime grooming, tacking, and untacking, use a cooler. Fold it forward over the crest of the neck as you work on the back half of the body, then double it back as you groom the front.

To Shoe or Not to Shoe

Some owners like to leave their horses bare-foot in winter, when hooves grow more slowly, and trim them less often to give the feet a rest. Letting old nail holes fill in strengthens the hoof wall, and letting the frog again have natural contact with the ground improves blood flow and toughens soles. This is a healthy practice if your horse has hardy hooves that don't crack or split and soles that don't easily bruise. It is not advised in areas where ice builds up to the point where a horse might slip and fall.

Winter riders usually have their horses shod with borium or caulks with bubble pads that prevent snow from balling up in the metal shoe and turning to ice. Special horse-shoe nails can also be used by your farrier. This nail has a head that extends beyond the plane of the shoe and is designed to provide extra grip, like a cleat, when placed near the rear of the horse's shoes. Traction devices like removable studs are another option, but sometimes they work too efficiently, causing unnaturally abrupt stops that can strain muscles, tendons, and ligaments. A hoof grip pad that goes under the shoe and attaches at the rear is another solution, especially in hard-packed snow. (See Chapter 17.)

Snowballs in the hooves are awkward and dangerous. Years ago farmers using horses in winter would clean the hooves out well with alcohol and then cover the sole and frog area with heavy grease. Some people use nonstick cooking spray, but I've never had much luck with it. One western farrier, who uses borium shoes without pads, as they do in the East, sprays liquid plastic Varath on the hoof, creating a slick, semihard surface on which snow can't stick. For the plastic to adhere properly, the hoof must be cleaned thoroughly with alcohol and allowed to dry before Varath is applied. After the application, the hoof must dry on a flat, hard surface. If done this way, the treatment will last three days. (Because the ingredients dry out the hoof, be careful about using Varath for extended periods of time.)

Rough Riders

It takes a lot of dedication and determination to don four or five layers of clothing on a freezing morning and leave the comforts of home to saddle up a mount more interested in munching hay than moving out. To stay as cozy as possible, you'll need to dress in layers, the number depending on how cold it is out there. Start out with long underwear, topped by a cotton shirt, followed by a wool sweater, a Polartec shirt, and finally a thigh-length waterproof down jacket or microfiber shell. Warm winter pants are available in many styles, and insulated waterproof thermobreeches can be worn with or without riding pants underneath.

Under insulated boots, you'll wear Polartec socks (footwear tested to 20 degrees below), and thin, insulated gloves with leather palms or riding mittens that keep the pinkie separate. After protecting your face and lips with industrial-strength lotion, top the outfit off with a hard hat and fleece ear warmers, a scarf across the mouth, and sunglasses both for brightness and to keep the eyes from watering. Throw a quarter sheet on your horse, and you're set.

Winter Wonderland

Sometimes the wonderful world of white is just too nasty to ride out in. My friends and clients suffering from cabin fever welcome these opportunities to get together and watch educational videos of recent interesting competitions. One of the riding organizations in our region has more than a hundred videos in its library, and area tack shops offer rentals too. A monthly get-together like this, along with a potluck supper, is a great way to drive the dreary winter blues away.

WELCOME SWEET SPRINGTIME

The first days of spring can be fickle, with temperatures plummeting from a high of 60 to 25 degrees in a single day. These wild fluctuations confuse internal equine thermometers and leave horses prone to colds and colic. Winter blankets, if left on in hot sunny weather, can heighten this vulnerability, causing profuse sweating that could make a horse sick. Listen to forecasts if you'll be gone for the day, and remove the blankets when temperatures are expected to soar.

Early spring is the best time to go over your tack, oiling, reconditioning, polishing, or repairing it in anticipation of the coming season. You may want to get loose stitches on the stirrup buckles repaired or saddle panels restuffed. And if you need new equipment, this is usually a good time to buy it. Many tack shops and catalogs offer terrific sale prices on everything from halters to fly repellent.

This is also the time to start thinking about showing, sending for prize lists and scheduling show dates. If your horse has been idle all winter, start conditioning slowly (see Chapter 30), and set the date for your first show realistically, when your horse will be in proper condition to compete.

Showing means trailering, so take a look at the trailer's floors and tires and have it thoroughly inspected by a knowledgeable mechanic. (See Chapter 34.)

When the weather stays well above freezing for a week or two and tulips start to poke up their heads, horses begin feeling their hormones along with their oats. A misbehaving mare may need a dose of Regu-mate (see below), and don't be surprised if your fifteen-year-old gelding acts like a stallion again, snorting and galloping around the pasture with his head and tail held high—the equine version of spring fever. No need to worry unless extremely muddy conditions might cause him to fall or skid into the fence when he tries to stop. Such accidents are hard to prevent, but it helps to turn the horse out in clean, protective boots, throw out plenty of hay to keep him busy, and resume a regular exercise program as soon as possible to take the edge off all that energy.

Check a rambunctious horse out carefully back in the stable. One sliding stop too many can strain or pull a tendon or ligament, and deep mud with stones beneath it is a perfect setting for bruises and can pull a horse's shoe off the same way it sucks off your boots.

When you bring these mud monsters in from the pasture, hose off the legs and dry them thoroughly with an old, clean stable towel or, better yet, a hair dryer. It's not only the manure and urine present in mud but its wetness that can bring on scratches and mud fever (to which white-legged horses are particularly prone). Even if you're not planning to ride, scrape all the mud off the horse with a metal curry or shedding blade, brush the face and back of the ears, and prepare to groom him. To minimize mud removal, turn your horse out in a light stable blanket. At least part of him will stay clean.

Spring Cleaning

Grooming your horse regularly promotes shedding and gives you a chance to check out his skin, head, legs, and hooves for any cuts or scratches that may have been hiding under all that hair. It removes dirt, sweat, glandular secretions, and dead skin cells, brings natural oils to the surface and gloss to the coat. At the same time it gives a horse mental and physical preparation for all the work he'll be doing in the weeks ahead.

When temperatures get above 50 degrees, your horse is ready to get rid of a winter's worth of dirt and grime with a bath—the first of only two or three he really needs before the cold weather returns. (See Chapter 13.) The spring bath is a big moment for your shaggy friend, who is about to be transformed into a clean, trimmed, shining example of what a domesticated horse ought to look like. Don't be surprised if he's not as enthusiastic about the results as you are. After all, he's put in many concentrated hours of rolling to reach this peak of perfection. Be sure to groom him thoroughly, getting out as much of the shedding coat as possible. And along with your assembled bathing items, make sure to have a clean wool cooler on hand to put on afterward so he won't catch a chill.

If the sun is strong enough, hand-graze your horse in direct sunlight to dry him out. When it's too cool for that, let him stand covered in the cooler in a draft-free place until dry. Carefully clean all the grooming tools, too.

When your horse is bathed, trimmed, and shining, he'll probably pick the muddiest part of the pasture to roll in when next turned out. Don't despair. A vigorous session with the currycomb followed by a good vacuuming will make him beautiful again.

> Spring has sprung
> The grass has riz
> I wonder where
> My sweet mare is

Early one May morning a panicked client phoned to tell me that her normally mild-mannered and well-trained mare, Ginger, had gone haywire on a trail ride, snorting, crow-hopping, and finally throwing her rider with a gigantic, twisting buck before taking off at full gallop to parts unknown. It took nearly an hour to catch the recalcitrant rogue, and the next day we had to use a chain shank to lead her from the pasture. The veterinarian was called out to examine the mare, making sure her obstreperous behavior wasn't caused by a tumor or other pathological condition. Then he put her on the oral hormone suppressant Regu-mate. Within four days Ginger was back to her old docile self again.

As soon as the days become long and warm, nearly all mares will come into heat (estrus) every three weeks for a period lasting twenty-one days. During this time they are susceptible to a stallion for seven days. This cycle is interrupted in fall and winter, a time called anestrus. A transitional period precedes estrus in early spring, at which time cycles are irregular, longer, and not always accompanied by ovulation. Regu-mate was developed to regulate the cycle during this period.

Mares in heat often behave as unpredictably as stallions. They show primitive herd instincts by whinnying constantly and becoming testy and balky at best. At worst they grow uncontrollably wild, giving their gender an undeserved "bad rep." I have three wonderful mares in my school string that don't need Regu-mate, maintaining an even temperament without it. Some mares need it occasionally, and others never do; but to forestall potential problems, serious competitors give the hormone suppressant to their mares during the show season. Those who want to breed mares early use it during the transition period to control ovulation. When the dosage is stopped, a mare will come back into heat and ovulate ten to fifteen days later.

Regu-mate is expensive and must be handled with rubber gloves because it can be absorbed through the skin.

In a season synonymous with heat, humidity, and flies, it's best to ride your horse early in the morning or evening, keeping him cool during the day in a shady, well-ventilated barn and turning him out at night. If you're not comfortable with an all-night arrangement, schedule turnouts for early morning and from late afternoon until dark.

Flies

In areas where flies thrive, horses must be protected with daily applications of repellent and kept clean and free of dried sweat. Their ears and eyes should be shielded with a bonnet or mask (available at tack shops). Masks and bonnets for turnout should be purchased in the correct size for your horse for a comfortable fit. If they're too large they easily slip off, and if they're too small they rub. Masks made of stiff material should be very carefully adjusted so that the convex area over the eye is truly centered over the eye and won't shift. Don't leave your horse out with one on for longer than a day without checking it to see if it needs readjusting. Regularly wash or clean them off so they won't irritate your horse's skin.

If your horse has extra-sensitive skin, you may want to invest in one of the many styles of lightweight summer fly sheets. Loose-fitting mesh leg wraps help minimize

SUMMER SUGGESTIONS

Fly Control Masks
and Bonnets Worn
in Pasture

stamping and kicking, which can loosen and pull shoes. (See Chapter 21 for more on fly management.) Carefully check your horse all over for ticks daily, if they are troublesome in your area. Make the removal of botfly eggs part of your regular grooming procedure. (See page 169.)

Ventilation

Keep the barn dark, and keep air circulating with large fans hung at intervals on the walls and an exhaust fan at one end to pull air through. To deter respiratory problems, sprinkle water or disinfectant on barn aisles after sweeping to keep dust down. Horses particularly sensitive to dust should have their hay wetted down.

Stall guards or screens help keep stalls from getting stuffy. Guards made of cotton, nylon, or Dynal webbing can be installed in twenty minutes. Screens made of lightweight steel that expand across half of the door (good for traveling), those with yokes cut out for the horse's neck, and full-length doors are also easy to install. (See Chapter 9.)

Water

Dehydration can cause tying up or colic, so make sure your horse has free access to plenty of clean water. Keep two full buckets in each stall and a full trough in pastures that don't have a natural water source. (See Chapter 7.)

When a horse doesn't seem to be drinking enough, adding an electrolyte solution of two parts table salt to one part Lite Salt to his grain will increase his water intake. An alternative is flavored electrolyte solutions, sold at most feed stores, which can be added to water, starting with a few drops and gradually increasing to recommended dosage. These taste disguises are also useful for persuading a fussy horse to drink the unfamiliar water at competitions.

Salt causes the horse to retain water and should be available in both pasture and stall at all times year round.

Feeding

Loss of appetite is a common reaction to a heat wave and no cause for alarm. If pasturage is inadequate, *keep plenty of hay available and gradually decrease the grain ration and increase the vegetable fat intake by an equal amount.* Start by adding a quarter-cup of corn oil to each meal, gradually increasing this over a two-to-three-week period to one cup and then two as you cut back on grain accordingly. Watch the horse's manure to make sure his system can tolerate this regimen. When grain is metabolized, it produces lactic acid that can cause cramping and soreness in active muscles. Vegetable fats don't do this and will keep a working horse healthier.

Workouts

Hot-weather workouts should be interrupted with frequent breaks, allowing muscles to dissipate heat. Any indications of stress—like foam between the hind legs, blowing, or reacting slowly to leg pressure—should signal an immediate ten-minute break. Get him in the shade right away, hosing or sponging when possible, or squirting his neck, back, and sides with an alcohol-water mix to keep him cool. Always have a spray bottle handy at ringside, filled with equal amounts of cold water and alcohol, plus a few ice cubes.

Cooling down after a summer workout is essential before grooming. Studies conducted for the 1996 Olympics found that the safest way to cool down a horse after strenuous hot-weather exercise is to sponge or hose down the large muscles in his hindquarters, neck, shoulders, and back with very cold, even icy water, then immediately remove any excess with a sweat scraper. Repeat the process on both sides of the horse until body temperature is brought down to normal. During exercise, large muscle areas generate a lot of heat, which is conducted to the surface of the skin as the horse sweats, helping the body to cool as it evaporates. But extremely hot, humid weather hinders evaporation, trapping all that heat in the muscles.

Feet should be checked regularly, particularly in unusually dry summers, when additional moisturizers may be needed.

Sun

Sunburn is a common problem in the Southwest, particularly for paints, pintos, Appaloosas, and white horses that have unpigmented skin areas or sparse coats on some parts of the body. Sunburn is prevented by keeping susceptible horses out of the glaring sun. (See Chapter 19.)

Too much direct sunlight also causes bleaching of black and dark brown coats, turning them a shade or two lighter. To avoid this, turn dark horses out in the morning and late afternoon or in a light sheet to avoid the midday sun. Any sweat left on the coat after a workout can also discolor or fade it.

Anticipate Autumn

Start in midsummer by sending your heavy blankets and cooler out for cleaning and repairs (if you didn't already in the spring). It can take up to three weeks. Tack shops sell inexpensive plastic storage bags for blankets, which should be stored in a dry, protected place where they won't get dusty or moldy. And if you need more winter blankets, order them now to make sure you get the style and size you want.

By late summer you should also have lined up your hay source, preferably going out to the field to judge the quality. Those who have the equipment can save money by trucking the bales directly from the field.

Hiring a Horse-sitter

When you're planning a vacation or even a short weekend away, a reliable horse-sitter is often harder to line up than a baby-sitter. When you do find someone to come in, make sure he or she is dependable and competent, able to follow a feeding schedule, mend a fence if necessary, and recognize unnatural behavior in your horse. Have the horse-sitter come by for a few days before you leave so you both can go over the routine several times. Leave the sitter the phone numbers for the veterinarian and for a neighbor who would be willing to help out just in case the fence breaks down and your horse escapes, and a number where you can be reached in case of a serious emergency, especially if you will be away for more than a few days. And to be sure of no mistakes in turnout procedures or feeding menus, *write things down.* Covering all bases is worth the time it takes.

If you prefer to leave your horse in a boarding stable, rates will vary according to where you live. Rough board, consisting of feed and turnout with a run-in shed, is the least expensive in any area. Stabling costs more, and charges for grooming and exercise are extra. Ask your trainer or local tack shop to recommend accommodations. Make a point of dropping in unannounced to see how things are normally run before you decide if this is the barn for you. After all, you want to enjoy your vacation, not spend it worrying about your favorite equine. Some of my clients arrange for qualified friends to exercise their horse if they plan to be away for more than a few days.

FALL

As soon as days shorten and nights become cool, equine coats begin to grow to winter length. To delay the process, increase blanket weight in keeping with dropping temperatures, and close the barn up at night to keep heat in. On deceptively balmy autumn days, when he works up a sweat, *dry your horse thoroughly before blanketing him* for the evening. Indian summer nights can get pretty cold. When weather is really oscillating from hot to cold, be sure your horse isn't sweating under blankets that are too heavy, especially if you're leaving him out all day.

As pasture becomes depleted, the horse will look for other things to munch on. These include trees, fence posts, and sometimes more dangerous cuisine, like poisonous weeds, leaves, or acorns, that would be ignored if grass were abundant. Check your pastures to make sure no toxic plants are present. Some common varieties are listed in Appendix B, and your local agricultural organization can help you identify other culprits.

If you plan to clip your horse, October is the month to do it. (See Chapter 15.) Don't clip too early, or you'll have to do it again in a few months. Make sure your clippers are in good working order with blades sharp, and blanket your horse appropriately when the job is finished.

Begin preparing outbuildings, barns, and other storage areas for winter.

Trail riders who live in the rural areas of the Northeast should be aware of hunting season. The first day of deer season, in particular, is not an ideal day for a peaceful trail ride. All too frequently there are many novice hunters out who don't know a deer from a goat, let alone a horse, and shoot first and look afterward. Many horror stories will verify that fact. City hunters, not noted for their stealth, tromp noisily behind trees or brush, emerging suddenly to terrify your horse. During the more active days of hunting season, we avoid going out. Eventually we venture forth in bright orange or red clothing, with wraps and a band of sleigh bells attached to one of the D's on the saddle. We haven't lost a rider yet.

You should take similar caution when turning a horse out, especially if the pasture is large and near a wooded and/or known hunting area. Cover your horse with bright-colored lightweight sheets for daytime turnout, or restrict turnout to evenings when weather is warm enough. One stable restricts turnout to Sundays, when there is no hunting.

Trailering Your Horse

Every riding horse will be taking a ride himself at some point in his showing or hunting career. To save your sanity and avoid spending many frustrated, anxious hours trying to get him in the trailer, it's essential to train your horse to load easily.

**TEACHING
LOADING**

If you have yet to invest in a trailer but have a new horse that doesn't truck well (or a young horse that has never been taught), try to borrow a two-horse trailer from a friend willing to park it in your pasture for a few weeks. If this is impossible, rent one for the training period. It's money well spent.

Leading Him On

Before you borrow, buy, or rent a trailer and set it up, give your horse some preliminary tutoring to help him learn loading skills. Your goal in these lessons is a horse that will load easily when pointed at the open door on the lead, walking into the trailer in a relaxed, orderly way as you toss the lead over his neck. You can accomplish this goal with progressive training and positive reinforcement.

When a horse "refuses to load," leading is almost always at the heart of the problem. He must learn to lead well in this special situation, walking forward briskly when you're at his shoulder, rather than in the usual position by the head, and continuing the forward momentum as you turn to face him. To reinforce and amplify his previous basic training, work your horse in a small circle on the lead rope, using a whip four feet or longer, with a partially inflated plastic grocery bag tied to the end. (Blow into it as you would a balloon, knotting the air in, then tying the bag to the end of the whip.) Allow him to examine this bag and be relaxed about it before you proceed to the next step. As he walks around the circle, keeping his body parallel to you as he would on the lunge line, tap him lightly with the bag high on the hindquarters to encourage a brisk forward movement. (Don't tap the stifle or hock, which might cause him to kick out in annoyance.) You want him to move forward immediately on command.

It may take some strong taps at first to get him started, but as soon as he begins to move out well, reward him with praise and a pat on the neck (not treats). As the lesson continues, lighter taps should produce the same desired result, but continue to reward him as before. After a few sessions, begin to circle him in both directions. This work should progress gradually, like any other training, and be reinforced regularly.

Training for the Trailer

When your horse's performance on the lead is satisfactory, simulate a loading situation in your ring or pasture to accustom him to the ramp and narrow trailer.

Novice loaders are often frightened by the sound of their hooves on the ramp and trailer floor. To get them used to this noise, lay a four-by-eight sheet of three-quarter-inch plywood flat on the ground, first taking

your horse around it, then leading him up to it, walking by his shoulder and using the bag-end whip. Allow plenty of relaxed time for him to examine the board, and again reward his compliance with encouraging words and a pat on the neck instead of treats.

When he gets used to the sight of the board, ask him to place a foot or two on the plywood sheet and let him stand there relaxed. Back him off, so that it's not a forced situation, then lead him on again, a little farther each time, until you gradually induce him to stand quietly with all four feet on the noisy board. Then walk him off it, using the whip lightly when needed. After he's done this calmly several times, ask him to walk all the way on and then back off the board, as he will from the trailer, making sure he goes straight and slowly. (Hurrying backward can cause many accidents.)

Once board walking and backing become routine for your horse, it's time to introduce the *chute*. Horses are naturally wary of walking into narrow enclosures. To simulate the entrance and walls of a trailer, set up two jump standards one or two feet from each corner of the plywood sheet—the distance will depend on their length—and extend ten- or twelve-foot rails between them, parallel to the sides. Resume the leading lesson through the chute as you did over the unenclosed board. When your horse seems comfortable with this phase, add a rail across the front,

Head Bumper
for Shipping

leading him to it and then backing him up a few steps. While you are standing on the outside of the rail (alternating sides), encourage him to back several steps, stand, and then move the same distance forward, rewarding him as you did before.

Dress Rehearsal

Once your pupil becomes blasé about the chute, you can put on his leg wraps (see Chapter 25) and bumper for the poll (if you use one), and repeat the lesson until he's relaxed and comfortable again. The high wraps used for shipping need some getting used to and may provoke a high-stepping stride the first time the horse wears them, but as he gets used to the loading boots, he'll resume his normal walk.

Command Performance

Now it's time to introduce the real trailer to the pasture. Park it in a central location, with the ramp, if there is one, down. Standing by your horse's shoulder, continue to encourage that brisk forward stride as you lead him past the trailer in both directions. Allow him to stop and look at it from a comfortable distance. If he steps back during this initial survey, step with him, speaking in a calm and friendly manner, never forcefully. Don't try to restrain him. Remember that this joint effort is an extension of a friendly relationship.

If your horse doesn't want to move toward the trailer opening, turn him away from it and repeat the forward-leading exercise described at the beginning of this section, still on the small circle using the bag-end whip. Gradually work the circle over to bring him back to the front of the trailer, and give him another chance to look. If he doesn't stand or go forward, resume the energetic circling.

Don't rush it. Give your horse plenty of time to look at the trailer before you ask him to move toward it, and reward him for each step he takes closer to the ramp or step up. Encourage him to place one front foot and then the other upon it. Allow him to stand and absorb this accomplishment for a few minutes before asking him to step back. Spending ample time on forward and back steps will keep him relaxed and confident.

When moving his front feet forward and back becomes routine, coax your horse to put one back leg on the ramp or to the step-up, by tapping his hindquarters with the bag-end whip. Continue the step-forward-and-back routine, this time involving the hind legs as well, and gradually move him farther up the ramp or step up until he is inside the trailer and standing quietly (with the rear bar down). Then have him back out slowly. Repeat loading and unloading until he walks into the trailer by himself when you lead him to the door, entering as easily as he walks into his stall.

This is the best way to train a novice loader and to retrain a horse with loading problems. Just remember to take your time and, above all, to avoid mistakes in handling that could cause an accident and/or make your horse afraid to load.

Another way to accustom the horse to the trailer is to set it up in your pasture or on an out-of-the-way flat surface with the ramp down and the partition either open or pushed to the side. Leave one stall accessible, without allowing enough room to turn in. Then begin feeding your horse all his meals on the ramp. (Obviously this will work better in the summer, when your horse is outside most of the time.) Nine times out of ten, the horse will go up the ramp to eat, following the feed dish and hay as you move it farther and farther up each day, until he is finally taking his meals inside. By the end of two weeks most horses fed this way can be led right into the trailer to eat breakfast or supper from the crib at the front. (A friend trained her horses this way so well that they go in by themselves when she opens the back door and back out at the end of the meal.)

When the loading lessons are finished, it's important to follow up with a quiet solo ride with an experienced driver at the wheel. One horse alone in a two-horse trailer gets a better ride on the driver's side. If you are driving with a trailer for the first time, practice for a few days before putting your horse aboard. (Maneuvering one when backing up is particularly tricky.) And always check to see that the brakes and the brake and directional lights are working.

After you dress your horse for the occasion with leg wraps and bumper, make sure everything is ready before bringing him around to the ramp. Hay should be in the crib, and the doors open (including the escape door, if there is one).

Either walk ahead of your horse into the trailer or, if you've developed a positive loading technique, lead him to the opening and point him at it. When he's standing calmly, put up the back chain or bar, go around to the hatch or door by his head, and secure him with either a slipknot or the safety snap on a trailer tie.

Always put the chain or bar up before tying or snapping the horse in. Otherwise he could pull back and panic, breaking his halter, lead, or both and possibly injuring himself. For the same reason the horse should always be untied before taking off the back chain or bar.

When unloading your horse, untie him through the hatch or escape door first, toss the rope over his neck, open the back door, and then drop the back bar or unhook the chain. Stand by the door and say "back," prepared to guide him down the ramp if he starts off at an angle and is in danger of stepping off crooked or too early. You can do this by putting a hand on his rump or holding his tail as he backs down. Horses that have had a bad experience unloading are less willing to climb aboard the next time.

When Loading a Horse into a Trailer

• Never wrap a rope around your hand, wrist, arm, or any part of your body to restrain the horse.

• Never stand in front of the horse and pull on his lead. He will only pull backward.

• Never run a rope or line behind the horse's rump and try to pull him in. The rope could get clamped under his tail, hurting and causing him to pull away from it in fright.

• Never tie the horse before he's completely loaded and the tail bar is hooked.

• Never put the ramp up or close the trailer door before hooking the tail bar.

If your horse is a difficult loader, take time well before the show or competition to retrain him with these techniques. Videos on this subject are available at most tack shops or through catalogs.

SELECTING A SUITABLE TRAILER

In late spring and summer, owners who are showing and on the road with their horses two or three days a week will want to make their equine passengers as comfortable as possible, so they aren't lathered up or stressed out on arrival.

Experts all seem to agree that horses ride better facing backward in their normal relaxed position, with head down over forelegs and hind legs resting. In a study conducted for her doctoral dissertation, Dr. Sharon Cregier found that forward-facing trailers don't conform to equine needs, forcing a horse to ride with head up, weight in the rear, and hind legs splayed out. Many horsemen attest that horses are easier to load when they will be taking a backward position, simply stepping up on the platform, turning around, and backing into the stall. Some owners report a complete change in attitude among formerly trailer-resistant horses when they switched to a rear-facing trailer.

Newly popular slant-load trailers, commonly styled for three or more horses, are said to provide a more comfortable ride, and bad shippers usually ride better in them. But they have at least one disadvantage—to reach a horse in the middle diagonal stall, the animals on either side have to be unloaded.

The less expensive stock trailers, once thought inferior to their expensive counterparts, are receiving new accolades for being lighter and better ventilated than the conventional types, with room enough to allow a horse to choose the most comfortable traveling position, usually backward. Most horses will willingly climb on board a four-horse stock trailer, which can be easily converted into two loose boxes and can be winterized with removable Plexiglas panel inserts.

Unfortunately it isn't possible to turn a horse backward in a front-facing trailer because it's designed to accommodate the redistribution of weight over the axles. So if you like this idea, be sure to buy one designed for the horse to face the rear.

Horses should never ride at an uphill slant, as they do in forward-riding trailers, without contemporary stabilizing devices. Most have enough difficulty balancing themselves on the level. An uphill slant puts stress on both legs and mind, upsetting the horse and causing him to move around nervously to retain balance, feeling to the nervous driver as if he's on roller skates.

High and Wide

Most trailers sold today are a minimum of seven feet tall and sixty-six inches wide. The extra height and width are worth the few extra dollars. Trying to squash a sixteen-hundred-pound, 16.2-hand warmblood into a narrow six-foot trailer is a good way to turn him off loading and traveling altogether. The minimum acceptable interior width for a two-horse trailer is sixty-six inches, but they are available in a seventy-six-inch size. If the width is greater than your truck, just be sure you can maneuver on narrow, curving, or wet roads and have enough room to turn around.

Terror-free Towing

It's frightening to drive down steep hills and around curves with a loaded trailer pulling you backward or pushing you forward. And nothing is more terrifying than a trailer that starts to shimmy and sway as you're driving downhill at fifty-five miles per hour on a highway. To avoid these experiences, take *weight, stabilization,* and *horsepower* into careful consideration while shopping for a trailer.

First consider the loaded weight of the trailer relative to that of the towing vehicle. A simple two-horse trailer weighs at least two thousand pounds—considerably more if it has deluxe accommodations like a dressing room. (The weight is stamped on the trailer, along with the serial number and the date it was made.) If you're transporting a twelve-hundred-pound warmblood, or maybe two, their weight will be added on, along with that of tack and equipment, to produce a gross weight of about 4,500 pounds, or two long tons. If the tow vehicle isn't heavy and powerful enough, of sufficient length and width, and correctly stabilized, flipping or jackknifing could occur, with possibly fatal results to you and your equine passengers.

Don't assume your pickup truck can do the job. The fully fueled towing vehicle must weigh *at least 75 percent of the gross trailer weight.* If the latter is four thousand pounds, your truck or jeep must weigh three thousand pounds or, better yet, be of equal weight. Selecting a trailer that is too heavy for the tow vehicle is unfortunately a common mistake (and one of the biggest a person can make).

My advice is to choose a truck or wagon that can handle the worst conditions you might expect to encounter, taking into consideration the type of terrain and the average distances you'll be traveling. If the tow vehicle is too light or out of balance, the loaded trailer will push it around on downhill stretches, compromising your steering—particularly dangerous when you're driving long distances at highway speed limits. Before you buy, discuss relative weight with a trailer dealer or trusted mechanic.

The stability of the entire rig will be affected by the towing weight, the length of the wheel base, the engine size, and the number of cylinders. Extra stabilizing features can be installed to reduce drag and sway and soften the suspension systems. Sway bars, air springs, or weight distribution bars can help to correct a trailer's tendency to push to the rear and balance the weight of a fully loaded rig. With these devices less weight is placed on the front of the vehicle, distributing the load more equally. They also allow better tire contact with the road, easier steering, and better positioning on the headlight beams. And less of the tow vehicle's surface is exposed to the wind.

Too narrow a wheelbase (the distance between front and back axles) will cause the trailer to sway and possibly jackknife at speed. The base should be at least equal to that of a full-size passenger car.

Make sure you have enough horsepower to carry your horse up steep hills and to maintain momentum when you're in passing gear. This isn't the time to think about smaller engines and fewer cylinders for better gas mileage. To pull a full load without straining and overheating, you need a big engine and all the cylinders you can get. Towing mileage usually isn't very great anyway, and a larger engine will save wear and tear in the long run.

Lastly you should consider standard versus automatic transmissions. I've always preferred the standard, which gives me better mileage and more maneuverability at low speeds.

Getting Hitched

Hitches come in bumper-pull and gooseneck types. They should be installed by a trailer mechanic or an RV specialist. Goosenecks attach to the inside of the pickup bed. Although they cost about 20 percent more, I've always found them much more stable, giving the horse a smoother ride with less sway on turns. They're also steadier on the open road and easier to maneuver in and out of tight places, like crowded horse-show parking lots. A two-thousand-pound trailer will need a class III hitch with a capacity ball of five thousand pounds and a one-inch shank.

Aluminum, Steel, or Fiberglass

The traditional steel trailer is being dropped in favor of lightweight counterparts made of all-aluminum, aluminum-steel hybrids, and fiberglass-reinforced plywood. Some trailers combine all three products. One borrows an innovation from the aircraft industry: honeycomb panels purported to be 40 percent lighter than fiberglass. Prices vary from $5,000 for a basic two-horse to a starting price of $25,000 for a gooseneck trailer complete with living quarters. In a recent survey by the All American Quarter Horse Congress, aluminum trailers got the best rating because they are rustproof and lightweight.

Extra Features

Tack rooms, dressing rooms, and even living quarters are available in trailers for your comfort, but think of your horse's well-being first. Select a model with plenty of natural light and ventilation. Interiors are frequently painted white to give a roomy appearance—a definite plus when loading. Floors are made of wood or metal, either of which must be kept clean and maintained to prevent rusting, corrosion, or rotting. A wooden floor is cheaper than metal and is easily replaced with sturdy, pressure-treated lumber.

Whatever the floor's construction, it will have to be covered with a rubber mat for better traction, with shavings on top to provide an additional cushion and protect the floor from urine. A friend who has a particularly tender-footed horse puts a thick layer of foam rubber under the rubber mat.

Partitions are either full-length or a pole between stalls. Some owners and trainers like the full partitions, which prevent fellow travelers from kicking each other. Pole dividers, on the other hand, allow a horse to spread his legs and maintain balance. Either type should have adequate padding and be easy to put in place.

You can also choose between ramp or step-loading types. Some trailers have entry doors on the driver's side. Metal doors are best for inclement weather or when trucking a sick horse. Recessed door handles are advisable if your horse will be tied to the trailer during an event.

Portable Corrals

Portable corrals that attach to trailers are popular items at show grounds in the West and Southwest. Some friends of mine who traveled from Colorado to New York State with their camper, towing their trailer with two horses behind it, tell me that an easy-to-assemble portable corral made the trip a real pleasure. It enabled the horses to relax at night and allowed my friends more options selecting camping sites.

An easily assembled corral made by Farnam consists of a lightweight and durable panel four feet eleven inches high by six feet long made of one-inch, fifteen-gauge steel tubing with cold-rolled steel rods for connecting pins. The panels are joined by offset drop-pin hinges that give strength and stability. Each corral comes with trailer mounting brackets for easy transport. Panels are coated with a rust-resistant black enamel paint. Eight panels make a twelve-by-twelve corral, and extras can be ordered.

AVOID SUDDEN STOPS. Stopping suddenly can cause a horse to lose balance and fall, making him fearful of trailering. Be especially observant, and prepare to stop slowly and gradually. If you cannot avoid a sudden stop, use the hand trailer break control, taking some of the stress off the tow vehicle. When traveling at high speeds, be sure to leave plenty of distance between yourself and other vehicles.

MAKE SLOW, LONG, GRADUAL TURNS. Turns are the most stressful part of travel for your horse, so accelerate gradually as you go into the curve.

REGULARLY MAINTAIN YOUR TOWING VEHICLE AND TRAILER. The trailer should be serviced and checked thoroughly once a year and inspected. Pay attention to the condition of the floor, lights, brakes, and electrical system at this time. Bearings should be packed and greased and new seals installed when needed. The trailer should be thoroughly cleaned after each use.

CHECK YOUR TIRES. Make sure they are sufficient for the weight and load they're carrying and have enough air before each trip. Use only all-weather, heavy-duty tires.

DOUBLE-CHECK THE HITCH. Check and recheck to be sure it's locked into place after the trailer is hooked up. I've heard horror stories about owners driving downhill and looking out to see their trailer passing them. A hitch that isn't locked on properly can easily pop off while going over a bump.

SECURELY LATCH DOORS. Make certain that the ramp *and* doors are securely latched. I once traveled with a friend who'd forgotten to do up one side of the ramp.

**TRAILERING
SAFETY TIPS**

We heard a horrible crash, then a scraping sound, and pulled over to see what had happened. The back of the trailer was wide open, the ramp dragging on the ground. Only the tail bar saved our terrified horse from backing onto the highway.

PLAN YOUR ROUTE BEFORE A LONG TRIP. Take major highways, which are better patrolled and marked. Take time beforehand to mark your route on a map.

DON'T TRAVEL ALONE. If at all possible, bring a friend, or try to travel accompanied by another vehicle in case of emergency. This is especially important on a long trip.

HAVE MAPS, DIRECTIONS, AND PHONE NUMBERS HANDY. Phone numbers should include those of your veterinarian, your destination, and your emergency road service. Travel with a cellular phone or CB. Either can be a life-saver.

Being stuck alone on the road with a flat tire and an impatient horse is a nightmare, even during the daytime. Before cellular phones, I once ran out of gas on a major New England turnpike en route to an event with my horse in tow and my fourteen-year-old daughter. Even in broad daylight, no one would stop. I was worried about leaving my daughter and horse alone while I tried to get a ride to the nearest service station with my gas can. Finally, after more than an hour, the driver of a huge stock trailer carrying fifteen horses stopped and took pity on us, giving me a ride to the station and back. It took another horseman to understand our dilemma and help out, despite the inconvenience to him.

FEED YOUR HORSE *LESS* GRAIN OR A BRAN MASH. Do this before leaving on a trip no matter how long or short the duration. Feed him at least an hour before starting out. For a long trip, cut the grain in half. Don't feed the horse grain while traveling in the trailer.

BRING PLENTY OF HAY AND WATER. Offer your horse a drink every few hours, and fill a hay net so he can munch en route.

When you reach your destination, unload your horse and walk him out, offering him a small amount of water and hay, or sometimes a little hand-grazing, to settle him down. Hold off on the grain for an hour or so.

PRECAUTIONS

No one likes to think about accidents, but they do happen, and you should be prepared should an emergency occur. Before leaving, learn how to apply a pressure bandage to stop the bleeding. Pack a couple of prepared syringes, loaded with proper amounts of the tranquilizers acepromazine and possibly Rompun, depending on what your veterinarian recommends. Have him or her show you how to give the shots when you pick up the prescriptions. Learn how to use a twitch in case you have to restrain your horse in an emergency.

Check your rig thoroughly before starting out, including all fluid levels, oil, radiator, battery, transmission, brakes, windshield wipers, tires, and spares. If you spend the night on the road, recheck the oil, water, and tires again before leaving in the morning.

What to Do in a Breakdown

Pull over and get as far off the road as you can safely manage. Set a reflective triangle or flare ten feet in front and at intervals of ten, one hundred, and two hundred feet behind to alert oncoming motorists. If you have stopped on a hill or curve, set a marker below the crest or beginning of a curve, to give plenty of advance warning.

If you're alone, without a phone or CB, it's better to wait for help than to leave your horse alone. Tie a white handkerchief to the antenna.

If it's a flat tire and you have someone with you to help, take your horse off the trailer with a shank over the nose (see Chapter 12), and let him eat some hay or grass. If he's extremely nervous, a shot of tranquilizer may be needed to calm him down.

Two experiences come to mind concerning a flat tire on a loaded trailer. The first time it happened, I was with two competent teenagers, and we were lucky to find a wide grassy shoulder to pull over on. The girls unloaded the horses and hand-grazed them while I changed the tire. In the second situation I was driving a four-horse gooseneck, with dressing room, on the New Jersey Turnpike when the tire blew. I had two young grooms with me and four Arabian horses under three years old. There was no shoulder, truck traffic was whizzing by, and unloading was out of the question. We put flares out and were able to change the trailer tire with horses inside and live to tell about it.

Emergency Checklist

- Large container of water (for horse and car)

- Buckets

- Hay and grain

- Hay net

- Extra halter and lead ropes

- Chain shank

- Bandaging materials

- Syringes with tranquilizer

- Swiss army knife (for cutting ties and ropes in an emergency)

- Flashlight and batteries

- Flares and reflective triangles

- Wheel chocks

- Spare tires (ready to go)

- Lug wrenches, jacks, and tire-change block

- Alternate-size sliding ball mount (for tagalong)

- Extra motor oil

- Jumper cables

- Maps, directions, and phone numbers

- Notepad and pencil

- Cellular phone or CB radio

- Cash and credit cards

- Horse's health papers

- Truck and trailer registration

Reflective Tape

Use reflective tape to define the perimeters of your trailer at night, assuring its visibility. (Government-sponsored studies have concluded that this practice has reduced horse trailer accidents by 22 percent.) In most states reflective tape is mandatory for the sides of trailers. High-intensity strips that focus and intensify light from oncoming headlights are available in mail-order kits.

Nowadays it's not uncommon for owners to take horses with them on vacation or to travel two to three days with them loaded behind. Trailers that include living accommodations make this very simple. But even without these extras, trailering a horse across country doesn't always require a professional vanning service. Many private barns, commercial stables, and fairgrounds offer overnight accommodations for horses on the move.

Here are some general tips for the long haul.

MAKE FREQUENT STOPS. This is probably one of the most important things to remember. It will give your horse the opportunity to relax, urinate, and drink water. For long trips plenty of *deep bedding* will make him more comfortable about urinating when a trailer is standing. Some horses may not be willing to urinate in the trailer and will need to be taken out and walked around at some relatively safe spot. That will also give them a chance to stretch their legs, recover their balance, drop their necks, blow out their lungs, and generally relax. The longer the journey, the more important this is. If your horse is an experienced traveler and/or has been taught to load and unload easily, this won't present a problem.

AVOID COLIC. The greatest danger to a horse on a long trip is impaction colic. It can be most easily avoided by making plenty of stops for watering, urinating, exercising, and careful feeding while on the road. Feed your horse plenty of good-quality hay while he's trucking. Do not feed him grain. Some seasoned travelers advise dropping the horse's grain ration several days before traveling and replacing it with good-quality hay. Keep the grain ration to a minimum during the trip, feeding him only at night at the layover.

CARRY LARGE CONTAINERS OF WATER. Some containers carry anywhere from fifteen to twenty-five gallons of water. For a horse that is finicky about the taste of different water (see Chapter 7), if you plan to add anything to the water to make it more palatable, start this gradually ten days before you plan to leave. Make sure you have easy access to water buckets. Smaller ones are easier to handle, especially if you have to hold them up for your horse to drink.

STOP EVERY FOUR TO FIVE HOURS FOR AN HOUR. Friends who frequently travel long distances with their horses claim that this helps them stay more alert when driving and allows the horse to let down. When weather is particularly hot, they travel in the evening and at night, resting during the heat of the day at an accommodation. While camping out with your horse, a portable corral is a marvelous asset, allowing him space to move around, recover from "trailer legs," stretch, roll, and just look around.

DO NOT LET YOUR HORSE TRAVEL WITH HIS HEAD OUT THE WINDOW. At fifty to sixty miles an hour, this is extremely dangerous. Another vehicle passing too close or anything blowing into his eyes could be disastrous.

IN COLD WEATHER PAY SPECIAL ATTENTION TO BLANKET WEIGHT. Some horses get nervous during hauling and can work up a sweat under the blanket. In that case a lighter blanket will be needed. Be sure to check your horse under the blanket as you are traveling, so you know his condition.

USE LEG WRAPS ONLY IF YOUR HORSE IS ACCUSTOMED TO THEM. Use a bumper for his head if he's tall or tends to throw his head around a lot.

If you are still gung-ho after these precautions and wish to vacation, camp out, or travel with your horse and need specific information, a directory published by the Equine Travelers of America (ETA) will give you specific information. (See Appendix F.) Membership fees are nominal and will get you an *Overnight Stabling Directory/Equestrian Vacation Guide* and access to a reservation and/or information service. (The guide and the service are also available to nonmembers.) Although you are well advised to talk to the state veterinarian for each state you will be visiting, the ETA directory does include a recent chart of the health requirements of each one.

The *North American Horse Travel Guide* also has a directory with similiar information, including the names and phone numbers of farriers and veterinarians nearest the area you'll be visiting. (See Appendix F.)

The *Overnight Stabling Directory* includes a state-by-state listing with addresses, phone and fax numbers, and available facilities. Besides all states a number of sites in Canada are also included. Some of the accommodations include bed-and-breakfasts, some are private farms and stables, and others are located on fairgrounds with nearby motels. A map of each state or province pinpoints locations and their nearest major highways (available through ETA).

TRAVEL INFORMATION

The Later Years

I have now lived in this happy place a whole year. Joe is the best and kindest of grooms. My work is easy and pleasant, and I feel my strength and spirits all coming back again. Mr. Thoroughgood said to Joe the other day:

"In your place he will last till he is 20 years old—perhaps more."

". . . My ladies have promised that I shall never be sold, and so I have nothing to fear; and here my story ends. My troubles are all over, and I am at home; and often before I am quite awake, I fancy I am still in the Orchard at Birtwick, standing with my old friends under the apple-trees."

Anna Sewell,
BLACK BEAUTY

Many years after Black Beauty went into literary retirement, his life expectancy has nearly doubled. Thanks to improved nutrition, healthier lifestyles, and advances in veterinary medicine, horses in their twenties and thirties, which in the past would have been retired or put down at the first signs of infirmity, are now able to lead active, useful lives.

A horse that was considered old at the turn of the century is just another kid on the block these days, when a life span of thirty-five is not extraordinary. At the time of this writing, three ordinary residents of my barn are the equine equivalents of people in their eighties. These old-timers, all over twenty, lead happy, healthy lives, and two of them put in full working days that include jumping lessons.

Though experts differ slightly on human-equine age comparisons, most would concur with this general estimate:

> First year = 12 human years (hy)
> Second year = 7 hy
> Third–Fifth years = 12 hy (four each)
> Each subsequent year = 2½ hy

Gauged this way, a horse will go through the "terrible twos" at a mere two months, galloping into adolescence by the end of his first year. By the second year a horse is a young adult, reaching early middle age by the age of five.

The care that a horse receives in these formative years is the primary promoter of

Schoolmaster

his longevity. While genetic heritage does play a role in the aging process, so-called "good" genes are no substitute for good nutrition and meticulous maintenance. A horse properly cared for from infancy is the most likely to enjoy a healthy old age.

This bonus in equine years offers a big human dividend as well: older, well-trained horses are ideal mounts for inexperienced child and adult riders—worth more than their weight to a novice, yet costing far less than an educated horse in its prime.

Years of experience have turned these seniors into fine teachers, usually possessed of mellow temperaments that build confidence. Many of today's leading dressage riders have started out on old "schoolmasters"—horses in their late teens or early twenties. With years of methodical training under their girths, they can teach a beginner how upper-level movements feel.

Even when these learned animals are no longer fit to compete, they can be comfortably maintained on low levels of medication, allowing them to do a few hours of work every day.

SIGNS OF AGING

Like some people, some older horses don't look or act their age, having the muscle tone, stamina, and sensory alertness of much younger animals. Because of the variation in individual aging patterns, "oldness" should be defined not by chronology but by signs of physical deterioration: decreasing agility and activity, failing eyesight, and poor hearing.

As cell growth slows with advancing years, the outer tissues lose their youthful mass and resiliency and begin to sag over stringy muscles. This process becomes apparent in drooping lower lips, hollows around the eyes, protruding withers, and a swayback. These changes usually show up by the twenty-fourth or twenty-fifth year and, excepting a swayback, don't affect performance. (Swaybacked horses can still be ridden, but only by lightweights and only for short periods of time.)

Because old cells are slow to regenerate, wounds heal more slowly and merit more medical attention. Reduced efficiency of the endocrine system makes it harder to keep body temperature up where it belongs and destabilizes chemicals secreted by the thyroid and pituitary glands. The digestive system's diminished capacity impedes the processing of protein, which can result in fragile bones, cataracts, and arthritis. All these changes affect the reproductive system—the reason why it's difficult to get older mares back in foal.

The immune system slows down with advancing years, leading to an increase in allergies, hypersensitivity to some feeds, and a high probability that pituitary and/or thyroid tumors will develop. Developing tumors, some still at subclinical stages, were found in 70 percent of a group of horses over age twenty, in a study conducted at the University of Colorado by veterinarian and equine geriatric specialist Dr. Sarah L. Ralston.

Clinical signs of tumors are failure to shed a winter coat, chronic infections, muscle wasting, and increased urination and water intake. Further complications in some horses are insulin-resistant diabetes and an increased tendency to founder. Although the condition is incurable, many horses with pituitary tumors survive for years after the first signs appear and can be helped by a low carbohydrate diet supplemented with extra B and C vitamins.

The most frustrating effect of aging is the decline in motor skills, beginning with loss of speed and followed by lessening agility, strength, and endurance. Physical deterioration cannot be stopped, but it can be slowed down by adjustments to feed, vigilant maintenance, and a carefully planned work schedule. Being aware of the aging process and offsetting it with proper care will add a decade or more to your horse's life span.

DIET AND DIGESTION

In general, the less active the animal, the less food it needs to maintain its ideal weight. This becomes a highly individual matter as a horse gets older. In the later years an appropriate diet will depend on age and condition as well as level of activity.

As inner tissues age, the digestive tract becomes less efficient at breaking down fiber and protein and absorbing and synthesizing nutrients, particularly calcium, phosphorus, and vitamins B and C. Consequently older horses often lose weight even when their teeth and overall health are good.

In a separate study of aged horses with good teeth and normal kidney and liver function, Dr. Ralston found that weight stabilized and body condition improved in those fed a diet high in protein (12 to 14 percent), digestible fat, and fiber, augmented with vitamins B and C. The horses were given sixteen to twenty pounds of "complete" feed daily, portioned at no more than five to six pounds at each of three feedings. If a horse has liver or kidney problems, protein content of feed should not exceed 10 percent.

Complete feeds are just that, formulated to give total nutrition without hay. They are more palatable, easier to chew, and highly nutritious. Most are also very moist, designed to thwart potential digestive problems. Food that is too dry can compact and become lodged in the esophagus, where it will impair swallowing (choke), or in the colon, impeding bowel movements (impaction colic). Small, dry stools are a result of food that is too dry and signal the need for a softer, more liquid diet.

Some precooked foods resemble dog food in texture and become highly digestible when mixed with water. All these special feeds contain most of the extra vitamins and minerals that an older horse needs. Those having trouble with chronic infections of the skin or respiratory system will need additional vitamin C. (Ten grams twice a day is the recommended dose.)

Wheat bran is an excellent bulk laxative, and when mixed with molasses, a little sweet feed, apples, and carrots, it makes a mash that improves digestion and lifts winter-weary spirits. (See Chapter 8.) Bran is also very high in phosphorus, and when mixed in equal amounts with calcium-rich beet pulp, it provides the optimum mix of these minerals. But because of the high mineral concentration, the amount of bran/beet pulp mix given should not exceed four or five pounds per day.

Wheat bran can be fed dry, but only in very small quantities so it doesn't dehydrate a horse. Beet pulp, which swells on contact with moisture, must be soaked in water before feeding. (See Chapter 8.) When hay can't be chewed properly, beet pulp makes a softer, equally high-fiber substitute, but it lacks the nourishment found in hay and will need added vitamin supplements.

Even when an older horse is getting complete feeds, you may want to augment the diet with some good-quality hay, just to give him something to do between meals. Pelleted foods are eaten quickly, leaving horses with a lot of time on their hooves in which to get bored.

DENTITION

A geriatric diet must be developed with equine teeth in mind. Aging horses get literally "long in the tooth" and suffer from loose and missing teeth as well, making it difficult for them to grind up and digest food efficiently. Partially chewed food doesn't release all its nutrients, and if it is too dry, it tends to "wad up," leading to weight loss and the digestive problems already mentioned. A show of hay and grain in the manure is a sure sign of dental problems.

Because older teeth become fragile and shallow-rooted, they can fracture easily when floated. You and your veterinarian may decide that poor dentition is preferable to the risk of losing teeth in the attempt to correct them.

Some older horses have a dental abnormality called *step mouth* or *wave mouth,* caused by the loss of one or more upper molars. It is so named because opposing teeth grow into the space in a steplike pattern, making chewing difficult. This condition can be improved, but rarely corrected entirely, by floating. Another common and irreversible condition is that of tooth surfaces worn perfectly smooth over the years by the grinding action of chewing, appropriately called *smooth mouth.*

In all these cases a moister and more nutritious diet is called for, in order to maximize digestive efficiency. One solution is the complete-formula pellets mentioned earlier. Another is high-quality extended feeds especially designed for senior stomachs, which contain extra vitamins and minerals to help break down food. These are soft enough to be chewed by bad teeth and sufficiently moist to be easily mashed into gruel for those nearly toothless old-timers who have to "gum it."

Where winters are hard, healthy seniors should be fed twice daily with a good-quality grass hay, supplemented with either linseed or soybean meal or one of the moist geriatric supplements. Alfalfa hay, fine for younger animals, has a high protein and calcium content that is hard on aging kidneys. In southern states, a product called Dengee Hay is available, cut into one-inch lengths for easier eating. (Make sure to get the Dengee oat grass, not alfalfa.) Never overfeed your horse. Remember that the amount fed must reflect the level of activity and the age and condition of the horse.

FITNESS

The horse that holds the world record for longevity spent most of his sixty-two years pulling canal barges in Lancashire, England. Old Bill, listed in the *Guinness Book of Records* as a Cleveland-Eastern breed cross who lived from 1760 to 1822, certainly had genetic heritage going for him. (Cleveland bays are notably long-lived.) But his job also kept him in top-notch condition. Several equine historians have expressed doubts about Bill's longevity, noting that a successor might have been given the same name. Even so, thirty-one was a long equine life back then.

The twentieth century's oldest horse to date was an Icelandic mare, who died in Denmark at age fifty-six. In this area a Quarter Horse named Amos became a testimonial to fitness, still going on trail rides well into his fourth decade. Had his career not been cut short by a freak accident, Amos might have beaten Old Bill's record; alas, at age forty-six he was struck down in his pasture by a lightning bolt.

These are extraordinary examples of longevity, of course, but the older residents of my barn testify to what ordinary horses can look forward to if properly cared for.

A fit horse of any age is lean and well muscled, with an even, shining coat. This condition is achieved only by appropriate diet, a regular deworming program, daily grooming, and regular exercise. When planning your horse's workouts, remember that advancing years first take their toll on speed, then on agility, strength, and endurance. So assess your horse's physical condition, and adjust the working schedule accordingly. Swayed backs and arthritic hocks cannot carry a lot of weight. A hunter that could go for hours in the field as a ten-year-old may be up for only a slow half-hour hack at age twenty-five. Try to schedule regular exercise, preferably at the same time and in periods of equal duration, the amount determined by individual capabilities.

Because aging muscles lose tone more quickly, it's very hard for an older horse to resume work after a long period of inactivity. A horse that has been idle for a long period because of illness or injury should resume activity gradually in increments of five to ten minutes, mostly at a walk, with a little trotting, working up to a quarter of an hour in the first week, half an hour in the second, and forty-five minutes in the third (if he is up to it). Trotting periods should be gradually increased and interspersed with a few minutes of walking. End each work session with a five-minute walk to cool the horse out. If you miss several sessions, working time should be decreased by ten minutes, then gradually increased again. Watch your horse's vital signs to determine how much is enough. (See Chapter 30.)

Even a lame horse can benefit from a routine workout. In a case of navicular disease, anti-inflammatory medication and corrective shoeing should allow the affected animal to continue with regular exercise.

Plan daily turnouts along with the work schedule. No horse should be stabled constantly unless it is necessary for medical reasons or because of inclement weather. Inactivity leads to a decrease in flexibility and range of motion in arthritic joints, while recreational exercise is essential to promote good circulation and relieve stiffness. Consequently the ideal stable arrangement for an elderly equine is a box stall adjoining a paddock, allowing him free access to turnout when weather permits. If this isn't possible, turn your horse out to pasture for at least two hours a day in the wintertime and all day during mild weather, even overnight if the pasture has shelter.

An important adjunct to exercise is daily grooming to help circulation, keep skin tone healthy, and shed out the coat when necessary. Often an older horse has difficulty shedding his winter coat. When extra currying doesn't do the job, a food supplement called MSM can help; speak to your veterinarian about it.

Grooming is a pleasant social interlude for horse and rider, also affording an opportunity to keep a close eye on your senior's behavior, attitude, and condition. Because of the weakened immune system and sluggish cell growth, even a hint of illness or injury merits veterinary attention.

PREVENTIVE CARE

The regularly scheduled preventive care that all horses should receive from infancy becomes particularly important with advancing years. Apart from the vaccinations necessary in your area and dental exams, an older horse should be dewormed every six to eight weeks to destroy intestinal parasites that sap the nutrients from food. (See Chapter 21.) Lost weight that can be fairly easily regained in an eight-year-old horse will be extremely hard to put back on a decade later.

Regular shoeing and hoof care is equally important. As feet are used less, they grow longer, and hooves are liable to split and crack more easily, placing abnormal stress on the legs and feet, which can lead to bruising and abscesses. Senior hooves should be trimmed or shod every month to six weeks, depending on the individual. (See Chapter 16.)

HUSBANDRY

Inappropriate equine companions and annoying human visitors can upset an older horse's stomach as well as his nerves, so stable and pasture accommodations should be arranged to maximize enjoyment and minimize stress.

The stall should be as comfortable as possible, picked out at least twice a day and given an extra layer of bedding at night to keep out chills and cushion old bones. Because an aging body's "thermostat" is less vigorous, the effort to keep warm burns up extra calories. Accordingly, the stall should be dry, draft-free, and preferably insulated in colder climates, to contain the body heat generated by its occupant.

Arthritic horses often have a hard time getting to their feet and do not move around much when they get there. Inactivity in the stable depresses circulation and, during the winter, increases the risk of hypothermia. In the pasture a horse could die if he lies down on snow and cannot get up again; the heat of the body will melt the snow to ice, pinning him down. Thus aching joints will need the protection of warm blankets inside and out.

Pasture space for a senior should be ample and fenced apart to keep him hassle free. Horses are highly convivial creatures, but like other members of the animal kingdom, they have a social hierarchy in which status diminishes with age. An old gelding would be miserable trying to defend his pasture space against an intruder half his age, while an arthritic mare wouldn't be able to defend it at all. In consequence, a senior's recreational surroundings should be as tranquil as possible—away from pushy equine companions and pesky children.

In general horses prefer the company of their own age group. When that cannot be arranged, a friend of another species can provide peaceful companionship.

PAMPERING

In the later years contrary behavior that would need correction in a younger horse can often be given free rein. And why not? After giving you years of riding pleasure, your old partner may have gotten a tad cantankerous. As long as this behavior doesn't endanger him or anyone else, go ahead and indulge his wayward ways. If his appetite gets finicky, tempt him with the treats he loves. If his whims are extra-dietary, cater to them.

A close friend who owns a dude ranch was dismayed when her formerly reliable trail horse, Gunsmoke, turned into a geriatric delinquent. Apparently weary of the same old routines, he began to balk at being confined to the paddock and rebelled against trails he didn't like, galloping away from the group and through the woods to a preferred route, with a terrified dude hanging on. By the time he was twenty-five, Gunsmoke had become an equine escape artist, able to break out of any pasture, often with the entire herd trailing in his wake. Being padlocked in his stall during trail rides caused him to work up such a lather that he had to be walked out and sponged off to cool down. Today, pushing thirty, a truce has been reached. Gunsmoke has his own way, roaming free around the stable area and allowed to tag along, riderless, on the trail rides. He's having the time of his life, and guests at the ranch adore him.

BLINDNESS

Although it's commonly assumed that horses who lose all or part of their vision are doomed to subsequent misery, knowledgeable horsemen and women know this isn't always the case. With careful management, many one-eyed or totally blind horses function surprisingly well, avoiding injury and continuing to be useful under controlled circumstances. Visually impaired horses are remarkably adaptive, able to sharpen and adjust their other senses to cope with their surroundings and communicate in new ways with other horses and human handlers. At first the conscientious owner will need to be a visual guide, working to establish a new riding and handling vocabulary. With patience, such guidance can forge a closer, more trusting partnership.

A former school horse of mine gradually lost her sight, over a four-year period, first in the left, then in the right eye. The cause was moon blindness, one of the many eye diseases that can afflict older horses. Amerah was a wonderful fifteen-year-old Anglo-Arab mare, an excellent trail horse who could do some dressage and jumped a steady course over fences. When her vision began to fail in the second eye, the jumping had to stop, but the rest of her activities continued until her twenty-third year, when she had to be put down because of other problems.

In Maryland a seven-year-old Shetland pony was given up for adoption when she became blind. She was placed in a new home by the agency HorseNet. Skipper now goes on trail rides, drives, and is learning dressage.

Horses adjust more easily to blindness when its onset is gradual and they are kept in familiar surroundings. It helps if they are confident, people-oriented performers with a fairly laid-back disposition. High-strung horses that are flighty and hard to work with often become dangerous when blind, although I've heard of several instances where horses like this calmed down after loss of vision, becoming more dependent on people. In another case, a horse that was increasingly skittish as visual deterioration progressed became placid when totally blind.

Horses gradually deprived of vision depend more and more on sound, smell, and tactile stimuli, developing individual techniques to expand and use the remaining senses—like cocking their ears toward walls to estimate distance by differences in the sound vibrations. Some develop unusual habits like tilting their heads or weaving and swinging them back and forth. Others will balk at any obstruction. In 1982 the Kentucky Derby had a one-eyed entrant named Cassaleria who became so agitated by the sensory deprivation of the box stall assigned to her that her handlers had to get permission to build one with a 360-degree view of Churchill Downs.

To compensate for loss of vision, some blind horses carry their heads unusually low or high, pricking or wagging their ears constantly and navigating by running their noses along fences or walls. This behavior seems to help them make a mental map of their surroundings. They often become so adept that observers are unaware of their condition.

In some social situations herd mates may take advantage of a blind horse, harassing or pushing him out of the group entirely. In these circumstances a horse could be hurt because he cannot see the signals, like laid-back ears and bared teeth, that would normally warn him of hostile intent. If you are planning to keep a visually impaired horse in pasture, be sure that the situation is safe.

In other instances blind horses have been known to devise an equine buddy system with sighted companions, keeping nose-to-tail contact and calling back and forth to avoid danger. A study of a wild herd in Utah, in which a genetic defect rendered many members blind, found that sightless individuals and their normal companions whinnied constantly to keep tabs on each other. Many owners attest that working with a blind horse leads to a rewarding relationship. Horse and rider develop a special command vocabulary of touch, pressure, and verbal cues to warn of hazards, creating a special bond of trust.

RETIREMENT

Sometimes an ailing senior can be invigorated by a change in environment. A twenty-six-year-old schoolmaster, owned by a friend, was getting stiff and having difficulty shedding his coat despite a hearty appetite and near-perfect teeth. When my friend had to move south for business reasons, she took her old pal along. She now reports that he's rejuvenated, with a gleaming spring coat and enough renewed agility to cavort with younger horses.

When a horse has to retire from work because of age or disability, the owner may not have the space for or be able to afford keeping both the pensioner and the new riding horse that has replaced him. In these cases a retirement home may be the answer.

More than a hundred agencies devoted to horse welfare are located in the United States alone. Some of them provide retirement facilities, while others place older equines in new homes as pleasure horses, schoolmasters, or companion animals. HorseNet, mentioned earlier, recently saved twenty-seven older horses from slaughter

after a riding stable in upstate New York closed down. With the help of the animal rescue agency Noah's Ark, in Stone Ridge, the redundant horses were relocated in new homes as distant as California, Oklahoma, and Arizona, with owners who paid from three to five hundred dollars for them.

HorseNet's many success stories include three Baltimore horses placed in homes where they will have new careers as beginner's mounts, and a neglected thirty-three-year-old show pony named Teddy Bear, who in earlier days had won ribbons in both English and Western classes for various owners throughout Florida. After a winning season with a new owner who subsequently lost interest, he was left without food in a filthy stall for months until a member of the local Pony Club learned of his plight and phoned HorseNet. When the rescuers arrived, Teddy Bear was half dead and barely able to stand. After a winter of rehabilitation by HorseNet director Ellie Powers, the pony was adopted as a companion animal by a retired woman whose hobby, coincidentally, is collecting teddy bears.

Many other retirement homes provide boarding and complete care for a minimal monthly fee. In Alachua, Florida, Peter and Mary Gregory share their 240-acre retirement home Millcreek Farm with seventy-three horses. A horse must be twenty years old to qualify for admission, and the monthly sixty-dollar fee is all-inclusive. The Gregorys are helped by student volunteers and a volunteer veterinarian.

These and other organizations will send information packets on request. A complete list of equine retirement homes in the United States, including several in Canada and England, is available from the American Horse Protection Association. (See Appendix F.)

The time comes to every creature when the miseries of declining health outweigh the value of continued life. Wild animals often sense when the end is near and wander from the group to die alone. Domestic animals, lacking this option, need human intervention.

SAYING GOOD-BYE

It's always a tough call and one that only you can make. This is a time when compassion and responsibility toward your horse must be foremost. Your love won't cure old age, and all the money in the world can't prevent natural physical deterioration. Put sentiment aside and consider the increasing pain suffered and the indignity of impaired coordination that makes it hard for the old fellow to lie down and get up again.

In reaching the decision to put a horse down, seek the counsel of your veterinarian, who can be relied on for candid, dispassionate advice. Euthanasia is a much more humane and practical alternative than a gradual and agonizing decline to death from "natural causes" in the stall or pasture. In the former case you might have to tear down the stall and possibly part of the barn to remove the body. In the latter instance you'd need a forklift. Should you decide to put your horse down, the veterinarian can help determine which method is best (usually a lethal injection, preceded by a tranquilizer and/or anesthetic) and can arrange beforehand to have the body removed immediately after death. (There are firms that perform this service for a modest fee.)

If you wish to bury the horse on your property (checking first to see if local zoning laws allow it and if your land survey shows the burial area to be free of pipes and groundwires), arrange in advance for a backhoe to dig the grave and stand by to fill it in when the job is done. (The horse should be put down as close as possible to the grave.)

However unpleasant this is to discuss, it is better to work out the details calmly in advance while you still have the opportunity to arrange the entire procedure with experts. I strongly advise that you not be present when the horse is put down. Better to remember your old friend alive and at his best.

PART XII

Getting Along Together

Go anywhere in England where there are natural, wholesome, contented, and really nice English people, and what do you always find? That the stables are the real center of the household.

—George Bernard Shaw,
HEARTBREAK HOUSE

Bad Manners Versus Vices

B ack when horses were the main mode of transport, human mobility depended on equine reliability. If a hack misbehaved, the behavioral equivalent of a garage mechanic was summoned to set things right. Known as "whisperers" because they mumbled secretively into the ears of obstreperous mounts, these sorcerers were believed to have a supernatural ability to tame and charm any horse, no matter how wild. Among the tools of their trade were talismans like toad bones, blanched and dried in an anthill; oil of burdock; and hooves from dead horses, which they nailed above the stable door. People with ill-mannered mounts paid high rates for the services of these "therapists."

What once passed for witchcraft was more likely compassion, patience, understanding, and discipline. Anyone who keeps a horse around the house will eventually practice some of this sorcery to forestall bad habits and manners and forge a happy and enduring relationship.

Horses are our fellow creatures, not sources of entertainment. They deserve sympathy and respect as well as firm guidance. But fond feelings cannot be allowed to interfere with discipline. Just as good stable manners should be rewarded with a pat, a kind word, or an occasional treat, a horse that behaves badly must be punished immediately. A spoiled horse is as annoying as a spoiled child—and twenty times as dangerous. Remember that you're the boss. He may be stronger, but you have the clear edge on brains.

Here are some of the more common bad manners that are not to be tolerated and should be corrected in any horse.

Biting

My students occasionally complain that their horses bite. When I ask if they ever hand-feed them, the answer is always yes. Hand-feeding is a sure way to teach a horse to bite, and if you have a horse that is "mouthy," stop!

A horse that is hand-fed learns to look for a snack and starts to nuzzle, push, and beg whenever his benefactor comes around. At first this may seem like an endearing trait, but sooner or later any horse accustomed to handouts will get annoyed when he isn't offered a snack and bite the hand that doesn't feed him. This could injure a child seriously, leading to a consequent fear of horses.

Should your horse try to bite you, the immediate punishment is a smack on the nose, accompanied by a sharp "no!" If done fairly and not too frequently, this rebuke won't make the horse head shy. Follow up by feeding him a snack from a feed dish or bucket. Even if the treat is only a carrot or two, cut it into strips and put it in an aluminum pie pan or his feed dish, not the palm of your hand.

Young horses—colts in particular—tend to be more oral than adults in their greetings, and biting is often an expression of their affection. If a one- or two-year-old tries to nip you, he's probably being playful, but you should discourage the act just the same. A horse of any age who tries to bite with his ears laid flat back doesn't have kind intentions.

Young horses will sometimes make a game out of punishment, trying to give you a nip and then pulling back before you can smack them. The best response to this youthful behavior is to stay out of biting range, warn others to do the same, and wait for your horse to outgrow it.

Cow-kicking

When a horse cow-kicks (kicks out sideways with a hind leg when you are grooming or mounting), he should be hit across the rump with a crop and given a sharp reprimand. Some authorities advise the more extreme punishment of kicking him back in the stomach with the side of your foot, but a crop is just as effective, and sometimes it just takes a firm "no!" You must let the horse know that this behavior is unacceptable. If you've been kicked while saddling or grooming, it may be your fault or the previous owner's. In the future take care and time to slide the saddle gently into place and tighten the girth slowly a hole at a time, interspersed with other grooming or tacking-up chores. When grooming with the curry, remember that your horse might be ticklish or sensitive. Watch his ears and expression, and take your time.

When I encounter this type of behavior, I treat the horse as if he were young. I go back to the basics of handling and gradually reintroduce him to currying, saddling, girth tightening, and mounting, areas in which the problem probably lies. (See Chapter 29.)

Crowding

In a stall crowding is an extremely disagreeable and potentially dangerous habit. In a straight stall a horse should immediately move over when you pat him on the rump and say "over." Don't enter the stall until he does. If the set of a horse's ears or a leg indicates that he has other ideas, speak firmly to him, and carry a crop where he can see it. When a bad actor finally does obey the command, give him a pat to encourage continued good behavior, or put a treat in his feedbox.

Cow-Kicking

When you enter a box stall, the horse should be taught to turn toward you. Swinging his rump around or crowding you is an unfriendly act, usually caused by rough or careless handling. In most cases such defiant behavior is a bluff, but if it isn't, you don't want to be on the receiving end. Move out of the way—but not in a frightened, jumpy manner that might scare your horse or show him that you're afraid. Be sure to speak to him.

Crowding when you enter with feed can be corrected with a little work. When you enter the stall, take your horse by the halter, put a hand on his chest, and say "back." Then bring in the grain. Hold him back from the feed dish as you pour the grain in. Before leaving the stall, turn him to face the doorway.

Many trainers feel that stall behavior is indicative of a horse's general attitude and conduct. At one stable that houses three hundred purebreds, horses are taught to stand in the middle of the stall as the attendant pours the grain, not approaching the feed dish until he leaves. This is considered routine good manners.

Owners often inadvertently cause bad stall behavior. I board a horse that has excellent stable manners, but he returned from a summer at home with a new habit of kicking out when his feet were picked up. It turned out that the young owner had been picking up his horse's feet in the pasture without tying him first. With nothing to stop him, the horse eventually started to walk away (reasonable behavior under the circumstances), becoming annoyed when the boy pursued him and tried to pick up his feet. The habit wouldn't have developed if the boy had just taken a few minutes to tie the horse properly. After three or four sessions we corrected the problem, and the horse again became his normal, well-behaved self.

Grazing During a Ride

As mentioned earlier, many ponies have very strong necks for their size. If a pony stops suddenly during a ride to graze, a young rider could be wrenched from the saddle. If he inadvertently steps on a rein, breaking it or the bridle and throwing his head up suddenly as the pressure is relieved, his rider could either be unseated then or fall off later as the pony races for home—a scary scenario in either case.

A horse should never be allowed to try to stop and graze with the bridle on, nor to graze while standing when you're in the saddle. To prevent this behavior, keep a firm hold on the reins and maintain a light contact with your horse's mouth at all times. If he keeps trying to graze, punish him first by voice, then by a smack on the rump with your crop. A pony that persists in this habit should wear an antigrazing sidecheck (available through tack catalogs).

Not Standing for Mounting

A horse that won't stand still for mounting is a nuisance to ride on the trail or in the ring, where he would be disqualified in a hack or pleasure class. Apart from that, it's awkward and undignified to hop after a horse with your foot in the stirrup. Teach your horse to stand still until you have adjusted the stirrup, gathered up your reins, and mounted, and to move out only at your command.

This problem could result from tugging on the saddle, sticking a toe in the horse's side as you mount, thudding down in the saddle, or trying to mount with long, loose, or uneven reins. If mounting is difficult for you, never pull on the saddle; rather, let your stirrup down three or four notches, and adjust it to the right length when you are mounted—acceptable procedure even in the show ring.

Using a mounting block is more comfortable for the rider and easier on the horse's back. An inexpensive, lightweight two-step block can be purchased at any tack shop or through a tack catalog, to make mounting a pleasant experience for you both.

Rubbing or Butting the Rider

After a ride a horse is usually hot and itchy and may, if allowed, try to scratch or butt his head against your shoulder as you lead him—behavior that's hard on you as well as your clothes. An equine head has a lot of weight behind it, enough to knock a child down and throw an adult off balance. A pleasant riding horse shouldn't treat people like trees and fence posts. If your horse tries to rub or butt, say "no" forcefully, and slap him on the neck.

Running Off in the Pasture

After leading your horse through the gate, say "easy" as you unsnap the lead, encouraging him to leave you in a quiet manner. You will thereby gain his trust and make it easier to catch him again.

If your horse pulls away while being led or when you're unsnapping the lead rope, the cause is poor handling sometime in his history. (Review the section on leading in Chapter 12.)

When you are leading your horse into the pasture, take him all the way inside, close the gate, and turn him to face you before you unsnap the lead or remove the halter. Children often unsnap the lead before the horse is all the way through the gate, but this will create a problem if he decides midway that he doesn't want to go in. (He can leave the child in the pasture while he takes off to explore elsewhere.)

Having to wrestle with a gate before turning a horse out is nerve-racking for both of you. A pasture gate should be lightweight, secure, and easily opened and closed with one hand. Many styles that suit different budgets can be purchased at your local farm supply store, an expenditure that will save a lot of aggravation.

By gaining a horse's confidence and handling him properly, you can easily train him to come to you. If he's at first difficult to catch, offer him treats or grain in a bucket for a few weeks to teach him to approach. And schedule riding for a certain hour of the day, so he'll get used to being caught at that time.

Don't follow the example of some inexperienced riders and run around the pasture after your horse shouting and waving carrots. This is a sure way not to catch him. Any horse will be frightened by the noise and activity, distrusting his pursuer and sensing that he's being treated as an object to ride. Horses are naturally gregarious, curious animals who enjoy company, but they also have an elemental fear of strange sights and noises—a trait that protects them in the wild.

When you go to catch your horse in the pasture, don't approach in a direct line. Instead, mosey out without looking directly at him, keeping him in your peripheral vision. Have the halter and lead over your shoulder to make them as unobtrusive as possible, and *take your time*. Ideally, when you get close, he should come to you. If that's not the case, approach him from the side, not the front, touching him first on the shoulder and then the neck so he won't be frightened. Then talk to him and pat him for a few moments before sliding the halter on.

Your horse will trust you more and enjoy being ridden more if you spend quality time with him in daily grooming and handling. He will demonstrate this trust by walking right up to you or standing still with ears pricked as you approach. (Some horses can be trained to respond to a whistle.) Whenever my husband or I went into the pasture to repair a fence, we always had a friendly muzzle or two at our shoulders, checking to see what was going on.

Leaving a halter on a pastured horse makes him easier to catch, but the dangers often outweigh the advantages. If a horse gets itchy and rubs against a branch or fence post, the halter could get caught. I've heard of a number of horses that were

badly injured when an unbreakable nylon halter got snagged. And a horse that scratches his ears with a hind foot, like a dog, is liable to catch it in the halter.

Halters can also get lost, buried in the mud, or chewed off by a buddy. I seldom turn a horse out with halter on, preferring to hang it near the pasture gate with a lead rope attached. Occasionally, when a new horse has a temporary attitude about being caught, I will turn him out for a few days in a breakable halter.

One exceptional incident comes to mind, when I was the newly arrived manager at an Arabian breeding farm. A beautiful, very high-strung yearling colt named Zatellite was presenting serious leading problems, or I should say, catching problems. (He had been extremely mishandled by the previous—nonhorseman—farm caretaker and consequently had never even been led from his paddock.) The first fruitless attempt to move him from paddock to barn took more than two exasperating hours. Instead of catching him, three of us finally ended up hazing him into the barn and then a stall.

Eventually, after many hours of slow, gentle handling, we were able to slip a halter on him. It was apparent that it would take a great deal of time and repetition to undo his trauma and fear and replace it with trust. I decided to leave a snug green halter on him all the time (by then he was relaxed when I touched the halter), place another halter over the green one when he was moved from the stall to pasture, and remove it when he was released and vice versa. By following this daily routine for several weeks, interspersed with many hours of TLC, he became a very sweet and obedient horse. He went on to become an Arabian National Top Ten Halter Gelding.

VICES

Some equine habits transcend bad manners to become serious personality problems called vices. Stall walking, weaving, digging, kicking, cribbing, striking, charging, chewing, and eating dirt are vices that develop when horses are stabled for long periods, standing idle with nothing to capture their interest. Some vices are damaging only to property; others are dangerous to horse and owner. High-strung, nervous horses are more prone to this type of behavior.

Charging

Some nasty horses will charge when you enter their box stall or pasture. A whip will help discourage this vice, which results from past mishandling. But rebuilding the horse's trust is the best route to a lasting cure.

Chewing

Unlike cribbers, who get their front teeth on wood and gulp air, chewers just gnaw away on it. It is equally dangerous because the horse may swallow sharp particles, get colic, wear down his teeth, or develop an infection from a splinter. If this vice is not nipped in the bud, it can become chronic or develop into cribbing.

Chewing is usually a result of boredom and/or stress, which can be caused by being stabled for extended periods, cold or wet weather, lack of exercise—or running out of hay to chew on. When researchers at the University of Illinois put video cameras in the stalls of chronic chewers, they found that they did most of their gnawing during the night (horses sleep only three hours a night, leaving a lot of time to misbehave), and that time they spent chewing decreased as their exercise increased. Horses receiving no exercise chewed considerably longer than those spending forty-five minutes a day on a mechanical walker followed by an equal amount of turnout time.

A separate study by the Illinois group suggests that hunger may be a contributing factor. Horses that were turned out at night continued to graze, even after dark, while those stabled began to chew several hours after the evening feeding, when they had finished their hay ration.

New antichew remedies have been developed to replace the old standby, creosote, which is carcinogenic and can burn lips and lungs if chewed or inhaled. One product has cayenne pepper as an active ingredient. We find that Tabasco or other similar hot sauces work very well. These remedies can also be used to deter horses from chewing cross-ties, bandages, blankets, and leg wraps.

Cribbing or Windsucking

When a horse grasps an object with the front teeth, pulling back and up with an arching movement of the neck and gulping air at the same time, this is cribbing. It is the most common of all the vices and is so called because hay cribs are usually chewed first.

Aside from being hard on stalls and pasture fences, this vice is easily picked up by stablemates—something to consider if you're thinking of buying a known cribber. The vice can develop when a horse needs his teeth floated, or it can be learned by watching other cribbers. To discourage this activity, you can put a cribbing strap snugly around the horse's neck when he is idle. It will press on the throat when he pulls his neck up in the act of cribbing. An alternative is to apply an anticribbing spray or paint to vulnerable surfaces.

Cribbing has been found to have a narcotic effect: it causes the brain to release substances called endorphins that produce feelings of euphoria and well-being. Researchers at the Tufts University School of Veterinary Medicine found

Cribbing Strap

that stressed horses became addicted to the endorphins, not to the cribbing, and that they ceased doing it after receiving narcotic-antagonist drugs that neutralized the euphoric effect. At this writing the cost of these drugs is too high to make them commercially practical.

Digging

Fortunately digging is a rare vice and can be stopped by putting the horse on a wood or asphalt floor. On a dirt or clay floor, a digger can scoop out huge holes, sometimes three feet deep—an obvious danger because he might fall into his excavation. Filling the holes with water is a classic remedy, but I think it would be easier to change the flooring—or sell the horse.

Drinking Excessively

Boredom sometimes drives horses to drink—water, that is—which they drink and drink. This causes them to urinate and urinate until their stall turns into a swamp. Horses that acquire this vice are usually confined to a stall or small corral with an automatic watering system. After testing him first to rule out diabetes, kidney disease, or other organic causes, water a heavy drinker the old-fashioned way—with a bucket—or take him out to water several times a day.

Eating Dirt

Eating dirt in the pasture can indicate a mineral deficiency, a parasitic infection, or the same kind of psychological stress that leads to nail biting in humans. The vice often leads to colic. Soaking a horse's favorite dirt spots with pine oil will discourage the habit.

Stall Kicking

Kicking at stall walls can become a vice unless it is corrected early. Not only is kicking rough on your stable, but the kicker can develop blemishes or damage his hocks and tendons. Some kickers seem to enjoy the noise they make, and stablemates overhearing it might decide to join in the fun. A smack on the rump with a crop will usually discourage this habit. I've also found it effective to just strike the side of the stall with a whip and say "no!"

Giving careful attention to daily exercise, and adjusting the grain ration to the amount of work being done, will usually stop this symptom of boredom. One of my boarders, who started stall kicking when he was stabled for several days after an ice storm, stopped as soon as his regular working schedule resumed.

If kicking is allowed to become a habit, it can carry over to the trailer, where it is both annoying and dangerous. I once trailered a client's horse with this vice, who started kicking the back door of the trailer when we stopped for a red light. I asked my assistant to run around to the back of the trailer, smack her on the rump, and shout "no!" It worked like a charm, keeping her quiet for the rest of the ride. I'm sure the wide-eyed elderly couple in the car behind us thought we were being terribly cruel.

Stall Walking

Horses with this vice have formed the habit of pacing or sometimes trotting around their stall or pasture for hours at a time, wearing a circular track in a dirt or clay floor and messing up the bedding, or tearing up the field and losing weight in the process.

A horse that is turned out daily or exercised regularly will probably not develop this vice. But pacing is sometimes a symptom of "separation anxiety," occurring when a horse accustomed to company is turned out alone or left in the stall without nearby companionship. Tranquilizing drugs can be used, under a vet's supervision, to treat this problem. Another approach, suggested by the Cornell University *Animal Health Newsletter,* is to wean a pacer from his companions gradually, leaving one in an adjacent stall when the others leave, then moving the other horse down one stall and then two, over a period of three weeks. If this fails, a companion animal like a pony or goat should keep a pacer calm. Stall walking can be often discouraged by placing obstacles like rubber tires or bales of hay in the pacer's path.

Striking

What often starts as simple pawing can develop into a habit of striking with a front foot. This can become a very dangerous and frightening vice if allowed to continue. Punish the problem horse by standing to his side and striking the offending leg with a whip or crop. This vice usually decreases as exercise is increased.

Weaving

Weaving is a common vice among high-strung fillies, caused by nerves and excess energy. A horse with this habit stands in front of a stall door or window and rocks, or weaves, back and forth on her front legs. (A Thoroughbred I once boarded did this all the time, and one of my students used to say she was dancing.) A weaving horse will lose weight from the increased exercise, and stablemates looking on will mimic the vice.

One veterinarian recommends hanging tires, chains, or water-filled cans from the stall ceiling, rigged so the weaver will bump into them. But he concedes that a chronic weaver will get used to the bumps and drips, working them into the routine. The best remedy is plenty of daily exercise and stimulating surroundings—like a window opening on the paddock yard to let the horse see what's going on.

TIPS FOR BEATING BOREDOM

When a horse has to be stabled for an extended period, stall toys are a useful diversion. Half of a rubber tire, a knotted burlap bag, a rubber ball, or a plastic bleach bottle with paper removed and some pebbles inside can be hung from the ceiling on an elastic string to give your horse something to butt around and chew on. Some breeding stables pamper their horses with all kinds of diverting toys. One trainer even put a mirror in the stall of a high-strung filly to give her the illusion of company. And a stable in Arizona soothes its air-conditioned occupants with piped-in music.

Among the commercial toys available is a large, red plastic apple that can be tied to the stall ceiling or given to the horse in the pasture. Many of these toys have thick unbreakable handles so that rambunctious equines can pick them up and toss them around.

Remember to never leave anything that you don't want chewed or played with around the stall or pasture. When my husband and I went out to mend fences one overcast day, he hung his expensive new mackintosh on a post in case of a sudden downpour. A few minutes later we froze to the unmistakable sound of tearing cloth and turned to see each of our two colts shaking a severed section of raincoat in his teeth.

If your horse does not have to be stall bound for health reasons, the best preventive against boredom vices is daily turnout and/or regular exercise, either riding or lunging.

HORSE SENSE

Some horses are smarter than others, but even those of relatively high intelligence are not, compared with humans, very bright. Horses have tiny brains, with approximately the same reasoning capacity and attention span as a child in nursery school. But their limited mental abilities are balanced by prodigious memories, making them quite easy to train.

Equine senses, however, are far better developed than ours. Their vision is superb. Like cats, they can see well in the dark and, except for a small blind spot, have a much wider span of vision than humans, able to see somewhat to the rear and side as well as the front.

As any equestrian knows, horses are frightened by loud or unexpected noises. Their hearing is particularly sensitive, and it's important to speak in low tones when working around them. A horse confronted by a shouting child will react with fear or visible annoyance.

Because horses have a highly developed sense of feeling, they can be trained to respond to the subtle riding aids of seat, leg pressure, and hands. The equine sense of taste is also quite refined, and some horses are very discriminating about changes in water or their choice of food, favoring entrées of sardines and artichokes over fodder. Others have more common tastes, going in for ice cream or hot dogs (a favorite of the famous racehorse Kelso).

The least developed of all equine senses is smell, but wild horses are still keen enough to smell water and stallions to scent mares in season. And any horse will react to the odor of a rider's fear.

By understanding a horse's intellectual and sensory capabilities and limitations, you can learn to behave in an appropriate manner around him. Make no sudden movements, and speak in a soft, relaxed voice. In new surroundings a horse should always be allowed to become familiar with the area by sight and smell before any demands are made of him. Before riding a strange horse, approach to let him see and smell you.

The Social Scene

Like all other animals, humans included, horses observe a social pecking order. In any large stable one horse will be the acknowledged reigning monarch of the pasture, with a descending hierarchy of lords, ladies, and serfs. As long as all the stablemates know their place, things will work out fine, but occasionally two horses will compete for top billing, and then there's trouble. Usually these disputes are resolved in a day or two, but if they drag on longer, the conflicting horses must be separated for their own protection.

In small pastures or paddocks of a quarter acre or less, no more than two compatible horses should be put together, both for their sake and the pasture's future. (See Chapter 11.) If you have the acreage and are introducing a newcomer to a pasture with several others, it's best to segregate him on the first day with your friendliest and most dependable horse, so the gang won't pick on him. After a few days move him in with the others, watching carefully for any signs of an uprising. The trouble often comes not from the kingpin but from the low man in the pasture, who sees the new horse as an opportunity to improve his social standing. One of my horses, an exceptionally mild-mannered gelding with no status at all among his peers and no apparent pretensions, spent a happy week lording it over a short-term boarder. The poor visitor cowered in the far corner of the pasture all day, while my horse, mad with newfound power, stalked up and down imperiously to make sure he stayed there.

Occasionally a horse who has had the room at the top in one stable finds himself on a different floor when sold to another. A beautiful 16-hand Thoroughbred gelding who once reigned supreme in my pasture ended up in the equine basement at his new home, where he was chased mercilessly around the paddock by a Shetland pony.

Just because a horse is loved by humans and horses alike when he's out on a ride doesn't mean he can be turned out indiscriminately. We have a beautiful quarter horse gelding in our barn, adored by his stablemates and human acquaintances, but in the pasture he always manages to get himself or another horse into trouble. He wants to play constantly, pestering his more sedate companions until they become fed up and start to bite or kick. Not even a fence deters him from playing chewing games—once he mischievously tore a fly mask off a pal on the other side.

GAMES HORSES PLAY

Being herd animals, horses naturally like company. With very close stablemates this can be a problem, particularly when one is left behind. Some horses get hysterical when their friends leave, breaking down stall doors and fences to follow them.

A former school horse of mine tried to kick out the door of his new owner's two-horse trailer when he was trucked to a show without his stablemate. In another instance a friend's Anglo-Arab, awaiting his class from a box stall outside the show ring, saw his companion competing and jumped over the Dutch door to join him, keeping pace outside the rails as the stablemate trotted within.

A Thoroughbred hunter I once had used to jump over the pasture gate whenever his stablemate was taken on the trail. He came from a big stable where he had constant company and had developed a real neurosis about being left alone. Actually, since he'd shown that he could get out at will, he was quite reasonable about it, hopping the fence not only to follow his friend, but also at dinnertime so he could amble over to the stable and peer across the feed room door to watch me scoop out the grain.

Situations like this can be avoided by separating stablemates frequently when they are young and not always taking them out together. A trail horse that constantly looks back and balks at moving out in front isn't a pleasant ride. And when you're miles from home, it's no fun to have a galloping stablemate suddenly appear on the horizon.

If you have only one horse and he looks lonely, you may want to get him a companion. Horses are fond of cats, dogs, chickens, ducks, and goats—and at my stable, even a raccoon. One friend has two stable cats that leap from the rafters to her horse's back, often stopping to nap there.

The racehorse Portico II was as renowned for her mascot as her prowess on the track. Her companion was a goat called Fainting Bill, so called because members of his breed often swoon from fright. Portico was very protective of her horned friend, carefully covering him with a blanket of straw every night when he lay down to sleep. If anyone disturbed the goat's blanket, she would get angry, tear it apart, and make another.

The famous Kelso shared his stall with a dog named Charlie, rubbing noses with him in greeting every morning. Nashua, a well-known track star in the 1950s, had a well-publicized friendship with a pony named Bill. His trainer recalls that the racehorse liked to come up behind the pony, grab his tail in his teeth until his hind legs

left the ground, and then let go.

Horses amuse themselves in all kinds of curious ways. In the winter it's not uncommon to see two stablemates basking in the sun on a snow-covered pasture, their muzzles touching. Most horses also enjoy playing the "scratching game," standing head to tail and scratching each other's withers or backs with their teeth, stopping once in a while to break into a contented horse laugh.

Horses in a group like to play running games like racing and tag. At game time they huff, snort, and carry their tails high, looking like graceful high-level dressage horses. Sometimes two young horses will line up side by side and race to the end of a field and back. Or one will tag the other with a bite on the rump and then race around the paddock until he is nipped in turn.

Don't be alarmed if you see two normally friendly horses rearing up at each other. Males, particularly colts, often stage ritual fights modeled after the real fights between stallions. They may try to grab a front leg with their teeth, coming down on their knees in what looks like a ceremonial bow, or they might strike out with their front feet as they rear. Although they are a joy to watch, sometimes they can get carried away and bang each other up. Separating them may be necessary.

One Quarter Horse filly I knew liked to chase her tail. Considering the short length of a yearling's tail, it was even more remarkable that she occasionally caught it.

One of the greatest delights in having a horse around the house is the pleasure of seeing him cavort with his stablemates or, as you sit on the terrace in the evening, watching him quietly graze. Add to this the satisfaction gained from working with

him day to day, grooming him and feeding him his meals, and hearing his enthusiastic nicker of greeting every morning. You'll no doubt agree with Robert Surtees that there is "no secret so great as that between a rider and his horse."

This anonymous poem, read every year at the closing ceremony of the Pacific National Exhibition in Canada, expresses the parting sentiments of horse owners everywhere:

> *Where in all the world*
> *Can one find nobility without pride,*
> *Friendship without envy,*
> *Or beauty without vanity?*
>
> *Here one finds gratefulness*
> *Coupled with power,*
> *And strength tempered by gentleness.*
>
> *A constant servant,*
> *Yet no slave.*
> *A fighter,*
> *even without hostility.*
> *Our history*
> *Was written on his back.*
>
> *We are his heirs,*
> *But he is our heritage:*

The Horse

Appendix A

For terms covering the parts of the horse not included here, see the endpaper illustration. For terms covering ailments, see Chapters 19 and 20.

Aged. A horse past the age of nine, as of January 1 of a given year. The term means "fully mature," not elderly.

Anglo-Arab. The offspring of a Thoroughbred sire and an Arab dam.

Appointments. Specific equipment and clothing required for a class, event, or style of riding.

Bag. The breast or udder of a mare.

Balance seat. A centered seat that can be used for all types of riding. The rider sits on seat bones in the center of the saddle with legs hanging in a natural, bent position, inside of legs against saddle, ankles flexed, balls of feet resting flat in stirrups, feet close to the horse's sides. The arms are bent at the elbows, and the reins are held over the horse's withers, with hands angled slightly inward at the top.

Bald. A large, uneven white mark on a horse's face that includes one or both eyes; referred to as a *bald face.*

Barrel. The trunk of a horse; the rib cage; the area between the shoulder and hindquarters.

Bars. Horizontal black marks on the legs, desirable in certain color breeds like buckskins. Also called *zebra striping.*

Bay. A horse of medium brown color with a black mane and tail and sometimes black points. There are light bays and dark bays.

Bedding. A material used to bed down the floor of a stall, such as straw, wood chips, or wood shavings.

Billet straps. Straps on an English saddle that attach the saddle to the girth. Sometimes called *girth straps.*

Blaze. A wide white mark running from between the eyes down to the muzzle.

Blemish. An unsightly mark or scar that doesn't interfere with a horse's serviceability.

Blistering. The application of a heating ointment to an inflamed area, usually a tendon, to heat it and draw blood to the injury, thereby speeding recovery.

Bloom. A term used by equestrians to describe an exceptionally healthy-looking horse, fit, with a good coat.

Boggy. A *bog spavin* is a soft swelling caused by inflammation of the bursa in the joint capsule at the front and sides of the hock. Also called *spongy.*

Bone spavin, or **jack spavin.** A bone enlargement that can be felt through skin in and around the hock joint. It usually causes lameness.

Boots. An article used in exercise and trucking to protect and prevent injury to a horse's lower limbs from the knee down.

Bottom line. The dam line of the pedigree of a horse. The *top line* is the sire's pedigree.

Breastplate. A leather piece across a horse's chest that attaches to the saddle and the girth to prevent the saddle from slipping back.

Bridle. A head harness that is used to control a horse. It usually includes a crownpiece, cheekstraps, throatlatch, headband, cavesson (or noseband), bit, and reins.

Bridoon. A small snaffle bit used in combination with a curb bit in a full bridle.

Broodmare. A female horse used for breeding.

Brown. A color often mistaken for black. The difference is that the flanks and muzzle are brown although the body color is black.

Brushing. A faulty way of going, in which the inside of a hoof brushes or interferes with the opposite leg, causing cuts and abrasions.

Buckskin. An overall beige color with a black mane and tail, and sometimes black points, bars, and dorsal strips.

Bursa. A fluid sac that surrounds a joint, ligament, or tendon.

Canter. A slow collected gallop; a three-beat gait that was originally called the Canterbury gallop.

Chestnut. A color of reddish brown. Also the semi-horny protrusion on the inside of a horse's upper foreleg and on the inside face of the hock. Believed to be rudiments of one of the digits that characterized the foot of Eohippus.

Cob. A stocky, short-legged equine of 15.1 hands or less, capable of carrying considerable weight for its size. Usually a type rather than a breed.

Crest. The top of a horse's neck.

Cribbing. A stable vice in which a horse chews the wood of his stall or pasture fence and swallows air. It is dangerous because wood splinters may be swallowed. It is considered an unsoundness.

Cross-ties. Two chains, ropes, or rubber leads, each about four feet long, hung from rings, about five feet high, opposite each other, used to secure a horse on each side of his halter.

Crownpiece. A piece of bridle leather that goes over a horse's head and attaches to the cheekpieces.

Curb. A type of bit used on both Western and English bridles, only in combination with a bridoon in the latter. Also: a swelling of the plantar ligament just below the hock, usually caused by overwork or poor conformation.

Curb chain or **strap.** A chain or strap used under the chin of a horse with a curb, Pelham, or Kimberwick bit, which gives a fulcrumlike action to the bit.

Cutting. A faulty way of going, in which the inside of a horse's hoof strikes the opposite diagonal leg, usually injuring it. Also called *brushing.*

Cutting horse. In Western riding, a horse trained to cut cattle out of a herd.

Dam. The mother of any horse, referred to on a pedigree as the *bottom line.*

Dapples. Patterned color variations on a horse, usually the size of a fifty-cent piece.

Diagonal. A term in English riding that refers to the rider's posting. When trotting inside a ring, the diagonal hind leg and foreleg of the horse strike the ground together. When the horse and rider are moving clockwise around the ring, the rider posts in rhythm with the horse's left front leg and is therefore on the left diagonal.

Direct rein. Use of the rein that displaces the horse's weight from the forehand to the hindquarters. It is most frequently used in English riding to decrease speed, turn, or back a horse. Pressure is never increased when it is used correctly.

Dorsal stripe. A dark stripe down the spinal column, extending from the withers to base of the tail. Also called a *zebra* or *eel* stripe.

Draft horse. A horse originally bred for farm work, especially plowing. Characterized by large bones and a powerful build.

Drenching. Giving a horse liquid medicine by elevating his head and pouring it down his throat in a bottle or syringe.

Dressage. The most refined form of flat riding, in which a horse is trained to move in perfect balance with the utmost lightness and ease.

Driving horse. A horse trained or bred to pull a wagon, gig, or sulky—such as a Hackney, Cleveland bay, or Standardbred.

Dun. A beige color, with a similarly colored or brownish mane and tale. Sometimes with a dorsal stripe.

Eohippus. The former name for the most ancient fossilized equine ancestor, the hypertheracium.

Equus caballus. The scientific Latin name for the modern horse.

Ewe-neck. A neck that is curved upward like a U (or upside-down neck). This conformation fault often interferes with performance.

Faults. In a jumping class, points taken off one's performance.

Field hunter. A hunter of any breed or cross that regularly hunts with a recognized club.

Filly. A female horse under the age of four.

Fittings. Accoutrements of an English saddle that can be separated from the saddle, such as stirrup leathers, stirrups, and girth.

Flat saddle. A saddle with a low or cut-back pommel

and no knee rolls. The term is used by Western riders when referring to an English saddle.

Flat. The term "riding on the flat" is used by hunter and jumper riders to refer to a ride at a walk, trot, and canter without jumping.

Flats. A Thoroughbred racetrack. Short for *flat racing*.

Flaxen. A chestnut-colored horse with a white or cream-colored mane and tail.

Flexion. The degree to which a horse can relax his jaw and bend at the poll and neck.

Floating. Filing down rough, irregular molars to give a smooth grinding surface to the teeth.

Foal. A newborn horse of either sex. The term usually applies until one year of age.

Forage. All types of horse feed, including hay, grass, grain, concentrates, and vegetable snacks.

Forehand. The forequarters of a horse, including the head, neck, shoulders, and front legs.

Forelock. Hair from the mane that hangs down over the forehead of a horse between his ears.

Forging. A faulty way of going, in which the rear hoof strikes the toe of a front hoof. It is most likely to occur at a trot and is caused by poor balance or overextending. It causes a clicking noise.

Founder (or laminitis). An inflammation of the sensitive laminae in the foot. In acute cases the sole drops down and separates from the wall.

Frame. The overall balance, head, and neck carriage when a horse is in motion. A hunter frame is more horizontal when viewed from the side (where the head and neck are carried naturally as the horse travels closer to the ground) than that of a dressage horse at FEI level (where the frame is squarer because the haunches are lowered, the back is lifted, and the head and neck are carried higher).

Gait. A way of moving forward, characterized by the sequence and speed with which a horse's feet leave the ground. The basic gaits are walk, trot, canter, and gallop. Other gaits, which certain breeds are either born with or easily trained to do, are slow gait, rack, pace, running walk, and foxtrot.

Gaited. Possessing one or more gaits either beside or instead of the usual natural three.

Gallop. The fastest gait of which a horse is capable—a full run.

Gelding. A castrated or gelded male horse.

Get. The progeny of any stallion.

Girth. A band of material that encircles the lower body of a horse and fastens the saddle to his back.

Grade. A horse of unregistered and/or uncertain ancestry.

Grain. The seed or seedlike fruit of a cereal grass like oats, corn, or barley, fed alone or in combination.

Green horse. Usually a young, unschooled, or partially schooled horse.

Green jumper. A horse that has just learned to jump. In most horse shows there are special classes for green jumpers or hunters.

Ground tying. The method by which a Western horse is trained to stand still after the rider dismounts and drops the end of one rein on the ground. The horse is taught to remain stationary and not to graze or move around.

Gymkhana. Informal games on horseback, like egg-and-spoon and relay races.

Hack. A light horse used for pleasure riding. Trail and pleasure riding or riding to a hunt meet are often referred to as *hacking*.

Half-bred. A horse with a purebred sire or dam.

Halter. A headpiece with noseband, attaching ring, cheekstrap, and occasionally a headband and ring under the chin, used for tying or leading a horse.

Hand. A standard unit of equine measurement. Four inches equals one hand. Therefore a 17-hand horse would be five feet eight inches, measured from the bottom of the front hoof to the top of the withers, when he is standing straight on flat ground.

Hard mouth. A mouth in which the nerves on the main bone or "bar" of the jaw have been deadened by harsh bits and mishandling.

Harness horse. A driving horse trained to pull a cart or sulky rather than be ridden. Such horses usually race in harness.

Hay. A variety of different regional grasses and legumes, such as timothy and alfalfa, that have been cured, dried, and baled to serve as the bulk of a horse's diet.

Hay crib. A trough-shaped, slatted, wooden structure used to hold hay in a field or stall.

Hay fork. A three-tined fork used for handling hay; not to be confused with a five-to-ten-prong (or more) manure fork.

Hay net. A rope or plastic fiber bag to contain hay, which is tied up or hung at shoulder height of the horse.

Headband. A piece of bridle over the horse's forehead that prevents the bridle from slipping back.

Headstall. The leather pieces of a bridle, not including the bit and reins.

Heat or **estrus.** The period of time during which a mare may be bred. It occurs at approximately three-week intervals during spring and summer and lasts from four to six days.

Heavy in the forehand. A horse that pulls with his head and neck, putting more than a normal amount of weight toward the front of his body. It is often a fault of conformation, caused by an oversize head and neck.

Heavyweight hunter. A hunter capable of carrying a rider weighing over 205 pounds.

Herring-gutted. A barrel that slants sharply upward from the forehand. This unattractive conformation fault doesn't interfere with function.

Hindquarters. The portion of the horse situated behind the barrel.

Horse. Any member of the species *Equus caballus* that measures over 14.2 hands. In the United States most equines of lesser size are called ponies.

Hot-blooded. Usually synonymous with *high strung,* the term describes purebreds of Oriental, Mediterranean, Thoroughbred, or Arabian ancestry.

Hunter. Originally, a horse of any breed used for fox hunting. Today, a horse that jumps in a certain style. A hunter course is series of fences in the ring or on an outside course, imitating the type met in the hunt field.

Hunter class. A class in which horses are judged on their style of jumping, either in the ring over a course of fences or over an outside course. They are judged on their manners, way of going, and sometimes their conformation.

Hunter seat or **forward seat.** A style of riding that is workmanlike in appearance and suited for jumping and hunting. It differs from the *balance seat* in that it has more ankle flexion, because the stirrup is shorter with more knee bend, and the rider bends his hips slightly at the trot, so that he posts with the motion of the horse. When the rider is seated in the center of the saddle, the heel, seat, and shoulder should be in line. The hands are carried in a closed but relaxed position, slightly tilted in off the vertical. The line between the bit, rein, hand, and rider's lower arm is straight, with a bend at the elbow.

In foal. A pregnant mare. The gestation period is usually 340 to 400 days.

In hand. Showing a horse without a saddle, with the rider leading at a walk and trot. The horse is usually shown in a bridle, in classes judged on conformation, fitting, and showmanship, or jogging out for soundness. Special show halters are used in some breed classes judged on conformation.

In season. The time when a mare ovulates and can conceive if bred. A mare starts this cycle in early spring. Also called *estrus* or *in heat.*

Indirect rein. Reining used to displace a horse's weight laterally from one side to the other. It is used most often in riding hunters and jumpers.

Inside. The inside of a circle or an indoor riding ring.

Interference. A faulty way of going, in which the horse's legs brush or interfere with each other at various gaits.

Irish hunter. Usually a cross of seven-eighths Thoroughbred and one-eighth coldblood (a draft breed like a Percheron) to produce a rugged mount with temperament and conformation suited to the rough terrain encountered on an Irish hunt. Now referred to as the Irish sport horse.

Jog. A very slow trot required in Western classes and most comfortable for Western riding, where the rider doesn't post but sits the trot.

Jointed snaffle. The mildest type of bit, consisting of two bars joined in the center. Also called a *broken snaffle.*

Jumper. A horse trained to jump, usually specializing in show jumping.

Knee roll. Leather or foam-rubber material used for padding in a saddle to help keep the rider's knees in place.

Laminitis. See *Founder.*

Lead. When cantering, a horse should be on his right lead going clockwise on a circle. He starts with his left hind legs, then his left diagonal pair (left fore and right hind), and then the right fore, followed by a hesitation where all four feet are in the air. *Also:* a rope, leather, nylon, or chain shank with a snap end, used to lead and tie a horse by the halter.

Leading. Walking a horse forward by standing at his shoulder, the lead line or reins in your right hand, and moving your left foot simultaneously with his right foreleg.

Leading rein. A rein that, when the rider is in the saddle, puts the weight of the horse in the direction of movement. It is a simple way to turn a young or green horse.

Leg wrap. A polo wrap usually used to protect a horse's legs in exercise. When added to a cotton or flannel wrap, used as a standing wrap.

Legume. A leafy grass high in protein and vitamins, like clover and alfalfa, the highest-quality hay.

Light horse. Any horse not of draft ancestry. Originally this term meant *light-legged.*

Lightweight hunter. A horse that can carry up to 165 pounds.

Limit class. A class at a horse show in which the entries may not have won more than six blue ribbons at a recognized show.

Lope. In Western riding, the canter, a slow, balanced, three-beat gait. It is a contraction of the word *gallop.*

Lunge line or **longe line.** A long line of canvas or nylon, about thirty feet long, that attaches to a halter, lunging cavesson, or bridle and is used for training and/or exercising a horse on a circle.

Lunge whip. A long whip used as an aid in training a horse on the lunge line. It never actually touches the horse but is snapped to reinforce spoken commands. A small *popper* on the end sounds like a cap gun when the whip is snapped.

Lunging or **longeing.** Training and/or exercising a horse with a lunge line, using a lunge whip and voice commands. Done on a circle in both directions. The horse is usually taught to walk, trot, canter, halt, and reverse on the lunge line before being mounted.

Maiden class. A class at a horse show open to entries who have never won a blue ribbon at a recognized show.

Manger. A wooden feeding box or slatted trough attached to the stall wall to hold feed and hay.

Manure fork. A fork with five, ten, or more prongs, used to remove droppings from a stall.

Mare. A mature female horse, over the age of four.

Martingale or **tie-down.** A device used to aid in keeping the horse's head in the correct position so he can be controlled. Some attach directly to the noseband (or cavesson), and some attach to the reins. It terminates at the girth and usually has a piece that goes around the neck.

Mature horse. Any horse five years or older.

Medicine hat. A rare coloration found on certain pintos, consisting of chestnut or black speckling around the ears, chest, barrel, legs, and rump on an otherwise white coat. Indians considered it extremely lucky.

Middleweight hunter. A hunter capable of carrying 185 pounds.

Milk teeth. In a young horse, the teeth equivalent to baby teeth in a human. They are lost and replaced by permanent teeth in a consistent order.

Model. A horse in a class judged on conformation.

Muzzle. That part of a horse's head that includes his nose, nostrils, lips, and chin.

Navicular disease. Disintegration of the navicular bone of the foot.

Near side. The left side of a horse, viewed from behind. Schooled horses are accustomed to being approached, mounted, led, haltered, and saddled from the near side, as opposed to the offside. The term stems from cavalry officers who carried their swords on the left hip, making it necessary to mount on that side.

Neck rein. A method of turning a Western horse or polo pony with reins in one hand, laying them across the side of the neck to turn in the opposite direction. (The reins on the left side of the neck would cause a horse to make a right turn.) Also called a *bearing rein,* it allows the rider to change direction without decreasing speed.

Noseband. A strap that goes over the nose, as part of the Western bridle.

Novice class. A class at a horse show open to entries who have not won more than three blue ribbons at recognized shows.

Offside. The right side of the horse when viewed from behind; formerly called the *far side.*

Open class. A class at a horse show open to any horse and rider in a given division.

Open jumper. A horse capable of high jumping in competition, scored only on jumping and/or time faults.

Opening rein. A rein used out to the side to guide a horse in that direction. Also called a *leading rein.*

Outside. The outside of the circle or ring in which a horse is turning.

Overtracking. A way of going in which the hind foot steps in front of the print of the front foot.

Paddock. A small, fenced area or enclosure. It sometimes adjoins a barn, allowing a horse to go in and out at will.

Parasites. The hundreds of worms, flies, lice, and so on, that live on or in a horse. If uncontrolled, they can permanently damage an animal's health.

Park horses. Horses formerly ridden or driven in the park, with animated gaits.

Park trot. A slow, animated, very collected trot with a lot of leg action, called for in the show ring. It is seen in all harness classes where hackneys or saddlebreds perform.

Pellet concentrates. A horse feed comprising small, compressed pellets that contain concentrated hay, grain, vitamins, and minerals, or a combination of these, all with a high nutrient value.

Piebald. A horse whose color is black and white; seen in pintos and paints.

Pigeon-toed. Standing with toes pointed inward.

Plantar ligament. A deep, short ligament extending from the point of the hock to the point below.

Pleasure horse. Usually, a horse that is quiet and tractable and performs willingly at all three natural gaits.

Pointing. A way of standing with weight on the back feet, indicating unsoundness, particularly founder.

Points. The muzzle, legs, mane, and tail; used to refer to their color.

Poll. The uppermost point of a horse's neck, behind the ears.

Polo pony. Any small, agile horse between 15 and 15.2 hands, capable of the speed, endurance, and quick turns demanded in polo. Usually polo ponies are one-half to three-quarters Thoroughbred.

Pommel. That part of the English saddle that fits over the withers.

Pony. Any equine under 14.2 hands, excepting breeds like the Arab and Thoroughbred, which can also measure under that. A small pony measures up to 12 hands; a large one runs to 14.2. In England a pony is any child's mount, no matter what size.

Post entries. Entries made on the day of a horse show. They cost a higher fee than those mailed in advance of the deadline.

Posting. In English riding, rising and descending with the rhythm of the trot (going up with one diagonal pair of legs and down with the other).

Pulley rein. A severe rein aid used for a sudden stop.

Purebred. A horse whose sire and dam are registered in a studbook.

Quarter Horse. A breed developed to race the quarter-mile.

Rack. A four-beat gait done at speed. Also called the *single-foot,* it is a strenuous acquired gait.

Refusal. When a horse stops or runs out at a jump instead of taking it.

Reining. A skill in Western riding where the horse performs complex patterns of turning at the lope.

Resistance. When a horse balks or evades what he is being asked to do.

Roan. A bay, black, or chestnut coloration, consistently intermingled with white hairs over the entire body.

Roaring. A defect in the respiratory system caused by paralysis of a vocal nerve, resulting in a roaring noise.

Rose gray. A gray horse with chestnut hairs mixed in.

Running walk. A slow gait resembling the regular flat-footed walk, but faster. The sequence of hoofbeats is a diagonal four-beat. This gait was developed primarily in the Tennessee Walker.

Saddle seat. A style of riding where the rider sits close to the cantle of the saddle, with very little bend of the knee. The toes and knees are in line, with feet parallel to the horse's sides. The hands are held even with the waist over the horse's withers.

Schooling. Basic or refresher training, or teaching new skills to the horse. It is most effective when done on a regular weekly basis. It leads into figures and other exercises and can include jumping.

Seat. Used with *proper* or good: the way a rider correctly sits his horse.

Shank. A lead line of leather, nylon, or other material with a chain in snap end.

Sire. The father of a horse; the *top line* in a pedigree.

Skewbald. A coloration like piebald, except that the colors are bay, chestnut, and brown on white or vice versa.

Slow gait. One of the two slower artificial gaits performed by an American Saddlebred five-gaited horse. It is usually a slow pace or stepping pace. Taken from a walk, it is a slow, ambling, lateral, almost four-beat gait—very easy and comfortable. Other slow gaits are the running walk and the foxtrot.

Snip. A white mark in the area between or including a horse's nostrils.

Sock. A white coloration on the leg, below the fetlock joint.

Sorghum. A genus of cereal grass used as animal feed, of which there are four distinct types. One of the best known is milo. Molasses is made from sweet sorghum.

Sorrel. See *Chestnut.*

Sound. Free from any abnormal deviation in structure or function that would interfere with usefulness.

Splayfooted. A way of standing with toes pointed outward.

Spook. A high-strung, unpredictable horse given to shying and bolting for no apparent reason.

Stake class. A class at a horse show that offers money prizes. The entry fees depend on the amount of the stake.

Stallion. A mature male horse, usually kept whole for breeding purposes.

Star. A small white mark between a horse's eyes. *Also:* a mark on the biting surface of a horse's teeth that helps determine age.

Stock seat. The correct Western seat. The rider sits on the seat bones with a slight bend at the knee, toes under the knee, and feet parallel to a horse's sides. Reins are held in one hand in a comfortable position over the withers.

Stocking. A white coloration on the leg, from the knee down.

Stocking up. A swelling of the legs or a filling of the tendons.

Straight stall. Usually an eight-by-five-foot enclosure in which a horse is tied in the front by the halter, with manger and bucket at his head. Also called a *tie stall.*

Stud. A place where stallions and mares are kept for breeding purposes. *Also:* a breeding stallion.

Studbook. The registry where all the purebred ancestors of a breed are recorded.

Switch. A matching hairpiece that ties into a horse's tail, matching his own color and texture, to add length or fullness.

Suppleness. The flexibility of a horse's body, his ability to carry and push from behind, using hip, stifle, and hock, which follows through to rounding the back and neck. *Also:* bending and balancing laterally.

Tack. Bridle, saddle, and other equipment used in riding and handling a horse.

TDN. The total digestible nutrients in any feed. In oats, for example, the TDN is the highest of all feed—80 percent.

Throatlatch. The strap on the bridle that goes under the throat. This part of the horse's anatomy bears the same name.

Thrush. A disease of the hoof characterized by black flaking of the sole and frog and a foul odor.

Tick. In jumping, the nick of a horse's front or hind legs on the obstacle without knocking it down.

Tie-down. A Western martingale, running from the cinch to the noseband, to keep a horse's head down in its normal position when working.

Tie stall. See *Straight stall.*

Top line. On a pedigree, a horse's sire lineage. Also: in dressage, the shape that the top of the neck, back, and croup take when a horse is using its hind legs actively.

Tracking up. A way of going in which the hind foot steps into the hoofprint of the front foot.

Trail horse. A horse used for pleasure riding or trail riding, not show. Often called a *hack* or *hacking horse.*

Tree. The wooden or metal frame on the inside of a saddle.

Trot. A natural two-beat gait in which the legs move in diagonal pairs.

Turnout. The overall general appearance of a tacked-up horse, including appropriateness, cleanliness, and condition. Turnout can also include the rider. *Also:* a heavy blanket or waterproof rug worn outside in cold weather, or *turnout rug. Also:* a horse in pasture, as in *daily turnout.*

Unsound. Unhealthy or with serious problems of wind or limbs; unserviceable.

Walk. A flat-footed four-beat gait; the slowest of the three natural gaits.

Watch eye. A blue eye circled with white, sometimes called a *glass eye.* The other eye is usually brown. The unusual coloration does not affect vision.

Weanling. A foal that has been weaned but is not yet a yearling.

Weaving. A stable vice in which the horse weaves rhythmically back and forth in his stall.

Western seat. See *Stock seat.*

Whistling. A mild form of roaring.

White coronet. Coloration with white bands on the coronet, just above the hoof. Sometimes the horse will also have white heels.

Wide behind. A horse whose hocks are not parallel, making him look bowlegged from the rear.

Wind puffs. Puffy, spongy swellings around the fetlock joints, caused by pockets of fluid secreted from the bursa.

Wind sucking. See *Cribbing.*

Yearling. A horse of either sex that is a year old on January 1 of a given year.

Appendix B

POISONOUS PLANTS

More than seven hundred species of plants in the United States and Canada are known to have caused equine illness at one time or another. Unfortunately no pattern of relationship, geographical distribution, habitat, season, or plant part can successfully be used to distinguish poisonous plants from harmless ones, and they are found everywhere.

Ideally your horse shouldn't be eating anything other than semidomesticated grasses planted in the pasture, which doesn't include weeds. Don't risk poisoning by turning your horse out in woodland or natural meadow, and when pasturage becomes sparse, be sure to provide enough hay to keep him from browsing on weeds.

Weather conditions can cause harmful concentrations of toxins in normally harmless plants. Cold, dark weather produces dangerously high accumulations of nitrogen in sorghum-Sudan hybrids, alfalfa, corn, and many grasses. Toxic concentrations of cyanide in sorghum and Sudan grass can be caused by drought or killing frost. If this forage is included in your grazing area, plan to take your horse off the pasture when unusual weather affects the growth rate. After a wind storm or heavy rain, it's a good idea to walk the pasture to make sure no dangerous plants have intruded. Many plants that are lovely in your garden can wreak havoc with your horse's stomach. Keep flower and vegetable beds far away from pasture fences. Horses are always tempted by the greens on the other side of the fence.

PLANT	POISONOUS PART	SYMPTOMS
Black locust	Bark, sprout, and sometimes foliage	Nausea, weakness, and depression
Cherry, wild or cultivated	Foliage, twigs	Released cyanide acts within minutes to produce gasping, excitement, then prostration
Elderberry	Root, mostly; berry least	Nausea, digestive upset
Oak	Fallen leaf and acorn or felled tree	Gradual kidney damage from large amounts

Wooded Areas

Baneberry	Foliage, irritant sap	Intense digestive upset
Bracken fern	Foliage mixed in hay or bedding	Nervousness characteristic of digestive upset
Mayapple	Foliage, root	Chemically related to opium—excitement, then prostration
Wild Dutchman's	Foliage	Oxalate crystals embed in tissues of tongue and mouth, resulting in intense burning irritation.
Jack-in-the-pulpit	Calcium oxalate raphide crystals	Death may occur from swelling in base of tongue, causing blocking of air passage.

Swamps and Moist Spots

Cocklebur	Seed, burr	Nausea, depression, weakness
Marsh marigold	Irritant sap	Intense digestive upset
Water hemlock	Fleshy root	Violent and painful convulsions

Fields, Meadows, Pastures

Buttercups	Foliage contains irritant juices	Digestive upset
Common agricultural crops	When spoiled; sweet clover hay, sorghums, Sudan grass, and some clovers	Digestive upset
Corn cockle, bouncing vet, cow cockle	Seeds and foliage	Injury to the wall of the digestive tract. Destruction of red blood cells, severe digestive upset, or death
False hellebore	Leaf contains alkaloids	Depressed blood pressure

PLANT	POISONOUS PART	SYMPTOMS
Horsetail	Foliage	Vitamin B deficiency and nervousness
Milkweed	Foliage	Poison symptoms usually appear within a few hours of ingestion
Nightshade, all members, including henbane, jimsonweed, and horse nettle	Foliage, particularly vine and green tissue, contains complex alkaloids	Intense digestive disturbances, nervousness. Cumulative effect
Poison hemlock	Foliage and seed contain at least five alkaloids	Excitability, staggering, depression of vital functions, and death
Pokeweed, dogbane celandine poppy	Foliage, root and berry (least)	Severe digestive disturbances
Pond scums (algae)	Bloom: dense mass of tiny organisms: water becomes paintlike, with millions of green or blue particles	Death
Sensitive fern	Foliage mixed in the hay	Brain damage and death
St. John's wort	Foliage contains pigment	Reacts with sunlight and causes blood vessels to leak; blood serum collects under skin, producing watery swelling and even killing skin, leaving raw, painful exposed areas.

Yard Plants, Bushes, Trees

Box and privet hedge	Clippings	Mild to severe digestive upset that may result in death
Christmas rose	Whole	Severe purgation
Dumbcane, caladium, philodendron	Needlelike plant crystals	Intense burning and irritation; death; tongue swelling blocks air passages
Foxglove	Whole, fresh, or in hay	Increased contraction in heart, irregular heartbeat and pulse, digestive upset, mental confusion.
Horse chestnut (buckeye)	Plant or nut	Irregular gait, excitement, loss of coordination
Iris	Flesh, underground portion	Severe digestive upset
Larkspur and aconite or monkshood	Cutting	Digestive upset; nervous excitement or depression

PLANT	POISONOUS PART	SYMPTOMS
Lily and the amaryllis groups; hyacinth, narcissus or daffodil, autumn crocus, star-of-Bethlehem, lily-of-the-valley, snowdrops	Bulb or tuber	Symptoms; intense digestive upset, nervous symptoms; lily-of-the-valley may affect heart
Lupines (wild in some northern areas)	Alkaloid of plant	Death
Mountain Laurel	Leaf	Nausea and colic, depression, difficult breathing, prostration
Oleander and poinsettia	Leaf	Affects heart; severe digestive upset
Ornamental sweet pea	Seed	Large amounts cause skeletal deformities
Poppies and bleeding heart or Dutchman's breeches	New growth in early spring before other foliage	Similar to that from morphine or opium; death from Dutchman's breeches
Yew	Foliage	Depressed hearing action, death

Vegetable Garden Plants

PLANT	POISONOUS PART	SYMPTOMS
Onions (in large quantities)	Whole	Destroy red blood cells
Potato	Sprout, vine, and rotted potatoes	Intense digestive disturbance, nervous symptoms
Rhubarb	Leaf	Toxic oxalic acid crystallizes in kidneys, ruptures tubules
Tomato	Vine	May be poisonous to livestock in large amounts

The National Animal Poison Control Center (a nonprofit source of information concerning potential toxins of horses and other animals) may be reached at (800) 548-2423. There is a minimal charge per case. Credit cards are accepted.

Appendix C

- Three sturdy lead ropes with strong, easy-to-snap clips
- Two halters
- Bridle
- Saddle
- Saddle pad
- Saddle cover (optional)
- Fly bonnet or mask
- Cross-ties with safety snaps
- Grooming tools (see Chapter 12)

- Stall cleaning tools (see Chapter 10)
- First-aid kit (see Chapter 18)
- Feed dish
- Two water buckets
- One wash bucket
- Hay net
- Hay fork (optional)
- Water tub (for pasture)
- Wire cutters (for hay bales)
- Tack cleaning equipment (see Chapter 27)
- Tool box (for emergency repairs)

- Hay and grain (see Chapters 7 and 8)
- Bedding (see Chapter 10)
- Stable and fence maintenance equipment (see Chapters 9 and 11)
- Inside stall and/or open shed (10 × 12 per horse)
- Pasture area (ideally two acres per horse)
- Fenced working ring (optional)
- Riding clothes (see Chapter 31)

- Turnout rug, cooler, cotton stable sheet, rain sheet, and/or quarter sheet
- Other blankets (see Chapter 25)
- One set (four) polo wraps
- Brushing boots

Appendix D

MAKING YOUR OWN HORSE OR PONY BLANKET, COOLER, AND SADDLE COVER

A Horse or Pony Blanket

Materials

- Three sturdy lead ropes with strong, easy-to-snap clips
- 4 yards (3.7 meters) of 45-inch (114.5-cm)-wide, machine-washable fabric with firm body. Denim is a good choice.
- 1 spool of thread of matching or coordinating color
- 5 to 6 yards (4.6 to 5.5 meters) of webbing for girth straps (available at tack shops)
- Twill or bias tape (doubled) or webbing made for upholstering or for hooked rug bindings
- 6 to 8 yards (5.5 to 7.4 meters of 2.5 cm) twill or bias tape for edges of blanket (optional)
- 2 overall buckles (or blanket buckles purchased from a tack shop or catalog for repairs)

Supplies

- Scissors
- Straight pins
- Pencil and chalk
- Iron and ironing board
- Tracing wheel and dressmaker's carbon
- Large sheets of brown wrapping paper
- Sewing machine
- Transparent tape

Making your blanket

1. Enlarge the pattern shown below, then tape together sheets of brown wrapping paper to make a rectangle at least 6 feet (1.9 meters) long by 4 feet (1.2 meters) wide. Mark the paper into a grid of 6-inch (15-cm) squares, then mark a series of dots on the grid to duplicate the outline of the blanket as shown on the pattern. Connect the dots to make a smooth, continuous line.
2. Fold the fabric in half lengthwise. Pin the pattern on the wrong side of the fabric, with the long edge of the pattern along the selvage of the fabric. Using a tracing wheel and dressmaker's carbon, trace the outline of the blanket onto the wrong side of both layers of fabric. Mark the position of the webbing.
3. Before cutting, check to see if the back curve fits the horse's back. Machine-baste across the back seamline. Drape the blanket wrong-side-out over your horse to see that it lies smoothly on his back. (If not, pin a new curve that fits.) Check the rest of the outline of the blanket directly on the horse to see that the size is correct. Any changes can be marked with a piece of chalk.
4. Add a half-inch (1.3-cm) seam allowance, and cut along the correct outline.
5. Sew the two pieces together along the correct back seamline. Press the back seam to one side, and finish it with a flat felled seam. Or zigzag-stitch both raw edges in place. Stitch slowly and carefully to make a smooth seam along the curve.

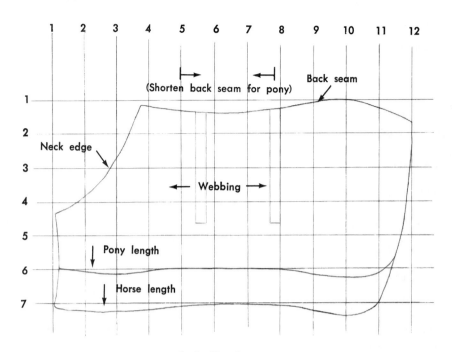

Scale: ⅜ inch = 1 foot

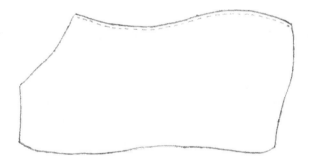

Blanket edges

1. Turn the edges twice (about a quarter-inch or 6 mm) each, and stitch them in place. Use a straight, zigzag, or decorative stitch.

2. Finish the edge with double-fold bias tape. Fold the tape over the edges of the blanket, and pin it in place. Using a straight or zigzag stitch, stitch through both layers of tape and blanket.

3. Finish the edge with a half-inch (1.3 cm) of twill tape. Fold, press, and pin the edges of the blanket a quarter-inch (6 mm) to the right or wrong side, depending on whether you want it to show. Pin the tape flat along the fold, covering the blanket's raw edge. Stitch along both edges of the tape, using a straight, zigzag, or decorative stitch.

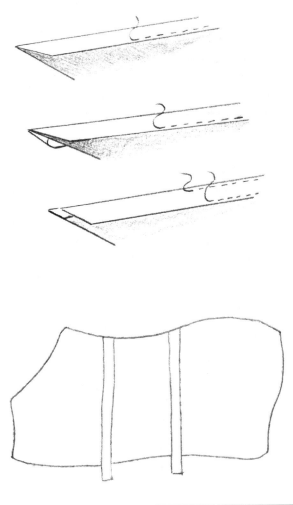

Attaching the webbing

Cut the webbing into two equal lengths. Fold each piece in half, and mark the fold with a pin. Place the pin mark on the back seam at the place marked for the webbing. Pin along the placement line to 15 inches (38 cm) from the bottom edge of the blanket. Do this for the webbing strips on the left and right sides of the blanket. Sew in place, stitching down both edges of the webbing and straight across at the 15-inch (38-cm) marks.

Attaching the overall buckles

1. Slip the ends of the webbing strips through the slots in the buckles, and pin in place. Put the blanket on your horse. Fasten the buckles, and adjust the webbing length to fit your horse. You might want to attach a strip of elastic tape between one end of the webbing and the buckles to allow more adjustment. Stitch the buckles in place.

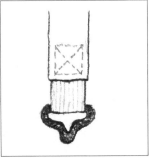

Making chest ties

1. By using leftover fabric, leftover tape, decorative trim, or Velcro, you can make ties to hold the blanket in place over your horse's chest. Buckles made just for this purpose are also available in tack shops. To tell how long the ties should be and where they should go, you'll need to try the blanket on your horse.

2. When making ties from leftover fabric, cut the material in strips 3 inches (7.5 cm) wide, to the desired length. Press the strips in half lengthwise with an iron. Then open and fold in the long edges to meet the center crease and press. Fold again, press, and pin. Top-stitch along both edges and across one end.

A Cooler

You can make a cooler for practically nothing by using an old blanket and dyeing it to freshen the color, or by buying a king-size blanket on sale. (A wool blanket isn't a good idea, because you want to be able to throw the cooler in a washing machine.) Several friends have picked up new, full-size acrylic blankets at white sales. The only other materials they added were bias seam binding and cotton roping. (Binding can be used instead of roping if you're using a contrasting color and want all your trim to match.)

1. If you're using a blanket, remove the satin binding at the top and bottom. Then place a saucer-size plate on each corner to give them a uniform curve. Trace with a pencil or pen, and cut on the line.
2. Start in the center of one of the short sides, and pin the binding around the edges of the blanket until you reach the beginning. Make sure to leave enough binding to overlap the beginning by 1 inch. Cut off the excess, then turn the raw edge under an eighth of an inch. Overlap the start of the binding, and stitch as close to the edge of the binding as possible, making sure you catch both sides.
3. Fold the blanket, or cooler, lengthwise, and mark the center front (head) and the center back (tail). For durability it's a good idea to overlap the tail end of the blanket. Use cotton cord or binding for the brow-band and tail tape. Cut one piece 14 inches long for the browband and a piece 24 inches long for the tail.
4. Lay the blanket out flat, and pin the ends of the cord to it 6½ inches from the center front for the brow-band and 11½ inches from the center back for the tail, on the wrong side of the fabric. Overlap the cord 1 inch over the edge of the blanket so the end can be stitched securely. Flatten out the cord slightly, cut 4 pieces of binding 1½ inches long, fold over the ends ¼ inch, and place over the ends of the cord. Stitch in place following the pattern indicated.

DIAGRAM OF A COOLER

5. For the ties, cut four pieces of binding 8 inches long. Turn under the raw edges a quarter-inch, and stitch. Place one set a third of the width from the bottom of the blanket and the other set a third of the width from the top. And that's it.

6. A rain cooler is also simple to make. Follow the same directions as above, but substitute heavy-duty sheet plastic (like that used for covering windows in the winter). Hem it on itself around the outside edge, using a zigzag stitch. You can sew the hem with a thread of your stable color to match the cording of the head and tail. Sew on felt initials, or glue them, for a chic effect.

A Saddle Cover

This easy-to-make, waterproof slip-over saddle cover with heavy-duty elastic all around is the best protection for your saddle when it isn't in use.

1. Waterproof canvas, nylon, Naugahyde, and similar vinyl materials are sold at larger fabric stores and often can be bought as inexpensive remnants. A friend used a vinyl tablecloth. Whatever your choice, you'll need 1 yard of 60-inch material and 3 yards, 8 inches of heavy-duty elastic (less than half an inch wide). Take your saddle pad and lay it out flat on a 36 × 60-inch sheet of paper. Trace around the pad with a bright-colored chalk or crayon, then add another 6 inches all the way around.
2. Place the pattern on the wrong side of the material, then trace around it with a crayon and cut on the crayon line. Do not pin the pattern to the material; water will penetrate the holes.
3. Fold the edges over by three-quarters of an inch, and stitch very carefully five-eighths of an inch from the edge to form a casing for the elastic. Use heavy-duty polyester or nylon thread, and leave a 2-inch opening to insert the elastic.
4. Pin a large safety pin to one end of the elastic, and insert it into the opening, pushing it through the casing to the other end. (Do not let the loose end go through the opening.) Now that you have both ends of the elastic outside each end, temporarily place the cover over your saddle. Pull the elastic until the cover fits snugly, and knot it permanently. Remove it from the saddle, push the knot into the casing, fold over the edge, and stitch. You now have a long-lasting saddle cover that shouldn't have taken more than forty-five minutes to make.

To make other items for your horse, tack, or English or Western riding, contact SuitAbility. (See Appendix F.)

COLLAPSIBLE SADDLE RACK

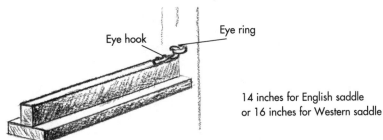

Eye hook   Eye ring

14 inches for English saddle
or 16 inches for Western saddle

Appendix E

KNOTS

Slipknot

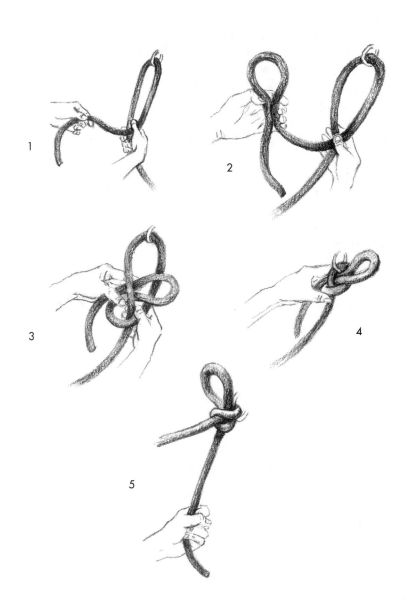

Halter Hitch

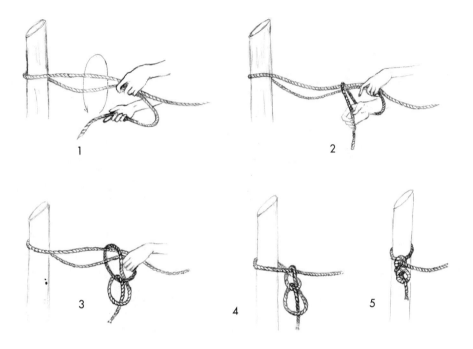

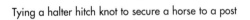

Tying a halter hitch knot to secure a horse to a post

Bowline Knot

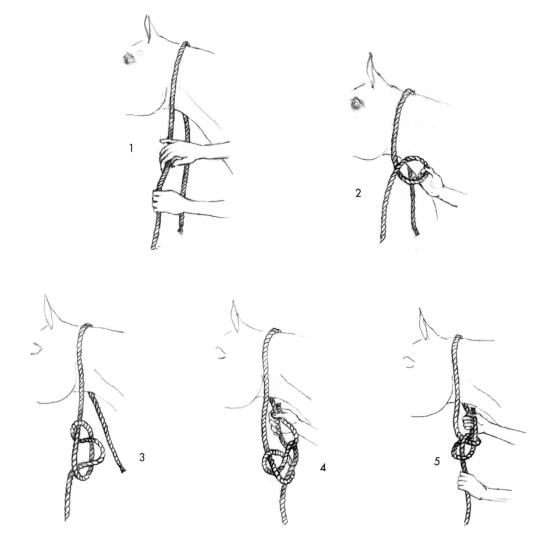

Tying a bowline knot for a horse trained to tie by the neck

Appendix F

Organizations

Adopt-A-Horse
Consumer Information Center
Pueblo, CO 81009
(800) 417-9647

American Association of Equine Practitioners
4075 Iron Works Pike
Lexington, KY 40511
(800) 438-2386
The brochure *Therapeutic Options: Considerations for Horse Owners* is available through AAEP-member veterinarians.

American Association of Veterinary Medicine (Herbology)
2214 Old Emmerton Road
Bel Air, MD 21015

American Horse Council
1700 K Street, N.W., Suite 300
Washington, DC 20006
(202) 296-4031
The directory is available by subscription.

American Horse Protection Association
1000 29th Street, N.W., Suite T-100
Washington, DC 20007
(202) 965-0500

American Horse Shows Association
598 Madison Avenue
New York, NY 10022
(212) 972-2472

American Medical Equestrian Association
103 Surrey
Waynesville, NC 28786
Phone and fax (704) 456-3392

American Paint Horse Association
P.O. Box 961023
Fort Worth, TX 76161-0023
(817) 439-3400

American Riding Instructors Association
Certification Program
P.O. Box 282
Alton Bay, NH 03810
(603) 875-4000

American Veterinary Medical Association
1931 North Meacham, Suite 100
Schaumburg, IL 60173-4360
(800) 248-2862
Write for names and addresses of alternative therapy associations.

Center for Equine Health
College of Veterinary Medicine
University of California at Davis
One Shields Avenue
Davis, CA 95616
(530) 752-6433

Cornell University
College of Veterinary Medicine
Office of Communications Services
Ithaca, NY 14853-6401
(607) 253-3747
Publishes *CCVM Annual Reports* and *CCVM Animal Health Newsletter*

Department of Animal Science
Texas A&M University
College Station, TX 77843
(409) 845-7731

Bureau of Land Management
U.S. Dept. of the Interior
Division of Wild Horses and Burros
18th and C Streets, NW
Washington, D.C. 20240
(202) 452-7736

The Equine Connection
Agricultural Division
Bayer Advertising
P.O. Box 390
Shawnee Mission, KS 66201
(800) 438-2386
Will provide a list of alternative equine therapists in your area.

Equine Research Laboratory
University of California at Davis
(916) 752-6433 (director)

Equine Travelers of America
P.O. Box 322
Arkansas City, KS 67005-0322
(316) 442-8131

International Livestock Investigations Association
4701 Marion Street, Room 201
Denver, CO 80216
(303) 294-0895

International Museum of the Horse
4089 Iron Works Parkway
Lexington, KY 40510
(606) 259-4231

International Veterinary Acupuncture Society
1132 North Main
P.O. Box 1478
Longmont, CO 80502-1478
(303) 682-1167

Keenland Library
4201 Versailles Road
Lexington, KY 40510
(606) 254-3412

National Sporting Library
P.O. Box 1335
Middleburg, VA 20118
(540) 687-6542 (director)

North American Horse Travel Guide
Round-Up Press
P.O. Box 109
Boulder, CO 80306-0109

Oklahoma State University
115 Printing Building
Stillwater, OK 74078
(405) 521-3864
Offers free booklets on *Use of Forages* (no. 3980) and
Managing Grazing Horses (no. 3981)

Pinto Horse Association of America, Inc.
1900 Samuels Avenue
Fort Worth, TX 76102-1141
(817) 366-7842

SuitAbility (Equestrian Patterns)
P.O. Box 3244
Chico, CA 95927-3244

TTeam Headquarters
P.O. Box 3793
Sante Fe, NM 87501
(800) 854-8326

United States Dressage Federation
U.S.D.F. Box 6669
Lincoln, NE 6805-0669
(402) 434-8550

United States Pony Club
U.S.P.C. 4071 Iron Works Pike
Lexington, KY 40511-8462
(606) 254-7669

Recommended Magazines

Chronicle of the Horse **(weekly)**
P.O. Box 432
Mt. Morris, IL 61054
(800) 877-5467

Dressage and CT **(monthly)**
P.O. Box 420235
Palm Coast, FL 32142-0235
(904) 446-6914

Equus **(monthly)**
656 Quince Orchard Road
Gaithersberg, MD 20878-1472
(800) 829-5910

Horse Journal **(monthly)**
P.O. Box 420234
Palm Coast, FL 32142
(203) 661-6111

The Horse: Guide to Equine Health Care
(bimonthly)
P.O. Box 4680
Lexington, KY 40544
(800) 582-5604

Horse Illustrated **(monthly)**
P.O. Box 6040
Mission Viejo, CA 92690
(800) 365-4421

Horse and Rider **(monthly)**
P.O. Box 921
North Adams, MA 01247-0921
(800) 358-6327

Practical Horseman **(monthly)**
P.O. Box 420235
Palm Coast, FL 32142
(800) 829-3340

Western Horseman **(monthly)**
P.O. Box 7980
Colorado Springs, CO 80933
(800) 877-5278

References

Dent, Anthony. *The Horse Through Fifty Centuries of Civilization.* New York: Holt, Rinehart and Winston, 1974.

Edwards, Elwyn Hartley. *The Encyclopedia of the Horse.* New York: Dorling-Kindersley, 1994.

Gianoli, Luigi. Trans. Iris Books. *Horses and Horsemanship Through the Ages.* New York: Crown Publishers, 1969.

Goodall, Daphne Machin. Trans. *The Flight of the East Prussian Horses.* New York: Arco Publishing Company, 1985.

Gould, Stephen Jay. *Hen's Teeth and Horse's Toes: Further Reflections in Natural History.* New York: Norton, 1984.

Gould, Stephen Jay. *Wonderful Life: The Burgess Shale and the Nature of History.* New York: Norton, 1989.

Hendricks, Bonnie L. *International Encyclopedia of the Horse.* Norman: University of Oklahoma Press, 1995.

Hooper, Frederick. *The Military Horse.* New York: Barnes, 1976.

Hayes, Capt. M. Horace. *Veterinarian Notes for Horse Owners: An Illustrated Manual of Horse Medicine and Surgery.* 16th rev. ed. New York: Arco Publishing Co., 1988.

Hyland, Ann. *Equus: The Horse in the Roman World.* New Haven: Yale University Press, 1990.

International Encyclopedia of Horses and Ponies. New York: Howell Book House, 1995.

Keith, Thomas B. *The Horse Interlude.* Moscow: University of Idaho Press, 1976.

Liedtke, Walter. *The Royal Horse and Rider: Painting, Sculpture, and Horsemanship, 1500–1800.* New York: The Metropolitan Museum of Art, 1989.

Maynard, Rick, Jennifer Maynard, and Marcia Hayes. *Horses in Focus.* Middletown, MD: Half-Halt Press, 1992.

von Nelson-Zerweck, Eberhard, and Erhard Schulte. Trans. *The Trakehner.* London: J. A. Allen, 1989.

Index

Note: Page numbers in *italics* indicate illustrations.

ABOUT THE AUTHORS

Patricia Jacobson is a professional horsewoman, teacher, trainer, and licensed AHSA judge in dressage. She has studied with a number of leading Olympic riders and has been an award-winning competitor in equitation, hunters, combined training, and dressage, on both her own and her clients' horses.

Jacobson has raised, bred, and trained her own horses as well as teaching all levels of riders in jumping and dressage. These experiences led her to develop a stable management program at her own barn and later to initiate an ongoing one at an upstate New York community college. In the 1980s she established and managed a world-class Arabian show and breeding barn. She frequently lectures on equine subjects and gives riding clinics in many areas of the United States. Currently she enjoys teaching and training riders and horses in upstate New York.

Under the name Pat Kelly she is an accomplished professional artist whose commissioned paintings of horses and dogs now hang in more than eighty corporate and private collections. She studied at the Art Students League and The Woodstock School of Art. She is a graduate of Stephens College in Columbia, Missouri.

Marcia Hayes worked her way through the University of Michigan as a medical secretary and student editor in the geology and forestry departments. She went on to work as a copy and production editor in the science books division of Prentice-Hall Publishers, then as a reporter, feature writer, rewrite person, and regional editor for *The Record,* a New Jersey daily, and thereafter as an assistant city editor for the *Kingston Daily Freeman.*

After winning a fellowship in science writing at Columbia Graduate School of Journalism and receiving her M.A., she freelanced as a syndicated science correspondent, feature writer, and investigative reporter for the old North American Newspaper Alliance and for Reuters News Service. During this time she also edited UPI's Illustrated Science Service, contributed to various national and international magazines, and wrote four books, this one the second.

The two coauthors met when Hayes and her two children took riding lessons from Jacobson. A year later, *A Horse Around the House* was born. Hayes has since coauthored a fifth book on horse photography and is currently collaborating on *The Museum Week,* a movie and television series set in New York City and London museums. She and her husband, the former Condé Nast art director and artist André Glatz, live and work in Roxbury, New York.

1. Withers
2. Cannon bone
3. Fetlock joint
4. Pastern
5. Coronet
6. Dock
7. Gaskin
8. Hoof
9. Chestnut
10. Ergot
11. Croup
12. Knee
13. Hock
14. Loin
15. Back
16. Crest
17. Point of hip
18. Stifle
19. Barrel
20. Muzzle
21. Girth
22. Tendons
23. Elbow
24. Shoulder
25. Gullet
26. Projecting cheekbone
27. Flank
28. Curb groove
29. Arm
30. Forelock
31. Forearm
32. Heels
33. Poll
34. Chest
35. Point of shoulder
36. Sheath
37. Throatlatch